Understanding Actuari~~al Man~~agement: the actuarial control cycle

Understanding Actuarial Management:
the actuarial control cycle

Second Edition

Edited by

Clare Bellis
Richard Lyon
Stuart Klugman
John Shepherd

SOCIETY OF ACTUARIES

Published by

The Institute of Actuaries of Australia

ABN 69 000 423 656

Level 7, Challis House, 4 Martin Place

Sydney 2000 Australia

Phone: +61 (0) 2 9233 3466

Fax: +61 (0) 2 9233 3446

Email: actuaries@actuaries.asn.au

Website: www.actuaries.asn.au

ISBN 978 0 85813 074 6 (volume and CD-ROM)

Cover design by Kirk Palmer Design, Surry Hills NSW

Typeset by Mercier Typesetters Pty Ltd, Granville NSW

Printed in USA on behalf of Ligare Pty Ltd, Australia

Copyright Acknowledgements

Extracts in Chapter 2 from AS/NZS 4360 reproduced with permission from SAI Global under Licence 0911-C006. The Standard can be purchased online at http://www.saiglobal.com.

Extracts in Chapters 2, 11 and 12 from the Australian Prudential Regulation Authority's website (© Commonwealth of Australia) reproduced with permission.

Extract in Chapter 2 from "Corporate Governance Principles and Recommendations" reproduced with permission as follows:

> © ASX Limited ABN 98 008 624 691 (ASX) 2009. All rights reserved. This material is reproduced with the permission of ASX. This material should not be reproduced, stored in a retrieval system or transmitted in any form whether in whole or in part without the prior written permission of ASX.

Extract in Chapter 6 from "Against the Gods: The Remarkable Story of Risk" by Peter Bernstein (© 1996) reprinted with permission of John Wiley and Sons, Inc.

Extract in Chapter 6 from the "Global Framework for Insurer Solvency Assessment" (© 2004), published by the International Actuarial Association (IAA), reproduced with permission. An electronic or hardcopy of the document is available for purchase from the IAA.

Extracts in Chapter 6 from the "Report on Special Purpose Entities," published by the Basel Committee on Banking Supervision BIS Joint Forum, reproduced with permission as follows:

> The BIS does not warrant or guarantee the accuracy, completeness, or fitness for purpose of the BIS material, and shall in no circumstances be liable for any loss, damage, liability or expense suffered by any person in connection with reliance by that person on any such material. The original texts are available free of charge from the BIS website (www.BIS.org).

Extracts in Chapter 12 from the Australian Accounting Standards Board's "Framework for the Preparation and Presentation of Financial Statements," paragraph 49(b) reproduced with permission as follows:

> © Commonwealth of Australia (2004)

> All legislation herein is reproduced by permission but does not purport to be the official or authorised version. It is subject to Commonwealth of Australia copyright. The Copyright Act 1968 permits certain reproduction and publication of Commonwealth legislation. In particular, s.182A of the Act enables a complete copy to be made by or on behalf of a particular person. For reproduction or publication beyond that permitted by the Act, permission should be sought in writing from the Commonwealth available from the Australian Accounting Standards Board. Requests in the first instance should be addressed to the Administration Director, Australian Accounting Standards Board, PO Box 204, Collins Street West, Melbourne, Victoria, 8007.

Extracts in Chapter 13 from Actuarial Standard of Practice No. 4 reprinted by permission of the American Academy of Actuaries. As the Academy may supplement, update, or amend such materials from time to time, parties should refer to www.academy.org (or http://www.actuarialstandardsboard.org/ as applicable) to confirm whether any changes or deletions have been made since the initial publication date.

All other quotes and extracts included in the text are reproduced with permission and sources are indicated.

Foreword

Understanding Actuarial Management: the actuarial control cycle was first published in 2003 by the Institute of Actuaries of Australia, in response to demands from Australian universities for a resource to support Part II of its education syllabus. Since that time, the Actuarial Control Cycle concept has been adopted as part of the education syllabus of many actuarial associations around the world, including the Society of Actuaries.

In planning this second edition, the Institute of Actuaries of Australia and the Society of Actuaries have partnered to produce a completely revised text, ensuring that the requirements of both professional bodies and those of the International Actuarial Association and the UK Actuarial Profession have been met. This collaboration has resulted in what we believe to be a global textbook, for a global profession.

The teams of editors, authors and reviewers who participated in this project were sourced from around the world, reinforcing the project's aims of global application. In particular, the commitment and dedication of the three editors of this edition, Clare Bellis, Richard Lyon and Stuart Klugman, have produced an extremely valuable resource for actuarial students in Australia, the US, Canada and around the world.

On behalf of the Institute of Actuaries of Australia, the Society of Actuaries and the rest of the profession, we offer our congratulations and sincere gratitude to the editors and authors of this second edition of *Understanding Actuarial Management: the actuarial control cycle*, for the exceptional contribution they have made to our future.

Bozenna Hinton   S. Michael McLaughlin
President   President
Institute of Actuaries of Australia   Society of Actuaries

March 2010

Contents

Foreword   vii

Preface   xxv

Chapter 1: Introduction   1
by the Editors

1.1	What this book is about	1
1.2	What is an actuary?	1
1.3	The control cycle framework	3
1.4	The structure of the book	4
1.5	An illustration of the Actuarial Control Cycle	5
1.6	Fred's coffee shop	6
1.7	Applying the control cycle framework	6
1.8	Communicating the results of actuarial work	6
1.9	Conclusion	7
CD Items		7
References (other than CD Items)		7

Fred's Coffee Shop – Risk Management Frameworks   9

Chapter 2: Risk Management Frameworks   11
by Ian Laughlin

2.1	Introduction		11
2.2	Risk management framework (RMF)		11
2.3	Large financial services providers		12
2.4	What is risk?		14
	2.4.1	Systemic and diversifiable risks	14
	2.4.2	Risk and reward	15
2.5	Types of risk		15
	2.5.1	Financial risks	16
	2.5.2	Non-financial risks	17
	2.5.3	Hazard risks and underwriting risks	17
	2.5.4	Formal definitions of risk types	18
2.6	What is risk management?		18
2.7	What is ERM?		18
	2.7.1	Defining ERM	19
	2.7.2	Forces supporting ERM	20
	2.7.3	Integration of ERM into planning	21
2.8	Risk management process		21
	2.8.1	Establish the context	22
	2.8.2	Identify risks	24
	2.8.3	Analyze risks	25
	2.8.4	Evaluate risks	29
	2.8.5	Treat risks	29
	2.8.6	Monitor and review	32

	2.9	Communicate and consult	32
		2.9.1 Documentation and reporting	32
		2.9.2 Risk management policy and/or strategy	34
	2.10	Execution	34
	2.11	Risk management interests, responsibilities and governance	35
		2.11.1 Shareholders	35
		2.11.2 Board of directors	35
		2.11.3 Board risk management committee and audit committee	36
		2.11.4 Senior management	37
		2.11.5 Chief Actuary	37
		2.11.6 Middle management and staff	38
		2.11.7 Customers (policyholders, bank depositors and borrowers, pension fund members etc)	38
		2.11.8 Regulators	39
		2.11.9 Service providers and intermediaries	39
		2.11.10 Employers as pension/superannuation fund sponsors	39
	2.12	Capital and risk management	40
	2.13	Critical success factors and causes of ERM failure	40
	2.14	Measurement of success	41
	2.15	Practical implications for actuaries	41
	2.16	Key learning points	42
	CD Items		42
	References (other than CD Items)		43
	Recommended further reading		44

Fred's Coffee Shop – Being Professional   45

Chapter 3: Being Professional   47
by Clare Bellis

	3.1	Introduction	47
	3.2	What is a profession?	48
		3.2.1 The characteristics of a profession	48
		3.2.2 The theory about why professions exist	49
		3.2.3 How the concept of a profession is changing over time	50
		3.2.4 How the concept of a profession varies from country to country	50
	3.3	The role of the professional body	52
		3.3.1 General comments	52
		3.3.2 The actuarial profession: the international level	53
		3.3.3 The national level	54
		3.3.4 Professional guidance	54
		3.3.5 Monitoring standards within the actuarial profession	56
		3.3.6 How do the codes apply to you?	57
	3.4	The regulatory role of the actuary	57
		3.4.1 General comments	57
		3.4.2 Prudential supervision	57
		3.4.3 Other customer protection	58
		3.4.4 Disclosure to third parties	59
		3.4.5 Examples of legislated roles for actuaries	59

3.5		Professional issues to consider while you work on any task	60
	3.5.1	Ethical behavior	60
	3.5.2	Conflicts of interest	61
	3.5.3	Consideration of other stakeholders	61
	3.5.4	Materiality	62
	3.5.5	Reliance on other experts	62
3.6		How to do a professional job	62
	3.6.1	Before you start	63
	3.6.2	Define the task	63
	3.6.3	Collect the information you need	63
	3.6.4	Check for reasonableness	63
	3.6.5	Communicating the results	64
3.7		Practical implications for actuaries	64
3.8		Key learning points	64
CD Items			65
References (other than CD Items)			65

Fred's Coffee Shop – The Need for Financial Products **67**

Chapter 4: The Need for Financial Products **69**
by Anthony Asher

4.1		Meeting needs	69
4.2		The financial life cycle	69
	4.2.1	Introduction to the financial life cycle	69
	4.2.2	Income	69
	4.2.3	Expenses	70
	4.2.4	Savings	70
	4.2.5	Different socio-economic classes	72
4.3		Risks and volatility in the life cycle	73
	4.3.1	Studies of household income, expenses and savings	73
	4.3.2	Income risks	73
	4.3.3	Expense risks	74
	4.3.4	Risks in savings	77
4.4		Business needs	78
	4.4.1	Equity or capital	78
	4.4.2	Managing risks	79
	4.4.3	Tax and regulatory arbitrage	80
4.5		Products designed to meet financial needs	80
	4.5.1	Monetary products	81
	4.5.2	Insurance	83
	4.5.3	Long-term savings products	90
	4.5.4	Retirement income products	95
4.6		Other sources of financial security	97
	4.6.1	Families	97
	4.6.2	Governments	98
	4.6.3	Employers	100
4.7		Practical implications for actuaries	101
4.8		Key learning points	101
CD Items			102
References (other than CD Items)			102

Fred's Coffee Shop – The Context of Actuarial Work   105
Chapter 5:   The Context of Actuarial Work   107
              by John Shepherd

        5.1   Why consider the context?   107
                 5.1.1   Introduction   107
                 5.1.2   Context: external forces   108
                 5.1.3   Context is not static   109
        5.2   Components of the context   109
        5.3   Two special components   111
        5.4   Government and judicial context   111
                 5.4.1   Government   111
                 5.4.2   Taxation   112
                 5.4.3   Social assistance and social insurance   112
                 5.4.4   Judicial decisions   113
        5.5   Physical environment   113
                 5.5.1   Climate and natural perils   113
                 5.5.2   Pandemics   114
                 5.5.3   Man-made disasters   115
                 5.5.4   Technological developments   115
        5.6   Economic and social environment   116
                 5.6.1   Economic conditions and trends   116
                 5.6.2   Demographic structure and trends 117
                 5.6.3   Work and employment patterns   118
                 5.6.4   Social factors and trends   119
                 5.6.5   Industrial issues   120
        5.7   Industry and business environment   120
                 5.7.1   Range of products and services offered   120
                 5.7.2   Convergence of financial institutions   121
                 5.7.3   Product distribution and intermediaries 121
                 5.7.4   Accounting standards and practices   124
                 5.7.5   Competition   124
                 5.7.6   Industry associations   125
                 5.7.7   Stakeholders   126
                 5.7.8   Corporate culture   127
                 5.7.9   Globalization   128
        5.8   Practical implications for actuaries   129
        5.9   Key learning points   129
        CD Items   130
        References (other than CD Items)   131

Fred's Coffee Shop – Applying Risk Management   133
Chapter 6:   Applying Risk Management   135
              by Stuart Wason

        6.1   Introduction   135
        6.2   Identifying risk   138
                 6.2.1   Identifying insurer risks   140
                 6.2.2   Identifying superannuation risks 147
                 6.2.3   Identifying funds management risks 149
                 6.2.4   Identifying banking risks   151

6.3	Risk assessment		152
	6.3.1	Quantitative versus qualitative assessment	153
	6.3.2	Experience data	153
6.4	Risk treatment		157
	6.4.1	Avoid	159
	6.4.2	Retain	160
	6.4.3	Reduce	162
	6.4.4	Transfer	162
	6.4.5	Exploit	165
	6.4.6	Reinsurance	165
6.5	Recent lessons learned		167
	6.5.1	Systemic connections more extensive than expected	168
	6.5.2	Misaligned incentives worsened the turmoil	168
	6.5.3	Insufficient consideration of extreme events	169
	6.5.4	Insufficient investor due diligence	169
6.6	Practical implications for actuaries		170
	6.6.1	Risk management is more than just risk models	171
	6.6.2	Each period of turmoil is different	172
6.7	Key learning points		172
	CD Items		173
	References (other than CD Items)		173

Fred's Coffee Shop – Regulation   **175**

Chapter 7:   Regulation   **177**
by Craig Thorburn

7.1	Introduction		177
	7.1.1	The sources of law	177
	7.1.2	Levels of regulation	178
	7.1.3	Types of law	179
7.2	The scope of laws that influence the financial sector and the work of actuaries		180
7.3	Types of regulation and the objectives of governments		181
	7.3.1	Taxation legislation	181
	7.3.2	The regulation of markets and companies	181
	7.3.3	Other objectives for regulation	184
	7.3.4	The regulation of specific types of business	185
	7.3.5	Prudential regulation	186
	7.3.6	Arguments for keeping regulation to a minimum	188
	7.3.7	Arguments in favor of regulation	189
7.4	International organizations that influence regulation		190
	7.4.1	International regulatory standards	190
7.5	Summary of core principles		192
7.6	Official roles for actuaries		192
7.7	The structure of regulation and supervisory institutions		193
7.8	Practical implications for actuaries		194
7.9	Key learning points		194
	CD Items		196
	References (other than CD Items)		196

Fred's Coffee Shop – Product Design   197

Chapter 8:   Product Design   199
              by Jeffrey Beckley
              8.1   Introduction   199
              8.2   Stage 1 of the product design control cycle   199
                      8.2.1   Identify the need for a new product   199
                      8.2.2   Develop a product strategy   202
              8.3   Stage 2 of the product design control cycle   207
                      8.3.1   Project management   207
                      8.3.2   Design features to control risks   209
                      8.3.3   Competition, the marketplace, and the pricing
                                 process   210
                      8.3.4   Stakeholder expectations   212
                      8.3.5   Deciding whether to launch the product 214
              8.4   Stage 3 of the product design control cycle   214
                      8.4.1   Distributing the product to our clients 215
                      8.4.2   Risk selection   218
                      8.4.3   Administration of the product   220
                      8.4.4   Asset-liability management   221
              8.5   Stage 4 of the product design control cycle   221
              8.6   Practical implications for actuaries   221
              8.7   Key learning points   222
              CD Items   223
              References (other than CD Items)   223

Fred's Coffee Shop – Modeling   225

Chapter 9:   Modeling   227
              by Andrew D. Smith
              9.1   Introduction   227
              9.2   Examples of models   227
                      9.2.1   Automobile insurance   227
                      9.2.2   Savings product with an investment guarantee   227
                      9.2.3   Fairness of insurance prices   227
                      9.2.4   Valuing pension benefits   228
                      9.2.5   Investment risks and returns   228
                      9.2.6   Setting dividend policy   228
                      9.2.7   Mortality improvement   228
                      9.2.8   Social behavior   229
              9.3   What is a model?   229
                      9.3.1   Case study – building a model of inflation and
                                 interest rates   229
                      9.3.2   Using a fitted model   236
                      9.3.3   Challenging a fitted model   237
              9.4   Normative approaches to modeling   238
                      9.4.1   Modeling in the physical and social sciences   238
                      9.4.2   Exploratory data analysis   239
                      9.4.3   Model calibration   240
                      9.4.4   Fit to evidence   241
                      9.4.5   Hypothesis testing   242

	9.4.6	Parsimony	244
	9.4.7	Fit to theory	245
	9.4.8	Computer technology development	247
	9.4.9	Using models for projection	248
	9.4.10	Bootstrapping	250
	9.4.11	Computational model classification	250
9.5	Limitations of the normative approach		253
	9.5.1	Practical difficulties	253
	9.5.2	Theoretical ambiguities	254
	9.5.3	Expecting the unexpected	255
9.6	Commercial modeling		255
	9.6.1	The role of modeling within the Actuarial Control Cycle	255
	9.6.2	Costs of models and data	256
	9.6.3	Robustness	257
	9.6.4	Governance and control	258
	9.6.5	Models for advocacy	259
	9.6.6	Models and markets	260
	9.6.7	Disclosure	261
9.7	Practical implications for actuaries		263
9.8	Key learning points		263
	CD Items		263
	References (other than CD Items)		264

Fred's Coffee Shop – Data and Assumptions   **265**

Chapter 10: Data and Assumptions   **267**
by Stuart Klugman

10.1	Introduction		267
10.2	Data		268
	10.2.1	Why is data critical to actuarial practice?	268
	10.2.2	Specifying data requirements	270
	10.2.3	Sources of data	272
	10.2.4	Obtaining high-quality data	273
	10.2.5	Data checks	274
	10.2.6	Data repair	277
	10.2.7	Missing or inadequate data	277
	10.2.8	Standards of practice and professional implications	277
	10.2.9	Challenges presented by limited data	278
10.3	Assumptions		280
	10.3.1	Why are assumptions critical to actuarial practice?	280
	10.3.2	The assumption-setting control cycle	281
	10.3.3	Identification of assumptions	281
	10.3.4	Quantifying assumptions	282
	10.3.5	Interdependency of assumptions	284
10.4	Practical implications for actuaries		284
10.5	Key learning points		285
	CD Items		285
	References (other than CD Items)		286

Fred's Coffee Shop – The Need for Capital   287

Chapter 11: The Need for Capital   289
            by David Knox

11.1   Introduction: what is capital?   289
        11.1.1   Types of capital   290
11.2   The reasons for capital   292
        11.2.1   Providing operational capital   292
        11.2.2   Withstanding fluctuations within ongoing operations 292
        11.2.3   Consumer confidence   292
        11.2.4   Withstanding unexpected shocks   293
        11.2.5   Ability to respond to future opportunities or capital
                  needs   293
        11.2.6   Credit rating   293
        11.2.7   Stability and confidence in the financial system 294
11.3   The need for capital: perspectives of different stakeholders 294
        11.3.1   Introduction   294
        11.3.2   The shareholders (ie the investors)   295
        11.3.3   The board and senior management   296
        11.3.4   Regulators   298
        11.3.5   Customers   298
        11.3.6   Rating agencies and market expectations   299
11.4   Financial institutions without shareholders   299
        11.4.1   Mutual organizations   300
        11.4.2   Superannuation funds   301
11.5   Risks and capital needs in financial institutions   302
        11.5.1   Asset risks   303
        11.5.2   Liability risks   305
        11.5.3   Asset/liability risks   306
        11.5.4   Operational risk   308
11.6   An overall company perspective   310
        11.6.1   Diversification benefits   310
        11.6.2   Economic versus regulatory capital   311
        11.6.3   Target surplus   312
        11.6.4   Capital allocation   312
11.7   Practical implications for actuaries   313
11.8   Key learning points   313
        CD Items   314
        References (other than CD Items)   314

Fred's Coffee Shop – Valuing Liabilities   315

Chapter 12: Valuing Liabilities   317
            by Richard Lyon

12.1   Introduction   317
        12.1.1   A brief history   317
        12.1.2   What are liabilities?   317
        12.1.3   Liabilities in the accounts   318
        12.1.4   Measuring liabilities   320
12.2   The nature of liabilities   320
        12.2.1   Short-term or long-term liabilities   321
        12.2.2   Types of liability   321

12.3	Measuring liabilities		323
	12.3.1	Best estimate liabilities	323
	12.3.2	Liabilities with margins	324
	12.3.3	Profit margins	325
	12.3.4	Market value of liabilities	326
	12.3.5	Calculation methodology	327
	12.3.6	Valuing guarantees and options	329
	12.3.7	Allowing for risk	331
	12.3.8	Other considerations	332
12.4	Profit and the liability valuation		334
	12.4.1	The valuation objective	335
	12.4.2	Liability valuation basis and total profit	340
	12.4.3	The accuracy of the valuation	341
	12.4.4	Intrinsic capital funding	342
	12.4.5	Liabilities and pricing	343
12.5	Practical valuation issues		343
	12.5.1	Materiality	343
	12.5.2	Sensitivity	343
	12.5.3	Data	344
	12.5.4	Projection assumptions	345
	12.5.5	Discount rates	347
12.6	Financial economics and discount rates		350
	12.6.1	Arbitrage-free pricing and state price deflators	350
	12.6.2	The risk-return trade-off: CAPM	351
	12.6.3	Actuaries and financial economics	353
12.7	Practical implications for actuaries		354
12.8	Key learning points		355
	CD Items		355
	References (other than CD Items)		356

Fred's Coffee Shop – Pricing 357

Chapter 13: Pricing 359

by Mark Rowley

13.1	Introduction		359
	13.1.1	What is pricing?	359
	13.1.2	Pricing process: application of the Actuarial Control Cycle	359
	13.1.3	What is covered in this chapter?	360
13.2	The environment in which actuaries operate		360
	13.2.1	Pricing objectives – competitiveness and profitability	360
	13.2.2	Stakeholders	361
13.3	Product design		361
	13.3.1	What is product design?	361
	13.3.2	Interaction of product design and pricing: an iterative process	361
13.4	Prices postulated		362
	13.4.1	Setting and testing prices	362
	13.4.2	Impact of prices and commission on sales	363
13.5	Modeling		363
	13.5.1	What is modeling?	364
	13.5.2	One pricing model	364

13.6	Assumptions	365
13.6.1	What are assumptions?	365
13.6.2	What process is used to set assumptions?	365
13.6.3	What is a margin?	366
13.7	Expenses	369
13.7.1	Analyzing expenses	369
13.7.2	Pricing for expenses	370
13.8	Profit objectives	372
13.8.1	What are profit objectives?	372
13.8.2	New business strain	372
13.8.3	Alternative profit measures	373
13.9	Profit testing	374
13.9.1	What is profit testing?	374
13.10	Sensitivity tests	379
13.10.1	What are sensitivity tests?	379
13.11	Pricing report	381
13.12	Product monitoring	382
13.13	Pricing for long-term commitments	383
13.13.1	What does it mean to price for long-term commitments?	383
13.13.2	Applying the Actuarial Control Cycle	383
13.13.3	Funding methods in general	384
13.13.4	Funding methods – accrued benefits	384
13.13.5	Funding methods – projected benefits	385
13.13.6	Funding methods – projected unit credit versus aggregate	385
13.13.7	Responsibility and authority for making choices	385
13.13.8	Wider applications	386
13.14	Practical implications for actuaries	386
13.14.1	What professional implications are most common in pricing?	386
13.14.2	Consideration of overheads in pricing	386
13.14.3	Actuarial assumptions and the future	387
13.15	Key learning points	388
	CD Items	389
	References (other than CD Items)	389

Fred's Coffee Shop – Assets   391

Chapter 14: Assets   393
by Richard Lyon

14.1	Introduction	393
14.1.1	What are assets?	393
14.1.2	Assets in the accounts	393
14.1.3	Asset valuation terms	394
14.2	Types of asset	396
14.2.1	Short-term or long-term assets	396
14.2.2	Non-investment assets	396
14.2.3	Investment assets	398
14.3	Valuing assets	402
14.4	Asset risks	405

14.5		Asset-liability management	409
	14.5.1	How assets relate to liabilities	409
	14.5.2	Basic asset-liability risks	410
	14.5.3	Cash flow matching	413
	14.5.4	Immunization	414
	14.5.5	"Appropriate" investment strategies	414
	14.5.6	Liability-driven investment	416
	14.5.7	Asset/liability modeling	417
14.6		Asset-liability management constraints	418
	14.6.1	Investment mandates	418
	14.6.2	Investment product offerings	418
	14.6.3	Legislative constraints	418
	14.6.4	Capital requirements	419
	14.6.5	Access to capital	419
	14.6.6	The impact of tax and fees	419
	14.6.7	The impact of negative returns	420
14.7		Practical implications for actuaries	420
14.8		Key learning points	420
CD Items			421
References (other than CD Items)			421

Fred's Coffee Shop – Solvency   423

Chapter 15: Solvency   425

by Shauna Ferris

15.1		Introduction	425
	15.1.1	Deciding on the acceptable level of solvency	425
	15.1.2	Solvency management and capital	426
	15.1.3	Three views of solvency	427
15.2		Cash flow solvency (or liquidity)	427
	15.2.1	Liquidity risk in normal conditions	427
	15.2.2	Liquidity risk in a crisis	428
	15.2.3	Managing liquidity risks	429
15.3		Discontinuance solvency and going-concern solvency: general approach	431
	15.3.1	Introduction	431
	15.3.2	Alternative forms of discontinuance	432
	15.3.3	Measuring discontinuance solvency	432
	15.3.4	Measuring going-concern solvency	433
15.4		Valuation of assets for solvency purposes	434
15.5		Valuation of liabilities for solvency purposes	435
	15.5.1	Methods for the valuation of liabilities	435
	15.5.2	Adjustments to reflect the impact of discontinuance on the liabilities	439
	15.5.3	Dealing with discretionary benefits	439
	15.5.4	How can we be sure that the value of liabilities is correct?	440
15.6		Capital requirements: the risk-based capital approach	440
	15.6.1	Introduction to risk-based capital	440
	15.6.2	Creating a risk-based capital standard	441
15.7		Risk-based capital: internal models	445

15.8   Integrating the capital management model into the
          control cycle   445
15.9   Assess the amount and quality of the capital   446
15.10   The role of risk management and market discipline in
          solvency regulation   449
          15.10.1   Introduction   449
          15.10.2   Internal risk management   450
          15.10.3   Reporting requirements and early warning systems   450
          15.10.4   Disclosure and ratings   451
          15.10.5   The role of the professional   452
          15.10.6   Financial condition reports   453
          15.10.7   Dynamic Solvency Testing   454
15.11   Responding to solvency problems   455
          15.11.1   Deciding when to intervene   456
          15.11.2   Deciding how to intervene   457
15.12   Guarantee funds   458
          15.12.1   Arguments for and against guarantee funds   458
          15.12.2   Design of guarantee funds   460
15.13   Practical implications for actuaries   462
15.14   Key learning points   462
          Answers to questions in Example 15.1   463
          CD Items   464
          References (other than CD Items)   465

Fred's Coffee Shop – Profit   469

Chapter 16: Profit   471

by David Service and Richard Lyon

16.1   Overview of profit   471
16.2   Profit measurement   472
          16.2.1   The traditional view of profit   473
          16.2.2   The modern view of profit   473
          16.2.3   Profit measurement versus solvency   474
16.3   The emergence of profit   474
          16.3.1   Sources of profit   474
          16.3.2   Timing of profit recognition   475
          16.3.3   Measurement issues   483
16.4   Profit versus value   484
16.5   Appraisal values   485
          16.5.1   Overview of appraisal values   485
          16.5.2   Components of an appraisal value   486
          16.5.3   Appraisal value as a profit measure   489
16.6   Practical implications for actuaries   489
16.7   Key learning points   490
          CD Items   490
          References (other than CD Items)   490

Fred's Coffee Shop – Monitoring Experience   493

Chapter 17: Monitoring Experience   495
by David Service

17.1	Introduction	495
17.2	Why do we analyze experience?	495
	17.2.1 Introduction	495
	17.2.2 Reviewing assumptions	495
	17.2.3 Providing understanding of the drivers of the emerging experience	496
	17.2.4 Developing a history of experience over time	496
	17.2.5 Aiding in an analysis of profit and its sources	496
	17.2.6 Providing information to management	496
	17.2.7 Providing information to shareholders and third parties	497
	17.2.8 Satisfying regulatory requirements	497
	17.2.9 Aiding public relations purposes	497
	17.2.10 Satisfying disclosure requirements in a listing or acquisition	497
17.3	What do we analyze?	497
	17.3.1 Introduction	497
	17.3.2 General insurance	498
	17.3.3 Life insurance	499
	17.3.4 Funds management	499
	17.3.5 Superannuation	499
	17.3.6 Banking	499
	17.3.7 Health insurance	500
17.4	How do we analyze experience?	500
	17.4.1 Introduction	500
	17.4.2 Product-specific	501
	17.4.3 Economic	504
	17.4.4 Investment performance	504
	17.4.5 Expenses	509
	17.4.6 Business volumes and business mix	518
	17.4.7 Profit and return on capital	519
17.5	Data issues	522
17.6	Practical implications for actuaries	523
17.7	Key learning points	523
	CD Items	525
	References (other than CD Items)	525

Fred's Coffee Shop – Responding to Experience   527

Chapter 18: Responding to Experience   529
by Bruce Edwards

18.1	Introduction	529
18.2	Role of the actuary	529
18.3	General considerations	530
18.4	Managing the business	531
	18.4.1 Business plans	531

	18.4.2	Financial control systems	531
	18.4.3	Audit controls	532
	18.4.4	Expense controls	533
	18.4.5	Claims controls	536
	18.4.6	New business and termination controls	537
	18.4.7	Capital management	538
18.5	Allocating interest to accounts		539
18.6	Unit pricing		542
18.7	Review of insurance pricing		544
	18.7.1	Pricing review cycle	544
	18.7.2	Pricing changes	544
	18.7.3	Pricing response	544
	18.7.4	Experience refunds	546
18.8	Defined benefit superannuation		546
	18.8.1	The actuarial review	546
	18.8.2	The pace of funding	547
	18.8.3	Responses to the actuarial review	547
	18.8.4	Returning excess funds to the employer	548
18.9	Participating life insurance		549
	18.9.1	The origins of the actuarial profession	549
	18.9.2	Participating policies	549
	18.9.3	Allocation and distribution of profit	550
	18.9.4	Allocation of profit	550
	18.9.5	Fair and equitable	550
	18.9.6	Distribution of profits	552
	18.9.7	Methods of distribution	553
	18.9.8	Asset share methods	554
18.10	Practical implications for actuaries		554
18.11	Key learning points		555
	CD Items		555

Fred's Coffee Shop – Applying the Actuarial Control Cycle   **557**

Chapter 19: Applying the Actuarial Control Cycle   **559**
by the Editors

19.1	Introduction	559
19.2	Advising on the viability and financing of a fiber optic cable project	559
	19.2.1 Background	559
	19.2.2 Developing a solution	560
	19.2.3 Comments on the fiber optic project	561
19.3	An application of the Actuarial Control Cycle to marketing problems	562
	19.3.1 Interview	563
	19.3.2 Comments on the marketing application	563
19.4	Risk management consulting	564
	19.4.1 Background	564
	19.4.2 Interview	564
	19.4.3 Comments on the risk management interview	566

19.5	A football tipping model		567
	19.5.1	Background	567
	19.5.2	Discussion	567
	19.5.3	Comments on the tipping example	570
19.6	Conclusion		570
	CD Items		571

Notes on Editors and Contributors   573

Glossary   581

Index   603

Preface to the Second Edition

The first edition of this book was published by the Institute of Actuaries of Australia (Institute) in 2003. It was written as a textbook for Part II of the Institute's education program but it has since been used around the world – especially by the Society of Actuaries (SOA), as a textbook for its Fundamentals of Actuarial Practice e-learning course.

A lot has happened since 2003 and it is now time for a new edition. This edition sees the following changes to the editorial team:

*   Clare Bellis has moved from Australia to the UK;

*   Australia-based Richard Lyon, who was a late addition to the editorial team for the first edition, has been involved in the second edition from the outset;

*   US-based Stuart Klugman has joined the team for the second edition; and

*   John Shepherd has retired and, apart from revising Chapter 5 as author, has not been involved in editing this edition.

The three editors for this edition therefore span the globe; regular editorial telephone calls took place in the afternoon (US Central Time), late evening (UK) and early morning (Australia).

We have taken the opportunity to revise the topics covered in the book. The number of chapters hasn't changed but we have added a chapter about Risk Management Frameworks (Chapter 2) and separated Data and Assumptions (Chapter 10) from Modeling (Chapter 9). At the same time, a single Assets chapter (14) replaces three investment chapters. One of the original investment chapters has been updated and is included as a supporting paper on the CD. In producing this new edition, we continued to take note of the IAAust's Part II (Actuarial Control Cycle) syllabus; and we also covered the equivalents in the International Actuarial Association (IAA), the Institute & Faculty of Actuaries and the SOA.

We have also added an index and a glossary.

Many of our original authors have returned to update their chapters but the addition of several new authors has allowed us to make the panel truly international. This, together with a range of backgrounds, means a diverse selection of examples.

As the chapters were written, they were extensively reviewed by experts around the world, as well as by current and recent students. We gratefully acknowledge the assistance of these reviewers, whose names are listed at the end of the book, and also the guidance provided by the members of the editorial steering committee. Any errors or omissions remain, of course, the responsibility of the editors and the authors of the individual chapters.

Finally, our thanks go to Carol Dolan, Actuarial Education Consultant at the Institute of Actuaries of Australia. Carol has overseen the project from start to finish and her patience, efficiency, creative suggestions and meticulous attention to detail have greatly lightened our load.

Clare Bellis, Richard Lyon and Stuart Klugman

March 2010

Chapter 1:   Introduction
by the Editors

1.1   What this book is about

In this book we explain the work of actuaries. We show how actuaries contribute to the design, construction and ongoing management of systems that provide a wide range of financial services. The typical reader of this book will be a student or actuarial trainee who has mastered the economic, financial, mathematical and statistical techniques of actuarial work. For these readers, we explain how actuaries use these techniques to provide advice to enterprises of many types, particularly in financial services. Readers from other backgrounds will also find the book useful for appreciating the work that actuaries perform.

Our emphasis is on the big picture of actuarial work, concentrating on the fundamental concepts that underpin actuarial work across both practice areas and countries. We do not cover the detail of laws, regulations, taxation rules, accounting standards and technical issues. Such detail is important for actuarial practice but not for our current purposes. You will build up your knowledge and understanding of the detail when you start to specialize in a particular practice area, either later in your studies or early in your working career.

Our overview of actuarial work will be structured around a framework called the Actuarial Control Cycle. The Actuarial Control Cycle represents the processes typically required in the ongoing management of a financial enterprise, product or scheme, and the relationships between those processes.

1.2   What is an actuary?

Chances are that you already have your own answer to this question. However, as it provides the foundation for this book, here is what three actuarial society websites say.

The Society of Actuaries (SOA, 2010) says:

> An actuary is a business professional who analyzes the financial consequences of risk. Actuaries use mathematics, statistics and financial theory to study uncertain future events, especially those of concern to insurance and pension programs. They evaluate the likelihood of those events and design creative ways to reduce the likelihood and decrease the impact of adverse events that actually do occur.

> Actuaries are an important part of the management team of the companies that employ them. Their work requires a combination of strong analytical skills, business knowledge and understanding of human behavior to design and manage programs that control risk.

The Actuarial Profession in the UK (AP, 2010) says:

> Most people will know something about the professions of accountants, doctors and lawyers. But tell someone you're an actuary and more than likely they will look at you blankly – never having heard of an actuary.

> If, however, they are aware of the work that actuaries do, they are likely to be impressed; being an actuary carries quite a reputation. This is partly due to the

difficult exams, but mostly due to the fact that actuaries are experts in a field that is renowned for its complexity and mathematical prowess.

Actuaries apply financial and statistical theories to solve real business problems. These business problems typically involve analysing future financial events, especially when the amount of a future payment, or the timing of when it is paid, is uncertain. A lot of actuaries' work might be thought of as 'risk management', assessing how likely an event may be and the costs associated with it.

Understanding how businesses operate, how legislation may impact and how financial economics can affect values are all vital skills for an actuary. But what differentiates actuaries is their core mathematical, economic and statistical understanding and their ability to apply this to real financial problems.

The Institute of Actuaries of Australia (IAAust, 2010) says:

Actuaries are among the brightest people in the business world. Actuaries apply their mathematical expertise, statistical knowledge, economic and financial analyses and problem solving skills to a wide range of practical business problems. Actuaries help organisations to understand the long-term financial implications of their decisions, many of which can affect individuals as well as the wider community.

Actuaries apply their skills in a variety of areas including:

- Measuring and managing risk and uncertainty
- Designing financial contracts
- Advising on investments
- Measuring demographic influences on financial arrangements
- Advising on a wide range of financial and statistical problems.

Leaving aside the sales pitch, it is clear that these three professional bodies all agree that actuaries solve business problems involving risk, particularly in a financial context.

Problem solving requires both a good understanding of the problem (and its context) and the tools to get the job done. Most readers of this book will already have the basic actuarial toolkit and will add to this toolkit throughout their actuarial education and beyond.

The actuarial profession has existed for over two centuries and originally concentrated on problems in long-term insurance and pensions (superannuation). For readers with an interest in the historical background, we have included on the CD some articles describing the development of actuarial science. Actuarial skills are, however, more widely applicable than just in the original areas of specialized practice. For example, solving problems involving the economics of distribution channels for any product is not really any different from solving problems connected with the economics of insurance sales.

Actuaries are also creative problem solvers. As the environment changes and new products are needed, actuaries are well-situated to adapt. The book includes examples of applications from a variety of practice areas and we encourage you to think, as you study each chapter, where else could these tools be applied? In the concluding chapter, we describe some applications from areas where actuarial skills would not have been applied even a few decades ago.

1.3 The control cycle framework

The Actuarial Control Cycle is a conceptual framework that is useful in describing the processes needed for the development and ongoing management of a financial enterprise, product or scheme. It is based on a simple problem-solving algorithm:

- define the problem;
- design the solution; and
- monitor the results.

The whole process, or control cycle, is conducted within an environment or context that shapes the decisions taken. The cycle is iterative: the three steps may be repeated or at any stage we may return to an earlier step.

This problem-solving process is universal. It applies to any field of activity. For example, a doctor will diagnose a patient's condition and recommend treatment. If the condition does not improve, the doctor will reassess the diagnosis and the treatment. The doctor's decisions will be shaped by the environment: the state of medical science, the availability of tests, drugs and procedures, the circumstances of the patient and so on. At each consultation, the doctor will make judgments about ongoing treatment, weighing up all the available evidence, including test results and the patient's progress since the last visit.

What makes the Actuarial Control Cycle distinctly actuarial is the nature of the work carried out at each stage of the cycle. The problem will usually (though not always) involve uncertain future cash flows. The process of defining the problem includes understanding the background, fully identifying all the issues and specifying them clearly to ensure that the client and the actuary agree on the work to be done. The design of a solution will almost always involve modeling. The actuary may have ongoing responsibility for monitoring the experience as it develops and advising on the response, or may seek to build flexibility into the solution.

Figure 1.1[1] The Actuarial Control Cycle

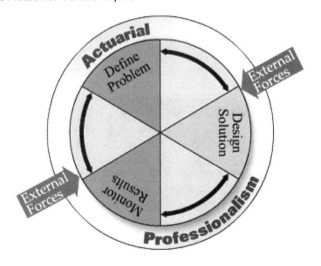

Figure 1.1 is a diagram of the Actuarial Control Cycle. In this diagram, we include the two components of the environment in which actuarial work is carried out. The actuary has to take account of external forces, such as economic conditions and the commercial setting. Then the whole process operates within the context of Professionalism, which is an inner guide to attitude and practice that governs the actuary in carrying out the work.

1.4   The structure of the book

The book contains seventeen chapters, each focusing on an aspect of the Actuarial Control Cycle, plus this *Introduction* and a final chapter on *Applying the Actuarial Control Cycle*. The order of the chapters roughly takes us round the cycle shown in Figure 1.1. However, the iterative nature of the cycle means that the topics are inter-related and we could easily have covered them in quite a different order. No topic can really be considered in isolation, so each author draws on concepts elsewhere in the book, both earlier and later. Generally, you should be able to understand each author's message without referring to the other chapters but the messages are likely to be clearer on your second reading of the book.

Chapters 2 to 7 cover the process of identifying and specifying the problem, including understanding the context. Our first topic, *Risk Management Frameworks* (Chapter 2), reflects the fact that actuarial problems typically deal with risk. A systematic framework helps us approach the problem, as well as helping the enterprises that actuaries advise to manage their risks. Next, *Being Professional* (Chapter 3) deals with the implications for an actuary of being a member of a profession. It is important that you understand these implications from the beginning, since they affect virtually everything an actuary does. *The Need for Financial Products* (Chapter 4) explains how products meet the needs of individuals and businesses. *The Context of Actuarial Work* (Chapter 5) describes how external forces must be allowed for by actuaries and the enterprises that they advise.

Next, we consider how businesses and regulators deal with risk. *Applying Risk Management* (Chapter 6) reviews how risk is managed in financial institutions, while *Regulation* (Chapter 7) discusses the impact of actions taken by governments, by courts and by other bodies that establish practices and accepted norms.

The next seven chapters cover the second stage: developing and implementing the solution. *Product Design* (Chapter 8) in some ways offers a solution: the development of a new product to meet some need. However, looked at from another perspective, the introduction of a new product is not an endpoint but the beginning of a whole new set of problems. How do we set a price for the product? How do we ensure that the product does not threaten the solvency of the provider? *Modeling* (Chapter 9), *Data and Assumptions* (Chapter 10), *Valuing Liabilities* (Chapter 12), *Pricing* (Chapter 13) and *Assets* (Chapter 14) provide the tools to help answer these questions. *The Need for Capital* (Chapter 11) comes in the middle of these chapters: you can think of this as representing the fact that capital is central to the Actuarial Control Cycle. Capital is needed to finance the cash outflows when expenses are incurred earlier than revenue is received and, most importantly for a financial institution, to absorb risks.

Four chapters cover the final stage of monitoring and responding to experience: *Solvency* (Chapter 15), *Profit* (Chapter 16), *Monitoring Experience* (Chapter 17) and *Responding to Experience* (Chapter 18). The Actuarial Control Cycle's feedback mechanism is explained, whereby monitoring outcomes leads to better understanding of both the problem and the solution, so that the solution can be improved.

Finally, we examine a number of examples from various types of actuarial work in *Applying the Actuarial Control Cycle* (Chapter 19).

Each chapter, covering a single topic, is written by a different author. As far as possible, we have allowed the author to speak in his/her own voice and to address the topic from his/her own perspective. This means that the writing style varies quite significantly. This presents challenges for the reader but reflects the realities of actuarial practice, where information must be gleaned from a variety of sources.

Throughout the book there are exercises to reinforce the concepts being discussed. Outline solutions can be found on the accompanying CD. The CD also contains articles for further reading. At the end of each chapter there is a list of the relevant items on the CD.

1.5   An illustration of the Actuarial Control Cycle

Let's review how the topics in this book fit together by considering a simple example. Suppose a life insurance company decides to sell lifetime annuities that increase in line with inflation. When the company sells an annuity, it immediately receives a large one-off payment (the single premium). Its commitment in return is to make regular, smaller, increasing payments for the lifetime of the customer. As this could be quite a long time, it is important that the company's risks are properly managed (Chapter 2). In particular, the actuaries advising the company have professional responsibilities (Chapter 3), because people will be entrusting a large part of their retirement savings to the company in exchange for a lifetime income.

What needs will these annuities meet and why will people want to buy them (Chapter 4)? What is the environment in which the company will offer these products (Chapter 5)? How are they taxed? Are competing products available? What is the outlook for interest rates, inflation rates and mortality rates?

The company must understand the sources of risk for these products, such as volatile inflation and increasing longevity (Chapter 6). And the regulators (Chapter 7) will also be concerned about risk.

The product has to be clearly specified (Chapter 8). Decisions are needed on design issues, such as whether or not the annuity has a guaranteed minimum payment period, what that period is and how inflationary increases are to be defined.

Once the product is specified, an actuary can develop a model to forecast the likely future cash flows for the product (Chapter 9). The actuary must analyze available data, both to shape the model and to help in setting assumptions (Chapter 10).

The model will be useful in a number of ways. First, it will help to determine the extent of the risk the company will face. The company needs to know how much capital (Chapter 11) to hold for these annuities, in case inflation is higher, or lifetimes are longer, than anticipated. The company needs to know the value of the long-term liability it will be taking on (Chapter 12).

Secondly, the model, including allowances for liabilities and capital, will help the company decide what prices, or premiums, to charge (Chapter 13) for the product, allowing for the risks involved and the interests of all stakeholders.

After meeting initial expenses, the balance of the single premium is invested in assets (Chapter 14) to generate income from which to make the regular annuity payments. The selection of assets must take into account the nature of the liabilities, so that the company meets its obligations and achieves its profit objectives without taking excessive risks.

At regular intervals, the company will compare its assets and liabilities to determine whether it has sufficient capital – in particular, whether it meets the capital requirements set by the regulators and is therefore solvent (Chapter 15).

Shareholders, and the taxation authority, will also be interested in how much profit (Chapter 16) is being earned from the lifetime annuities.

In designing, pricing and managing the product, the company will need assumptions about investment earnings, inflation rates, mortality rates and expenses in the future. Over time, the actual rates experienced will be compared with those assumed. Any differences must be analyzed and understood (Chapter 17). An actuary will advise the company how to respond in the light of trends and changes emerging from this monitoring of experience (Chapter 18).

In the control cycle framework, the feedback process closes the loop. In addition, at any point in the cycle, there can be a return to a previous step. For example, if the modeling process shows that the annuity product involves too much risk, the product design stage could be revisited, to seek an alternative product design that could meet the customers' needs at less risk to the company.

1.6   Fred's coffee shop

The example in Section 1.5 is a simplified description of a typical actuarial problem. To help guide you through this book, we have invented another, atypical, example: Fred's coffee shop.

Fred is an actuary in a large financial institution. He enjoys his job but he also wants to try something new. He has recently decided to resign and set up a coffee shop.

We introduce each chapter with a discussion of how it relates to the coffee shop. We have chosen a coffee shop because the situation should be familiar to every reader – and, because it is not a financial services example, it should help you to appreciate how the Actuarial Control Cycle is applicable outside the financial services industry.

1.7   Applying the control cycle framework

The control cycle framework can be applied to the management of an entire financial institution. It can also be applied to subdivisions of the whole, such as subsidiary companies (eg a reinsurance subsidiary or an overseas company), business units (eg funds management), operational functions (eg claims handling), product groups (eg retail banking products) and, of course, individual products (eg disability income insurance). You will recognize cycles within cycles in many situations.

1.8   Communicating the results of actuarial work

It is not the role of this book to discuss the principles and practice of good communication. This does not mean, however, that they are not important for actuaries. An effective actuary needs more than just technical knowledge and skills and experience in applying them.

An actuary might produce technically superb models, projections, estimates and analyses, but whether or not they lead to good decisions, sound strategies, appropriate solutions and effective plans depends on two things. Did the actuary fully understand the client's (or employer's) real needs? Did the client fully understand the actuary's advice? If both answers are "yes," then sound technical work will make a difference.

Both good listening and strong oral and written communication skills are essential for an actuary. An actuary has to communicate effectively with clients and employers – and also with other professionals, such as accountants, lawyers, marketers and IT specialists. Many projects on which actuaries work generate questions that actuaries are not qualified to answer, so advice must be sought from someone who is qualified to give it.

1.9   Conclusion

The Actuarial Control Cycle is a useful framework but it should not be viewed as a template for every piece of work. Some roles that actuaries fulfill deal with only one stage of the cycle, or may not seem to have any direct connection with the cycle. Nonetheless, within this framework you will find principles that will be applicable to all actuarial work.

CD Items

The Actuarial Profession (AP) 2009, History of the Actuarial Profession, www.actuaries.org. uk.

Mitchell, R. B. 1974, Excerpts from *From Actuarius to Actuary, The Growth of a Dynamic Profession in Canada and the United States*, Society of Actuaries.

References (other than CD Items)

The Actuarial Profession (AP) 2010, What is an Actuary?, http://www.actuaries.org.uk/careers/actuaries, accessed January 13, 2010.

Institute of Actuaries of Australia (IAAust) 2010, Frequently Asked Questions, http://www.actuaries.asn.au/AboutTheInstitute/FAQ, accessed January 13, 2010.

Society of Actuaries (SOA) 2010, What is an Actuary?, http://www.soa.org/about/about-what-is-an-actuary.aspx, accessed January 13, 2010.

Fred's Coffee Shop – Risk Management Frameworks

In the rest of this book, we will be introducing each chapter with a brief explanation of how it fits into the Actuarial Control Cycle. As Chapter 1 explained, we will be illustrating the principles by following the story of Fred's coffee shop.

The chapter you are about to read covers the use of a framework to manage risk. This chapter comes early in the book, because risk management is what the Actuarial Control Cycle is all about. The chapter introduces the idea of Enterprise Risk Management (ERM). As you will see, the important thing about ERM is that the enterprise, and the risks it faces, should be considered and managed as a whole.

In Fred's case, when we talk about an "enterprise," we are talking about Fred, his financial situation and personal life, his family if he has one, and even his connections and responsibilities to the wider community. He is planning a move from a salaried job working in an office to running and owning a small retail business. What risks will this bring? What factors should Fred take into account in considering what level of risk is acceptable?

Think about these questions for a few moments; then read on.

The financial risks include: not making enough money to live on; potentially losing the money put in to set up the business; not having any money coming in if Fred gets sick; and getting sued for large amounts if someone slips in some spilt coffee. Lifestyle risks include having to work long and unsociable hours.

How much Fred worries about these risks will depend on their impact, which is specific to his own circumstances. Earning a reasonable income is essential for the average person with children or other dependents. It may not be as important to someone with no responsibilities, or who has just won the lottery.

When he thinks about the risks, Fred also has to consider the benefits. He will gain the freedom and satisfaction of being his own boss. Perhaps he can give up commuting and become a part of the local community.

He has to think about the alternatives as well. Are there other forms of work that will offer the same benefits but fewer disadvantages?

Fred will also consider how he may be able to manage some of the risks. He can, for a price, insure against disability and liability claims. He could avoid the risk of investing in the business by assisting at or managing a coffee shop owned by someone else. Overall, Fred's decision whether to go ahead with his plans will depend on his risk appetite. If he is a cautious person, with dependents, he may decide that he should stick with a job that pays a regular salary. If he is much more adventurous then a coffee shop is unlikely to be the sort of high-risk, high-reward activity that he would enjoy.

There is a lot for Fred to think about. Having a framework will help him to organize his thoughts, identify the important risks and have a consistent method to deal with them. It will help him adapt quickly to change, including taking advantage of opportunities that may come along.

Chapter 2: Risk Management Frameworks
by Ian Laughlin

2.1 Introduction

This chapter begins with an explanation of what we mean by a risk management framework. To give context for what follows, it then gives an overview of entity structures and governance. It considers definitions of risk and its various types and introduces the concept of Enterprise Risk Management (ERM), and then the risk management process is discussed in some detail. This leads to discussion of stakeholders and responsibilities, and some of the tools and techniques used to support a risk management framework.

Note that there are no widely agreed definitions or taxonomy in the field of risk management, though there are many examples (including Kamiya et al, 2007) with consistent themes. In this chapter, for illustration we generally will use one or two of the definitions or terms available (noting sources where appropriate).

There are many different types of enterprise that operate in our community. Some are one-person businesses and others very large. There are enterprises whose main aim is to make money for their owners, while others, such as charities, exist for the benefit of third parties. Still others, such as clubs, exist for the benefit of their members.

These enterprises are structured in a variety of ways, but most of any size will have full-time management staff and some sort of oversight committee such as a board of directors. All of them are exposed to risks of one sort or another and so have an interest in risk management. For our purposes we will focus on risk management in large financial services providers (insurance companies, banks, pension/superannuation funds etc). However, much of what we cover is relevant for large and small enterprises of all types and even for individuals.

2.2 Risk management framework (RMF)

At the extremes, risks can be managed:

- in an ad hoc way – as and when some issue is looming or something actually goes wrong (which may or may not be done well); or

- systematically – proactively, based on a thorough understanding of risks, processes, controls, responsibilities etc.

The complexity and variety of risks inherent in the operation of most large businesses (particularly financial services providers) are such that they can only be managed effectively with the application of strong process and considerable discipline. To do this, there needs to be a clear risk management framework, based on a robust model, and clear supporting processes and reporting in place.

As the name implies, an RMF is the "system" in which risk management takes place in an entity and so has multiple elements.

It is useful to consider a number of views that support this idea:

APRA (2007) defines the RMF for an insurer as:

the totality of systems, structures, processes and people within the insurer that identify, assess, mitigate and monitor all internal and external sources of risk that could have a material impact on an insurer's operations.

AS/NZS 4360 states that the RMF is:

the set of elements of an entity's management system concerned with managing risk.

NOTE 1: Management system elements can include strategic planning, decision making, and other strategies, processes and practices for dealing with risk.

NOTE 2: The culture of an entity is reflected in its risk management system.

The FSA (2006) does not define an RMF as such, but states that:

A *firm* must take reasonable steps to ensure the establishment and maintenance of a business plan and appropriate systems for the management of prudential risk.

The IAIS (2008) states that:

1. As part of its overall governance structure, an insurer should establish, and operate within, a sound Enterprise Risk Management (ERM) framework which is appropriate to the nature, scale and complexity of its business and risks.

2. The ERM framework should be integrated with the insurer's business operations and culture, and address all reasonably foreseeable and relevant material risks faced by the insurer in accordance with a properly constructed risk management policy.

Note the all-encompassing nature of these definitions and comments. Our references to an RMF are made in this context.

2.3   Large financial services providers

Most financial services providers have shareholders (that is, owners), but many are "mutual" in structure, in that they have no shareholders and they exist purely for the benefit of their members/customers. Mutual enterprises include company pension/superannuation funds, some building societies (savings and loan societies) and some insurance companies.

To give context as we discuss risk management, it will help if we first outline in simple terms how large businesses are typically organized and managed. For our purposes, we will focus on entities with shareholders, but the principles hold for mutuals (with members in place of shareholders and sometimes trustees in place of a board of directors).

Table 2.1   Typical corporate structure

Board of Directors (the *board*)	Represents interests of shareholders. Directors elected by shareholders. Large businesses usually have a majority of non-executive (or outside) directors. Board oversees management's performance; hires and fires Chief Executive Officer (CEO); approves strategy; responsible for overall governance.
CEO/Managing Director/President	In charge of running the business and responsible for its overall performance; accountable to the board.
Senior Management – business unit/line managers	Responsible for the performance of a subset of the overall business (eg motor insurance business) or a country's business. Report to CEO.
Senior Management – function heads/staff managers (human resources, information technology, finance, actuarial, risk management etc)	Provide support to business units and to wider entity. Examples include Chief Financial Officer and Chief Information Officer. Report to CEO.
Middle Management	Report to senior management and generally responsible for day-to-day operations.
Staff	Report to middle management and provide the "manpower."

The framework for the working relationships in this sort of structure is often referred to as *corporate governance.*

According to the OECD (2004):

> Corporate governance involves a set of relationships between a company's management, its board, its shareholders and other stakeholders. Corporate governance also provides the structure through which the objectives of the company are set, and the means of attaining those objectives and monitoring performance are determined. Good corporate governance should provide proper incentives for the board and management to pursue objectives that are in the interests of the company and its shareholders and should facilitate effective monitoring.

According to the European Central Bank (2004), corporate governance involves:

> Procedures and processes according to which an organization is directed and controlled. The corporate governance structure specifies the distribution of rights and responsibilities among the different participants in the organization – such as the board, managers, shareholders and other stakeholders – and lays down the rules and procedures for decision-making.

According to the Australian Securities Exchange (2007):

> Corporate governance is "the framework of rules, relationships, systems and processes within and by which authority is exercised and controlled in corporations". It encompasses the mechanisms by which companies, and those in control, are held to account. Corporate governance influences how the objectives

of the company are set and achieved, how risk is monitored and assessed, and how performance is optimized. Effective corporate governance structures encourage companies to create value, through entrepreneurialism, innovation, development and exploration, and provide accountability and control systems commensurate with the risks involved.

It is clear from this that good corporate governance demands that a business have clearly articulated objectives, with a robust framework to support those objectives.

Inevitably, there are risks to achieving those objectives. Some risks are taken deliberately in the sense that they are inherent in the venture and the business is seeking the rewards that potentially flow from those risks. Other risks are unwanted. Both types of risk need to be managed to achieve the optimal outcome – the first type to maximize the reward for the risks taken and the second to mitigate the risk as much as practicable.

Later on, we will discuss where responsibility lies for risk management. First, however, we need to better understand what we mean by risk and risk management.

Exercise 2.1

From the internet, obtain a copy of an annual report of a major financial services provider that you are familiar with and review the comments on structure (management and board) and what they say about their corporate governance.

2.4   What is risk?

At a simple level, we all operate in a world of uncertainty, because the future cannot be accurately predicted. Uncertainties that could lead to an adverse outcome are *risks*. Many (though not all) such risks can also lead to positive outcomes. Modern risk management is concerned with both positive and adverse consequences of risks.

More formally, *risk* can be (and is) defined in a variety of ways. Sometimes the definition used depends on the context. For example, if the focus was on investment then the definition may refer to investment results that differ from those expected. Often there will be reference to impact and likelihood. For our purposes we will use the definition in AS/NZS 4360: "the chance of something happening that will have an impact on objectives."

You will see the close link in this statement to the importance placed on objectives in the discussion of corporate governance above.

For some other useful definitions of risk (and of the various risks that we discuss in this chapter), you could refer to the internet, including Investopedia and Investorwords.

2.4.1   Systemic and diversifiable risks

Some risks are *systemic* in nature in that they are inherent in a particular "system." For example, the risk of failure of the banking system as a whole and inflation risk are *systemic risks*. If there is exposure to the system in question then there is exposure to the risks to that system. Systemic risks cannot be reduced by diversification.

Likewise, investment in a particular market (for example, the US stock market) results in exposure to the risks inherent in that market (for example, a decision by government to increase corporate taxation) and cannot be reduced by diversification within that market. This sort of risk is called *market* or *systematic* risk.

Other risks can be mitigated by diversification. For example, investing in the shares of a particular business has a risk that it will perform poorly relative to other businesses – that is, there is risk that is specific to the individual business. This risk may be mitigated by investing in more than one business, as each business will be exposed to different risks that are unlikely to occur at the same time. That is, the risk can be reduced through diversification and is thus a *diversifiable risk.*

2.4.2   Risk and reward

Some risks are taken deliberately – for the potential reward. All business ventures have such risks and shareholders provide capital hoping to gain the rewards from these risks. An example of such a risk might be the expansion of a business to a new country. This could be quite expensive and may not work for a variety of reasons, but there may be substantial rewards if it succeeds.

It is important to understand that, by and large, the market works in such a way that the larger the potential reward, the higher the risk – that is, the probability of not achieving the reward is also higher. If this did not occur, then inevitably capital would be drawn to higher returns without consideration of risk. In other words, there is a trade-off between risk and reward. One of the challenges for any business is to get this balance right.

The importance of the opportunity inherent in many risks is supported by AS/NZS 4360, which notes:

> Although the concept of risk is often interpreted in terms of hazards or negative impacts, this Standard is concerned with risk as exposure to the consequences of uncertainty, or potential deviations from what is planned or expected. The process described here applies to the management of both potential gains and potential losses.

Of course, higher risk does not necessarily indicate a higher potential reward. Indeed, for some risks there is no potential reward at all. Rather they only expose the business to financial costs or other adverse outcomes. A simple example of this would be an administrative error that leads to a product being sold for an incorrect price.

2.5   Types of risk

There are not yet universally accepted classifications of risks, so care needs to be taken with terminology and interpretation.

At the highest level, there are financial and non-financial risks. Each of these can be further broken down into lower-level risk types.

2.5.1 Financial risks

2.5.1.1 Credit risk

Most businesses extend credit to customers and other parties – for example, allowing 30 days for a customer to pay for goods or services. Some businesses, such as banks and building societies, provide credit as a fundamental part of their business – for example, lending for home purchase, or for a business purpose, or providing credit card services. Provision of such credit involves risks that interest won't be paid as required or the loan amount won't be repaid in full and on time. This is called *credit risk.*

This is an example of a risk that offers a reward – for example, a bank expects to make a profit from its lending activities. The subprime lending behind the global financial crisis of 2008 vividly illustrates that the risk/reward balance can get out of control if poorly managed.

Investments (for example by a pension fund) in fixed-interest securities such as company or municipal bonds also involve credit risk.

2.5.1.2 Market risk

Any investment is carried out in the context of a market of some sort. For example, there is the stock market, or the property market, or the fixed-interest securities market, or the currency market. Any investment thus carries a risk that the relevant market will perform poorly, irrespective of the merits of the individual investment. Thus an investment in the shares of IBM, for example, necessarily involves exposure to the US stock market. This is called *market risk.*

Market risk is another example of a risk that offers reward. In contrast to credit risk where the reward is generally clear, the reward for market risk can vary greatly.

2.5.1.3 Liquidity risk

A business has income from its activities (eg sales proceeds for goods it makes and sells) and it has outflow (eg costs of its raw materials, and staff wages). The resultant cash flow can be irregular and at times negative, even for a successful business. Any shortage of cash can be addressed in a variety of ways – eg by capital provided by the owners, by credit provided by suppliers, by credit provided by banks, or by long-term loans provided by banks or other investors. However there can be occasions – because of market conditions, or perhaps because of worries about the particular business – when sources of cash dry up, causing real problems. The global financial crisis of 2008 generated massive liquidity issues for many companies. This is known as *liquidity risk.*

Exercise 2.2

Consider a retail bank that accepts deposits, operates checking accounts, lends for house purchases and business purposes, issues credit cards etc. What liquidity risks is such a business exposed to and how do you think it might manage such risks? What particular aspect of its business model caused problems for the UK bank, Northern Rock, when it found itself in financial difficulty in 2007?

2.5.2 Non-financial risks

2.5.2.1 Operational risk

Any enterprise is supported by its staff, the processes they follow and the systems they use in its operation. This may not always go as planned – mistakes can be made, accidents occur, systems can fail, etc – and this can cause damage in one way or another. This may be a function of people, process, or systems.

The enterprise also has to respond to external events such as government decisions, or changes in market conditions, any of which may have positive or negative consequences.

These are all *operational risks*.

Most operational risks do not offer any reward for the risk taken.

2.5.2.2 Strategic or business risk

A well-run enterprise will have a clear strategy for outperforming its competitors and achieving its objectives. This might include, for example, a focus on niche markets for its services; being a "first mover" in its field in adopting new technology; or having a lower cost base than its competitors. Clearly, some strategies will work better than others and some will not work effectively at all. This is called *strategic risk* or *strategy risk* or *business risk.*

2.5.2.3 Other risks

Various other risks (often included in operational risk) include:

- *application* or *implementation risk*. This is the risk that, while the theory or intent behind a decision or action may be appropriate in the context of an entity's governance, strategy and/or risk management objectives, the implementation of the decision fails;
- contagion and related party risk;
- competition risk;
- reputational risk;
- legal and judicial risk;
- regulatory and/or political risk;
- technological change risk;
- extreme events risk;
- social attitudes change risk; and
- environment change risk.

This list above is not exhaustive and its components are not necessarily mutually exclusive. It does, however, provide a useful foundation for our purposes.

2.5.3 Hazard risks and underwriting risks

Sometimes, a subset of the operational risks above is classified as *hazard risks*. These would normally include fire, natural perils, crime, injury and liability. Some insurance companies are in the business of providing financial protection for individuals or enterprises against hazard risks. This requires considerable expertise and there is a risk (called *underwriting risk*) that it will not be done as well as it should be. For example, the premium rate for a particular hazard could be set too low, or claims might be paid or denied inappropriately.

2.5.4   Formal definitions of risk types

There are various sources of more detailed and formal definitions of the various risk types, including:

- Casualty Actuarial Society (2003);
- International Actuarial Association (2004);
- Basel Committee on Banking Supervision (2006), known as "Basel II"; and
- CEA and Groupe Consultatif Actuariel Europeen (2007), the glossary for what is known as "Solvency II".

Exercise 2.3

Do a search on the internet and find out what you can about the underlying reasons for the 2008 global financial crisis. What types of risk were of most consequence?

2.6   What is risk management?

Again there is no generally accepted definition of risk management, but usually a definition would have at its heart a systematic (as opposed to ad hoc or reactive) approach to managing the impact of risks to the achievement of the business's objectives. This typically includes steps like identifying, analyzing, evaluating and treating risks.

AS/NZS 4360 defines risk management as:

> the culture, processes and structures that are directed towards realizing potential opportunities whilst managing adverse effects

Less formally, AS/NZS 4360 states "Risk management involves managing to achieve an appropriate balance between realizing opportunities for gains while minimizing losses." This supports the point made about the risk/reward balance in 2.4.2.

So it is important to note that risk *management* is much more than risk *avoidance* or risk *reduction.*

We will explore risk management throughout the rest of this chapter.

2.7   What is ERM?

The concept of ERM is gathering momentum around the world, in both financial services and the broader business community. It is rising on the agenda for company boards, including in their capacity as employers and pension fund sponsors.

The fundamental idea is that:

- an enterprise faces a wide (and potentially evolving) variety of risks to successful achievement of its objectives;

- these risks need to be managed in a way that reflects not only the individual risks but their cumulative impact on the business; and

- risks should be managed to maximize the value generated for shareholders given the risks to which it is (or would like to be) exposed.

This implies the need to understand not only each risk in isolation but also its interaction with other risks and risk types and events, so that the overall behavior of the business can be properly managed in accordance with its strategy and objectives. Some benefit may result from this because of the lack of correlation amongst some of the risks, or there may even be negative correlation in some cases, which may provide a natural hedge. For example, rather than just looking at operational risk and market risk separately, they would also be considered together, their interaction understood and their management coordinated to ensure an optimal outcome.

Concentration of risks (such as a geographic one for a property insurer) is in some ways the antithesis of diversification and should also be understood and managed.

Maximizing value for shareholders includes understanding and exploiting the diversification of risks (as we discussed in 2.4.1) and ensuring that rewards are appropriate for the risks taken.

The idea of managing a portfolio of disparate risks holistically is relatively new and still developing – and it is difficult to implement well. Not only is there a wide range of risks to consider but an understanding of the interactions between different risks is needed in the context of the entity being managed. Further, ERM can involve significant change in thinking and priorities, and any wide-ranging change in an established large organization can be quite difficult to execute. This might be because of complexity, bureaucracy, lack of commitment, general reluctance to change or other reasons. Given that many (but not all) financial institutions have survived, and indeed thrived, over relatively long periods, there can be some resistance to the need to adopt ERM. The state of ERM implementation thus varies considerably from enterprise to enterprise.

Further discussion can be found in Tripp et al (2008) and Section 1.3 of IAA (2009).

2.7.1 Defining ERM

There are various formal definitions of ERM but, as suggested above, common features include a holistic approach to risk across the entity and a focus on value optimization rather than risk reduction.

This definition from the Casualty Actuarial Society (CAS) is a good example:

> ERM is the process by which organizations in all industries assess, control, exploit, finance, and monitor risks from all sources for the purpose of increasing the organization's short and long term value to its stakeholders.

The following is taken from the Committee of Sponsoring Organizations of the Treadway Commission (COSO):

> Enterprise risk management is a process, effected by an entity's board of directors, management and other personnel, applied in strategy setting and across the enterprise, designed to identify potential events that may affect the entity, and manage risk to be within its risk appetite, to provide reasonable assurance regarding the achievement of entity objectives.

The definition reflects certain fundamental concepts. Enterprise risk management is:

- A process, ongoing and flowing through an entity
- Effected by people at every level of an entity
- Applied in strategy setting
- Applied across the enterprise, at every level and unit, and includes taking an entity level portfolio view of risk
- Designed to identify potential events that, if they occur, will affect the entity and to manage risk within its risk appetite
- Able to provide reasonable assurance to an entity's management and board of directors
- Geared to achievement of objectives in one or more separate but overlapping categories

2.7.2 Forces supporting ERM

Forces driving support for ERM are both internal and external to entities and include:

- sharper focus on ERM by rating agencies, as evidenced in Standard & Poor's (2007);
- regulatory change, including:
  - ○ internationally – for example, Basel II for banking around the world, and Solvency II for insurance companies in Europe;
  - ○ nationally – for example, APRA and FSA regulations in Australia and the UK respectively;
- specific laws – for example Sarbanes-Oxley legislation in the US;
- listing requirements of stock exchanges, which highlight the importance of risk management – for example the Australian Securities Exchange (ASX) or the New York Stock Exchange (NYSE);
- losses generated by many more complex organizations in recent years as a direct result of poor or inadequate risk management across the business;
- growing appreciation of the value that can arise through controlled risk taking;
- increasing recognition of the complexity and interdependency of markets and risks, accentuated by increasing globalization and the pervasive impact of technology;
- rapid development of financial products, such as derivatives, and their use in retail products as well as in financial risk management;
- improved understanding of risk-based capital and its use by regulators;
- understanding and use of risk-adjusted returns; and
- increasing sophistication of risk management techniques.

The management and quantification of certain financial risks lies at the core of actuarial work. However there is a wider universe of risks, which interact with each other and which affect the success of entities. These are all managed under the ERM banner. This means that actuaries need to acquire a well-developed understanding of modern methodologies, techniques and thinking, including the broader and more qualitative aspects of risk management.

2.7.3 Integration of ERM into planning

A well-run organization conducts detailed planning and then manages its business around those plans. These plans set out what the business is trying to achieve and how it intends to get there. Typically, there are higher level plans – strategic plans – and lower-level plans – operational or business plans. These plans are usually reviewed each year. It is critical that the plans address the major risks to the business. Without this, they could completely misrepresent the likelihood of achieving the business objectives. The concept of ERM, with its holistic approach, lends itself well to strategic and operational planning, which also necessarily addresses the complete enterprise.

Following any strategic planning exercise something significant in the business may change. For instance, the company may choose to develop new products, expand into other markets, change the operational model of the business or launch something completely new.

Any change to a business brings risks with it. Equally, deciding to operate the same business model without change can bring risks as changing market conditions render obsolete business models that were previously effective. Whenever business objectives are set or changed as part of a strategic planning exercise, it is prudent to conduct a risk assessment of the objectives and their effects upon the business.

Thus it can be seen that ERM is an important part of any strategic planning exercise and should be embedded in the planning process.

Exercise 2.4

As an extension of Exercise 2.3, find out what is said about risk management, and consider how consistent it is with the concept of ERM.

2.8 Risk management process

Another key element of an RMF is a disciplined risk management process. This ensures that the entity's people are clear on what they need to do to fulfill their ERM duties.

There are several established risk management process models in operation around the world including ones from FERMA (2002) and from COSO (2004). Another commonly used in Australia, and having considerable recognition overseas, is AS/NZS 4360 (2004). AS/NZS 4360 was the first official risk management standard in the world and has been adopted not only in Australia and New Zealand but by government agencies in Canada and the UK, and as the stated basis for the CAS risk management process.

An international standard, ISO 31000, is in the process of development at the time of writing. The ISO 31000 process model is partly based on AS/NZS 4360.

The AS/NZS 4360 risk management process is set out in Figure 2.1 below.

Figure 2.1   AS/NZS 4360 risk management process overview

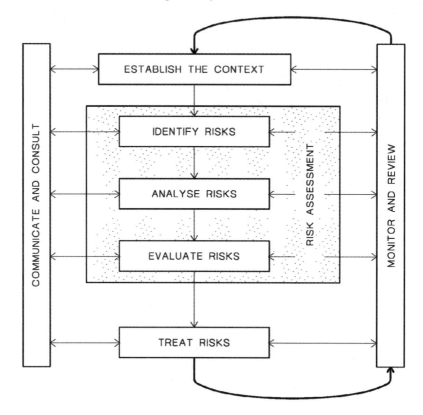

A summary of the seven elements in the AS/NZS 4360 process is provided in the following sections together with commentary on certain important aspects in each step.

Note the inherent use of a cycle – a high-level application of a control cycle. The issue is identified and characterized, solutions are put in place, and then results are monitored and changes made as required.

Exercise 2.5

Map each step in the AS/NZS 4360 process against the Actuarial Control Cycle. Are they consistent?

2.8.1   Establish the context

AS/NZS 4360: Establish the external, internal and risk management context in which the rest of the process will take place. Criteria against which risk will be evaluated should be established and the structure of the analysis defined.

To ensure a robust footing for risk management, it is essential that the overall context for risk management is well understood and accounted for. This includes the external environment, the internal environment and the context for the particular risk management exercise being addressed.

The external environment includes anything of relevance to the risk management of the business. Major examples include:

- the legal and regulatory framework – particularly important in the financial services industry, which is heavily regulated;

- social expectations – regarding the physical environment, climate change etc;

- the market in which the business is operating, its competitors etc;

- the state of the economy; and

- relationships with other stakeholders.

The internal environment includes everything within the business of relevance to risk management. Major examples include:

- the objectives and strategy of the business;

- the resourcing and capabilities of the business – people, systems, capital etc;

- the risk appetite and risk tolerance (see below) set down by the board and senior management; and

- attitudes of internal stakeholders.

Finally, the circumstances of the particular risk management exercise need to be considered. For example, risk management of a large project might need to take account of:

- project scope;

- project objectives, time frame etc;

- budgeted costs and margins;

- resourcing; and

- roles and responsibilities.

Once the context is clear, it is necessary to establish what elements of the context are most important from a risk management perspective – in other words, the criteria for assessing risks for the particular risk management exercise. These could range from simple (eg purely financial) through to a complex set of criteria based on multiple aspects of the context. This could include, for example, reputation; compliance with regulations; achieving budget; and meeting timetable.

It may be that the criteria emerge over a few iterations of the process (note the feedback loops in Figure 2.1).

2.8.1.1   Risk appetite and risk tolerance

Risk appetite and *risk tolerance* are two particularly important criteria.

As mentioned earlier, shareholders place their capital at risk in a company with the aim of achieving a satisfactory return.

But how much risk are they prepared to take? What is their *risk appetite*?

One of the jobs of the board (as representatives of the shareholders) is to answer this question in a pragmatic way so that management can run the business accordingly. This is far from a simple task. It needs to reflect information previously provided to shareholders about the company, feedback from shareholders and the board's own views. It then needs to be translated into clear and unambiguous language.

Usually, risk appetite is specified at a high level. This may be qualitative (eg it might include something like "we have a low appetite for financial risk") or quantitative (eg "it is essential that we maintain an A rating"). Ideally, the statement of risk appetite should not encourage an unduly conservative approach – for example, a property company might make it clear that "we are in the business of property development and recognize the risks that this poses, particularly in an economic downturn." The example given above could be extended along these lines: "it is essential that we maintain a rating of at least A but we do not seek a rating as high as AAA."

Usually, the focus is on shareholders when risk appetite is set. However, for financial services providers and their intermediaries, it is also necessary to consider the risk appetite of customers. History is littered with examples of people losing substantial proportions of their savings through events whose risk was either hidden or poorly disclosed.

Often, the high-level risk appetite is supported by quantified tolerances for particular risks or parts of the business. This helps translate the risk appetite into meaningful limits for operational purposes. For example, there might be no tolerance for a negative return on an investment portfolio more frequently than one year in ten, or no tolerance for a negative return at all. In both cases, the expressed tolerance will clearly dictate the nature of the assets in the portfolio and how they are to be managed, leading to very clear guidelines for the responsible staff.

The requirements of regulators and the criteria used by rating agencies will also generally be taken into account in setting the risk appetite and risk tolerance.

Further discussion may be found in Bennet and Cusick (2007).

2.8.2   Identify risks

> AS/NZS 4360: Identify where, when, why and how events could prevent, degrade, delay or enhance the achievement of the objectives.

Having established the context and in particular the strategic objectives, it is then necessary to identify the risks within the scope of the risk management exercise. At first this may seem trivial but this is far from the case, because:

- some risks will be obvious to some people and not to others – perhaps because of differing experiences or knowledge;

- risks change over time – perhaps because of changing market conditions;

- new risks emerge – perhaps due to changes in the market, technology, business model, competition etc;

- some risks are there but are simply missed or glossed over – an example of this is the impact of the sharp reduction in credit availability in 2008 on businesses that were unprepared for such an issue; and

- some risks are acknowledged but poorly understood.

So it is essential that there is a rigorous process of identifying risks on a regular basis. The first time this is done requires most effort of course, but subsequent iterations are just as important, not least because of the danger of familiarity undermining the process.

There are various ways of identifying risks and various parties who can sensibly contribute. The main thing is that there is a rigorous process for identification, that the right people are involved and that there is appropriate challenge and review.

It is useful to have both top-down and bottom-up exercises. So, for example, senior management (and possibly the board) could engage in a brain-storming session to capture the major risks from their perspective. At the same time, middle management and their staff could be asked to identify all of the risks that they can think of in relation to their particular responsibilities. They are closest to the action and often have the deepest insights into what the risks are and how well they are controlled.

These two perspectives then need to be brought together. The top-down outcomes are likely to inform those doing the bottom-up work and vice versa, so a further iteration may be necessary to ensure consistency.

Sometimes consultants are engaged to contribute as they may have a broader perspective and be aware of what other companies consider to be their major risks.

As part of the identification process, each risk should also have noted:

- a clear explanation of the risk;
- the controls in place to mitigate the risk;
- the effectiveness of these controls;
- the person(s) responsible for exercise of the controls; and
- the checks and balances to ensure that controls are exercised as planned and that they work as intended.

2.8.3 Analyze risks

> AS/NZS 4360: Identify and evaluate existing controls. Determine consequences and likelihood and hence the level of risk. This analysis should consider the range of potential consequences and how these could occur.

Armed with the information gathered in the identification process, management can then analyze the risks. This is about understanding, for each significant risk, the likelihood of the risk eventuating – and, in that event, the impact on the business.

Together likelihood and impact give an assessment of the significance or level of a risk. Sometimes this is represented as follows:

> risk = impact × likelihood

Both impact and likelihood can be considered qualitatively and quantitatively, or somewhere in between. A quantitative analysis provides most useful information, but often it is not possible or practicable to do the calculations. This is where a qualitative analysis by knowledgeable and expert people can be very powerful, as often they are able to bring a deep understanding to the process.

A simple qualitative approach might involve classifying risks along these lines:

> impact: high, medium or low

> likelihood: likely, medium or unlikely

A combination of "high" impact and "likely" likelihood might be rated as a high risk overall; a medium/medium, low/likely or high/unlikely as medium overall; and low/unlikely as low overall; etc.

A semi-quantitative approach would build on this by giving a numerical range for each rating. For example, a high impact might be $10 million to $50 million, a medium impact $1 million to $10 million and a low impact less than $1 million.

A more complete quantitative analysis involves a detailed assessment of impact and likelihood, as shown in Figure 2.2 (sometimes called a *risk heat map*). The shading indicates the overall risk rating; white is a high rating. Because it is not practical to quantify some risks in financial terms (eg reputational damage or human safety), another means of rating the impact is needed. There might be a few headings under which such impacts are considered, such as regulation, staff, customers and reputation, with impact defined on a five-point scale. For example, Level 1 impact under reputation might be "no adverse publicity at all" and Level 5 might be "prolonged and extensive very adverse publicity in the national press." As another example, Level 1 impact under staff might be "no widespread concern amongst staff at all" and Level 5 impact might be "loss of a number of key executives; staff turnover above X%; or loss of life."

It is helpful if both financial and other types of impact rating can be shown on the risk heat map to give a complete picture, as illustrated below.

Figure 2.2   A sample risk heat map

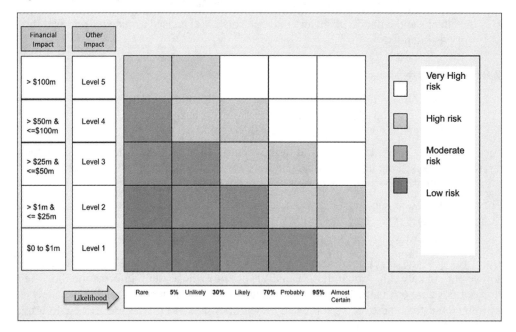

2.8.3.1   Other quantitative risk measures

The measures above are inadequate or inappropriate for some risks. For example, the discussion so far has assumed that for each risk there is a single impact amount. In fact, there is a distribution about that single figure and for the larger risks it may be possible to estimate that distribution. This will help greatly in deciding how acceptable a risk might be, as it gives much greater insight. For example, while the average impact amount may be acceptable, there may be unacceptable outcomes with a reasonably high probability. This is illustrated in the following diagram.

Figure 2.3   Illustration of risk impact ranges

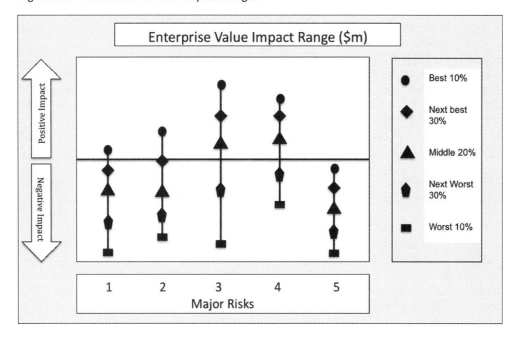

Diagrams like Figures 2.2 and 2.3 can be useful in reporting to management and the board. We will consider this further in section 2.9.1.

2.8.3.2   Modeling

Some risks, or indeed the whole business, may be modeled to help quantify the risks to the business. Such modeling can be very complex but can give powerful insights and understanding about possible outcomes. For example, a book of insurance business backed by a portfolio of shares and fixed interest securities could be modeled stochastically. Amongst other things, the distribution of returns of the assets would be inputs to the model. The model would show the distribution of profits and so give a very good understanding of the riskiness of the overall business.

Deterministic modeling can also be very useful in estimating expected outcomes. It is also possible to compile a set of input parameters for such models to represent a range of scenarios.

Scenario modeling involves the identification of a set of circumstances that could occur and working through all the aspects of the business, risk management plan, strategic plan etc to determine what could happen to the business if this scenario came to pass. An important issue to consider in this context is that of management action. For example, if the scenario being modeled is a drop in values in an investment portfolio, both the action taken by management (for example, sale of shares as the market falls) and the timing of this action are critical to understanding the likely impact. In a scenario of deteriorating claims experience on a trauma insurance product the question may be how much premium rates will be increased and when.

Great care should be taken with models, as it is easy to rely too much on what they produce and in practice there may be considerable uncertainty over the results being produced. This might be because of weaknesses in the model itself, inappropriate or inaccurate parameters, poor data or human error.

2.8.3.3 Stress testing

Scenario modeling can be particularly helpful in stress testing the business, by considering very adverse scenarios and assessing how the business might cope. These sorts of circumstances, which can threaten the very existence of a business, can be difficult to allow for properly in stochastic modeling.

An example from recent history is the 2007-08 credit/financial crisis. If a risk manager had considered the possibility that a credit crisis (or a major market downturn, or a global recession) could occur when assessing and analyzing the company's risk profile, the relevant risks would have been identified and appropriate management or mitigation strategies put in place to allow the company to cope if these circumstances did arise.

2.8.3.4 Analysis and ERM

If risks and/or risk types are analyzed in isolation then good ERM practice would demand that there is further work to understand how the various risk types interact with each other and how they may be managed to produce an optimal outcome for the whole business. Modeling of the business lends itself well to this, but this still requires considerable understanding of the risks and their interaction if the modeling is to be of value.

2.8.3.5 Unmeasurable, unknown, omitted and emerging risks

Some risks may not be measurable. Examples include the impact of a damaged reputation and the entry of a new competitor. The question then becomes how to address risks that cannot be measured. Of course, the impact of such risks cannot simply be disregarded as they may be very significant. This may be a matter of judgment by management and the board.

Other risks may be unknown, or simply not thought of when going through the risk identification process. Again, it is not appropriate that these risks be ignored in the process. Rather, the board and management, having satisfied themselves that the risk identification process has been exhaustive, must acknowledge the possibility of unknown or omitted risks and ensure that appropriate processes are in place to quickly and appropriately address any such risks should they materialize.

Also, there are new risks emerging through changes in the environment, as well as changes in the consequences of identified risks. To presume that all relevant risks can be identified (let alone measured and mitigated) is to presume that no new risks will emerge. This is clearly a dangerous and inappropriate perspective to take. For example, consider the changes in financial risks due to new investment vehicles being developed; the impact of technology and the globalization of investment markets; the rise of longevity risk; the growing awareness of the risks of climate change; and the worldwide rise of identity theft and money laundering.

2.8.4 Evaluate risks

> AS/NZS 4360: Compare estimated levels of risk against the pre-established criteria and consider the balance between potential benefits and adverse outcomes. This enables decisions to be made about the extent and nature of treatments required and about priorities.

Now that the risks have been identified and they and their potential consequences are well understood, it is necessary to decide what to do about them and what the priorities are for this work.

To do this, we must return to the context work and the criteria that were identified then for assessing the risks – in particular risk appetite and risk tolerance (as discussed above in 2.8.1.1) – and the risk analysis work (see 2.8.3).

It can help if the risks are grouped along these lines:

- Strategic or business risks inherent in the venture and consistent with the organization's risk appetite and strategic objectives, where the potential rewards justify the risk being taken.

- Those risks that are acceptable.

  These might include risks that are reasonably small, or where there is no economic justification for addressing them, or where there is a low priority.

- Those risks that are completely unacceptable and need treatment irrespective of cost or other consequences.

  These include:

  ○ risks that are inconsistent with the risk appetite statement and in particular outside a specified risk tolerance; and

  ○ risks that fall into the high category following the analysis – see the white area in the risk heat map in 2.8.3.

- Those risks that need to be managed in a balanced way, involving consideration of treatment options and costs – and striking an acceptable balance.

2.8.5 Treat risks

> AS/NZS 4360: Develop and implement specific cost-effective strategies and action plans for increasing potential benefits and reducing potential costs.

Evaluation of the risks prepares the ground for their treatment.

There are various options for risk treatment, namely:

- reduce;
- avoid;
- transfer;
- retain; and
- exploit.

In this section, we discuss these options, the associated issues and the nature of the risk remaining after treatment.

2.8.5.1   Reduce the risk

If the risk is considered too high relative to the risk appetite or tolerances, then the first step is to consider ways to reduce likelihood or impact, or both. This would normally be through the application of controls (for example, comprehensive testing could be introduced into a process) or other actions (for example, reassigning responsibility to a more experienced person or changing the price of a product).

A good example of reducing the impact of a risk is the insurance of a building against fire. This has no impact on the likelihood of a fire, but significantly reduces the financial impact.

An example of reducing likelihood of a risk is a bank setting a high income requirement for anyone wanting a home loan, so default on the loan is much less likely.

2.8.5.2   Avoid the risk

If the risk is simply one that the business is uninterested in taking, or if the risk cannot be reduced to acceptable levels, then the business may choose to avoid the risk altogether. For example, it might decide to cease operating in a particular country altogether because political risk was too high and could not be reduced satisfactorily.

2.8.5.3   Transfer the risk

A risk might be one that can't viably be reduced but which the business does not want to avoid altogether. For example a property insurer might willingly provide comprehensive insurance in a particular market but be uncomfortable with the risk posed by cyclones in the area concerned. It could then reinsure the risk of cyclone damage and hence transfer that risk. As another example, a pension fund might have a sum invested in the stock market but be concerned that the risk of a substantial fall in that market is increasing. Rather than sell some of its shares, it might choose to use derivatives to reduce its exposure to a fall.

There is usually a cost to make such transfers and, importantly, a new risk usually emerges: *counterparty risk*, being the risk that the transferee fails to meet its obligations.

2.8.5.4   Retain the risk

A risk might be quite acceptable as it is. For example, an insurance company might invest some of its funds in the stock market and fully understand and accept the risk that this poses. At a more basic level, there might be a modest risk of a low-impact operational error, which would be too expensive to eliminate or reduce.

2.8.5.5   Exploit the risk

As already mentioned, every business takes certain risks with the intention of gaining rewards from those risks. Following an analysis of all of its risks, a business might find that it is being rewarded particularly well for a particular risk and so decide that it should increase its exposure to that risk to exploit the opportunity. For example, it might decide to increase its operations in a foreign country because of success to date, recognizing that there are risks in doing so because of an unstable political situation.

2.8.5.6   Risk treatment issues

The challenge is to decide the most appropriate treatment for each risk selected in the evaluation step. A host of factors might be considered in making this decision, including views of various stakeholders; consistency with business objectives and plans; available resources; possible side effects such as new risks; durability of treatment; effectiveness and robustness of controls; and legal issues.

The availability of capital can be a very important consideration, particularly in accepting or exploiting a risk. Capital is provided by shareholders to finance the operations and development of the business. Capacity to take business risk may be constrained by the supply of capital or borrowed funds, as we shall see in Section 2.12.

It is then a cost/benefit exercise – understanding the benefits of the various treatment options and their respective costs and choosing a treatment (or set of treatments) that produces the optimal outcome with an acceptable residual risk level. This does not necessarily mean a comprehensive cost/benefit analysis for every risk, as knowledgeable and experienced staff will often be able to identify the best way forward quite quickly. However, there should be clear reasons for the treatment chosen and a target risk level outcome identified.

Sometimes the cost/benefit analysis will be a quantification exercise. At other times, it will be qualitative work.

Exercise 2.6

Consider an insurance company that has found that a particular feature in one of its products is generating much higher claims than planned. However, the feature is important from a marketing point of view, so the company doesn't want to simply remove it from the product. Review the company's various options for treating the risk of ongoing excessive claims.

2.8.5.7 Inherent versus residual risks

It is important to recognize that the behavior and relative importance of net or *residual* risks (those risks present after mitigation and controls are in place) may be very different from the behavior and relative importance of the underlying gross or *inherent* risks (those risks present before mitigation and controls are in place). If we refer to Figure 2.2, effective controls might shift a risk from right toward left, or from top toward bottom, or both. For example, an insurer may be exposed to losses of hundreds of millions of dollars if a hurricane were to occur in the Gulf of Mexico. However, appropriate reinsurance might restrict total losses from any one hurricane to, say, $50 million. In this case, the risk might move from the top toward the bottom of the diagram but not move from right to left.

In the context of AS/NZS 4360 and Figure 2.1, the net risks are those that remain after the "treat risks" step has been executed.

Thus, all steps must be repeated once the treatment has been agreed and implemented. The feedback loop in Figure 2.1 reflects this iterative process.

Exercise 2.7

Consider a bank which lends to businesses and so is exposed to significant credit risk. Try to think of controls or other mitigating actions that might reduce both the likelihood and impact of losses from credit risk (refer to Figure 2.2).

2.8.6   Monitor and review

> AS/NZS 4360: It is necessary to monitor the effectiveness of all steps of the risk management process. This is important for continuous improvement. Risks and the effectiveness of treatment measures need to be monitored to ensure changing circumstances do not alter priorities.

Having been through the processes of identification, analysis and treatment, one might think that the process would be finished. However, much will have been learned, circumstances may have changed as a consequence of the process to date (for example, controls may have been put in place when a risk became better understood) and treatment may not be implemented or work as intended.

The risk management processes must not be treated as distinct from normal business. Rather, they must be embedded in the business thinking and operations. Thus, as the business changes and evolves, risk management will be addressed and changed accordingly.

The risk management function should continually monitor the workings of the risk management process to ensure that it is operating as intended; all parties are carrying out their responsibilities; controls are working as intended; reporting of issues and failures are being made as required; etc.

Regular audits of the operations of the business also play an important role by checking the effectiveness of controls and other aspects of the risk management process. Special audits of the risk management process may also be carried out.

All of this work needs to be fed back into the risk management process, so that it is changed and improved as required. This is reflected in the feedback loops in Figure 2.1.

2.9   Communicate and consult

> AS/NZS 4360: Communicate and consult with internal and external stakeholders as appropriate at each stage of the risk management process and concerning the process as a whole.

While we have presented this as the last step in the risk management process, in fact communication and consultation with relevant stakeholders must take place throughout the process. Indeed, this should also be the very first step in the process.

We have explained that there are various stakeholders in an organization's risk management. Each should be consulted in a manner consistent with their interests and responsibilities. This will ensure that knowledge and experience of all stakeholders is exploited and that there is buy-in to the overall process.

This is an iterative process, which is reflected in the feedback loops in Figure 2.1.

2.9.1   Documentation and reporting

Much of what has been discussed above should be documented in a formal way for the record and to help with communication. Timely, informative and appropriate reporting is critical to sound risk management. The "monitor and review" and "communicate and consult" elements of the AS/NZS 4360 process require a form of reporting.

The format that this reporting should take depends on the size and complexity of the business in question. Commonly used report types include:

- *risk register* – that is, a description of all relevant risks identified for the business;

- *incident register* – a record of what has gone wrong over time, setting out identified causes, costs etc;

- *key risk indicators* – measures that are monitored to highlight levels of risk; and

- various ways to provide information about the specific risks facing the business.

These last range from detailed information about each of the significant risks (eg context, explanation, history of incidents, controls in place, plans for improvement and target residual risk) through to summary reports like that shown below in Figure 2.4. This is a version of the risk heat map shown in Figure 2.2, with two risks shown for illustration – typically it might show the top 10 risks. This is a particularly powerful form of reporting because it is rich in information.

Figure 2.4   Sample residual risk heat map

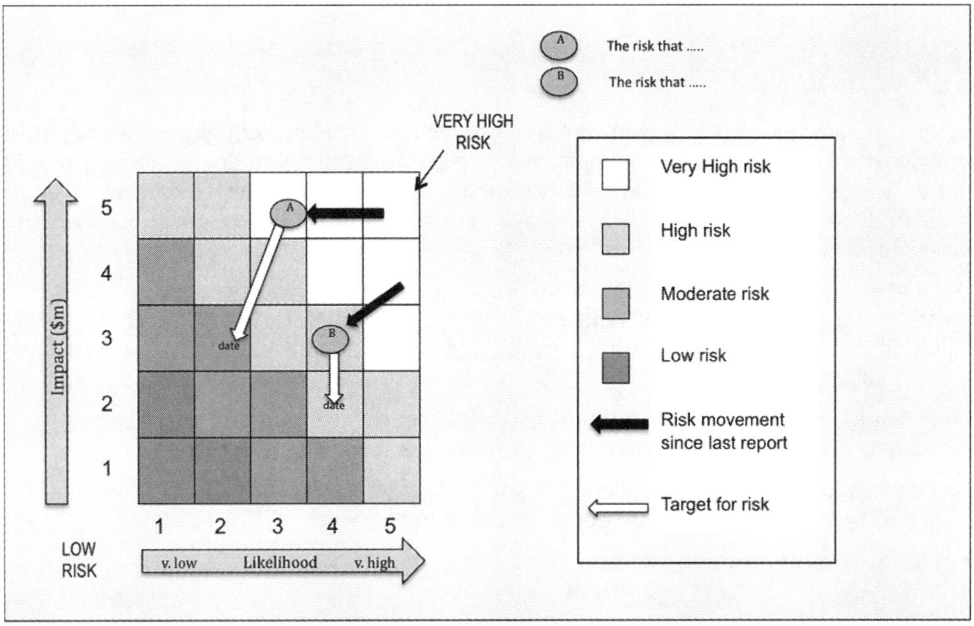

Another example of this sort of reporting is given in Section 6.2 of IAA (2009).

These reports need to be considered by the appropriate people. This may include centralized risk and business unit risk management functions, as well as management at appropriate levels within the company. This will culminate in the major risks being considered by the board – eg where there is potential brand damage. The nature of the reporting will vary, depending on the audience, with management, risk, actuarial and financial staff considering much more detail than the board.

2.9.2   Risk management policy and/or strategy

A major component of documentation is the *risk management policy*. This should be approved and issued by the board, so that it starts at the top and covers the whole business.

The risk management policy would normally include:

- background and context, including the connection to the business objectives and strategy;

- risk appetite and risk tolerances as set by the board;

- the risk management process to be used;

- how the company assesses its key risks;

- the respective responsibilities of the board, senior management, relevant committees and front-line staff;

- how risk management performance is to be monitored; and

- the nature, frequency and timeliness of reporting.

Sometimes the *risk management policy* is a higher-level document and more of the detail is provided in a document called the *risk management strategy*.

2.10   Execution

In many ways, effective implementation of the risk management policy is the most problematic aspect of sound risk management; and the difficulty in doing this well should not be underestimated. There are many examples in the 2008 global financial crisis of businesses with well-crafted risk management policies but whose risk management execution failed badly when it most counted.

An understanding of the importance of – and a belief in – the benefits of sound risk management must be embedded in the business at multiple levels. This is not easily achieved and is ultimately reliant on strong and ongoing leadership from the board and senior management.

Performance of the people in an entity is fundamental to successful ERM and is very difficult to get right. Let's consider why, by looking at a sporting analogy.

Many of us follow sporting teams of one sort or another. Most of us would agree that, for a team to be successful, it needs something along the lines of:

- good people – talented, capable;

- clear roles – each team member allocated a position in the team and playing accordingly;

- good management and training – the coach is capable, understands the game and his or her players, improves their skills and is able to get the best out of them;

- good leadership – the team captain gives direction, motivates, makes good decisions etc; and

- commitment – players have a positive attitude and a belief in the team and its goals.

Successful implementation of ERM is very similar and each of the points mentioned for the sporting team applies equally to ERM in an entity. Staff involved in risk management need to be capable; have clear responsibilities; be properly trained and managed; be well led; and be committed to high-quality risk management. It is very difficult to achieve this across a complex financial services business. However, failure in any of these areas can undermine the whole risk management process.

It also takes time for ERM to be operating successfully, even if implementation is managed very well. This is because there will often be significant change in responsibilities, procedures, reporting etc, as well as a marked shift in attitude to risk management.

It is critical that risk management reporting is clear and unbiased, so that senior management and the board have sound foundations for making decisions and running the business. To help with this, it is now common in financial services organizations to have a specialist risk management function (explained in more detail below) and for both internal and external audits to include risk management within their scope.

2.11 Risk management interests, responsibilities and governance

A robust ERM governance framework will have clear roles and accountabilities for the various parties, including the board, board risk committee, senior management, central risk management function and business unit staff.

Nearly all the parties involved in a financial services provider are exposed to its risks of one sort or another and so have an interest in the quality of the company's risk management. At the highest level, each stakeholder is responsible for managing the risks to which he or she is exposed. However, many of these risks affect more than one party; and often one party depends on the risk management of another (so that the first party has a counterparty risk).

2.11.1 Shareholders

2.11.1.1 Why shareholders have a stake in risk management

Shareholders provide the capital to support an enterprise. This capital is knowingly put at risk with the aim of reaping the rewards from the enterprise's success. So they are exposed to both strategic risk and implementation risk. Shareholders are "at the bottom of the food chain" and so are most at risk if things go wrong.

It is the nature of financial services providers that their shareholders are exposed, to varying degrees, to all of the financial risks mentioned above.

They are also exposed to most of the non-financial risks mentioned above in Section 2.5.2.

2.11.2 Board of directors

2.11.2.1 Why the board has a stake in risk management

The board represents the interests of shareholders, so directors are indirectly exposed to the same risks as shareholders.

The board also has moral and legal obligations to customers and these too are exposed to risks.

In their own right, directors are exposed to various risks, including personal financial liability in certain circumstances, eg negligence.

2.11.2.2   Board responsibilities

The need for risk management to be "driven from the top," the need to have clear risk management processes and reporting, and the need for a risk-aware culture are in the first instance a responsibility of the board. In many countries, this is strongly reinforced by regulation. For example, APRA (2007) says that:

- the board is ultimately responsible for the risk management framework of the life company;

- the board is responsible for the risk management framework whether or not risk management and business operations are outsourced or are part of a corporate group; and

- the board must provide APRA with a risk management declaration, relating to each financial year of the life company, signed by two directors stating that, to the best of their knowledge and belief, having made appropriate enquiries:

   o   the life company has systems in place for the purpose of ensuring compliance with relevant legislation;

   o   the board is satisfied with the efficacy of the processes and systems surrounding the production of financial information at the life company;

   o   the life company has in place a risk management strategy, developed in accordance with the requirements of the Prudential Standard; and

   o   the systems that are in place for managing and monitoring risks, and the risk management framework, are appropriate to the life company, having regard to such factors as the size, business mix and complexity of the life company's operations.

Beyond the regulatory requirements above, best ERM practice requires that the board sets the tone for "the way we do things around here" – that is, the culture. If the board shows little interest in the risks and the way they are managed, chances are that risks will be managed poorly. Conversely, if there is keen interest and understanding of the risks and their management, supported by tight and clear risk management processes and regular monitoring by a dedicated committee, and if senior management rewards are linked to effective risk management, then risks are much more likely to be managed well. A related point is that the key risk management jobs must be resourced appropriately in terms of both quantity and quality – ie enough people who understand the business and are not afraid to speak up.

We discussed the risk management policy and risk management strategy – the formal record of the board's views and guidance – in Section 2.9.2.

2.11.3   Board risk management committee and audit committee

Often a board will appoint a subcommittee of itself to oversee risk management. This recognizes the importance of the board's role in risk management and helps to ensure that appropriate attention can be given to it. The risk management committee would normally deal with senior management and the risk management function on all matters to do with risk management, reporting to the full board as required.

Usually, the board will have an audit committee to oversee internal and external audit activities – and sometimes the risk management committee and the audit committee are one and the same.

Internal and external audits play an important role in risk management – for example, the adequacy and effectiveness of risk and financial controls would normally be checked as part of a regular audit. Also, it has become common for audits to be risk-based, in that time and resources are devoted to those areas of most risk, and this ensures a focus on risk management.

2.11.4 Senior management

Flowing on from the board-approved risk management policy, a key responsibility of senior management is to implement and operationalize this policy into day-to-day actions, limits and expectations for all employees. At a cultural level, senior management needs to ensure that the right messages with respect to risk management are sent throughout the entity, in line with board expectations. Senior managers need to ensure that:

* bad news gets passed up the chain in a timely fashion so that problems can be headed off before they grow in size – shooting the first messenger might not be smart;

* business growth doesn't become stifled through excessive risk avoidance;

* front-line staff are clear which risks are acceptable and which are not;

* appropriate rewards are given for "good" risk taking; and

* there is no perception that "risk management is someone else's job."

Increasingly, senior management teams within financial services providers now include a Chief Risk Officer (CRO) role. The CRO leads the central risk management function. The role is quite broad, but a key function is coordination of risk management activity across the whole company. It is critical that there is no perception within the firm that "the CRO is managing risk, so I don't need to."

The CRO role has emerged in the last ten or so years for similar reasons to those for the existence of specialist risk committees of boards. Risk management has become more complex and time demanding for the reasons given previously. In most cases, risk management at the senior executive level cannot be managed appropriately by other executives, such as the CEO or CFO, if they are to execute their other responsibilities properly. The CRO is needed to share this workload and give risk issues the attention that they deserve.

A risk management function also plays an important role in terms of independent reporting, as this function can have a more objective view of the risks facing a unit than its management.

It is also common to have a committee or series of committees (each considering different risk types, such as operational, financial, legal and compliance) of senior management to provide oversight of risk management.

2.11.5 Chief Actuary

In insurance companies and in some pension funds, there is usually a senior actuarial role. Sometimes this has particular responsibilities dictated by regulation (eg in Australia, the Appointed Actuary role for insurance companies or, in the UK, the With-profits Actuary and the Actuarial Function Holder). For our purposes, we will refer to such roles as the Chief Actuary.

If the Chief Actuary is a member of the senior management team that reports to the CEO, he or she will have the same responsibility as other managers for the risk management culture. In addition, it is very likely that the Chief Actuary will have particular responsibilities for aspects of risk management. These will be a function of the particular job, but may also include regulatory responsibilities. For example, in Australia, the Appointed Actuary for an insurance company must include an assessment of the suitability and adequacy of the risk management framework in the Financial Condition Report.

Different views exist as to whether the Chief Actuary can or should also be the CRO in an insurance company. For instance, does he or she have sufficient time to fulfill both roles? Or is there any conflict of interest in one person holding both positions? These questions have not yet been answered definitively.

2.11.6   Middle management and staff

This is where much risk management occurs operationally and so is critically important.

Risk management processes must be well thought through, absolutely clear and well documented. Job descriptions should include risk management responsibilities and performance appraisals should give appropriate weight to the performance of risk management duties.

They must then be carefully managed to ensure their proper operation and effectiveness.

If risk management is given lip service here, it will surely fail.

2.11.7   Customers (policyholders, bank depositors and borrowers, pension fund members etc)

Customers have a direct interest in their financial services provider's risk management, with risks including:

- direct exposure to the financial risks listed in Section 2.5.1 above through many products (eg mutual funds or defined contribution pension funds);

- underperformance of their product (eg investment performance of a mutual fund relative to peers);

- poor service (eg administrative errors);

- failure of the entity, so that contractual obligations (such as guaranteed benefits) are not met; and

- for members of defined benefit pension funds, failure of the sponsoring employer in various ways.

Customers have a responsibility to choose the services and the provider of those services carefully. However, it is often not possible or practicable for this to be done thoroughly and they should be able to rely on the "system" to provide some protection. Regulators have an important role here, as can be seen below.

2.11.8 Regulators

Both prudential and market conduct regulators have a keen interest in the risk management of a financial services provider, as can be seen from their responsibilities:

- Prudential regulators have an obligation to financial services customers to operate a regulatory regime that provides a high degree of confidence that a financial services provider will always have adequate resources to meets its obligations to customers.

- Market conduct regulators have an obligation to protect customers from inappropriate practices by financial services providers. They reduce fraud and unfair practice in financial markets and financial products; protect and enhance market integrity; and provide customer protection, including ensuring proper and timely disclosure of information, fair treatment and adequate redress to complaints.

Financial services regulators set down a wide range of requirements for the entities they license. These usually include rules for risk management and for the capital required to support the risks in the business. Regulators are responsible for the effectiveness of the regulations and for supervising the licensed entities in the application of those regulations, to ensure a stable and fair market, balanced with the need for competition, innovation and good service. The events of 2008 suggest that there have been some failures in this process.

It is important to note that regulators only have an indirect responsibility in the risk management of a particular financial services provider. The direct responsibility lies with the board and management.

2.11.9   Service providers and intermediaries

Service providers for financial institutions – such as administrators, investment managers, insurers and consultants – also have an interest in the institution's risk management:

- Administrators are exposed to operational risk, both in their own right and on behalf of their clients, both of which may be impacted by the financial institution's risk management.

- Advisers are exposed to reputational risk if their advice is poorly implemented.

- Intermediaries (such as insurance agents) may be heavily reliant on the success of the financial institution, the quality of its products and supporting material etc.

2.11.10   Employers as pension/superannuation fund sponsors

Employers as pension/superannuation fund sponsors have an interest in the fund's risk management, because:

- they typically have a range of regulatory obligations, for example payment of contributions in a timely manner;

- they are exposed to counterparty risks, particularly with respect to the trustees, whose decisions can have a direct financial impact on the employer. That is, the employer can have indirect exposure to the fund's financial risks; and

- their reputation as an employer can be adversely affected by the performance of a fund that they sponsor.

2.12   Capital and risk management

Every company requires capital to allow it to operate. Many financial services businesses (such as insurers and banks) require a good deal of capital to be held in the company to ensure that they can provide their customers with the security that they demand.

The providers of this capital, whether it be debt or equity, expect a reasonable return for the risks they face by investing in the company rather than investing it somewhere safer, such as a bank deposit.

The main risks faced by capital providers are that part or all of their capital is lost; that the capital is not available (or returned to them) when it is required; or that the return achieved on that capital is not as high as expected or required. Thus, the riskier a business is seen to be, the higher the expected return required by providers of capital for them to risk their capital.

2.12.1   Economic or risk-based capital

This principle is inherent in the concept of *risk-based* or *economic capital*. Economic capital is essentially the capital theoretically needed to support a venture, given its risk profile. With the use of this concept the parts of a business that are riskiest have a higher allocation of capital for management purposes than less risky parts. This in turn means that they need to generate a higher profit to service this capital.

The use of risk-based capital is a key way for the board to focus the business on risk and reward relationships, through both:

- demanding a higher return on riskier parts of the business; and
- incentivizing management to reduce risk and therefore make the return hurdles easier to achieve.

2.13   Critical success factors and causes of ERM failure

In our discussion so far, we have given an overview of the most important aspects of risk management. We will now highlight some of the points that are most critical to successful enterprise risk management.

Earlier in the chapter, we emphasized the importance of the culture of an organization to the success of its risk management. This in turn is driven by the attitude and commitment of the board and senior management. Together, these form the bedrock of sound risk management and, if they are not right, then all of the processes, systems, calculations and reporting that might otherwise be done will count for little.

The board and senior management must also agree and clearly communicate their risk appetite to provide appropriate direction for the rest of the organization – and we have noted that this is far from simple. This, then, can be a point of weakness and at worst can undermine the whole process. Done well, though, it can add great clarity of purpose and direction.

There is, therefore, a need for a structured process and supporting systems. A formal process like AS/NZS 4360 provides considerable structure and discipline and a consistent framework for use across an enterprise.

Simply adopting a formal process means little. Staff and management need to have appropriate risk management skills and understanding of the business to ensure that the process will work and they must embrace risk management. They must then be rewarded in a way that encourages appropriate risk management to reinforce the desired behavior. It is worth noting that there is a view that one of the causes of the 2008 global financial crisis was remuneration that encouraged key staff in some organizations to take inappropriate risks.

Lastly, risks must not be managed in silos but a holistic approach taken – as per the concept of ERM.

2.14   Measurement of success

ERM is a rapidly evolving field and assessment of its effectiveness is in its infancy.

Nonetheless, effective risk management has a significant impact through more effective use of capital, lower costs, deeper understanding of the business and more stable financial results. And this should manifest itself in performance against the enterprise's objectives – eg improving the value of a business to its shareholders through profit and share price. These are measurable outcomes, though unambiguous attribution of benefits to risk management may be difficult.

There have been some analyses done of the relationship between the quality of risk management and business performance but it is early days in this process. From a different perspective, it is very likely that analysis will, in due course, show that the cost of risk management failures in the financial crisis of 2008 has been enormous.

Of course, while risk outcomes within an organization's tolerances give a positive indication, this is not enough to demonstrate that its risk management is actually working well. It might simply be a reflection of luck or a relatively benign environment. A much better indication usually emerges in harsh conditions, when the organization is under stress.

2.15   Practical implications for actuaries

The actuarial profession has its roots in the management of certain risks within insurance companies, pension funds and other financial enterprises. It has been very successful in this over a long time.

However, risk management has evolved rapidly in recent years, with the development of new thinking, concepts, tools and techniques. This is amply demonstrated by the rising importance of ERM in the eyes of regulators, boards and senior management. In the modern world, it is critical that actuaries have a broad perspective and deep understanding of ERM, so that:

- they understand how their work contributes to the overall risk management of an enterprise; and

- they are able to embrace opportunities for and competently carry out roles in risk management as they emerge and develop.

2.16   Key learning points

- Emphasis on corporate governance has increased significantly in recent years.
- Robust risk management is fundamental to sound corporate governance.
- This in turn requires a comprehensive risk management framework.
- The culture, driven by the board and senior management, is absolutely critical.
- Many parties have a role in risk management – and responsibilities need to be clear and staff properly trained and rewarded.
- There is a trade-off between risk and reward and one of the challenges for management is to manage this balance to get the best possible outcome.
- There is a variety of risk types. Some are taken with the aim of reward and others are not. Some are systemic and some are diversifiable.
- The risk management process involves a number of steps with multiple feedback loops and risks can be treated in a number of ways.
- Enterprise risk management (ERM) involves a holistic approach to risk management (with an understanding of how the various risks interact with each other) and a focus on managing for value.
- ERM has widespread support by regulators, rating agencies and risk management experts, and is generally regarded as best practice.
- ERM is still evolving.
- There is great potential for the actuarial profession in ERM, but this too is evolving.

CD Items

Barker, M. 2009, Some Further Thoughts on Systemic Risk – And How to Control It, *Actuary Australia*, August 2009, Institute of Actuaries of Australia.

Canadian Institute of Actuaries ERM Applications Committee 2008, Enterprise Risk Management: Should You Be Doing It?, Canadian Institute of Actuaries.

Waite, J. 2009, ERM – Black Swans, Fat Tails and Spherical Cows, *Actuary Australia*, April 2009, Institute of Actuaries of Australia.

Wolf, R. 2008a, The Evolution of Enterprise Risk Management, *The Actuary*, June/July 2008, Society of Actuaries.

Wolf, R. 2008b, The Birth, Death and Resurrection of Dynamic Financial Analysis, *The Actuary*, Oct/Nov 2008, Society of Actuaries.

Wolf, R. 2009a, Expert Input on the Current Financial Crisis: Did ERM Fail? *The Actuary*, Feb/Mar 2009, Society of Actuaries.

Wolf, R. 2009b, Seeing the Big Picture: ERM in the Health Care Industry, *The Actuary*, Apr/ May 2009, Society of Actuaries.

Wolf, R. 2009c, Getting Up To Speed: ERM in the Life Insurance Industry, *The Actuary*, Oct/ Nov 2009, Society of Actuaries.

Wolf, R. 2009d, Doors of Opportunity: ERM in the Broader Economic Sector, *The Actuary*, Dec 2009/Jan 2010, Society of Actuaries.

Chapter 2 Exercise Solutions

References (other than CD Items)

Australian Securities Exchange (ASX) Corporate Governance Council 2007, *Corporate Governance Principles and Recommendations*, 2nd edition, Australian Securities Exchange.

Australian Prudential Regulatory Authority (APRA) 2007, Prudential Standard LPS 220 – Risk Management, APRA.

Basel Committee on Banking Supervision 2006, International Convergence of Capital Measurement and Capital Standards, A Revised Framework, Comprehensive Version, Bank for International Settlements.

Bennet, C. & Cusick, K. 2007, Risk Appetite: Practical Issues for the Global Financial Services Industry, Institute of Actuaries of Australia Biennial Convention.

Casualty Actuarial Society Enterprise Risk Management Committee 2003, Overview of Enterprise Risk Management, Casualty Actuarial Society.

CEA and Groupe Consultatif Europeen 2007, Solvency II Glossary.

Committee of Sponsoring Organizations of the Treadway Commission (COSO) 2004, Enterprise Risk Management — Integrated Framework Executive Summary, COSO.

European Central Bank 2004, Annual Report, European Central Bank, Germany.

Federation of European Risk Management Associations (FERMA) 2002, A Risk Management Standard, FERMA, Belgium.

Financial Services Authority (FSA) 2009, SYSC 14.1.18 R (31/12/2006), *Handbook*, UK.

International Actuarial Association (IAA) Insurer Solvency Assessment Working Party 2004, A Global Framework for Insurer Solvency Assessment, IAA.

International Actuarial Association (IAA) 2009, Note on Enterprise Risk Management for Capital and Solvency Purposes in the Insurance Industry, IAA.

International Association of Insurance Supervisors (IAIS) 2008, Guidance Paper on Enterprise Risk Management for Capital Adequacy and Solvency Purposes No. 2.2.5, IAIS.

International Organization for Standardization 2009, *ISO 31000 Risk Management – Principles and Guidelines*.

Investorwords, www.investorwords.com, accessed January 30, 2010.

Investopedia, www.investopedia.com, accessed January 30, 2010.

Kamiya, S., Shi, P., Schmit, J., & Rosenberg, M. 2007, Risk Management Terms, CAS-CIA-SOA Risk Management Section Research Team.

OECD 2004, Principles of Corporate Governance.

Rech, J. E. 2005, Enterprise Risk Management for Insurers: Actuarial Theory in Practice, *Contingencies*, Nov/Dec, Washington.

Risk and Insurance Management Society (RIMS) 2008, 2008 Global Financial Crisis: A Wake-Up Call for Enterprise Risk Management, RIMS.

RIMS and Marsh 2008, Viewing Risk Management Strategically: Excellence in Risk Management V – An Annual Survey of Risk Management Issues and Practices, Marsh Inc.

Standards Australia 2004, *AS/NZS 4360:2004 Risk Management*, Standards Australia.

Standard & Poor's 2007, Summary Of Standard & Poor's Enterprise Risk Management Evaluation Process For Insurers, *RatingsDirect*, November 26.

Tripp, M. H., Chan, C., Haria, S., Hilary, N., Morgan, K., Orros, C. G., Perry, G. R. & Tahir-Thomson, K. 2008, Enterprise Risk Management from the General Insurance Actuarial Perspective, presented to the Institute of Actuaries (UK), 28 April.

Recommended further reading

Many actuarial bodies have ERM or risk management sections on their websites and these will usually have useful reading lists and/or links to documents and other websites. In addition, the following are recommended:

Association of Superannuation Funds of Australia 2005, Best Practice Note 19: A risk management framework for superannuation funds, ASFA, Australia (available to members).

Association of Superannuation Funds of Australia 2005, Best Practice Note 23: Risk treatment tools and resources, ASFA, Australia (available to members).

Deighton, S.P., Dix, R. C., Graham, J. R. & Skinner, J. M. E. 2009, Governance and Risk Management in United Kingdom Insurance Companies, Presented to the Institute of Actuaries (UK), 23 March.

Financial Services Authority (FSA) 2006, The FSA's Risk Assessment Framework, FSA, London.

Financial Services Authority (FSA) 2009, FSA Financial Risk Outlook 2009, FSA, London.

Fred's Coffee Shop – Being Professional

We now turn to the subject of professionalism. We have placed it early in the book, because a professional attitude should underpin all actuarial work.

As an actuary, Fred is already a member of a profession, so he will be familiar with the concept of professionalism. His new line of work may not satisfy all the requirements to be considered a profession in the same sense as traditional professions such as law and medicine. However, he will find that acting in a professional way is still very important. He must be competent at what he does, or most of his customers will not return. He should seriously consider undertaking a barista course, perhaps even earning the Certified Coffee Specialist designation. He is likely to have more success if he treats his customers with respect (and a smile) and behaves ethically. For example, if that milk is just past its use-by date, it is probably best not to use it, even if it smells OK.

It is likely that Fred will look for similar behavioral traits in any staff that he hires. He may well find that he develops a basic code of practice, even if he doesn't write it down.

When you read Chapter 3, think about Fred and think about other ways in which the chapter can be applied to his new venture.

Chapter 3:   Being Professional
by Clare Bellis

3.1   Introduction

When you decided to become an actuary, you were not just choosing a career. You were entering a profession. We hope that throughout your career you will find opportunities for interesting and rewarding work. These opportunities will be open to you, not solely because of your own qualities, but also in part because you are a member of the actuarial profession. You will have a good reputation even before you start to prove yourself. People will be inclined to trust your opinion and to rely on your advice when making decisions. You will be able to draw on an accumulated body of science and practical solutions, and to learn and develop with the support of a network of peers.

These benefits have been earned by actuaries over long periods of professional work done with integrity and high standards. In return, you are expected to conduct yourself in a way which justifies the trust placed in you, and which contributes to the reputation you share with other actuaries. That means approaching your work with a professional attitude. In this chapter, we will look at what being professional means:

- 3.2 considers what we mean when we say that some occupations are *professions*.

- 3.3 describes how actuarial organizations support actuaries in working professionally.

- 3.4 explains certain regulatory roles which are entrusted to the actuarial profession.

- 3.5 sets out some professional issues to bear in mind when working as an actuary.

- 3.6 offers some practical advice about doing a professional job.

Please note that this chapter can only scratch the surface of what you need to know about being professional. Your actuarial professional body will probably require you to attend one or more short courses concentrating on professionalism before you can work as a fully qualified actuary. Such courses deal in depth with examples of the professional issues you may meet in practice. Our goal in this chapter is to help you to understand the concept of professionalism and how it shapes the way in which actuaries work, and to guide you in developing a professional approach.

Exercise 3.1

Before you go on to read any further in this chapter, think of three occupations which you feel sure are professions. Then think of three occupations which you feel sure are not professions. Don't agonize over your choice – just list those which come quickly to mind.

For example, some people might say that accountants are definitely professionals, and checkout operators are definitely not. Other people would disagree. What do you think?

Exercise 3.2

Write down the characteristics which you think distinguish a profession from an occupation which is not a profession. For example, most people would say that a professional occupation requires a lengthy period of specialized training/ education. You might find it helpful to think about the differences between the two sets of occupations which you listed in your answer to Exercise 3.1.

3.2 What is a profession?

3.2.1 The characteristics of a profession

Defining a *profession* is not a simple task. Different people use the term to mean different things. Attempts to define a profession often start by making a list of characteristics or essential features, as you were asked to do in Exercise 3.2. If we were to compare all the lists of characteristics of professions that have ever been written down, we would find that most of their elements fall into three main categories: knowledge-related, value-related, and organizational elements.

- *Knowledge-related*: A profession is based on a specialized body of knowledge. Members of the profession undertake lengthy training in the science and its practical application.

- *Value-related*: The members provide a service which is valuable to society, and live up to a high standard of ethical behavior.

- *Organizational*: The members belong to an organization which supports the knowledge- and value-related elements.

In this chapter, we will call the version of the definition of profession which has all three strands – knowledge-related, value-related and organizational – the *full version*. There are other less comprehensive definitions in common use. This is one reason why it is difficult to pin down any discussion of professionalism. Some people use *profession* to describe any knowledge-related occupation, and therefore would consider computer programming, for example, as a profession. Teaching has knowledge-related and value-related aspects, and some people would include teachers in their list of professions but exclude computer programmers. Other people would exclude teaching if teachers were not considered to have a controlling professional body, as distinct from a trade union, ie if teachers were not considered to possess the organizational characteristics.

Exercise 3.3

For each characteristic on the list which you drew up in Exercise 3.2, consider whether you can fit it into one or more of these categories: knowledge-related, value-related, or organizational.

Does this tell you what concept of a profession you were using when you made your list?

The way in which actuarial work is carried out in much of the world, including the US, the UK, Australia, Canada and many other countries, meets all the characteristics of the full version of a profession. There is a lengthy period of training in actuarial science, as you have no doubt discovered! The work which actuaries do can be very important to the financial security of many people. Also, actuaries in these countries have to belong to a professional actuarial body and conduct themselves according to its standards.

In some other countries, actuarial work may not fit the full version of the definition of a profession. This is discussed further in 3.2.4 below.

3.2.2   The theory about why professions exist

There are benefits to being a member of a profession. These include:

• members gain status and respect as professionals;

• legislation or accepted practice may specify that certain jobs are only done by members of the profession;

• governments may listen to opinions which are expressed by the profession as a whole in their area of expertise; and

• there is mutual support between the members.

Because of these benefits, occupations may organize themselves into societies and try to gain recognition as professions. They can get the benefit of mutual support, if they are able to attract enough members, but they cannot gain the benefits listed in the first three bullet points above, unless the wider community recognizes them as a profession.

Theorists have tried to understand why some occupations gain this recognition, while other occupations do not. One theory which gives a plausible explanation is as follows: to be recognized as a profession, the occupation must provide a service which has the following characteristics:

• The service offers solutions to problems that society considers to be important.

• The quality of the service cannot easily be assessed before it is performed, and sometimes the quality cannot be assessed even after the service is performed.

• The service cannot be delivered by applying a standard set of rules. Instead, an expert has to bring a broad and deep practical knowledge and theoretical understanding to determine the best solution to fit the specific case.

In these circumstances, it is important but difficult for the consumers to ensure the quality of the services. To some extent, they have to take the work of the expert on trust. The theory postulates that the concept of a profession evolved as an answer to this problem. All individual members of the profession are expected to carry out their work in a way which lives up to the trust placed in them. They share a joint reputation, which means it is in the interests of the professionals, as well as the consumers, that they perform their work to a high standard. In the full version of the concept of a profession, this is backed up by the actions of the professional body. The professional body will set out what is expected and will enforce this by disciplinary powers. Members of the profession are also expected to guide other members, and if necessary, report any unprofessional conduct to the professional body. Finally, the requirement that professionals meet a high standard may have legal force. For example, if you are considered to be a professional person and you do not carry out your work with due care and competence, then you can be sued for professional negligence.

So, according to the theory, an occupation is recognized as a profession because doing so provides benefits for the consumers, who are able to rely on the service.

Governments also often rely on professions to apply their skills in a regulatory role. For example, suppose that you are unable to work because of illness. You would need to see a doctor and get a medical certificate to qualify for any sickness benefit. In this case, the medical profession is acting as part of society's regulatory system, by ruling on what is sickness and what is health. The doctor's professional service in filling out the medical certificate is performed on behalf of society as a whole, and not for your benefit as the patient. (Of course, if you really were sick, the doctor should also provide treatment of the illness for your benefit.)

Actuaries fill some regulatory roles, particularly because they tend to work in parts of the economy which, for reasons discussed in Chapter 7, are highly regulated. We will discuss regulatory roles further in 3.4.

3.2.3   How the concept of a profession is changing over time

Society is less trusting of professions than it used to be. For example, in the past, professions were able to persuade society that they needed certain restrictive trade practices, such as fee-fixing and a ban on advertising, in order to maintain the quality of their services. Professions were often specifically exempted from legislation which banned other people from such anti-competitive activities. This is no longer the case. Professions do still have a monopoly over provision of some services, but they are always under pressure to demonstrate that they are not abusing this monopoly. At an individual level, practitioners have to justify their advice. It is no longer possible to dismiss concerns by saying, explicitly or implicitly, "Trust me, I'm the expert." Communication skills are becoming more and more important.

The role of professions in regulation has also changed. Governments, which have historically delegated many decisions to the discretion of individual practitioners, now require more formal standards of practice. The standards may be drawn up by the professional body, so in this sense the profession is still in control despite the loss of autonomy of individual practitioners. However, government officials will be involved in negotiating the standards. More recently, it has become common to have standard-setting bodies that are separate from the professional body, and which include representatives who are not members of the profession.

Thus on the one hand, the willingness of individuals and regulators to entrust decisions to professions has reduced. On the other hand, the ever-increasing complexity of our modern world means there is a great need for expert advice. In some ways, professions are more important than ever, but they have to be more open to scrutiny, with more formalized codes and standards.

3.2.4   How the concept of a profession varies from country to country

The full version of the concept of a profession is strongly located in an Anglo-American context. In fact, some theorists think that in its most traditional form it is specifically English. Burrage (1990) uses political history to explain the different development of professions in England, France and the US, and in the other parts of the world which those countries influenced.

When we turn to consider actuaries around the world, the historical differences we can see in the organization of actuarial work fit well with Burrage's observations about professions in general. We can make the following broad generalizations about actuarial work:

- In the UK, and in other countries such as Australia and South Africa which derive their institutions from England, the actuarial occupation is well organized, with a large extent of self-regulation, and with the education and examination of students firmly under the control of the profession itself. In these countries, the governments have historically left considerable authority to the actuarial organizations and to individual actuaries in matters such as the valuation of life insurance liabilities.

- In western continental Europe, actuaries have been regulated more by the state than by their own organizations, and education and examination are also under the control of the state-run universities.

- In the US, the situation lies between the UK model and the continental model. The governments of the individual states have historically retained more control over regulation of life insurance, for example, and the actuarial bodies are segmented. Canada in turn lies somewhere between the UK and US models.

This is the historical position, but the international differences are narrowing. In North America, regulators are moving toward allowing more scope for professional judgment. Thus the UK and North American models are converging. In Europe, the move to harmonize credentials under the European Union (EU) has been reducing the differences between the UK and continental European models. For example, in some European countries where the education of actuaries used to be entirely left to the university system, a professional body has been formed and has either influenced the university syllabus or introduced its own post-university education and examination process.

As actuarial services emerge in economies that had not previously seen a need for actuarial science, the users and providers of these actuarial services are influenced by the model of established actuarial professions in other countries. Here are some comments from Chris Daykin, a past President of the UK Institute of Actuaries and past Chairman of the International Forum of Actuarial Associations,[1] who has been active in work to extend the practice of actuarial science to many countries that had not previously had a tradition of either actuaries or professions, or where such traditions had been suspended. The international bodies he mentions are discussed further in 3.3.2 below.

> It has been encouraging to observe the establishment, or in some cases re-establishment, of the actuarial profession in the countries of central and Eastern Europe and in China, after a period when professions were not recognised and private associations could not be set up. Indeed, self-regulation and control of ethical standards by independent private entities were alien concepts for centrally planned economies.
>
> Actuarial science represented a new and potentially challenging application of mathematics and statistics, which formed the background for most of the new

---

[1] The International Forum of Actuarial Associations was a predecessor organization to the present International Actuarial Association (IAA), which is discussed further in 3.3.2.

actuaries [in these countries]. There was a need for those with a good theoretical background in mathematics to learn more about economics and finance, with applications in insurance, pensions and investment. Then actuarial associations began to develop and to aspire to become professional bodies, inspired by the traditions in countries with a long history of professions and by the international coordination entities for the profession – the International Actuarial Association (IAA) and the European Actuarial Consultative Group (known as the Groupe Consultatif).

Even among the original members of the European Union there had been significant differences in the role of actuaries and the way in which the profession was organised. In some countries actuaries were regarded as technical experts rather than as independently-minded professionals. Some actuarial associations were more in the nature of clubs of individuals with common interests, not responsible for providing initial actuarial education, setting professionalism requirements or for awarding any designation. This has changed considerably since the early 1990s, with full membership of the Groupe Consultatif requiring the adoption and implementation of a code of conduct from 1992 onwards and similar requirements at the global level with the formation of the International Forum of Actuarial Associations (IFAA) in 1995 and the reconstituted IAA in 1998.

There are inevitably some differences in the approach to professional issues, rooted in social, cultural and legal differences between countries. However, this has not so far led to any insuperable obstacles to the adoption by new associations of a code of conduct meeting the minimum requirements of the IAA, so that they can aspire to be admitted as Full Members.

The leaders of new associations have been keen to welcome public interest roles for individual actuaries, such as the Appointed Actuary of an insurance company. They recognise that their young organisations must take responsibility for the maintenance of standards of competence and for enhancing the reputation of members of the profession, and they see the need to contribute to debate on public and social issues. Although this has been more difficult to achieve in some countries than others, the developments have been encouraging, and suggest that the established concept of a profession can be implemented into almost any market economy.

One important area where there is scope for differences of emphasis arising out of culture is the balance between the individual actuary's fiduciary responsibility with the client and the public or corporate interest. However, with increasing globalisation and with actuaries working for companies and consulting firms whose operations span the globe, it is important that we should continue to work towards a common understanding of what the principal stakeholders expect of our profession.

3.3   The role of the professional body

3.3.1   General comments

We have noted above that the full version of a profession has organizational elements. These are conducted through a professional body. Usually there is only one such body in a jurisdiction – a state or provincial body if this level of legislation is important, otherwise a national body. This enables the professional body to serve as a channel for discussion between the government and the profession. Sometimes though, for historical reasons, there will be more than one body. This is a natural situation if the different bodies cover different specialisms; then really we could think of each specialism as a separate profession. For example civil engineers and electrical engineers might have separate bodies, or these occupations might find they have enough in common to combine into one body. In some countries there are separate associations for actuaries working in life insurance, non-life insurance and those advising employer-sponsored retirement benefit plans. If there are two or more bodies whose members provide the same service, this tends to be an unstable situation. One organization will probably become dominant and will eventually absorb the others, or the bodies may become very similar to each other, and work together in many ways.

We will now consider how the actuarial profession is organized.

3.3.2   The actuarial profession: the international level

The actuarial profession is more international than many other professions. Most professions have multinational conferences and educational societies to develop their science, but generally their services are provided only in their local environment, and therefore any standards of practice they develop only have to apply to the local jurisdiction. Doctors, for example, usually only treat patients in their local area. But some professions, notably actuaries and accountants, may be involved in advising corporations that operate in many countries. The International Actuarial Association (IAA) serves as a forum to enable the actuarial profession to deal with issues at the international level. It is the umbrella association for professional actuarial bodies around the world.

The criteria for an organization to become a full member of the IAA encapsulate some of the key features of a professional body. For full membership of the IAA, a professional actuarial body must have:

- an acceptable code of conduct;

- an acceptable disciplinary procedure;

- an acceptable procedure for drafting and enforcing standards of practice, if these are issued; and

- a commitment that the education of its fully qualified members at least meets the minimum education guidelines set out by the IAA. (To give you an idea of this minimum standard: if you study this book as part of a practical actuarial course after completing a set of courses in technical actuarial material, your education will probably meet those education guidelines.)

The IAA has no power over the individual national bodies, but its criteria are influential. Associations have made changes to the way they are organized to ensure that they meet the criteria for full membership. Actuarial associations which do not meet the criteria can be Associate members of the IAA.

Another important international actuarial organization is the European Actuarial Consultative Group (known as the Groupe Consultatif). It was formed to represent the actuarial associations in the European Union in discussions about EU legislation that has an impact on actuarial work. The Groupe also now provides a forum for discussion among all actuarial associations throughout Europe. Thirty-five actuarial associations from thirty-two European countries are represented on the Groupe.

3.3.3   The national level

The IAA website, at www.actuaries.org, lists the bodies which are full members of the IAA. This is a useful way of seeing which professional bodies operate in which countries, and finding their websites.

You will see that in most cases there is only one professional actuarial body in each country. There are a few exceptions.

The UK has two bodies, the Institute (based in England) and the Faculty (based in Scotland), but in recent years they have combined for many of their activities, and at the time of writing they are discussing a merger.

The US has several different bodies. The background to this situation is explained in the historical article "From Actuarius to Actuary, The Growth of a Dynamic Profession in Canada and the United States," on the CD. The American Academy of Actuaries was established to provide a single voice for the whole US profession in dealing with government and making statements on matters of public interest.

There are also many actuarial organizations which are not professional bodies as such, but exist to facilitate discussion. These include students' societies, local societies, and associations of consulting actuaries or other groups of actuaries with special interests in common.

Although professional bodies which aspire to full membership of the IAA must commit to the minimum education guidelines, this does not mean that every full member body organizes its own pre-qualification education. For example, the Actuarial Society of Hong Kong admits as Fellows those who are Fellows of the Institute or Faculty of Actuaries, of the Society of Actuaries or Casualty Actuarial Society, or of the Institute of Actuaries of Australia. The Canadian Institute of Actuaries admits as Fellows those whose educational qualifications meet the level of a Fellow of the Society of Actuaries or Casualty Actuarial Society, but also requires completion of a course specifically on Canadian legislation and practice. There are also "Mutual Recognition Agreements" between actuarial bodies, to recognize each other's qualifications. Many bodies, particularly in Europe, admit as fully qualified actuaries those who have completed approved actuarial degrees at university.

3.3.4   Professional guidance

Code of conduct

The professional actuarial body will have a code of conduct, sometimes referred to as a *professional conduct standard* or *code of ethics*. This sets out broad principles of how actuaries should behave, in any area of actuarial work.

Some examples of codes of conduct which are current at the time of writing are included on the CD.

A fundamental part of all the codes of conduct, whether explicitly stated or not, is that actuaries should only take on tasks which they are competent to perform. Whether or not there are any formal requirements for specialist qualifications or prior experience in a particular area of work, individuals must apply their own professional judgment to assess whether they have the necessary knowledge, skills and practical experience.

Exercise 3.4

Consider the following scenario:

You have produced a sophisticated and lengthy analysis and report for a client. As you are delivering an oral report of the results of your analysis to the client's board of directors, a director asks you a particularly insightful question. As you ponder your response, you suddenly realize that you failed to take into account the issue the director raised, and your conclusion may be materially incorrect.

Obtain the code of conduct for the actuarial body you belong to, or are likely to join. Describe how the Code would guide your actions in responding to the scenario.[2]

Other professional guidance

In addition to the code of conduct, there are usually written standards of practice covering different aspects of actuarial work. These may be issued by the professional body, or a separate actuarial standards body, usually after consultation with the wider profession.

The absence of a *written* standard does not necessarily mean that there is no agreed standard for a particular area of actuarial work. If all members clearly agree, through the formal education process and through formal and informal discussion among themselves, on how a certain task should be done, then there may be no need to have a written standard about that task. However, there are advantages in having a written standard:

- A written standard protects the client, and others who may indirectly rely on the actuary's work, by ensuring the actuary does a complete and thorough job using appropriate methods.

- The professional body will have a solid case if it has to discipline any member for not following good practice.

- The standard provides a useful checklist of what should be done, and since it reflects agreed practice, it will not constrain competent and conscientious actuaries from doing what they would have done anyway.

- A client cannot pressure the actuary into omitting essential parts of a task in order to save time or money, or into using unacceptable methods in order to arrive at the answer the client would like (particularly when carrying out work that will be relied upon by third parties).

- The actuary has some protection from allegations of unsatisfactory performance, since the standard sets out a minimum standard of work.

- Regulators can be satisfied that actuaries will perform a task to a given standard.

---

[2] Scenario from Ryan, Bakos and Bloom (2003).

Note that although it may sometimes help actuaries to set out good actuarial practice in the form of written standards, the primary purpose of standards is always to protect the users of actuarial services.

The disadvantage of having a written standard is that it is difficult to specify methods which apply in every situation. Remember that the very purpose of a profession is to deal with problems calling for discretionary judgment, which cannot be reduced to a set of rules. Standards are usually therefore written in fairly general terms, with a requirement on the actuary to consider what methods and assumptions are appropriate to use in the particular case. An actuary who does not take the steps a reasonable actuary should have in a particular case, will not escape blame just because the standard did not specifically say that those steps should be taken.

The professional body may also issue other documents which guide actuaries in their work in particular areas, but do not have the force of standards which *must* be followed.

3.3.5 Monitoring standards within the actuarial profession

All actuaries have a joint responsibility for the standards of the profession. This means that you not only have to make sure that your own behavior is up to standard, but you must also take steps if you see other actuaries failing to meet the standards. You don't have to manage this responsibility alone. You can consult other members of the profession in confidence. The professional body will usually have a professional guidance committee whom you can ask for advice, but as a first step you can talk the issue over with any experienced member of the profession.

In the past, most professional bodies generally relied on self-monitoring and the threat of disciplinary action to ensure that members followed the standards. In recent times there has been pressure for more formal monitoring. This can be done in different ways.

One method of monitoring is a requirement to submit to the professional body a self-assessment of compliance after a piece of work is completed. The Canadian Institute of Actuaries has had this requirement for some years for actuaries who have a legislated role in life insurance. Some actuarial bodies require members to report each year that they have complied with the requirements of a continuing professional development standard.

Another possibility is peer review, requiring members to check that they are in line with common practice by submitting their work for inspection by other members of the profession, ideally actuaries from a different employer, but at least not someone under the first actuary's direction. This might be required before or after the work is released to the client, and might be for all work or for a random sample, and might cover all types of work or only specific types, such as work performed in statutory regulatory roles.

Note that formal peer review does not mean checking the data and calculations in a piece of actuarial work. (Such checking should be done, as a matter of course, but usually by someone other than the peer reviewer.) Formal peer review means checking whether the correct approach and methodology has been used and the standards of work met – including whether sufficient checking of data and calculations has been carried out. Peer review is a positive component of professionalism, and actuaries should consider whether it is appropriate to seek peer review of their work, whether or not there is any formal requirement to do so.

3.3.6 How do the codes apply to you?

It is likely that you must already comply with a code of professional conduct, even if you are not yet a fully qualified actuary. The codes of the UK and Australian bodies specify that they apply to student members. Candidates for the examinations of the Society of Actuaries (SOA) and the Casualty Actuarial Society can sit their examinations before becoming members. These Societies therefore have codes of conduct specifically for candidates. Whether or not you are studying for the SOA examinations, you should read the SOA Code of Conduct for Candidates, which is contained on the CD, as it makes it clear what sort of behavior is expected of all entrants to the actuarial profession.

Exercise 3.5

Read the SOA Code of Conduct for Candidates (on the CD).

(a) Summarize what you see as the three most important points.

(b) Whom do you think the Code is intended to protect?

Another important issue is knowing which codes apply to you. If you have your primary actuarial qualification from an organization based in one country, and work in another country where there is also an actuarial professional body, you are still held to the first body's code of conduct. However, you will also be expected to familiarize yourself with local legislation and practice and abide by the standards of the second body.

3.4 The regulatory role of the actuary

3.4.1 General comments

We mentioned above that professions often play a part in the regulatory system, and this is particularly true of actuaries. Different countries will have different roles for actuaries set out in legislation. Legislated roles are most common in life insurance, but are also found in other areas of insurance and in employer-sponsored retirement benefit plans. In some countries, actuaries may also be allowed, because of their actuarial qualifications, to give investment advice or other financial advice to individuals without meeting some of the licensing requirements for these services.

In 3.4.2 to 3.4.4, we consider some of the broad functions provided by actuaries. In 3.4.5 we look at a few specific examples. You should not rely on this chapter for a definitive description of regulatory roles, because the legislation varies from country to country, and changes over time.

3.4.2 Prudential supervision

Prudential supervision, which is also referred to simply as *supervision*, means that regulators watch over financial institutions to try to ensure that they are operating sensibly, and to reduce the risk that policyholders, depositors and other vulnerable individuals will suffer losses from the collapse of an institution. Chapter 7 will discuss why some types of financial institutions, such as insurance companies and banks, are considered to need prudential supervision.

If you look at the Actuarial Control Cycle, you will see that much of it can be applied to keeping a financial institution from failure. The institution needs to understand the risks it is taking, and not rashly sell products or otherwise take on commitments which may expose it to unexpected problems. It needs to charge sufficient prices or otherwise generate sufficient cash inflow, and then set aside sufficient assets, suitably invested, to cover the liability for its commitments plus a margin for safety. To do all this, it needs to analyze its experience and build models of the future.

Regulators may control many of these things by rules. For example, banks have often had limitations placed on the types of products they can offer, and what assets they can invest in, and have been required to use specific formulae to calculate a sufficient safety margin. Banks may be allowed to use their own models in some circumstances, but regulators will generally be closely involved in considering the suitability of the modeling process.

In other cases, regulators may delegate some or all of the activities that support prudential supervision to actuaries. The directors of the financial institution may be required to seek actuarial advice when designing products, setting prices, and/or when determining what amount of assets should be held, or, indeed, they may be required to have an actuary's overview of the whole of the operations of the institution. The actuary may have to approve what is done, or simply provide advice, which the directors can choose to take or to ignore. In the latter case, the directors may be held accountable for losses resulting from ignoring the actuarial advice.

3.4.3   Other customer protection

Ensuring that financial institutions operate prudently is obviously a key part of protecting customers. However, there are other aspects to customer protection. Financial institutions often provide products that are difficult for their customers to compare, or which contain areas where the institution can apply discretion. Actuaries may be given a regulatory role to protect the customers from unfair treatment in these areas. Here are some examples.

Actuaries may be required to certify not only that insurance premiums are not too low (which could endanger the solvency of the insurance company, as discussed in 3.4.2), but also that the premiums are not too high. This would apply particularly in cases where purchase of insurance was compulsory.

Long-term savings products may be sold on the basis of projections of the final benefit. These projections, or illustrations, depend on the assumptions made and could easily mislead by using over-optimistic assumptions. Actuaries may be required to ensure that the illustrations are reasonable and that the uncertainty about the final outcome is made clear.

Situations where an actuary may be required to determine discretionary amounts include the following:

*   With-profit (or participating) life insurance provides for the policyholders to share in the future profits, either by way of extra benefits or by premium reductions. The life insurance company will usually be required to follow actuarial advice in deciding how profits are allocated to each policy.

- The amount paid as a surrender value when a policyholder cancels a long-term insurance contract may be calculated at the discretion of the insurance company acting on actuarial advice.

- The rules for benefits payable from employer-sponsored defined benefit retirement plans may be defined only for standard cases, such as taking a pension on retirement at a specified age. In other circumstances, such as early retirement or exchanging part of the pension for a lump sum, the rules may state that the benefit will be calculated by an actuary to be equal in value to the standard benefit. The same may apply when a cash sum is paid to transfer entitlements to another plan.

3.4.4   Disclosure to third parties

The measurement of profit will be discussed in depth in Chapter 16, but you can probably understand that the profit an insurance company reports in any year is affected by how much it sets aside at the end of the year to cover its liabilities. If the liabilities are understated, the profits will look good at first, but eventually when the true costs emerge, the profits will be depressed, and indeed can turn into large losses. This would be very unfortunate for anyone who had relied on the reported profits, for example in deciding to invest in the company. To improve the quality of disclosure, regulators may require insurance companies to use actuaries to determine the amount of money to set aside for the insurance liabilities. This will particularly apply for life insurance business and for types of non-life insurance business where there is a lot of uncertainty about the amount and timing of the outstanding claim payments.

Any company that sponsors a retirement benefit plan for its employees may also be required to report an actuarial assessment of the plan, so that investors and other interested parties can have an informed view about the payments the company is likely to make to the plan in coming years.

In many cases the actuary's role will not be set down in regulation, but the organization that is disclosing financial information will choose to have an actuary involved for its own good management and so that third parties can have confidence in the information.

The accounting profession has standards for the disclosure of financial information which actuaries must take into consideration, as well as legislative requirements and actuarial standards.

3.4.5   Examples of legislated roles for actuaries

In some jurisdictions, regulators have created special legislated roles for actuaries. The legislation creating the role will typically:

- Specify who is qualified to fill the role; this may require credentials or experience on top of the standard actuarial qualification.

- Set out the responsibilities (some examples are given below).

- Clarify the process for reporting on these responsibilities. For example, the legislation may require that the actuary must have direct access to the board of directors of a financial institution to provide advice. Sometimes the actuary may have the final decision on some matter, or the role may be to ensure that the board has good advice in making the decision. In other cases, the actuary may make a report to the regulator or to policyholders.

- Empower the actuary to obtain from the institution whatever information is necessary to fulfill the role.

In some situations, the legislation will require the actuary to inform the regulator if the actuary feels that intervention by the regulator is necessary. This is called a *whistle-blowing* role.

A few examples of legislated roles are given below:

- Syndicates writing general insurance business in the Lloyd's specialist insurance market must appoint an actuary (the "Syndicate Actuary") to provide an annual opinion on the adequacy of their worldwide technical provisions.

- US life insurers must appoint an "Illustration Actuary" to certify that illustrations of benefits under policies comply with the standards.

- UK insurance companies and friendly societies with with-profits insurance liabilities must appoint a "With-Profits Actuary" to provide technical advice to the institution's board of directors focused on the fair treatment of policyholders.

- US defined benefit retirement plans must appoint an "Enrolled Actuary" to monitor their compliance with levels of funding required by the regulators.

Some legislated roles can be quite narrow and specific, for example certifying values for taxation purposes or making calculations for the purpose of dividing up the rights to retirement benefits in divorce cases.

Other roles can be wide-ranging. For example, in Australia every life insurance company must at all times have a single individual who takes overall responsibility for actuarial advice across several areas. This role is called the "Appointed Actuary" and is described in more detail in Section 15.10.5. Other jurisdictions have similar roles, which may be called Appointed Actuary, "Responsible Actuary," or some other term. The scope of the role will vary from country to country. The principle behind having a single individual taking the role is that the Appointed Actuary can see the whole picture, instead of having several different actuaries each focusing on different aspects. In practice, for a large institution the Appointed Actuary will have to delegate much of the work to other actuaries, but will still retain the overall responsibility.

3.5 Professional issues to consider while you work on any task

3.5.1 Ethical behavior

Everyone, not just members of a profession, should behave with integrity and respect for others. We're not suggesting that professionals are somehow more ethical than people who are not members of a profession. But being professional means that you have to meet higher standards, because that is what is being assumed by those who know that you are a professional.

For example, if someone tells you something in your non-professional life, it would be quite reasonable to use that information or pass it on. But if you are told in your capacity as a professional, then you have to meet a higher standard of confidentiality.

Again, there is no law against selfishness, but in your professional life, you have a responsibility to your client ahead of yourself. You must take care to avoid conflicts of interest that could affect your independence, or appear to do so.

In some situations it is easy to know what the ethical thing to do is, although it may be hard to actually do it. If you feel uncomfortable about some action you are contemplating, ask yourself: How would I feel if my family knew about this? How would I feel if my actions were reported in the newspaper headlines? Or, in the case of a complex issue which would be difficult to explain to non-experts, how would I feel justifying my actions to a fellow actuary whom I respect?

In other situations it may not be clear, and you may find yourself in a difficult position, choosing between least worst alternatives. Then it can help to seek advice from other members of the profession.

3.5.2   Conflicts of interest

As professionals, actuaries have a duty to put their clients' interests first. The only exception is in the whistle-blowing role mentioned in 3.4.5, where the actuary has a higher responsibility to the public interest. Actuaries must always look out for areas where the clients' interests may conflict with their own interests, or indeed where the client may have a conflict of interest.

While ideally you would avoid conflicts of interest, this is not always possible. For example, suppose you are advising both sides in a transaction. You might be the only available person with expertise to provide advice. Whenever you are aware of a conflict of interest, you should have regard to your code of conduct. This may say that you can proceed to give advice even if a conflict of interest exists, as long as it is disclosed to all parties involved.

3.5.3   Consideration of other stakeholders

In many situations where actuaries are giving advice, there are stakeholders other than the direct client. You need to be aware of their interests. Some of the regulatory roles make this explicit. For example, an Appointed Actuary in a life insurance company has to consider the interests of the policyholders as well as the interests of the shareholders.

You must always be aware that advice you provide may be relied upon by third parties. For example, suppose that you are consulted by a company set up to grow olive trees. This sort of operation is not generally covered by prudential regulation. You consider all the aspects of their planned operation: how much money they intend to raise in the form of equity and debt, how the operation will be managed, the projections for harvests and sales of olives, and the risk management procedures in place, and conclude in your report that the proposal is sound and that there is little risk that the debt cannot be repaid. You then discover that the company is approaching potential lenders and quoting the professional opinion of an actuary that the debt is very low risk. You would be particularly alarmed if you now remember that, since you know nothing about the likely harvest per tree or future prices for olives, you relied entirely on the company's own figures for your projections. When you prepared your report you should have taken into account exactly this possibility, that the company would be using your words to persuade others.

Exercise 3.6

In the situation of the olive tree farm described above, what steps should you have taken to avoid the potentially misleading use of your report?

3.5.4   Materiality

Materiality means how much something matters, or how much difference it will make to the final outcome. For example, if you are calculating the present value of cash flows of millions of dollars payable over the next decade, the choice of discount rate is very material. The materiality of your work is always an issue you should bear in mind. While you must follow the professional standards, this can involve more or less work to suit the materiality of the task. It would be ridiculous to spend hours selecting a possible model for discount rates if you were calculating the present value of a cash flow of one dollar in one day's time. It would also be unprofessional to charge the client for your time doing such research.

Having regard to materiality will also involve your professional judgment as to which parts of the task will require the most attention in the context of the particular job.

3.5.5   Reliance on other experts

You should be prepared to call in an expert to provide advice in areas in which you don't have expertise. Don't be overconfident. Knowing your limitations is a key to being professional; giving advice or opinions where you are not capable is unprofessional.

In carrying out a task, an actuary may have to start with work done by others. You should disclose this. The professional standard will usually say that you can take data which has been audited as reliable.

There are special considerations when using models designed by others. The US actuarial standard on this (Actuarial Standards Board, 2000) provides some useful guidelines:

*   your effort to understand and evaluate the model should be consistent with the materiality;

*   you should consider the expertise of the model designers;

*   you should have some idea of how the model works and how it has been tested, validated and calibrated;

*   you should consider whether the model is appropriate for your purpose; and

*   as always, you should check results for reasonableness.

3.6   How to do a professional job

When you are performing actuarial work, you should be conscious of the issues of professionalism such as those outlined in 3.5 above. You should also bear in mind that the penalties for unprofessional work can be severe.

We will now discuss some further practical aspects of how you should approach your work as a professional. We will refer to the person or organization for whom you are providing an actuarial service as your "client," whether this is a client in the more traditional meaning (a person or organization who obtains a professional service from a practitioner for a fee) or your employer.

You should take account of all professional standards and guidance. Apart from covering the essential technical matters, these will usually expand on the points mentioned below.

3.6.1 Before you start

We have noted above that it is fundamental to being professional that you only take on actuarial tasks which you are competent to perform. You must have up-to-date knowledge of relevant legislation and standards, technical and practical skills, and the necessary experience. If you are inexperienced you may work under the guidance of a more experienced actuary. In fields where actuaries have not worked before, you will have to use your judgment about whether your knowledge and experience in related tasks equip you to provide a professional service.

You must also be sure you have the time and any other necessary resources to complete the job within the required timeframe.

3.6.2 Define the task

The next step is to make sure that you understand what is required, and your client knows what you will deliver as a result of your work. Communication is a very important part of actuarial work, and it starts right at the beginning of the job.

In many situations of actuarial work, it is not enough just to listen to what your client is asking you to do. You also have to understand your client's background and the issues the client is facing. This is vital so that you can interpret your client's instructions and requests correctly. Clients aren't always good at explaining what they want done. But even if the instructions are clear, you have to stop and think: Is your client asking the right question? Also, if you are being asked to do a limited part of a larger job, does your client understand the limitations of your work?

In defining the task, be clear about whether you are expected to simply calculate the numbers needed, or if you are to create a final report/presentation to deliver to the client. The difference between the two can greatly affect the amount of time needed to complete the project.

3.6.3 Collect the information you need

The need for quality data is emphasized in later chapters. We will simply mention here that this is one of the biggest areas where pressure is placed on professionalism: data is always difficult and expensive to obtain in a timely manner and you will often be pressured to come up with answers from inadequate data. Be careful! Even where you think this is not a problem, check the data for reasonableness and set out in your report what data you have used and the checks you have made.

The information you need will also cover issues such as establishing your client's attitude to risk, and what form your final report will take.

Be sure to review the data as soon as you receive it. If the first time you look at it is when you need to use it, you may find a problem and need to request new data. This could take some time and potentially delay the entire project.

3.6.4 Check for reasonableness

We have mentioned above that you should check for reasonableness when you receive data, and when you rely on the output of models provided by others. Naturally, you must also check the results of your own work, at intermediate stages and at the end of the job. It is worth emphasizing this point, as it is easy to lose sight of the meaning of your answers in the complexity of doing the work. A few simple checks may save you from a serious blunder.

3.6.5 Communicating the results

Once again, communication is very important. Actuarial work often involves dealing with very uncertain cash flows, which may have to be reduced to a single number or range of numbers. You need to communicate the variability surrounding any answer you give, as well as setting out clearly the relevant information about the data, the assumptions and the methodology used in arriving at the answer. What is relevant will vary with the circumstances.

Communicate the results in the appropriate format. If you have been working on a large, detailed project, a formal report and/or presentation are necessary. If the client has asked you a quick question, a short email may be more appropriate. Also, keep the intended audience in mind. If the client has no actuarial background, do not use technical terms without explanations of their definitions and importance.

3.7 Practical implications for actuaries

Being a member of a profession is very important for any actuary. Some aspects of behaving in a professional way are quite obvious, such as complying with all the relevant professional standards. Other issues, such as being sensitive to conflicts of interest, or thinking about the impact of our work on all stakeholders, are more subtle. For this reason, actuarial bodies run courses on professionalism which explore the issues in depth. This chapter is only an introduction to the area, but we hope it serves the purpose of alerting you to the need to be professional.

3.8 Key learning points

*   A profession exists to provide an important service, the quality of which cannot be easily judged before, or sometimes even after, the service is performed.

*   Professionals do work which cannot be managed by applying a set of rules to every case. However, there are professional standards about the way in which the work should be done.

*   The actuarial profession is more international than many other professions. There is usually an actuarial professional body at the national level. The International Actuarial Association (IAA) is an umbrella association of professional actuarial bodies around the world, which serves as a forum to enable the actuarial profession to deal with issues at the international level.

*   The professional actuarial body will have a code of conduct, which sets out general principles on how actuaries should perform their work. A fundamental part of all the codes of conduct is that actuaries should only take on tasks that they are competent to perform. In addition to the code of conduct, there are usually written standards of practice covering different aspects of actuarial work.

- All actuaries have a joint responsibility for the standards of the profession. If you have concerns, you can talk the issue over with any experienced member of the profession. Peer review is a positive component of professionalism.

- It is likely that you must already comply with a code of professional conduct, even if you are not yet a fully qualified actuary.

- Professions often play a part in the regulatory system, and this is particularly true of actuaries. Actuaries play a regulatory role in prudential supervision, customer protection, and disclosure.

- A professional approach to your work begins before you start, and carries on throughout your work on the task. Communication skills are very important in many aspects of actuarial work.

CD Items

Actuarial Society of India 2009, Professional Conduct Standards Ver. 3.00, effective December 1, 2009, http://www.actuariesindia.org.

American Academy of Actuaries 2001, Code of Conduct, effective January 1, 2001, http://www.actuary.org.

Canadian Institute of Actuaries 2006, Rules of Professional Conduct, effective July 2006, http://www.actuaries.ca.

Institute of Actuaries of Australia 2009, Code of Conduct, effective January 1, 2010, http://www.actuaries.asn.au.

Mitchell, R.B. 1974, Excerpts from *From Actuarius to Actuary, The Growth of a Dynamic Profession in Canada and the United States*, Society of Actuaries.

Society of Actuaries 2008, Code of Conduct for Candidates, effective December 1, 2008, http://www.soa.org.

The UK Actuarial Profession 2009, The Actuaries' Code, effective October 1, 2009, http://www.actuaries.org.uk.

Chapter 3 Exercise Solutions

References (other than CD Items)

Actuarial Standards Board 2000, Actuarial Standard of Practice No. 38, Using Models Outside the Actuary's Area of Expertise (Property and Casualty).

Burrage, M. 1990, Beyond a Subset: The Professional Aspirations of Manual Workers in France, the United States and Britain, in Burrage, M. & Torstendahl, R. (eds), *Professions in Theory and History*, Sage Publications, London and Newbury Park, California.

Compliance/Peer Review Working Party 2000, Monitoring Compliance with Professional Guidance, *British Actuarial Journal*, 6, II, pp. 365-431.

Daykin, C. D. 2009, Private communication.

Financial Reporting Council 2008, *Discussion Paper: Promoting Actuarial Quality*, London.

Foley, P., Shaked, A. & Sutton, J. 1982, *The Economics of the Professions*, LSE, London.

Hickman, J. 2004, History of Actuarial Profession, in *Encyclopedia of Actuarial Science*, John Wiley & Sons, 2004.

Ryan, A.W., Bakos, T. & Bloom, L. 2003, Case Studies in Professionalism, SOA/AAA/CIA Annual Meeting, Session 731F, Orlando.

Fred's Coffee Shop – The Need for Financial Products

There is one area where Fred's role as an actuary and his role as a coffee shop owner intersect. As an actuary, Fred worked for a company that supplied financial services. Now, as the owner of a retail business, Fred will be a consumer of financial services. He has a good starting point because he has been able to save some money and has only ten more years of mortgage repayments before he owns his home. But he may need financing to set up the shop and there are both personal and business risks in his future.

On the personal side, he is aware of risks such as:

- early death, permanent disability or costly illness;
- not having enough funds available to retire at a reasonable age; and
- the costs of raising children or taking care of elderly parents.

On the business side, consider:

- changes in the economy, including interest rates, inflation and the prices of his supplies, versus the ability and willingness of customers to pay for his products;
- damage to his property, such as fire or water;
- lawsuits from injuries to customers, such as slipping in the store on spilt coffee, being burned by hot coffee, or suffering food poisoning;
- changes in government regulations regarding the workplace environment;
- competition from an international chain of coffee shops placing a shop nearby; and
- a medical discovery that coffee, even in small quantities, is a health hazard.

Are there any additional risks you can add to these lists?

Fortunately, various financial products are available to meet some of Fred's needs. Suppliers include:

- banks, which can provide loans and other means of raising capital;
- life insurance companies, which can provide death and disability cover as well as retirement savings vehicles;
- general insurance companies, which can provide cover for physical damage and liability;
- health insurance companies, which can provide cover for illness; and
- government social programs, including tax or other incentives.

In Chapter 4, you will learn about a wide variety of specific products that help individuals and businesses meet their financial needs and reduce their risks. As you read the chapter, think of Fred and the various products he may want to consider as he gets ready to open his business.

Chapter 4:   The Need for Financial Products
by Anthony Asher

4.1   Meeting needs

The social purpose of any organization is the meeting of some human need. In order to fulfill its purpose, the organization offers products and services that meet these needs. Private companies make a profit if they meet enough of people's perceived needs to generate revenues greater than expenses. In the case of governments and non-profit organizations, the link between meeting needs and revenue is not direct, and those with managerial responsibilities have to find other ways of measuring their success. In some cases, individual organizations form part of a larger system and meet the needs indirectly by providing intermediate goods or services to other parts of the system.

As we have seen, actuaries' professional work is within the broader financial services system – particularly in financial security systems. This chapter looks at the needs served by these systems and the products and services that have been developed to meet them. Many of these needs are for protection against the risks that are also faced by the financial security systems. Designing optimal ways of meeting these needs without imperiling the safety of the system and its component organizations is an actuarial task. The work of actuaries described in the rest of the book is the detail of this task; it is easy to see in product design and pricing, but it also applies to all the components of risk management.

It is important to separately identify the needs, the products, the measures of success in meeting needs and the responsibilities of managers and experts such as actuaries. Actuaries can best serve their employers or the organizations they manage – and their ultimate clients – if they are able to test the results of their work against the needs of the clients for appropriate financial instruments and for financial security.

In this chapter, we look at how financial products meet these needs. First, we look at the needs in detail. Then, we consider the products and services that have been developed to meet these needs. Finally, we consider other sources of financial security.

4.2   The financial life cycle

4.2.1   Introduction to the financial life cycle

The financial life cycle provides a framework for considering the needs of individuals as buyers of financial products at different stages through life. The basic idea of the financial life cycle is spelled out in Modigliani's (1986) Nobel lecture. The elements of the cycle have been intensively investigated in the economics literature. Polachek and Siebert (1993) give an excellent coverage of factors affecting income, and Bodie, McLeavey and Siegel (2008) provide an outline of the investment issues relating to savings. Cooper (2002) uses the framework to analyze the savings needs of British households.

4.2.2   Income

Incomes depend significantly on education levels and age:

- For educated men, income rises with age until the late forties (later in organizations with promotions based on seniority), and then levels off.

- Non-skilled men's incomes peak at around age 30.

- Single women's incomes largely follow the pattern for single men.

- Married women's incomes drop at the birth of the first child, and they seldom catch up.

- Married men appear to have the highest incomes. They have partners who are likely to take a disproportionate share of domestic chores that enables them to work harder. They also incur additional expenses that make more work necessary.

Section four of Asher (2009) shows how these patterns are similar in many different countries over the past 30 years. The income cycle has been explained by *human capital* theory, of which Gary Becker (1983) is the originator – and for which he received a Nobel Prize. Human capital is the accumulated set of skills, knowledge and experience that equips us to earn our income. It is created, or at least supplemented, by education and training but it depreciates over time. As people age, they slow down their investment in new human capital, as they have fewer working years over which to amortize any investment.

4.2.3 Expenses

Expenses have a different pattern:

- Education is a major cost in childhood and young adulthood.

- Setting up house – and buying cars – is expensive. This is aggravated if children arrive early.

- The cost of children generally rises with age and drops when they leave home.

- Medical costs are more or less proportional to the number of people in the household until retirement, after which they rise rapidly.

- Other expenses reduce after retirement, more so as health deteriorates.

4.2.4 Savings

Savings depend on the interaction of income and expenses.

The following simplified model of middle-class wage earners in a nuclear family[1] provides an initial framework of how savings progress:

- Twenties: complete education; start work; marry or live together and set up a separate household; have children. If possible, save for deposit on a house. Depending on time and place, this can vary from a few months' to a few years' income.

---

[1] A *nuclear family* is a household/economic unit that consists of a couple and their children while the children are growing up. Adult children leave the household to set up their own nuclear families. It contrasts with the *extended family*, where several generations live together, and other social arrangements where parents are not solely responsible for raising their children. The nuclear family remains the critical financial unit for many people. This is especially true when younger children are involved. In the 16 countries he investigated in the early 1990s, Andersson (2002) found that between 79 percent and 97 percent of the children under 15 were living with both their natural parents – of whom at least 90 percent were married to each other. Sweden was an exception, as there only some 80 percent were still married.

People can be liquidity constrained when they start work. This means that their consumption is constrained by their inability to borrow enough to live at a level that is likely to be justified by their future earning power. Fears of moral hazard[2] and the lack of the ability to insure risks lead to reluctance on the part of lenders. Student loans may offer the best opportunity to borrow. Banks hope to attract profitable clients for the future, and find that a tertiary education and professional status reduce the moral hazards. Governments may also make loans available in the expectation that their future tax revenues will be enhanced. In many cases, however, young people will be limited to loans secured by their cars and some consumer credit.

- Thirties: Buy a house by borrowing a maximum of some four years of income, secured by a mortgage over the house. Repayments will take 20 percent of earnings over about 20 years. (You should always check numbers like this to ensure that you understand, and that they are correct. A good actuary is a perpetual numbers checker.) House prices can be so high as to price lower income earners out of the market even when both spouses are working. They may rent – but this is unlikely to be much cheaper – or share accommodation; when house prices are high, the trend is for adult children to stay at home for longer.

  Paying off debt as soon as possible is usually prudent. Saving for retirement can then begin. The requirement to contribute to compulsory pension schemes at an earlier age often means that retirement provision begins before debts are repaid. Modeling of the process can show that it might be reasonable to start retirement savings later if a house has been purchased.

- Forties and fifties: planned saving towards a comfortable retirement provision. A retirement income of say one half of final salary may require about one quarter of earnings over the preceding two decades.

- Healthy over-sixties: Depending on finances and inclination, these people can choose to work, or retire, or some combination of the two. Schulz (2002) points out, however, that they normally face obstacles to staying in the formal workforce, not least because of attempts to make job opportunities for younger people.

- Unhealthy over-sixties: These people will not be able to work. As they become frail, they will increasingly need help in their activities of daily living. Included in these activities is the management of their finances.

The cycle is effectively normative: deviations from the norm can be costly. For instance, too little saving may lead to financial hardship in retirement. On the other hand, excessive saving at any point may create unnecessary reduction in consumption at that time. This may not be immediately obvious, but the difficulties faced by young families trying to meet mortgage payments are well known.

Government intervention, in the form of compulsory savings for instance, can create distortions. Subsidies and tax concessions can, on the other hand, change the optimal pattern of savings.

---

[2] For example, the lender may fear that the borrower will default without the capacity to repay the loan, because the consequences do not seem too severe.

The determinants of saving in the economy as a whole constitute a major debate in economics. Smith (1990) provides a useful review that looks at the effects of increases in income and self-employment, tax incentives, income volatility etc.

4.2.5 Different socio-economic classes

The financial life cycle differs between cultures and between socio-economic classes, but can be said to start when individuals begin to accept financial responsibility for themselves.

The major exceptions to this simple model are the rich, the poor and entrepreneurs:

- Those with significant personal assets clearly do not need to save for retirement.

- Low levels of income, and unemployment, disrupt the chances of marriage and separate household formation, and make saving difficult. People in this position are unable to make prior provision for retirement and are likely to work for as long as possible and then rely on support from family members or from society (charity or state benefits).

- Entrepreneurs will often need capital for their businesses, which inevitably makes them save a considerable proportion of their income (Smith, 1990). This is desirable to the extent that the return on capital in their enterprises is greater than the cost of capital they would otherwise have to raise. The concentration of their assets in their own businesses represents, however, a risk that they may be left destitute if their businesses fail.

Exercise 4.1

(a) Develop a simple human capital model of income progression from ages 25 to 65 on a spreadsheet. Assume that 25 percent of income is "invested" in accumulating human capital. Assume that it yields a return of 5% per annum that is added to salary. Accumulate the investment but depreciate it (declining balance method) at 5% per annum. See if this corresponds with any examples of income progression over the lifetime that you can find.

(b) How do you expect your own financial life cycle to work out? Develop a workbook of spreadsheets that allows you to experiment with different scenarios of income, expenses and savings. Make plausible assumptions about the unknown.

- The spreadsheet should give details, by year, of income and expenses broken down into regular and irregular spending. It should separately consider at least housing, transport, rates and taxes, recreation, medical costs and schooling. Include borrowing, saving and the accumulation of assets and liabilities.

- Graph the results showing income, expenses, assets and liabilities from age 20 through to 90.

(c) What income do you think you would need in a comfortable retirement? Think about the expenses you will no longer incur – and the extra expenses you may incur – when you are no longer working. Using your spreadsheet, see how much you have to save to provide this retirement income.

(d) How might the spreadsheet change for someone earning a very low wage?

(e) From your spreadsheet, do you look as if you will be liquidity constrained at first? Test this by setting your expenditure so that your assets are more or less exhausted by age 90. You probably will find that your spreadsheet tells you that you would have to go into more debt at younger ages than a bank is likely to lend you. Does this mean you should borrow more? See what happens if you are retrenched and take early retirement at 50.

4.3   Risks and volatility in the life cycle

4.3.1   Studies of household income, expenses and savings

Much intriguing data on the volatility of income, expenses and savings has come from the Panel Study on Income Dynamics started in 1970 by the University of Michigan. Duncan et al (2004) provide a fascinating report on some of the findings in the first 30 years. The study has been copied widely in developed countries. The Institute for Social and Economic Research (ISER) at the University of Essex, for instance, runs the British Household Panel Survey. The Australian equivalent is The Household, Income and Labour Dynamics in Australia (HILDA) Survey, based at the University of Melbourne.

The results that have emerged appear to be similar in all countries.[3] Relatively few families remain persistently in poverty but the actual progress of income from year to year can be described as "chaotic" and a third or more of the population can suffer unexpected and significant drops in income at some point in a decade. The particular challenge to actuaries, and one crucial to our social role, is to discover ways of ameliorating the consequences of these drops in income.

Changes to family composition (particularly divorce) prove to be the major contributors to financial instability. Young adults leaving home frequently see a dramatic drop in their standard of living. Also of interest is the spread and volatility of income progression in the light of changes to inflation and other economic variables.

The financial risks encountered by individuals in the course of the life cycle can be analyzed into the categories discussed in 4.2: risks to income, risks from expenses, and risks in saving.

4.3.2   Income risks

What are these risks? Family income can be reduced by two obvious life contingencies (death and disability) and by unemployment.

Death

If some family members are fully or partly dependent on income earned by other family members, the lives of the income-earners should be insured.

The most obvious need is for the support of orphans. The presence of children in a household not only increases expenses but also diverts time from parents' opportunities to

---

[3]   Details can be found on the website http://www.iser.essex.ac.uk/ulsc, which has links to initiatives in other countries.

earn. Most poverty, worldwide, is experienced by single parent families (most often headed by mothers) with young children.

Disability

Where disability leads to a loss of income, there is a need for income replacement – whether the disability is temporary or permanent, total or partial. This can be provided by insurance.

Disabled people need rehabilitation, either to aid recovery or to mitigate the effect of permanent disability. Some return to the workforce and "normal" life is almost always a possibility – and is generally recognized as the best treatment. Rehabilitation may require special equipment or other provision and needs special effort from family, employer and insurance provider. Rehabilitation may be difficult and even painful for the disabled person. It is, however, not only superior from a human point of view but likely to be less costly in the long run.

Ill health does not necessarily lead to the inability to work. Many people who have lost, or lost the use of, limbs, eyes or ears are able to live very productive lives. Others with debilitating conditions, such as schizophrenia or high blood pressure, can similarly continue to work. Such people may, however, be at greater risk of becoming unemployed – especially when jobs are scarce. Smith (1998) provides details of a study that suggests that ill health has a long-term negative effect on assets and earning power. This is more difficult to insure but part of the need might be met by the critical illness insurance described in 4.5.2.4 below.

Unemployment

The most important cause of income reduction recorded in the panel studies is reduced employment (normally in overtime, which often makes up a significant proportion of the wages), or total unemployment.

There are indications that unemployment may become more of a problem in the future than it has been in the past. The greater efficiency of manufacturing industries worldwide, rapid technological change and policies encouraging free trade create pressures on companies to be globally competitive. This often means laying off staff in order to cut costs. The need for some insurance against unemployment is probably greater than previously.

Unfortunately, insurance is not always possible – as we will see in Section 4.5.2.3 below. Without private insurance, people will need to find other sources of support and reduce their expenses. Support can come from family, state assistance or the drawing down of assets, possibly in the form of an early retirement.

4.3.3 Expense risks

Expense risks include:

• divorce, resulting in the need to set up separate households;

• damage to property, or to other persons, who then claim compensation;

• medical expenses;

• the cost of frail care, especially for the elderly;

- interest charges, on housing loans particularly;
- inflation; and
- longevity risk, being the risk of outliving one's retirement savings.

Some of these risks are discussed below.

Divorce

This is a major source of financial hardship and is probably uninsurable. The law may compel the better-off partner, probably the non-custodial parent if there are children, to contribute to the support of the poorer partner – overwhelmingly the mother.

Property

People normally accumulate tangible assets as they age. The most serious loss would be significant damage to a house. Losses to cars, household appliances and furniture are likely to be less significant, but might still be worth insuring. Insuring against the damage that one's own car might do to other people's property and person is likely to be compulsory in the form of public liability insurance.

It is worth remarking that people are not always logical and can both under-insure and over-insure. Arguably, one should only buy insurance against losses that would be significant. This can be achieved through the use of *excesses* where the people insured pay for smaller claims themselves and pay the first part of large claims. It is, however, sometimes difficult to find an insurer that will offer a sufficiently large excess.

Medical costs

Medical expenses can be divided into several different categories for the purpose of examining their impact on people's financial security. At one end, there are smaller costs – such as visits to the family doctor – that are unimportant financially to most people. At the other end there are cosmetic operations and time in luxury hospitals that can be paid for if people have the money.

In the middle are expenses that are necessary, but cannot be paid out of normal income. They can, however, be covered by medical insurance. Medical insurance pools the risks, thus turning irregular and potentially crippling costs into easier regular payments.

The level of costs differs significantly from country to country, but costs have risen dramatically as a proportion of GDP in most countries. Statistics in OECD (2009) show that health care expenditure averaged nine percent of GDP in 2007 in the 26 of 30 countries surveyed for which data was available.[4] Costs have been rising on average by 2% per annum faster than GDP (over periods that range from 15 to 45 years) with no signs of abating. The main reason is that technological change continues to add new medical services: machines, drugs and procedures. The increase may therefore be not so much an increase in costs as an improvement in quality. It is expensive, but we would want as many people as possible to have the benefits of new technology.

---

[4]   This is a simple average, which does not allow for differences in population and GDP. It is noteworthy that the US figure is almost 16 percent.

Medical costs also increase as people age – for obvious reasons (and the aging of the OECD populations also plays a role in the increase in medical costs as a percentage of GDP). Some other expenses reduce as people age but the two seldom match exactly: medical costs are incurred disproportionately in the last year of life rather than rising gradually with age. There is, therefore, the need to include some allowance for increased medical costs when looking at the life cycle described in Section 4.2 above.

The level of medical care that can be offered appears to have almost no limits and might be regarded as effectively arbitrary. Even short-run usages fluctuate significantly and medical insurers can face large changes in their financial results. They manage these by increasing contributions or restricting their reimbursement of expenses. In national health schemes (ie where medical services are provided by the state, either free or at subsidized prices), control is maintained by explicit rationing or by requiring people to queue.

Private insurance, in countries where it is not compulsory, can be vulnerable to *anti-selection*. People can, for instance, remain uncovered by medical insurance and then opt to take out cover in the year before they have a baby. They can then claim for a variety of expenses where they have some control of the incidence: dental treatment, new spectacles and minor surgery. This anti-selection is worse where legislation restricts underwriting.

Interest

Changes to interest rates become a problem when relatively high and volatile inflation leads to dramatic increases in mortgage repayments. *Variable* or *floating rate* mortgage loans allow the lender to change interest rates after a short period of notice. If a mortgage loan has a long outstanding term (say, over 20 years), a significant proportion of the remaining repayments will be interest. A 50 percent increase in the interest rate will therefore translate into a substantial increase in the mortgage payment – typically, well over 25 percent and possibly over 40 percent.

As lenders may allow installments of up to 30 percent of a person's before-tax income, such increases can lead to severe hardship. Mortgage interest rates in South Africa, for instance, moved from 12% to 18% between 1989 and 1990 and from 18% to 25% between 1998 and 1999. Both periods saw high levels of bad debts amongst the lenders and many people evicted from their houses.

Mortgage loans in the US have traditionally been fixed for the full term of the loan, which provides protection for the borrower against rising interest rates. These loans normally include an option to refinance at no penalty should interest rates decline. In other countries, interest rates can be fixed often for shorter periods and sometimes with significant repayment penalties if interest rates decline.

Inflation

People may be retired for 30 years or more, over which period it is clearly necessary to allow for many unexpected changes in the general level of prices.

Figure 4.1 gives a 90-year history of US inflation. Even this, the world's largest and most stable economy, has suffered three bouts of significant inflation over the period. The chart shows that wages (for which per capita income is an estimate) more than kept pace except during the Great Depression. Those most at risk of inflation are those on a fixed income such as pensioners. By inspecting the graph, you can see that the value of a fixed pension for someone retiring in 1940 would have halved by the mid-1950s and halved again by the mid-1970s.[5]

Figure 4.1   US inflation[6]

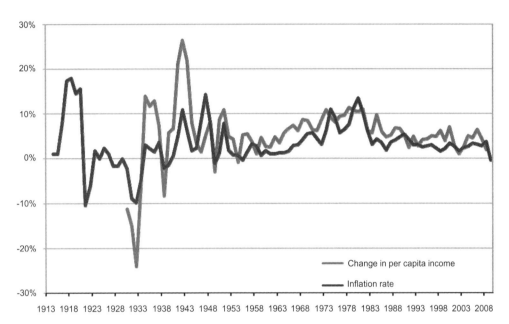

4.3.4   Risks in savings

Issues of investment risks are dealt with in more detail in Chapter 14. At this stage we note the significance of investment risk to the average person. The worst situation is when negative real returns occur close to – or after – retirement, as there is then little opportunity to add to savings. It will become clear in later chapters that these risks create major imponderables in future planning because the confidence interval for future real investment returns is very wide.

Volatility of real returns is an issue even with well-selected, diversified portfolios of investments. For a typical consumer, there are other greater risks. Indeed, there are many ways of losing one's entire life savings: embezzlement by a fraudulent adviser; collapse of a financial institution from which one has purchased savings products; concentrating one's savings in one risky venture that then fails; and political risks such as war or confiscation of property by a revolutionary government.

---

5   It is possible to do quick calculations of this sort if you know the rule of 72, which gives a quick approximation to how long it takes for money to double (or halve):
   $(1+f)^n = 2 \rightarrow n \ln(1+f) = \ln 2 \rightarrow n = .72/f$ (.72 more or less correct for f = 7.5%)
6   Created from US Census and Bureau for Economic Analysis Data obtained from ftp://ftp.bls.gov/pub/special.requests/cpi/cpiai.txt and http://www.bea.gov/regional/spi, both accessed January 27, 2010.

Chapter 7 on regulation and Chapter 15 on solvency are related directly to these issues. However, it could be said that the whole work of actuaries revolves around seeking solutions to these problems, directly or indirectly.

Exercise 4.2

(a) Using the workbook you created earlier, experiment with income, higher expenses or different investment returns.

(b) List the different insurance cover you want at different times of your life. If you expect to be liquidity-constrained at some point, what insurance would a bank want before it lent money to ease your constraints?

(c) We have mainly considered a middle class, nuclear family unit. Many people of course do not live this way. Consider how the income and expense risks may vary for people in other situations. A single person with no dependents, for example, does not need life insurance but may have greater need for disability insurance, to cover household expenses and pay for the sort of assistance a spouse might otherwise provide. Give some other examples.

4.4 Business needs

There is also a financial life cycle of businesses, which begins with their formation and the raising of funds. Various financial instruments have been developed in order to assist in raising these funds and protecting them against risk.

4.4.1 Equity or capital

With some exceptions (such as terminating building societies[7]) businesses are meant to exist in perpetuity – although their mortality (in the form normally of takeover or insolvency) is high. The normal intention is for the initial funding to continue to be available. Funding can be in the form of borrowing or equity, with some equity or capital (or an equivalent guarantee to creditors) always required to absorb possible losses, and ensure that the creditors can be paid.

The form of the equity depends on the legal form of the business. Economically developed societies allow for a range of different business structures. Most simple of the forms are individuals operating as sole traders or in a group as partners. In such cases, equity comes directly from the owners of the business, but is normally kept in separate accounts – if only for tax purposes.

More sophisticated businesses are separate legal entities, where the owners have a limited liability to make good any losses. Non-profit businesses (and here we might include trusts

---

[7] These are temporary bodies that collect deposits from their members and allocate loans on a lottery basis to the members. They are disbanded when all the original members have bought houses and repaid their mortgage bonds.

set up to own assets for other people) will receive an injection of capital that will be reflected in their accounts, with the rights of the donors and other stakeholders included in the constitution (also called the articles of association).

Since the late 18th century, when developed countries passed enabling legislation, the most common form of commercial enterprise is the limited company. Internationally, however, various different legal structures are possible: trusts, companies created by statute or under simplified legislation, different types of association, etc. Such separate entities need some founding capital before they can begin operation.

Incorporated sole proprietors can operate similarly. Where more than one party provides capital, there will be a need to keep account of their different shares. The shares (called common stock in the US) can be subject to restrictions posed by the constitution, and are not necessarily entitled to equal shares in the profit, or equal rights to vote at general meetings of shareholders that elect directors of the companies. Preference shares, for instance, are normally entitled to a fixed rate of dividend and do not include the right to vote, unless their dividends are unpaid.

Public companies list their equity on one or more stock exchanges to allow owners of equity to buy and sell easily. These companies are subject to the rules of the stock exchange, which typically require disclosure and provide other protection to owners of equity against unfair behavior by management and controlling voting blocks of equity.

4.4.2 Managing risks

Businesses face the risk of losses that will reduce their capital to a level where it is no longer sufficient to continue trading. The management may also be concerned with large fluctuations in profit that reduce confidence in the business. For our purposes, we can divide the risks taken by businesses into three types.

Insurable risks

Businesses face physical risks to assets, liability risks that might arise from tort claims (where the directors or the business is found to have been negligent and caused harm to employees or customers), the risks of internal or external fraud and risks from external events that might lead to loss of revenue or additional costs (such as drought or hail). It is usually possible to buy insurance to cover the financial effect of these risks.

Hedgeable risks

Businesses are also exposed to unexpected price movements unequally affecting their revenues and costs, leading to unexpected (and potentially unaffordable) losses. If their prices are closely linked to those of traded commodities, it may be possible to hedge these risks using derivative instruments that are based on the commodity prices.

Other risks

There are other risks that are neither insurable nor hedgeable. These can arise from the business plan or from the capacity of the business to compete in its market (such as technical changes that make its product irrelevant). In both cases, the risks have to be actively addressed by the business's management and cannot be taken by outside parties.

4.4.3   Tax and regulatory arbitrage

Both individuals and businesses are entitled to organize their affairs in such a way that they pay as little tax as possible, provided that they are honest.

Because different financial instruments can attract quite different tax treatments, tax management plays a particularly important role in the financial structuring of companies. *Tax arbitrage* can happen if it is possible to make a guaranteed reduction in tax by changing some element of the company's operations.

Regulatory arbitrage arises if it is possible to reduce legal restrictions on the company's operations or the capital required by changing the legal nature of the business or changing regulatory regimes – if that capital is not really needed for solvency purposes.

From a private perspective, failing to take advantage of honest tax arbitrage opportunities can be seen as making a donation to government revenue. They may not be socially desirable activities, but the onus is on tax collectors to limit the possibilities and regulators to make them unnecessary.

Exercise 4.3

(a) Can you list the types of business form that exist in your country?

(b) "Tax planning is made possible because governments want to encourage certain business practices." Would you say that this statement was true? What might it be missing?

4.5   Products designed to meet financial needs

Having considered why people and businesses need financial products, we now turn to the various financial products and services[8] that have been developed to meet these needs. These can be grouped into four categories:

*   monetary products, including money itself;

*   insurance;

*   long-term savings; and

*   retirement income products.

Note that Chapter 6 (Applying Risk Management) discusses issues around dealing with risk in the provision of financial products.

---

[8] There are not generally well-defined distinctions between "financial products" and "financial services" and variations such as "financial services products" are also common. In this book we use the terms interchangeably.

4.5.1   Monetary products

4.5.1.1   Money or transaction services

Cowry shells and the like, which were used as an intermediate store of value to simplify barter transactions, were probably the first financial services product. Davies (2002) suggests that banknotes were next, preceding the development of coinage. Receipts for grain stored in the palaces of ancient Mesopotamia could be used for the purchasing of other goods. Given that they used clay tablets, "banktablets" would perhaps be a more descriptive term.

Perhaps the most basic form of money today, called or forming part of *M0* or *M1*, is the notes and coins issued by central banks. Its value is guaranteed by *legal tender* legislation that requires everyone transacting business in a country to accept it – although this does not prevent inflation eroding its worth.

The next layer of money supply, which goes under a variety of names including *M2*, *M3* and *M4*, includes all sorts of easily-negotiable financial instruments.

Most commonly used are *current*, *cheque* (*checking*) or *money market* accounts with banks (in which we include similar institutions such as building societies or credit unions). These can be accessed by methods including:

*   checks – pre-printed instructions for the bank to pay to another;

*   debit cards – where vendors can draw directly from the accounts of their customers when presented with the plastic card;

*   debit orders – where service providers (such as utility suppliers and insurance companies) electronically instruct the bank to pay them from their customers' accounts;

*   standing orders – where the accountholder can instruct the bank to pay a regular amount to a service provider;

*   a variety of computerized or internet banking options (including more old-fashioned telegraphic transfers to foreign countries) – where the accountholder can instruct the bank to transfer money to another account; and

*   a bank branch or automatic teller machine (ATM).

Also included in money are all sorts of short-term bank deposits, negotiable certificates of deposit issued by banks, and short-term securities issued by government or other corporations. The latter are mainly used by businesses, which also need most of the transaction services listed above.

4.5.1.2   Short-term savings products

The line between money for transaction purposes and savings through bank deposits is blurred. In some countries, current accounts earn interest. Accounts with longer notice periods, or *term deposits*, will normally pay higher rates of interest. The notice periods or terms can be as much as five years in some environments. The rate of interest payable will normally be pre-determined; in order to cover initial expenses (and defer tax), it may well be *stepped* – ie increasing over time.

Other short-term savings instruments include *money market funds* or *cash management trusts*, which allow unitholders to participate in a portfolio of short-term investments that may well include some higher-yielding but riskier loans.

4.5.1.3 Borrowing instruments

Individuals

There are four main types of loan used by individuals:

- *Hire purchase* is for a relatively short term, secured by the item purchased and attracts high rates of interest. The legal position is that the goods sold remain the property of the seller until all payments have been made. The item is hired, until it is purchased. It is mainly used for cars and large items of household furniture.

- Other *consumer credit* consists of *credit cards* normally managed by banks or *credit* or *accounts* with retailers. If the balance outstanding on credit cards is paid off monthly, no interest will normally be charged. Retail credit may be advertised as interest-free, but discounts are often obtainable for cash. The interest rates charged are high both because the small size of the loans means that administration charges are proportionately high, and because risks are high given that there is no collateral.

- Banks offer *mortgage loans* to finance house purchases. These loans can be of a much longer term and, because of their size and security, come at a lower interest rate.

  The problems associated with fluctuating-rate mortgages were discussed in 4.3.3 above. The obvious solution is a fixed-interest mortgage as in the US. It is, however, not clear that such contracts would be attractive to borrowers without the option to repay without penalty, or attractive to investors without a government body to underwrite the risks.

  An alternative is a *dual indexed mortgage*, where one index refers to the rate at which installments are increased – often in line with average salaries – and the other index is the interest rate used to determine the amount of loan outstanding. Another alternative is *salary-linked home finance* described in Asher (2009), which are instruments where the installment is fixed in advance as a percentage of income. (The fixed percentage could be determined by dividing the amount to be lent by the term of the loan and again by current salary.) In addition to protecting borrowers against fluctuations in interest rates, these instruments could provide investors with an investment that grows in line with salary inflation.

- Banks also offer their wealthier customers the option of an *overdraft*, which means that the balance on their current accounts can be negative – up to predefined limits. Interest rates here will depend on the customer's creditworthiness, but will be higher than mortgage rates.

Businesses

Businesses can raise funds using most of these methods – and two more.

Larger companies can issue *debentures* or *bonds* that may be traded and listed on a bond or stock exchange. The rate of interest can be fixed or floating, depending either on what the company thinks offers the best value at the time or the nature of the cash flows that will be used to pay the interest. As with mortgages, interest can be capitalized.

The business can sell an asset that is created through *securitization*. Where businesses are in receipt of cash flows that are readily identified and are not much exposed to moral hazards, the cash flows can be "securitized" and sold directly to investors. The cash flows are purchased by a *special purpose vehicle* (SPV), the funders of which accept all profits and losses from the cash flows.

The SPV will normally be funded by different tiers of capital that take on different layers of the risk: first losses will be taken by an "equity tranche," with the most senior debt often enjoying AAA status. The originating business may take a share in the equity and junior tranches of the SPV, or provide some guarantee in order to show its goodwill and reduce moral hazard. SPVs may also take out credit insurance (or credit enhancement) as this can raise their credit rating to that of the credit insurer, which can reduce their cost of borrowing.

Securitization has given rise to a significant number of new financial instruments, the most important of which are shown in Figure 4.2, taken from IMF (2008). The derivative elements are discussed in more detail in Section 4.5.3.6 below, but full and largely reliable descriptions of most of these instruments can be found in online encyclopedias.

Figure 4.2   Modern credit instruments

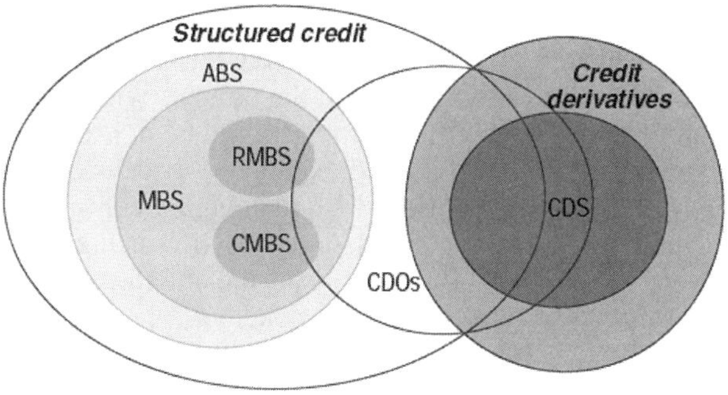

4.5.2   Insurance

4.5.2.1   Life insurance

Life insurance generally provides a cash lump sum (the *sum insured*) in the event of the death of the *life insured*. In the case of *joint life* policies, payment can be made on the death of either the *first-to-die* or the *last-to-die*. Life insurance comes in a range of different packages of cover, investment and additional options (*riders* or *supplementary benefits*).

Some products discussed in other parts of this chapter may be regulated as life insurance. For the purposes of this section, we are only concerned with products that pay benefits on the death of the insured.

Term insurance

Term insurance contracts pay on death before the end of a fixed term. They can offer level or decreasing cover, the latter being suitable to cover a decreasing debt. Generally, a level premium is payable over the term of the contract.

Yearly renewable term insurance (YRT) is the dominant term insurance product in Australia and is found in other markets. Premium rates change each year over the term of the policy, to reflect the relationship between age and mortality risk. Most YRT policies in Australia advance some or all of the sum insured on the diagnosis of a terminal illness – ie when the insured is expected to die within 12 months.

Family income benefits are a variation of *decreasing term insurance*, offering an income to the beneficiaries from the death of the life insured until the end of the fixed term. Family income benefits are, in some ways, the ideal cover to replace the lost income of a breadwinner. However, they have not been widely sold, largely because the income benefit is usually taxable, while lump sums are normally received free of tax. Other variations of decreasing term products are designed to repay a mortgage or other decreasing debt with a lump sum.

Whole life insurance

Term insurance premiums have to be increased at the end of the term if cover is to be maintained at the same level. This is purported to be a marketing problem, although in most cases, the need for cover should reduce with age. *Whole life insurance* contracts offer permanent life cover for a level premium that obviously starts at a much higher level than term policies.

Many policyholders were historically sold whole life contracts on the basis of the permanent cover and level premium. Life insurers preferred the policies with greater premiums and a larger investment component as they provided opportunities for greater profits and reduced the risks posed by variability in mortality and expenses – because some of the risk could be borne by the policyholders. These policies also paid higher commissions to salespeople. These are, however, poor reasons for customers to buy life insurance. It is interesting to note that the Life Insurers Fact Book (2008) confirms the ongoing swing to term insurances in the US, which also appears to be occurring elsewhere.

Unlike term insurance contracts, whole life insurance contracts achieve a *surrender value*, ie an amount for which the contract can be cashed in. Over the long term, this can represent a reasonable return on premiums paid. However, insurance is the primary purpose of the contract.

There are many other types of life insurance contracts that are designed as long-term savings contracts; in fact there are some products classed for legal or taxation purposes as "life insurance" that do not have any actual insurance element at all. We will come back to these products in Section 4.5.3.

4.5.2.2 Disability insurance

Definitions of disability

Disability is normally defined as inability to work. Three types of occupation-based definitions can be used:

*   *own occupation* – no longer able to perform one's normal occupation;
*   *own or similar occupation* – no longer able to perform an occupation for which one is fitted by training and experience; and
*   *any occupation* – no longer able to perform any paid work.

Disability can be *total* or *partial*. There is no universal definition of total disability. Some companies will allow the claimant to be able to work a few hours a wcck and still be considered totally disabled, while others relate the concept to "important duties" or earnings. There is also often an effective difference in the definition of total disability between income and lump sum products, as we will see below.

To provide cover for people who don't work – eg the retired, unemployed or homemakers – some companies use alternative (and far more stringent) definitions of disability, including paraplegia/quadriplegia and an inability to perform more than a few *activities of daily living*, such as bathing, eating, dressing, toileting and transferring from bed to chair.

Disability income insurance

Disability income insurance (DII), *permanent health insurance* (PHI) or *income protection* provides an income stream should the life insured become temporarily unable to work in normal employment because of sickness or injury. Benefits are paid monthly, not as a lump sum. The amount of cover purchased is usually restricted to a percentage, such as 75 percent, of monthly income in order to limit moral hazard.

The period over which claims can be paid is known as the *claim benefit period*. This could be two years, five years, or until retirement. There is a *waiting period* before a claim will be paid, the most common periods being 30 or 90 days – depending often on sick leave entitlements.

In many markets, benefits will normally only be payable if the disability is total. Partial benefits may become payable as the insured recovers and is able to begin work on a part-time basis. This is highly desirable from the point of view of rehabilitation. In other markets, products may pay partial benefits without an initial period of total disability.

The amount payable on total disability depends on whether the policy is an *indemnity* policy or *agreed value*. Under an indemnity policy, benefits are limited to the agreed percentage of the level of income shortly before disablement, while the benefit on an agreed value basis is locked in.

Lump sum disability

Total and permanent disablement (TPD), also known as *accelerated benefits*, *disability cash* or *capital disability* cover, provides a lump sum payment that can only be paid after permanent disability is proven. Payments are normally made only on total disability. These covers are normally added as supplementary benefits to life policies.

Single TPD is effectively an advance payment of the equivalent amount of life cover and the underlying policy will continue with the cover reduced by the TPD payout. *Double TPD* payouts do not affect the life cover – so this benefit is more expensive. Some companies offer benefits on the *continental* scale that pays a portion of the lump sum on various events, eg 50 percent for loss of an eye and five percent for loss of a toe.

Waiver of premium

This is another common supplementary benefit, which pays the premiums on a life insurance policy in the event of the disability of the *policyowner*, who is responsible for the premium payments. The premium will also be waived on death if the owner is not the life insured.

Managing claims

The rate of claim on disability insurance contracts is particularly subject to moral hazards and tends to rise with higher *payout ratios* (benefit as a percentage of income before disability) and in times of higher unemployment, especially for causes related to mental health and back pain. The more difficult it is to find a suitable job and the more attractive the disability benefit, the more likely a claim will be made. This is why disability income contracts normally limit claims from all insurers to a maximum payout ratio.

The purpose of insurance is to pay benefits when they are needed, but it is also necessary to contain costs. Disability insurance management requires an extremely difficult balance between concern for people's feelings, rehabilitation, cost control and the reputation of the insurance provider.

4.5.2.3 Unemployment insurance

Unemployment benefits that replace a portion of the lost income can be provided to cover unpredictable and unmanageable events. Such losses can occur for many reasons; most can be categorized into either temporary events that affect small groups of people or permanent technological or demographic changes, which may have a significant impact on the employment rate of the country. The former are insurable, but companies are naturally reluctant to offer much cover for the latter – and because it is difficult to distinguish between the two in practice, very little unemployment insurance is offered by the private sector.

Unemployment insurance bears many similarities to disability insurance, not least because it is those who are least fit who are most at risk of retrenchment. Finding new employment is difficult and even traumatic, especially when there is a shortage of positions. The same balance is needed as in managing disability claims.

In practice, most countries' social security systems provide a basic level of unemployment insurance and private insurance is often limited to a component of *credit insurance* – ie insurance sold by banks to cover the repayments on loans.

4.5.2.4 Medical costs insurance

Medical cover comes in a variety of forms and is normally intended to supplement whatever medical services are provided by the state. It is often used in travel, as foreign visitors are often not entitled to care in state hospitals.

Medical insurance (also called private health insurance or medical aid)

This cover is of indemnity to the life insured for the medical expenses incurred by his or her immediate family. The cover may be for all medicines, consultations, procedures and hospital visits. There may be maximum annual limits to the overall claims, or claims in each category. There may also be *deductibles* (also known as *excesses*), where a fixed amount or proportion of each item must be paid by the insured. These obviously protect the insurer, as the deductibles reduce the moral hazard.

Critical illness insurance (also called trauma or dread disease)

These are not indemnity contracts but pay out a pre-determined amount in the event of the diagnosis (or treatment) of one of a number of conditions listed in the contract. These lists were relatively short when these contracts were introduced in the mid-1980s, but have increased to hundreds of conditions in some cases. These policies are less expensive to administer than more comprehensive medical cover, as they only pay for the larger costs.

These contracts could replace medical insurance, but this is often not permitted by legislation that requires a version of indemnity cover. In such cases, the justification for these policies has to be that the conditions covered can have a debilitating effect on the ability to earn income and may give rise to significant expenses not directly related to treating the condition. The policies can provide funds for rehabilitation or enable the insured to modify his or her future lifestyle as well as compensation for the unpleasantness of a major illness.

Hospital cash

This is the simplest form of medical cover, paying a fixed amount for each day the insured spends in hospital. These contracts fulfill a need to the extent that the more significant medical costs are related to stays in hospital. They may be less relevant in light of the modern medical practice of returning people to their homes as soon as possible after hospital treatment.

Health maintenance organizations (HMOs)

These are a mainly US development, and are a response to rising medical costs and the problems of *third party payment*. The parties are the patient, the health care professional and the insurer. Where medical expenses are fully covered, there is no incentive for the first two parties to reduce costs, particularly if this will impair the quality of care.

In HMOs, the health care professionals are paid a *capitation* amount for each person covered. Their incentive is therefore to keep people healthy so that they do not have to be treated. This may, however, lead to experimentation with cheaper forms of care, which may cause insecurity on the part of members. There have been successes in containing costs, but HMOs are not a panacea.

Long-term care insurance

This covers the costs of assistance with the needs of everyday living, which is a need mainly of the frail aged. Frailty is usually determined by reference to the ability to perform certain activities of daily living. The cover is expensive and not easy to contemplate at a young age; in the US, the Life Insurers Fact Book (2008) reports that, while most purchasers are over 65, the trend is towards younger purchasers – especially the 12 percent of the workforce not covered by employer-based insurance. It also reports that policies are now designed to cover services that promote independent living in addition to institutional care.

It may be appropriate or efficient for care to be provided in an aged care institution, at a cost. It is widely accepted that it is desirable for people to remain outside formal institutions for as long as possible, but increasing numbers will inevitably require admittance.

4.5.2.5   General insurance

This is called *property and casualty insurance* (P&C) in North America, and can also be called short-term insurance because the contracts are reviewed annually – or even after shorter periods. General insurance policies are indemnity contracts.

In most cases, each policy has a *sum insured* on which the premium is based and which places an upper bound on the claim. The insurance, however, only indemnifies the policyholder against financial losses, so the actual claim amount may be smaller than the sum insured. If the sum insured is less than the *maximum loss* possible, then the policyholder is under-insured and the insurer will apply *average* and reduce the claim in the ratio of the sum insured to the maximum loss.

To reduce the level of claims, and virtually eliminate small claims, there is likely to be an *excess*, or *first amount payable* by the insured (also called a *deductible*). Many products, particularly motor insurance, will also qualify for a *no claims discount* (also called a *no claims bonus*) that can see premiums reduced by half or better.

Insurance may be for all *perils* or provide *exclusions* for one or more of: fire, flood, theft, civil commotion, accidents or landslip, which would include earthquake. The excluded events are regarded as uninsurable either because of their potential catastrophic impact on the insurer's solvency or because of moral hazards: the insured either knows more about the risk than the insurer or may lose the incentive to take proper precautions if the insurer bears the risks.

We now discuss the three major *personal lines*, ie types of cover sold to individuals, plus the common types of *business insurance*.

Home insurance

This includes homeowners and householders (or building and contents) insurance. They cover the house or apartment itself and its contents respectively. More valuable personal items such as jewelry may need to be covered separately and present more difficult moral hazards: how do you prove you have lost the diamond out of your engagement ring?

These general insurance contracts are often long and complicated and it is difficult for the insured to understand the extent of their cover. For instance, flood damage may be excluded if it arises from rising water levels but not from falling rain. The challenge is to find ways of providing clients with the necessary cover at the right price. In the case of flood exclusions, the reason may be the difficulty of identifying low-lying properties that are particularly exposed. Arguments can be made that charging them the much higher premiums that would be necessary to give adequate cover would be unfair; a counter argument is that not telling the owners that their properties are at significant risk is also unfair!

Motor

This can cover loss or damage to the policyholder's car and any damage to the person or the car of any *third party. Compulsory third party* (CTP) insurance to cover death, disability and medical insurance is commonly required by governments – perhaps because motor accidents are potentially lethal and a properly-designed scheme can reduce wasteful litigation as to blame and quantum of damages.

In some countries, CTP insurance is subcontracted to private companies. In others, the costs are included in the price of fuel, on the basis that a driver's risk is related to the distance driven.

Personal accident

This is strictly life or disability cover, but limited to losses caused by accident. Short-term insurers can offer it because the risks do not generally increase with age. It may, however, be difficult to integrate with insurance for other causes (such as sickness), leaving people with insurance gaps or excessive entitlements for benefits arising from the accident.

Business insurance

Common types of insurance bought by businesses include:

- *marine insurance* – covering ships, aircraft and goods in transit;

- *fire* and other *property* cover – with the obvious meaning;

- *business interruption insurance* – cover against loss of revenue arising as a consequence of other losses;

- *liability insurance* – cover against claims arising as a consequence of unsafe workplaces or products or negligent practices. This includes *professional indemnity* and *directors and officers* insurance that provides cover against claims for work-related negligence;

- *credit insurance* (or *trade credit insurance*) – cover against debtors failing to make payments, which is especially attractive for exporters who cannot analyze their customers' creditworthiness easily;

- *surety bonds* – insurance purchased by securitized vehicles seeking to enhance their credit ratings; and

- *reinsurance* – insurance for insurers.

Organizations sometimes buy insurance cover that does not appear to be strictly necessary given the risks to which they are exposed:

- Tax and regulatory arbitrage can be a motivation. Insurance premiums can often be paid to companies in low tax jurisdictions that may also require less capital for the same risks. The international conglomerate, which may well own the "captive" insurer, thus earns a higher profit on lower capital.

- Insurance can also be a form of outsourcing: the insurer may know a lot more about the evaluation and management of the risks concerned, leaving the company's management free to concentrate on the job they do best.[9]

- Most countries require employers to take out *workers compensation* insurance to provide life, disability and medical cover for job-related injuries. The objective is to protect workers and employers who might otherwise have to meet very large claims. As with compulsory third party motor insurance, such schemes can also reduce unfruitful litigation, but invariably fail to provide cover for other causes of injury or death.

---

[9] Worldwide reinsurers, particularly, are likely to collect a wider range of statistics than companies have available, and to analyse them in more detail. Technical support provided by reinsurers can, in this way, provide benefits to entire industries. Stephen Bates, an engineer working for an international underwriter, reports that the reinsurers' engineers, informed by their claim statistics, were able to provide significant assistance to companies operating in such various fields as tunnelling and the manufacture of electricity generators. Also gratifying was support on safer construction methods for rebuilding houses in Afghanistan after an earthquake.

4.5.3   Long-term savings products

As we discussed in Section 4.2, the primary purpose of long-term savings is to secure a comfortable retirement. Products designed for long-term savings generally reflect this, although they can often be used for other purposes.

We start this section with traditional life insurance products, and then consider superannuation and various forms of investment-linked contracts.

4.5.3.1   Traditional life insurance savings products

Traditional life insurance savings products dominated the long-term savings market in the 19th century and for much of the 20th century. In exchange for a level premium payable for a fixed term (generally the term of the policy), these products generally pay a *sum insured* at the end of the policy term or on the earlier death of the insured. These products are often *with-profit*, or *participating*, meaning that they share in the distribution of profits, allocated largely at the discretion of the company.

Where traditional policies share in profits, the usual mechanism is to add *bonuses* to the sum insured. These bonuses can be *reversionary*, meaning that they are permanent additions to the sum insured, or *terminal*, meaning that they only vest in the policyowner on the termination of the contract. Often, bonuses are paid in cash (*dividends*) or used to reduce the premium. The identification and distribution of profit is discussed in Chapter 16.

Three main forms of traditional savings policies are offered:

*   *endowment insurances* – that pay the sum insured on death or on survival to the end of the policy term;

*   *pure endowments* – that pay the sum insured on survival to the end of a fixed term and usually give a return of premiums with interest on earlier death; and

*   *deferred annuities* – that pay an annuity when the annuitant reaches a pre-determined age. Today, many versions of this contract operate with the option to take cash at maturity rather than the annuity, effectively making them primarily an investment product.

4.5.3.2   Superannuation funds

Superannuation funds, also called pension or provident funds, are savings vehicles established for the purpose of providing lump sums or pensions at retirement. The practice of granting pensions to retiring employees arose in the 19th century and in 1898 Bismarck introduced the first government-funded national scheme for Germans over the age of 65. In earlier centuries, however, retirement was the prerogative of the wealthier classes.[10]

Superannuation funds – of many different kinds – are now very common. This reflects the continued growth in living standards, the increased length of healthy retirement and the tendency to treat superannuation contributions made by the employer as deferred pay.

---

[10] The Oxford English Dictionary gives 1529 as the first time that the word pension was used to refer to a retirement benefit. The author, Cardinal Wolsey, did not, however, enjoy much of a retirement, as it appears that he died at about 55, on his way to be tried for treason.

In most countries, saving via superannuation funds has tax advantages, generally in exchange for constraints such as limited access to the money before a reasonable retirement age and the requirement to take most of the benefit as an annuity.

Defined benefit or defined contribution?

Many funds, internationally, provide *defined benefits*, generally in relation to the employee's length of service and his or her salary at retirement – for example, a lump sum of 15% × years of service × final salary or a pension of 1/60 × years of service × final salary.

Defined benefit funds usually also pay benefits on death, disablement, early retirement, ill-health retirement, resignation and redundancy. The basis for calculating each benefit is defined in the scheme's rules or trust deed. Some benefits may be expressed as an accumulation of contributions with interest.

Benefits based on salary may be calculated with reference to the average salary over a period. Many other variations are also possible.

From an employee's perspective, the value of a defined benefit fund is that the employer takes the risk that extra contributions will be required to meet the promised benefits. However, it is hard to know what the superannuation is worth to the employee, especially because resignation benefits are often very much less generous than retirement benefits.[11]

Many employers and employees now treat superannuation as a form of deferred pay. This being the case, it makes sense to operate the superannuation fund as a vehicle to invest this deferred pay. In this structure, apart from insurance benefits (whose cost may be met either by the employer or by the employee), benefits are usually the accumulated value of contributions, being the employer's *defined contributions* and any contributions from the employee, whether defined or voluntary. This structure is also known as *money purchase*.

For the same level of contributions, a defined contribution structure can be expected to support higher resignation benefits and lower retirement benefits than a typical defined benefit structure. Therefore, when defined contributions replace defined benefits, either the cost of the fund (level of contributions) will increase or the retirement benefits will become less generous.

Employer-sponsored superannuation funds

A superannuation fund established and sponsored by an employer can be structured as either defined benefit or defined contribution and may well have elements of both styles. For example, a company's superannuation fund might have a defined contribution section for the commissioned sales force (whose income is very variable) and a defined benefit section for the rest of its staff. In countries where there has been a strong move to defined contribution structures, public sector employers (governments, statutory authorities, etc) are often slower to make that change, perhaps because the retirement benefits of at least some public sector employees are relatively generous when compared to either resignation benefits or salaries.

---

[11] In many defined benefit superannuation funds, resignation benefits may simply be the return of the employee's own contributions, with interest. Even in Australia, where minimum benefits are somewhat higher, it would be usual for the resignation benefit to have a lower funding cost than the retirement benefit.

Industry or multi-employer superannuation funds

In many countries, *industry funds* or *multi-employer funds* have grown up to manage the superannuation of employees in specific industries. Typically, trade unions representing employees in such industries have negotiated agreements with the employers so that the employees have a right to have contributions paid to the industry fund. This enables a worker to change employers without having to change superannuation arrangements.

Public offer superannuation funds

In many countries, individuals are compelled or offered tax concessions to make their own retirement arrangements. In Australia, individuals can direct the contributions made on their behalf into *public offer funds*. These are run by a separate trustee company, often owned by a large financial institution. In other countries, they can be called *retirement annuities*, *personal pensions* or, in the UK recently, *stakeholder pensions* (with fees limited by law). In the US, *401(k)* plans fulfill a similar purpose.[12] In all countries, the funds are normally invested in *investment-linked* arrangements, which are discussed in Section 4.5.3.3 below.

4.5.3.3   Investment-linked arrangements

Various products have been developed in more recent times to give customers access to the investment performance of asset portfolios.

Unit trusts

Unit trusts (called *mutual funds* in the US) are legal trusts that pool investors' interests in assets determined by their constitutions or trust deeds.[13] Typically, the investment profile of the trust will be one of:

*   *diversified* – active investment management across a range of asset sectors in accordance with stated aims and constraints;

*   *indexed* – an attempt to match the performance of an index, such as the S&P 500 Total Return Index;

*   *sector* – active investment management within an asset sector such as *cash* or *domestic equities*, again with stated aims and constraints; and

*   *specific purpose* – the trust is established to invest in a specific asset such as an office building or an infrastructure project.

Investors participate in the trust by means of *units*, which define their share of the trust. Units are frequently revalued and may be sold back to the trust (for *unlisted*, or *open*, trusts) at the market value of the underlying assets. *Listed* or *closed* trusts, which are called

---

[12] 401(k) plans are also designed to encourage investment in the individual's employer, but of course this exposes the employee to the risk of losing both job and savings if the company fails. This famously happened to Enron employees, for example.

[13] Unit trusts can be managed by a commercial manager, with a separate trustee with particular powers to look after the interests of investors. In Australia, the roles of manager and trustee have been combined into one role, the *single responsible entity*, but the obligation to abide by the rules of the unit trust still applies.

investment trusts in some countries, are bought and sold on the stock exchange at prices that might differ from the underlying value. For both types, there are periodic distributions of investment income and these must be reported in the investor's tax return.

For investors, the major benefit of this pooling of funds is the ability to diversify their investments or access specific opportunities with relatively small holdings.

Investment-linked life insurance policies

Life insurers recognized that unitization was an efficient mechanism for passing pooled investment performance through to individual policyowners. This gave rise to *investment-linked* life insurance policies (called *variable life* in the US) that operate in a similar manner to unit trusts and provide similar advantages.

The key difference is that the pooling mechanism is within the policy and therefore does not necessarily give rise to periodic cash distributions to the policyholder. Unit prices are generally calculated at least weekly, often daily, and the change in prices reflects all sources of investment return, including unrealized gains. Unit prices also reflect the tax payable by the life insurer in respect of the investment return credited to these policies.

Investment-linked policies generally offer a choice of several investment options, often including funds managed by managers unconnected to the life insurer. Policyholders may switch managers at little cost.

Being life insurance policies, these contracts may also include *rider benefits*, such as term insurance.

Pooled superannuation trusts

In Australia, *pooled superannuation trusts* (PSTs) operate like unit trusts, except that the units accumulate value net of tax at the rate applicable to superannuation funds. They are available only to superannuation funds, and usually also offer a range of investment options.

Master trusts

A master trust is a unit trust that only invests in other unit trusts. As public offer funds and other investment-linked products developed, the range of available investment options was generally limited to those available from the product provider – eg the life insurer. In order to access the investment performance of another fund manager, the investor had to take his or her money out of one product and reinvest it in another. This could be very expensive in exit and entry fees and could also create a tax liability.

With the introduction of *master trusts*, it became possible to access a wide range of investment options, provided by various fund managers.

Wrap funds

A wrap fund, or service, achieves the same effect as a master trust, but the investor holds the underlying assets in his or her own name. It provides a sophisticated administration system, usually for wealthier clients.

4.5.3.4   Other long-term savings products

There are various other designs for long-term savings products, some of which are discussed below.

Investment account policies

These life insurance policies are more like bank deposits and are capital guaranteed rather than unitized. In the US, they are called *guaranteed investment contracts* (GIC). Interest rates may be predetermined or, like bonuses, can be credited to the policy on the basis of profits earned by the life insurer from time to time. Over the long term, the policyowner can expect to receive a rate of return equivalent to that earned by the supporting assets less fees, taxes and a charge for the capital guarantee.

Group versions are called *deposit administration* (DA) contracts in some countries. Individual versions (including *unitized with-profit* or *accumulation account* contracts) may have greater equity backing and pay terminal bonuses if market conditions are favorable.

Universal life

This product, which was developed in the US, unbundles the savings and insurance components of traditional life insurance policies. It is effectively an investment contract, often with a guaranteed minimum interest rate, combined with a (generally large) term insurance rider.

4.5.3.5   Direct investment

Long-term savings products are all ways to enable the individual to access the investment returns from a pool of assets. Sometimes the link is very clear, while at other times it is hidden behind capital guarantees, company discretions or opaque distribution mechanisms.

The alternative of investing directly, through stockbrokers, is available to an increasing number of individuals as transaction costs fall and education and awareness increase. While direct investment is not a topic of this chapter, it is important to be aware that product issuers and sellers are in competition with all reasonable alternatives.

4.5.3.6   Derivatives

Derivative instruments, whose cash flows are based on the price of some underlying asset or index, have become particularly popular in the past 30 years. While they can perform much the same function as insurance contracts, they are included in this section because they are invariably seen as investment instruments. They are used to enhance investment returns (with an increase in risk) and as tools for risk reduction.

- *Futures contracts* have a long history of use in agricultural markets,[14] where farmers have wanted to reduce their exposure to commodity fluctuations, and consumers have been happy to lock in acceptable prices. They have expanded to mining commodities and oil for the same reasons, while burgeoning foreign exchange futures contracts

---

[14] The origins are lost in time, but Aristotle (around 350BCE) tells the story of Thales, who successfully speculated on the future price of olive presses. The intention of Thales was not to become wealthy but merely to demonstrate that philosophers were smart enough to do so if they wanted to!

have made it possible to make currency conversion rates more predictable for users of these products. Traded futures contracts are standardized, making trade in them much easier and safer as the exchange provides some guarantees of counterparty risks.

- *Option contracts* are perhaps no less ancient, but trade in options did not take off until the creation of the standardized, listed stock or share options on the Chicago Board Options Exchange in 1973. Options can provide producers with a more secure hedge than a future as they protect from situations where production fails for some reason (such as drought).

  Options are often used in investment markets. One use is to provide short-term hedges to protect funds in transition between one investment strategy and another. They can also be used to provide guarantees that investments will not lose value, without giving up some opportunity for upside profits greater than that earned on interest-bearing assets. They have gained particular popularity in providing the basis for investment guarantees that provide investors with a return somewhere between that of equity and fixed interest portfolios.

- *Contracts for difference* (CFDs) pay out on the movement in the underlying price, enabling the purchaser to obtain the performance of an asset for a fraction of the outlay and without incurring the transaction costs associated with buying and selling the underlying asset. CFDs can be used to hedge portfolios in a similar manner to futures contracts.

- *Swaps* and *swaptions* are used to convert borrowings to a structure that is likely to be less expensive or has become more appropriate to the borrowers' and investors' needs. The most common swaps are of fixed for floating interest payments, but there is also a large market in *credit default swaps* that indemnify the investor against particular credit losses.

- *Exchange-traded funds* (ETFs) are derivatives that are equivalent to a unit trust passively invested in a particular index. They are available in many stock markets to cover both the entire market and various sectors. ETFs often have a cost advantage over unit trusts in that there is no cost of trading the underlying assets, although the providers are likely to want to hedge their position and therefore face these costs themselves. There is also no "basis error" or "cash drag" because they can exactly match the index.

Investment options invariably replicate an alternative strategy that holds the underlying assets, but are used because of greater liquidity in the derivative markets, or for reasons of tax or reduced costs of trading. The greatest users for hedging purposes are the trading desks of banks who cannot trade in the underlying instruments (because they are unlisted arrangements with their banking clients), and who use the derivatives to reduce their exposure to interest rate, foreign exchange and credit risks. Derivatives provide a quick and inexpensive manner of dividing these risks amongst the international banking industry.

4.5.4 Retirement income products

Savings for retirement are built up during the working life. A person reaching retirement needs products that convert these saved assets into an income. Annuities convert lump sums into regular payments. They can be divided into *immediate annuities* that commence when the lump sum premium is paid, or *deferred annuities* that will commence payment at a later date (often chosen to be the retirement date) and that can be funded by regular or single premiums.

4.5.4.1 Term certain annuities

Term certain annuities provide a guaranteed regular income for a fixed term, in exchange for payment of a lump sum. The income is typically paid monthly and may be fixed or periodically (usually annually) increased. Typically, the increase might be:

- at a fixed rate (eg 5% per annum);

- indexed to inflation (generally a price index such as CPI); or

- determined as a share of investment profits.

In Australia, the purchase price may be returned at the end of the term, in which case this product is identical to a deposit or debenture but can be classified as an annuity by the regulations governing eligibility for the social security age pension.

4.5.4.2 Lifetime annuities

Lifetime annuities provide a guaranteed regular income for the remaining life of the annuitant, in exchange for payment of a lump sum. As with term certain annuities, the income is typically paid monthly and may be fixed, indexed to inflation (generally CPI) or annually increased at a fixed rate. When payments are made to a couple, the annuity may reduce to a set proportion (eg two-thirds) on the death of either annuitant. Often, the annuity provides for a guarantee period (typically five or 10 years) during which the annuity will be paid regardless of whether the annuitant is alive.

Lifetime annuities obviously protect against the risk of living too long. They are, however, not popular in many countries, which has puzzled economists: people seem to be acting illogically.

There are a few possible explanations, apart from the possibility that many people are indeed shortsighted when estimating their life expectancies, including:

- incomplete markets – because insurers have not historically differentiated by state of health, those with lower life expectancies have avoided the poor value offered by annuity policies;

- desire for control – older people want control of their money for unpredictable expenses; and

- the bequest motive – people want to leave money to their children, or at least to be able to promise benefits to children in exchange for care and love.

Wadsworth et al (2001) discuss the problem and suggest some solutions, based on an extension of the principles of *variable annuities*, which are discussed below.

4.5.4.3 Variable annuities

Variable annuities (usually called *allocated annuities* in Australia) are investment-linked policies that provide income from assets held on behalf of the policyholder. The value of these assets increases with investment income and capital growth and is reduced by fees and annuity payments. Eventually, the assets will be exhausted but the annuitant hopes to receive more than from other annuities because of an expectation that the investment returns will be higher than those effectively provided by the other annuities. Allocated annuities are also called *allocated pensions*.

The returns from variable annuities can be guaranteed in a variety of ways, including:

- Guaranteed Minimum Death Benefit (GMDB);
- Guaranteed Minimum Accumulation Benefit (GMAB);
- Guaranteed Minimum Income Benefit (GMIB); and
- Guaranteed Minimum Withdrawal Benefit (GMWB).

Where a variable annuity is sold as a deferred annuity, much of the focus may be on the accumulation phase and, like many deferred annuity policies nowadays, the proceeds are often taken as a lump sum rather than as an income stream.

Exercise 4.4

(a) Draw up a table that links the needs and risks set out in Sections 4.2 and 4.3 with the products set out in Section 4.5.

(b) Find out what products are sold by a few of the financial institutions known to you. See if you can match them to the descriptions in Section 4.5.

(c) Can you identify any products in Section 4.5 which are not widely available in your country? Why do you think that they are not available?

Hint: Is there a need? Is it met in some other way? Is there another reason?

(d) Give some examples of when you would think it would be appropriate to use derivative instruments rather than insurance or a replicating portfolio of the underlying assets.

4.6   Other sources of financial security

The institutions providing financial security other than through the sale of financial products to individuals can be viewed collectively as a country's social security system. It is important to understand their role when considering how financial products can meet the needs of consumers.

4.6.1   Families

The family acts as an important source of financial security for many people. This is both true for the immediate family (spouse, parents and children) and for the extended family (including grandparents, adult brothers and sisters, cousins and their various permutations). The family appears to become less important as insurance markets develop, and people become wealthier. This has enabled individuals to provide specifically for their dependents, for their own disability and retirement, and to borrow to make major purchases such as a house.

The wealthy often seem to want to create a dynasty, and the *bequest motive* (discussed in 4.5.4.2) drives much of their financial planning. The poor, on the other hand, are often reliant on their children to maintain them in their old age. Regardless of income, as older people lose their ability to look after themselves, so families normally play a greater role in caring for them.

The three main intergenerational flows appear to be:

•   from parents to children until they leave home;

•   from children to old and frail parents; and

•   from parents to children as loans or bequests.

The other major type of flow, not necessarily intergenerational, is from the wealthier to the needier members of the immediate or extended family. These flows may take the form of loans or donations.

Strains can exist in these financial relationships, especially where the cost feels high or unaffordable. Families are probably more secure if they can transfer some of their risks to other institutions. There is an important role for the state and the private sector to help to provide this security.

4.6.2   Governments

This chapter discusses the role of direct state provision of insurance and other financial products. Its other role in regulation and consumer protection is discussed in Chapter 7.

Money and banking

Most governments retain a monopoly on the issue of money through their central banks,[15] which are also lenders of last resort. Bailouts in 2008 showed that they are also providers of bank equity in times of significant stress.

Governments may also intervene to provide low-cost savings accounts to poorer people (through the post offices in a number of countries).

Political pressures make it difficult for governments to collect bad debts; they therefore often make unprofitable loans. A common example is the offering of loans for tertiary education that relieve liquidity constraints on the really young. These loan programs usually replace alternative schemes that require outright subsidies, so cost is not always a major concern.[16]

---

[15] Visitors to Scotland could, however, be surprised to be given banknotes issued by three private banks.

[16] Milton Friedman suggested in the 1940s that the repayment of educational loans could be made income contingent. All graduates would repay the same percentage of their income for a period. This would mean that the better-paid graduates would subsidise those less well off, but the loss in utility would be more evenly spread. If the percentage and term of repayment were set appropriately, the return to the lender could be made acceptable. Yale University tried a variant of this approach with some success in the 1970s. Other variants are used by the HECS-HELP scheme in Australia, and the TEFSA scheme in South Africa. The salary-linked mortgages discussed in 4.5.1.3 are closer to human capital contracts, which are available to fund more lucrative degrees in some countries.

Social assistance

The dividing line between the extended family and the community is blurred, but members of communities have presumably always entered into mutual arrangements that incorporated some risk sharing. These arrangements were formalized over time. In the UK, local parishes were made legally responsible in the early 17th century for the local poor. The benefits were never generous, but there was still a tendency for poor people to select parishes with better benefits. For this and other reasons, these responsibilities have been centralized over time.

Today, probably all governments provide some grants designed to prevent destitution. They are paid out of general tax revenue, or perhaps foreign aid. Payments can be made on an ad hoc basis – such as after floods, fires or droughts. They can also be structured and paid to all people in a category likely to be needy. Thus benefits can be paid to caregivers of young children and the disabled, to the unemployed, older people (whether healthy or frail) and to the disabled.

Social assistance payments relate to need, not to the contributions of the beneficiaries. For instance, a fixed amount might be paid to a single person, slightly less than twice as much to married couples and less, pro rata, to larger families. They may, however, depend on length of residence in the country.

Government grants are usually means tested; the amount paid depends on the *means* (income and assets) or needs of the beneficiaries. This is intended to reduce the cost and target the poorest. The difficulties of auditing the income of poorer people are, however, immense. One just has to think of determining income from odd jobs and the renting of rooms, and irregular interest, pensions and transfer payments from other family members. Transfer payments can be one-off gifts, but migrant laborers will often send large portions of their income to their families at home.

Statutory insurance schemes

Governments can set up a variety of insurance schemes with benefits that depend on compulsory contributions. They can be administered by government or by specially licensed providers. Typically, contributions are deducted by employers before paying salary or wages – eg National Insurance contributions in the UK and the Medicare levy in Australia. A further form of statutory insurance cover is legislated minimum payments by employers in certain circumstances, such as parental leave.

Contingencies that may be covered in this way include:

- parenthood – parental leave;
- unemployment – minimum redundancy payments (but note that government payments are generally paid out of consolidated revenue and are therefore covered under "social assistance" above);
- medical costs – public medical insurance; and
- death or injury in workplace or road accidents.

The contributions may be *actuarially fair* – ie equal in present value to the expected benefits – or there may be cross-subsidies. Generally, there will be intentional cross-subsidies from rich to poor and from low risks to high risks, but other less justifiable cross-subsidies can also arise. One of the roles that the actuarial profession plays in many countries is to help identify these cross-subsidies, which may be unintentional but will often be enthusiastically supported by the beneficiaries.

Retirement provision systems

In developed countries particularly, governments will have designed a retirement provision system. In addition to pensions provided out of consolidated revenue as part of "social assistance" discussed above, most governments also act to compel or encourage additional retirement contributions, either from employers or individuals. Many countries operate earnings-related pay-as-you-go schemes where current contributions go to pay current pensions with little or no accumulation of assets. In a growing number of cases, there is also compulsory investment in money purchase arrangements.

Issues of fairness and cross-subsidies also apply to both benefits and taxation arrangements, and actuaries frequently play an important role in debating these issues. Barr and Diamond (2008) provide an insightful review of the major issues, while Asher (2007) applies the ideas of this chapter in more detail.

4.6.3 Employers

We have already seen that employers may be used by governments to collect premiums for statutory insurance and retirement savings schemes. Employers also have the option to provide non-statutory benefits.

Group superannuation and insurance

Employers can offer a more attractive remuneration package by allowing their employees to participate in a company superannuation fund or a group insurance scheme. These have several advantages over individual products,[17] including:

- cheaper administration – almost all the information required for administration can be obtained from the employer's personnel records and contributions can be collected in one monthly amount from the employer. Large superannuation funds are also able to negotiate lower investment management fees. James et al (1999) gives some indication of comparable cost levels;

- life, disability and health insurance without medical questions – if every employee is covered by the group scheme, there is no opportunity for anti-selection, so these questions are not required. This also represents a cost saving; and

- salary-linked benefits – if the superannuation fund is a defined benefit fund, it will usually provide retirement benefits related to members' final salaries. This feature is not available under individual life insurance contracts.

Keeping charges low, or rather ensuring value for money, can make a difference of 20 percent or more to the eventual retirement incomes. You can check this by considering the

---

[17] Note that the benefit may only be achieved if membership of the scheme is compulsory – eg group life.

long-term benefit of reducing fees by one percentage point (eg from an average of 2% to an average of 1%).

Other cover

Employers may also offer other types of insurance cover. However, this will generally be provided by individual policies either tailored for the company (eg to cover specific risks) or offered at a discount achieved through the employer's purchasing power.

Exercise 4.5

(a) Find out what social assistance is offered by the government in your country or state, and the rules that are used for determining who is entitled to what – especially any means tests.

(b) In future, is the role of the family in the provision of social security likely to be greater or smaller? Give reasons.

(c) Do you think that businesses, run to achieve a profit, can provide social security as well as, or better than, government? Give reasons.

(d) "Individual choice is to be preferred notwithstanding the cost savings available from group contracts." Discuss.

4.7   Practical implications for actuaries

As we said at the beginning of this chapter, actuaries work in managing financial security systems that provide people with appropriate financial products. Many countries require insurance premiums and pension contributions to be calculated by actuaries, but actuaries may play a variety of other roles in the design, production and distribution of these products. Whatever their involvement, they are likely to be more productive if they understand the purpose for which the products will be applied, and have an idea of the different types of product that are available – both locally and in other countries. This understanding will help to suggest new ideas, to adapt product features so that they are more likely to be attractive and useful to consumers and investors, and to design products so that they give the best value for money – and produce the greatest profits.

4.8   Key learning points

In this chapter, we have looked at the following elements of the financial services system:

- The financial life cycle provides a framework for understanding that the needs of individuals for insurance and savings products change over their lifetime. Young adults are more likely to need insurance cover for their incomes and to borrow money. As they age, saving becomes more important and they are more likely to need property insurance cover.

- The need to raise and preserve capital drives the needs of businesses for different financing instruments and for insurance.

- Different products have been developed by insurers to meet the needs for insurance of income against death and disability, the loss of property and medical costs.

- Different financial instruments and banking, investment and superannuation products have been developed to meet needs for borrowing and saving.

- Families also play a role in meeting financial needs over the life cycle by sharing resources and risk.

- Group schemes run by employers or government can provide insurance, savings and other assistance – with government help especially for poorer people less likely to have been able to provide for themselves.

CD Items

Abbey, T. & Henshall, C. 2007, Variable Annuities, Staple Inn Actuarial Society.

Asher, A. 2000, Draft Standards for the Development of Spreadsheets.

Asher, A. 2007, Pension Benefit Design: Flexibility and the Integration of Insurance over the Life Cycle, *South African Actuarial Journal*, vol 7: pp 73-115.

Banks, J. 2004, Signs of Ageing, *The Actuary* October 2004, Institute of Actuaries.

Cooper, D.R. 2002, Family Fortunes: A Guide to Saving for Retirement, *British Actuarial Journal* vol 8, no 5, pp 849-885.

Galabova, T. & Lester, R. 2001, Is Insurance a Luxury? *The Actuary* December 2001, Institute of Actuaries.

Varughese, M., *Financial Lifecycle.xls*.

Wickham, D. 2007, It's Time to Abolish Retirement (And Here's How To Do It), Institute of Actuaries of Australia Biennial Convention, Christchurch, NZ.

Chapter 4 Exercise Solutions

Chapter 4 Exercise 4.1 Solution Spreadsheet

References (other than CD Items)

(Recommended texts are starred *)

Andersson, G. 2002, Children's experience of family disruption and family formation: Evidence from 16 FFS countries, *Demographic Research [Online]* 7: pp 343-364, http://www.demographic-research.org/Volumes/Vol7/7, accessed on January 27, 2010.

Asher, A. 2009, Salary Linked Home Finance: Reducing interest rate, inflation and idiosyncratic salary risks, Institute of Actuaries of Australia Biennial Convention, Sydney, http://www.actuaries.asn.au/IAA/upload/public/Con09_paper_Asher_%20Salary%20Linked%20paper.pdf, accessed on January 27, 2010.

* Barr, N. & Diamond, P. A. 2008, Reforming Pensions, *MIT Department of Economics Working Paper* No. 08-22, http://ssrn.com/abstract=1315444, accessed on January 27, 2010.

Becker, G. S. 1983, *Human Capital: A Theoretical and Empirical Analysis, with Special Reference to Education*, 2nd edition, University of Chicago Press, Chicago.

Bodie, Z., McLeavey, D. & Siegel, L. B. (editors) 2008, *The Future of Life-Cycle Saving and Investing*, Research Foundation of CFA Institute.

Davies, G. 2002, *A history of money from ancient times to the present day*, University of Wales Press, Cardiff, brief summary at http://projects.exeter.ac.uk/RDavies/arian/origins.html, accessed on January 27, 2010.

* Drucker, P. F. 1977, *Management*, Pan, London.

* Duncan, G., Hofferth, S. & Stafford, F. 2004, Evolution and change in family income, wealth and health: the Panel Survey of Income Dynamics 1968–2000 and beyond, in *A Telescope on Society: Survey Research and Social Science at the University of Michigan and Beyond*, ed. J. House, T. Juster & R. Kahn. Ann Arbor: University of Michigan Press, http://psidonline.isr.umich.edu/Publications/Papers/tsp/2002-01_Evolution_and_Change.pdf, accessed on January 27, 2010.

IMF 2008, Global Financial Stability Report, *International Monetary Fund*, http://www.imf.org/external/pubs/ft/gfsr/2008/01/pdf/text.pdf, accessed on January 27, 2010.

ISER, Institute for Social and Economic Research, http://www.iser.essex.ac.uk/survey/ulsc, accessed on January 27, 2010.

James, E., Smalhout, J. & Vittas, D. 1999, Administrative Costs and the Organization of Individual Account Systems: A Comparative Perspective, in *New Ideas about Old Age Security*, ed Holtzmann, R. & Stiglitz, J. 2001, World Bank, http://www.oecd.org/dataoecd/7/55/1816059.pdf, accessed on January 27, 2010.

* Levitt, T. 1975, Marketing myopia, *Harvard Business Review*, Sept-Oct.

Life Insurers Fact Book, 2008, American Council of Life Insurers, 1001 Pennsylvania Ave, NW, Washington D.C. 20005-2599, US, http://www.acli.com, accessed on January 27, 2010.

Modigliani, F. 1986, Life Cycle, Individual Thrift and the Wealth of Nations, *American Economic Review*, Vol 76(3) pp. 297-313.

OECD 2009, OECD Health Data 2009, http://www.irdes.fr/EcoSante/DownLoad/OECDHealthData_FrequentlyRequestedData.xls, accessed on January 27, 2010.

Polachek, S. W. & Siebert, W. S. 1993, *The Economics of Earnings*, Cambridge University Press.

Schulz, J. H. 2002, The evolving concept of retirement: Looking forward to the year 2050, *International Social Security Review* vol 55, no.1, pp. 85-105.

Smith, R.S. 1990, Factors Affecting Saving, Policy Tools and Tax Reform: A Review. *IMF Staff Papers* vol 37, no.1, pp. 1-70.

Smith, J.P. 1998, Socio-Economic Status and Health, *American Economic Review,* Vol 88, no. 2, pp. 192-196.

Wadsworth, M., Findlater, A. & Boardman, T. 2001, Reinventing Annuities, Staple Inn Actuarial Society, Staple Inn, High Holborn, London, January, http://www.sias.org.uk/siaspapers/listofpapers/view_paper?id=ReinventingAnnuities, accessed on January 27, 2010.

Fred's Coffee Shop – The Context of Actuarial Work

In Chapter 5, you will learn how important it is to consider the context in which you are working. The *context* can also be referred to as *external forces*; these are things that are outside your control but that you must take into account. The chapter discusses many examples that affect the work of actuaries but no list can cover every possible aspect. You will need to develop your own understanding of the relevant context for each work situation.

Let's apply the idea to Fred's coffee shop. There are external forces that will influence how he should run the shop. One major area is regulation. Is it even legal for Fred to set up a shop? Does he have to get permission and meet certain standards? Regulation is usually such a significant part of the context for actuarial work that we have a chapter devoted to it, Chapter 7. Other than regulation, what are some of the other external forces that Fred has to take into account?

Think about this for a few moments; then read on.

Fred needs to take account of the market that he is entering. The local culture will be an important factor – do people in the area like coffee? Is the demand for expensive, high-quality products or for low-cost basics? This may depend on the state of the economy, so he needs to be aware of the economic outlook. The economy will also affect the cost and availability of financing. The middle of a credit crunch may not be the best time to raise money for a new business.

What is the competition?

When is income tax due, how is it calculated and will Fred be liable for any sales taxes? The tax system will not only affect the viability of his business but also influence what records he needs to keep.

He has to be aware of the available technology and the directions in which this may develop. Should he take cash payments only or invest in the necessary equipment and contractual relationships to take credit/debit card payments? Can the coffee-making equipment be updated for new styles of drink?

The physical environment will also be important. Fred will need compact equipment if space is restricted. He needs to consider access and safety – for himself, his employees and his customers.

These are just some of the many factors that Fred has to be aware of and take into account in his planning. He also has to be aware that these things are all subject to change, so his solutions need to be as flexible as possible. For example, it may be better to rent premises on a short-term lease with an option to renew, rather than enter into a long lease or buy a site. Think about the context in which Fred's shop operates as you read Chapter 5.

Chapter 5:   The Context of Actuarial Work
by John Shepherd

5.1   Why consider the context?

5.1.1   Introduction

Consider the following headlines. They appeared in one issue of a major city newspaper (SMH, 2008) early in 2008.

*   Economic growth is expected to be slower

*   Growing number of people in mortgage stress

*   HIV rates to soar

*   Elderly suffer long wait for home care help

*   Huge number of Texans cast early Presidential vote

*   Researchers cast doubt on mega-tsunami theory

*   Higher interest rates here to stay

*   No end to selling on Wall Street

*   There's an inconvenient truth about rising immigration

*   Subprime worsens for major bank

Each headline highlights a story that is potentially relevant to the work of some actuaries. In any newspaper in any big city on any day we could identify a similarly diverse set of stories reporting events, developments or trends likely to impact actuarial work.

Most actuarial work concerns a risk-bearing entity like an insurance company or a retirement benefit plan. Actuaries provide solutions to risk-related problems and those solutions have to work in a particular context. We have to know the context, because it is part of understanding the problem. Understanding the problem is the first step in designing a suitable solution. We have to also know how the context has changed in the past, because that influences how we use past experience as a guide in developing a model of the risk process. The model captures and represents the most critical elements of the real world processes (ie the context) that affect the risk-bearing entity. The model is used to project what may happen in the future.

We have to understand the context so we can anticipate how it might change in the future. This will help us to build better models of the future. It will also help us to recognize risks and opportunities that may arise from changes in that context.

Even the most sophisticated model can never fully capture the complexity of the real world. The context, or environment, is made up of a diverse and intricate array of elements (or external forces). The context changes over time. The context varies from country to country. Within a particular country, the context differs from practice area to practice area. For a given practice area, the context differs from company to company and from client to client.

For example, suppose you are a consultant who performs actuarial reviews for several defined benefit retirement plans. You must know the environment or context within which all the plans operate (eg relevant legislation, regulations and taxation rules, current economic conditions and trends, actuarial practice standards, etc). This environment or context is common to all the plans you review. However, you must also know each plan and its particular circumstances (eg its trust deed or other defining document, its benefit structure, its size, the demographic profile of its members, the nature of the work performed by members, the attitudes of the trustees, the sponsoring employer's outlook and concerns, etc).

Exercise 5.1

For each of the ten headlines listed above, write a brief note on how you think the underlying event, development or trend might impact on the work of actuaries. Identify and explain one impact for each headline.

Because the context varies across many dimensions, there is no all-purpose, black-and-white, standardized recipe for actuarial work. If we are going to have a framework such as the Actuarial Control Cycle we have to keep it flexible. We have to define the framework in terms of the basic principles of actuarial work. That is why this book focuses on the basic principles. In practice, every actuarial problem or task is different. Textbook solutions and processes rarely match neatly a set of real-world circumstances. What we need is a thorough understanding of the basic principles of actuarial work, enhanced by the experience of applying those basic principles in a range of different situations.

5.1.2   Context: external forces

Another way to think of the context is in terms of the *external forces* that affect the product, service or scheme on which an actuary is working. These forces are external in the sense that they are usually outside the actuary's control or sphere of influence. In a dynamic world the forces change over time. Such changes can create downside risk (threats) or upside risk (opportunities).

For example, one element of the context – one of these external forces – is government policy. Suppose the government of a developing country announces that it is considering introducing a new law to make third party personal injury liability insurance compulsory for all motorists. This would be seen as an opportunity (upside risk) for general insurers to participate in a potentially profitable new market.

On the other hand, the same government may decide also to fix the maximum premiums that can be charged for the new compulsory insurance. If these maximum premiums are believed by general insurers to be inadequate to cover expected claims then the risk will be seen as downside.

Being able to recognize, understand, anticipate and allow for external forces is a critical capability for an actuary. In this chapter we identify common elements of the context of actuarial work, or common external forces and discuss how these elements or forces may affect the work we do as actuaries.

5.1.3   Context is not static

The iterative nature of the Actuarial Control Cycle reminds us that the context is never fixed. The context changes over time. Each time an actuary investigates a retirement benefit plan's finances, or estimates the outstanding claims of a portfolio of home insurance policies, or reviews the premium rates for term life insurance policies, the task becomes a new problem to be solved, because the context has changed. The degree of change can vary from slight and insignificant to considerable and material.

Changes in the context generate new problems and challenges for actuaries. Such changes can bring upside or downside risk. They can generate new kinds of risk requiring new approaches to analysis, quantification and management.

The feedback mechanism in the Actuarial Control Cycle framework is needed to deal with the impact on our work of the changing environment. Economic conditions change, new legislation is passed, social attitudes shift, technology evolves, consumers become more discerning, or a host of other factors vary. If we could predict such change, our Actuarial Control Cycle would not need a feedback mechanism. There would be no point in comparing emerging experience with what was assumed, because they would be identical. Change in the real world is unpredictable. This produces the future uncertainty that creates the need for actuarial expertise. The feedback mechanism represents a learning process for the actuary and for the company or scheme being advised.

The problems that actuaries tackle are rarely one-dimensional. Like most real-world problems, they can be viewed from a number of perspectives. The actuarial perspective has been primarily a financial and a mathematical one. Most problems also have social, cultural, psychological, historical, industrial, political, geographical and other dimensions. The actuary who is aware of these perspectives, and who allows for them in developing problem solutions and recommendations, will give better actuarial advice to employers and clients.

Such an understanding of the broader context can lead to wider application of actuarial skills. For example, some Australian consulting actuaries have advised clients in an environment that may seem unusual for actuaries – the electricity market. During the late 1990s, some previously government-operated electricity industry functions were privatized, leading to the development of a market in which the price of electricity is set in (almost) real time, according to supply and demand. Wholesale prices can be very volatile. Actuarial skills have proved to be valuable to electricity generators, distributors and regulatory bodies, in a number of different ways outlined in Hinton (1999).

5.2   Components of the context

Table 5.1 is a summary of components of the context of actuarial work. It is not exhaustive. Other items, not listed here, will sometimes be important. The listed items will not all be important in all circumstances. The components are not separate and independent, but interconnected and interwoven. They do not form a static backdrop like the scenery on a stage. Instead they make up a dynamic, multi-dimensional environment which both affects and is affected by actuarial practice. Other schemes might be used to group the components; they are interrelated and can be viewed from other perspectives.

In the rest of this chapter we discuss some of the listed components, one by one. We must remember, however, that they are not separate and unrelated. They often interact and they sometimes create conflicts or pressures for an actuary.

Table 5.1   Summary of components of the context of actuarial work

Broad category	Components	Chapter/Section
Professional context	• Code of conduct • Practice standards	Chapter 3
Regulatory environment	• Laws of the country and/or province • Supervisory authorities • Regulations	Chapter 7
Government and judicial context	• Government policy • Taxation • Social assistance and social insurance • Judicial decisions	Section 5.4
Physical environment	• Climate and natural hazards (eg storms, earthquakes) • Pandemics (widespread, severe outbreaks of disease) • Man-made disasters • Technological developments	Section 5.5
Economic and social environment	• Economic structure, conditions and trends • Demographic structure and trends • Work and employment patterns • Social factors and trends • Industrial (labor union) issues	Section 5.6
Industry and business environment	• Range of products and services offered • Convergence of financial institutions • Product distribution and intermediaries • Accounting standards and practices • Competition • Industry associations • Stakeholders • Corporate culture • Globalization	Section 5.7

Exercise 5.2

Think about the components of the context (or external forces) listed in Table 5.1 above. Can you think of other ways of classifying or summarizing the components into groups?

5.3 Two special components

Two major elements of the context of actuarial work – professionalism and regulation - are so fundamentally important that we give them their own chapters in this book.

In most countries, an actuary is recognized as a professional, with special privileges and responsibilities. The implications of this for an actuary's approach to and conduct of his/her work is very important. We have discussed these implications in depth in Chapter 3, so they will not be specifically discussed here, except perhaps where it interacts with other aspects of the actuary's working environment.

It is worth noting, however, that familiarity with the context of the work being done can be seen as a professional responsibility for an actuary. For example, Professional Standard PS300 of the Institute of Actuaries of Australia deals with the valuation of general insurance claims and states (paragraph 5.1.2) that an actuary performing such a valuation must consider "the relevant economic, legal and social environments and trends."

Governments often regulate financial institutions and their activities. Regulation may be imposed through a combination of legislation (laws passed by parliament) and supervision by statutory bodies known as *supervisory authorities*, or *regulators*. These are given specific responsibilities and powers. The regulatory environment has a major impact on actuarial work. It is also an area where many actuaries work. Regulation is discussed at length in Chapter 7.

5.4 Government and judicial context

5.4.1 Government

Changes to a nation's laws can have an impact on areas where actuaries are involved. For example, the introduction of compulsory wearing of seat belts in motor vehicles, or the random breath testing (for high levels of alcohol) of motor vehicle drivers, may have a dramatic effect on both the incidence and the severity of motor vehicle accidents. This in turn may impact the cost of motor vehicle insurance claims, as well as the cost of claims under medical and other classes of insurance.

Changes to laws can often be anticipated because they tend to flow directly from the policies of the government of the day. Being aware of government policy as it evolves and understanding the forces shaping it can help an actuary to advise clients or employers on possible future legislative, regulatory and other changes and their likely impact. Similarly, it can be useful to be aware of the policy platform of political parties which are not in government but which may win government, or may attain a position of influence in future.

For example, New Zealand held a general parliamentary election in November 2008. Prior to the election the major opposition party, the National Party, announced that, if elected, it would investigate the desirability of privatizing some parts of the country's Accident Compensation Corporation (ACC) scheme. Such privatization would be likely to create opportunities for general insurance companies.

Actuarial professional associations monitor government policy development. They often participate in public debate on policy directions and provide advice to politicians and public servants on issues related to actuarial work. Actuaries often serve on government advisory bodies, actuarial standards boards, committees of inquiry and boards of regulatory and supervisory authorities, where actuarial expertise is relevant.

Governments in different countries take widely varying approaches to regulation. In some countries insurance companies have little or no flexibility in product design, in pricing and in valuation of liabilities because the government (or the regulator empowered by the government) mandates standard policy wordings, controls premium rates and prescribes valuation methods and assumptions. In other countries insurers have freedom to make their own decisions on these and other aspects of the business.

5.4.2   Taxation

Taxation is nearly always part of the context of actuarial work. There are very few examples of financial products, schemes or arrangements where taxation is not an important consideration for all parties involved. Governments sometimes encourage certain financial behavior by corporations or individuals (eg personal saving during working lifetime for retirement) by giving favorable taxation treatment to such behavior. Such favorable treatment does not necessarily mean a complete absence of taxation, although retirement funds in the UK and the US accumulate on a basis that is almost tax-free or tax-deferred.

Financial institutions, like other business enterprises, are subject to the taxation regime of the countries or states in which they operate. Some measure of company earnings is usually the basis for taxation, but the measure can vary widely from country to country.

The nature, extent and operation of taxation are usually defined by legislation, supplemented by a set of regulations and interpreted by a host of rulings from taxation tribunals and courts. Taxation is discussed further in Chapter 7.

As well as understanding and allowing for the implications of current taxation law and regulations, an actuary should aim to be aware of possible future changes to taxation regimes. Such changes are often flagged well in advance, when governments initiate reviews of taxation, either across the board or as it affects particular parts of the community. Following and understanding the public debate associated with such reviews may help actuaries to bring to the attention of their clients and employers the sensitivity of their forecasts and projections to possible future changes.

Taxation can affect product pricing, valuing policy or scheme liabilities, determining profit, analyzing expenses and projecting likely future cash flows – in short, just about every job an actuary undertakes. Taxation considerations can be important for product design. The customer, or even the provider, may benefit from a tax break (eg by paying or incurring less tax) if a product is designed in a certain way. For example, in the US there are adverse tax consequences for a universal life policyholder if contributions (premiums) are too large.

5.4.3   Social assistance and social insurance

Governments often provide social security benefit programs such as old age pensions, disability pensions, free or subsidized health care, unemployment benefits and work injury benefits. In some cases, workers are required to make some individual contribution toward the cost of the benefits provided. In other cases, benefits are financed from taxation revenue.

Social insurance is usually a government-sponsored scheme that involves contributions by (or on behalf of) the person who is covered. For *social assistance* (or *social protection*), however, there are usually no contributions required. Social assistance benefits are designed to address needs and eligibility is based on need.

The availability, nature and extent of social security benefits can impact the demand for financial services. From time to time, governments come under pressure to decrease (or increase) the relative level of social security benefits. (In fact, such pressures may conflict because people often want both higher benefits and lower taxes!) If benefits are reduced, individuals tend to turn to financial service providers to enhance their personal financial security programs. If benefits are raised, the opposite effect may result.

Different approaches to social security have been used in different countries. In China, until the movement toward free enterprise in recent decades, many millions of people were protected by a "cradle-to-grave" system of social security (ie protection for the whole of life, from birth to death). Most economic enterprises were state-owned. A very high proportion of the total population was either employed by state-owned enterprises (SOEs) or was a dependent of an SOE employee. Each SOE was responsible for the welfare of its own employees and their dependents for life. This included provision of old age pensions to retired workers on a pay-as-you-go basis.

From time to time a government may expand or contract the range of social security benefits it provides. This is likely to reduce or increase the opportunities for banks, insurers and other financial institutions to offer products and services meeting those needs.

5.4.4 Judicial decisions

Judicial decisions are rulings made by judges in courts of law. In countries with a common law system (discussed in Section 7.1.1) judicial decisions can be particularly important when new legislation is enacted, in determining just how the new legislation is going to work. The interpretation of an insurance policy's wording may become the subject of a judicial ruling. For example, suppose a life insurance company markets a critical illness insurance policy designed to provide a cash payment if the insured is diagnosed with a serious illness like pulmonary hypertension or cancer. The critical illnesses are listed in the policy. The premium is set on the assumption that the policy covers only the set of medical conditions listed. If that set of conditions is not precisely and carefully worded, a court may subsequently rule that the policy covers a condition that the company never intended to be included. The resulting unanticipated claims could damage the financial soundness of the life insurance company.

Judges' (or juries') decisions on the amount of damages payable often have a large impact on insurers, affecting the amounts of claim payable. Levels of claim payments in the liability classes of general insurance (eg public liability, product liability, professional indemnity and employer's liability or workers compensation) are particularly impacted by judicial decisions.

5.5 Physical environment

5.5.1 Climate and natural perils

Natural perils have an obvious impact on general insurance, in particular, and on other insurance classes as well. Earthquakes, cyclones, bushfires, floods, droughts, hurricanes, typhoons and tornadoes often lead to catastrophic events that generate huge claim costs for insurers. There has been growing concern that global warming and climate change may lead to an increase in the frequency and severity of severe natural hazards.

Providing insurance against the financial impact of some of these perils can be problematic. For example, earthquakes are known to be very likely to occur in certain identifiable locations, and extremely unlikely to happen elsewhere. People who live in high-risk locations may want insurance against earthquake; those who live in low-risk locations will not be interested. Such a risk cannot be spread across a sufficiently wide spectrum of the community through private insurance. Government may decide to intervene and provide ad hoc payments after earthquakes occur, financed by the whole community through tax revenue.

Earthquakes and floods, for example, are not a problem for insurers until people want to live or work in affected areas and request insurance cover against those perils. In pricing such insurance actuaries will need to estimate the extent and the cost of possible damage. This will depend on the building regulations for affected areas. Economic and demographic forces are likely determinants of whether people want to move there while legislation determines the building codes for earthquake- and flood-prone areas. This is a good example of how elements of the context (in this case, the physical, economic, social and regulatory environments) interact.

Some actuaries have worked together with climatologists, seismologists and other scientists to develop improved models for measuring the risks associated with natural hazards. For example, de Alba et al (2008) reported the development of a composite model to estimate the probable maximum loss and the risk premium for earthquake cover by a Mexican general insurance company. The overall model combined models of seismic activity, local geological conditions and building structural vulnerability with the insurer's actual portfolio of insured buildings to generate a distribution of possible earthquake damage outcomes. Allowance was also made for various forms of reinsurance. This is a good example of how actuaries often need to work with experts in other fields to develop solutions to the problems they tackle.

5.5.2 Pandemics

A *pandemic* (derived from two Greek words meaning "all peoples") is an epidemic of infectious disease that spreads globally, or on a very wide geographical front, through human populations. Throughout recorded history there have been many pandemics.

In recent times the most serious pandemic has been HIV, the virus that causes AIDS. HIV spread from Africa to Haiti, then to the US and then to much of the rest of the world. Projections of worldwide deaths from AIDS have numbered from tens of millions to hundreds of millions. Africa has been particularly hard hit by HIV. For example, the Actuarial Society of South Africa (2008) estimated that 5.6 million South Africans were HIV positive in 2008.

Since the outbreak of HIV there have been several pandemic concerns. In 2003 SARS (Severe Acute Respiratory Syndrome) – an atypical form of pneumonia – triggered rapid action by health agencies. In 2005 the avian flu (H5N1 virus) showed signs of spreading across species barriers and cases were found of humans being infected (with high fatality rates). In 2009 the outbreak and spread of a new strain of influenza A (H1N1 virus) was declared a pandemic by the World Health Organization.

Pandemics affect actuarial work. Health insurance companies can expect much higher claim costs. Life insurance companies may experience greater numbers of deaths as well as more and higher disability claims. Lenders may find repayment defaults increasing. Asset values may fall. Financial institutions may suffer from the absence through illness of key staff – a form of operational risk.

5.5.3 Man-made disasters

Not all disasters can be regarded as natural. Acts of terrorism and war are obvious examples of man-made disasters that cause loss of life, injury, disability and extensive property damage. In addition, large numbers of deaths and injuries, as well as serious damage to property, occur each year around the world in man-made incidents like fires and explosions in oil refineries, mines and chemical plants (Swiss Re, 2008a). Transport disasters (aircraft crashes, train crashes and derailments, and shipping disasters) are other examples. Outer space can also be the setting for disasters involving space vehicles or satellites. If insurers are to insure the resulting deaths, injuries, disabilities and property damage, actuaries must find ways to quantify the risks involved.

5.5.4 Technological developments

Technological development, especially in computing and communications, has had a major impact on actuarial work since the early 1970s. Until then, many developments in actuarial science were focused on finding better ways to calculate the present value of expected future cash flows. Improvements in the storage capacity, processing speed and cost of computers, and the development of easy-to-use software like spreadsheets, has meant that what was once the cornerstone of actuarial work (commutation functions, assurance and annuity functions and a complex system of symbolic notation) has almost disappeared from use.

Technological change influences product design and product improvement. Take, for example, the development of unit-linked life insurance policies. Regular revision of unit prices, and their use in determining the number of units purchased by additional premiums and in calculating policy cash values, became feasible only when fast and powerful computing technology became available. Also, as communications technology improved, unit prices were revised more frequently.

Marketing and sales techniques have also been greatly affected by technological developments. The direct marketing of financial products aims to reduce new business acquisition costs. It depends heavily on technological support no matter what distribution channel is used. Use of the internet for financial product promotion, marketing, quotations and sales is now established and will no doubt grow.

Technological change can have a major effect on mortality and morbidity. The development of new drugs can significantly reduce risks of sickness, disability and death from particular causes. New machines and technologies for diagnosis, for surgical procedures and for treatment can have similar effects. New treatments can become available for previously untreatable conditions.

Developments in medical technology are clearly important for life insurance and annuity business. Improving diagnosis, treatment and medication means increasing longevity which means reducing life insurance claims and greater annuity costs. However, for medical and hospital expenses insurance the overall impact is less clear. Newer technologies tend to be more expensive and can lead to increases in claim costs but improved treatment may lead to reduced need for treatment.

Technological development brings with it a wide range of new physical assets to be insured (eg space satellites, rockets and other space vehicles). Insurers have to decide how to price and underwrite insurance of these new assets, usually with no prior experience or data to work from. Technological change also makes many items obsolete and so creates difficulties in valuation and replacement for insurance claims management.

5.6   Economic and social environment

5.6.1   Economic conditions and trends

Actuaries' employers or clients are often financial institutions or schemes whose future experience will be greatly affected by economic conditions and their changes over time. To forecast future cash flows arising from the business, assumptions are needed for a range of factors including economic variables like investment earning rates and inflation rates. Current economic conditions and likely future trends will influence the choice of assumptions.

Some areas where economic effects are of great importance are obvious: investment returns for investment and savings products, salary inflation for defined benefit retirement plans and expense inflation for long-term fixed premium insurance policies.

Other influences can be less obvious. Insurance claims, for example, are significantly affected by economic factors. Changing demand and supply conditions affect the prices of goods and services, which influence the cost to the insurer of claims for the repair or replacement of damaged or stolen property. Economic boom-and-bust cycles are important. In times of recession, which tend to lead to increased unemployment, claim costs for personal injury under workers compensation insurance may rise because injured employees cannot be brought back to work on alternative duties. Periods of recession may also lead to business failures and higher interest rates, which may encourage more theft, fraud and arson.

The economic structure of a country's population is an important aspect of the context. For example, countries with a high proportion of middle income families will support a diversity of financial service providers. Consumers likely to move into higher income bands will have different and increasing needs during their lifetime. Although India's population includes a relatively small proportion (about 25 percent) of economically active citizens, foreign insurers are interested in India's newly deregulated insurance markets because 25 percent of more than a billion people constitutes a very large market.

Exchange rate movements can affect the cost of claims on property insurance policies. For example, consider motor vehicle insurers in Singapore that may insure cars imported from Germany, Sweden, France, Japan and Italy. The Singapore insurers will be faced with claims based on repair costs that depend on currency exchange rates, because replacement parts for the imported vehicles will have to be imported from overseas.

Economic conditions are also related to demographic trends. For example, researchers have reported that mortality rates appear to increase when incomes fall following an economic crisis. Cutler et al (2002) found that, during periods of economic crisis in Mexico during the 1980s and 1990s, mortality rates increased for the elderly and for the very young. They suggested that economic crisis leads to reduced incomes, which means less spending on food, medical services and medication, leading to poorer nutrition, poorer health and higher mortality.

Exercise 5.3

Suppose you are the actuary responsible for setting premium rates for motor vehicle insurance. (Assume for the purpose of this exercise that only property damage is covered – damage to the insured vehicle and to third party property. No liability or medical coverage is provided.) The insurance company's Chief Financial Officer (CFO) asks what you think are the three most relevant components of the context in which you operate. Draft a one page memo to the CFO listing and explaining your choice.

5.6.2 Demographic structure and trends

Demographic structure and trends influence the types of product and service that financial institutions can market.

Demographic structure and trends affect the choice of assumptions for actuarial projections of future cash flows. Current levels of, and future changes in, fertility, migration, mortality, disability and unemployment are important factors when investigating the financial condition of a national old age pension scheme, for example.

A current demographic trend often mentioned is that of the ageing population, seen as an important issue in most developed countries. In such countries, fertility rates and mortality rates are falling. People are living longer. Therefore, in future there will be relatively fewer persons in the working age groups and more in the retired age groups. If current economic and social security structures continue unchanged in a country with an ageing population, the costs of old age pensions, health care and aged care (as a percent of GDP) will grow, and tax revenue (as a percent of GDP) will fall. The extra cost to governments of this fundamental demographic change is projected to be significant (though varying from country to country). There will be implications for many areas where actuaries work.

Partly in response to concerns about ageing populations and increasing costs of state-provided age pensions, many governments have moved to equalize (at the older age) male and female eligibility ages for commencement of age pensions. For example, both Australia and the UK decided to change gradually the female eligibility age from 60 to 65. In both countries, the male eligibility age has been 65 for many years. A second external force at work in this trend has been the desire to remove discrimination by sex. This is another good example of how external forces can interact.

Brown et al (2002) developed a model relating the expected age at retirement for workers in Canada to a Wealth Transfer Index (WTI). Retirement age is the age at which workers cease to be economically productive. The WTI, which is expressed as a ratio of consumption demand to labor productivity, represents the demand for wealth placed on the labor force from the aged, the young and the unemployed. The authors suggest that, from a macroeconomic viewpoint, average age at retirement varies in such a way as to allow an acceptable level of transferred wealth from workers to dependents. They argue that retirement age can be regarded as a balancing item in an economic subsystem that continually seeks equilibrium. Where will the additional production of goods and services, to support the growing proportion of retirees, come from? It will be produced, suggest the authors, by workers who remain longer in the workforce. They forecast, for Canada, a general decrease in median retirement age until 2017, followed by an increase during the period 2017-34.

Exercise 5.4

You are advising the government department responsible for primary school education (ages five to 11) in your state, province, territory or country. You are asked to summarize the external forces likely to impact the demand for trained teachers over the next 50 years. Make a list of the major external forces and briefly explain why each one will be important.

5.6.3 Work and employment patterns

In most industrialized countries, it was not uncommon until relatively recently for employees to spend a full working lifetime with one employer. However, in recent decades, there has been a trend toward greater job mobility, at least for people with developed and valued skill sets or qualifications. It is now often regarded as desirable for employees to experience several jobs in different organizations in order to develop their skills and gain wider experience. Also, as the incidence of corporate downsizing, mergers and acquisitions increases, the likelihood of forced job changes becomes greater.

Traditional defined benefit retirement plans, designed to fit a working lifetime with one employer, failed to meet the needs of more mobile workers. They also did not serve the needs of lower skilled and unskilled workers. Changes like *compulsory preservation* have been introduced in response to these needs. Preservation rules require an individual's retirement benefits to be accessible (in cash) only after the individual has reached preservation age (typically 55 or 60). This eliminates the possibility of workers cashing in their accumulated funds each time they change employers.

In some countries (eg Australia), legislation against age-discrimination has made it illegal to specify a maximum retirement age. This effectively means that mandatory retirement is out of the question (except in certain exempted professions and occupations). This has obvious implications for the design of retirement benefit plans.

Employment patterns are closely linked with other components of the context, such as economic conditions and structure, cultural factors, social attitudes and conventions, demographic characteristics and technological change. Encouraging workers to postpone retirement (ie increasing the average age at retirement) is a tactic sometimes used by governments seeking ways to lessen the impact on public finances of an ageing population.

The concept of *retirement* as a distinct life event occurring upon attainment of some typical retirement age, marking the end of a full-time working-for-income phase and the beginning of a full-time retirement phase, is under challenge. The practice of gradual or phased retirement, where workers reduce their hours worked as they get older, is becoming more common and is likely to continue to do so.

However, before gradual or phased retirement can become the norm solutions will have to be found to some of the existing legal, economic and cultural barriers to gradual retirement. For example, social security rules and superannuation scheme rules may need to be modified to recognize, encourage and support phased retirement. Employers, as well as workers themselves and their families, may have to change their attitudes to retirement.

For some time now many countries have experienced significant growth in female participation in the workforce. This trend has had an impact on many areas of actuarial work. New savings, investment and insurance products have been designed to meet the needs of working women. More flexible and more equitable retirement saving schemes have been developed to allow for the fact that many women experience breaks in their working careers while bearing and raising children.

5.6.4 Social factors and trends

Here are some examples of how social factors (eg community values and attitudes, cultural factors), and changes in them over time, can impact on actuarial work:

- the preference shown by retiring workers (noted over several generations in some countries but not necessarily prevalent in all countries) for a lump sum benefit rather than an income benefit (which affects the design of retirement benefit plans);

- community disapproval of discrimination based on sex, marital status, religion, disability, race and other factors has led to anti-discrimination legislation in many countries, and ongoing public debate questions the right of life insurers and retirement benefit plans to be exempted from such legislation (eg in order to use sex as a rating factor for life insurance pricing, and in order to provide different benefits for males and females making the same superannuation contributions);

- calls for de facto partners and same-sex partners to be recognized, along with married opposite-sex partners, for benefits payable to spouses from health or retirement benefit plans;

- constraints on the questions that insurers can ask applicants for insurance (eg sexual orientation or sexual preference);

- the development in low-income markets within emerging or developing economies (eg India) of *microinsurance* and *microfinance*, under which very small amounts of insurance cover or loan are provided in return for very small amounts of premium or repayment;

- the shift in Western culture toward a greater focus on the rights and the welfare of individuals and away from traditional systems of pooling and sharing. This is seen in some countries in the demise of mutual enterprises (mutual life and general insurance societies, friendly societies, building societies) and the rapid move toward an individual account format for savings through life insurance and through retirement benefit plans (this shift may be attributable to economic as well as cultural forces);

- the attitude of members of the community to insurance, and especially to claiming (for example, people who think of, say, their home insurance as an arrangement whereby "their" premiums are being accumulated for "them" by the insurer, so that they have a right to some return of their outlay, in the form of an overstated loss when they make a claim);

- the extent to which people believe that under-insuring (nominating a sum insured that is lower than the true value of the property being insured) is a prudent method of reducing their expenses; and

- the level of criminal activity, such as burglary, other theft and fraud, in a community has an obvious impact on the level of general insurance claims.

It has been estimated (Swiss Re, 2008b) that approximately 1.5 billion Muslims throughout the world are underserved by insurance providers. Islamic law scholars regard conventional insurance as inconsistent with the shariah (Islamic law), so various forms of Islamic insurance have emerged. The most common form is known as *takaful*. The underlying basis of takaful is mutual assistance and joint risk bearing, so it has a lot in common with mutual associations like friendly societies. Policyholder (takaful) funds are kept separate from shareholder funds and investments are made on a shariah-compliant basis (avoiding companies engaged in inappropriate activities and avoiding interest payments). Islamic banks also operate on shariah-compliant principles. For further information read the article "Takaful: An Islamic Alternative to Conventional Insurance Sees Phenomenal Growth" on the CD.

Exercise 5.5

Suppose you are advising the Government of the People's Republic of China on financing and providing retirement incomes for its older citizens, now and in the future. Research the context and make a list of what you think are the most important elements of that context (ie the critical external forces) that will impact on this task. Briefly explain each element.

5.6.5   Industrial issues

Industrial issues are matters over which there is dispute between employers and representatives of employees (eg labor unions). Such disputes may be industry-wide, or restricted to a particular business enterprise. Employee benefits, such as superannuation, death or disability insurance, and medical or dental cover, may be the subject of negotiation from time to time. An actuary may be asked to advise one or other of the parties to the dispute, or to recommend a solution which is acceptable to both parties.

Industrial pressure from labor unions can lead to increased wage and salary levels, which in turn impacts on the cost of retirement benefit plans.

The involvement of labor unions adds an extra stakeholder perspective to the financial management of superannuation schemes. For example, Ferris et al (1995) pointed out that actuaries might find their work for retirement benefit plans being subjected to close scrutiny by labor unions. The authors explained that the development of industry-based retirement benefit plans, and the emergence of large surpluses in some of these plans, has helped to bring retirement benefit plan finances to the attention of unions. Increased scrutiny of the work of actuaries is to be welcomed. Appreciating the perspective of the unions and providing valuable advice to all parties requires actuaries to have good listening, understanding and communication skills.

5.7   Industry and business environment

5.7.1   Range of products and services offered

Since much actuarial work is concerned with financial products and services, these form a key part of the actuarial work environment. Chapter 4 described the range of financial products and services and discussed the consumer needs they are designed to meet. Some of the external forces we are identifying in this chapter impact the needs of consumers and hence also influence the products and services developed to meet those needs.

5.7.2 Convergence of financial institutions

Convergence is the term used to describe the trend observed in many countries since the 1980s for previously distinct classes of financial institution to become similar. This trend has come about as each class has broadened the range of financial products and services it offers. The aim has been to provide one-stop shopping for customers, by attempting to meet all their financial needs. This full-service approach is sometimes known by the German word *allfinanz*. Banks have added life and general insurance, and retirement benefit and funds management to their traditional product range. Life insurance companies have introduced general insurance and reinsurance, as well as banking products (deposits, loans, credit cards, etc) and funds management.

The trend has created financial service institutions that consist of units and subsidiaries in a variety of specific businesses. Recognizing and analyzing the risks faced by a full-service enterprise, as well as the interdependencies and correlations between them, is a challenge for managers, investors, rating agencies, regulators and actuaries.

5.7.3 Product distribution and intermediaries

Financial products and services are made available to consumers through a range of distribution channels or intermediaries. The mix of channels, and their relative importance, varies between countries. Actuaries who design or price products need to take account of the distribution channels to be used. For example, direct distribution tends to work better for simple products (like term life insurance) because the consumer can understand the product and does not need an intermediary (agent or adviser) to explain it. More complex products can be more difficult to understand so an agent or adviser is more likely to be needed to explain the product to the client. Further, lower expense assumptions can be used when pricing directly distributed products because there will be no commission to be paid to an intermediary.

5.7.3.1 Sole agents

Sole agents are sales intermediaries who represent and sell the products of just one product provider. They are also known as *tied agents*, or *captive agents*. Usually, they are extensively trained by the company they represent and are paid largely on a commission basis in proportion to the amount of new business they sell. Sole agents may have other jobs, or, at least, work only part-time (eg many life insurance agents in Japan are also housewives).

Sometimes, sole agents are authorized to sell the products of one or two other companies as well. This is likely when the company to which they are tied does not offer a full range of products (eg no annuities, or no income protection insurance). Sole agents are representatives of the company providing the product.

5.7.3.2 Multi-agents

These are individuals or firms who are authorized to sell the products of a number of product providers. Successful, well-established tied agents will often make the move to set up their own multi-agency practices. Their successful past performance enables them to obtain agency agreements with several companies. Like sole agents, multi-agents usually receive commissions from the companies whose products they sell and are regarded as representatives of the company.

5.7.3.3 Brokers and financial planners

Brokers are intermediaries who provide advice to consumers of financial services or financial instruments. Stockbrokers provide advice to clients on investment in shares or other financial instruments. Insurance brokers provide advice on insurance, savings and investment products. Stockbrokers receive a fee or commission from their client, while insurance brokers may receive commissions from the companies providing the products they sell.

Financial planners provide advice to their clients across the whole spectrum of financial planning needs. They focus on providing an individual, a family or even a small business with a comprehensive financial plan. Such a plan may include recommendations on an insurance program, financial planning for retirement, a savings and investment program, tax minimization, estate planning and so on.

In some countries insurance brokers and financial planners are increasingly choosing to charge their clients on a fee-for-service basis. For example, planners may charge a fee of $500 to $1,000 for the first consultation and preparation of a financial plan. Additional advice will carry an additional fee. Suppose the client agrees to a plan that includes the purchase of products on which the product provider pays commission. The commission received from the provider may be offset against the adviser's fee (so the client pays less to the adviser), or the full commission may be passed on to the client (with the client paying the full fee to the adviser). Either way, all fees and commissions should be fully disclosed.

Insurance brokers and financial planners are representatives of their clients (not representatives of the companies providing the products and services).

Agents, brokers and financial planners (all types of intermediary) usually have to be licensed or registered. They may also be subject to regulation and supervision on matters such as the adequacy of their knowledge and experience for acting in that capacity, the handling of client moneys and the nature and quality of the advice they give. They commonly are required to disclose fully to their client all fees, commissions and charges they will either receive or charge.

Some actuaries have developed successful practices as financial planners. An actuary's education in recognizing and quantifying risk provides a good platform for the role of financial planner.

5.7.3.4   Commissions and sales

For as long as intermediaries (agents, brokers and other advisers) have been paid commissions for selling insurance and other financial products there has been controversy over the extent to which commissions influence what products are sold. Ethical advisers will always put the needs of their client (the consumer) first, even if it means recommending a product with a lower commission. Unethical advisers put their own interests ahead of those of their client, in several possible ways including:

- recommending products with high commissions even if they do not fit the client's needs;

- encouraging an unnecessary change of product or fund so that they can receive a commission; and

- recommending a higher premium product because it pays a higher commission.

Many countries have introduced extensive legislation and regulations designed to improve the quality of advice and service provided by intermediaries to their clients. Some of the measures used are minimum standards of education and training for advisers, requiring advisers to be licensed, forcing disclosure of commissions and other remuneration, requiring standard processes (eg written analysis of client's needs), introducing *cooling off* periods (ie a period – perhaps two to four weeks – during which a consumer who has agreed to buy a product can change her mind, cancel the purchase and receive a refund of any money paid), minimum standards of product information disclosure and requiring advisers to provide written statements of advice.

5.7.3.5   Direct distribution

Any distribution method that does not involve an intermediary is known as direct distribution. The obvious attraction for product providers is that there is no commission payment required rewarding an intermediary for time and effort. The costs of selling the product are significantly reduced.

Direct distribution has three basic forms:

- personalized contact, targeted to an individual (eg direct mail, telephone marketing);

- advertising designed to elicit a response (eg a newspaper, magazine or television advertisement inviting customers to "ring this number," a poster in a bank branch); and

- customer-initiated contact, usually the result of general brand advertising, word-of-mouth recommendation, convenience of branch location, etc (eg customer phones a large, well-known company to buy term life insurance, or accesses a website to arrange motor vehicle insurance through the motorists' association he belongs to, or walks into a bank branch to open an account).

The internet plays an important role in direct distribution for relatively simple products like term life insurance, motor vehicle insurance and home insurance. Many insurers use websites to provide information, including premium quotations. Comparison websites are popular with many consumers because they help to find the lowest premium for the desired cover.

5.7.4   Accounting standards and practices

Company accounts have to be prepared in accordance with accounting standards (called Generally Accepted Accounting Principles (GAAP) in some countries and Financial Accounting Standards (FAS) in others). Accounting standards affect virtually all types of actuarial work. They may set out the general nature, to a greater or lesser degree, of the assumptions to be made when performing a valuation of almost anything whose value is included in financial statements. This includes, for example, the liabilities of a retirement benefit plan and the outstanding claims of a general insurance company.

For example, in Australia the accounting standard AAS25 specifies the types of assumptions that must be used in liability and asset valuations shown in retirement benefit fund accounts. An actuary may choose to use different assumptions in performing an actuarial review for funding purposes. However, the actuary will need to explain to the trustees and sponsoring employer why the accounts show different values to those in the actuary's report.

Accounting standards may address the way in which insurance companies report their activities. In general insurance, for example, aspects affected are likely to include the definition of premiums, accounting for deferred acquisition costs, accounting for reinsurance payments, apportioning management expenses and determining outstanding claim liabilities (Hart et al, 1996, p. 26). If prudential regulations for general insurers call for a different approach to estimating outstanding claim liabilities, then a different value will be determined from that appearing in the published accounts.

A movement toward global accounting standards has been gathering momentum for some years. The International Accounting Standards Board (IASB) has developed International Financial Reporting Standards (IFRS). At the time of writing, these standards have been adopted by more than one hundred countries including those of the European Union, Russia, South Africa, Singapore, Turkey, Australia, Hong Kong, Malaysia and Pakistan while Japan, India, Canada and the US are all moving toward adoption.

5.7.5   Competition

The clients and employers that actuaries advise often operate in a commercial environment where competition is strong. This may result in pressure on actuaries involved in product pricing to recommend premium rates that are competitive, perhaps at the expense of profitability or even adequacy. Ferris et al (1995) identified other situations in which actuaries may feel such pressure. The existence of actuarial professional standards, however, does help to mitigate these pressures.

In some classes of general insurance, an absence of adequate, relevant and reliable data may mean that expected claim costs and even expected management expenses cannot be known with any reasonable degree of certainty. In these circumstances people in the company who want to argue for competition-based pricing may feel that they have a strong case. However, in these circumstances an actuary should be careful to suitably qualify a pricing report in the light of the uncertainty arising from the data.

Competition can be strong in some life insurance product markets. De Ravin (1996) surveyed actuaries with pricing responsibilities at 24 Australian life insurance companies, operating in very competitive markets. One of the survey questions was "Would you say that in the past year you have felt more pressure to achieve profits or sales?"

Eleven respondents (46 percent) said "About equal," while seven (29 percent) said "Profits," and six (25 percent) said "Sales."

Competition can also be strong across (not just within) financial market sectors. For example, in recent decades, competition for savings products from banks, mutual funds, unit trusts and other savings vehicles has had a profound effect on the life insurance and superannuation sectors.

5.7.6 Industry associations

In many countries industry-based associations of companies have been formed in the finance sector to promote the role and collective interests of their members to government, to the media and to the community. On behalf of their members, these not-for-profit organizations take part in debates on public policy, make submissions to government on matters like regulation and taxation, liaise with regulators and publish research reports. Table 5.2 provides examples of industry bodies from a number of countries.

These associations may also be providers of education, training and accreditation for people working in the industry. The industry base may be life insurance, general insurance, banking, funds management, retirement benefits or any other financial sector.

The activities of industry associations may affect actuarial work in several ways:

- member companies may adhere to voluntary codes of conduct in areas such as customer service and sales;

- associations sometimes provide data collection and reporting services to members and this aggregated data can be useful for pricing products and valuing policy liabilities; and

- they may set up mutual emergency funds or levy agreements whereby all members make a commitment to help to support a fellow member that encounters financial difficulties.

The mission statement of the Insurance Council of Australia is fairly typical of industry bodies of this type:

> The Insurance Council of Australia's mission is to influence ethically, and expertly, the political, social and economic environment, in order to promote members' roles in providing insurance protection and security to the community.

In some countries an insurance industry association may have a quasi-regulatory role. For example, membership of the industry association may be compulsory for all licensed insurers and members may be obliged to use standard policy wordings and standard minimum premium rates for a particular class of business (say, homeowners insurance).

Table 5.2   Examples from several countries of financial sector industry bodies

Country	Industry	Industry bodies
Australia	• Banking	• Australian Bankers' Association (ABA)
	• Life insurance, reinsurance and funds management	• Investment and Financial Services Association (IFSA)
	• General insurance and reinsurance	• Insurance Council of Australia
	• Insurance education and training	• Australian and New Zealand Institute of Insurance and Finance
	• Superannuation	• Association of Superannuation Funds of Australia (ASFA)
Canada	• General insurance (non-government)	• Insurance Bureau of Canada (IBC)
	• Life insurance and health insurance	• Canadian Life & Health Insurance Association (CLHIA)
	• Banking	• Canadian Bankers Association (CBA)
Hong Kong	• General insurance, life insurance and retirement provision	• Hong Kong Federation of Insurers (HKFI)
Singapore	• Life insurance based financial planners (agents)	• Insurance and Financial Practitioners Association of Singapore (IFPAS)
	• Life insurance	• Life Insurance Association of Singapore (LIA)
	• General insurance	• General Insurance Association of Singapore (GIA)
UK	• Banking	• British Bankers Association (BBA)
	• Wholesale general insurance and reinsurance	• International Underwriting Association of London (IUA)
	• Insurance and pensions	• Association of British Insurers (ABI)

Exercise 5.6

Choose a country not already listed in Table 5.2 and compile a list of its financial sector industry bodies. Include two additional columns – one describing each body's mission and objectives and another outlining its major activities.

5.7.7   Stakeholders

Broadly speaking, actuaries – whether they work as employees or as consultants – provide advice to risk-bearing entities. The entities may take the form of companies, government departments, non-governmental organizations, friendly societies, retirement benefit funds, etc. The stakeholders in these entities are important elements of the context of actuarial work. A stakeholder in an entity is any individual or organization that is affected by the activities of that entity.

In the case of a (non-mutual) company the primary stakeholders are the shareholders (the owners of the company), management (who run the company on behalf of the owners), the employees and customers. In the case of an insurance company the primary customers are the policyholders. Other stakeholders include reinsurers, competitors, banks and other lenders who provide the company with credit, various arms of government (eg financial supervisors, taxation authorities), financial analysts, rating agencies, trade unions (representing the interests of employees) and suppliers of goods and services (eg owners of rented office space, IT service providers). Some people argue that every entity should consider both the wider community and the environment to be stakeholders.

Another important stakeholder is the actuarial profession itself. Each member of the profession benefits from the profession enjoying a high reputation. Thus it is important (to each member) that all other members maintain, and even enhance, that reputation.

Often the interests of different stakeholders will conflict. For example, shareholders may see their short-term interests best served by higher prices, to generate higher profits and thus higher dividends and share prices. Customers (policyholders) will want prices to be as low as possible without unduly risking insolvency. The shareholders, however, will usually recognize that a strategy focused on short-term profits might jeopardize their ability to continue to earn profits in the longer term.

Exercise 5.7

List the stakeholders in each of the following entities that an actuary might advise:

(a) an industry superannuation fund established to provide retirement benefits in the form of accumulated contributions for workers in the construction and building industry;

(b) a prudential regulatory authority empowered by government to supervise banks, insurers, superannuation funds and all other financial institutions; and

(c) a country's Treasury Department which is considering introducing a loan scheme for university students under which students can borrow the cost of their tuition fees and repay them gradually through the PAYE (pay-as-you-earn) tax system after graduation when their annual income reaches a minimum level.

5.7.8 Corporate culture

The culture of the organization within which an actuary works is also an important ingredient of the context. Corporate culture has been explained as "the way we do things around here." It consists of the combination of beliefs, values, ethics, rules, procedures and processes of the organization. Elements of corporate culture range from the basic vision, mission and philosophy set by a firm's founders to written standards of practice for writing a report, building and documenting a spreadsheet model, peer reviewing the work of colleagues and meeting with existing or prospective clients.

Since the organizational culture is outside the control of an individual actuary but affects the actuary's work, it is an external force in the sense of this chapter. Corporate culture is not always positive. Since its spectacular failure in 2001 the US company Enron has been cited often as an example of a company whose culture turned sour. On the surface its corporate values were stated to be respect, integrity, communication and excellence. In reality, according to many critics, its activities were high-risk, ruthless and deceptive.

Corporate culture is not necessarily uniform throughout a whole organization. Different subcultures may be discernible at different levels in the organizational hierarchy or in different functional areas (eg actuarial and marketing). The risk of a clash of cultures is often raised as a potential problem area when two companies merge.

5.7.9   Globalization

In terms of economic and financial conditions and trends in particular, no country can regard itself as being immune from the effects of international events and changes.

Consider the year 2001, for example. Global economic growth was slow around the start of the year, following the collapse of the high-tech bubble, and it worsened as the year progressed. The realization grew that Japan's economy, one of the world's largest, was in recession. Predictions for US and world economic growth were cut back. Then the terrorist attacks of September 11 disrupted the normal operation of financial markets everywhere, creating great uncertainty, heightening risk aversion and lowering consumer and business confidence. The attacks themselves led to the largest ever claims on the international insurance market and produced solvency concerns for some insurers. Later, the major US energy company Enron filed for bankruptcy and the government of Argentina defaulted on its debt (the largest ever sovereign debt default).

These events, and others, helped to focus attention in all countries on the importance of contingency planning, disaster recovery, sound corporate governance, effective auditing and improved regulatory supervision. Nevertheless, less than a decade after the turbulent year that was 2001 the world was rocked by the financial and economic upheaval of 2007-09. The chain of events that unfolded was another dramatic reminder of the complexity and interdependence of the global environment.

Housing and credit booms in the US came to an abrupt end. Defaults occurred on mortgages classified as subprime because the borrowers had little or no creditworthiness. Investors lost confidence in the value of large quantities of complex financial products designed to securitize subprime mortgages and other debt. Asset values fell. The global financial system came under great stress. Key financial institutions failed, were bought at deep discounts or needed large injections of capital to survive. Some governments became bankrupt and many others ran up huge debts. Stock markets crashed and became very volatile. There was a widespread decline in economic activity. The loss of jobs, wealth and economic output was enormous.

This is not the place for an analysis of the causes of this global financial crisis. Many causes have been cited and given varying weights by analysts. From the perspective of this chapter we note that:

- economies and financial markets are closely interrelated across national borders;
- many investors do not properly assess risk in times of sustained market growth;
- financial products can be very complex and difficult to understand;
- regulation does not always keep pace with innovation; and
- most economic forecasters failed to predict the worst financial crisis since the Great Depression.

For some time financial regulation has been developing a global dimension. In 5.7.4 we noted the trend toward global financial reporting standards (IFRS). Banking regulation is also moving toward global standards. The Basel II Accord aims to establish an international standard for specifying the amount of capital banks are required to hold. Basel II takes a risk-based approach to determining the amount of capital. In a similar vein is Solvency II (often referred to as "Basel for insurers") – a set of standard regulatory requirements for insurance companies operating in the European Union.

Finally there is the rapid development toward a global actuarial profession. There are agreements in place between several pairs of national actuarial bodies to recognize each other's full professional qualifications. In addition, the International Actuarial Association (IAA) has adopted a minimum common core educational curriculum. In order to be recognized as full members of the IAA, national actuarial organizations must demonstrate that their actuaries satisfy at least this minimum curriculum in the process of their qualification.

5.8   Practical implications for actuaries

Widely respected UK actuary Frank Redington (1968) said:

> As a profession we are apt to be accurate, cautious, consistent and reticent, and in these lies our strength; but if they do not leave enough room for impulse and imagination, they can be a weakness. The actuary who is only an actuary is not an actuary.

How does this relate to this chapter? Redington's observation emphasizes the need for an actuary to be able to see various dimensions of a problem or task and the external forces that operate in each dimension. It is not good enough to see only the financial or mathematical aspects without also being aware of the other relevant aspects.

This does not mean that every actuary needs to be also an economist, a sociologist, a lawyer, a medical practitioner, a geneticist and so on. However, it does imply that an awareness of all these perspectives and a willingness to seek advice (where appropriate) from others who are experts in those areas will often help an actuary to devise better solutions to problems.

Actuaries have much to gain by learning to work together with experts from other fields (for example, statisticians, economists, geneticists, climatologists, environmentalists, engineers and health professionals) in developing better models that better represent the complex world in which actuaries aim to "make financial sense of the future" (The Actuarial Profession, UK).

5.9   Key learning points

The main point of this chapter is *not* to identify all the components of every context in which actuarial work might take place – *all* of the external forces. The main point is for you to see that if you are to become the best actuary you can be you need to develop for yourself the capability to analyze the context of each project you tackle and each job you undertake and to recognize the critical components.

Actuarial work never happens in a world as simple as that implied by the assumptions and methodologies that underpin most of the models used by actuaries.

Other key learning points arising from this chapter are:

- Problems and tasks that actuaries tackle always have a context.

- Within that context, external forces (outside an actuary's control) affect both problem and solution.

- The context is not static; the external forces change over time.

- Therefore an actuary cannot rely on standardized solutions and techniques.

- Knowledge of standard actuarial techniques is necessary but not sufficient.

- An understanding of the underlying principles of actuarial work is also required.

- Allowing for possible change in the context is critical to finding a good solution to a problem.

- External forces are not always easy to identify or to understand.

- Being able to see a problem from different perspectives is a valuable skill for an actuary.

- Being able to work together with experts in other fields greatly enhances an actuary's value.

CD Items

Ahmad, H. 2009, Takaful: An Islamic Alternative to Conventional Insurance Sees Phenomenal Growth, *Actuary Australia*, Institute of Actuaries of Australia, August 2009, pp. 8-10.

Coleman, A. 2009, The Global Financial Crisis: An Actuarial Perspective, *Actuary Australia*, Institute of Actuaries of Australia, May 2009, pp. 11-13.

Elliott, M. 2009, 2020 Vision, *The Actuary*, December, Staple Inn Actuarial Society, London, pp. 20-22.

Freeman, M. 2008, Life Insurance in Japan, *Actuary Australia*, Institute of Actuaries of Australia, December 2008, pp. 8-10.

Fulcher, G. 2009, Non-Life Road to Recovery, *The Actuary*, October, Staple Inn Actuarial Society, London, pp. 22-23.

Gutterman, S. 2010, Growing Up Obese: A National Health Challenge, *Contingencies*, American Academy of Actuaries, Jan/Feb, pp. 20-27.

Hinton, B. 1999, Energy Market Actuaries, *The Actuary*, March, Staple Inn Actuarial Society, London.

Kelly, E. 2009, Same, Same ... but Different – Living and Working in India, *Actuary Australia*, Institute of Actuaries of Australia, May 2009, pp. 19-21.

Miles, S. 2009, Living With Even Lower Interest Rates, *Actuary Australia*, Institute of Actuaries of Australia, April 2009, pp. 19-21.

Ngwenya, M. (Convenor) 2009, Discussion: Longevity Risk, *The Actuary*, December, Staple Inn Actuarial Society, London.

Rudolph, M.J. 2007, Pandemic Influenza's Impact on Health Systems, *Health Watch*, Society of Actuaries, January, pp. 14-15.

Tindall, J. 2008, Managing the Weather, *Actuary Australia*, Institute of Actuaries of Australia, July 2008, pp. 12-14.

Wood, M. 2009, Looking Back ... On the Future, *Actuary Australia*, Institute of Actuaries of Australia, July 2009, pp. 4-5.

Chapter 5 Exercise Solutions

References (other than CD Items)

Actuarial Society of South Africa 2008, The Actuarial Society of South Africa sets the record straight on HIV statistics, Press release (May 6, 2008).

Brown, R. L., Damm, R. & Sharara, I. 2002, A Macroeconomic Indicator of Age at Retirement, Presented at Retirement Implications of Demographic and Family Change Symposium, Sponsored by the Society of Actuaries, Chicago.

Cutler, D. M., Knaul, F., Lozano, R., Mendez, O. & Zurita, B. 2002, Financial crisis, health outcomes and ageing: Mexico in the 1980s and 1990s, *Journal of Public Economics*, 84, pp. 279-303.

de Alba, E., Zúñiga, J. & Ramírez-Corzo, M. A. 2008, Measurement and Transfer of Catastrophic Risks: A Simulation Analysis, *IIPR Technical Report 2008-03*, University of Waterloo, Waterloo.

De Ravin, J. W. 1996, Munich Reinsurance 1996 Pricing Survey, *Quarterly Journal of The Institute of Actuaries of Australia*, Part 1, December.

Ferris, S. D., Finnis, D. J., Munns, M. A. & Shuttleworth, D. 1995, Pricing: Theory, Practice and Control, *Transactions of The Institute of Actuaries of Australia*, pp. 765-795.

Hart, D. G., Buchanan, R. A. & Howe, B. A. 1996, *Actuarial Practice of General Insurance*, The Institute of Actuaries of Australia, Sydney.

The Institute of Actuaries of Australia 2002, *Guidance Note (GN353): Evaluation of General Insurance Technical Liabilities*.

Redington, F. M. 1968, On the presentation of Institute Gold Medal, *Journal of the Institute of Actuaries*, Vol 94, pp. 345-348.

SMH 2008, Selection of headlines (some modified slightly) from the edition of Monday, March 3, 2008, *The Sydney Morning Herald*, Fairfax Media Publications Pty Ltd, Sydney.

Swiss Re 2008a, Natural catastrophes and man-made disasters in 2007: High losses in Europe, *Sigma*, No 1/2008, Swiss Reinsurance Company Ltd, Zurich.

Swiss Re 2008b, Insurance in the emerging markets: Overview and prospects for Islamic insurance, *Sigma*, No 5/2008, Swiss Reinsurance Company Ltd, Zurich.

Fred's Coffee Shop – Applying Risk Management

Chapter 6 is devoted to applying risk management to the operation of financial services firms. As such, this chapter does not directly relate to Fred. However, there are a few general ideas that apply to all businesses.

One idea is to prioritize risks and, in particular, identify those risks with a high severity when they occur. Should such risks occur, they are likely to ruin the business; thus, they should receive high priority. Risks with a low frequency and low severity may be ignored. High frequency risks can be part of the budget process, although a high frequency risk where there is a possibility of high severity should be given special attention.

For Fred, a top priority risk might be the possibility of a lawsuit filed by a customer. He will need to take steps to minimize that possibility and also buy insurance against this risk.

Another example is the possibility of theft. If Fred anticipates that it will be a frequent but low-cost occurrence, he might just invest in more security and improved locks and window bars. If theft is potentially a very expensive occurrence, he should seriously consider also buying insurance.

A financial services firm will be asked by various parties such as regulators and stockholders to quantify the risks that it faces. While Fred may get the urge to apply his actuarial skills to quantifying the risks facing his coffee shop, it is unlikely that he will have the data to assess the specific risks to his shop. On the other hand, there may be small business associations in his area or an insurance broker who can help him understand the magnitude of the risks.

As you read Chapter 6, can you think of other risks that should be a high priority for Fred? What might he do to mitigate these risks?

Chapter 6:   Applying Risk Management

by Stuart Wason

6.1   Introduction

"All of life is the management of risk, not its elimination," is a quote widely attributed to Walter Wriston, former chairman of Citicorp. Indeed, risk is inherent in all areas of human endeavor. We readily identify the presence of risk in developing a space program and launching both equipment and humans into outer space. Equally however, risk is present in everyday commercial and personal activities. Risk results from the presence of more than one potential outcome from a course of action.

In his book *Against the Gods: The Remarkable Story of Risk*, Bernstein (1996) tells the story of a group of thinkers who showed the world "how to understand risk, measure it and weigh its consequences [and by so doing] converted risk-taking into one of the prime catalysts that drives modern Western society." Bernstein argues that, without the development of the instruments of risk management (eg probability theory), our complex and highly integrated world could not function. Liquid capital markets, insurance, pensions, engineering achievements and many more examples could not exist without risk management.

Claridge and Griffin (1997) point out that risk includes both upside as well as downside effects. This point was also made in Chapter 2 (eg 2.4.2).

Despite this, many risk management processes and techniques tend to be aimed at minimizing downside risk.

It is human nature to be averse to outcomes that are, in our view, less favorable than desired. In fact, we are prepared to reduce the expected (*mean*) outcome of a venture in order to reduce the likelihood of an unacceptably adverse outcome. This is the basis on which insurance is possible, given that the cost of insurance (the premiums) exceeds the expected value (in claim payments) by the insurer's loading for expenses and profit. Indeed, insurance is a tool for risk management.

Some risks cannot be insured, or the cost of insurance is higher than a business or an individual is prepared to pay. Other forms of risk management are therefore required. We discuss some of these in this chapter, in the context of financial services businesses and their customers.

There are many different definitions of risk. Claridge and Griffin define risk as follows:

> Risk is the possibility of failing to meet objectives. [...] Degree of risk can be measured by the likelihood and extent to which objectives will not be met and is affected by, amongst many other factors, constraints imposed upon the entity. (p 144)

Claridge and Griffin assert that risk only has meaning in the context of objectives. By implication, there can be neither success nor failure for an entity with no objectives. While this may appear to be a strange concept, consider how you would assess the success or failure of an activity such as an evening at the casino. Even without any statement of the objectives, you will form a view of what these would be (eg "do not lose more than I can afford"). In fact, individuals and businesses always have objectives, even when they have not been explicitly stated.

For effective risk management, we need our objectives to be clearly stated. We also need to understand how and when we intend to achieve these objectives and what our underlying assumptions are. The better we understand all this, the greater our chances of managing the risks and achieving the objectives.

In a business, some readily identifiable objectives (eg "achieve $X billion funds under management within three years") will be supported by business plans setting out how they will be achieved and highlighting the key assumptions and risks. Other, often more fundamental, objectives may simply be implicit, eg "remain solvent." Individuals are frequently advised to set goals and map out how to achieve them. This is simply the personal equivalent of a business plan and the first step toward personal risk management.

Claridge and Griffin also assert that constraints are a prerequisite for the existence of risk. Trivially, this must be true because an entity with no constraints will always be able to achieve its objectives.

In practice, constraints always exist and the valuable insight is that two entities with the same set of objectives but different constraints will be exposed to different types or degrees of risk. For example, if both entities aim to achieve a 15% return on capital by selling similar investment products, but one is restricted to operating in one state while the other can sell nationwide, then the former will be exposed to greater risk.

To be effective, a risk management process must be continuous and fully integrated into the structure of the entity. Risk management must have the active support and encouragement of the entity's most senior management, including its board of directors (the *board*).

Boards have a fundamental concern for the future of the organizations they serve. They continually assess the competence and good judgment of the senior management group that will develop, execute and amend strategy. Management is all about making decisions in the face of uncertainty. Best governance practices in many countries now require boards to ensure an effective risk management process is in place in their organization.

Risk management should occur at all levels in an organization, by both management and employees. For the most part, risk will be managed through the organization's normal command and control structure and its attendant standards, policies and operating procedures.

Some organizations structure this process with more formality than others, but all organizations manage risk in this multi-step process whether they recognize it directly or not.

The feedback loop for a continuous risk management process might be as illustrated in Figure 6.1. Note the similarity to the Actuarial Control Cycle and the importance of communication throughout the risk management process.

Figure 6.1   Risk management process

Exercise 6.1

Imagine that you are a loan officer at a bank responsible for mortgage lending to homeowners. Describe the risk management process according to the diagram outlined in Figure 6.1.

For maximum effectiveness, all participants in the risk management process must share a common understanding of the risks to which their business is subject. Important in developing this common understanding is the use of common terminology for describing risk types. Unfortunately, while there is some degree of standardization in terminology, there remain many different ways of identifying types of risk. In this chapter, we shall use a framework proposed by Jorion (2001).

Jorion takes all of the enterprise-wide risks to which a company is subject and divides them into *business risks* (those which are directly related to the products sold by the company) and *non-business risks* (those not directly related to the products sold). Non-business risks are those related to the running of the business in general and not to the specific products sold by the company. Non-business risks include *event risks* and *financial risks*. A portrayal of Jorion's general view of enterprise risks is illustrated below.

Figure 6.2   A general view of enterprise risks

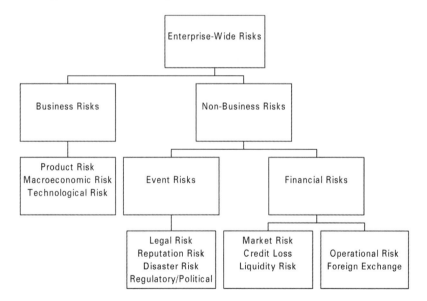

Exercise 6.2

The following list shows some of the activities of a financial institution. How would you classify them in the context of Jorion's risk management framework?

(a) Marketing activities, including the design and pricing of products.

(b) Distribution, including the development and management of sales channels.

(c) Underwriting, being the assessment and acceptance of risks.

(d) Customer service and other administration.

(e) Claims management.

(f) Financial management, including financial reporting and expense control.

This chapter illustrates the application of the risk management process in a range of commercial situations in the financial services sector including life insurance, general insurance, superannuation, funds management and banking. Many concepts introduced within the insurer section are also applicable more broadly to other businesses or areas of practice. This chapter presumes the prior establishment of an appropriate governance structure for risk management with the firm (eg including board responsibility for overall risk appetite and limits).

Section 6.2 discusses different types of risks for various applications in the financial services sector. Although the classifications used come from a different source, it is useful to consider how the categories match up with Figure 6.2.

Section 6.3 discusses the next step in the risk management process, risk assessment. Risk assessment refers to the measurement of a risk's impact on the business.

Section 6.4 discusses the methods for treating or managing risk providing examples from the financial services sector.

In this chapter, we refer to the worldwide financial turmoil that began in 2007 as the *global financial crisis* (GFC). Section 6.5 discusses the lessons learned from the GFC.

Finally, Section 6.6 discusses the practical implications of this chapter for actuaries while Section 6.7 summarizes the chapter.

6.2   Identifying risk

Before we can manage risks, we must identify them. Once identified, these risks can be incorporated in the risk management process and their impact on the entity or process can be optimized. At this stage of the process, we must also prioritize the risks.

Some of the most important risks for an organization are the ones that it has not yet identified. It is easy for an organization to be lulled into thinking that nothing has changed in its business and hence to overlook changes to its risk profile. There are many examples of organizations that did not fully identify all their risks (eg Claridge and Griffin note that Barings, which collapsed in February 1995 under the losses accumulated by rogue trader Nick Leeson, would have been solvent had the loss position been identified just two months earlier).

It is important to continuously consider the possibility of new or emerging risks as well as the continued relevance of previously identified risks. The GFC also demonstrated the difficulties involved in identifying risks arising from increasingly complex securities in which the ultimate investor is considerably distant from the original borrower (more on this later in this chapter). Many investors in these securities relied upon others (eg rating agencies) to inform them of the risks. It is now apparent that use of the work of others in identifying or assessing risk is not a substitute for the investors' own due diligence.

It is also important to note that risk mitigation techniques (to be discussed later in this chapter) are used to manage risk. However, in many cases the risk mitigation technique used does not simply remove risk; rather it transforms the risk in some fashion or even exchanges the current risk for other types of risk depending on the technique used. For example, reinsurance is used by life insurers to remove mortality risk from their books but the insurer assumes a counterparty risk exposure to the reinsurer.

The identification and prioritization of risks begins with the gathering of information from individual employees/team members about their concerns, uncertainties or issues regarding the entity or process under review. These views should be supplemented with feedback from relevant stakeholders who contribute to, participate in or make use of the process under review. A unique risk identifier should be assigned to each risk along with a clear statement of the risk that describes:

- the circumstances causing uncertainty;

- the tangible outcome of that uncertainty; and

- any risk dependencies within the entity or process.

In describing the circumstances causing uncertainty, sufficient context should be provided to enable others to clearly understand the risk.

Identify Risks
Objective:
Identify and prioritize the key risks
Methodology:
Brainstorming
Focus groups
Interviews
Periodic risk reporting
Surveys
Deliverables:
Statement of prioritized key risks

The following sections provide examples of identified risks for insurers, banks, fund managers and superannuation funds. These examples of the risk identification process for some specific businesses can be useful to a risk manager in other types of endeavor in illustrating the risk identification process.

6.2.1   Identifying insurer risks

The International Actuarial Association (IAA) and the International Association of Insurance Supervisors (IAIS) have developed similar views of the key risks faced by insurers. In particular, they are working together to develop a common glossary of insurance terminology. The glossary is maintained by the IAIS but can be accessed by connecting links from either the IAA website (www.actuaries.org) or the IAIS website (www.iaisweb.org). Foundation work by the IAA on a risk assessment framework for insurers was published in 2004 (*A Global Framework of Insurer Solvency Assessment* – informally referred to as the "Blue Book").

Insurer risks could be categorized under six major headings, namely:

* underwriting risk (sometimes called insurance risk);
* credit risk;
* market risk;
* operational risk;
* liquidity risk; and
* strategic/event risk.

This list is not necessarily a complete list of the risks to which an insurer is exposed – for example, it does not address the significant risks in distribution processes. Nevertheless, it does represent a growing global consensus on the categorization of the most significant risks faced by insurers.

The extent to which an insurer is more greatly exposed to these categories of risk depends very much on the nature of the business undertaken by the insurer. For example, an insurer selling long-term or savings-related insurance products will be more subject to market and credit risk (eg permanent life insurance or payout annuities) than an insurer selling short-term products for which the obligations are likely to be extinguished within a year (eg auto insurance).

It can be challenging to identify the true source for a risk. For example, adverse underwriting experience could be due to a variety of causes such as:

* incorrect pricing;
* risk profile of business assumed varying from that assumed in its pricing;
* underwriting practices actually used varying from those expected in the pricing;
* actual risk experience of the business assumed varying from that assumed in its pricing; and
* faulty claims management.

In this example, the adverse underwriting experience could well emerge as a result of a number of operational risks (eg underwriting practices and claims management) in addition to the traditional sources of underwriting risk (eg incorrect pricing and variance of experience from that expected in pricing).

These high-level categories of risks (though not their exact nature) are also faced by the banks, although much of underwriting risk is unique to insurance.

Insurer risk management seeks to address all six categories of risk. Insurance regulators are similarly concerned with an insurer's management of all of its risks but only some categories may be appropriate for capital requirements (typically the first four) while the others would be addressed by other forms of supervisory review.

It is worth repeating that, while risk management is about managing the upside as well as the downside potential of risks, certain insurer stakeholders (such as regulators) will naturally tend to focus on the downside of risks.

Each risk is listed as if it existed in isolation, independent of the other risks. However there are situations, for example in life insurance, where products are specifically designed and managed with the asset and liability risks modeled together in an integrated fashion. In addition, there are important considerations for combining the impact of the various risks across the whole company.

Exercise 6.3

The following list shows some of the activities of a financial institution. How would you classify them in the context of IAA/IAIS categories of risk?

(a) Marketing activities, including the design and pricing of products.

(b) Distribution, including the development and management of sales channels.

(c) Underwriting, being the assessment and acceptance of risks.

(d) Customer service and other administration.

(e) Claims management.

(f) Investment management.

(g) Financial management, including financial reporting and expense control.

Underwriting risk

Insurance companies assume risk through the insurance contracts they underwrite. The risks within the *underwriting risk* category are associated both with the perils covered by the specific line of insurance (fire, death, motor accident, windstorm, earthquake, default) and with the specific processes involved in the conduct of the insurance business. The Blue Book chose not to list all the specific hazards, but rather to focus on more generic risks that are applicable to all (or at least most) lines of insurance.

These risks, which generally fall into the category of *product risk* in the *business risks* section of Jorion's risk framework (Figure 6.2), are:

- *underwriting process risk* – risk from exposure to financial losses related to the selection and approval of risks to be insured;

- *pricing risk* – risk that the prices charged by the company for insurance contracts will be inadequate to support the future obligations arising from those contracts;

- *product design risk* – risk that the company's insurance contracts expose it to risks that were not anticipated in the design and pricing of those contracts;

- *claims risk* (for each peril) – risk that many more claims occur than expected or that some claims that occur are much larger than expected, resulting in unexpected losses.

This includes both the risk that a claim may occur, as well as the risk that the claim might develop adversely after it occurs;

- *economic environment risk* – risk that the environment will change in a manner that has an adverse effect on the company;

- *net retention risk* – risk that higher retention of insurance loss exposures results in losses due to catastrophic or concentrated claims experience;

- *policyholder behavior risk* – risk that the insurance company's policyholders will act in ways that are unanticipated and have an adverse effect on the company; and

- *reserving risk* – risk that the provisions held in the insurer's financial statements for its policyholder obligations (also *claim liabilities*, *loss reserves* or *technical provisions*) will prove to be inadequate.

Credit risk

Credit risk is the risk of default and change in the credit quality of issuers of securities (in the company's investment portfolio), counterparties (eg on reinsurance contracts, derivative contracts or deposits given) and intermediaries, to whom the company has an exposure. This category, which largely corresponds to *credit loss* in the risk framework, includes:

- *business credit risk* – risk that a counterparty fails to perform an obligation. This includes the risk that a reinsurer fails to meet its obligations to the company under a reinsurance contract;

- *invested asset credit risk* – risk of non-performance of contractual payment obligations or adverse changes in creditworthiness of invested assets;

- *political risk* – risk that changes in government policies or actions affect the creditworthiness of financial instruments held by the insurer; and

- *sovereign risk* – risk of default or adverse change in creditworthiness of securities issued by governments or government entities. Although sovereign risk could be included with invested asset credit risk, it is often separately identified due to its importance.

Market risk

Market risk arises from the level or volatility of market prices of assets. It involves the exposure to movements in the level of financial variables such as share prices, interest rates, exchange rates or commodity prices. It also includes the exposure of options to movements in the underlying asset price. Market risk also involves the exposure to other unanticipated movements in financial variables or to movements in the actual or implied volatility of asset prices and options. This category, which corresponds to *market risk* in the risk framework, includes:

- *interest rate risk* – risk of exposure to losses resulting from fluctuations in interest rates;

- *spread risk* – risk that interest spreads will fluctuate;

- *equity and property risk* – risk of exposure to losses resulting from fluctuation of market values of equities and other assets;

- *currency risk* – risk that relative changes in currency values decrease values of foreign assets or increase the value of obligations denominated in foreign currencies;

- *basis risk* – risk that yields on instruments of varying credit quality, liquidity, and maturity do not move together, thus exposing the company to market value variation that is independent of liability values;

- *reinvestment risk* – risk that the returns on funds to be reinvested will fall below anticipated levels;

- *concentration risk* – risk of increased exposure to losses due to concentration of investments in a geographical area or other economic sector;

- *asset/liability management (ALM) risk* – risk that fluctuations of interest and inflation rates have different effects on the values of assets and liabilities; and

- *off-balance sheet risk* – risk of changes in values of contingent assets and liabilities such as swaps that are not otherwise reflected in the balance sheet.

Operational risk

Operational risk, which broadly corresponds to the equivalent item in the risk framework, is the risk associated with events such as fraud, systems failure, litigation or regulatory breach within the company. Loss data for this risk can be difficult to obtain since it has not been required in the past for risk modeling. Capital management focuses significantly on those operational risk events that are infrequent but of high severity. More frequent operational risk events (which tend to be smaller) can be significantly mitigated or exacerbated by the quality of internal controls and guidelines. Operational risks include:

- *human capital risk* – risk that the insurer will not be able to obtain and maintain sufficient well-trained personnel;

- *management control risk* – risk that the insurer fails to have appropriate management discipline or internal controls resulting in inappropriate actions by the insurer or its representatives;

- *system risks* – risk that computer systems failures impair the company's ability to conduct normal business; and

- *strategic risks* – risk that arises from the company's inability to implement appropriate business plans, to make decisions, to allocate resources or to adapt to changes in its business environment.

Liquidity risk

Liquidity risk is the exposure to loss in the event that insufficient liquid assets will be available from amongst the assets supporting the policy obligations to meet the cash flow requirements of the policyholder obligations when they are due. This category, which corresponds to the equivalent category in the risk framework, includes:

- *liquidation value risk* – risk that unexpected timing or amounts of cash needed may require liquidation of assets when market conditions would result in loss of realized value;

- *affiliated company risk* – risk that investments in affiliated companies may be difficult to sell or that affiliated companies may drain financial or operating resources from the company; and

- *capital market risk* – risk that the company will not be able to obtain sufficient funding from capital markets.

Event risk

Event risks are risks outside the control of the enterprise, which can have a significant negative impact on the enterprise. In some classifications, some specific event risks are separately identified. This category, which matches the equivalent one in the risk framework, includes:

- *legal risk* – the risk that unforeseeable lawsuits or adverse judgments can disrupt or otherwise negatively affect the operations or condition of the company;

- *reputation risk* – risk that negative publicity, whether true or not, causes a decline in the customer base, costly litigation and/or revenue reductions;

- *disaster risk* – risk that a major external event such as earthquake, fire or flood can have a negative impact on the systems of the company that impairs the ability of the company to conduct its business in an orderly manner;

- *regulatory risk* – risk that legislative actions, tax changes, court decisions or regulatory rulings will alter markets or competitive abilities; and

- *political risk* – risk that actions by governments or government entities will impair the company's ability to conduct business.

As mentioned earlier, insurers are subject to additional risks. Two further categories of risk are discussed below.

Distribution risk

Distribution risk covers the risk to which distribution channels expose the business. This risk can be considered to fall into three categories, namely:

- volume of business sold – generally, the risk is that sales volumes are low and, hence, cost per sale is high. However, if new business creates a cash flow strain on the company then high volumes are also a risk;

- nature of business sold – a number of risks have been identified under *underwriting risk* above. Distribution is the entry point for these risks, which will be reduced if the distribution channels are likely to reach the "right" customers; and

- reputation/compliance – many of the compliance issues and other risks to a company's reputation arise around the point of sale.

Expense risk

All businesses face the risk that expenses are too high, with an adverse effect on profits. This can generally be managed by a combination of budgeting, expense control, *expense analysis* – gaining an understanding of what drives the level of expenses – and specific cost-cutting projects. Often, scale can be the issue, especially for a small insurer that seeks to offer a wide range of products.

A more subtle expense risk is the risk that expenditure is too low in certain areas where it adds value. For example, a reduction in underwriting or claims management expenditure may lead to higher claims costs.

6.2.1.1 Life insurance risks

The degree to which insurers are exposed to each of the risks described above will vary depending on the specific nature of the insurance business conducted. Life insurers tend to engage in the sale of products affording financial protection of various sorts to their customers or policyholders. The significance of the savings element versus the pure protection element varies greatly from product to product. Consequently, some products with a very high savings element (eg some types of deferred annuities or variable annuities with guarantees) can be quite similar to, and share many of the same risks as, financial products sold by banks or other fund management businesses.

Because the products offered by life insurers are frequently long-term in nature, there could be an additional risk that the definitions of claimable events will become obsolete. If the life insurer cannot change these definitions, the cost of claims could increase very significantly. For example, the conditions covered by *trauma* insurance are intended to be traumatic events, often requiring major surgery, which have a significant impact on the insured's life and lifestyle. Advances in medical science mean that some conditions that would have met these characteristics a few years ago now only require minor surgery without even an overnight stay in hospital. Similar advances can be expected in future.

The long-term nature of some life insurance products (eg lifetime annuities or long term care insurance) exposes the insurer to considerable reinvestment risk since the contracts may have single or fixed premiums even though suitable assets with sufficient duration to match the future contractual obligations are not available when the product is sold.

A significant life insurer risk is that of changes in policyholder behavior. The withdrawal behavior of policyholders in the presence of significant financial options (such as can be embedded in universal life and variable annuity products for example) under varying future economic scenarios can result in significant financial uncertainty to the insurer.

Unique to life insurers, their retirement income products carry *longevity risk*. With lifetime annuities, the longevity risk is held by the life insurer (and its reinsurer, if applicable), while with term certain annuities and some forms of variable annuities, the annuitant takes the risk.

6.2.1.2 Health insurance risks

Where prospective customers can be underwritten, the risks in offering health insurance are similar to those in other *short-tail* insurance products, ie those whose claims are generally settled quickly, such as term insurance, home insurance and automobile insurance.

In many cases, however, there is little or no scope to underwrite each person applying for health insurance. In this situation the key risk is *anti-selection*. Anti-selection occurs when persons in better health opt for cheaper or less comprehensive forms of coverage while those in poorer health will remain covered and are insensitive to premium increases.

Health insurance products are also subject to the future evolution of health care (eg costs, types of procedures, utilization patterns, medical inflation, health care financing and changing consumer perceptions about health care).

6.2.1.3 General insurance risks

General insurance provides coverage for a wide variety of risks including home, automobile, commercial and professional liability insurance. Most commonly, general insurance is written for a one-year term. Some types of coverage provide mostly for high-frequency but low-amount claims. Significant components of both home and automobile insurance provide for these types of claims. General insurance also provides protection against catastrophic losses, such as from earthquakes or floods.

Important specific risks in the management of general insurance are *volatility risk*, *uncertainty risk*, risk of *extreme events* and *super-imposed inflation*.

Volatility risk

Volatility risk is the risk that, given the probability distribution of total claims, the total amount of claims will differ from its expected value. Volatility risk is caused by the randomness of frequency, severity and time to payment of claims and related expenses. The volatility risk of a portfolio is higher if the range of insured amounts is higher, as more variability in insured amounts leads to a higher degree of randomness in the severity of individual claims. Also heterogeneity in policyholder characteristics (eg kilometers driven each year, alcohol consumption patterns) contributes to volatility.

On the other hand, volatility risk relative to the portfolio size decreases if the size of a portfolio is increased. This can be explained by the law of large numbers. However, volatility risk may not vanish entirely with increasing size of a portfolio owing to correlations between policyholders.

Uncertainty risk

The *uncertainty risk* in the general insurance claims process can be divided into three parts. First, the parameters of the distributions used are prone to misestimation. Such misestimation can be quantified using statistical theory.

Secondly, the parameters driving the claims process are not constant over time. They may fluctuate as a result of changes in the environment – legislation, weather and climate conditions, rising expenses, etc. For instance, in a dry summer, there will be an increased frequency of fire incidents. The fluctuation of parameters over time can be observed through previous experience. However, modeling such fluctuations ranges from straightforward to very complex. For instance, weather conditions can often be modeled reasonably well, but changes in a legal system cannot.

Thirdly, there is *model risk* – the risk that the chosen distribution and other model assumptions are not correct. Although it is not easy to further quantify model risk (another model would be needed for it), it can be said that some risks can better be modeled than others. Hence, there is more model risk for risks that cannot be modeled well (eg the changes in a legal system as mentioned above).

Extreme events

Extreme events are events occurring with a low frequency and a high severity. Because of the low frequency of catastrophes, catastrophe risk cannot be estimated on the basis of statistical evidence dating back only a few years.

Estimating the total risk of a portfolio based solely on statistical evidence of a number of past years may ignore extreme event risk if no extreme events have occurred in those years and thus underestimate the total level of risk. If an extreme event is included in the experience data, estimating risk and expected liabilities on the basis of that experience may lead to an overestimation of both.

Estimation of natural catastrophe risk is extremely difficult, as detailed and specific knowledge about the stochastic nature of such catastrophes is in most cases unknown. The dependency structure between the individual risks is important but almost always unknown. Because of the scarcity of experience data, the parameter uncertainty and model risk are usually large.

General insurance risk management frequently relies on layers of reinsurance coverage to manage extreme event risk. This can expose the general insurer to significant counterparty risk in the event that a reinsurer fails.

Super-imposed inflation

The risks discussed above can apply to all general insurance products. There is another specific risk for *long-tail* business. Long-tail claims are those that generally take a long time to settle. Indeed, some of them may not be known to the insurer until years after the claim event – examples include asbestosis claims and some medical indemnity claims. *Liability* and *indemnity* covers are the main types of long-tail business.

While the costs of most claims can be expected to increase with inflation, the cost of long-tail claims can be very significantly affected by *super-imposed inflation*. This extra growth in claims costs can come from various sources including increases in the levels of damages awarded by courts.

6.2.2   Identifying superannuation risks

As specialists in the financial measurement and management of risk and contingent events, actuaries are also actively involved in the operation of superannuation funds. As with any business, risk is inherent in the operation of superannuation funds. This section will touch on some of the unique aspects of risk management in a superannuation fund, particularly one offering defined benefits.

Risks can arise from any part of the management of a superannuation fund, including:

*   plan design;
*   investment policy;
*   asset selection and allocation;
*   asset/liability modeling;
*   plan valuation;
*   plan administration – including, for example, commutation of pension entitlements;
*   member education;
*   compliance and tax filings;
*   financial management, including pension accounting;
*   performance assessment; and
*   plan funding.

The two basic forms of superannuation fund are defined benefit and defined contribution funds. Defined benefit funds require the plan administrator or the trustee to constantly assess whether the combination of current assets, future rates of contribution (from both the fund sponsor and the members) and future plan experience (including investment performance and expense levels) will be sufficient to provide for the defined benefits. Defined contribution schemes require an assessment of whether the investment options provided to fund members represent an appropriate range of choices with acceptable rates of investment performance.

Defined benefit fund risks

The main objective of a defined benefit fund might be stated as being to provide reasonable benefits at a reasonable cost (ie employer contribution rate). Provided that the benefits are reasonable and the employer remains in business, the major risks faced by the fund member (employee) relate to his or her career with the employer, including the cost (in benefits forgone) of resignation. Therefore, we shall consider the employer's risks.

In essence, the key risk is that the cost of the fund is excessive and affects the viability not just of the defined benefit plan but of the sponsoring employer. Past financial crises have resulted in substantial pension plan funding shortfalls that, in some cases, significantly contributed to the insolvency of the sponsoring employer. This may happen through adverse experience in:

- investment performance – poor investment performance will result in higher rates of contribution by sponsors of defined benefit funds. Poor performance can be the result of several factors, including asset allocation, reinvestment rate of return and asset default experience (*credit risk*);

- salary inflation – rapid growth in salaries, particularly those of higher-paid and longer-serving employees, will increase the cost of benefits;

- pension inflation – pensions are usually linked to a price index such as CPI, so high inflation (at least relative to investment returns) will increase costs;

- pensioner longevity – higher than expected rates of mortality improvement result in higher costs; and

- other experience – various other factors can affect the cost of the fund, although they will not generally be as significant as those listed above.

Employers (and fund trustees) manage these risks by setting contribution rates, monitoring experience and reviewing the funding. The role of actuaries is critical in this process.

Different approaches to funding the benefits carry different risk profiles. Funding methods are discussed in a subsequent chapter, but it is worth making some brief observations at this stage.

First, it is important to understand that risk depends on our perspective. Reducing risk in the superannuation fund may vastly increase risk to related parties outside the fund. For example, making excessive contributions to the superannuation fund will greatly increase the security of benefits in the fund, but it will reduce the company's profit and may even lead it into insolvency. In turn, this presents a larger risk to the members of the fund (the employees of the company). Also, providing lump sums rather than pensions transfers longevity, investment and price inflation risk to retiring members.

Secondly, the fundamental rationale for funding is that the investment earnings on contributions will exceed the growth rate of benefits (ie salary inflation). In times of high inflation or low investment earnings or in jurisdictions with high tax rates (or no tax concessions) this may only be achievable within the fund by taking significant investment risks (ie by taking the risk that investment performance will be well below what is required).

Combining these two observations, there may be circumstances in which the *lower* risk option for the fund, in the context of its environment, is to make relatively low contributions. A form of this approach is practiced in many public sector superannuation funds that are *pay as you go* (PAYG) – ie contributions are merely sufficient to meet current benefit payments and expenses.

Note that we do not advocate PAYG funding or any particular funding approach. The discussion above is to highlight that the issue must be viewed in context.

Defined contribution fund risks

By fixing the contribution rate, the impact of adverse experience falls on the members of a defined contribution fund. The question for each member – whether in a company-sponsored fund, an industry fund, or a personal superannuation fund – is "what retirement income will my accumulated fund purchase compared with my needs or my pre-retirement income?"

It is arguable that the members should manage this risk in a similar way to the sponsor of a defined benefit fund. That is, they should determine the contribution rate (or shape of rates) as part of a financial plan that is expected to meet their current and future lifestyle objectives and then monitor the progress of the fund (and their overall circumstances), reviewing their financial plan from time to time. This is not common practice at present but the increased reliance on defined contribution funds means that there is a strong need. Eventually, advisers (including actuaries) will find a way to meet that need and get adequately remunerated for doing so.

Within the general class of investment risks for members of these funds, a specific risk is that of poor selection of investment strategy or investment manager. We shall consider this risk in the next subsection.

6.2.3   Identifying funds management risks

Chasing superior performance

Fund managers, including life insurers as managers of savings and retirement income products, typically generate most of their profit from the difference between fee income and expenses. Expense risk is similar to that for insurers (6.2.1), particularly in relation to scale.

A key driver of fee income is the volume of *funds under management* (FUM), so the fund manager's objectives will usually focus on growing FUM.[1]

FUM, in turn, is driven by three factors:

*   inflows – investments from new and existing customers increase FUM;

---

[1] Similar issues apply to master trusts and other retail fund administration vehicles, where the driver of fee income is *funds under administration* (FUA). For the purposes of this subsection we will discuss FUM and assume that this expression incorporates FUA.

- outflows – when customers draw down or transfer their funds or payments are made on retirement income products, FUM is reduced; and

- investment performance – growth in the investments, whether income or capital gains, increases FUM.

Investment performance can also have a powerful indirect effect on FUM. If investment performance is poor, especially relative to competitors, inflows will reduce and outflows will increase. If the fund manager is a sector specialist, then other sectors are "competitors" – eg poor stock market returns will induce investors to switch to cash or fixed interest assets.

This central importance of investment performance means that the fund manager is likely to pursue any opportunity to improve or enhance its performance. This clearly opens the door to all manner of risks, of which the following are the more obvious:

- Assets that offer the potential for additional return have a downside risk as well. That risk is all the more dangerous if it is not apparent. For example, some highly rated tranches of securitized mortgages proved to have unexpectedly high risk under the stress of the GFC.

- The pursuit of extra performance may lead the manager to invest in assets that are not allowed under its *investment mandate*, the rules by which it has agreed to operate.

- Despite the risks, the manager may be lucky for a considerable period of time. If this good fortune is perceived to be the result of skill, the manager will be blind to its investment performance risks and slower to take remedial action when its luck turns.

Asset/liability mismatch risk

Issues in relation to the mismatch of assets and liabilities are discussed in Chapter 14. For now, the key point to make is that the existence of any form of guarantee may be expected to make the investment more attractive. However, this is only of real benefit to the fund manager if the true cost of offering the guarantee is lower than the value placed on it by the investor.

For example, investment banks have often constructed products, based on derivatives, that offer the investor a proportion of the gain in a stock market index and an underlying capital guarantee. For the investor, the effective cost of the capital guarantee is the proportion of the index gain forgone (plus any dividend yield if an accumulation index is not used). This charge must cover the actual cost of the guarantee plus the investment bank's other expenses and profit requirements and may even have to cover distribution costs – and yet there are times when people are prepared to buy these products.

Therefore, the risk to consider is that any performance guarantees in the products have been retained by the manager and have been mis-priced. Indeed, an important subset of this risk is that guarantees exist that have not even been identified.

Customer expectation risks

Fund managers make their money from the difference between asset fees and expenses. This difference can be expected to be greater when there are more funds under management. Therefore, the loss of customers is a significant risk. Accordingly, fund managers should be aware of the risk that customers experience investment returns that are below their expectations.

A fund manager's customer, whether an individual or an entity such as a superannuation fund, selects an investment strategy and one or more investment managers to implement that strategy. Usually, this is done by selecting from the pooled investment funds operated by different managers but the risks are similar if the manager has been given a specific mandate.

Other than risks relating to the general performance of asset sectors, the risks include:

- that the investment strategy does not suit the customer's objectives – perhaps the best way to manage this risk is for the customer to ensure that he or she gets good advice and that it is discussed and understood;

- that the implementation of the strategy does not suit the customer's objectives – fund managers measure success in terms of relative performance against benchmarks, before tax and fees, whereas the customer experiences investment performance after these deductions and may have the objective of beating salary inflation by x%. This can lead to the situation where the manager is proud of achieving a gross return of -5% against a benchmark of -10% – but the customer receives -6% after tax and fees and compares this with salary growth of 4%. If the customer had more direct control over the investment decisions, it is likely that these decisions would give more weight to issues such as the tax effect of the decision and the likelihood of negative returns; and

- that the fund manager selection was poor – generally, you might expect this to become obvious through poor investment performance, but short-term performance is not a reliable indicator of the quality of the manager. The real issue is whether the manager's internal processes, including its methodology for selecting assets, are likely to add value. Customers can manage the risk of selecting a poor manager by reviewing external ratings of the manager and by use of expert advisers.

6.2.4 Identifying banking risks

The risks faced by banks depend on the businesses in which they operate. Typical types of business within a global bank include:

- domestic banking;
- international banking; and
- capital markets.

Domestic banking

Domestic banking might focus on customer segments such as retail, small business and commercial, as well as credit card operations and mutual funds. The dominant risk faced in domestic banking arises from the credit risk inherent in loans of all types (eg mortgages, credit cards, lines of credit, home equity lines of credit and commercial loans). These operations are also subject to market risk as a result of any mismatch between the term of their assets and liabilities. A key challenge for this business is to maintain an adequate spread between the interest earned on the assets versus that paid out on the liabilities (eg demand deposits and GICs).

International banking

International banking would include the local banking operations in foreign markets. It faces similar risks to domestic banking but within the foreign markets in which the bank has operations. Overall the global bank would face currency risks from conducting its foreign operations. It may also face additional operational and regulatory risks from those operations.

Capital markets

Capital markets might focus on businesses such as corporate loans, derivatives, special asset classes, broker services and investment banking. Through its operations in these businesses, the bank is subject to *warehousing risk* (risk of loss from securities it has created but cannot be sold to investors) as well as *underwriting risk* (risk of loss through providing a guaranteed price when new securities are underwritten and issued publicly).

The Basel Committee on Banking Supervision (BCBS) has developed views of the key risks faced generally by banks.

For the purposes of this chapter, banking risks can generally be categorized under five of the six major headings in Section 6.2.1, namely:

- credit risk;
- market risk;
- operational risk;
- liquidity risk; and
- strategic/event risk.

This list is not necessarily a complete list of the risks to which a bank is exposed; nevertheless, it does represent a global consensus on the categorization of the most significant risks faced by banks.

6.3   Risk assessment

Having identified the key risks of a business, an important next step in applying risk management involves risk assessment. Risk assessment refers to the measurement of a risk's impact on the business and should not be confused with a subsequent step in which the treatment or management of the risk is considered.

Assess Risks
Objective:
Assess exposure to loss from key risks
Understand risk dependencies
Methodology:
Qualitative models
Quantitative models
Deliverables:
Understanding of gross and net risk exposures
Development of risk models for scenario testing

While the topic of risk assessment is introduced in 2.8, three aspects of risk assessment will be examined in this section to highlight their application in risk management. These aspects are:

* quantitative versus qualitative assessment;

* experience data; and

* design of a risk model for decision making.

6.3.1   Quantitative versus qualitative assessment

It is normally preferable to be able to quantify the frequency and severity of each risk to the greatest extent possible. However, for some risks this is not fully practical (eg impact of a product recall on the reputation of an organization). In this situation it is preferable to use a qualitative approach to risk assessment rather than relying on a few opinions. A qualitative technique for assessing the key risks illustrated in Chapter 2 is the heat map which uses individual and group ratings of each risk according to agreed scales of frequency and severity.

Wherever possible, it is important to attempt to assess both the quantitative and qualitative aspects of risk. For example, the assessment of credit risk is frequently conducted using sophisticated risk models based on substantial amounts of underlying experience data. Such assessments can be quite complex and require significant technical expertise. The results of such models need to be considered along with qualitative judgment on topics such as model risk, controls, expertise and external market information.

6.3.2   Experience data

Risks vary in their impact as a result of differences in their probability of occurrence as well as in their severity. These in turn are derived by studying the underlying experience data related to the risk exposures and the resulting losses.

Example 6.1

Credit risk: The probability of default of a rated security will tend to vary depending on the rating and prevailing economic conditions. The severity of loss given default will also vary with the prevailing economic conditions.

Underwriting risk: For disability income insurance, the probability of disablement varies considerably due to risk factors such as age, sex and occupational class. The severity of the loss depends on the length of time the claimant remains disabled and unable to return to work. This in turn will depend on the policy definition of disability and the economic conditions.

Risks that are frequent in their occurrence (eg certain types of medical reimbursement claims such as prescription drug and dental claims) will have considerable claim data from which to assess the probability of their occurrence. Other risks occur so infrequently (eg major earthquake) that their probability of occurrence may be difficult to estimate and require models and/or regulatory or professional guidance for their estimation.

Even when loss experience data does exist (for probability of occurrence as well as severity of loss) the risk manager must assess the credibility of the data for the risk being assessed.

If the business does not have sufficiently credible experience of its own, it may be appropriate to consider relevant industry or market data. Life insurers can make use of relevant industry mortality and lapse experience to supplement their own. The risk manager must take care in using such supplemental data to ensure that it is indeed appropriate for the intended purpose. The use of population mortality in place of insured lives mortality, for example, could represent a significant difference in loss experience and result in incorrect risk management decisions.

Sufficient or credible volumes of loss experience data can also be gained by using a longer study period. However the use of a longer period has a number of pros and cons that the risk manager must weigh. If the longer study period involved life insurance mortality, these might include:

- period now includes an unusual flu epidemic;

- length of period masks an underlying mortality trend of mortality improvement;

- period masks a change in the product mix, target market or sales distribution;

- period contains claims of unusually large amounts; and/or

- longer period serves to smooth out volatility in experience by claims year.

Exercise 6.4

A general insurer is reviewing its motor vehicle damage claim experience for the most recent calendar year. You have been asked to comment on the pros and cons of using experience over a longer period of time (eg two full calendar years) to re-price this insurance product. What would you say?

Insurers frequently make use of reinsurer experience, as a supplement to their own, in the design and pricing of new products if that reinsurer has proven expertise and experience with the risks inherent in those products.

Risk models

A very important tool in the application of risk management is the development of a risk model. For example, risk models are in common use by banks and insurers for risk and capital management. While the following paragraphs use insurance reference materials to describe risk models, many of the concepts are equally applicable to other types of businesses as well.

A risk model is frequently called an *internal model*, which is defined in the joint CEA, Groupe Consultatif Glossary for insurers as follows:

> An internal model is a risk management system of an insurer for the analysis of the overall risk situation of the insurance undertaking, to quantify risks and/or to determine the capital requirement on the basis of the company specific risk profile.

Risk models are used for a variety of purposes within an insurer, including:

* valuation of insurance liabilities;

* financial condition analysis;

* stress and scenario testing;

* analysis of asset/liability investment practices and policies;

* analysis of market risk;

* pricing of insurance products;

* evaluation of reinsurance programs; and

* evaluation of various management strategies.

Risk models used by insurers can also be complicated by the presence of significant dependencies between financial market performance, insurance risk, operational events and management options. The nature of these dependencies may change significantly in times of stress.

In the design of a risk model, it is important to have a framework for risk management with:

* time horizons;

* risk measures;

* confidence levels; and

* terminal provisions.

Time horizon

In assessing risk, it is necessary to define the time horizon over which extremely adverse experience is assumed to occur. This should not be confused with the need to consider the full time period of risk exposure. The time horizon is typically established based on regulatory or accepted reporting practice, and reflects some reasonable time frame during which management and/or supervisory action is expected. For example, in formulating a capital requirement, a supervisor will take into account the time horizon between the date when the insurer's financial statements are prepared and the expected date by which a supervisor could take effective action if this was deemed to be necessary. Since this time horizon depends upon local business practices, the supervisor's resources, legislation and the legal system, this horizon may vary from one jurisdiction to another. For example, European supervisors have chosen a time horizon of one year for Solvency II.

In some cases the time horizon is set to longer periods or even the entire lifetime of the risks. A time horizon longer than one year may be useful when assessing the impact of risks that may take some years to fully emerge (eg a full economic or underwriting cycle) or for management's response to changing circumstances. For example, some supervisors require insurers to conduct a multi-year future financial analysis involving adverse scenarios. Regardless of the length of the time horizon, the remaining risks beyond the time horizon according to the stressed assumptions (ie assessed in the light of the projected experience in the time horizon) will often be provided for through a present value amount or terminal provision.

Risk measure

Figure 6.3   An illustration of VaR and TVaR

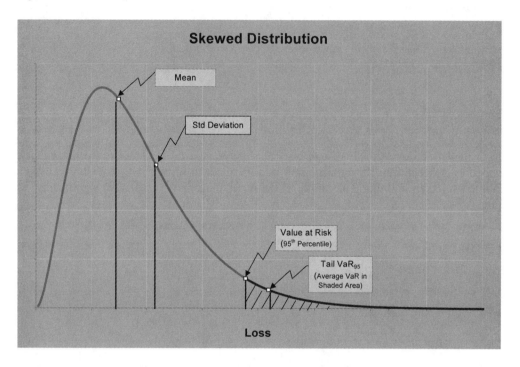

A risk measure is a numeric evaluator that can be used to help determine the financial impact of the risk. The most useful risk measures for solvency assessment will exhibit a variety of desirable properties (eg consistency). Of course, one risk measure cannot adequately convey all the information necessary for the management of a particular risk. A risk measure that exhibits several desirable properties for various (but not all) risks is *tail value at risk* (TVaR), also called *TailVar, conditional tail expectation* (CTE) or even *policyholders' expected shortfall*. In many situations, this risk measure is better suited to insurance risks than *value at risk* (VaR), a risk measure commonly used in banking, since it is common for insurance risk distributions to be skewed with lumpy or fat tails. An advantage of using TVaR as a risk measure is that, given an appropriately represented risk distribution, it provides an indication of the potential size of catastrophic losses above a certain confidence level when distributions are not normal. This is illustrated in Figure 6.3.

While the insurance regulator will specify the risk measure(s) to be used for assessing regulatory capital requirements, the insurer may well set up its own measures to fit its risk management objectives.

Confidence level

The selection of an appropriate confidence level for an insurer to use in an internal model will depend on the specific use of the model, its time horizon and choice of risk measure. In the design of an economic capital model, the insurer may be guided by the work of rating agencies in assessing insurers and the substantial volume of credit rating and default data available from these agencies. In the case of internal models used for regulatory capital requirements, the insurance regulator will generally specify a confidence level for the industry to use.

It is important to note that the degree of protection afforded by a given confidence level needs to also consider the length of the time horizon over which it is to be applied. For example, a 99% confidence level measured over a one year time horizon with what would be a current estimate terminal provision after one year (in the hypothetical circumstances then relating to that confidence level) may be a weaker requirement than a 95% confidence level measured over the entire lifetime of the remaining risks. It is generally accepted that the confidence level required will decrease as the time horizon lengthens.

A challenge in the use of higher confidence levels is that, by definition, they are considering increasingly rare events for which there may be little experience data or knowledge of risk dependencies under extreme circumstances.

Terminal provision

A terminal provision must be calculated whenever the time horizon is shorter than the full lifetime of the insurer's obligations. It can represent a very material portion of the total balance sheet requirement, particularly when the time horizon is short compared to the ultimate runoff (eg a horizon of one year for most life insurance products). The considerations involved in determining the terminal provision at the end of the time horizon may vary by the specific use of the internal model, but typically include:

- conservatism – depending on the use to which the measurement framework is being put (eg for capital requirements), it should include an appropriate level of conservatism (in excess of the then current estimate at the end of the time horizon) to allow directly or indirectly (eg by calculating a cost of capital) for the uncertainty or volatility of the current estimate. The method and amount of the conservatism may differ depending on whether the model is being used for regulatory or economic capital purposes;

- reflecting the position at the end of the time horizon – the risks allowed for in each terminal provision should be assessed in the light of the relevant (potentially stressed) assumed conditions at the end of the time horizon as well as including provision for subsequent future risk; and

- risks that do not fully develop within the time horizon – life insurance risks take years to develop (eg a deteriorating mortality trend), or develop quickly but take years to have a significant impact (eg product guarantees). The terminal provision should make appropriate allowance for risks that could develop or otherwise have an impact after the time horizon. There is a need to consider any correlation of adverse outcomes within the time horizon to adverse outcomes beyond the time horizon. Such a material correlation is common for claim liability estimates for property/casualty business.

6.4   Risk treatment

Following the identification and assessment of all the known risks to a business, the next step in applying risk management is to consider the appropriate treatment of those risks.

Deciding on the appropriate treatment requires the development of appropriate risk management strategies. These strategies would be developed within the organization's overall risk appetite and risk tolerances.

Risk Treatment
Objective:
Execute the optimal risk management strategy
Methodology:
Project implementation best practices
Deliverables:
Action steps for executing strategy including goals, responsibilities, resources, reporting, scope, schedule etc

Assigning responsibility for dealing with risk within an organization can frequently be a challenge by itself. Those assigned responsibility must have the requisite knowledge, experience and authority to execute those responsibilities. Their risk management responsibilities must be aligned with their goals and responsibilities within the organization. Assigning responsibility for risks ensures that no known risks are ignored and that the most effective resources within the organization are selected.

Risk managers need to be aware of the risk management strategies they are permitted to use, as well as the scope allowed for their actions. For example, in a financial services institution, is the use of derivatives to hedge foreign currency risk permitted? Are there appropriate limits placed on their use?

The objectives in selecting risk management strategies include:

- consider the important risks first;
- ensure that the consequences and sources of risk are well defined;
- ensure that risk dependencies are considered;
- design strategies that minimize risk and cost while maximizing opportunity and value;
- ensure that the strategies considered take into account the risk implications of the strategy itself;
- select the optimal strategy from among the prioritized strategies;
- consider risk management process improvements; and
- develop a work plan for implementation.

Each strategy for the treatment of risk has its own risk implications. Frequently the inherent risk is transformed or exchanged for another risk or set of risks in some way. This can leave the business with residual risks and/or with additional risks. For example, the outsourcing of administration to a third party, while removing the primary burden of administration from the business, introduces the business to counterparty risk as well as potential risks to its reputation in the event that the outsourcer fails to perform as expected. In the end, the principal business remains responsible to its customers.

Strategies for managing risk fall into the following major categories:

- *avoid* – eliminate, stop, prohibit or sell the risk exposure;
- *retain* – accept and self-insure the risk exposure, eg by integrating it with other risks or by diversifying risks;
- *reduce* – mitigate or cap portions of the risk exposure;
- *transfer* – insure, hedge, securitize or outsource the risk exposure; and
- *exploit* – expand and diversify the risk exposure.

Risk management process improvements should include techniques for monitoring risks and the effectiveness of risk treatment (also called risk mitigation) strategies on a regular basis.

The remainder of this section on risk treatment expands and provides examples of the application of these risk strategies and concludes with a discussion of reinsurance, a special type of risk treatment used significantly by insurers.

6.4.1 Avoid

Any business can seek to eliminate its exposure to certain risks by simply avoiding them.

For example, the political risks associated with a particular country can be avoided by not operating in that country. The risks associated with certain businesses, products or asset classes can similarly be avoided by a deliberate decision to avoid them. Not all risks can simply be avoided. All businesses are subject to trends in our economic environment (eg inflation, economic growth, broad equity growth, interest rates and savings patterns) that impact all businesses.

Insurers can also seek to avoid risks through prudent product design, underwriting and business acceptance processes. Through these actions, insurers seek to focus their sales on a portion of the total insurance buying market in order to avoid certain types of risk. For example, life insurers can avoid risks associated with lifetime benefit periods for income protection policies by not offering such an option. General insurers can avoid certain risks or levels of risk by providing for exclusions in their contracts (eg damage to homes caused by floods).

A superannuation fund or fund manager can seek to minimize its risks by avoiding investment in certain asset classes. For example, ethical funds may refuse to invest in certain industries such as armaments, tobacco or liquor.

Banks may choose to avoid the risks associated with investment banking and focus their business on personal and commercial banking instead.

Some reasons for seeking to avoid certain risks are:

- risk appetite – the risks in question are not within the risk appetite set by the board;
- strategic plan – the risks in question are not within the strategic plan developed by senior management;
- financial capacity – the organization lacks sufficient financial capacity (eg capital and liquidity) to withstand the risk;
- skills – the organization lacks sufficient internal resources to identify, assess and treat the risk; and

- effective processes – the organization lacks appropriate processes to identify inappropriate risk management decisions sufficiently early that remedial action may still be affordable.

The desire to avoid certain risks is frequently complicated by the actions of competitors who accept such risks and appear to be successful in managing them and earning a profitable return. Each organization must weigh the benefits of competing head to head with its competitors (ie riding with the herd) versus striking an independent path for reasons such as those mentioned above.

Exercise 6.5

You are Chief Risk Officer for ABC Life Insurance Company. Your CEO has asked your advice about entering a new product line that your nearest competitor has been selling in great volume for the last year. Your CEO complains that ABC's sales are falling due to the competitor's new product. This new product includes complicated market options which the insurance consumers love. However, you know that the recruitment of specialized and highly technically trained staff, not to mention new processes and capital requirements will be needed. Outline what you might say to your CEO about the pros and cons of avoiding this new risk.

6.4.2 Retain

Businesses are formed to bear risk and earn a profit (hopefully) in doing so. It is therefore likely that they will seek to retain risks that are core to their business expertise.

Among the reasons for a business to retain risk would be the opposite of those mentioned in the previous section:

- risk appetite – the risks in question *are* within the risk appetite set by the board;
- strategic plan – the risks in question *are* within the strategic plan developed by senior management;
- financial capacity – the organization *has* sufficient financial capacity (eg capital and liquidity) to withstand the risk;
- skills – the organization *has* sufficient internal resources to identify, assess and treat the risk; and
- effective processes – the organization *has* appropriate processes to identify inappropriate risk management decisions sufficiently early that remedial action may still be affordable.

Benefits of retaining risks, especially across similar or complementary businesses, include:

- diversification – if the risks in question are uncorrelated then the benefits of risk diversification can be achieved; and
- economies of scale – a focus on similar businesses can be of assistance in developing a tightly focused business strategy and develops economies of scale in business operations.

For example, general insurers can diversify the risks associated with natural disasters by assuming insurance coverage from a wide variety of geographic regions. Life insurers can seek to diversify the risk of mortality improvement in their retirement products by also selling life insurance products. Individual asset credit risk or equity market risk exposures held by superannuation funds, fund managers, banks or insurers can be diversified by holding a wide variety of these instruments.

Note that a business holding these assets remains subject to a general deterioration in credit quality or market risk across the market. Insurers who underwrote substantial volumes of variable annuity business with substantial market guarantees discovered in 2008 that these risks were not diversifiable – the general market decline increased the "in the money" position of each and every contract. The same story held true for pension funds holding significant volumes of equities in their portfolios. This substantially worsened the funding position of these pension plans and placed an additional financial burden on their sponsoring employers who were already struggling with the GFC.

Businesses can decide to retain risks that are beyond their risk appetite or tolerances as long as there are acceptable ways of immediately transferring some of that risk (as we shall see in 6.4.4) at an acceptable price to others.

Insurers attempt to narrow the range of insurance risk that they assume through a deliberative process of underwriting new insurance risks that assists the insurer in pricing the risk appropriately. Insurers conduct regular studies of their emerging experience and use that information to modify their product design and/or pricing.

In many cases, however, insurers have little or no scope to underwrite, in which case the key risk is anti-selection. Ways of managing this risk for health insurance, for example, include:

- broad coverage – if most people are insured, the average cost becomes more predictable and more manageable. However, the better risks need to be encouraged to stay, which is one reason for seeking government action to keep a high proportion of the population in health funds;

- exclusion periods (ie avoid) – health funds generally apply exclusion periods before they will pay certain claims that are largely under the control of the customer;

- ancillary benefits – by offering discounts on fitness club memberships or on certain sporting goods, some health funds seek to attract and retain better risks (ie healthier or younger members); and

- complex products – health insurance products often include long lists of claimable events. This can reinforce the sense that the products represent good value and it can make the likely cost of claims more predictable.

Obvious risk management approaches to treat risk once it has been retained include "reduce," "transfer" and "reinsure" (a form of "transfer"). These are discussed in the coming sections of this chapter. For example, in general insurance there may be the need for some or all of: premium increases; reinsurance; active claims management; close monitoring and frequent review of outstanding claims provisions; and the avoidance of long-tail classes. Less obviously, the company or the industry can seek to influence the cost of claims by lobbying governments to make favorable changes to legislation.

6.4.3 Reduce

Businesses can reduce their risk exposure in the event that the inherent risk retained is beyond their risk tolerances. The risk reduction can be accomplished in many different ways depending on the objectives of the business, including:

- disposition/sale – the inherent risks can be reduced through sale of a part of the business; and

- new business reduction – a reduction in the amount of new business should reduce the risk being assumed.

Superannuation funds could reduce their exposure to equity markets by disposing of a portion of their equities and reinvesting in alternative asset classes such as fixed income securities. Of course, any such disposition will have risk/reward trade-offs for the superannuation fund, its members and the sponsoring employer that need to be considered.

Insurers can also reduce their exposure to certain products by reducing the volume of new sales. This can be accomplished through a combination of a more stringent selection process and re-pricing/redesign of the product (eg by introducing limits into the product design).

The sale of a business unit that no longer fits with the strategic plan, or that poses significant risks, can free up capital and resources for the primary objectives of the overall organization.

Risk reduction can also occur through improvements in operating practices. The use of improved information management systems can improve claim costs.

6.4.4 Transfer

The most common way for businesses to treat risk that is beyond their tolerances or capabilities is to transfer that risk. We shall discuss reinsurance in Section 6.4.6. Other means of accomplishing this transfer include:

- sharing experience with customers – contractual agreements with financial services customers that some part of their plan performance (eg investment return) will be borne directly by them rather than being guaranteed by the financial services provider;

- *hedging* – using derivatives or other financial instruments to offset market risk; and

- *special purpose entity (SPE)* – a legal entity used for a specific business purpose, while protecting the parent entity from excessive risk.

Sharing experience

Certain types of financial/insurance products are designed to share emerging experience with the customer in some defined manner. In the case of mutual funds (for banks) or variable annuities (for insurers), there is direct sharing of investment performance with the customer. Some of these products may also provide the customer with various options and/or floor guarantees. In the case of participating life insurance products, the customer shares in emerging experience through a scale of policyholder dividends or bonuses, which is adjusted on an annual basis.

Hedging

Hedging is used by financial services providers to offset a variety of market risk exposures. It is important to note that the degree to which the inherent risk is mitigated depends on the specifics of the hedging program. For example, the hedging of long-term equity exposure using short-term puts still leaves the business exposed to a variety of risks including basis risk and increased operational risk required for managing the hedged portfolio.

Special purpose entities

Increasingly, businesses are transferring some of their assets and liabilities into a special purpose entity (SPE), also known as a special purpose vehicle (SPV). An SPE has limited liability (usually in the form of a limited company), so its losses do not directly affect the originating institution. SPEs are usually sufficiently separate that they are also not affected by the originator's performance. Risk managers need to carefully consider the risks actually transferred, the permanence of those transfers and under what conditions the risk might revert back.

Thus, an SPE can be a risk management tool for an originating institution or for others who wish to invest in a specific aspect of the institution's business without being exposed to the whole institution.

The Joint Forum (2009) discusses SPEs in some detail, with examples of their uses including:

* securitization of assets for external investment – including Residential Mortgage-Backed Securities (RMBS), Commercial Mortgage-Backed Securities (CMBS) and Collateralized Debt (or Loan) Obligations (CDOs, CLOs);

* joint ventures, especially those carrying high risk;

* quarantining assets for tax or regulatory reasons – for example, it can be beneficial to hold a specific asset in a separate company so that it may be more readily traded; and

* risk-linked securities, particularly insurance-linked securities known as Catastrophe Bonds (CAT Bonds).

The following example, drawn from the Joint Forum paper, describes the operation of CAT Bonds.

Example 6.2 Catastrophe Bonds (CAT Bonds)

A relatively recent innovation in the market for structured finance has been the use of SPEs by insurance firms for the purpose of transferring certain insurance risks, whose potential losses would have historically been either absorbed by the firm's capital position or transferred to a third party via a reinsurance contract, into the broader financial market. The first transactions came to market in the mid 1990s and since that time the market has shown steady, if not dramatic, growth. The earliest of these bonds, so called "CAT bonds," or "act of God" bonds were designed to allow insurers a mechanism to manage catastrophic risk of loss, eg hurricanes, earthquakes, etc.

Structurally, these transactions appear very similar to most structured finance: a bankruptcy remote[2] SPE is created, assets are held by the SPE and notes are issued into the financial markets. Figure 6.4, which comes from Swiss Re Capital

---

[2] A *bankruptcy remote* company within a group is one which could become insolvent without affecting any other company in the group.

Markets, shows a simplified form of a typical structure. In this structure, the SPE conducts two actions simultaneously. It issues notes to investors②, and it enters into a reinsurance contract with the client①. The proceeds from the notes issued are invested in high quality, short-term securities and deposited in a trust account collateralizing the transaction③. The actual returns generated from this account are swapped with a highly-rated swap counterparty④. Through the swap mechanism, the bonds become floating rate notes from which interest rate risk is largely removed. Over the term of the bonds, the periodic interest payments paid by the SPE to the investors consist of two parts: the premiums paid by the client and the floating-rate returns earned by the principal which are guaranteed by the swap counterparty. At the conclusion of the bond term, if the covered events have not occurred, the principal is returned to investors.

Figure 6.4   Insurance securitization structure

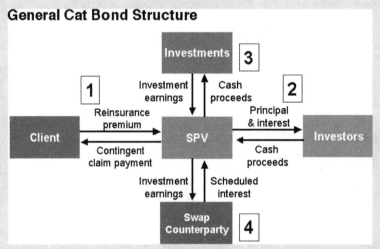

What makes these insurance securitizations unique is the nature of the transfer involved in these transactions. Unlike an asset-based securitization where physical and legal ownership of a portfolio of assets is transferred to the SPE, in an insurance securitization, what is being transferred, to all intents and purposes, is a potential insurance liability.

The securitization notes define the conditions for the SPE to provide funds to the direct insurer in the event of a loss and the amount of these funds. The amount of risk is defined by the trigger point and exhaustion point specified in the notes.

Investors in insurance securitizations are attracted to the relatively high yields offered by these securities, and are especially attracted to the fact that there is almost no correlation with most existing portfolios of financial assets. That is, whether or not an earthquake occurs in Europe is not correlated with overall business cycle activity, unlike the risk in most corporate security portfolios.

Finally, these securities allow investors to participate in the market for insurance risk and return opportunities without having to be exposed to the general overall risk of an insurer, as they would be if they were buying its debt or equities. Many investors find this attractive.

Exercise 6.6

As the regulator for insurance companies, you have become concerned at the aggregate level of market risk assumed by one of the companies you supervise. The market risk is inherent in the design of a large block of variable annuity products with substantial accumulation and income guarantees. The CRO of the insurer has indicated that a hedging program has been introduced to mitigate some of the risk. In preparation for a meeting with the CRO, you are preparing a list of questions to ensure that you fully understand the effectiveness of the hedge in mitigating risk. What questions would you ask?

6.4.5 Exploit

A risk may represent an opportunity. This could be a clear opportunity for the outcome to be more favorable than anticipated or it could simply be an opportunity to exploit a relative advantage, eg the cost of accepting a particular risk may be lower than it would be for some or all of the competition.

Where an opportunity exists and the insurer has the capacity to exploit it, then it probably makes sense to do so. One example might be the active pursuit of riskier, capital-intensive business on the basis of access to cheaper capital.

6.4.6 Reinsurance

Reinsurance refers to insurance purchased by an insurer to provide protection against some or all of certain risks of the insurance policies issued by the insurer. In exchange for the assumption of these risks, the reinsurer receives payment in the form of reinsurance premiums or allowances from the direct writer of the business, the insurer. This section draws on CAS (2001) and on Tiller and Tiller (1995).

From the perspective of the insurer, the direct writer of insurance policies, reinsurance provides for a transfer of risk to the reinsurer. The extent of the transfer depends on the specifics of the reinsurance agreement or treaty. It is important to note that reinsurance also creates risk for the insurer. Reinsurance exposes the insurer to the risk that the reinsurer defaults on its obligations through insolvency. Depending on local legislation or case law, the insurer may find that many other classes of creditors will rank higher for distribution of proceeds from the liquidated reinsurer. Additionally, the terms of the reinsurance agreement may not match exactly those of the underlying insurance contracts. Heavy reliance on reinsurance may expose the insurer to increased costs in tightening reinsurance markets. The insurer must evaluate these risks.

Beyond all of the risks normally associated with being an insurer, a reinsurer faces some unique challenges. Reinsurance products are difficult to price (especially in the general insurance market, where there are often complicated layers of reinsurance cover) owing to the limited data available on which to base the pricing. Additional risk arises in general insurance from the low claim frequency and high claim severity of many reinsurance coverages and from the lengthy time delays between the occurrence, reporting and settlement of many covered loss events. It is especially important for the reinsurer to understand the insurer's target market, its pricing and all of the layers involved in its reinsurance program. In addition, the reinsurer is exposed to the risk of default by the ceding insurer. Depending on local legislation or case law, the reinsurer may find that many other classes of creditors will rank higher for distribution of proceeds from the liquidated insurer. Potentially critical to the reinsurer in this circumstance is the legal right (allowed in some cases) to offset any funds it owes to the liquidator by the amounts that the ceding insurer owes it.

Reinsurers must monitor the profile of their insurance risks very carefully, for precisely the reasons that they were ceded in the first place. They will often *retrocede* a high proportion of the risks and, in turn, accept retrocessions from other reinsurers. Some of the most complex and significant risks thus become spread over a very large number of reinsurers. This is why major disasters seem to affect all major reinsurers, no matter where they are based.

Reasons to purchase reinsurance

Reinsurance is one of the most important risk management tools available to all types of insurers. In a reinsurance arrangement, the insurer *cedes* risks to the reinsurer. Reinsurers can do the same thing by a *retrocession* to other reinsurers, including their parent company. Reinsurance is purchased for reasons that include:

- increasing new business capacity – one of the most common reasons for the purchase of reinsurance is to enable an insurer to issue larger insurance policies than it would prudently issue on its own, since the reinsurance will reduce the impact of several large claims occurring in a short period of time;

- limiting catastrophic claims – catastrophic coverage generally provides for the reinsurer to pay claims in excess of a certain limit, subject to a minimum number of claims and subject to a maximum amount of reinsurance per event. This coverage provides protection against concentrated claims arising from a single event (eg storms, earthquakes, plane crashes, etc);

- limiting total claims – some insurers, especially smaller ones, need stop loss reinsurance to limit the aggregate cost of claims in a given year;

- transferring investment risk – insurers may reinsure a block of business to effect a transfer of investment risk from the insurer. This can occur because of the growth of interest-sensitive life and annuity products, either to take advantage of reinsurer asset management capabilities or to avoid a large concentration of assets arising from a single product or annuity;

- gaining product expertise – upon entering a new line of business, product or territory, an insurer may request the assistance of a reinsurer with existing experience in that market. In exchange for their advice, the reinsurer will participate via reinsurance in the future profitability of the business sold;

- gaining underwriting advice – one benefit provided by reinsurers is their experience in underwriting. This can prove valuable during the design, pricing and underwriting of products, especially new, novel, large or complex ones;

- divesting a product line – an insurer wishing to exit a certain business, product or territory may choose to cede that business by means of an assumption reinsurance agreement or through indemnity reinsurance; and

- financial results management – insurers may be able to use the financial reporting impact of reinsurance agreements to achieve earnings and surplus objectives and also to minimize taxes.

Types of reinsurance

A reinsurance agreement between an insurer and a reinsurer is called a *reinsurance treaty*. The treaty defines the type of reinsurance being undertaken. The most important types of reinsurance are:

- *indemnity/assumption* – most treaties are called *indemnity agreements*. Such agreements are binding only for the companies. The policyholders of the insurer have no contractual relationship with the reinsurer. On the other hand, *assumption reinsurance* entails the permanent transfer of insurance liabilities to the reinsurer. Policyholders are notified that the assumption reinsurer has assumed the legal responsibility for the business and that all future premiums and claims are to be the responsibility of the assumption reinsurer;

- *proportional/non-proportional* – reinsurance may be offered on either a *proportional* or a *non-proportional* basis. Proportional reinsurance provides for the *cession* of a portion of the coverage by means of a formula based on the *ceding* insurer's retention limit (eg all amounts of life insurance in excess of the insurer's retention limit will be reinsured). Common proportional reinsurance techniques would include: *traditional coinsurance*, used for life insurance products with a savings element whereby all risks and policy elements are shared with the reinsurer, including the investment risk; *modified coinsurance*, similar to traditional coinsurance except that the insurer retains the investment risk; and *yearly renewable term* (YRT) cover, whereby the insurer reinsures a specific risk, such as mortality, in exchange for a YRT premium. Non-proportional reinsurance provides protection that depends on the claims amount experienced (eg *stop loss* or *catastrophe* reinsurance);

- *automatic/facultative* – an *automatic* reinsurance treaty[3] allows an insurer to cede risks in excess of its retention limit automatically to its reinsurer subject to pre-determined conditions. *Facultative* treaties require that the reinsurer approve each risk before it assumes any liability for the risk. These latter treaties tend to be used for the larger, more-complex-to-underwrite risks; and

- *excess/quota share* – *excess* treaties provide for risks in excess of the schedule of retention limits to be reinsured. *Quota share* treaties provide for a fixed percentage of each risk to be reinsured.

6.5   Recent lessons learned

The GFC has had very serious implications for the risk management practices of the entire financial services sector. In a July 2009 speech to the Reserve Bank of New Zealand, Howard Davies commented on the wide range of blame that the public attributes to the sources of the GFC. He also provided a useful summary of the economic events that detailed the steps in the crisis. In a February 2009 speech entitled "Why banks failed the stress test," Andrew Haldane of the Bank of England outlined some risk management lessons learned from the financial turmoil. Some of the lessons from both Davies and Haldane include that:

---

[3] Confusingly, automatic reinsurance is often referred to as "treaty," even though facultative reinsurance is generally also governed by a treaty.

- systemic connections were more extensive than expected;
- misaligned incentives worsened the turmoil;
- there was insufficient consideration of extreme events; and
- there was insufficient investor due diligence.

6.5.1   Systemic connections more extensive than expected

According to Davies and others, the origins of the GFC had been building for some time in the US, owing to:

- a decade of economic prosperity;
- the housing boom;
- lenient residential mortgage lending practices;
- originate-to-distribute mortgage lending;
- low prices for credit risk; and
- a boom in the credit default swap market.

However, the speed with which the GFC unfolded within the US and around the world was unprecedented. The bursting of the real estate bubble and the consequent collapse of the market for credit derivatives severely affected the US banking system. The collapse of Lehman Brothers created a crisis of confidence that led to tight credit markets and a sharp decline in equities worldwide. Consumer confidence fell to historic lows resulting in lower demand for goods and services worldwide and widespread reductions by manufacturers such as car makers. Global trade fell, unemployment rates rose and GDP growth turned negative in many countries.

The GFC demonstrated how tightly inter-connected and reliant our world has become. For example, insurance giant AIG was hobbled by its subsidiary credit default swap operations in the UK. While our sophisticated world has taken giant strides forward with enterprise risk management (ERM) to identify and manage risk, the focus has tended to be on managing risk at the regulated entity level without adequate consideration to systemic implications of our business activities as part of our surrounding economic, social and political environment, both locally and globally.

6.5.2   Misaligned incentives worsened the turmoil

Incentives drive behavior. One type of incentive is remuneration. Remunerating CEOs on the basis of short-term performance has been well documented as a cause for company actions that leveraged short-term earnings rather than addressing longer term risks. The earnings model for originate-to-distribute mortgage lending and structured financial products are other examples.

There are other types of incentives that do not involve remuneration. For example, the form and style of insurer regulation and supervision serves to influence company behavior. There is a global trend toward principles- and risk-based regulation and supervision of insurers to encourage insurer best practices and the protection of policyholders. This is a significant improvement over rules-based approaches that tend to encourage "gaming of the rules" to the detriment of the long-term interests of the financial markets and policyholders.

However, principles-based approaches rely on the use of sound professional judgment by insurers and regulators alike. The implementation of modern risk-based solvency frameworks such as Solvency II in Europe will make increasing use of this professional judgment and the actuarial profession will need to ensure that it is ready for the challenge.

Yet another type of incentive arises from the natural desire to condense all the information needed to assess risk (as per Section 6.3) into one metric. A recent North American study (Rudolph, 2008) indicates that risk managers frequently use only one risk metric in their ERM. The metrics most frequently used were TVaR and VaR. There can be a temptation to use the new Pillar 1 regulatory capital requirements being developed in various jurisdictions as a good assessment of risk (or proxy) that can be used for a variety of risk management purposes. Such views are dangerous in that risk cannot be viewed in one dimension. Several perspectives are needed before pricing, assuming and managing those risks.

6.5.3 Insufficient consideration of extreme events

The GFC has called into question the adequacy of pricing for financial risks and the provisioning for these risks in the balance sheets of insurers. The stresses exerted by the turmoil have been much more severe than was generally anticipated, as evidenced by two quotations reported in the New York Times[4] and widely quoted elsewhere.

> "It is hard for us, without being flippant, to even see a scenario within any kind of realm of reason that would see us losing one dollar in any of those transactions." Joseph Cassano, a former AIG executive referring to AIG's credit default swap business in August 2007.

> "Almost no one expected what was coming. It's not fair to blame us for not predicting the unthinkable." Daniel Mudd, former chief executive of Fannie Mae, discussing the impact of the GFC in 2008.

In Section 6.3 we noted the challenges of choosing experience data but Haldane suggests that a human failing he calls *disaster myopia* is at least partly to blame. Haldane suggests that in choosing stress scenarios we have been too strongly influenced by favorable economic data in recent years. A simple example of this myopia occurs when we drive down the highway and pass an accident that has occurred. We react by slowing down and exercising caution, at least for the next few kilometers. However, as the distance from the accident increases, our feeling of confidence increases and our speed increases. Similarly as our distance increases from a previous crisis, our belief that those problems are behind us and the solutions found will continue to protect us, blind us to new and different dangers building around us.

6.5.4 Insufficient investor due diligence

As a result of investor demand in recent years, the asset securitization market in the US has flourished and grown dramatically. Securitization (mentioned in Section 6.4.4 as a way of transferring risk) has given institutional and individual investors the opportunity to participate indirectly in various types of lending that they might not be able to do

---

[4] http://www.nytimes.com/2008/09/28/business/28melt.html and http://www.nytimes.com/2008/10/05/business/05fannie.html

directly. In particular, mortgage lending was a prime candidate for such securitization that involved packaging the original loans and using them as collateral for securities (called mortgage-backed securities) to be sold to investors. Collateralized mortgage obligations and collateralized debt obligations took the packaging process one step further, pooling mortgage-backed or other debt securities and parceling the interest and principal payments into different tranches with varying risk/reward characteristics. These securities were often credit-enhanced through external means (such as pool insurance provided by mortgage guaranty insurers, financial guarantee insurance products or credit default swaps) or through internal means (eg *overcollateralization*, which means that the face value of the collateral exceeds that of the securities that it is supporting). Additional parties included rating agencies and other service providers. At the very end of the process were institutional and individual investors.

Davies (2009, slide 8) shows the spectacular rise in the global issuance of structured products in recent years. As a result of demand from investors for more structured products as well as an increasing supply of mortgages from aspiring homeowners, the overall market for these products grew tremendously in recent years. However, as originate-to-distribute mortgage brokers saw the profits of sourcing such lending without being responsible for the ultimate losses, lending practices became more lenient. Subprime lending began. Loan losses escalated and caused significant losses to investors, financial guarantors and mortgage insurers. The rating agencies have received their share of the blame in this subprime turmoil as many of the rated entities in the securitization process have been downgraded.

A lesson to be learned from these securitizations is that they built in layers of complexity between the original borrower and the ultimate investor. This complexity masked the risks faced by the investors and they were forced to rely on the work of rating agencies and the good names of financial guarantors and mortgage insurers. In the future, investors and risk professionals assessing such structured financial products need to ensure they have performed their own due diligence and should be wary of product complexity unless they can evaluate all of the inherent and net risks.

6.6   Practical implications for actuaries

As we have seen in this chapter, and especially as a result of the GFC, much is expected of the risk management professional in applying risk management. Indeed, these expectations have been rising rapidly in recent years. Risk management professionals, including actuaries, are facing increasingly tough questions and scrutiny about their risk management roles and actions. Life as a risk management professional is now much more exciting and demanding.

Actuaries need to be able to demonstrate their in-depth technical knowledge of risks and their ability to look across an organization at all its risks. They must also be able to translate their technical expertise into practical, easily understood language that enables the management of an organization to manage its risks effectively.

In particular, actuaries need to consider that:

*   risk management is more than just risk models; and

*   each period of turmoil is different.

6.6.1 Risk management is more than just risk models

The GFC has served to highlight the relative effectiveness of the ERM capabilities of insurers. ERM was clearly not as effective as it should have been for a number of insurers. Boards, investors and regulators were caught by surprise. Improvements need to be found throughout the ERM process. Actuaries can play a key role in this but it also needs improvements at the top, at the board level and throughout the ERM governance structure.

During the GFC, even insurers with advanced risk management practices did not necessarily have appropriate governance structures in place. Reports such as a *future financial condition report* (similar to an ORSA[5] report) can be most useful in identifying insurer sensitivity to the important risks such as those that unfolded during the GFC. However, there have been some examples where the key representatives of risk governance within the insurer did not have an adequate understanding of their most important risks. Insurers should consider ways in which they can further strengthen risk governance in this regard. Boards need to assume ownership of ERM.

Best practices for ERM require organizations to establish their risk appetite as well as clear roles and responsibility for risk taking. It seems clear that insurance giant AIG did not expect that its global solvency would be affected by its credit derivatives operations. In a hypothetical example, if an insurer has a large market risk position then we would expect the insurer to consider appropriate risk mitigation for that risk. Failure to commence such risk mitigation would have exposed the insurer and its financial strength during the recent turmoil. If this happened then the regulator would have reasonable grounds to wonder if the underlying risk was underpriced and question how the risk governance process, especially the setting of the risk appetite, actually worked at that insurer.

Philipp Keller (2009), a Swiss mathematician and actuary, talked about insurer ERM and paraphrased Donald Rumsfeld's now famous quote as follows:

- things that are known – high frequency, low impact risks;
- things that are known to be unknown – eg the impact of the next financial market bubble, natural catastrophes, terror events;
- things that are believed to be known but are actually unknown – eg operational risks, financial market risks;
- things that are preferred to stay unknown – company-dependent and part of the risk culture (risks that would force a change in the business model); and
- things that are unknown to be unknown – unknown by definition.

Keller suggests that insurers are typically very comfortable dealing with the first two but that what frequently gets them into trouble is actually the fourth – things that are preferred to stay unknown.

Embedding ERM within the decision-making processes of an insurer requires the adoption of an appropriate risk culture in the organization. The adoption of a compliance mentality by the insurer when dealing with the regulator regarding risk management issues can

---

[5] *Own Risk and Solvency Assessment*, a requirement of the "Solvency II" regulations governing insurers operating in the EU.

be very troubling and can cause the regulator to question the insurer's ability to manage its risks.

There are many ways in which a compliance mentality can creep in. For example, in the future financial condition report used in Canada, the base scenario in the report should represent the company's business plan. The adverse scenarios are selected by the actuary to represent tail (but yet still plausible) events. The goal of the report is to discuss with the board how the company would manage with these adverse scenarios. It was designed to form part of the strategic decision making of the company. Unfortunately, there can be a tendency for insurers and their actuaries to consider this report as a compliance exercise. Consequently, this can result in reports that feature little imagination, use similar language from year to year and receive very brief airtime in front of the board. Risk managers must be wary of this tendency and seek ways to strengthen the role of this report within the risk management of the insurer.

We must always remember that risk management is much more than just models. We should not be so in love with our models and their theory that we lose sight of the inherent risks if the assumptions do not hold up. Scenario testing and supplemental capital provide a check on model optimism.

6.6.2   Each period of turmoil is different

Each period of financial turmoil of the past has taught us valuable lessons. Our economies, products, risk management, etc evolve over time. For example:

- the stock market crash of October 1987 resulted in the birth of VaR;
- the failure of hedge fund Long Term Capital Management (LTCM) in 1998 gave impetus to stress testing; and
- the market meltdown that began in 2007 will give impetus to various reforms.

As actuaries, all we can say for sure is that the next period of turmoil, when it does occur, will be different. We can learn the lessons from the GFC but we need to be more vigilant than we have been in the past for the signs – perhaps hard to decipher – that the pressures leading to a new crisis are building once again.

6.7   Key learning points

- The generalized risk management process was reviewed.
- Within the risk management process this chapter focused on applying risk management through risk identification, risk assessment and risk treatment.
- Risk identification examples were provided for insurers, superannuation funds, funds management and for banks.
- Risk assessment was shown to require both qualitative as well as quantitative review. Quantitative review requires the selection of appropriate risk measures, confidence levels, time horizons etc.
- Several methods of treating risk were explored including to avoid, retain, reduce, transfer or exploit.
- Lessons from the recent financial turmoil were explored, including that:

- ○ systemic connections were more extensive than expected;

- ○ misaligned incentives worsened the turmoil;

- ○ there was insufficient consideration of extreme events; and

- ○ there was insufficient investor due diligence.

- • Some practical implications for actuaries were examined including:

- ○ that life as a risk management professional is now much more exciting and demanding;

- ○ the caution that risk management is more than just risk models; and

- ○ that the causes of the next turmoil will be different from past ones.

CD Items

Davies, H. 2009, *The Financial Crisis Whodunnit?*, Reserve Bank of New Zealand, speech and slides, http://www.rbnz.govt.nz/research/workshops/75thpubliclecture/3713648.html.

Haldane A. G. 2009, *Why Banks Failed the Stress Test*, Bank of England.

Rudolph, M. J. 2008, Emerging Risks Survey, Joint Risk Management Section: Society of Actuaries, Casualty Actuarial Society and Canadian Institute of Actuaries.

Chapter 6 Exercise Solutions

References (other than CD Items)

Bernstein, P. 1996, *Against the Gods: The Remarkable Story of Risk*, John Wiley & Sons.

Casualty Actuarial Society 2001, *Foundations of Casualty Actuarial Science*, Fourth Edition, Casualty Actuarial Society.

CEA, Groupe Consultatif Glossary for insurers.

Claridge, J. B. & Griffin, K. 1997, *An Introduction to Holistic Risk Management*, Institute of Actuaries of Australia.

IAA 2004, *A Global Framework of Insurer Solvency Assessment*, International Actuarial Association.

Joint Forum 2009, *Report on Special Purpose Entities*, Bank for International Settlements.

Jorion, P. 2001, *Value at Risk*, McGraw-Hill.

Keller P. 2009, *Stress and Scenario Testing for Insurers*, Financial Stability Institute.

Tiller J. E. Jr. & Tiller D. F. 1995, *Life, Health & Annuity Reinsurance*, Second Edition, ACTEX Publications Inc.

Fred's Coffee Shop – Regulation

We come now to the topic of regulation. Take a moment to think about all the sorts of rules and regulations Fred may face.

These include: protection for customers against unhygienic food, unfair measures or misleading advertising; health and safety for employees and people passing by; and minimum wage and other conditions for employees. Depending on the jurisdiction, Fred's shop may be periodically visited by health and safety inspectors and he may be required to purchase unemployment insurance and workers compensation insurance on behalf of his employees.

Generally, the regulations are there to protect the vulnerable.

Sometimes, authorities use rationing and price-fixing to try to ensure that everyone can afford essential items like food. But the current view is that such actions distort the market and are counter-productive – less food will be produced if the price is artificially low. Everyone may be better off if the market is left to operate freely. A lot of regulation will then be based on ensuring that the market does work properly. For example, an efficient market needs informed buyers. So the law may say that Fred mustn't label his coffee as organic if it isn't.

When you read the following chapter, you will see that many of the regulations in the financial world are about protecting the vulnerable and ensuring free markets. These regulations shape the financial products that are available to Fred. For example, all building insurance contracts may be required to provide cover (at a fixed cost) against flood, even if the building is on the top of a hill.

Other regulations governing Fred's coffee shop relate to the contribution that Fred and his employees are expected to make to the provision of government services through taxation. Fred will be required to pay tax on his profits and his own income and to withhold estimated income tax from his employees' wages. He probably lives in a country or state where some form of tax must be paid on his sales (eg Australia's GST) and there will be several other taxes, levies and charges.

Yet more regulations may require Fred to make contributions to state or private retirement funds on behalf of his employees. In the UK, for example, part of National Insurance contributions is used to fund state pension benefits. In Australia, the Superannuation Guarantee levy is directed by the employee to his/her chosen fund. In the US, there are mandatory employer and employee contributions to Social Security and Medicare.

The complexity of all the regulation that Fred must comply with means that he will need to have adequate accounting and filing systems and appropriate expert help.

Major companies have the same requirements, albeit on a different scale. And actuaries provide part of the expert help.

Chapter 7:   Regulation
by Craig Thorburn

7.1   Introduction

This chapter examines an important part of the environment in which much of the work of actuaries is conducted: the regulatory environment. *Regulation* is used here to include all actions taken by governments and by official bodies constituted by them, and the operation of courts and other bodies that can have the effect of establishing practices and enforceable norms. Sometimes a distinction is drawn between *regulation* as the making of rules and the imposition of requirements, and *supervision* reflecting the monitoring of compliance with these rules. Increasingly, this distinction is becoming less relevant as supervisory authorities are provided with rule-making powers, but it is worth noting that these terms can be used and intended to imply a clear distinction.

The aspects of regulation that can be relevant for actuaries extend well beyond the most obvious ones relating to institutional solvency or soundness. Examples range from laws related to revenue-raising by the authorities, to aspects of social laws such as anti-discrimination regimes and family law.

The aims of this chapter are to:

* provide students with an awareness of the importance of the legal and regulatory environment to actuarial work;

* introduce the legal system;

* discuss the types of laws that are relevant to actuarial work;

* examine the objectives of regulation;

* outline the influence of international bodies in financial regulation;

* outline the specific roles that actuaries may be given by regulators; and

* discuss the structures of supervisory authorities.

7.1.1   The sources of law

For actuaries, it is important to be familiar with legal requirements that impact on their work. In order to grasp the detail of any regulation, interpret it soundly, and understand the implications for actuarial work, it is important to understand the source and context of the regulation.

In any jurisdiction, laws and customs exist for the good order of the society. In general terms, the source of authority is provided for in the constitution or other fundamental documents of the jurisdiction. There are then several levels of regulation, as described in 7.1.2 below.

The way in which the broad structure of law-making is conducted in most countries falls into one of two main traditions. These are the *common law* system and the *civil code* system. The common law system evolved in England over many centuries, and influenced the legal structures of countries with an English heritage, including the US and Commonwealth countries such as Australia, Canada, South Africa, and India. The *civil code* system originated in ancient Rome. The ancient Roman structure formed the basis for the French system, which Napoleon introduced into much of continental Europe. From there it spread to other regions such as Latin America. Systems of law based on a civil code are also referred to as being based on *Roman law* or the *Napoleonic code*. Some jurisdictions combine both systems. For example, the state of Louisiana in the US and the province of Quebec in Canada, although operating within a common law framework at the national level, have legal systems based on the Napoleonic code because of their French heritage. The European Union also brings the two systems together. Some countries, particularly in Asia, have systems that reflect a mixture of local traditions and common law or civil code.

Documentation of the laws of many countries can now be found on the internet, although it is important to ensure that the information is current. The most reliable websites will usually be those that are maintained by the national governments or other institutions, such as those associated with the legal profession, that have a particular interest in providing accurate and up-to-date information. Where websites are not available, governments tend to provide access to laws through publishing services. Legal firms and other consultants may also provide information about current laws, commentary on proposed amendments, and discussion of their implications. It is important for actuaries working in a particular field of practice to understand the laws that are in force at the time, and also the manner in which laws can be changed, so that they can monitor developments and keep up to date.

7.1.2 Levels of regulation

The main levels of regulation in most jurisdictions are as follows:

Primary legislation (Acts, laws)

This is law developed by the relevant legislative body (for example, the national, regional or provincial parliament) under the authority of the constitution of the jurisdiction. Primary legislation can take varying forms depending on the customs of the country and the nature of the issue being regulated. In some cases, the law itself is very detailed and specific. In other cases the primary law represents a general framework and provides the authority and powers to make subsidiary legislation to cover the detail.

Under the civil codes, primary laws tend to be more elaborate than under common law systems. Actuaries familiar with civil code laws may find common law documents vague and lacking specificity. For example, there may be a general requirement to be "prudent" with little elaboration. Actuaries with a background in common law systems may find civil codes verbose and seemingly restrictive. It is important that actuaries recognize the nature of the legal system to understand fully the implications and interpretation of the primary laws.

Subsidiary legislation (regulations, standards)

Primary legislation may provide for other documents to be prepared which have the force of the primary legislation. These are issued by the delegated authority following the proper, sometimes specified, process.

These regulations or similar documents provide additional detail beyond the Act itself. They are made effective by the elected assembly or sometimes the head of state on the advice of the relevant government ministers.

Standards or circulars can also be issued under the authority of the primary legislation by an official body. These documents may have the force of law.

The process for altering a regulation or a circular or standard is usually easier than the process for altering a law. As a result, subsidiary legislation can be the preferred method (over primary legislation) for requirements that may need to be adjusted to reflect changing conditions or for technical documents. Much legislation that is relevant to actuaries can be technical. By setting out the detailed requirements in subsidiary rules or regulations, the legislators can more easily respond to market circumstances and make changes.

In many jurisdictions, official pronouncements that are less formal than regulations and standards may also have force. For example, taxation rulings, press statements, and speeches made by high ranking officials can carry weight. These can help to determine how the law is to be interpreted or provide guidance on the acceptable practices in particular cases.

Court decisions and precedent

Inevitably, there are disputes or uncertainties arising under the law or over the precise meaning of the law in a particular situation. These may be referred to the courts for decision. The courts may have a practice of recording decisions that provide precedents for future cases of the same or similar nature. In this way, laws and practices continually evolve as new cases are subject to rulings of courts. The precedent-making nature of court decisions is part of common law and is not a strong feature of legal systems based on the Napoleonic code.

Self-regulatory organizations

Self-regulatory organizations can play a role in regulation, particularly in the financial sector. One example would be industry complaints-handling operations. Another example would be organizations that oversee markets, such as stock exchanges, where it is common to monitor the practices of market participants. A third type of self-regulatory organization is a profession (actuarial, accountancy etc). A profession, among other things, establishes membership criteria, education and qualification systems, codes of conduct and standards of practice for members. These organizations may be given their role or recognition in the legal framework. In addition, the organizations may have the power to apply limited sanctions for breaches of their codes and standards or may refer matters to an authority that has greater official status for investigation or sanction. The various standards and rules issued by self-regulatory organizations would also represent part of the legal framework in those jurisdictions where they have a defined role. In particular, for actuaries, professional association standards, codes of conduct, and discipline procedures are key examples.

7.1.3 Types of law

In common law systems there is a distinction within the legal system between *criminal law*, *civil law* and *equity law*.

Criminal law is usually related to particular crimes against "the people" or the state. The penalties for breach of these laws can include imprisonment or fines. Criminal law does not usually provide for specific recompense to the party that has been harmed. Instead, the crime is an offence against the fundamental premise on which the state is established and the community operates. This is why the penalties such as the payment of fines to the state itself or imprisonment are normally imposed by the state.

Civil law, by contrast, can provide for compensation through the payment of damages to the party that has been harmed. Civil law actions are usually brought to rectify a private wrong. As a result, there is no official role for the state in the action. Government bodies may be the plaintiff or defendant in a civil dispute, and supervisory authorities may have the power to take civil law actions against the entities that they supervise. A usual feature of this type of law is the need for liability or injury ("harm") to exist as a basis for damages to be awarded.

In *equity law*, one party can restrict or force the actions of another party. For example, party X may seek an injunction securing a court order that party Y must stop doing something that is violating X's legal rights and causing harm to X. Unlike criminal or civil law, equity law can provide a basis for intervention before the particular damaging action or harm actually happens.

7.2   The scope of laws that influence the financial sector and the work of actuaries

Laws influence many aspects of the financial sector and the work of actuaries, including:

- the operation of a company, through both the general company laws, and those specific to the type of business that the company undertakes. The areas affected include registration, corporate governance, financial reporting and accounting standards, standards for establishing technical provisions and reserves, and restrictions aimed at ensuring that the company operates soundly;

- maintaining competition in markets;

- the selling of financial products. These laws apply particularly to agents and brokers, financial advisers and other representatives;

- the conduct of business with customers, both at and before the point of sale as well as whilst the product is in force or associated with claims settlement;

- the content of contracts of financial products, particularly insurance contracts, and in many cases contracts for products that provide credit;

- particular classes of insurance that may require special treatment;

- providing for the operation of supervisory oversight of institutions and other activities;

- fiduciary or trustee-related obligations and responsibilities on institutions, providers or benefits, or on professionals such as actuaries to act in the best interests of others;

- taxation, duties, levies and other charges;

- government provision of social security benefits, which will affect the design of financial products; and

- the indirect effects of broader social legislation, such as anti-discrimination laws and family law.

There are specific laws made for all or a specific part of the financial sector and laws that apply more generally. Both types are relevant to the work of the actuary.

7.3 Types of regulation and the objectives of governments

7.3.1 Taxation legislation

One objective of taxation legislation is to raise revenues to meet the cost of providing government services. Other objectives are to encourage behavior that the government wishes to advance or to discourage other behavior. Examples include: lighter taxation of long-term financial products to encourage long-term savings, the application of a heavier tax on fuels that are more polluting, and taxes on tobacco and alcohol to discourage consumption of these products.

The taxation of investment returns, particularly the relative treatment of various classes of assets or of income and capital growth, is relevant to the investment strategies for most institutions.

Institutions that offer financial products will take account of the taxation legislation, ensuring that their products comply with any rules to qualify for favorable taxation treatment. The cost of paying taxes and duties must be included in any modeling, for example when setting prices.

Taxes and duties can influence not only activity levels, but also commercial structures. For example, suppose that investment-related transactions are subject to a tax unless they are conducted within a dedicated investment trust. Then it can be expected that larger investors will establish trusts to conduct their investments, in order to avoid the tax.

Apart from taxation legislation, another form of revenue-raising legislation covers *levies*. A levy is a fee or charge imposed under legislation. Whilst they may appear to be taxes by another name, levies are often established under separate legislation to taxation laws and are introduced to fund a particular activity on a user-pays basis. Some activities may be subject to levies to recover costs, whereas others may not, on social access rather than pure cost recovery grounds. For example, a business that applies for a license to operate may have to pay an application fee, whereas services providing consumer information access may be provided free of charge.

7.3.2 The regulation of markets and companies

The argument is often made that for an efficient financial sector, governments should allow financial markets to operate freely. Carmichael (2002) provides a useful summary of this argument which is expanded in more detail in Carmichael and Pomerlearno (2002).[1] He argues that, apart from legislation to raise revenue and achieve social goals, regulation of the financial sector is aimed at addressing market failure, ie dealing with situations where markets do not operate efficiently and competitively. Some commentators reject this view that addressing market failure is the main objective of regulation, and emphasize the primacy of consumer protection. They consider that there is no reason to believe that the market would provide the level of consumer protection that is desirable. Even if this is true, the "market failure" framework is a useful starting point for analyzing some of the main types of regulation. Other regulatory issues that do not fit well within this framework are discussed in later sections of this chapter.

There are four main sources of market failure: anti-competitive behavior, market misconduct, asymmetric information, and systemic instability.

---

[1]   Refer, in particular, to Chapter 2.

Anti-competitive behavior

The prevention of anti-competitive practices can be considered equally relevant for financial markets and for other markets. As a result, the regulator for anti-trust or anti-monopoly regulation may have authority across all markets or may have responsibility for the financial sector or parts of it.

Retail markets for some financial products may be less subject to competitive pressures than other markets. Reasons include:

- Some products can be compulsory. A common example would be the types of insurance described in 7.3.4 below, where customers have to purchase the product no matter how expensive it is relative to the intrinsic value.

- Market entry can be limited or subject to high barriers. Financial institutions usually require minimum capital levels, high establishment costs, and license approval.

- Substitutes for the product may not be available or permitted. An example is life insurance, which may be legally restricted to life insurance companies as providers.

As a result, the financial sector may have specific regulation to promote competition and to limit market concentration.

In addition, opportunities to change from one provider to another may be restricted by practicalities: taxation consequences or administrative complexity; terms of the contract; an absence of secondary markets; or legislative constraints. An insurance policyholder may not be able to change insurers as readily as changing the provider of a savings account or a phone service. This issue will also arise where a company provides long-term contracts with discretion over the terms offered on cancellation prior to the end of the term. There is commonly a very limited secondary market in products such as life insurance policies. A policyholder wishing to surrender must in effect sell the policy back to the issuing insurance company. As another example, individuals whose retirement savings are organized through employer-sponsored plans may be unable to move their savings to another institution while they remain in the service of the employer, and may receive less than a proportionate share of the promised retirement benefit if they leave service before retirement.

Therefore regulations may prescribe minimum termination values, and may provide a right for employees to opt out of employer-sponsored plans.

Regulation to enhance the financial security of long-term contracts and retirement benefit plans can also be seen as, in part, a response to this source of market failure. This type of regulation is often called *prudential regulation*, and is further discussed in 7.3.5 below.

Market misconduct

Secondary markets, ie markets for buying and selling existing financial securities,[2] are regulated to minimize market manipulation and fraud.

Primary markets, involving the issuing of new financial securities, are subject to market disclosure rules to ensure that potential purchasers can make informed decisions. Individuals who purchase financial products are generally considered to be particularly

---

[2] Note that here we would consider financial securities to have a broad definition and include financial instruments and insurance policies.

in need of protection. Disclosure regulations are often specific for distribution channels (direct sales, insurance agents and brokers etc) of institutions offering retail products rather than wholesale products.

Regulation may also be related to the *fitness and propriety* of those that participate in the markets. In this context, fitness and propriety means:

- ethical standing;

- financial standing;

- competence in understanding the features of the products being provided; and

- competence in making any recommendations about which products are suitable for the customer's requirements.

The disclosure regulations may include prescription of the way in which information is disclosed, in order to improve the ability of less financially literate customers to make comparisons. For example, companies that publish projections of future benefits may be required to use standard or otherwise limited or guided assumptions.

The wording of contracts needs to be sufficiently clear. Customers must not be deceived about their entitlements, or caught out by important details hidden in fine print. Regulation may be tailored to particular types of financial products or it may be covered by general contract laws that seek to prevent unfair contract terms.

Asymmetric information

In some cases, even with extensive disclosure of information, buyers and sellers of financial products may not be on an equal footing.

It is difficult for an ordinary customer to assess the level of security offered by complex financial institutions. This is particularly so for long-term savings and life insurance contracts, where the security would have to be evaluated over the prospective term of the contract. This is one reason for regulation aimed at ensuring that the providers of these products operate soundly.

Asymmetry of information can also occur where the buyer has more information than the seller of a financial product. This is particularly the case in insurance when the prospective policyholders may know more about their dangers, habits and health than the insurer. Thus insurance contracts are usually covered by legislation that goes beyond normal contract law to require disclosure of all facts material to assessing the risk. For actuaries, understanding the quality of the underwriting of risks is important. As such, this area of law is critical to ensuring the credibility of any underwriting and risk management process. This underpins the effective delivery of insurance to the market and, for actuaries, effective pricing and underwriting.

Distributors can also have considerable informational advantages over clients who are less informed or financially literate. This may be perceived as an information asymmetry. Alternatively, if it leads to bad sales practices or to poor recommendations of products, it can be seen as an example of market misconduct. Either way, it is usually subject to oversight and control.

Systemic instability

System-wide instability can damage otherwise sound institutions, because of loss of confidence in the sector as a whole, or contagion from one institution to another via the payments system causing loss of liquidity. For banks in particular, there is a risk that the failure of one bank will lead to further collapses. While effective prudential supervision, as described in 7.3.5 below, reduces the risk of systemic instability by reducing the risk of individual bank failures, it can be necessary to have other processes in place to limit the spread of instability.

One method is to provide some *last resort* support. This is most often the role of the central bank. The central bank, with its substantial balance sheet strength and reputation, can be used to support an institution at risk. The objective of forestalling or minimizing the effect of a run is to maintain the reputation of the institution, and the industry, and the country's financial system, so as to prevent major crises. Guarantee funds and protection schemes may also be considered to provide some form of last resort support.

7.3.3 Other objectives for regulation

There are broader social reasons for regulation in circumstances where it would not be justified by the various purely economic rationales set out above. Governments will usually be concerned to protect consumers, from motivations of social justice or to avoid the political embarrassment when consumers suffer from mis-sold products or failed institutions. There is no certainty that market mechanisms will achieve the desired level of consumer protection, or act in the interests of consumers.

In a truly efficient market, new companies enter with relative ease and the less successful companies fail and go out of business. Most insurance regulatory regimes are designed to prevent the latter and to inhibit the former. Market realities also oblige long-term providers of financial security to remain in the market, at least to some extent, rather than leave at the first sign of a downturn. A life insurer or pension provider is obliged by the nature of its business to take long-term decisions and make long-term promises to clients, so exiting the market and re-entering is not a viable choice.

Competition between life insurance companies in a free market can operate to increase commissions, as companies compete to build up a larger and more effective sales force and hence sell more business and make more profits. Anti-competitive measures, such as restrictions on commissions, may be necessary for the protection of consumers.

A government may have a social objective to ensure access to particular products, such as types of insurance or simple savings products, that it sees as essential for all or most members of the community. In some jurisdictions, particularly developing economies, the government may attempt to stimulate competition, ensure availability of products, ensure reasonable prices, or improve access to insurance services, by setting up a state-owned company or scheme. Even in developed economies, the prices for these products may be subject to regulation to ensure affordability.

A government may have economic objectives in regulation. The need to raise revenue has already been mentioned. Other economic objectives may include:

- to favor local companies at the expense of foreign-owned companies, for example by restricting the entry of the latter into the market;

- to encourage the growth of a strong financial industry in the nation;

- to strengthen local capital markets;

- to ensure that the government debt can be financed (eg by requirements to invest a minimum proportion in government securities);

- to control currency movements; and

- to integrate the overall structure of social security, especially old-age pensions.

A government may have objectives in regulation that are not specifically related to the financial sector, but the regulations may have implications for the financial sector and the work of the actuary.

One example of such laws is anti-discrimination legislation, which can have the effect of restricting the ability to charge differential premiums by sex or other characteristics such as race or disability. In some jurisdictions, such discrimination may be prohibited, whilst in others it may be permitted only where there is credible statistical data to support differential prices. Another example is the influence of family and divorce law on products, particularly the design of retirement funds where the treatment of benefits on the breakdown of marriage will be relevant.

7.3.4   The regulation of specific types of business

There are some types of business where governments do not rely on the natural operation of competitive forces. Examples include compulsory products, and products that are considered to be so important that the government intervenes in the market to ensure access for all.

Examples of compulsory financial products include insurance providing for liability to third parties for injury caused by motor vehicles (sometimes called *compulsory third party* or CTP insurance) and insurance for liability of employers for compensation of employees for injuries and death associated with employment (*workers compensation* or *employers liability* insurance). Governments often make it compulsory for the driver or employer to take out these types of insurance rather than self-insure, and benefit entitlements may be specified in legislation.

The compulsory nature of this insurance creates the opportunity for anti-competitive behavior, because customers have to purchase the product even if they consider it to be poor value. In addition, as the government provides this compulsion, it may feel the need to ensure that there is a greater certainty than normal market forces provide that the insurance company will be able to deliver the benefits. (This is one reason for tightening the prudential regulation of retirement funds if governments introduce compulsory retirement systems and contributions.)

Furthermore, when a company writing such business fails, there are more parties affected than those that made the original decision to purchase the contract. The injured third party is most likely to be financially dependent on the insurer despite having had no say in the purchase decision, whereas the purchaser of the insurance has little incentive to consider quality (ie the security of the insurance company) as well as price. Where benefits are prescribed and identical from one company to another, then market shares may largely depend on price levels. It is common for such products to be subject to regulation of premium rates to ensure that premiums are not too low, which would be unsafe, nor too high, which would make the cost of compulsory insurance excessive.

Finally, a government may still need to provide some mechanism to address cases where there is an eligible claim to be made but the insured party, or the insurer, cannot be determined, or where the compulsory insurance has not been properly put in place. The usual example of this situation is a hit-and-run accident victim where the insurance policy cannot be identified, if it exists at all.

The second situation mentioned above where governments do not rely on the natural operation of competitive forces is in the case of products that are considered to be so important that the government intervenes in the market to ensure that the products are widely available at affordable prices. An example is health insurance. If the market was left to operate freely, insurers would charge premiums that reflected the risk, and people with ongoing health problems requiring expensive treatment would be faced with unaffordably high premiums. Governments have introduced various measures to address this problem.

7.3.5   Prudential regulation

Prudential regulation means regulation that tries to ensure that the regulated institutions are operating soundly. It is aimed at reducing the probability of failure of a financial institution to an acceptable level and minimizing the losses to the most vulnerable parties (typically, depositors, policyholders and beneficiaries of third party insurance) when failures do occur.

Prudential supervisors are regulatory bodies responsible for overseeing the financial institutions and administering the prudential regulation. Prudential supervisors have various regulatory tools. A supervisor can sometimes use the authority of its position to achieve its objectives without strict and formal legal action. This tool, termed *moral suasion*, can be effective, but needs to be supported by the recognized alternative of more severe action and the credibility that the supervisory authority maintains amongst supervised institutions. It relies on the supervisor having independent powers to act and being respected within the financial sector.

The provision of financial support as a last resort to institutions in difficulty was mentioned in 7.3.2. Prudential supervisors that are not part of the central bank tend not to have the financial resources to enable them to take this action, so they will coordinate their responses with the central bank and other government agencies.

Regulatory tools include laws that control the conduct of business covering:

*   requirements on corporate governance;
*   fitness and propriety of owners, shareholders and senior managers;
*   the quality and quantity of capital;
*   accounting standards;
*   levels of disclosure so that the company can be exposed to market discipline;
*   restrictions on the nature of corporate structures; and
*   rules that impose limitations on the level of risk that can be taken on and the proper management of those risks that are retained.

Companies can be required to provide information to supervisors on a regular basis, be subject to inspections to assess their current and prospective viability in detail, and may have restrictions imposed on their activities through legally enforceable directions from the supervisor.

Rules limiting risk can vary in how restrictive they are. Consider the rules limiting asset risk. There may be specific rules ensuring that high-risk assets cannot be held and setting specific limits for assets in order to ensure diversification. Alternatively, there may be a more general requirement that the assets held should be consistent with how a prudent expert would invest. The transfer of risk (ie reinsurance, in the case of insurers, and securitization, more generally) can be subject to detailed supervisory review and approval. In some cases, product terms and conditions and prices may be subject to greater regulatory oversight and even prior approval by the supervisory authority.

Rules can ensure orderly entry into the market by requiring providers to be licensed. License applicants need to convince the authorities that they can comply with the ongoing requirements and manage the business effectively and prudently. Detailed submissions are required from the license applicants to demonstrate the merits of the proposed operation and should include detailed financial projections and information about key owners, management, and operational plans.

Rules to ensure orderly exit are also important, because the owners of the company may wish to withdraw, while customers expect, and in many cases have a contractual right, to continue their contracts. Rules can require approval of change of control of companies to ensure that licensed companies do not pass to the control of owners who would be rejected if they applied for a license on their own merits.

In some cases, the supervisor rather than the owners of the company can initiate an orderly exit. The failure of a financial institution may not be generally recognized by the community. Instead, the supervisory authority may intervene so that the company is merged, acquired by a stronger institution or sold to another organization which restores its capital position. It is difficult for the wider community to distinguish between this activity and the more conventional merger activity that takes place without intervention. Supervisors, desiring to maintain market confidence, are unlikely to point out the extent of their involvement. In other cases, particularly in a time of financial turmoil, institutions can be acquired into public ownership for a period until they are recapitalized, stabilized and returned to private ownership. Other mechanisms to ensure orderly exit include partial public sector support of one form or another.

The extent to which managed mergers take place depends on the tools available to the supervisor. It also depends on the availability of stronger institutions to act as the merger partner. As a result, very large institutions are more likely to present difficulties to the supervisor. Smaller markets can deal with this problem by seeking the participation of larger institutions from other jurisdictions. However, the rescue of companies in difficulty also acts to limit the degree of concern that may be experienced by company directors and management about the extent to which they take on risk. Management might take on less risk if they are aware they are liable for the consequences, such as public disgrace, attached to failure. Customers, in the absence of public failures, may think that these companies are guaranteed not to fail because of the presence of the supervisory authority or another government sponsored entity. When failure is a possibility, even if remote, the marketplace does impose a discipline on companies that assists supervisors in their task. As a result, the likelihood that a supervisory framework will let a company fail varies from jurisdiction to jurisdiction. In the US, there appears to be a liberal approach to this issue. There are very many companies in the US market, so this approach leads to a reasonable number of publicly visible failures that can be studied. Consistent with this approach, the US has consumer protection schemes which provide a great deal of protection to retail customers. The argument in favor of a fully liberal approach is that customers are more aware of the possibility of failure, take more care in choosing their products, and this exercises some market discipline on company strategies.

Consumer protection once failure has occurred may be offered by schemes such as deposit insurance and policyholder guarantee funds, which compensate customers for some or all of the losses suffered.

Another area of legislation is that governing the wind-up and liquidation of failed entities and the role and actions of supervisors in these circumstances.

Actuaries and auditors can be assigned official roles in regulatory and supervisory arrangements. This is discussed further in 7.6 below.

7.3.6   Arguments for keeping regulation to a minimum

Arguments for keeping regulation to a minimum include:

- Inflexibility: regulation can be difficult to change in response to market developments. Financial sector regulations enacted by parliaments have to be amended by parliaments. It can be difficult to secure time on the parliamentary agenda for what, in the wider context, appears to be a technical issue. As a result, regulation is reinterpreted to fit the circumstances in a way that is less optimal than if the opportunity to alter it is available.

- Cost: regulation comes with direct costs including the requirement for an infrastructure to maintain it, to monitor compliance and to enforce breaches. Indirect costs fall on institutions and individuals because of compliance costs or the cost of additional capital required by the regulations.

- Unforeseen implications: well-meaning regulation can have effects that are unforeseen and undesirable. For example, suppose that there is a restriction on investment choices aimed at reducing exposure to risky assets. The restriction may also create an automatic market demand for securities that would otherwise be held to a lesser extent. This would allow suppliers of such securities to benefit from an effective subsidy on the cost they pay for funds.

- Reduced care/compliance orientation: investors may assume that licensed providers must be safe. Advisers or providers can develop a box-ticking attitude, and are more concerned to comply than to serve the customer, manage risk effectively or conduct operations prudently.

- Market interference can introduce inefficiency. For example, the reduced competition resulting from barriers to entry may increase costs to consumers in a protected market. Innovation in product design may be stifled.

- Regulation may remain in force even if it has ceased to be useful. In many jurisdictions, whilst it is difficult to secure the attention of the legislators to make appropriate financial sector regulation, it can be even more difficult to get their attention to abolish it. Many jurisdictions, therefore, have a good deal of regulation that seems to serve no relevant purpose at all even though it did at the time it was introduced, that still requires the effort of compliance. This contrasts with the first point above where the regulation is still relevant but is not optimal.

7.3.7 Arguments in favor of regulation

Proponents of deregulation consider that the power of the market is sufficient, with the support of a sound disclosure regime, to ensure informed markets. World regulatory practice, as expressed in the various codes and standards as well as the practices of jurisdictions, is strongly in favor of a degree of regulation rather than complete reliance on disclosure. Reasons why disclosure alone is not accepted include:

- The effectiveness of disclosure depends on consumers and investors having the power to act on their observations and conclusions. If they do not have the power to move their money, because of institutional constraints or the costs involved (directly or indirectly, for example through the taxation effects) then the potential for the market pressure to lead to behavioral change in management risk-taking is limited.

- *Operational risks*, ie the risk of such events as rogue traders or the failure of computer systems, are difficult to address through disclosure. It is difficult for customers to assess the risk of such events. Whilst some theoretical approaches are being developed in this area, it is insufficient for customers to assess the risk.

- Full disclosure can be voluminous and filled with technical information that is difficult for lay persons to understand even if they have the stamina to wade through it. As a result, disclosure suffers from being misunderstood or not even read.

- Supervisors have tools that may be more effective at restoring the situation and improving the future outlook. In some cases, disclosure of the situation might hasten the demise of an entity. Compulsory transfers of business to other parties or the sale of companies can be executed while there is still some effective value in goodwill. In a full disclosure environment, by definition, this value of goodwill would reduce to nil if it was felt that the company was going to fail.

- Disclosure can be too late to solve problems. In particular, early preventative intervention can be based on anticipated activity that would not normally be disclosed due to its commercial sensitivity. An independent supervisor can act in advance of mistakes being made. Disclosure, it is argued, may only reveal problems made rather than offer the opportunity to address them before they get out of hand.

- Disclosure can lead to a *flight to quality*. If it becomes known that the risks at a particular financial institution are high then consumers, acting on this information, may move to safer institutions. This action, of itself, can exacerbate the problem. For example, unfounded rumors against a bank can lead to a run even where it is denied by the bank management (ie the market is correctly and fully informed by the organization) so that the bank becomes illiquid and has to realize assets at fire sale prices. It is argued that a flight to quality discourages market development and innovation because individuals are less able to absorb risk than diversified companies and favor less innovative companies.

- Several instances of financial mismanagement and fraud that have arisen in less-regulated segments of the financial markets have caused significant harm to retail investors and/or have contributed to the destabilization of broader global markets. This has led to calls for increased regulation of these segments, and has reduced the pressure for further deregulation of regulated markets.

In most jurisdictions, a balance is struck between market disclosure and specific regulation, and between prescriptive and more general structures. Readers can examine the regulation in their own environment and consider where the balance lies.

7.4 International organizations that influence regulation

As markets become more global, the role of international organizations influencing the existence, the form and the content of regulation has grown. These organizations produce papers that survey practices in particular regulatory areas, provide guidance as to how issues might be addressed, and in some cases set standards against which the regulations of an individual jurisdiction may be benchmarked.

7.4.1 International regulatory standards

There are several bodies setting international standards in the financial sector that are relevant to the work of actuaries and the institutions that they advise. The longest-standing of the standard-setting bodies is the Committee on Banking Supervision at the Bank of International Settlements (BIS), often referred to as the Basel (or Basle) Committee after the name of the city in Switzerland where it is headquartered. This committee continues to work on the enhancement of the supervision of banks. Also in Basel is the International Association of Insurance Supervisors (IAIS) that seeks to improve insurance supervision and regulation. Basel also hosts international organizations covering deposit insurance, payments systems and other financial sector global groupings. Similarly, the International Organization of Securities Commissions (IOSCO) focuses on the supervision of securities dealers and markets.

These organizations produce Core Principles, Standards and Guidance as well as research into current practices and developments. These influence individual jurisdictions because they establish accepted international benchmarks of practice and encourage dialogue on developments. They help developed markets expand beyond national boundaries and provide a general framework for supervisors and regulators in underdeveloped markets to develop a regulatory system. They define globally-accepted practices on such issues as prudent risk management, capital, and corporate governance. They define expectations of effective supervision that guide legal and supervisory practices globally. As global financial conglomerates reach across borders, they encourage the regulatory and supervisory regimes to become more consistent.

Also, some regulatory and supervisory requirements may be put in place in line with guidance, standards, or even binding treaties at higher levels. For example, the European Union directives are relevant for EU member states; the National Association of Insurance Commissioners (NAIC) in the US produces model laws that guide state insurance legislation; banking regulation in a group of Caribbean states is handled regionally rather than in each country separately through the East Caribbean Central Bank; and insurance supervision in west Africa is coordinated through the Inter-African Conference on Insurance Markets. Actuaries in these jurisdictions would need to be aware of both the local requirements and the developments at the level of the higher groupings of jurisdictions.

The International Accounting Standards Board (IASB) issues internationally applicable accounting standards described as International Financial Reporting Standards (IFRS).

Other international organizations also help to develop regulation and supervisory practices although they are not generally considered to be standard-setting bodies.

To enhance the coordination of the three standard-setting bodies – the Basel Committee, the IAIS and IOSCO – a forum of all three was established. This joint forum started work on the supervision of financial conglomerates with participation in more than one sector and has since carried out further studies on issues of comparability of approach in each sector. It is also particularly interested in the potential for risk transfer and arbitrage between sectors. The resulting research papers encourage greater consistency between sectors.

The Organization for Economic Co-operation and Development (OECD) takes an active role in the development of financial sector regulation. Before the existence of the IAIS and IOSCO, it provided a more important forum for the exchange of views and the development of best practices in the areas of insurance and securities. In addition, despite the small membership of the OECD in proportion to all countries, it tries to maintain contacts with all countries by sponsoring forums, educational seminars, and the publication of technical papers.

Although of less direct relevance to most actuaries, there is a set of principles produced by the Financial Action Task Force (FATF) dealing with regulation against money laundering and other financial crime. These place responsibilities on financial institutions and a range of law enforcement agencies from those involved in border protection to those overseeing financial institutions.

The World Bank and the International Monetary Fund (IMF) were both established after World War II. Since various financial crises in the 1990s, these two organizations have been involved in a Financial Sector Assessment Program (FSAP) which, in part, assesses the extent to which a jurisdiction conforms to the various standards and codes established by the standard-setting bodies. The FSAP assessments also address vulnerabilities in the financial sector and the developmental problems. Both of these organizations, along with other development agencies, provide technical assistance to countries seeking to develop further their regulatory and supervisory structures.

A more recently constituted group of senior regulatory officials and central bank governors is the Financial Stability Board (FSB). This organization is small but has considerable influence. It acts as a forum for issues to be raised and for research to be instigated. In the global financial crisis that began in 2007, it has served as a focus for action and response at the international level in support of major governments and was reconstituted and renamed as part of the response of governments recognizing its important role. As a result, it influences the agenda and priorities of other bodies.

Another body that influences regulation and markets is the World Trade Organization (WTO). Until the late 1990s, financial services were specifically excluded from the treaties of the WTO. Since then, work has progressed on a new round of agreements that would include financial services but with a *prudential carveout*. A prudential carveout means that restrictive rules would be permitted but only on purely prudential grounds, rather than as barriers to trade entry. Two particular consequences of this direction are that non-prudential barriers can be expected to be removed over time and that, at some point, there will be WTO actions taken that will further define the meaning of what is and what is not a purely prudential rule. One key area under consideration is the insurance sector where many jurisdictions favor reinsurance with locally licensed rather than offshore reinsurance companies and some do not permit the licensing of branches. Another area will be retirement benefit fund administration where there is some pressure to allow funds to contract administrative services offshore. A third area would be differential controls on market entry between locally owned institutions and foreign institutions (whether as branches or locally incorporated subsidiaries).

7.5 Summary of core principles

The various core principles issued by the international bodies provide a standard for regulation in the financial sector, particularly from the prudential supervisor's perspective.

The core principles provide for:

- the establishment of a supervisory authority that has operational and political independence from the government of the day. In particular, this independence is supported by specific and secure funding of operations, transparent appointment of office bearers that provides an element of security to the senior officers, and ability to make decisions free from the political process and industry lobbying;

- a regime for licensing new entrants that considers the adequacy of corporate governance, capital, risk management, internal controls, fitness and propriety of those in control of the entity and the soundness of the proposed business plan, and that regulates subsequent changes in control of the regulated entity;

- ongoing rules for corporate governance, corporate structures, internal controls and rules for the fitness and propriety of owners, directors and senior managers;

- accounting standards, including adequate, transparent and comparable valuation of assets and liabilities. These standards cover the treatment of approaches such as marking assets to market values, use of book values or amortized values, liabilities with margins at a particular level, and allowance for recoveries or transfer of risk such as through reinsurance for insurers and securitization of loan portfolios for banks;

- rules requiring a minimum level of capital (sometimes called the solvency margin) including minimum absolute capital amounts, use of methods that reflect the underlying risk levels in the organization, suitable types of capital instruments that can count toward meeting the requirement, particular assets that cannot count toward meeting the requirements such as loans to directors or affiliated companies or goodwill, and the treatment of capital in conglomerates that would lead to double counting of capital in a corporate group;

- powers of inspection and investigation, sanctions, and the capacity to deal with orderly processes for market exit;

- rules for market conduct including the treatment of customers and the regulation of distributors; and

- other rules for the prevention of money laundering, transparency of regulatory and supervisory processes, and disclosure by companies to markets and customers.

7.6 Official roles for actuaries

Particularly with respect to prudential aspects of operations, the actuary can have a legislated role and higher responsibility.

Some supervisory regimes prescribe an official role for actuaries. Whilst this practice is of longer standing for life insurance companies and defined benefit retirement plans, it is becoming more common that there will also be an official role for actuaries in non-life insurance and in health insurance.

The actuary usually has a role in the regime for prudential supervision. The official role of the actuary is related to the financial condition of the entity under supervision. Actuaries may have other roles in these entities but these may not be a requirement of the supervisory or regulatory structure. Actuaries who have a statutory role and other commercial roles must ensure that commercial considerations do not influence their statutory duties.

In defining the official role of the actuary, legislation or regulations often define:

- who can be an official actuary (requirements as to fitness and propriety, including experience and professional qualifications);

- what the official actuary is required to do;

- what obligations the official actuary has to report to the company and to the supervisor;

- what topics and areas the official actuary has responsibility to cover in these reports; and

- whether the official actuary has powers to obtain information needed for the task, powers to obtain access to the people to whom they have a responsibility to report, and protection from their efforts being frustrated.

In these cases, the actuarial professional body may support official actuaries in the conduct of their responsibilities. The professional body may provide peer review and support on technical issues such as the development of mortality tables; set professional standards and guidance on how to perform the particular tasks; deal with complaints against members; and investigate and, if appropriate, discipline those found to have failed in their duty. In some jurisdictions the professional body will provide a *practicing certificate* to those actuaries whose experience and education is deemed to fit them for a statutory role.

7.7 The structure of regulation and supervisory institutions

The structure of regulation and of the institutions that enforce it can be organized by type of institution, by areas of concern or by some blend of these two. In the first case, laws are passed and an authority is established for each institutional type (eg banks, insurance companies, retirement benefit plans). The authority is responsible for the regulation of all relevant aspects of the particular institutional type. In the second approach, an authority is established for each regulatory area (eg prudential regulation, disclosure requirements, etc) with scope to regulate and supervise across all institutional types.

It is important that actuaries, particularly those with legislated responsibilities, understand who is the relevant "policeman" for the particular responsibility. As noted earlier, senior officials or the organization as a whole can have a regulatory function by producing subsidiary rules, by guidance or simply by making public statements on issues.

Consider the following two examples of how a statement from a supervisor can be effective. First, suppose the chief of insurance supervision indicates his or her concern about premium rates for term insurances. An actuary pricing or valuing liabilities for such products has to consider whether the assumptions are realistic, reasonable and defensible in the light of the supervisor's view of the market. In other words, an approach weighted toward the actuary's perception of market practice may need caution. The actuary may even consider an informal discussion with the supervisor, recognizing that this is an area of particular interest. Secondly, suppose the supervisors indicate that they have conducted a series of on-site inspections and found a particular practice was poor and another was "best practice." Then where the poor practice exists for the entity being advised, action might be required to correct the poor practice to protect stakeholders.

7.8   Practical implications for actuaries

It is a fundamental requirement of professional practice that actuaries carry out their roles with a proper understanding of the environment, and a fundamental part of that environment is legislation. Legislation can impact implicitly on the nature of the risks that actuaries are estimating or assessing, or explicitly on the advice itself.

Actuaries should be aware of the professional and legal obligations attached to their work. If they are giving advice required under laws or regulations, they should be familiar with the requirements and also any professional standards of practice. Actuaries are rarely qualified lawyers. There may be times when an actuary has to seek advice from and collaborate with lawyers to ensure that his or her work reflects the legal situation and to consider any trends that may have implications for his or her work. Regardless of the situation, when an actuary takes on an official role, just as with all roles, the actuary should only act if he or she has the capability to fulfill the obligations of that role.

7.9   Key learning points

- Actuaries need to understand the environment in which they are working, and the issues that this may raise for the work that they are doing. The legal system and regulation are part of the environment in which actuaries work.

- Depending on the nature of the legal system and the problem being addressed by the actuary, relevant regulation can include primary laws, subsidiary rules and regulations, circulars from other government agencies, court decisions, documents issued by self-regulatory organizations or international organizations, and professional guidance and standards.

- Understanding the rationale for regulation includes understanding the objectives of regulation, the arguments in favor of more or less regulation, and the basis of the legal system itself. A basic understanding of these issues assists the actuary to identify areas of law that are relevant to a particular situation.

- The regulator and supervisor are usually important participants in the market for regulated financial products, both as an influence on regulation and to explain how the regulations are interpreted and enforced. Being able to identify the relevant supervisory agency for whatever particular regulations are relevant may be as important as identifying the regulation itself.

- International organizations influence legal systems in all countries. They influence the content of laws and provide guidance on best practices that may be relevant or useful to the actuary (even when there are no local legal requirements).

- Actuaries can have designated responsibilities under the law. When this is the case, the actuaries need to understand their higher and more complex obligations and responsibilities.

Exercises

7.1   Where relevant, consider a particular jurisdiction, perhaps the one where you work or hope to work in the future, when answering these questions:

(a) Review the primary and subsidiary legislation and become familiar with the structure and scope of the regulations in each part.

(b) Identify the sources where you can find the primary laws most relevant to the life insurance, non-life insurance, banking and private retirement income markets; the source of those laws (national or sub-national) and the names of the primary laws.

(c) Identify the supervisory authorities responsible for the oversight of these laws, particularly those responsible for prudential oversight, systemic stability, accounting and valuation, revenue raising, and market conduct.

(d) List the areas where these supervisory authorities have rule-making powers for one of these selected laws.

(e) What are the stated objectives of the organizations identified in (c)? How do these objectives match with the overall objectives of regulation identified in this chapter?

7.2   By reviewing either the Basel Committee on Banking Supervision or the International Association of Insurance Supervisors' Core Principles, how would you assess the independence of the supervisory authorities in your country? With respect to one selected authority, state the challenges and rationale for your assessment succinctly in not more than one page whilst still identifying the strengths and weaknesses of the system that is in place.

7.3   You have been approached by entrepreneurs who operate a chain of retail department stores in your country. They wish to provide financial products to their customers to improve services and increase profit and are considering a range of alternatives. Prepare a summary of the requirements that would apply in your jurisdiction regarding obtaining any necessary licenses and providing capital if they were to:

•   provide mortgages and term deposit accounts to clients by starting a bank;

•   provide car insurance by starting a subsidiary non-life insurance company; and/or

•   sell one or more existing insurer's life insurance product.

7.4   In your jurisdiction, what official roles are provided for actuaries that are mandated by laws or other legislation? What specific responsibilities does the actuary have in each case (such as valuation, capital certification, determining prices, solvency management, etc)?

7.5   You are the actuary of a small life insurance company writing endowment insurance savings contracts. You are responsible for establishing the provisions and reserves and reporting to the company's board of directors on the financial condition of the business.

(a) Identifying the role of actuaries in your jurisdiction, where such an official role exists, including the part played by the actuarial professional body in supporting this role, list the relevant obligations imposed on this role. What other laws and regulations would also be relevant to consider?

(b) You identify that the provision should be $12 million. The company's board, led by the major shareholder who is also the chairman and CEO, has amended your proposal to $6 million and put this in the accounts and has, as a result, reported a profit of $1 million, a dividend of $750,000 and a capital position of $5 million. You have considered a more optimistic valuation that would suggest $10 million instead of $12 million but you know this would leave no margins at all in the valuation. What concerns do you have and what action should you take?

CD Items

Chapter 7 Exercise Solutions

References (other than CD Items)

Basel Committee on Banking Supervision 2006, *Core Principles for Effective Banking Supervision*, Bank of International Settlements, Basel.

Carmichael, J. 2002, Experiences with Integrated Regulation, *APRA Insight*, 1st Quarter, pp. 3-7.

Carmichael, J. & Pomerlearno, M. 2002, *The Development and Regulation of Non-Bank Financial Institutions*, The World Bank, Washington DC.

International Association of Insurance Supervisors 2003, *Insurance Core Principles and Methodology, October 2003*, Basel.

Organization for Economic Co-operation and Development (OECD) 1999, *Insurance Regulation and Supervision in Asia*, OECD, Paris.

Organization for Economic Cooperation and Development (OECD) 2002, *Insurance Solvency Supervision: OECD Country Profiles*, OECD, Paris.

Richardson, J. & Stephenson, M. 2000, Some Aspects of Regulatory Capital, *FSA Occasional Paper Series*, No 7.

Fred's Coffee Shop – Product Design

Fred is considering what products to sell in his coffee shop. He probably has some general ideas, because his initial research should have identified a gap in the market that he will seek to fill. However, he now has to consider all the details, such as how he will make and present the products. Thinking about all the product design issues will help him to firm up his plans.

The physical premises will shape his product design decisions. For example, if he doesn't have adequate facilities, he will be unable to prepare food on the premises. This doesn't stop him buying food in for resale, such as cakes, sandwiches, salads and even certain hot meals that can be reheated in a microwave or under a small grill. However, it clearly restricts his options.

Fred's options are also limited by his prospective customer base. If his customers will be particularly price-sensitive, he probably shouldn't be planning to use expensive coffee beans. If price is less of an issue, he might consider offering a range of different beans or using more expensive (but higher-quality) equipment.

Fred will need to decide what coffee styles he will offer (eg cappuccino, latte and espresso) and whether to offer hot chocolate and various teas. He will find that customers expect a certain range of options but he may decide on a more extensive range.

Even the décor of the coffee shop, the cutlery and crockery, the disposable takeout cups and the way the staff dress are part of the product design. Think of different coffee shops that you have used and consider how they vary and how the differences affect your attitude to them.

So, as simple a product as coffee has many design options. However, there are also very many core features (such as the basic range of coffee styles) that are the same in all coffee shops in one region or country.

The same applies to financial products such as life insurance. When designing life insurance products, the customer appeal of a feature has to be balanced against the cost of providing it, including the impact on risk. From a product design perspective, the ideal feature is one that adds very little cost but is highly appealing.

As you read the chapter, think of features that might be considered in financial products and why they might (or might not) work. You might be able to find ideas from non-financial products. There are also different ways of achieving a desired outcome. The CD article about Islamic Insurance provides an interesting example.

Another issue is product distribution channels. In Fred's case, the two obvious delivery channels are in-store and takeout. To maximize sales through these channels, he needs to get people into the shop, perhaps by advertising and having an attractive shopfront that stands out.

What other distribution channels are available to Fred? Think for a moment before you read on.

Fred could operate a delivery service to local businesses, taking orders by telephone or the internet. It is likely that the demand for this service would overlap with the walk-in business but it would also reach different customers. He could reach another set of customers by equipping a van and selling coffee at the beach at weekends.

Another distribution channel is to establish several coffee shops under Fred's brand. One benefit of this is that a person away from home will be more likely to buy coffee from a familiar brand – Fred's. You can probably think of a franchised version of this model, with a worldwide presence.

Distribution is about reaching customers. To be profitable, it has to be efficient and effective. Most businesses that have been around for a while have major distribution channels that have been proven to work.

However, when reading the chapter, remember that most distribution channels don't reach all potential customers (or don't do so efficiently). Also, the economics can change; think how the banning of commissions would affect the distribution of investment products through financial advisers, for example.

Therefore, companies always need to consider other potential channels, both for now and for the future. As you read the chapter, think of ways in which non-financial products are distributed and whether financial products could be distributed in similar ways.

Chapter 8:   Product Design
by Jeffrey Beckley

8.1   Introduction

The process of product design can be viewed as one step in the Actuarial Control Cycle. Product design has its own control cycle, with four stages.

- Stage 1: Identify the need for a new (or modified) product and develop a product strategy.
- Stage 2: Develop the product.
- Stage 3: Manufacture and distribute the product.
- Stage 4: Gather and monitor experience.

The process forms a cycle as the fourth stage often leads to the identification of the need for a new or modified product.

We will use this framework to discuss product design, considering the various steps to be completed at each of the four general stages of this control cycle. We will conclude with an overall comment on the practical implications for actuaries working in product design.

8.2   Stage 1 of the product design control cycle

This first stage involves identifying the need for a new (or modified) product and developing a product strategy.

8.2.1   Identify the need for a new product

Identifying the need for a new product can occur in several ways. We will consider five examples:

- innovation;
- response to changes in regulation or tax law changes;
- entry into a new market or distribution channel;
- updating an existing product to reflect relevant experience; and
- market research.

8.2.1.1   Innovation

True innovation occurs when a product that is unique or considerably different from existing products is introduced. Innovation often occurs as the result of one person's insightful analysis of the market or as the result of looking at a market need from a different view than that of other people. This is a skill that is difficult to teach or develop.

Innovation, in and of itself, does not assure success. An innovative product may not meet a market need or it may be too expensive compared to alternatives. For example, alternative fuel automobiles have been available for many years. However, it can be argued that these cars have never been successful. First, they have generally been considerably more expensive to buy and often more expensive to operate than their gasoline-powered competitors. Only recently as gasoline and diesel fuel prices have reached high levels have consumers been able to justify financially such innovative cars. Secondly, these cars have lacked critical features necessary to be successful. For example, the power, range, top speed of these cars and the availability of refueling are often limited, resulting in their use outside an urban setting being impractical.

However, an innovative product that meets a market need can often command a premium over the price charged for competing products. The iPod is an innovative product that has been able to maintain a pricing premium over its competitors. The innovative iPod captured a dominant market share which it has been able to maintain for an extended period of time while still charging a price that is higher than that of its competitors.

Innovation in financial services also occurs frequently. For example, most derivatives are developed as a result of innovation and are frequently designed to meet a specific unserved market need. Innovation in derivatives has been possible in the past as derivatives have not been highly regulated.

Innovation in the insurance industry has been less common. Most life insurance and annuity products are identical to other products in the marketplace. Even when there are changes in insurance products, these changes tend to be minor alterations that are evolutionary. One major reason is that insurance is a highly regulated industry. It is often difficult to develop innovative products that will comply with the existing regulations. A second reason is that, unlike manufactured products, product innovations in insurance have historically not been patented and are copied quickly by other companies. Therefore, the financial motivation and competitive advantage of innovation has been muted. A third reason is the administrative complexity of insurance products. Non-incremental change requires a significant investment in systems making the cost of failure relatively high.

Over the last ten years, some insurance companies in the US have successfully sought patents covering the inner workings of a product and the computer systems used to administer that product. During 2009, Lincoln National Life was awarded a US$13 million settlement in a patent infringement lawsuit. The success of such patents could significantly change the competitive advantage and financial reward for innovation in the insurance industry. Furthermore, the actuary for an insurance company will need to verify that any design element is not patented, and if not, to consider whether to apply for a patent. For more information, see "Product Patents and their Impact on the Life Insurance Industry" on the CD.

Example 8.1

An example of innovation in insurance products was the introduction of universal life insurance in the US in the late 1970s. Prior to universal life, permanent life insurance sales consisted of whole life and endowment contracts. Universal life unbundled the elements of the whole life and endowment contracts. This permitted the universal life product to provide significantly more flexibility as well as enhancing the understanding of the product. As a result, universal life products captured and have maintained a significant market share.

8.2.1.2   Regulation or tax law changes

A change in regulation or tax may create new market needs, and thus create the opportunity to sell new products to meet those needs. Or the change may require modification of an existing product to meet the new environment. For example, changes in the tax and regulatory environment in the US and Australia have been one of the reasons why most retirement plans have moved from defined benefits to defined contributions.

Many financial products, including insurance products, are designed and marketed to take advantage of provisions in tax law. For example, derivative assets are often used to replicate more traditional assets because the derivatives are taxed differently than the traditional asset. The use of derivatives may allow an investor to mirror the results of the traditional asset in a more tax efficient way.

Regulation and tax laws also influence product design outside the financial services industry. For example, many of the innovations in automobiles have been driven by regulatory requirements with regard to passenger safety or the reduction in pollutants.

8.2.1.3   Entry into a new market or distribution channel

If a company wants to enter a new market or distribute its products through a different distribution channel, product design is likely to be necessary. Products targeted to one market or distribution system will generally not work in another market. At the very least, commission schedules usually differ between the various distribution channels. The company will conduct market research to determine the appropriate products for the new market. While market research is discussed below, one particular step of that process is to identify competitors and the products that are sold by competitors. Many times, when entering a new market (or to remain competitive in an existing market) companies merely copy the products of competitors. Sometimes this occurs because the company does not have enough experience or knowledge to price and market a new product with innovative features. Therefore, they enter the market using a competitor's design and benchmarking against a competitor's rates, trusting that those in the business are participating reasonably. The article "Variable Annuities" on the CD discusses one example of product designers in Europe (including the UK) taking inspiration from a product that has been successfully introduced in the US and Japanese markets. Another example is given in the article "Takaful" on the CD which describes how insurance contracts can be adapted to comply with Islamic law.

Other methods of gaining knowledge and expertise in order to enter a new market would include hiring a consultant or consulting firm with expertise in that market, entering the market through a joint venture with a partner (such as a reinsurer) who has the expertise, or hiring expertise from a competitor.

Copying successful products of competitors is common in all industries. In 1983, Chrysler Corporation introduced the minivan to the US automobile market. The minivan was an instant success in the marketplace. Other car companies developed minivans to compete with Chrysler.

8.2.1.4   Updating for experience

A common reason for product design is to update the product to reflect experience. The experience that needs to be reflected may be related to the consumers (for insurance, this would be the policyholder and would include persistency and loss experience), to the economic environment (interest rates for example), or to the company (for example, expenses of producing and administering the product).

When a product is first designed, several questions will arise, as summarized below in 8.3.5. These questions can often only be answered by making assumptions. Once a company has been selling a product in the marketplace, actual data can be gathered to replace the assumptions in answering these questions. This will generally result in the need to redesign the product.

Products that a company has been selling for an extended period of time may need to be updated for more recent experience as the environment changes. For example, new competitors may enter the market. The automobile industry in nearly every country has gone through drastic restructuring as foreign car companies entered the domestic market.

As another example, since mortality has generally improved over time, life insurance and annuity products need to be updated periodically to reflect current mortality. If the life insurance products are not periodically redesigned to reflect current mortality, the price of the product will become uncompetitive. For immediate annuities, if the product is not redesigned to reflect current mortality and the latest information about projected future improvements, the product will become unprofitable.

8.2.1.5 Market research

One of the major tools in identifying the need for a product is market research. Market research:

- identifies a market need or confirms that a market need exists;
- confirms that your company has the resources necessary to meet the market need; and
- identifies competitors and competing products.

Market research can take many forms and may itself lead to the identification of market needs. Market research on existing products may also indicate the need for new product designs in order to compete with the products that are being offered by competitors. Examples of market research would be industry surveys of product offerings and common features, as well as focus groups of consumers and marketers of a company's products.

If the market research does not support the perceived market need, it is prudent to reach that conclusion early in the process, as the "develop product" stage and "manufacture and distribute the product" stage are both expensive.

8.2.2 Develop a product strategy

A product strategy is necessary so that you can assess whether your company can benefit from meeting the need. A product will seldom be successful even if it meets a market need unless an appropriate product strategy is developed. A product strategy will:

(a) discuss how the product fits into the company's strategic plan and current product portfolio;

(b) discuss the specific markets being targeted;

(c) discuss the method of distributing the product;

(d) discuss the competitive advantages of the company;

(e) develop sales and profit expectations for the product;

(f)   discuss the risks associated with the product and the ability to mitigate these risks; and

(g)   discuss the resources necessary for a successful product and evaluate the company's capacity to meet those needs.

While all of these are important, we will focus below on the three areas (c), (f) and (g).

8.2.2.1   Distribution method

A company that produces products, financial or otherwise, generally has the choice of distributing those products through multiple distribution channels. Products can be sold:

*   through retailers;

*   directly to the consumer through factory stores, mail order, or the internet; and

*   by representatives through door-to-door sales, to employees at their place of employment, telemarketing, or even through parties.

Most companies rely primarily on a single method of distribution, but often utilize other methods as secondary distribution channels. Within a given industry, different companies will often utilize different distribution channels as their primary channel.

Cosmetics are a good example. You can buy cosmetics in retail outlets such as department stores as well as discount stores. In addition, you can buy cosmetics via the internet. Finally, cosmetics are sold door-to-door or through parties where a representative presents the products to guests at the party.

Financial products, including insurance products, are distributed through several different distribution channels. Companies must find efficient and productive methods for distributing their products in order to be successful. The main distribution channels for financial products are described in Chapter 5.

There is an old saying that life insurance products are sold, they are not bought. This basically means that even if an insurance product addresses a market need, if the consumer does not understand how the product addresses that need, the product will not be purchased. This is one reason why many insurance products are sold by an intermediary.

The point-of-sale contact for the financial services company performs other functions for the company in addition to the sales function. For example, the agent for an insurance company performs the initial underwriting function for the company. Underwriting is discussed fully later in this chapter. Similarly, the point-of-sale contact in the application for a mortgage loan performs an initial evaluation of the creditworthiness of the applicant.

Distribution through intermediaries does have limitations. Agents are high-cost and only reach a fraction of the population, so other channels are required in order to reach the rest. For example, simple insurance policies, with limited underwriting, are commonly sold by direct marketing, often from brochures included with other mailings such as credit card statements. There is also an increasing volume of business being done over the internet.

The distribution channel for a product affects the product design as well as the pricing and experience of the product. Therefore, the design of a product that aims to address a specific market need may vary depending on its intended distribution channel. Stated another way, a product developed for a specific market need that is successful in one distribution channel may not necessarily be successful in another distribution channel. For example, financial products sold through direct sales must be simpler and easier to understand than products sold through agents. The agent can act as an intermediary and explain the product to the consumer, which permits a more complicated product to be designed.

Another reason that product design is likely to vary by distribution channel is that each such distribution channel has a unique cost structure. For a product to be properly priced, the product must reflect the cost structure of the distribution system.

The final reason that the same product cannot be sold through multiple distribution channels is that each distribution channel will generate different patterns of experience. For example, insurance products sold through direct sales typically will have different patterns of persistency and loss experience than products sold by agents. If these unique persistency and loss patterns are not reflected in the product design and pricing, the risk exposure for the insurance company will be unacceptable.

8.2.2.2   Identify risks and evaluate the ability to mitigate them

Chapter 4 introduced common financial products and Chapter 6 discussed the risks of these products from the providers' standpoint. In the product strategy, the provider must consider the risks involved, its ability to mitigate them, and its ability and willingness to accept the remaining risk.

In Section 8.3.2 below, we will see how stage 2 of the product design process can reduce the risk by contract design. Section 8.4.2 describes how risk can be reduced in stage 3 of the product design process by choosing carefully which business will be accepted. Additionally, risks may be mitigated through internal or external hedging or reinsurance. The ability to hedge a risk at a reasonable cost will lead to offering product design features that the provider would not be willing to offer under other circumstances.

Example 8.2

An example of internal hedging, which is also a form of diversification, would be for a life insurance company to issue both life insurance and immediate annuities. With life insurance, the company will suffer losses if the insured dies more quickly than expected. With annuities, which make payments for as long as the annuitant is alive, the company will suffer a loss if the annuitant lives longer than expected. If overall mortality is heavier than expected, some of the losses encountered on the life insurance would be offset by profits on the annuities. Similarly, if the mortality is less than expected, the gains on the life insurance will help offset the losses on the annuities. While such hedging is very imprecise, these offsets may lead a company to offer both products to take advantage of these offsets.

Exercise 8.1

Why is such hedging imprecise?

Many financial products involve investment risks, which are discussed further below in Section 8.4.4. These risks may be mitigated externally by the use of hedging instruments such as derivatives, or internally by choosing assets that are appropriate for the liabilities. For example, if long-term fixed-interest investments can be bought, a provider may be more willing to offer long-term savings products with a guaranteed interest rate. If no long-term investments exist, the provider will be exposed to the risk that reinvestment will have to be made at lower than expected rates in the future. So the availability of suitable investments influences the product strategy.

An example of external hedging occurs when life insurance companies offer certain guarantees on investment-linked products. For example, a variable (investment-linked) product may provide a guarantee that if the product is held until death, the policyholder will receive a return of at least 5% per annum. This guarantee is typically provided for an additional fee. The fee can be used to purchase derivatives to hedge the risk that the linked investments will return less than 5% per annum. However, there is still risk involved for the provider. If the linked investments lose most of their value, then the fee, which is typically a percent of the assets, will reduce substantially at the same time that the guarantee is "in the money." You might ask why an insurance company would provide such a benefit and expose itself to the additional risk. The answer is that these products have been very popular in the market. Purchasers of variable products now expect these types of guarantees if they purchase the products. This is an example of market needs driving product design.

Example 8.3

Availability of reinsurance often influences product design by insurers. In the 1990s and early 2000s, mortality reinsurance for term life insurance in the US was available at a very low cost. The cost of the reinsurance was so inexpensive that the reinsurance premiums being charged were lower than the mortality costs many insurance companies were expecting to incur. As a result, many insurance companies ceded 80% or 90% of the mortality risk to reinsurers, which mitigated almost all their mortality risk. This influenced product designs in several ways.

- Companies who would not have been willing or able to accept the mortality risk associated with significant volumes of term insurance were able to enter the term insurance market.

- Term insurance products with longer terms were developed. Many companies offered 30-year term products. Some companies even offered 40-year term products. Without reinsurance, it is unlikely that companies would have been willing to offer term products that exceeded 20 years.

- Companies were willing to offer products where the premiums were guaranteed for all years. Once again, since the reinsurance locked in the mortality costs, the risk of providing long-term premium guarantees was minimized.

- Reinsurance companies were pursuing market share aggressively. Therefore, in addition to lower cost, they readily agreed to help direct writing companies to enter the market by sharing mortality experience in the term market. This allowed companies that would have been reluctant to enter the term market, because of their lack of experience data, to enter without significant risk.

8.2.2.3 Identify the resources required and available

Resources include access to sufficient capital and access to experience information.

Capital requirements

You will learn more about the need for capital in later chapters, but for now, suffice it to say that when an insurance company issues an insurance product, it will need capital to finance the initial expenses until they are recouped from premiums, and to absorb unexpected losses. So for every product that the insurance company sells, it needs to have some capital to support the product. The same applies for most financial providers. For example, a bank has to have capital to support each mortgage loan it provides to a borrower, to absorb larger than expected losses from default.

The amount of capital needed will be larger for products that involve more risk, and for those with heavy initial expenses that are recouped slowly. For particular products, there may also be regulations that require the amount of additional capital set aside to be very high. The need to provide the extra capital will result in a higher price to the insured (in order to provide a return on the capital) or a lower profit for the provider. Therefore, capital requirements encourage product designs that find a way around these issues.

Exercise 8.2

Which of the following products requires more capital and why?

- Non-participating life insurance versus participating life insurance.

- Private motor vehicle insurance versus product liability insurance.

- Loans to commercial property developers versus loans to government agencies.

Example 8.4

A provider may be able to meet its capital needs externally. During the 1990s and 2000s, the capital requirements in the US for universal life with secondary guarantees[1] were specified by certain formulas. In many cases, insurance companies felt that these requirements were too strict and led to excessive capital requirements. While the company could minimize the impact of these requirements through product design, many insurance companies used a combination of reinsurance and financial markets to reduce the capital requirements. For example, the insurance company ceded the business to a reinsurer who was not a US company, and therefore not subject to the same capital requirements. However, in order for the direct writing company to reduce the amount of capital required and still satisfy the regulator, the reinsurance company had to provide collateral. This was often done using letters of credit as collateral. These letters of credit were relatively cheap and lowered the cost of these secondary guarantees. However, in the second half of 2008 the credit markets constricted significantly. Letters of credit became much more expensive. This increased the cost of these secondary guarantees that the insurance companies had sold. This example illustrates the risk of offering certain product designs without the ability to lock in appropriate hedges.

---

[1] A universal life contract without a secondary guarantee remains in force, even if premiums cease or are less than the charges for death cover and expenses, for as long as the account value or surrender value remains positive. A universal life contract with a secondary guarantee will remain in force, ie will pay the sum insured in the event of death, even if the account value or surrender value is negative, provided that some specified minimum amount of total premiums has been paid.

Company experience

The prior experience that a company has with a product will influence product design in two ways.

First, if a company has significant experience with a given product, then it will be able to estimate more reliably the costs of various potential options and features it might include.

Secondly, the company is likely to know the perceived value in the marketplace of any additional features. The perceived value will be a function of both the value to the agent selling the product as well as the value to the ultimate consumer. Therefore, the product design will be influenced by the trade-off between the actual cost and the perceived value: the ideal extra design feature from the company's point of view is one that costs very little but that the customer perceives as being very valuable.

When a company has limited or no experience with a product, the company must use industry data, if it is available. If industry data is not available, then product design decisions will reflect the company's best estimate of expected experience. Decisions based on industry experience or best estimates contain more risks as experience usually varies considerably by markets, by distribution system, and by administrative or claim practices.

Exercise 8.3

Read the paper "Innovation in Retirement Incomes" on the CD. After you have read this paper, answer the following questions:

(a) Discuss the specific market being targeted and the distribution channel being discussed.

(b) Discuss the risks being addressed by the retirement income products from the consumer standpoint.

(c) Discuss the risks from the standpoint of the provider.

(d) Discuss how this paper identifies the need for a new product or product design as discussed in 8.2.1.

8.3 Stage 2 of the product design control cycle

We are now at the stage of developing the product. In this section we discuss:

* the concept of project management;

* how the design of the product can affect the risks we discussed above in 8.2.2.2;

* how design takes account of competition and the marketplace, including the pricing process;

* meeting the expectations of all stakeholders; and

* the decision whether to launch and the various assumptions that will be required.

8.3.1 Project management

Design of a new product in any industry is a major project with significant implications and costs for the company. Therefore, project management principles should be followed in most product design projects. Project management includes:

- development of objectives and expectations for the project;

- ongoing evaluation of the financial implications of the project;

- development of a timeline for each step of the project;

- assignment of responsibilities for each step of the project; and

- ongoing monitoring of progress with communication between all parties.

8.3.1.1   Develop objectives and expectations for the project

Before beginning any project, it is important to understand and articulate the objectives and expectations of the project. The objectives and expectations of all stakeholders need to be identified and agreed upon by all principals involved in the project, and communicated to all parties working on the project.

8.3.1.2   Financial implications of the project

The financial viability of the project must be evaluated. This is not a one-time process, but must be done on an ongoing basis as the project progresses. Additional information will continue to become available throughout the project. If at any time the project is no longer financially viable, then the project should be stopped at that point.

Various methods are used to evaluate the financial viability of a project. Some methods use quantitative analysis based on known or expected cash flows or profits. Many times, there are benefits or costs that are difficult to quantify. In these circumstances a more subjective approach is often used to supplement the quantitative analysis. For example, a cost-benefit analysis can be completed. Such an analysis may be as simple as comparing lists of the positives and negatives of the project. A more sophisticated and less subjective approach is to put a financial value on the positives and negatives and include those financial values in the quantitative analysis. Finally, real option theory is another method that could be used.

8.3.1.3   Timeline, responsibility, and communication

A major project is often overwhelming due to its size and scope. Project management takes the overall project and breaks it down into small tasks that are more manageable. The interdependencies of the various tasks must also be specified. Once these smaller steps are identified, then specific target dates for each task are assigned keeping in mind the overall time frame for the entire project. The smaller tasks within the project are assigned to specific individuals who are responsible to ensure that the task is completed within the time frame. The project manager has overall responsibility for monitoring each smaller task to assure that it is completed on time.

Frequent communication between all parties involved in the project is required for a successful project. The communication will identify tasks that have been completed. This is important as recognition that those responsible have met their objective. It also allows those responsible for tasks that are dependent on the completed task to know they can now start their task. Just as importantly, the ongoing communication must identify tasks that have not met the timeline and identify those that are responsible. This allows those involved to address missed deadlines and seek solutions to allow the project to get back on schedule. While many times the delay is beyond the control of the individual responsible for that task, this communication also acts as a strong incentive for all participants to complete their tasks on time. If they do not, they know that they cannot escape responsibility. No one wants to be identified as having let down a group of peers by not completing his or her job.

8.3.2 Design features to control risks

In Section 8.2.2.2, we discussed some resources that may mitigate risks, and enable products to be sold that would otherwise be too risky for the provider. The provider can also control the risks it accepts by careful product design.

For general insurance, products often contain a deductible or a coinsurance so that the insured shares in the risk with the provider. With a deductible or coinsurance, the insured will pay a portion of any loss suffered along with the provider. These features align the interest of the insured with the interest of the provider and prevent a situation under which the insured could actually benefit from suffering a loss. Deductibles also provide administrative savings by discouraging trivially small claims.

As another example, a life insurance policy insures the policyholder against the risk of early death. However, an insurance company cannot insure all risk of early death. If the applicant for insurance is ill and expected to die shortly, then the insurance company cannot accept this risk. The fact that the insured would be highly motivated to purchase insurance to the detriment of the company is called *adverse selection*. Therefore, the insurance company must control the risks that it accepts. The company typically controls the risk through the use of underwriting, which is discussed in 8.4.2. However, some life insurance products are sold without underwriting or with very limited underwriting. When this is the case, the insurance company could remove the risk of early death claims by including a policy condition stating that the policy will not pay a death benefit during the first two years. This would be an example of controlling the risk through product design.

Of course, there are limits as to the ability of the insurance company to control or eliminate risk in product design. First, there may be legal or regulatory restrictions. However, more importantly, if the product design is such that reasonable risks are not transferred to the insurance company, then the insurance company will be unable to sell its products.

In the above example, it is reasonable for an insurance company to eliminate the risk of paying out on early death when that death is foreseeable (eg the insured is in very poor health). However, if the insurance company eliminated all risk of payments on early death, it is unlikely that the potential policyholders would be interested in the policy. It is therefore usual that a policy that does not pay out on early death from illness will pay out on early death resulting from an accident.

Exercise 8.4

The table below lists some examples of product risks and design features that are used to control risk. For each feature, explain how it can work to control risk.

Products	Risks	Product Options
Life insurance (risk products and savings products)	• Investment • Mortality • Expense • Lapse	• Limited death benefit in early years • Non-guaranteed premiums • Non-guaranteed expense or mortality charges • Surrender charges • Market-value-adjusted surrender values • Investment-linked • Participating or with profits
General insurance	• Severity • Frequency • Investment	• Short term contracts • Experience refunds • Deductibles and coinsurance • Maximum benefits

---

8.3.3　Competition, the marketplace, and the pricing process

Product design cannot be done in a vacuum. You need to take account of what is happening in the marketplace. The pricing process will also have regard to what your competitors are doing.

8.3.3.1　Pricing the product

Pricing a product is both an art and a science. Pricing must consider the cost of producing a product. This is generally the science part of pricing. If a physical product is to be manufactured, cost accounting methods can be used to identify the costs of producing the product. To the manufacturing costs, distribution costs and profit margins are added to arrive at an initial cost.

If the product is an insurance product, a similar approach is used. However, the "manufacturing costs" are not as easily measured and are generally quantified using an actuarial model. Often more than one actuarial model can be used to develop the costs associated with an insurance product, so the first task is to identify the appropriate model to use. Additionally, the assumptions and inputs into the model often are subjective and determined using actuarial judgment. Therefore, the cost of "manufacturing" an insurance product is generally determined with less precision than the cost of a physical product. As with the physical product, the company still has to incorporate the distribution costs and profit margins.

Pricing must consider the cost of similar or identical products being offered by competitors. If there are identical products being sold by several companies, these products are generally considered to be commodities and will compete primarily on price. There may be other factors considered such as the financial strength of the manufacturer, but these are usually secondary. For example, a consumer loan is usually considered a commodity because the primary, if not only differentiating factor, is the price (interest rate) on the loan. On the other hand, if a product has features that differentiate it from its competitors, price competitiveness, while still important, will not be as critical.

Determining the final price at which to sell your product is often an art, and involves many factors of which the manufacturing costs and competition are just two. The reason for calling this an art is because the determination of the final price often involves considerable subjectivity. Of course, the final price must be consistent with the product strategy.

Modeling is discussed further in Chapter 9 and pricing of products is discussed in detail in Chapter 13.

8.3.3.2   Competition and the marketplace

Competition and the marketplace have a strong influence on product design. In designing a product for any industry, knowing the design of competing products is critical. If a competitor is offering product designs that are in demand, it will be difficult to compete without similar features.

Example 8.5

The downside of competitive pressures can be seen in the financial crisis that began in 2007. From 2000 to 2003, certain mortgage loan providers offered mortgage loans to borrowers who did not meet conventional credit assessment standards. These loans were known as *subprime* loans. As a result of competition, other mortgage lenders also entered this market and subprime mortgages became readily available. By 2006, these loans were 25% of the mortgage market in the US.

These loans were often packaged and sold in the secondary market. Many financial institutions purchased these subprime mortgages as investments. These investments paid a higher return assuming default experience was in line with recent experience. Once again, because competitors were purchasing these subprime loans in a securitized form, companies that were initially not very comfortable with the risks associated with the mortgages began to purchase mortgages as assets in order to achieve the higher purported return.

However, in 2007 and 2008, a high level of defaults began to occur in the subprime mortgages. This caused major losses to occur within the firms holding the mortgages, even in tranches that had been rated AAA. Further, it resulted in a significant tightening of credit in the financial markets and helped to facilitate a worldwide recession.

Understanding the needs of the marketplace will provide the opportunity to earn additional market share. Apple has consistently demonstrated the ability to understand the needs of the marketplace, and sometimes this understanding has resulted in significant market share. One example of success was discussed above with the iPod; another example is the iPhone.

8.3.4   Stakeholder expectations

In the product design process, the interests and expectations of the various *stakeholders* must be considered. The stakeholders are all the parties who have a financial or psychological interest in the product design. Clearly, the provider designing the product and the potential consumer of the product will be stakeholders. In addition, there may be several other parties who have a direct or indirect interest in the product such as:

- retailers, who will make a profit by selling the product; and

- government, who will be interested in the safety of the product even if the product is not directly regulated.

The interests and expectations of each stakeholder play an important role in product design. The interests and expectations of different stakeholders are often in conflict. Sometimes there are conflicting interests even within a single stakeholder.

8.3.4.1   The provider

The provider, as a stakeholder, consists of different parties such as stockholders, members of the board, and employees. Many of the interests of these parties are aligned. For example, all parties want the company to be profitable. The stockholders and the board clearly benefit from the company's profitability. However, the employees also benefit directly or indirectly. The employees may benefit directly if their compensation is related to profitability. Even if it is not, the employees still benefit, as without profits, the company will not remain in business and the employees will no longer be employed.

For insurance companies, the expectations include:

- Products will be designed to be profitable.

- Product design will eliminate, hedge or diversify risks that cannot be managed or mitigated.

- Product design will consider administrative requirements.

- Product design will consider the interests of the other stakeholders.

Exercise 8.5

Why does product design need to consider administrative requirements?

The interests of various departments within a company often appear to be in conflict. For example, let's look at the interests of the marketing department versus the actuarial department. The marketing department is responsible for selling the products of the company, and its compensation is often tied directly to sales. In order to accomplish their charge (and maximize their compensation), members of the marketing department want the most competitive premiums with the best product design.

On the other hand, the actuarial department is responsible for the profitability of the products and its compensation may be based on profitability (and will seldom be based on sales). Therefore, it wants to maximize profits (requiring higher premiums) and sell product designs that minimize risk, which means the designs may not be as rich in features and guarantees as some others in the market.

In reality, these conflicts between departments result in a healthy discussion and are resolved through compromise. The marketing department realizes that in the long run, products must provide a reasonable profit, so a design with unreasonably low premiums, or that accepts unmanageable risks, is not in its best interest. Similarly, the actuarial department knows that a product must sell for the company to make a profit, so uncompetitive premiums and product designs are not acceptable.

8.3.4.2   The consumers

The consumers of products expect that the product will perform as expected. The expectations are based on the stated functionality and the advertising used to market the product.

The policyholders of an insurance company have certain expectations. Among those expectations are:

- The product design will not be misrepresented in the sales process.
- The company will be able to provide the benefits promised by the contract.
- The company will provide reasonable service over the life of the policy.
- The product will provide a reasonable relationship between benefits and cost.
- Product design will consider the interests of the other stakeholders.

8.3.4.3   Retailers

The retailers of products expect that the products will be competitive from both price and quality standpoints with other products in the market. They expect the product to be safe and to perform as expected. They also expect the provider to back up the product with service and warranties if there are any problems with the product.

For insurance companies, the retailer is the company's distribution system. Among the expectations of the distribution system are:

- The company will provide a product that competes well in the marketplace.
- The company will be able to provide the benefits promised by the contract.
- The company will provide reasonable service in supporting the sales process and to the policyholder over the life of the policy.
- The product will provide a reasonable relationship between benefits and cost.
- Product design will consider the interests of the other stakeholders.

8.3.4.4   The regulators

The final stakeholder we will discuss is the government and its agencies, which will be referred to as regulators. Some products are highly regulated while other products are not subject to specific regulation. For all products, the regulators have certain expectations such as safety. Additionally, the regulators will expect the product to comply with any general laws and regulations. For products that are regulated, there will be laws and regulations that apply directly to those products.

Insurance companies are highly regulated and the regulator plays an important role in product design. The regulator's responsibility is to:

- assure the financial stability of the insurance company for the benefit of the policyholders;
- protect the consumer from misleading or improper marketing methods; and
- prohibit misleading or financially irresponsible product designs.

Among the expectations of the regulator are:

- The product will comply with applicable laws, rules and regulations.
- The product design will not be misrepresented in the sales process.
- The company will be able to provide the benefits promised by the contract.
- The company will provide reasonable service over the life of the policy.
- The product will provide a reasonable relationship between benefits and cost.
- Product design will consider the interests of the other stakeholders.

Exercise 8.6

For each stakeholder, we have stated that they expect the interests of other stakeholders to be considered. Why?

8.3.5   Deciding whether to launch the product

At each point in the stage of developing the product, the company should make a conscious decision to continue the development process. At the completion of this stage, the company must decide whether it will actually launch the product. In making these decisions, the company will consider questions such as:

- Do we still believe that this product will address a market need?
- What will be the costs (production, distribution, capital, etc)?
- How many products will be sold?
- What price will purchasers be willing to pay?
- What is the best distribution system for the product?
- Does it meet profit objectives?

If at any point in the development process the company believes that it cannot produce a competitive product that will generate an acceptable profit,[2] then the company should stop development.

8.4   Stage 3 of the product design control cycle

The third stage involves the manufacture and distribution of the product. For financial products, there are generally three steps within this stage:

---

[2] Note that the "acceptable profit" may be a loss. A company may decide to issue an unprofitable product if it contributes to the overall company strategy, for example as a loss leader to capture market share and lead to sales of other, profitable, products. Obviously the company has to be careful. The important point is that the company will have expectations from the product, and will stop development if it believes these expectations cannot be met.

- distributing the product to clients;

- selecting the acceptable risks; and

- administering the product and managing the assets and liabilities that result from selling the product.

8.4.1 Distributing the product to our clients

We have discussed the possible channels of distribution above in 8.2.2.1. Now we will look at the process more closely.

Potential customers have to be moved to buy the product. The first step of this process is to develop documentation that specifies what the product is, ie to draft the contract and sales material. The second step is marketing to the customers, whether by using intermediaries in the distribution channel, by advertising of various forms, or a combination.

8.4.1.1 Contract and Sales Material

For financial products, the product is a contract (policy) that the provider enters into with the consumer. The wording of the contract specifies the agreement between the parties to the contract. In the case of insurance, the insurance policy states the obligations of the company and the policyholder. The policy will state the exact circumstances under which the insurance company is obligated to make a payment. It will also state the financial obligations of the policyholder such as the obligation to pay premiums on a timely basis. The contract will also lay out the non-financial obligations of the parties. For example, the policyholder is obligated to notify the insurance company of any claim within a certain time frame. Similarly, once notified of a claim, the insurance company has a stated time to determine if the claim is valid and to pay the claim if it is valid.

Actuaries as well as lawyers are generally involved in the writing of the insurance contract. The wording of the contract is very important as the contract will be a primary determinant of the obligations of each party. Clear and concise language is critical. In the case of disputes, the parties will refer to the contract language. If the language is ambiguous, then the contract may be interpreted by the courts to require payment by one of the parties that was not intended, and that was not considered when setting the price for the product.

In addition to clear and concise language delineating the obligations of each party, an insurance policy is also subject to regulatory requirements. The insurance laws and regulations of each jurisdiction[3] where the policy will be sold must be reflected in the policy. In most cases, prior to sale of a new product, the generic insurance policy must be approved by the regulatory officials. This approval process confirms that the policy meets the laws and regulations of the regulatory jurisdiction. The regulatory review process is not intended to verify that the product language is clear and concise.

However, most of the time, the customer purchases financial products based on an illustration provided and the representations made by the company's agent in addition to the contract. In reality, the customer rarely sees the contract prior to making a decision

---

[3] Regulatory jurisdiction varies by country. In most countries, there is a single national regulatory body. In other countries, there are multiple regulatory bodies. For example, in the US, each state regulates the insurance products sold in that state.

to buy. Many times the illustrations and representations are as important as the contract. Therefore the advertising material, including illustrations, needs to be clear and to fully disclose the limitations of the financial product as well as the benefits.

For products that do not provide guarantees, the policyholder may not understand that benefits shown are not guaranteed. The agent and the company must be careful to explain fully which benefits are guaranteed and which are contingent upon current experience continuing. In the US and the UK, there have been many legal cases involving the deceptive and misleading marketing of insurance products. In the UK, with-profit endowments were sold as repayment vehicles for house mortgages on the assumption that the bonuses would be at levels that seemed reasonable in the 1980s. After a period of low investment returns, many of those policies matured with payouts that were not sufficient to repay the mortgage. In the US, universal life products sold in the 1980s were often sold under the assumption that premiums could be discontinued after they were paid for five to ten years. The assumption was that high interest rates would continue and the excess investment earnings would be enough that additional premiums would not be necessary. However, as interest returns dropped, continuing premiums were required and numerous lawsuits were instigated. The article "'Vanishing Premium' Litigation: the Plaintiff's Perspective" on the CD provides more details.

The law regulating insurance companies in the UK requires that companies have regard to *Policyholders' Reasonable Expectations* (PRE). However, there is no definition of PRE in the legislation. PRE has generally been considered to be what the policyholder could reasonably expect to receive based on:

- the contract;

- illustrations and representations made at the point of sales;

- actual experience with regard to investments, mortality, etc;

- the company's stated philosophy with regard to bonuses or dividends;

- the history and past practice of the company; and

- standard practice within the insurance industry.

PRE should also include fair and equitable distribution of profits among cohorts of policyholders as well as to stockholders.

Given that PRE is not defined by law and is a somewhat nebulous concept, it will eventually be clarified by case law. The concept of PRE was the centerpiece of a lawsuit in the Equitable (UK) case that is discussed in "The End of the Equitable" on the CD.

Keeton (1970) put forth the *Doctrine of Reasonable Expectations* with regard to insurance contracts in the US. The concept has been the justification for court decisions in the US. The concept is similar to that of PRE.

Actuaries are generally charged with assuring, to the extent within their control, that PRE is met once the policy is issued. There is guidance in actuarial standards of practice and guidance notes.

While the discussion with regard to PRE has centered on participating (with-profit) policies, the concept can be applied to all policies. For example, policyholders develop expectations with regard to the redetermination of premiums on in-force policies such as term policies. In the US, universal life policies have non-guaranteed elements such as interest rates credited and mortality and expense charges. Companies should be aware of policyholder expectations when changing these non-guaranteed elements.

The bottom line is that the contract, the illustration, other point-of-sale marketing material and the representations made by the company's agent all form the policyholders' expectations. Therefore, it is important that appropriate resources are devoted to developing a contract and sales literature that are clear and concise. Additionally, the marketing representatives of the company must be properly trained and supervised to prevent mis-selling or misrepresentation.

Exercise 8.7

The suitability of financial products for a particular consumer is another important aspect of marketing financial products. Identify at least three suitability issues. Describe each issue.

8.4.1.2 Marketing

As discussed in 8.2.2.1, the choice of distribution channel affects product design in various ways. If a company uses intermediaries, the type of intermediary will also influence product design and cost. For example, when a company markets through brokers, it is competing with all other companies represented by that broker. In order for the broker to pick a particular company's product, the product or company must provide an advantage to the broker. The advantage can take one of four forms:

*   the product is superior for the consumer because it provides a lower price or better benefits or service;

*   the product provides higher compensation to the broker;

*   the company provides superior service to the broker; or

*   the company has superior financial strength or reputation.

The distribution channel will also affect the quality and quantity of the product sold. Companies can try to influence the quantity of sales by recruiting more intermediaries or by increasing advertising for direct marketing. However, depending on the distribution channel, the success of such a strategy may be limited. For example, if a company markets through sole agents, there is a significant period of time between the agent being hired and when he or she becomes productive. As mentioned in Chapter 5, sole agents are extensively trained by the company and may have other jobs. Therefore, no increase in sales will occur until the new agent is trained. Furthermore, hiring and training new sole agents involves substantial upfront expense which is only repaid over time. On the other hand, the sole agent sells for just one company so the success of the company is important to the long-term success of the agent. Therefore, the sole agent will often produce a high quality of business.

We can contrast this situation with a company using brokers. The cost to a company of a broker is generally just the commissions that are paid on business sold. Therefore, if the company recruits more brokers to sell its products, sales will go up and there will be no disproportional increase in costs. Additionally, since the brokers are generally experienced sellers of the product, they can begin selling products immediately. Offsetting this advantage is the fact that brokers represent many companies. They will only sell a company's product if there is a reason for them to do so. Additionally, brokers are not tied exclusively to one company so their interests do not necessarily align with the interests of the company. Therefore, the quality of the business that is generated by brokers may be inferior to that of sole agents.

When products are sold through direct marketing, sales are clearly linked to advertising costs or number of contacts (eg number of direct mailings or telemarketing calls). Even when sales are through intermediaries, advertising directly influences sales. Advertising is often used to generate leads for the intermediaries. Additionally, advertising often aims to raise brand awareness which helps to increase the number of sales. Finally, through advertising a company can target certain markets. For example, advertising during a family television show targets the middle income family market whereas advertising during a financial news show targets an upper income market.

The concepts in this section have been discussed primarily from the standpoint of a financial services firm. However, the concepts apply to non-financial products as well. For example, Firestone tires are sold by Firestone stores (sole agents) as well as tire stores that represent multiple tire manufacturers (brokers). If Firestone wants to increase sales, it can open more Firestone stores. However, this is expensive as it must build the store and train employees prior to any sales. Additionally, there will be a lag prior to new sales as the store is built and employees trained. Alternatively, Firestone can convince additional tire stores to carry its tires. This should result in immediate additional sales as these are established stores. However, it may be expensive as the independent tire stores would want incentives to sell Firestone tires. Another approach would be to seek a greater share of tire sales from independent stores by reducing price or by advertising to end-customers so that they seek out Firestone.

Just as a financial services company can influence sales with advertising, so can other firms. For example, if Firestone wants to encourage the sale of high-performance tires (high-performance tires have higher profit margins), it will target advertising to certain markets. For example, sponsorship of racing teams and events will target auto-racing fans, who tend to buy more high-performance tires.

8.4.2   Risk selection

Risk selection is a primary tool used to mitigate certain risks identified above. Risk selection is used to control risks including:

- mortality risk on life insurance products;
- severity and frequency risk for general insurance; and
- credit risk on loans.

Risk selection (also often called *underwriting*) is the process that insurance companies and lenders use to differentiate between the risks that they are willing to accept and those that they are not willing to accept. Additionally, risk selection is used to classify and determine the price for those risks that are accepted.

Risk selection for loans involves evaluating the credit risk. This generally consists of an evaluation of the creditworthiness of the borrower as well as the value of any collateral for the loan. The creditworthiness of the borrower is evaluated based on past credit history (often represented by a credit score), income, wealth, and other credit obligations. The lender may also require an appraisal of the collateral used to back the loan such as an independent appraisal of the house upon which a mortgage is being taken.

The process of risk selection for insurance will vary with the type of cover, as discussed further below. However, for all types of insurance, the process will check for *insurable interest* and will probably involve *financial underwriting*.

Insurable interest means that the person buying insurance will suffer a loss if the insured event occurs. Usually the loss will be financial, but in the case of life insurance, the loss can be an emotional one, so that for certain family relationships, an insurable interest for life insurance is presumed. For example, a parent is assumed to have an insurable interest in a child. For long-term life insurance, insurable interest must exist only at the time of application. For example, a husband has an insurable interest in his wife and can purchase a life insurance policy with the wife as the insured and the husband as the beneficiary. The policy can be continued even if the two are subsequently divorced.

Financial underwriting means verifying that the amount of insurance being bought is reasonable relative to the potential loss. For example, for property insurance, the amount of coverage sold should not exceed the value of the property, as otherwise the owner of the property could be financially motivated to destroy the property and profit as a result.

Each type of insurance product also has specific forms of underwriting. For example, risk selection for life insurance involves evaluating the health of the proposed insured. When a person applies for life insurance, he or she will usually have to complete an application form that will ask a series of questions about that applicant's current and previous health, and may also ask about any dangerous hobbies or activities. Also as part of the underwriting process, insurance companies may seek additional health information. For example, the insurance company may contact the applicant's doctor or require the applicant to submit a blood or urine sample to test for diseases or drug or nicotine use. Additionally, if the amount of insurance being applied for is large enough, the insurance company may require the applicant to have a physical examination by a doctor of the insurance company's choosing. All of these tools are used to segment the applicants into those that the company is willing to insure at standard rates, those that it is willing to insure but only at rates that are higher than standard, and those that it is not willing to insure at any rate.

Exercise 8.8

The application form for life insurance will often ask if the applicant's parents and siblings are still alive. Also, if they are deceased, the application form will ask for the cause of death. Why would such information be used in risk selection?

As another example, premium rates for automobile insurance generally vary by factors such as the type and age of automobile, age of driver, miles driven each year, number and severity of traffic violations, where the owner lives, and whether the automobile is garaged or parked on the street. The risk selection process will also look at an applicant's past claims and accident history to determine if insurance coverage will be offered and at what rates. An applicant with recent accidents will be charged a higher premium than an applicant with no recent accidents. Actually, if the applicant's accident history is bad enough, the insurance company will decline to offer coverage.

Through risk selection, insurance companies are able to stratify risks so that similar risks are grouped together and charged the same premium. This stratification prevents excessive cross-subsidization between different risk groups.

On the other hand, it can be argued that the primary purpose of insurance is to facilitate subsidization through the pooling of risk. In other words, insurance is of value because it allows risk to be diversified or shared across a group of insureds. Stratification reduces the extent of risk sharing, and can make insurance prohibitively expensive for high-risk individuals. For an interesting alternative viewpoint to the above discussion on risk classification, you are encouraged to read "Some Novel Perspectives on Risk Classification" on the CD. This article argues that:

• From a public policy standpoint, adverse selection is not really adverse.

• Theoretical models of risk classification may exaggerate the significance of adverse selection.

• There are psychological perspectives on decision-making that explain why phenomena predicted by adverse selection models are often difficult to observe.

• Risk classification at times promotes policies that are contrary to public policy involving the same cohort of individuals.

8.4.3 Administration of the product

For products in the financial services arena, once the product has been sold, the company must still administer the product. This is unlike most other products where once the product is sold, other than warranty or liability claims, the producing company no longer needs to worry about the product. For insurance products (and most other products sold by financial services companies), the company must continue to service the product for its remaining lifetime.

For loans, administration includes sending notices of payments due on a periodic basis. This requires maintaining current information about the customer such as address. Once the borrower has made all the payments, the lender must release the collateral. Additionally, if the borrower defaults then the lender must enter legal proceedings to collect overdue payments or to foreclose on the collateral. If the lender becomes the owner of the collateral, then there are many additional administrative responsibilities that are assumed until the lender sells the collateral.

For insurance products, administration includes collection of premiums, payment of claims, maintaining current information on the policyholder (such as address for billing purposes and beneficiary in the case of life insurance), calculation and maintenance of reserves (a purely actuarial function), as well as many other functions.

Proper administration of products of financial services companies is critical to the long-term profits of these products. For example, if the company does not provide good service, then persistency of the product is likely to be impacted. Policyholders are more likely to lapse their policy if they feel that they are not receiving good service. Additionally, if the company does not pay the correct amount on claims, there will be considerable ill will. Further, if the company overpays the claims, it is unlikely that it will be able to recover the overpayments. Finally, even if the company makes claims payments that are for the correct amount, but does not pay claims on a timely basis, the company can be subject to regulatory actions (including significant fines) as well as policyholder lawsuits.

The administrative needs of a product must be considered in the product design process. We discussed in 8.2.1.5 that market research can confirm that your company has the resources necessary to meet the market need. One of the necessary resources is the ability of the company to administer the product being designed. If the company does not have the administrative capability necessary for a product then the administrative capability must be developed or the product should not be designed. It is highly preferable to develop the administrative capability prior to designing the product. For example, there is no need to consider design of a variable or unit-linked product if the company's administrative system does not have the ability to determine product values based on unit prices.

8.4.4 Asset-liability management

An institution that issues financial products will end up with both liabilities and assets. These must be managed in a coordinated way. It is essential to have a strategy for asset-liability management throughout the lifetime of the product, from the very beginning of the product design process.

For example, when an insurance company sets insurance premiums, it will make assumptions about the rate of return it will achieve by investing those premiums until claims are paid. If it assumes a rate of return of 5% per annum, say, then it must have an investment strategy that will ensure, to an acceptable level of certainty, that it can earn at least 5% per annum and that the investments can be converted to cash when it is time to pay claims.

Similarly, when a bank makes a loan, it must have a financing strategy that provides an acceptable level of certainty about continued access to funds at a cost that is less than the interest rate it can charge on the loan.

The process of asset-liability management is described in more detail in Chapter 14.

8.5 Stage 4 of the product design control cycle

The final stage involves gathering and monitoring experience. This step is important for any product, but it is particularly important for financial products such as insurance. Further, as indicated in the introduction to this chapter, this fourth stage often leads to the next product design cycle, as it can identify the need for a new or modified product. Furthermore, it will even more frequently identify that changes to the pricing of the product are necessary.

The process of monitoring experience is discussed in detail in Chapter 17.

8.6 Practical implications for actuaries

When advising a company on product design, the actuary must ensure that the provider understands the risks and the implications for capital requirements. The actuary may have professional responsibility to other stakeholders in the product design, and can be placed in a position of an arbitrator between the conflicting interests of the various stakeholders.

In 8.4.1 above we saw that insurance policies sometimes give the provider some discretion over the distribution of future profits or other non-guaranteed elements. Professional standards may place a responsibility on the actuary to ensure that these discretions are exercised in a way that treats the customers fairly. The actuary should consider, as part of the product design process, whether this can be managed practically over the life of the policy.

Actuaries will often be involved in drafting illustrative material, including projections of possible benefits. It is essential that any assumptions are reasonable and that the illustrations are not misleading. It is important that the customers understand that an illustration is subject to uncertainty, and the actuary should consider how to convey an idea of the level of uncertainty.

It will often be the responsibility of the actuary to provide accurate information to regulators who will review and approve the product being designed. If the actuary intentionally provides inaccurate or misleading information to the regulators, he or she will be subject to disciplinary action.

Finally, the actuary must document the work carried out in the product design. Professional standards require full and complete documentation of work done. For many actuaries, having the discipline to document one's work once the project is completed in other aspects is difficult. However, this is critically important and not just because it is a professional responsibility. Documentation serves as a roadmap to the work done and often provides a shortcut in the development of similar products. Documentation also permits other actuaries to utilize the work that was completed.

8.7   Key learning points

- Product design is a cycle within a cycle with stages being:
  - Stage 1: Identify the need for a new (or modified) product and develop a product strategy.
  - Stage 2: Develop the product.
  - Stage 3: Manufacture and distribute the product.
  - Stage 4: Gather and monitor experience.
- A new product can be identified through:
  - innovation;
  - response to changes in regulation or tax law changes;
  - entry into new market or distribution system;
  - updating product for relevant experience; and
  - market research.
- A product strategy is critical to the success of a product. Among other items, the product design must consider the company's distribution method, the risks of the product and mitigation techniques, and the resources necessary.
- Project management helps to achieve a successful product design by developing expectations and objectives; establishing financial objectives, timelines and responsibilities; and facilitating communication.
- Product design can be used to control risk.
- Competition and the marketplace must be considered in product design.

- Product design must consider stakeholders' expectations. Stakeholders include the provider, the customers, the distributors, and the regulators.

- Once the product has been designed, it must be manufactured and distributed. This involves distributing to the client using acceptable sales material and contract documentation, and selecting appropriate risks.

- Once the product has been sold, the provider must administer it, manage the assets and liabilities that result, and gather and analyze experience to determine if product design changes are necessary. These requirements must be taken into account in the initial design process.

- During the product design cycle, the actuary must always keep in mind the actuary's professional responsibilities.

These stages form the product design control cycle. The product design control cycle applies to all products. Additionally, while most of our discussion was around financial services products, most of the concepts discussed in this chapter are applicable to any industry.

CD Items

Ahmad, H. 2009, Takaful, *Actuary Australia*, August, pp. 8-10.

Bakos, T. & Hamann, B. 2007, Product Patents and their Impact on the Life Insurance Industry, Society of Actuaries Annual Meeting, Washington DC.

Ferris, S. 2001, The End of the Equitable, *Actuary Australia*, March, pp. 12-13.

Heyman, L. & Hickey, J. 2007, Innovation in Retirement Incomes, Institute of Actuaries of Australia, Biennial Convention, Christchurch, New Zealand.

Loh, M. & Gosden, M. 2007, Variable Annuities, *The Actuary*, June, Staple Inn Actuarial Society, London.

Phillips, R. 1996, 'Vanishing Premium' Litigation: The Plaintiff's Perspective, Presentation for the Mississippi Bar Summer School for Lawyers, July 9, http://www.smithphillips.com.

Thomas, R. G. 2007, Some Novel Perspectives on Risk Classification, *The Geneva Papers*, 32, The International Association for the Study of Insurance Economics, pp. 105-132.

Chapter 8 Exercise Solutions

References (other than CD Items)

Bakos, T. 2009, Lincoln National Wins $13M Jury Verdict in GMWB Patent Lawsuit, www.insurancenewsnet.com/article.asp?a=top_news&id=103773, accessed November 7, 2009.

Brown, R. L. & Gottlieb, L. R. 2007, *Introduction to Ratemaking and Loss Reserving for Property and Casualty Insurance*, Third Edition, Actex Publications Inc, Winsted, CT.

Chrysler minivan history – Dodge Caravan, Plymouth Voyager, and Others. Allpar has Dodge, Chrysler, Plymouth, and Jeep car, minivan and truck information, http://www.allpar.com/model/m/history.html, accessed March 20, 2009.

Jones, H. 2005, *Principles of Insurance: Life, Health, and Annuities*, Third Edition, LOMA.

Keeton, R. 1970, Insurance Law Rights at Variance with Policy Provisions: Parts One and Two, *Harvard Law Review*, 83, 961 and 1281, Harvard Law Review Association, Cambridge, MA.

Knox, D. 2002, Policyholder Reasonable Expectations and Consumer Responsibilities, Session 5.2, July 2002 Training Course, The Australian APEC Study Centre.

McDonald, R. L. 2006, *Derivatives Markets*, Second Edition, Pearson Education, Addison-Wesley, Boston, MA.

Pentz, M. C. & Evans, J. A. M. 2008, United States, Insurance and Transport, How To Avoid Getting Whacked By The Doctrine Of Reasonable Expectations – Foley Hoag LLP – 10/11/2008 11:39:01, Insurance, *Articles on All Regions, Law, Accountancy, Management Consultancy Issues*, http://www.mondaq.com/article.asp?articleid=60776, accessed March 25, 2009.

Vaaler, L. J. F. & Daniel, J. W. 2009, *Mathematical Interest Theory*, Second Edition, MAA Textbooks, Washington DC.

Fred's Coffee Shop – Modeling

Fred is very familiar with actuarial models, so he appreciates the value of models in decision-making.

At this stage, Fred has done lots of thinking and research about his planned coffee shop. He probably has a fairly clear idea of how he wants to proceed. Before he does so, however, he should build a model to help him to understand the implications of his decision.

Fred knows that his model won't be entirely accurate – indeed, it is likely to be highly simplified – but it must have sufficient detail to help him to decide whether it is worth investing his savings in this venture. And after the shop opens, his model may help him to monitor its success.

Before you read on, stop and think about Fred's model. What does he need to test?

Fred will have both financial and non-financial objectives. Ideally, he will have set these out in a *business plan*, a document describing how a business intends to achieve its objectives. He needs to test whether he can expect to achieve these objectives and what the key risks are.

Financially, Fred is likely to want to know:

- how much he needs to invest to establish his coffee shop;
- what further investment may be needed in the early days while he builds up his customer base;
- when he can expect to *break even*, which means having income at least equal to outgo;
- if he has to borrow money, when he can expect to repay the debt; and
- when the coffee shop is well established, what annual income he can expect to earn.

Fred's non-financial objectives are likely to influence the model rather than being direct outputs from the model. For example, Fred may wish to use only "fair trade" coffee (which you can look up on the internet) and this might affect his assumptions regarding the cost of the coffee and the price that he can charge.

Modeling is an area where Fred's actuarial skills can be directly applied. He can build a spreadsheet with future cash flows based on assumptions about salaries, cost of supplies, price of drinks and sales. Part of his model will be the relationship between price and sales.

Fred will need to check that the results make sense and that they respond sensibly to changes in assumptions. For example, if he expects to serve an average of 100 customers per day, a projected annual profit of $250,000 implies almost $10 profit per customer. This seems too high and should be investigated.

Having established that the model works properly, Fred will want to investigate what happens if his assumptions turn out to be wrong. He will be particularly keen to understand the consequences of adverse variation. For example, if his business plan involves serving 100 customers per day, what would happen if he only got an average of 50 per day? How many customers does he need in order to achieve his objectives?

Finally, Fred must effectively communicate the results of his model, particularly when he approaches a bank for a loan.

In Chapter 9, the author deals with rather more complex models than Fred's. However, it is worth bearing Fred's business plan model in mind as you read the chapter.

Chapter 9   Modeling

by Andrew D. Smith

9.1   Introduction

This chapter examines what a model is, why models are useful and how models are selected in actuarial work. Starting with an example model, we move on to consider how, in theory, models ought to be built and used. We then move on to the business issues affecting models, including their place in the control cycle.

9.2   Examples of models

9.2.1   Automobile insurance

Drivers in most countries must purchase insurance. To calculate premiums, insurers try to evaluate how likely each driver is to make a claim and how big the claim might be. That is why applicants have to answer so many questions – not only about their driving history but also their occupation, address, type of car driven, whether the car is garaged or not and so on. Insurers build models which use the answers to questions such as these for estimating likely claims cost.

Two actuaries responsible for such calculations are debating whether men or women are the safer drivers. One argues that women are safer because they make fewer and less costly claims on motor insurance policies. The other argues that men incur greater claims because they tend to drive longer distances in larger cars that cause more damage in the event of an accident. These factors, he argues, and not the sex of the driver, explain the greater average claims for males. To resolve this issue, the actuaries have to build a model that relates insurance claims to the characteristics of each driver.

9.2.2   Savings product with an investment guarantee

An insurer has designed a savings product in which policyholders invest in a portfolio of bonds. The insurer also provides a money-back guarantee in the event of falling bond markets, so that investors cannot lose their initial investment provided the insurer remains solvent. This guarantee has proved to be expensive in an environment of falling bond prices. The insurer has the idea of switching policyholders into another product design based on investments in shares, but with no money-back guarantee. This change cannot legally be imposed on policyholders without the approval of the regulator. The insurer wants to persuade the regulator that the switch leaves policyholders no worse off, on the grounds that shares have historically provided superior investment returns compared to bonds. To make this case, the insurer needs a model describing future returns on different investments.

9.2.3   Fairness of insurance prices

The Japanese subsidiary of a multinational insurer provides insurance to the Russian subsidiary. Tax rates are lower in Russia than Japan, and the Japanese tax authorities suspect that this insurance is deliberately under-priced in order to transfer profits from Japan to Russia so as to minimize tax – which would be illegal under Japanese law. The Japanese tax authorities engage actuaries to demonstrate that the insurance premium is insufficient for the risks covered, and therefore that the Japanese subsidiary is understating its taxable profit in Japan. This requires a model of how insurance is priced in relation to the claims covered.

9.2.4 Valuing pension benefits

A retirement benefit plan promises employees a pension on reaching retirement age. The annual pension amount is calculated based on how long an employee has served and on the employee's career average salary. An employee who leaves employment before retirement age is offered a cash value in lieu of the pension to which she is no longer entitled. The pension plan retains an actuary who certifies that the cash value offered is fair compensation for the lost pension entitlement, using a model that describes the cost of the benefits foregone.

9.2.5 Investment risks and returns

An investor wishes to construct a portfolio of assets that is expected to provide a good return while maximizing the probability of being able to pay a stream of future obligations. He constructs a model of the risks and returns on different investments, which he then optimizes to find a mix that maximizes the probability of meeting the obligations given the initial investment amount available.

9.2.6 Setting dividend policy

A bank has made a profit of $100 million in a given year. The strategy department wants to retain the profit to build up a fund that will be used to acquire a competing bank, leading to economies of scale and better scope for long-term growth. The finance director argues instead that paying an $80 million dividend would boost the share price, and so serve shareholders better in the short term, as well as providing a boost to executive compensation which is linked to the share price. The finance director builds a model to describe the likely effect of dividend policy on share prices over the medium term, to support the dividend decision.

9.2.7 Mortality improvement

A writer of life annuities is concerned that lifestyle improvements, greater access to medical care and technological developments may cause pensioners to live longer, increasing insurance payouts and making its product unprofitable. The firm constructs a model of pensioner mortality, analyzing past data to quantify the effect of mortality improvements in the past. It is found that the cohort born in the 1930s (and retiring in the 1990s) has shown particularly strong improvements. The model is used to analyze whether the improvements are explained by factors in the early years of life (such as growing up during an economic slump) or changes later in life (such as a reduction in smoking). This is used as an input into pricing and underwriting decisions.

9.2.8 Social behavior

A government is concerned about the rates of pregnancy among teenagers. It proposes a program of sex education in schools, including provision of confidential advice on contraception. Some religious groups argue that such education merely normalizes sexual activity among teenagers, leading to a greater rate of pregnancy rather than the reduction intended. The government commissions research to build a model explaining the rate of teenage pregnancy in different communities, relating it to the nature of education provision and surveyed levels of sexual activity.

9.3 What is a model?

Models are widely used for many purposes within financial institutions.

A model is a mathematical representation of a real world phenomenon. Models enable analysts to reduce complex problems to manageable terms. They must be well understood and used with care.

Models invariably involve making simplifying assumptions about the real world. By expressing the phenomenon in terms of a simplified representation we make possible calculations, simulations and predictions about the real world while hopefully retaining enough detail of the underlying processes to realistically represent the real world. Examples of the types of simplifying assumptions are:

- assuming a quantity is constant over the period of the model;

- assuming we know the statistical distribution of a quantity;

- assuming some aspects of the model are not influenced by (or are independent of) other aspects;

- assuming some aspects of the real world have an insignificant effect on what is being modeled; and

- assuming all financial instruments are always priced so as to preclude risk-free arbitrage profits.

Models are usually implemented in computer software. The software implements a series of mathematical formulas, using inputs and producing outputs.

The intended representation of something out there in the real world is a vital aspect of modeling. Model evaluation involves comparing aspects of the model to empirical observations. We do not consider a computational tool that implements formulas to be a model itself. A theoretical hypothesis of how the world might work is not a model either. It becomes a model when implemented in formulas and calibrated against the real world phenomena it is attempting to represent.

9.3.1 Case study – building a model of inflation and interest rates

9.3.1.1 The business problem

In many economies, older employees retire from work and receive an income of a certain amount per month. Sometimes this income comes from an *annuity*, that is, an insurance contract purchased with a lump sum at the date of retirement and paying a steady income for the remainder of the policyholder's life.

One possible problem with annuities is that they provide no protection against inflation, that is, increases in the price of goods. With inflation a constant annuity income buys less with each month that passes. To overcome this problem, other product designs exist. Some of them use payments that are recalculated regularly to reflect inflation. Most governments publish regular inflation statistics that can be used for this purpose. In this section, we consider how such products come to market, with a particular focus on the role of models.

9.3.1.2   The actuarial problem

Within an insurance company or financial institution, the starting point is usually one or two individuals within a product development team. Their objective is to design new products, get them through a number of internal checks and then launch these products onto the market.

Suppose an actuary within an insurer's product development department has an idea for a new product. The idea is this: in exchange for a single premium paid at retirement, the insurer promises a regular income until death, rising (or falling) in line with inflation.

9.3.1.3   The question to be answered

As part of the design process, the actuary notices that times of high inflation have often also been associated with times of high interest rates. He seeks to explore this relationship further and use the results as input to proposed pricing for the annuity. For example, if the actuary can show that interest rates are usually two percent above inflation, this could imply a pricing strategy where policyholders are promised inflation-linked cash flows and the insurer earns two percent more than inflation. That two percent margin provides funds to cover expenses, can be used as a source of profit, or may be passed to the customer in the form of a lower initial premium.

9.3.1.4   Data sources

A starting point is to investigate the relationship between inflation and interest rates by gathering relevant data. In the past, that may have involved difficult searches in libraries, but now much of the relevant data is published online. In the UK, the retail prices index is available from the Office of National Statistics. Inflation data since 1947 is available from their website, http://www.statistics.gov.uk.

There are many different kinds of interest rates, including yields on various bonds issued by governments and companies, rates at which banks lend to each other and rates embedded in other trades such as interest rate swaps and repurchase agreements. In the UK, the longest historical data is available on the Bank of England rate. This is the rate at which the Bank of England, acting as lender of last resort, would normally lend to other banks (subject to various other conditions).

Data on this rate is available as far back as 1700, on the Bank of England website, http://www.bankofengland.co.uk.

With the two key data elements in hand, it is now possible to investigate the hypothesis that there is a relationship between inflation and interest rates.

9.3.1.5   Exploratory data analysis

The two series, from 1948, are shown in Figure 9.1.

Figure 9.1   Historic inflation and interest rates

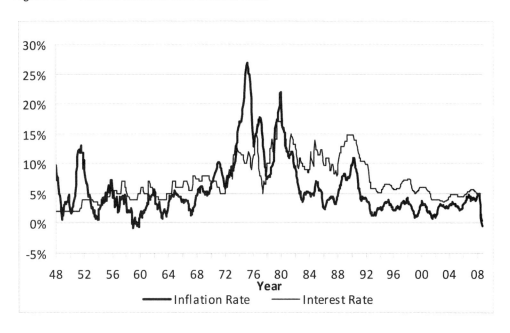

9.3.1.6   The first model

The actuary begins with a hypothesis that interest rates are a fixed margin above inflation. In other words, he constructs a model of the form:

$$\text{interest}(t) = \text{inflation}(t) + \text{real return}$$

He wants to test whether the real return is constant. Demonstrating a constant real return on cash deposits would be a useful contribution to demonstrating profitability of index-linked pensions.

Figure 9.2 shows the real return data, that is, the interest rate at a point in time minus inflation over the previous year.

As this chart is not constant, this immediately disproves the model of a constant real return. Instead of arguing that real returns are constant, the actuary has to propose a statistical argument, that real returns are sufficiently predictable to form a sound pricing basis. A key decision when using historical data is how far back in time to go. It appears that the series is moderately stable from 1979 onward and for the rest of the analysis only those data points will be used.

Figure 9.2   Difference between interest and inflation rates

For example, the actuary may look at the historic distribution of real returns, as shown in the histogram in Figure 9.3.

Figure 9.3   Histogram of differences

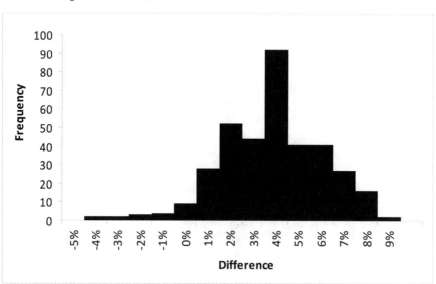

The model could then be written in the form:

interest(t) - inflation(t) = real return(t) = mean real return + error(t)

It is natural to estimate the mean real return as the sample average over the period. The error terms can now be analyzed statistically. They are found to have a sample mean of zero (this follows by construction – as the mean real return was estimated from the same sample) and a sample standard deviation of 2.2 percent.

For the purpose of product design, a forecast is needed of how these error terms might behave in future. Can we assume these are normally distributed (the histogram is slightly skewed left, but maybe not enough to cause concern)? One way to find out is to use the sample mean and standard deviation as estimates of the underlying parameters. Then construct a graph that shows the actual data alongside a simulation from the normal distribution model.

Figure 9.4 shows the historic path of real returns, with simulated future returns, according to a normal distribution, and assuming independent observations from one month to the next. This appears to be a poor model, as the simulated outcomes look completely different than the historical data to which they were supposedly calibrated.

Figure 9.4   Simulated path using independent normal variables

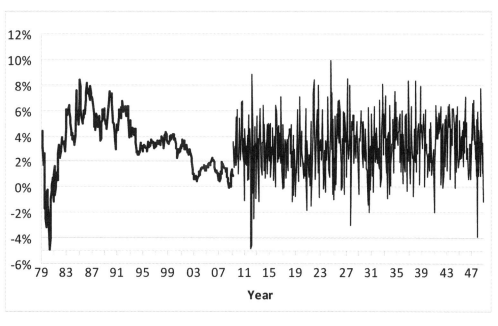

9.3.1.7   The second model

In the historical data, there are periods of high real returns and periods of low real returns. In a period of high real returns, the next real return is also likely to be higher. One way to investigate this is to construct a scatter plot with real return at time t on the y axis, and real return at time t-1 on the x axis. This is shown in Figure 9.5.

Figure 9.5   Scatterplot of year *t* difference versus year *t*-1 difference

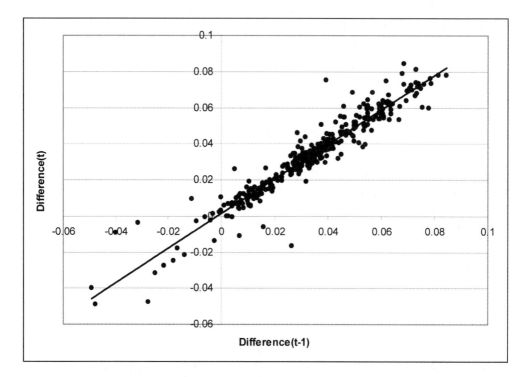

The regression line suggests a possible model of the form:

real return(t) = A × real return(t-1) + (1-A) × mean real return + error(t)

This is known as an *autoregressive model* in which real returns in one period depend on values in previous periods. The error terms (which are different from the variable of the same name in our previous model) are modeled using independent zero-mean normal variables whose common standard deviation is estimated from the historic data.

The result of regression is the estimated parameters $A = 0.958$ and a mean real return of 0.0313. The sample standard deviation of the errors is 0.0065. One indication that this may be a better model is the smaller standard deviation of the error term.

Assuming a normal distribution, this provides a possible model for projecting real returns into the future. Figure 9.6 shows the historic real returns and a randomly generated projection.

On visual inspection, this looks more promising. The projected outcomes visually resemble the past data, and represent plausible continuations of the patterns in that data set.

Figure 9.6   Simulation using the autoregressive model

Exercise 9.1

The data for this case study are in the Excel file "Chapter 9 Exercise 9.1 Data Spreadsheet" found on the CD. Verify the numerical results of the regression analysis. You may have learned other tests besides the simulation projection presented here. Conduct those tests and then decide if this model is appropriate for use.

Starting in 1979 was a qualitative decision based on observing the pattern of differences. Conduct a sensitivity analysis by using other starting years. For this situation, is the choice of starting year influential on the model choice? Do you recommend a different starting year?

A slightly more complex autoregressive model is one based on the real returns in each of the prior two years (an AR(2) model). It is defined as:

$$\text{real return(t)} = \text{constant} + A \times \text{real return(t-1)} + B \times \text{real return (t-2)} + \text{error(t)}$$

Using the starting year you just selected, fit this regression model and determine if it is an improvement over the previous model.

Write a brief memo supporting your chosen model. Assume the reader of your memo is familiar with such models but is many years removed from doing statistical analyses.

9.3.1.8   Further discussion

This model illustrates some important lessons:

- A solution to a problem may require investigation of more than one model. In the case study above, the actuary built a preliminary model to investigate the relationship between interest rates and inflation. This model will support decisions regarding input parameters into the final pricing model.

- Model building is an iterative process. The simulated outcomes from the first model were completely different from the historical output, indicating that the initial model did not capture the behavior of this series. Thus the model was modified and the check on the second model indicated that this new model is much more reasonable. In practice, the actuary may conduct several further iterations until the model is deemed satisfactory. At this point the actuary is ready to apply the model.

- Statistical theory and its appropriate application play an important part in building models which are easy to follow, understand and use.

Exercise 9.2

Obtain a paper or report in which a model is proposed. Read it critically to determine if the author has presented a convincing argument for the recommended model. Comment on what was done well and what could be improved. If you are unable to locate a paper or report, consider the paper by Hardy (2001) that promotes the regime switching lognormal model. It is available on the CD.

9.3.2   Using a fitted model

Having fitted a model,[1] the analyst can apply it to the problem in hand. This means turning a statistical forecast into a business proposition for launching inflation-linked annuities.

The development actuary uses the model to advocate the product launch. In our example, this advocacy might involve the following four steps:

(a) Proposal of a pricing basis for the product, for example based on providing customers with a real return of one percent per annum. This also requires assumptions about other risks such as mortality; larger firms often have standards for how these assumptions are derived for pricing purposes.

(b) Analysis of the product's expected profitability, together with an investigation of the likely demand for the product, leading to a business plan including likely volumes sold and other distribution costs, such as commission and advertizing.

(c) Analysis of the product's risks – what might go wrong, for example if there is a change in market behavior and the historical analysis turns out to have been a poor guide, and how much capital must the insurer put aside to cover a bad scenario? These capital requirements are considered over the product's lifetime.

---

[1]   When an appropriate model has been determined, it is customary to refer to it as having been "fitted." This is shorthand for "fitted to the data."

(d) Confirmation that the profit in (b) is sufficient given the capital required in (c). This is usually achieved by comparing the return on capital to a hurdle rate set by company management.

The intended audiences for this presentation are the insurer's pricing and risk committees.

By this stage in the process, the product development actuary has invested significant time and energy into this product. If he is convinced of the product's viability, he will be seeking to persuade the risk and pricing committees, not merely to lay unbiased information in front of them.

In addition to the scientific content, presentation and communication are important in business situations. For this reason, the actuary may rehearse the presentation in front of colleagues, not only checking content but also carefully crafting the arguments to make them as compelling as possible. He may research the individuals on the committee, arranging face-to-face meetings in advance of the presentation in order to identify and address any of their particular concerns. Even such details as arriving in good time, in a freshly pressed shirt, are important.

Throughout the process, the actuary will need to deal with many groups of people including:

- the marketing team – to gain an understanding of competitor prices and product features, customer needs and price sensitivity;

- the operations team – to understand product costs to be built into the expense budget;

- the sales team – to understand commission structures and expected target sales volumes; and

- the management team – to gain approval of the final product.

9.3.3 Challenging a fitted model

The risk and pricing committees have different functions. The pricing committee wants to ensure the product is as profitable as possible, so that appropriate consideration has been given to the profit margin, taking into account that pursuit of higher margins is likely to lead to lower transaction volumes. The committee is unlikely to have any idea what the right answer is. Instead, it polices the product developer's process, ensuring the calculations are logical and sufficient market research has been undertaken.

In the current example, the pricing committee might challenge the product developer over the interest series analyzed. The bank data has the advantage of a long history, but it relates to a lending rate for the Bank of England, which is not necessarily the rate at which an insurer could invest. The product developer would be expected to justify the choice of data period and the way he had gone about fitting a model. All these aspects must be documented.

The role of the risk committee is to understand the risk to the insurer if the pricing assumptions should turn out to be invalid. How much could be lost in a disaster scenario? And how likely is that scenario?

A starting point for these questions could be the fitted probability model. The risk committee will look beyond the fitted model to consider, for example, whether the estimates of various parameters are reliable and how alternative values would affect the modeling. They may consider stress events, such as possible defaults on the cash deposits. Depending on their investment knowledge they may also ask how the proposed pricing basis compares to market prices of inflation-linked government bonds.

They will also try to consider wider aspects of product design. For example, although the insurer has a standard set of pensioner mortality assumptions, the risk committee may be concerned about adverse selection – that super-healthy pensioners are more concerned about inflation over the long term, and so may find inflation-linked annuities particularly attractive, meaning that the insurer's standard assumptions are not valid for this product.

Depending on the insurer's organizational structure, the risk committee may investigate these items in some depth, or alternatively may require the developer to answer a standard set of questions and confirm that a list of items has been considered.

At the end of this process, there may be agreement to proceed to the marketing phase of a product launch. In that case, the product developer has met his objectives. This example shows a common aspect of actuarial models: that, although the matter for debate is the long-term future, those engaged in negotiations may be more concerned about short-term outcomes, such as whether a product launch is a success or a flop. The product developer may be concerned about the medium term, to the extent that he needs to develop credibility with the risk and pricing committees. That credibility could be undermined by a series of models whose forecasts turned out to be badly wrong. There is a limit in any organization to how many times an analyst can credibly attribute inaccurate forecasts to bad luck.

Exercise 9.3

The Excel file "Chapter 9 Exercise 9.1 Data Spreadsheet" found on the CD has a more detailed description of the proposed inflation-linked annuity product. A worksheet has been developed based on the first-order autoregressive model for the real interest rate. Certain assumptions have been made (detailed on the spreadsheet) that relate to topics covered later in the text (in particular, the measurement of liabilities and of profit). There is also a summary of what the actuary plans to report based on this model. As a member of the pricing and then of the risk committee, what questions do you have for the actuary?

9.4   Normative approaches to modeling

9.4.1   Modeling in the physical and social sciences

Normative theory means a theory of how something *should* be done. There is a large body of normative theory as to how models should be built. As with most sentences containing the word "should," there are different views as to how models should be built. The major fault line lies between the social and the physical sciences. Actuarial work is caught in the middle.

Social sciences address questions of human behavior. The systems analyzed are complex and there is little hope of finding a set of equations that describes everything. Furthermore, controlled experiments, which are fundamental to the physical sciences, may be impossible or unethical in social science. In a democracy, no government would survive an experimental raising of interest rates by two percent, four times a year, just to investigate what happens to unemployment or trade surplus.

Within the social sciences, models are used as a way of organizing hypotheses, revealing their logical dependencies. A hypothesis about how the world works is then expressed as a model. Observations are useful for calibrating the model, that is, choosing and setting assumptions. Models may then be ranked in their ability to predict different phenomena, or usefulness for a certain purpose. Being useful is not considered to imply that a model is right in any absolute sense, and there is some tolerance for models that explain an aspect of particular interest while shedding no light on other aspects deemed less important for the application in hand.

Within physical sciences, there is more often an implicit conviction that models are capable of describing reality very accurately, and that the purpose of science is to discover such models. Diligent scientists spend time devising harsh tests for any hypothesis and constructing experiments to validate or refute any assumption. This is the basis of the mathematical discipline known as *statistical inference*. In the following sections, we will describe statistical inference in more detail.

These two approaches to modeling collide in actuarial work. Differences in approach can lead to many misunderstandings and fruitless conversations between actuaries, economists, statisticians and other quantitative analysts.

9.4.2 Exploratory data analysis

In the framework of statistical inference, a starting point for model building is collection and analysis of data. The idea is to use data to form hypotheses about appropriate models. As more is discovered about the data, the process of model construction can become more formal.

The least formal, yet important, stage is called *exploratory data analysis*. In effect, this means examining the data and looking for patterns. This is often approached graphically. An analyst tries to spot patterns, for example whether one data item appears to depend linearly on another. If no pattern emerges, data may be transformed in different ways, for example by taking logarithms of a positive data item.

Despite its informality, exploratory data analysis can have a strong influence on model results, because it is at this stage that major choices are made regarding model structure.

The result of exploratory data analysis is a formula to be estimated, containing observed data, unknown parameters and random noise.

In our example relating to real returns, the proposed formula was:

real return(t) = A × real return(t-1) + (1-A) × mean real return + error(t)

Here, the real returns are the data, while the mean real return and A are parameters to be estimated.

In many actuarial examples, there are well established conventions for model choice. Error terms in theory appear everywhere, but in practice are often not written down. This can be interpreted as saying the error terms are implicit, but given the common understanding of their existence it is considered unnecessary to write them down every time.

For example, a model of insurance claims for 40-year-old females might be written as:

number of deaths = death probability × exposed to risk

The *exposed to risk* is the number of insured lives that would have been counted as deaths if they died. The error term, resulting from the randomness in which individuals die, is often omitted. This could be for clarity of notation or because it is not believed to be material.

In this case, the formula used is well established – numbers of deaths are invariably compared to exposed to risk. There are a number of possible reasons for choosing a model of this form.

First, there may be statistical evidence that exposed to risk does predict the number of deaths, and does so better than other predictor variables. There may also be statistical evidence in support of a proportional relationship.

Secondly, there may be an assertion that the relationship is a matter of common sense. In a fundamental sense, it seems likely that doubling the number of lives doubles the number of expected deaths. Underlying this is an implicit assumption about the relationship between different lives. For example, if there was a particularly nasty life-threatening infection that is only likely to reach epidemic proportions in populations exceeding 50 individuals, then doubling the population size might not double the number of expected deaths. It is very unusual in practice to see such extraordinary scenarios listed and then dismissed. The "obvious" relationship is more often justified in terms of "common sense," "general reasoning," "professional judgment" or other similar terms.

Thirdly, familiarity may favor a particular model. The analyst may have successfully used this model before. Success may be measured in a number of ways, from the purely statistical (the model accounted for the data) to the more commercial (my audience was pleased with the model output, or application of the model resulted in a reported profit last year). Familiarity may alternatively stem from a belief that competitors or peers use this approach. It might appear in published papers or textbooks, or be easy to use in a particular piece of software than happens to be available.

Given the importance of model choice, financial firms are placing increasing emphasis on the processes used to choose models. It is good practice to document the decisions taken, including the reasons for these decisions and so subject any significant areas of judgment to some form of review.

9.4.3 Model calibration

Model calibration means estimating the uncertain parameters in a model.

Statistical theory provides several techniques for parameter estimation. The most popular method is called *maximum likelihood*, often abbreviated to ML or MLE. The maximum likelihood estimate is the choice of parameter value that maximizes the probability of observing the actual data. It is plausible, but not obvious, that this method produces the best parameter estimates. It is not even obvious how to define what makes an estimate a best one. Nevertheless, there are some mathematical results (eg Stuart and Ord, 1984) that relate maximum likelihood estimates to definitions of good estimates, and for this reason maximum likelihood is widely regarded as theoretically the best approach.

Maximum likelihood is sometimes described as choosing the "most likely" set of parameters. However, that is a misrepresentation; the method says nothing about the likelihood of parameter values, it looks only at the likelihood of a particular outcome given the parameters. The framework, often called *frequentist* or *classical*, therefore treats the parameters as fixed and data as the random variable. To some analysts, this seems intuitively the wrong way around. We will revisit this aspect when we consider errors in model projections.

The *Bayesian* method is an alternative approach that treats parameters as being uncertain. Here, the analyst specifies a *prior distribution* capturing a subjective view of where he expects parameters to lie. The distribution of outcomes given the parameters is given, as in the classical framework. The Bayesian method proceeds from *Bayes' theorem* to deduce the conditional distribution of parameters given the data.

Both the classical and Bayesian methods encounter significant obstacles in terms of computation. Probability densities are often defined by complicated formulas. Likelihood maximization is a difficult numerical task. Quite apart from the difficulty of identifying a best fit when it exists, problems also frequently arise where no optimum exists, or it exists but is not unique. Bayesian analysis is also more difficult than it may seem at first sight. The numerical application of Bayes' theorem is often challenging. For these reasons, practical work often entails a number of approximations, shortcuts and compromises. Recent computational breakthroughs, particularly the application of Monte Carlo Markov Chain algorithms, have driven a renaissance in Bayesian approaches.

Results of fitted distributions are not always intuitively easy to explain. For example, consider fitting a lognormal distribution to the five observations $\{0.01, 0.1, 1, 10, 100\}$. It can be shown that fitting by maximum likelihood is equivalent to taking logarithms, and then fitting a normal distribution with the same mean and variance. However, this fitted distribution has a theoretical mean in excess of 200, which is larger than any of the observations used in calibration.

Most data sets contain an element of noise, that is, apparently random terms not explained by any plausible model. This means that, although we can try to estimate parameters, our ability to do this is limited by the noise in the data. There is almost no chance that our estimated parameter value is exactly the correct value underlying the data. The best we can hope is that the estimated value is close to the true underlying parameter value. Our chances of achieving this improve if we have more data, and if a good statistical estimation method is used.

9.4.4   Fit to evidence

With data, equations, parameters and error terms, we have a possible model. What we lack is evidence as to whether this model is correct or useful.

The next step is to show that the model adequately accounts for the history used for calibration. An example of such a test is to consider extreme events that occurred in the data series, and check to see whether the model gives an appropriate probability to events of that severity or greater. Another check is to examine key properties of a model (such as means and variances), checking that these correspond sufficiently closely to means and variances of the calibration data.

These and similar approaches are generically known as *back testing*. While not a formal statistical test, back testing is a popular tool because it is relatively straightforward to communicate and the results seem easy to interpret. However, the test is easily fooled by over-fitting, that is, by having a model with so many parameters that it captures every aspect of the past history. In that case, the back testing appears to work well but this does not imply that the model will capture likely behavior outside the data sample to which the model was calibrated. The analysis can be made more rigorous by the use of out-of-sample or blend-test evaluation, where some recent data is set aside during the calibration process and then used for testing.

An alternative method of testing models is to generate several random future projections from the model, including all the error terms. This test was performed in our real return example. The test is a visual inspection of the projected future outcomes in comparison with the historic observations. If the projections look very different from the past, this raises important questions about how well the model captures the data.

Many models describe how variables move over time, and in this case testing is particularly subtle. It is useful to distinguish between *longitudinal* analysis that follows the progress of one simulated path over time, compared to *cross-sectional* analysis that looks at a fixed future time horizon across many simulated outcomes. When it comes to measures of variability, there is no reason for longitudinal and cross-sectional measures to be equal. For example, a longitudinal measure of inflation variability is often far greater than a cross-sectional measure with a one year horizon. This is because retail prices tend to change gradually but cumulative changes can come over a number of years.

9.4.5   Hypothesis testing

At this point in the process we want to see whether the model captures important aspects of historical data. This usually involves inspection by eye rather than a formal statistical test. The reason is that for most models there are no statistical tests of goodness of fit. This fact is not widely appreciated – for most model classes encountered in practice, there is no absolute measure of fit that enables analysts to determine whether an estimated model is a good fit to the data or not.

Consider for example the estimation of a straight line fit by linear regression. Linear regression minimizes the sum of squared differences between the data and the model's fitted values. But there is no absolute threshold in this sum of squares that defines a boundary between a good fit and a poor fit.

Statistical theory does offer tests of one model compared to another. In the typical situation, an analyst wants to compare two hypotheses, conventionally called the *null hypothesis*, written H_0 and an *alternative hypothesis* H_1. In the usual set up, H_1 corresponds to a broad class of models and H_0 corresponds to a narrower class of models within H_1. These examples, and virtually all practical applications, are *compound hypotheses*, that is, both H_0 and H_1 contain more than one parameter combination.

For example, consider a linear regression, with points (X_i, Y_i). The null hypothesis might be that the Y_i are independent identically distributed normal variates. The alternate hypothesis is that

$$Y_i = a + bX_i + \text{error}_i$$

The compound alternative hypothesis allows a and b to be any real value. The null hypothesis is the compound subset where $b = 0$ and a can be any real value. Statistical tests then consist of estimating b and asking whether the estimated value is significantly different from zero. In other words, is an estimated value of b so close to zero that maybe the true value really is zero and the estimate is an artifact of random noise? To perform these tests in practice, further assumptions are required, for example that the error terms are independent identically distributed normal variates with mean zero.

We can write the two hypotheses as in Table 9.1.

Table 9.1   Hypotheses for a linear regression problem

	H_0	H_1
Name	Null hypothesis	Alternate hypothesis
Mathematical formulation	$b = 0$	$b \neq 0$
Supportive test result	Estimated b is not significantly different from zero.	Estimated b is significantly different from zero.

Ideally, a statistical test supports H_0 when H_0 is true, and supports H_1 when H_1 is true. However, like all else in statistics, hypothesis testing is subject to uncertainty in the presence of noisy data. Table 9.2 shows two types of error classically considered in statistics.

Table 9.2   Type I and II errors in hypothesis tests

	Test result supports H_0 (rejects H_1)	Test result supports H_1 (rejects H_0)
H_0 is true	Good outcome Probability $1-\alpha$	Type I error Probability α
H_1 is true	Type II error Probability β	Good outcome Probability $1-\beta$

A Type I error is rejecting H_0 when it is true. The probability of this is traditionally denoted by α. The value is usually specified by the user – and called the *size* of the test. A small value of α means a small probability of rejecting H_0 when it is true. Unfortunately, this may mean a large probability β of accepting H_0 when it is false. So the users of hypothesis tests face a trade-off. It has become common practice to set $\alpha=0.05$, so that H_0 is falsely rejected with a one in 20 probability. However, there is no fundamental reason why this is the right significance level to use – it merely represents one possible way to trade off the conflicting requirements of low probabilities for both Type I and Type II errors. In theory the chosen value of α should depend on the nature of the problem in hand. For example, in criminal justice H_0 could be that the defendant is innocent while H_1 is guilty. The choice of α, the probability of locking up the innocent might reflect society's view of how this compares to the alternative of criminals roaming free.

There are good ways to construct tests and bad ways to construct tests. For example, if we had a large data set, we could test a hypothesis in a way that ignored half the data. The folly of this approach shows up as a larger-than-necessary probability β of Type II error given the Type I error probability α. The best test, the one with the smallest possible β for a given value of α, is called the *most powerful* and can be interpreted as using the available data in the most efficient manner. In many practical situations, a most powerful test does not exist, because the Type II error probability β is different for different underlying parameters within H_1.

A further complicating factor is the difficulty of determining the size α of a test for arbitrary underlying distributions. Expressions for α are known when the underlying models take the form of straight line fitting (or higher dimensional equivalents) and all the error terms are normally distributed. There are also some limiting theorems that say this normal result is approximately true if the data set is large enough. For moderate-sized data sets, the use of statistical tests requires an act of faith that the number of observations is large enough for the limiting regime to apply. *Non-parametric* tests are less reliant on strong distributional assumptions but are also less likely to reject a hypothesis even when it is wrong.

Exercise 9.4

In Exercise 9.1 you were asked to perform additional tests on the model. Re-examine either your tests or the ones provided in the solution and comment on how they relate to the ideas presented in the previous two sections.

9.4.6 Parsimony

We have discussed model fit to data. Good data fit becomes easier as more parameters are added, but adding parameters without limit may violate the principle of *parsimony*. Parsimony means using only as many parameters as necessary to fit a model.

Parsimony is often applied informally as follows. A simple model is constructed as a first guess at what may be driving the data, and parameters estimated. Standardized residuals are then calculated by dividing the difference between each data point and the model prediction by some measure of prediction standard error. These residuals are then examined by eye, plotted against various possible explanatory variables. Where a pattern is spotted, a new term is introduced to the model designed to explain this pattern. The process continues until no further patterns are observed. In that case the residuals appear random, which offers support to the idea that all the patterns are captured within a model.

A limitation of this approach is the subjective nature of the decision whether a pattern exists or not. For example, a pattern may exist where residuals depend on several variables taken together but none individually. Such patterns are notoriously hard to spot in graphical plots. On other occasions a pattern may be spotted but deliberately ignored because the additional effort of modeling it is not deemed worthwhile. An example could be deliberately ignoring seasonal effect in inflation figures (due for example to cheaper fresh fruit in summer), if the objective is inflation projection for many years into the future.

On the other hand, there is a human tendency to spot some sort of pattern even in data that is in fact random. This tendency is well illustrated by the linking of stars into named signs of the zodiac.

The process of adding parameters can be made more rigorous using hypothesis testing. As each parameter is added, the new model with the additional parameter is tested as H_1 against the null hypothesis that the original model H_0 was valid. The process stops when H_0 cannot be rejected.

An alternative approach to this problem is to use an *information criterion*. Suppose we have fitted a model with k parameters to n data points, by the method of maximum likelihood, and the maximized likelihood is L. As additional parameters are added, the maximized likelihood L naturally increases, as adding further variables to an optimization problem can only improve the optimum achievable.

Two examples of information criteria are:

$$\textit{Akaike Information Criterion } (\text{AIC}) = 2k - 2\ln L$$

$$\textit{Bayes Information Criterion } (\text{BIC}) = k\ln n - 2\ln L$$

These criteria are both increasing functions of the number of model parameters, minus twice the log likelihood. Models are selected by minimizing an information criterion, which has the effect of penalizing the use of excessive parameters. For moderate-sized data sets, the BIC imposes a heavier penalty on additional parameters (if $\ln n > 2$) and therefore tends to produce more parsimonious models than AIC, with correspondingly worse fit to the data. Compared to repeated application of hypothesis tests, AIC tends to produce more parameters while BIC produces fewer.

The information criteria recognize the fact that better apparent fits will be achieved by any additional parameters, even if that parameter was absent from the true underlying model (a *noise parameter*). The information criteria seek to include additional parameters only when the improvement in fit is better than would be expected from a noise parameter.

A more difficult aspect to control is the multiple testing of many model formulas. This does not show up as an increase in parameter count, but picking the best fit from a large number of model families could inspire greater confidence in model fidelity than is truly deserved. It follows that an important diagnostic in validating a proposed model is the *graveyard*, a term used for the collection of models tested and rejected.

A common bias in the use of theory is double counting of evidence. A particular data set may be examined in an exploratory fashion, resulting in a hypothesis regarding possible model approach. Subsequent more formal testing confirms the appropriateness of the approach. However, this is in effect double-counting the information content of a single data set.

To avoid such double counting, we need to examine the graveyard in more detail. We can think of the model graveyard as consisting of several layers. The top layer consists of alternative models with alternative parameter values to those arising from the best fit, and is exposed using sensitivity tests. The next layer consists of models with more or fewer parameters. Further down lie different model formulas entirely, but still tested in-house. Further down still are models that might have been tested and rejected on previous occasions and therefore given low priority. At the lowest level are models that were never tried, but are either overlooked or deliberately excluded.

Exercise 9.5

In Exercise 9.1 you were asked to fit a second, more complex, autoregressive model. Using the two formal criteria presented in this section, which model should be selected? Does this differ from your previous choice?

9.4.7 Fit to theory

In most cases, data alone cannot drive model choice. There are very many competing sets of mathematical formulas that might describe a situation; testing all of these formally is practically impossible.

Choosing a model structure may then make an appeal to theory. For example, Fisher (1930) suggested modeling interest rates as a sum of inflation and a real return, with the real return being stable over time. So, in our real return example the chosen model structure could be justified by reference to theory.

There are a number of theories about the operation of financial markets, some of which are more controversial than others. An example of a more controversial theory is that of efficient markets, ie that market prices already reflect all available information. Making an assumption about efficient markets reduces the range of models that might be used to describe market prices. In particular, efficiency excludes models where past price movements are useful for predicting the direction of future movements. Market efficiency is also consistent with some theories of what constitutes optimal investor behavior. Market efficiency could be used as a criterion to distinguish between models with similar ability to explain historic data. Of two models with an equally good historic fit, the model consistent with market efficiency or rational investor behavior might be preferred. Such an appeal to theory is controversial, because the criterion is acceptable only to the extent that the underlying theory is accepted.

Another way of expressing the conundrum of market efficiency is to observe that some models are *self-referential*, that is, they describe the behavior of other agents who are also using models. The presence of a model can change the behavior of the phenomenon being modeled. Efficient market models have the property that, even if all other participants believed the model, their optimizing behavior would not change the nature of the model. Such a thought experiment cannot prove or disprove market efficiency (which is an empirical question) but it does explain why efficient market models have a certain stability that other models lack. This issue is peculiar to finance. Self-reference is much less of a problem in the physical sciences – the existence of an earthquake model does not cause earthquakes.

Some references to theory are very explicit. For example, there is a well-known theory of option pricing due to Black and Scholes (1973). This model is very widely quoted and used. A modeler making use of this prior material is effectively taking on all the assumptions made by Black and Scholes in developing their theory. Consistency with Black-Scholes theory could be used as a criterion for choosing a pricing model.

In other cases, references to theory may be implicit. For example, a model may be fitted to a mathematical form such as an exponential growth curve, with no explicit reference to the theoretical construction that would imply that form. Where a formula is proposed prior to data fitting, there is inevitably some theory, implicit or explicit, leading to that formula. However, there will be differences in the extent to which that theory has been documented or subjected to empirical testing.

In any theoretical work, there is a natural preference for elegant and concise theories. In physics, it is difficult not to be impressed by the elegance of Newton's laws of mechanics or Maxwell's electrodynamic equations. It is common to hear arguments that a theory is more likely to be true, simply because it is mathematically elegant and quite aside from experimental support. Similar arguments may be made in favor of economic concepts such as market efficiency, or elegant mathematical results such as the Black-Scholes formula.

Elegant models typically have other advantages too. Algebraic elegance often enables quick numerical implementation, with fast run times. For example, manipulations of normal distributions often lead to tractable formulas that can be explained quickly and implemented reliably within fast-running code. However, many actuaries have been quick to criticize certain branches of economics (sometimes called *financial economics*) that are seen as placing too great an emphasis on model elegance at the expense of empirical support. This remains an active controversy, particularly when the alternative models are more difficult to estimate, implement and validate.

9.4.8 Computer technology development

It is one thing to build a set of mathematical formulas, and quite another to turn these into a working computer model. The missing step is turning the model formulas into computer code to solve a specific problem.

While statistical theory is concerned with random errors, modelers also need to guard against the more mundane errors that come from human mistakes. In some situations (for example in website design) it is advisable to guard against deliberate or malicious users as well as the innocent mistake-prone.

To guard against mistakes, it is important that mathematics is validated and software tested. One approach to this is to have experts check mathematics and computer code line by line, seeking any mistakes. Unfortunately, mistakes are extraordinarily difficult to spot in this way. Any experienced modeler will recall examples of code that, after checking and re-checking, still failed to perform as intended.

Here are some more proactive ways to look for errors:

- In a long step-by-step mathematical derivation, verify intermediate equations numerically by substituting values into the left and right hand sides. It is often useful to perform this test with randomly generated variable values. If an equation fails to produce equality of the left and right hand sides, this indicates a mistake has arisen between this equation and the previous equation tested. Testing next an equation partway between these two equations provides a binary section algorithm that can quickly locate mathematical slips.

- Where a particularly complex mathematical operation is required, such as a Fourier transform or integration, then numerical checks are a valuable way to validate algebra.

- Sense-check model outputs. Test for different sets of inputs and ensure that sensitivities can be satisfactorily explained in a business context. Compare results to other analyses, studies and reports that may be available and investigate any apparent inconsistencies.

- Re-test software functionality with many inputs, including both expected and unexpected (wrong or meaningless) inputs. Step through code line by line and verify that data fields are correctly populated after each step.

- Where routine outputs have known properties, test these. For example, test a matrix inversion routine by verifying that a matrix, multiplied by its inverse, gives the identity. Test a routine for generating gamma-distributed random variables by using a goodness-of-fit test.

- When a new version of the model is released, apply *regression testing*. Regression testing involves using a large number of test input sets and ensuring that the new and old versions' output is consistent.

- If your mathematics or code solves a problem that others are likely to encounter, consider making the model widely available via the internet, providing a facility to report bugs. This increases the number of testers and thus helps with timely reporting of bugs, but may fall foul of an employer's IT policy.

- Document the tests performed to avoid repeated testing effort.

- Be aware that mistakes may not be purely down to your code. Some compilers, operating systems and math processing chips have known problems. This emphasizes the importance of testing real model output and not relying only on proven mathematical theorems.

Many model development projects embark on coding too early, on an unstructured basis. The developer may then be condemned to months of tracking down and fixing bugs, only to find that each new bug fix generates further problems. There are some well-established tools for dealing with this situation, generically known as *defensive programming*. Some of these are listed below:

- Break software down into pieces that can be checked individually. Where possible, design components that can be re-used, particularly for common tasks such as random number generation, solution of linear equations, matrix inversion and so on.

- Document model components in plain language, with a complete description of inputs, outputs and algorithms used. Use meaningful variable names.

- Ask colleagues to review or audit the code, focusing on completeness of documentation and ease of relating the documentation to the implemented model.

- In simulation models, use pseudo-random number generators that can be seeded with a starting point. This ensures reproducibility of a set of random numbers for later testing.

- Reduce code complexity as much as possible. Clever tricks that shave a small margin off run time while making code unreadable are rarely a good idea. Use plenty of comments in the code to explain the purpose of each section, referring back to the component documentation.

- Use version control. Release updates in a disciplined manner with each new release numbered and changes since the previous release documented.

- Write code to handle unexpected conditions. For example, if a particular algorithm requires positive inputs, check the inputs are positive and report an error if not.

9.4.9   Using models for projection

Most models involve producing forecasts of the future. These may be point estimates or probability distributions. Projections may also be associated with a stated degree of confidence. Statistical textbooks often emphasize the value of accompanying every estimate with a measure of its uncertainty. The standard tool for this is the notion of a confidence interval, which in this context is commonly understood as an interval with a certain probability (for example, 95 percent) of containing the future outcome. Confidence intervals are open to back testing, that is, analysis of the frequency of *exceptions* where actual outcomes lie outside the claimed 95 percent confidence interval.

Modelers need to be aware of several causes of error in projections. If insufficient account is taken of all these causes, then back-testing reveals an exception rate in excess of the permitted five percent, leading to a questioning of the statistical methodology. On the other hand, where regulators or other bodies take a particularly close interest in exceptions, firms may deliberately err on the side of prudence in constructing confidence intervals, in order to reduce the obligation to report exceptions.

These causes of error may include: process error, parameter error, model error, calibration error, survivorship bias and operational errors.

Process error is that part of the randomness that the model is supposed to capture. Quantifying the process error involves an examination of the errors in fitting of past data and extrapolating these probabilistically into the future. In our real return example, the simulated paths take into account process error only. Because other forms of error are ignored, 95 percent confidence intervals constructed from this model would produce exceptions more frequently than one in 20.

Parameter error arises from errors in the estimation of the parameters underlying a model. These can also be estimated statistically, using techniques similar to those in hypothesis testing. Statisticians may talk of a "95 percent chance that the mean lies within a confidence interval," giving the impression that the underlying mean parameter is stochastic and is 95 percent certain to lie within a defined range. Within a Bayesian framework, where parameters are treated stochastically, this makes sense. Under the classical framework, interpretation is more subtle than this – as seen for example in situations where two 95 percent confidence intervals for the mean do not overlap. If the confidence interval represented a range for a random parameter then two 95 percent confidence intervals must overlap with a common range of at least 90 percent probability. The lack of overlap exists because, in the classical framework, the parameter is considered an unknown constant. The limits of the confidence interval are stochastic, and the 95 percent probability of containing the true mean is contingent on the underlying model being correct. Two 95 percent confidence intervals for the mean from different models can fail to overlap if the models cannot simultaneously be true.

Within statistical inference, model error occurs when a model uses the wrong functional form for its underlying formulas. An example of a model error could be an assumption of a normal distribution when in fact the underlying process is driven by a fat-tailed distribution. Another example would be a failure to allow for climate change in models extrapolating historic experience of insured damage from storms. Given that no model will ever be correct, some degree of model error is inevitable. This is difficult to quantify, but indications can come from trying plausible alternative models.

Within the social sciences, the concept of model error is less relevant, as there is no concept of a correct underlying model that explains everything. Instead, there is a concept of omitted variable bias. It occurs when a simplified model with a small parameter count does not account simultaneously for all input data. This is a special case of model error, where the functional forms and distributions are agreed upon, but the set of input variables is not. For example, analysts might use the Black-Scholes model to price a complex financial derivative. However, as Black-Scholes is a simple model with a small number of parameters, it is not possible to capture all input prices simultaneously with the parameters available. This then leads to some degree of mispricing, even of the known price inputs.

Survivorship bias happens when models are selected from a range of possibilities. For example, an insurer may wish to identify the ultimate value of claims arising from a block of policies insuring employers against payouts for negligence toward employees. This business is subject to substantial uncertainty, and for a premium of $50 million the projected losses could be anywhere between $20 million and $100 million depending on the modeling approach adopted. For any value in this range, a case could be made consisting of data analysis, modeling, associated statistical tests and projections. You can imagine a shelf of 81 equally persuasive reports, arguing for projected liabilities of $20 million, $21 million, and so on until $100 million. It then emerges that the business plan profit was 12 percent of premium, so the management selects the report ending with $44 million of claims. Future calculations are done using this model while the remaining 80 reports remain on the shelf collecting dust.

Operational error arises because of mistakes and oversights during the modeling process. This can include inaccuracies in input data, software bugs, incorrect copying of information from one source to another, deliberate mis-statement and typographical errors.

Exercise 9.6

In your development of a model for inflation and interest rates have all of the error sources mentioned above either been eliminated or measured? If not, what additional steps do you suggest?

9.4.10   Bootstrapping

Bootstrapping[2] is a powerful but labor-intensive test. The name refers to the illusion that someone might be able to lift themselves into the air by tugging on their own bootstraps.

The idea is to take a fitted model, taken to be "correct," and use this, with a random number generator, to produce random data sets according to that model. Each of these simulated data sets is then used in a model estimation, fitting and testing exercise. The hope is that most of these tests will result in a reconstruction of the original model, with more or less the same parameters.

This is a useful exercise, because it simultaneously tests many parts of the modeling process. If the model is not reproduced, this may indicate a large degree of statistical uncertainty, leading to a degree of caution in interpreting the model. It may alternatively point to mistakes in the model coding. In some cases, it may be appropriate to fine-tune a chosen information criterion. For example, if the bootstrap systematically results in a simpler model than that generated from the data, this may indicate the penalty for parameter counts was too light.

In real examples, there is a shockingly low chance of correctly reconstructing the original model, even under the favorable conditions of a bootstrap where a correct model is known to the experimenter. To draw comfort from bootstrapping, the acceptance criterion has to be broadened. In addition to accepting an accurately reconstructed model, we may also be satisfied with an incorrect model whose predictions for the problem in hand are reasonably close to the output from the correct model. In other words we have to be satisfied with a model that is useful rather than right.

9.4.11   Computational model classification

Models in actuarial use are diverse and there are many ways to classify them. For example, models could be classified by their field of application, by the alternative ways in which

---

[2]   This is one application of the bootstrap. You may have learned others that rely on simulations from the empirical observations rather than from the model.

assumptions are derived, or by the model's purpose. In this section, we classify models according to the computational algorithms embedded within them.

The first step in the model hierarchy is to distinguish between deterministic and stochastic models.

A deterministic model applies a set of formulas without introducing any randomness. In an actuarial context, deterministic models are used for forecasting cash flows. For example, we might model a life assurance business with the following properties:

- This is a start-up company with no existing policyholders.

- At the start, 10 customers each purchase whole of life assurance. They each pay premiums of $1,000 per annum throughout their life, with a sum assured of $8,000 payable at the end of the year of death.

- Each year, one-tenth of the current customers die.

- Ten more identically situated customers join at each year-end.

It is then a straightforward matter to project this population of insurance policies, keeping track of the number of policies, the premium income, the claims outgo and so on. It is easy to see that the population tends to a steady state of 100 customers, of which the 10 deaths every year are replaced by 10 more new entrants. Each year the premium income is $100,000 and claims are $80,000 leaving $20,000 profit.

Models in real life are more complex than this. Models would allow for: investment income; administrative expenses; more frequent cash flows; policyholders failing to keep up premium payments; mortality varying by policyholder age and/or time elapsed since policy inception and perhaps splitting by other attributes such as smoker/nonsmoker status. Putting all these equations together produces what is sometimes called a *model office*, that is, a computer model of the financial statements and cash flows of an insurance operation.

We could debate the role of probabilities in this model. Although there are no explicit probability references in the model, actuaries would concede that the actual number of deaths in a given year is random. There is some recognition of this in a common actuarial convention, that the projected numbers of lives and deaths are not constrained to be integers. If the assumption of one-tenth of the population dying leads to a fractional number of deaths, this fraction is left in the model, and allowed to accumulate into future projections, despite the physical fact that any one individual is 100 percent alive or 100 percent dead. A justification for this convention is an interpretation of model output as the expected number of lives and deaths. In other words, the model output is implicitly an average of many plausible scenarios, even though the precise projected scenario could not in fact happen because of the fractional deaths. A probabilistic setting has been transformed into a deterministic model by replacing all random items by their expected values.

Despite the underlying references to probability, there are many questions that this model cannot answer. One obvious question to ask is the probability that the insurer runs out of money, that is, the probability of experiencing aggregate claims in excess of the accumulated premiums. On a deterministic model, this ruin cannot occur because the premiums assume an eight-year lifetime but the underlying model assumption is an average lifetime of 10 years, so the insurer continuously accumulates profits. It would be possible to investigate alternative stress tests – for example, how does the insurer fare if 15 percent of lives die each year rather than 10 percent? The answer, in this case, is that the insurer is doomed because the premiums are inadequate. But such a stress test tells us nothing about how likely ruin is.

To answer this question, a stochastic model is required, that is, a model with explicit reference to different probabilities. For example, it might be assumed, going back to the original parameters, that every life, independent of history and of other lives, has a 10 percent probability of death in a given year. This then provides a stochastic model, that is, an explicit probability model.

There are several computational ways to analyze stochastic models. One method is analytical and employs explicit calculation of probabilities. In our example, hand calculations immediately give us a warning that the business model may be less than robust. If two or more deaths occur in the first year then the insurance scheme is unable to pay all claims. According to the binomial distribution, this failure has a probability of 26 percent. This is likely to be an unacceptably high risk.

In our example, for each future time step, there is a minimum number of lives (zero) and a maximum number of lives (if nobody has died). There are also minimum and maximum fund balances. It is possible to enumerate all possible outcomes and assign probabilities using a probability tree. This process is tedious by hand, and there is a limit to this calculation even on a computer because it is unlikely that all the myriad possible paths can simultaneously be stored. Just as importantly, explicit calculations grow substantially in complexity if more factors are made random – the number of new entrants each year, for example. Nevertheless, explicit calculations are often a good way to investigate a stochastic model. In our case, the explicit calculations for the first year quickly reveal the project is not viable, and so a more sophisticated approach is not required.

Further progress can be made using a number of mathematical devices. Discrete probability distributions have a property called the *probability generating function* from which it is possible to evaluate means and variances explicitly. In our simple example, the probability generating functions for the number of lives and the total fund balance can be calculated explicitly. This gives a more compact way of calculating future outcomes than using explicit probabilities. However, even more than explicit probability calculations, probability generating function techniques rely on particular analytical forms for probability models. They are a powerful tool, but only in tractable special cases – some would say, only in contrived examination questions.

An alternative to explicit calculation is Monte Carlo simulation. This tool simulates many thousands of scenarios at random according to the assumed probability law. Probabilistic questions are then addressed by analyzing the simulations. For example, to investigate the probability that the insurer runs out of money within 500 years, one could simulate a million scenarios and count the proportion resulting in ruin. This is an estimate of the probability of failure for the original problem. The calculation (which results in a roughly 36 percent probability of survival after 500 years) runs in a few seconds on a modern computer, making Monte Carlo simulation a highly efficient way to answer this particular question.

There is always a danger in Monte Carlo models of being blinded by the apparent sophistication of the model, and to believe that the presence of millions of scenarios implies all risks have been taken into account. In fact, only those risks explicitly modeled have been taken into account. For example, making mortality stochastic does nothing to address uncertainties in the number of new entrants each year, nor the possibility that the initial 10 percent mortality estimate was wrong.

Monte Carlo methods inevitably entail some sampling error. If the true probability of survival is 36 percent, then out of one million independent samples we might hope to find 360,000 simulations resulting in survival. But as the simulations are generated randomly, we are unlikely to observe exactly 360,000 successes. Purely as a result of randomness in the sampling, our estimate might be inaccurate by a thousand or two. As this affects only the third significant figure in our probability estimate, we may consider that a million simulations gives sufficient accuracy. This could, however, be deemed insufficiently accurate in relative terms if the probability of failure were much smaller. And, remember, our example is a very simple business model. A typical model of an insurer could take more than an hour to run a single scenario, in which case it is not practical to run a million simulations.

Monte Carlo is a powerful and flexible tool, but there are some questions which are difficult to answer. For example, a regulator might permit an insurer to remain open only if the insurer can demonstrate at least a 98 percent probability of being able to pay all claims for the next 10 years. Suppose this is a new rule, and there are transitional arrangements which have the effect of deferring this test until five years after the law is passed.

Our example insurer is interested in the probability of being able to survive the test, applied in five years time. In other words, the insurer is required not only to pay all claims over the next five years but to do so with sufficient accumulated profit that, at the end of the five-year period, a 98 percent survival probability can be demonstrated until 15 years from now (and 10 years from when the test is applied).

To solve this problem with Monte Carlo, we need to calculate simulations within simulations. This is sometimes called *nested Monte Carlo*, or *Monte Carlo squared*. There is a set of *outer simulations* for the first five years, as before. After five years, each outer simulation must split into, for example, 1,000 inner simulations in order to calculate the conditional survival probability from that point on, given the known history up to year five. Thus, if there are 500 outer simulations, and 1,000 inner simulations for each outer simulation, this implies 500,000 simulations in total. However you look at it, this is a large amount of computation. Detailed analysis is worthwhile to ensure the best use is made of available resources – for example, with capacity for 500,000 simulations in aggregate, would a more accurate estimate be obtained by performing 100 outer simulations and 5,000 inner simulations per outer simulation?

The increased use of Monte Carlo stochastic models and nested stochastic models has spawned new techniques for handling what would otherwise be exploding run times –such as variance reduction techniques, use of closed form approximations in the inner stochastic loops, representative scenarios and importance sampling. The text by Glasserman (2004) provides a useful overview.

9.5 Limitations of the normative approach

9.5.1 Practical difficulties

The normative approach lays out procedures to be followed, but these procedures are far from prescriptive and permit many interpretations. This means that a model presented as the result of rigorous analysis may represent only one possible set of conclusions. For reasons that we will explain, in a business context, it would be naive to suppose that the presented model has been selected at random or toward the center of the possible outcomes.

First, there are practical difficulties in applying the normative approach. For example, maximum likelihood estimation may fail to converge, with the likelihood ever increasing as fitted parameters race off to infinity or zero. Even where an optimization algorithm appears to converge, the final point may not be an optimum. Testing of multiple hypotheses may lead to apparently contradictory results, with different models resulting from adding parameters in a different order. Tests might show that a set of parameters improves the fit when added simultaneously while none offers a significant improvement when taken individually. Given the combinatorial difficulty of scanning all possible combinations of including and excluding parameters, it is likely that potentially good models are overlooked. These problems are particularly acute for small or poorly understood data sets. A candid statistician might protest that no conclusions can be drawn from such unpromising inputs, but the actuary has to report model results despite these difficulties.

In some cases, aspects that improve model fit may be omitted because a better model may have little impact on decisions using the model. For example, insurance analysts commonly assume that claims arise as a Poisson process where the time interval between claims has an exponential distribution. At the detail level, this model could easily be disproved by aspects such as fewer claims notifications at night compared to day time, by multiple claims in short succession arising from a single incident, or by the fact that a given vehicle is unlikely to give rise to further claims while off the road for repair. However, if the purpose of the model is to predict aggregate claims over a full year, such short-term fluctuations are irrelevant even if clearly present in the data. The lack of statistical fit does not, in this case, make the model less useful. The same effects could be important for other purposes, however, for example in planning staffing levels in call centers and claims handling departments.

9.5.2   Theoretical ambiguities

More generally, theory tells us how to test competing hypotheses but does not tell us how to construct the hypotheses for testing. Any model can be made to look good in comparison to a sufficiently implausible alternative. On the other hand, given that a hypothesis test at five percent entails a five percent chance of rejecting a correct model, simply testing against 20 or more alternatives provides a good chance of a statistical rejection – at which point, of course, the other 19 alternatives are quietly forgotten. The process of constructing hypotheses therefore involves a degree of skill and judgment that is difficult to verify from a physical science perspective. From a social science perspective, experience, skill or judgment is used to refine the universe of models under consideration, in preference to throwing random hypotheses at a set of data until one sticks. The often-quoted facetious observation that "you can prove anything you want with statistics" has substantially devalued statistical testing in the minds of many managers. For this reason formal statistical tests feature less prominently in commercial negotiations than might at first be thought.

In this context, Box's dictum is often quoted – that all models are wrong but some are useful (Box, 1979). To put this in terms of hypothesis testing, this means that our biggest problem is the Type III error, where neither H_0 nor H_1 is correct but we have to pick one anyway. This has some subtle effects on hypothesis testing. In theory we would like to see the process of adding further parameters terminating at a correct model, with enough data available to distinguish important from unimportant parameters. In actuarial work, in the presence of a Type III error, it is more common to see an apparently inexhaustible supply of significant further parameters, each of which improves model fit while chipping away at parameter estimate reliability. The decision to stop adding parameters is frequently pragmatic, for example due to reporting deadlines, rather than statistical.

9.5.3   Expecting the unexpected

A key part of financial planning in most businesses is stress testing against past scenarios. Firms might consider how their business strategy might fare in a repeat of the UK 1974 equity crash, Hurricane Andrew, the Russian debt crisis of 1998, the 2001 World Trade Center attack, and so on.

Calibration to past data is in the nature of statistical models. As a result, events that have never happened are usually ascribed a modest probability. In a data set of modest size, rare but extreme events are over-represented if they appear and under-represented if they do not.

Practical examples of this problem include:

- evaluating the cost of earthquake or flood insurance for a building in a location with no recorded past earthquakes or floods;

- evaluating insurance against events that have occurred in the past but which reforms (supposedly) exclude in future. What effectiveness should an insurer ascribe to reforms introduced in the wake of market crashes or accounting frauds?

- evaluating liability insurance in respect of a nuclear power plant, whose only past claims have been in relation to minor injuries from slips and falls; and

- evaluating risks in the presence of uncertain trends, for example old-age mortality or risks affected by climate change.

Techniques for estimating such tail events include:

- the fitting of a distribution to historic data, based on a particular functional form. This form is then extrapolated to rare events outside the historic data;

- an analysis of extreme but painful outcomes may make use of data on near misses. For example, financial firms are interested in the frequency of events severe enough to cause ruin, but by definition these events are excluded from the history of a solvent firm. However, there may be clues in accounts of losses whose severity fell short of being ruinous; and

- exposure-based analysis looks at the drivers of potential losses even when no claims have been made. For example, a mining company examining the cost of accidents may have no data on a particular kind of loss, but exposure measures such as the number of employees exposed to a particular hazard can be combined with measures of likely costs of compensation or remediation as relevant factors in consideration of future risks.

9.6   Commercial modeling

9.6.1   The role of modeling within the Actuarial Control Cycle

Some models are used once and then thrown away. In a business context, this is usually regarded as inefficient investment of effort. Models are designed to be used over and over. The shelf life of a model may vary from a few weeks to many years.

The fact that a model is re-used does not mean that it does not change over that period. Instead, most models are continually updated, improved and enhanced. Model forecasts are compared to observed outcomes. Any discrepancies are then fed back into the modeling process to improve the model's forecasting ability.

We might hope for a smooth progression of ever-improving models on a happy trajectory to perfection. Each new piece of emerging new information leads to improved estimates and the model becomes an ever more effective forecasting tool. Reality is not usually this simple, and the modeling process usually involves blind alleys, that is, promising modeling approaches later abandoned. Data may confirm the existing model, or may alternatively discredit a model entirely. Catastrophic events such as market crashes, earthquakes, floods, epidemics and man-made disasters may have a huge human cost but also act as stimuli for new directions in modeling.

9.6.2   Costs of models and data

Statistical theory has a great deal to say about optimal estimates. In many contexts, an additional factor comes into play, which is the cost of building a model and using the output. These costs include:

- costs of data collection, cleaning and processing;

- costs of estimating model parameters;

- costs of model testing and validation;

- hardware and software costs of computer implementation; and

- costs associated with the use of model outputs, including communication.

We now consider examples of these costs and how they affect model choice.

Collecting data can be expensive. For example, consider a pension plan that wants to improve the accuracy of mortality estimates by reflecting levels of obesity. Statistically, this is very likely to improve forecasting accuracy, as obesity exacerbates many medical conditions. There may also be a social benefit, in that obese members confronted with the longevity implications may take steps to lose weight.

But the practical costs of collecting that data are severe. Quite apart from the logistics of tracking down and weighing a large number of pension plan members, willing cooperation is by no means assured. There may be legal obstacles to asking members about their weight, and members may have a legal right to refuse to share the information. Data reported by members may suffer a number of biases. Data storage requires appropriate security and compliance with privacy legislation.

Model estimation is made more complex by the use of additional data. For example, an important actuarial task in motor insurance is the forecasting of claims ultimately arising from a collection of policies. This issue is subtle because insurers may not be immediately notified of the loss on an insurance policy when an accident happens. There may be delays in reporting of accidents, and various elements of negotiation as a claim proceeds. The last claims to be settled are subject to greatest uncertainty, for example in relation to the cost of ongoing medical care for a faultless party injured in an accident. It is currently standard practice within the industry to estimate the ultimate losses by plotting claims notifications and payments cumulatively as a function of time since policy inception. This produces a sigmoid ("s"-shaped) curve that may be extrapolated using various curve-fitting techniques.

There is the possibility, however, of making use of more granular data broken down at the level of individual claims. It is then possible, for example, to detect whether an unexpected flurry of payments is due to new notifications of accidents, or a deterioration in the financial positions of claims already recognized. There may be evidence of data changes at a granular level which are invisible, or only visible later, in aggregate patterns. Granular data may also give better insight into estimation uncertainty. One of the effects of developing information technology is to reduce the cost of data processing and analysis, with the result that the use of claim-level data is becoming more widespread in loss estimation.

It is common in modeling to group input data. For example, in a database of insurance policyholders with ages between 40 and 50, a model might instead assume that all policyholders are aged 45. Plainly this simplification makes the model output less accurate, but it is also likely to reduce by a factor of ten both the input data storage requirements and the calculation run time. If the loss of accuracy is not significant, then the data grouping is justified by reference to the cost savings.

Many models start their lives as computer spreadsheets. Spreadsheets make many things easy, including manipulation and graphical display of moderate-sized data sets. Popular spreadsheet packages are widely used and understood. Most analysts will have access to a desktop computer with spreadsheets already installed.

Although many spreadsheet packages have basic statistical functionality, there comes a point in some models where a specialized statistical package is required. However, the process for an analyst to obtain access to that package may not be straightforward. Common difficulties include obtaining authorization for the cost of software licensing, arrangements for training, and support in the absence of in-house expertise. Organizations are likely to also require extensive testing of new software in the context of existing technology infrastructure. A quick way to become unpopular is to download a piece of clever software from the internet that causes a substantial slowing of network traffic.

For all these reasons, it is common to see models analyzed and fitted in spreadsheets, using intuitive and informal methods even when superior statistical tools are available in specialized software. From a purely statistical perspective, this may not be the best course of action. However, the benefits of greater statistical sophistication are outweighed by other costs associated with model sophistication.

Finally, we can consider the costs of use of model output. Senior executives in large organizations may prefer not to spend their time understanding the models embedded within their organization or waiting for output of complex number crunching. As a result, models presented to senior management are often simplified to a level that management can grasp within an allotted 30-minute presentation, including time to re-run under alternative hypotheses. It is good practice for analysts preparing such simplified models to compare the output to more theoretically justifiable models, ensuring that key messages are not lost.

9.6.3 Robustness

It is common to see models described as *robust*, with this term intended to denote a good thing.

So what does robustness mean? In plain English, it means a robust model can stand up to challenge. It signals confidence in assumptions, in the mathematical formulas and in the software implementation. There is also a precise, but different, statistical meaning of robustness, defined in terms of estimator sensitivity to outlying observations. In this section we use the broader definition rather than the statistical one.

In a business context, modelers may face difficult timing decisions in relation to the disclosure of model results. These decisions are not purely statistical, but also arise from information asymmetries within commercial organizations.

For example, suppose a model initially produces results that nobody believes. The search for an explanation picks up first the most flagrant mistakes – for example an input in millions that should be in thousands. Attention then moves on to other variables whose value might be subjective and could be varied to move the answer in the right direction. When the model produces the previously expected answer, particularly if a reporting deadline is looming, modelers might call off the search for further mistakes.

Such a process is unlikely to lead to a robust model, but how can management evaluate that risk? The recipient of modeling output tries to evaluate several things at once:

• the answer to the problem posed;

• the quality of project management; and

• the quality of the modeling.

Project management is about planning, organizing and managing resources to complete a project successfully. A piece of good statistical analysis may still be a poor example of project management – for example, because it was delivered late or the budget was overspent. Every project sponsor's fear – particularly for technically complicated projects – is a series of reassuring interim reports followed by a failure to achieve any of the project's objectives. For this reason, most project plans involve the reporting of milestones, including intermediate results. Analysts may feel under pressure to release results early, perhaps before the proper statistical and quality controls are in place.

Quality of modeling includes an assessment of whether modeling has been competently executed, with sufficient checks and reviews in place. One possible indication of poor quality is output results that fluctuate wildly between one report and the next – for example because of mistakes in data or coding which are then rectified. There are also legitimate reasons for results to fluctuate; for example, most analyses of the risks of corporate bond investment produce dramatically different results after a year of bad credit experience. The difficulty from the recipient's perspective is that these explanations for volatile results are difficult to distinguish, so clear communication from the modeler is vital. There are usually many factors that contribute to fluctuations in results, and it is understandable that explanations from modelers themselves tend to give greater prominence to those causes, such as moves in market data, for which the modeler is unlikely to be blamed. For this reason, modelers are often reluctant to release early model results until thorough testing has been done, lest subsequent revisions undermine the modeler's reputation for good quality work.

9.6.4   Governance and control

The multiplicity of approaches to model building can lead to unpredictable output or unpredictable changes in results from one period to the next. Organizations can seek to manage this volatility in two ways: governance and information technology.

Governance is the process of oversight in decision making. Where modeling decisions affect the way a business works or reports, inputs need to be validated with the relevant business units and the conclusions need to be brought to the attention of a suitably senior person. Governance includes the structure of financial reports, the distribution lists of people who receive them, the process for numbers to be signed off, as well as the processes for establishing and maintaining documentation relating to the models themselves.

Information technology can be both a blessing and a curse in model control. Without computers, most of today's modeling would be impossible. Model users often value flexibility – the ability to run many different models, and experiment with data sets, assumptions, outputs and so on. This flexibility can create dangers for the integrity of financial reporting. For example, suppose an actuary experimented with alternative mortality tables ("what happens if everybody dies at age 70?") and then forgot to reset the table prior to a financial reporting run. To mitigate this risk, most business systems impose a series of locks and approvals to limit users' ability to make changes to business-critical processes. There are also processes to migrate models from an experimental spreadsheet environment during development to a more disciplined environment sometimes described as "business as usual." These controls, however, bring their own frustrations, for example when an important bug fix is delayed because the approval is stuck in the in-box of a colleague who is on holiday or an untested fix is forced into production because of an important subsequent change to the same code.

9.6.5 Models for advocacy

In many actuarial applications, the modeling purpose is close to what the textbooks assume – to produce the best forecasts of real world events. For example, the purpose of a mortality investigation is to develop tables that can be used to forecast deaths in future. Analysis of borrowers' defaults on credit card debt, as a function of borrower attributes such as income, occupation or age, are built with a purpose of predicting future defaults and (from a lender's perspective) avoiding the advance of money to borrowers who are unlikely to pay it back. In these cases, the modeling comes first, and whatever conclusions are drawn are then supported with reference to the modeling effort.

Constraints of time and money may limit the amount of modeling that can in practice be performed, and good modelers develop a strong sense of where time and money can be best spent. With experience, they may also develop a sense of the kind of investigations that are a waste of time and money, that is, which bring little incremental insight for the effort put in.

On the other hand, many modeling projects are commissioned for the purpose of advocacy, especially in long-term actuarial work. Actuaries are in the business of long-term financial projections for long-term purposes such as multi-year life protection and long-term savings. In any contract, lawyers will attempt to foresee a range of possible events and capture in the contract the rights and obligations of each party under a nearly exhaustive list of circumstances. However, the longer the term of the agreement, the wider the range of possible outcomes and the more likely a chain of events not foreseen in the original contract. Examples of this include the various circumstances under which an arrangement, such as a retirement benefit plan or a policyholder fund with profit-sharing provisions, may be wound up or restructured.

There is a way of dealing with such situations, where legal uncertainty arises from contracts failing to anticipate all future eventualities. The business solutions invoke notions of fairness, and compliance with the intention of the original agreement. There is often a consumer protection concern, with either a court or regulator appointing an independent expert whose role is to ensure the interests of plan members or policyholders are appropriately represented.

In this situation, an insurance company or retirement benefit plan sponsor must try to convince the members' representative that its proposed solution is fair. For example, it may argue that a restructuring to simplify the operation of a profit-sharing fund can provide a cash benefit to shareholders while leaving policyholders no worse off in terms of their expected benefits. Other cases where fairness may need to be demonstrated are in the justification for discriminatory insurance pricing, or that a proposed merger does not impair competition. Banks may wish to argue to a regulator that they can exploit new growth opportunities in exotic financial products or emerging markets without adversely affecting depositors' security.

Where fairness is to be demonstrated, the project sponsor clearly desires a particular model outcome. A model that demonstrates the fairness of the sponsor's approach is a good outcome. A model that demonstrates the opposite is a waste of money, from the sponsor's point of view. The dilemma for the business is how to plan expenditure to ensure value for money, when the results of modeling are not known in advance. This is a vitally important area for actuaries, bringing together questions of statistics, economics and business ethics. We consider these issues in the next section.

9.6.6 Models and markets

Economists since Adam Smith have tried to understand the *invisible hand*, that is, the mechanism by which markets direct production and consumption with minimal external planning or control. As well as being a way to describe the world about us, models are a tool by which some earn their living, which makes models open to study as an economic good. There is a market in models, which can lead to supply and demand for models rather different from those arising from normative principles. The way in which managers source model output to support their arguments is subtle, delicate and seldom discussed. This section gives an introduction to some of the tools available to study model selection.

Analysts very seldom receive requests to prove a statement that everyone knows to be false. Compliance with such a request would be not only unethical but also damaging to the analyst's reputation. For example, there is practically no research now published demonstrating health benefits from the smoking of tobacco. However much the tobacco manufacturers might like such research to exist, they are also realistic about the prospects of any credible research coming to that conclusion. So there is some self-censorship by management in proposing only those positions that have some chance of credible defense.

The market in models is of particular interest where data is scant, ambiguous or open to several interpretations. In that case, normative principles may be inconclusive, leaving a greater role for the market in model selection. Prior to commissioning research, management may try to become familiar with the various possible methodologies in order to understand approaches that are likely to lead to the desired conclusions.

Modelers may also develop knowledge of the relationship between prior views, approaches adopted and modeling conclusions. This knowledge may be developed at first by the labor-intensive approach of trying out many alternatives and logging the results. Published literature surveys may also help in developing a sense of what techniques lead to what conclusions, and why. Expert modelers with knowledge of available data and commercial operation of a particular market often develop a fine intuition in relation to modeling approaches.

From management's perspective, hiring an expert has the clear advantage of reducing the uncertainty in model outcome. The procurement process for commissioning models provides ample opportunity for modelers to signal in advance the likely outcome of their investigations, without the sponsor having to demand explicitly a certain set of conclusions. Research papers supporting certain commercially expedient conclusions are more widely quoted and more effectively disseminated than papers proposing the opposite. Analysts with a good understanding of management's objectives are able to deploy limited resources more productively – a key requirement for promotion in most organizations.

The operation of this market does not imply that management or researchers are being dishonest or otherwise unethical. An accountant may observe that the lower the value he puts on a liability, the happier his clients are. If a button on the computer program has the effect of doubling the stated liabilities, the accountant soon learns not to press that button, just as laboratory rats learn to avoid the corridor that leads to an electric shock. A simple process of learning from client feedback leads to a preference for certain methodologies and avoidance of others. It is easy to interpret a happy client as a signal of intellectually superior work. There need be no conspiracy to drive down stated liability values.

It might be tempting to draw the sad conclusion that the only stable situation is of shoddy work producing conclusions to order, with elastic moral principles the primary requirement for a profitable actuarial career. That conclusion would offend the high principles of many actuaries and in any case is wrong because of the feedback mechanism of reputation. Most analysis ultimately seeks to persuade, and that persuasion is most effective when it builds on the author's reputation for integrity. For this reason, individuals, corporations and professions invest in their own reputations by refusing to sign statements that may later be proved false. Fears of litigation, professional censure or reputational damage combine with ethical principles to encourage good quality work. For this reason, aspects such as consensus and authority of the author sit alongside statistical tests in many model evaluations.

9.6.7 Disclosure

According to the best practice in scientific methodology, hypotheses should be subject to harsh tests and independent verification before they can be regarded as knowledge. Such testing works best in an environment where data and models are published and debated openly. For this reason, it is usually good practice to document models fully, so that another analyst, faced with the same data, can reproduce the model results.

In commercial practice, full and open disclosure is not the norm, and it is important to understand why. The first reason relates to intellectual property and the second to the negotiation process.

To understand the intellectual property issue, let us consider the example of natural catastrophe models. Insurers have an interest in forecasting events such as storms, tsunamis and hurricanes that may give rise to insurance claims. However, few insurers have the geological and meteorological expertise in-house to develop credible models in this area. Instead, a small number of specialized teams of scientists carry out the necessary research and generate their income by licensing to the insurance community software that encodes the results of the research, allowing insurers to enter the geographic coordinates and values of insured property and providing as output a distribution of catastrophe losses.

Unfortunately, it is in the nature of information that once you have given it away, it is much more difficult to use that information to earn continued income. For this reason, catastrophe modelers may be evasive about the exact data and assumptions that underlie the model. Such secrecy may also reduce the scope for disputes, but this creates a difficult situation for customers, that is, insurers. They may be unclear how much reliance they can place on black-box models. It is difficult to calibrate allowances for effects such as climate change if the model builder is secretive about the extent to which the model already allows for these effects. There is some scrutiny after events have happened; for example following events such as Hurricane Katrina, insurers evaluate how well the model captured their loss experience and the model builders rush to patch any exposed model weaknesses.

Another reason for withholding modeling information is the process of negotiating. For example consider the sale of a business unit from one insurer to another. The seller naturally wants to achieve the highest price possible, but it will have in mind a walk-away price at which there is no further interest in selling. The buyer wants to achieve a low purchase price, but also has in mind the highest price it is prepared to pay.

Negotiations do not typically follow a series of numerical bids and offers. Instead, models and discussion of model results are an important part of the process. The purpose of the modeling is not merely to provide work for actuaries (although that is an incidental benefit) but reflects the role of information in negotiation. At the start of negotiations, the seller has more information about the business than is available to the buyer, although the buyer may have information about possible synergies with its own business, affecting the price it is prepared to pay. Information asymmetries act as a hurdle to transactions, as each party fears signing up to a deal that turns out to be different from how it originally seemed.

As part of the negotiation process, each side seeks additional information that may give it a pricing advantage. Information is traded against price – for example, the buyer may point to a particular area of uncertainty as an obstacle to raising its bid; the seller then discloses aspects of its own models in the hope of securing a higher price.

One of the most persistently difficult elements in negotiation is understanding the model graveyard, that is the modeling approaches that were tried but later abandoned. In negotiation each party is keen to show its proposal in the best possible light, so models that might not support the desired conclusion are censored. On the other hand, each party will try hard to dig into the other party's model graveyard in order to discover any business risks that may otherwise not emerge until after the deal is signed. A policy of openness is clearly not an optimal negotiating strategy.

Disclosure is about sharing models and assumptions with other parties. However, even within organizations, openness and transparency may not be the norm. Management is increasingly alert to the risks this brings, and may seek to mitigate the risks by ensuring knowledge is broadly spread and that documentation is accessible, comprehensive and up-to-date. Analysts, however, may see a career advantage in being one of a small group that understands a business-critical modeling process. Sharing that knowledge may increase the risk of employment being terminated at a later date. There may also be risks of documenting models in the event of a discovery process. This is a legal process where one party may have access to another party's working documents in the event of a dispute.

To conclude this section, in many circumstances clear documentation and open discussion are inherently good things. Free dissemination of good modeling and analysis can contribute to the public good with benefits to society as a whole. However, appropriate mechanisms for getting to that position remain a matter for debate. Producing models and analysis is expensive, and in many negotiation situations the private gain from access to confidential information remains a powerful motivation for producing that information in the first place.

9.7 Practical implications for actuaries

Models are an integral part of the management of any modern financial business.

There is a large body of theory in statistics and computer science relating to models. This theory is a source of good practice for designing, building and operating actuarial models in a business context, even when data and computational power are limiting factors. However, practical situations frequently require compromise and there is often room for debate regarding the best modeling approach.

The commercial environment adds complexity to actuarial modeling. Good project management imposes budget and timescale constraints. There may be a preference for a particular model outcome, for example to support a particular argument. Such commercial pressures can bias model output in many ways of which the recipients of model output need to be aware. For this reason, model experts need skills in communication and negotiation in addition to technical statistics and computing expertise.

Many insurers have experienced a proliferation of thousands of models as technology has enabled these to be created in greater volume and variety than ever before. The next decade is likely to see substantial investments in computer systems and procedures to bring these models more substantially under management control and to minimize any threats to the integrity of financial reporting and business management.

9.8 Key learning points

- Models are essential to actuarial work.
- Models represent reality with the degree of accuracy required depending on the application.
- There are formal, statistical approaches to constructing and validating models.
- There is a difference in how the social and physical sciences approach the modeling process.
- Parsimonious models are generally preferable.
- Documenting and communicating all steps in the modeling process is critical.
- Computers and information technology play a significant role in the modeling process.
- Modeling may be part of an advocacy process.

CD Items

Ferris, S. 1998, Greenslips in the Red, *The Actuary*, July 1998.

Hardy, M. 2001, A Regime Switching Lognormal Model of Long-Term Stock Returns, *North American Actuarial Journal*, 5(2), pp. 41-53.

MacDonald, A.S. 1997, Current Actuarial Modeling Practice and Related Issues and Questions, *North American Actuarial Journal*, July 1997, Vol. 2, No. 2, pp. 24-37.

Salmon, F. 2008, Recipe for Disaster – The Formula That Killed Wall Street, *Wired.com*, February 23, 2008.

Chapter 9 Exercise 9.1 Data Spreadsheet

Chapter 9 Exercise Solutions

Chapter 9 Exercise 9.1 Solution Spreadsheet

References (other than CD Items)

Black, F. & Scholes, M. 1973, The Pricing of Options and Corporate Liabilities, *Journal of Political Economy*, 81(3), pp. 637-654.

Board for Actuarial Standards 2009, Modelling Standard, http://www.frc.org.uk/bas/ publications, accessed on January 28, 2010.

Box, G. 1979, Robustness is the Strategy of Scientific Model Building, in *Robustness in Statistics*, R.L. Launer and G.N. Wilkinson, eds., Academic Press, New York.

Cairns, A.J.G. 2000, A Discussion of Parameter and Model Uncertainty in Insurance, *Insurance: Mathematics and Economics*, 27, pp. 313-330.

Fisher, I. 1930, *The Theory of Interest*, Macmillan, New York.

Glasserman, P. 2004, *Monte Carlo Methods in Financial Engineering*, Springer.

Stuart, A. & Ord, K. 1984, *Kendall's advanced theory of statistics, 6th edition*, Arnold Publications.

Fred's Coffee Shop – Data and Assumptions

Fred needs data to help him to set the assumptions for his business plan model. He will also need data and assumptions when he sets his prices, which we will cover in Chapter 13 (Pricing). Finally, he will need to collect data on the operation of his business so he can track experience and make changes as needed.

What data do you think that Fred might be able to gather for his business plan?

Fred has many options for gathering data. For example, he could:

- count how many other coffee shops there are in the area where he intends to operate. He could visit similar areas and count the coffee shops there, to see whether his patch appears under-serviced;

- investigate the local office buildings where his potential customers work to estimate the total amount of occupied office space within striking distance of his proposed coffee shop;

- visit the local competitors, as a customer, to check their products, prices and the pattern of usage;

- undertake market research by handing out survey forms;

- obtain demographic data (ages, incomes, etc) from the Census Bureau or local civic association; and

- gather data on costs such as rent, utilities (electricity, gas and water) and labor.

Having obtained his data, Fred can use it to help him to set the assumptions for his model. He must understand that much of the data he has collected is unreliable (people do not respond truthfully to surveys, demographic data may be outdated, etc) and so the basis for his assumptions may not be as accurate as he likes. He may have to make some assumptions with no data at all. Even where data is plentiful and accurate, Fred will need to exercise judgment in using it to set assumptions. For example, if demand has been unusually high due to unseasonal weather, or if Fred's proposed offerings are markedly different from the current products, the data from current providers may not be a good guide to his future sales. He may choose pessimistic assumptions so that results are more likely to be better rather than worse than projected.

Once his business starts up, Fred must have a plan for continuing to collect data. Some will be necessary for accounting and tax statements. In addition, he will want to have data available to revise his business plan and its assumptions. By deciding his data needs in advance, he can ensure that it is collected in a timely and reliable manner.

Chapter 10: Data and Assumptions

by Stuart Klugman

10.1 Introduction

The quality of actuarial work depends on the quality of the data and assumptions used. Consider the following list of factors that can hinder the development of the best possible solution:

- lack of time;
- lack of resources (computer time/power, assistance, etc);
- lack of data (quantity);
- lack of relevant data (quality); and
- lack of knowledge about key factors.

The first two are realities of working life. Every aspect of actuarial work discussed in this text is constrained by time and resource limits. The last three are more specific and are the subject of this chapter.

Much, if not all, actuarial work involves considering the effects of uncertain future events. In fact, the slogan of the UK Actuarial Profession is "making financial sense of the future." Since we can't *know* what the future will bring, we need to make assumptions. We also need data, for three reasons. First, we must have data about the present, to give us an accurate starting point for projecting into the future. Second, we will usually require data about the past, to use as a guide in constructing models and setting assumptions about the future. Finally, knowledge about key factors is essential. This knowledge will determine our approach to the whole problem, including dealing with any weaknesses in the quality and/or quantity of the data, and deciding how much weight to give to past data when setting assumptions.

To see how data and assumptions are necessary and intertwined, consider the owner of a professional sports team that is about to move from a covered stadium to an open air venue. The owner is concerned that on rainy days some ticket holders may choose to stay home (in this sport, games are always played whatever the weather, and most of the tickets are sold in advance). The owner gets to keep the money from tickets sold in advance, but will not make money from selling food, drink, souvenirs and parking. The owner would like to estimate the revenue to be lost in the coming season and has hired a consultant to provide the answer.

The consultant has various sources from which to obtain data and set assumptions. The following possibilities are typical of such assignments:

- Facts that are known with certainty. Here that might be the seating capacity, the number of tickets already sold for the upcoming season, and the prices to be charged for the various items purchased by those attending games.

- Reasonably accurate data. It should be possible to get data on the past frequency of rain from the weather service. There should be data from the owner concerning sales of the various items in the season just ended. There should also be historical data from teams that play outdoors regarding the number of no-shows on rainy days.

- Assumptions based on the data combined with judgment. Because the future circumstances differ from the present, it may be necessary to adjust the data-based results. For example, it is possible that customer buying patterns will differ once the team moves outdoors.

It is possible to use data directly without making explicit assumptions (the implicit assumption is that the future will look exactly like the data). However, when doing so, careful thought should be given before proceeding. For example, if an actuarial student has passed the first four Society of Actuaries examinations on the first try, the data would indicate that all future examinations will be passed on the first try. Unfortunately, many actuarial students have proved this assumption to be unsound. Or, suppose 1,000 people age 58 are observed for one year and 48 die, and then 1,000 different people age 59 are observed for one year and 45 die. If one-year term insurance premiums are based directly on these observations, a 59 year old customer will pay a lower premium. This would be contrary to large amounts of previous actuarial experience which strongly indicate that in this age range, mortality increases with age.

While the terms *data* and *assumptions* are familiar to almost everyone, the Merriam-Webster Online Dictionary (2009) defines them as follows:[1]

Data: factual information (as measurements or statistics) used as a basis for reasoning, discussion, or calculation.

Assumption: a fact or statement (as a proposition, axiom, postulate, or notion) taken for granted.

Actuaries may find the phrase "taken for granted" a bit extreme when their assumptions are questioned by regulators or in the courtroom. But once an assumption is set (keeping in mind that the assumption may be a probability distribution or a range of values), it is indeed taken for granted as the basis for further work and the conclusions that follow.

In this chapter we will first look at data. Aspects include types of data, quality of data, data checks and repair, standards of practice and challenges when data are limited. Once the problem has been defined and the objectives determined, the next step is to decide what data is required, how it will be obtained, and what steps are required to ensure its validity. It is tempting to start collecting data at the onset of a project, but the actuary's work will be most successful when data issues are informed by the objectives of the project so that the most useful information is collected.

The second part of the chapter will cover assumptions, including a description of an assumption-setting control cycle; choosing and quantifying assumptions; and the interdependency of assumptions.

10.2   Data

10.2.1   Why is data critical to actuarial practice?

Data is important both to know where we are today and where we might be tomorrow. For the former, it provides the starting point for any analysis. As an example, in a retirement

---

[1]   Less relevant definitions have been omitted.

benefit plan the composition of the covered employees (including those currently receiving benefits, those who are no longer employed but who may receive benefits in the future, and current employees who may receive future benefits) is needed. Information needed for the plan will depend on the terms of the plan, but may include age, gender, salary history and years of employment. A second example is valuing a block of insurance policies for sale or purchase. The first step is to know the characteristics of the policies in the block. It may appear that gathering and verifying such data is trivial, but mistakes happen and there can be surprising difficulties. In one real-life example, when a retirement benefit plan administrator computerized the employee data, data on years of service prior to plan inception was not transferred. Fortunately this caused the valuation numbers to be significantly out of balance with regard to what had been expected and a diligent search eventually uncovered the problem. Another real-life example was a class action lawsuit against an insurance company. The issue was deceptive sales practices that occurred decades in the past. Only paper application records were available and it was not always possible to determine which policies fit the criteria to be in the class.

The second use for data is to aid in the development of a model for what might happen in the future. Actuaries do not have the luxury of predictability that is common to the physical sciences. For example, a physicist can tell you how long it will take a 20 pound ball to fall from a height of 100 feet and would also know how fast it will be going at impact. A chemist knows what will happen when two chemicals are mixed and knows that the same thing will happen the next time.

Actuaries face a more difficult situation for two reasons. First, the future is random (if it were not, there would be no need for actuaries). That means the goal is either a probability distribution or characteristics of a probability distribution. The second is that the probability distribution or its characteristics are rarely known with certainty.

For example, consider the number of claims a 27 year old male driver in an urban location will make in the next year under an insurance policy that pays benefits each time the driver is involved in an automobile accident. A Poisson or negative binomial distribution may be appropriate, but a lot of data will be needed to set the parameters and aid in deciding which distribution to use.

Insurance companies have long recognized the need to acquire large amounts of data and often do so by collaborating in its collection. Such collaboration might be viewed as anti-competitive. In the US, the McCarran-Ferguson Act allows this collaboration by exempting insurance companies from certain provisions of anti-trust laws.

And even if the actuary knew enough to make a highly accurate estimate, the appropriate formula will change each year as driving habits, safety measures, policy wordings and laws change. This means that data-based models may need to be altered to reflect changes in the environment. So, while physicists, chemists, economists and actuaries all have theories about how the world works, only the first two have the luxury of working in a reasonably stable and predictable environment.

The ability to process more numbers at greater speeds continues unabated. As a result, the actuary has more and more information available. But this makes it even more important that data be valid for its intended purpose. Here is an example (from Squire, 1988) where there was an abundance of data, but it was of little value for making predictions.

Example 10.1

In 1936 the *Literary Digest* magazine mailed 10 million poll ballots asking the respondent to indicate if they would vote for Roosevelt or Landon in the upcoming US presidential election. 2.4 million ballots were returned and accurately counted, showing Landon the winner 55 percent to 41 percent (with other candidates getting some votes). The election turned out to be 61 percent to 37 percent for Roosevelt. They had accurate data. What happened?

It turned out that there were two problems. First, the poll was mailed to lists of telephone and automobile owners, a subpopulation that tended to view Landon more favorably. Second, it turned out that those who returned the poll ballot were more likely to be Landon supporters.

Actuaries similarly have to recognize that observations from the past may or may not be representative of the conditions which will apply in the future. For example, the time period over which data is collected should be long enough to capture a variety of environmental conditions. Or, sometimes it is just a matter of being sure to understand exactly what each field in a data set represents. For example, a field may indicate whether or not an insured life is a smoker. Without knowing the definition of being a smoker (current or former, regular or occasional, etc) the results of any analysis will have little value.

10.2.2   Specifying data requirements

Data does not appear on demand. It must be collected, perhaps from a company's own records, perhaps from a statistical agency, or perhaps from a government agency. Regardless of the source, the first step is to determine what data to collect. Although the Actuarial Control Cycle suggests that solving problems is an iterative process, it can be very costly if additional data needs to be requested. Although the solution cannot be obtained until after the data is collected, it is important not only to understand the problem, but to have a very good idea of the nature of the solution in advance of data collection. It is also beneficial to consult with the data sources to know what might be available. For example, in a study of joint life mortality it would be ideal to have the date of death of both lives. While it is clear that the age of the second death in a policy that pays at the first death will not be available, it may not be obvious that the age of the first death in a policy that pays at the second death will not be available. The company may only note that the first death occurred. Since no payment is made, the date of the death is not relevant to company operations.

In the discussion above it is assumed that the process is already underway and the only data that will be available is that which has been collected. At times the actuary has the luxury of being part of the process when a new product or system is introduced. This provides an opportunity to request data fields that may be useful for future analyses. While it appears that there is little to risk in not getting it right, on December 31, 1999 the entire world was concerned about just this issue. Many databases recorded dates using only the last two digits of the year. What would happen at midnight when 99 became 00? Calculations done on these dates might be producing negative numbers and odd results. Companies spent millions of dollars leading up to this date investigating what became known as the Y2K problem to find any programming errors. There was a concern that power grids, airplane guidance systems, and anything on a timer might fail. People in the US watched the New

Year's Eve celebrations in Sydney not to see Australians welcome in the New Year but to see if the city was still functioning. When midnight passed in Australia without incident, it could then be reasonably assumed that the US was not at risk.

The key point of the above example is to be thinking not only of today's task but also of data needs for the future. As another example, it may not be clear today what rating factors might be used (or allowed) in the future.

Example 10.2

Consider a defined benefit pension scheme. At retirement, the benefit is based on the number of years of service and the average salary over the five years prior to retirement. At retirement, employees may choose from several annuity types, but they are all actuarially equivalent (that is, the actuarial present value at the time of retirement is equal for all choices). Employees contribute a fixed percent of their salary to the plan and the employer funds the difference. In addition, employees who leave the company prior to retirement age are entitled to benefits earned as of the time they leave employment. One of the tasks of an actuarial consultant to such a plan is to determine the actuarial present value of all promised benefits. What data is needed to perform this task?

As noted earlier, initial data is needed to understand the employee group. For each employee, the following is the minimal amount of information required:

- date of birth;
- date hired;
- current status (employed, previously employed but not receiving benefits, currently receiving benefits);
- salary history (only last five years needed and only for those not receiving benefits); and
- benefit amount and annuity choice (for all but those currently employed).

The projections may be improved with additional information, such as:

- gender; and
- job classification and time in that job.

These may help because mortality and retirement rates may differ by both these factors. Future salary values may differ by job classification and time served in that position.

In order to construct a model (deterministic or stochastic) for future behavior, it is not always necessary to collect data. In a case such as Example 10.2, models for mortality, retirement, and salary increases may be available from industry studies or from government agencies. However, if the plan has been in operation for some time, there will be data available from prior reviews. This can be used to modify assumptions (as discussed in Chapter 17) to reflect differences inherent in this employee group.

Exercise 10.1

Your company operates in a jurisdiction where reserves may be calculated using mortality tables based on your company's own experience. You have been asked to collect experience data from the past five years on your company's universal life policies. You are about to ask the IT department to provide data on all policies that were in force during that period. What data items should you request?

When collecting data, there is a choice between individual and grouped data. Individual data means that the entries for each person (or each policy, or each loan, etc) are kept separate throughout – think of it as one spreadsheet row for each person. Sometimes it is convenient to group data. For example, instead of using the entries for each term insurance policy separately, results could be grouped by age. The record would show the totaled amounts for male, nonsmokers, age 36-45; male, nonsmokers, age 46-55 ... etc. All policies in a single group are treated as if they are identical, with each measurement based on an average (possibly a weighted average), such as using ages 40.5, 50.5 and so on in the above example. The advantage is that significantly less computer work, both in storage and run time, will be needed. When doing stochastic simulations, the savings can be considerable. The trade-off between the accuracy of individual data and the simplicity of grouping will be determined by the resources available and the materiality of not grouping. Before considering whether to use grouping it is a good idea to do some preliminary analyses using individual data to verify that the grouping is not creating distortions. While it seems like grouping would rarely create distortions, consider the case of endowment policies maturing at age 65. With five-year age groupings, the projected maturity benefits will be paid every five years (for example, if everyone currently aged 58-62 is treated as age 60, they will be projected to receive their endowment in five years, with no one receiving endowments in the two years before or the two years after), creating unrealistic cash flow projections.

10.2.3 Sources of data

There are various sources of data. The next three paragraphs discuss some of the choices we have over sources of data.

10.2.3.1 Internal versus external

Data may be classified as being internal (collected by the company on its own business) or external. Some relevant data can be available from both sources and then a decision about relative weighting must be made.

10.2.3.2 Whole population (census) versus sampling versus survey

A whole population study, or census, is a complete enumeration of all members of the relevant population. Sampling selects a subset of the population for study. The subset is selected so that each population member has a known random chance of being picked. Survey data is based on questionnaires being sent to selected members of the population, but depends on their cooperation to return them. Actuarial calculations for a retirement benefit plan will normally use the data from the whole population of the plan's members. Auditing of processing of health insurance claims often uses stratified sampling (where large claims have a higher probability of being selected). This is necessary due to the cost of auditing every claim. Surveys are more likely to be used for market research or to gauge customer satisfaction.

10.2.3.3   Cross-sectional versus longitudinal

Cross-sectional data arises when observations from numerous subjects are collected at one point in time. An example would be claim payments made in respect of automobile accidents during a fixed time period. Longitudinal data refers to observations collected over time on the same entity. Monthly returns on a stock market index is an example (such data is often referred to as a time series). Of course, both can be present in one data set (for example, several years of automobile accident claims on a block of policies with characteristics varying from one policy to another). In statistics this is referred to as panel data. Challenges can arise with panel data when characteristics change over time. For example, in determining loss reserves the speed with which claims are settled can change over time. In life insurance mortality studies conducted over longer periods of time some contributing companies may drop out in mid study while others may join in.

10.2.4   Obtaining high-quality data

It is obvious that high-quality data is preferred over low-quality data. There are three steps in improving data quality:

- Prevention: this step is done in advance, with a goal of eliminating errors before they enter the database. For example, consider an application for a life insurance product. A form containing relevant information about the applicant as well as characteristics of the product being purchased must be completed. This may be a paper form that is later copied into electronic form or may be directly filled in on the agent's computer or on the internet by the applicant. The system should be programmed to reject obvious errors such as non-existent categories (eg gender not M or F) and inconsistent dates (eg application date prior to birth date).

- Detection: the next step is to study the collected data in a search for errors. This will involve simple checks such as those applied in prevention, as well as other investigations. Section 10.2.5 discusses in detail the sorts of checks that can be applied.

- Treatment: the final step is dealing with the errors which have been detected. It may be possible to repair the data, as described in Section 10.2.6, or we may be faced with deciding whether to proceed with less than perfect data, as discussed in Section 10.2.7.

Further reading on these issues can be found in Herzog, Scheuren, and Winkler (2007).

It is important to carry out the steps of detection and treatment before the data is used. This may seem obvious, but is not always done in practice.

Example 10.3

In a real-life consulting assignment, calculations were to be done on 60,000 policies. A unique rate of interest reflecting past investment earnings was to be assigned to each policy. This seemed to be straightforward because another party had already calculated the rates. (Section 10.2.8 points out that there are often standards of practice for relying on data supplied by others.) Thus, prevention was not an option. While an examination of 60,000 numbers was not feasible, a detection step might include calculating summary statistics such as minimum, mean, and maximum. Had this been done, the assignment of a 20,000% interest rate to one of the policies would have been identified as an error, alerting the parties involved to examine the data further. This was not done, and only when the results (the product of numerous calculations) were significantly out of line with expectations was the search for the cause undertaken. The repair was made, but with significant extra time expended.

10.2.5   Data checks

Appropriate data checks will always depend on the characteristics of the problem at hand. Nevertheless, it is possible to construct lists of items to consider. One such list was compiled by Mailander (2000) and is summarized below. The full article "Some Guidelines on Data Quality Verification" can be read on the CD.

(a)   Know where the data comes from.

(b)   Know why and how the data was originally captured.

(c)   Understand the incentives inherent in the data's original use.

(d)   Examine several randomly selected records.

(e)   Have an expectation of the distribution of the data.

(f)   Look for blanks and duplicates.

(g)   Ask for the definition of the critical data items.

(h)   Develop some ways to verify the data.

The first three items seem trivial, yet it is easy to end up with the wrong data, with incomplete data, or with data collected in an inappropriate manner.

Data checks may be deterministic or exploratory. *Deterministic checks* look for specific errors that are likely to occur. An *exploratory check* examines various global characteristics of the data to see if anything unusual has been recorded. Deterministic checks are completely dependent on the specific problem, and thus can only be discussed in generalities here and then illustrated with an example. Some general categories are:

*   entries are restricted to a specific list of possibilities, such as Male/Female, or Smoker/Nonsmoker, or Urban/Suburban/Rural;

*   entries are restricted to certain numerical ranges, such as a range of allowable ages at issue or of policy amounts; and

*   entries must bear a specific relationship to other entries, such as current date must be later than issue date, which in turn must be later than birth date, or surrender value

must be less than death benefit. Another example is that if one entry or combination of entries have certain values then another entry is restricted (for example, only certain age ranges or benefit amounts allow non-medical underwriting).

Exploratory methods extract certain characteristics of the data. Examples include calculating the maximum, minimum, and average values. A histogram or box plot may also give an indication of whether the items are distributed as expected. For example, when a histogram is made of the number of people at each age in a government enumeration of its population, there will be more people than expected at ages ending in 0 or 5 (due to people who are unsure of their age tending to report a round number). Adjustments can then be made before using the data. A histogram may quickly reveal some high or low values that need further investigation.

At times there is an additional option: reconciling the data against other sources. For example, when doing a valuation on a block of insurance business or a pension plan, there may be summary totals from the company's sales records or from the plan sponsor's payroll records. For quantities calculated each year, the previous year's value, properly updated, may provide a good indication regarding this year's number. This may seem trivial, but sometimes it is the only way to detect major errors such as using the wrong data set. Examples of incorrect data sets include extracting the wrong month or year or extracting the wrong type of claims.

Exercise 10.2

From the list of eight items taken from Mailander, which are deterministic checks, which are exploratory, which are both, and which cannot be categorized as either?

Example 10.4

This example is paraphrased from the Society of Actuaries' "1986-2002 Credit Risk Loss Experience Study." Data from *private placement bonds* was collected in order to learn more about credit risk event rates. Private placement bonds are loans made by insurance companies to corporations. They are not publicly traded, so little information about them is available. A *credit risk event* was defined as failure to make any payment which was due under the terms of the contract. Rates were to be calculated in terms of both counts (number of events divided by number of bonds) and amounts (amounts lost due to event divided by value of bonds). Only one event per bond was allowed.

As a result, for each bond, the following information was required:

- the date of the credit risk event;

- the value of the bond just prior to the event, discounted at current interest rates appropriate for a bond of its characteristics prior to the event. This calculation used the contractual cash flows;

- the value of the bond after the event, discounted at current interest rates appropriate for its characteristics after the event. This calculation used the revised cash flows, taking account of the event; and

- the book value of the bond at the time of the default. In this case, book value meant the value of the contractual cash flows discounted at the interest rate in effect at the time of issue.

The original data set, from which the above were calculated, was examined for inconsistencies. These included bonds having a positive book value on dates after complete default or after maturity; book values being negative; bonds continuing in the database after a credit risk event; bonds leaving the database for no reason; and cash flows that appeared to be normal bond activity even though a credit risk event is stated to have occurred. All changes were made to a copy of the original submission to ensure that the supplied data remained intact. (Details of this process are on pages 140-142 of the report.)

Once the data was cleaned, the key quantities were calculated. Additional checks were then made such as comparing the stated book value to the future cash flows discounted at the original interest rate; identifying bonds where the bond value after the credit risk event was equal to or exceeded the bond value prior to the event; and checking bonds with zero value after the event (while possible, it is unlikely).

At both stages, when anomalies were discovered, the contributing insurance company was asked to check the data it had provided.

Exercise 10.3

You have been asked to perform a mortality study on policyholders who have converted their retirement plan benefit into a life annuity. For each policy being studied, you want to obtain the following information:

- policy ID number;

- date of annuitization (all dates are in yyyymmdd format and annuitization must occur on or after age 40);

- amount of single premium used to purchase the annuity;

- monthly annuity payment;

- annuity form (allowable values are 1, 2 and 3);

- gender (M or F);

- date of birth; and

- date of death (0 entered if annuitant is alive at the end of the study).

The file "Chapter 10 Exercise 10.3 Data Spreadsheet" on the CD contains 1,000 records that were collected for the study. Determine which of the records contain data that warrants further investigation.

10.2.6 Data repair

In Example 10.4, one common method of correcting errors was employed: return to the source and determine what went wrong and then make the correction. At times it is not necessary to return to the source, as it is possible to make the corrections based on internal consistencies or obvious changes, for example, changing cents to dollars or months to years, or filling in a blank data field for gender if the other characteristics point to the data being only for males.

If the correct answer is not obvious and it is not possible to return to the source, then an alternative way of continuing the analysis must be found. One such method is called *imputation*. This is commonly used in government census work to fill in missing values. By looking at records with complete data, an inference can be made about the missing field based on those fields that are filled in, for example, by regressing the missing item on the other variables. Most applied statistics texts offer methods of dealing with missing data.

If the record cannot be repaired then it may have to be deleted, or at least not used for those analyses that make use of the entry known to be defective. However, this in itself may lead to further problems, as discussed in the next section on missing or inadequate data.

10.2.7 Missing or inadequate data

Much of the above discussion concerns the data you have and assumes that except for small mistakes it is the data you wanted and is appropriate for the task at hand. On occasion, some data that was expected is not present. The reconciliation checks mentioned earlier may help to identify such a situation. Regardless, it is always a good idea to regularly ask whether you have all the data that was requested.

Sometimes it is not possible to obtain the data you need to do a proper analysis. For example, when a company changes administrative systems, its actuaries may believe that all relevant data has been transferred to the new system. It may turn out later that calculations require historical data that was not captured. In such cases the likely possibilities are either to spend the resources to obtain the data or to do the best possible analysis with the available data. In the latter case it is essential to document the shortcomings of the subsequent analysis.

In Exercise 10.4 an example of the challenges of incomplete data is presented.

10.2.8 Standards of practice and professional implications

Some of the national actuarial associations have developed standards of practice with regard to data quality. The CD contains "Actuarial Standard of Practice 23 – Data Quality" from the US Actuarial Standards Board and "Standards of Practice – Section 1530 – Data" from the Canadian Institute of Actuaries. The UK and Australia do not have a specific standard regarding data quality, but data issues are mentioned in the context of other standards. Some extracts from the UK standards are provided on the CD. Whether or not the country in which you practice has data quality standards, these provide excellent guidance for good practice. The following points summarize the key items in the US and Canadian standards, but those practicing in the two countries represented should read the standard and not rely on this summary.

- The actuary should communicate and disclose all data issues and in particular any data limitations.

- Data should be appropriate for the scope of the assignments and the intended use of the analysis.

- Accuracy and completeness of data supplied by others can be relied upon, with the following precautions. There must be disclosure, that is, all reports must identify the supplier and the manner in which the data was relied upon; and, while a complete audit is not required, such data should be reviewed for reasonableness, consistency and questionable values.

- The actuary must decide if the data is sufficient and is fully useful; is usable, but must be qualified; or is unusable.

The following view from outside the profession is also helpful. The Australian Bureau of Statistics (2009) has a data quality framework which lists seven dimensions of quality. While designed for use by government statistical agencies, they are applicable to all who use data.

(a) Institutional environment: the production of data should be impartial and objective; conducted by independent professionals; carried out with adequate resources; and controls must be in place to ensure confidentiality.

(b) Relevance: the data should be adequate in scope and coverage; should be collected over an appropriate time frame; and should measure those qualities it is intended to measure.

(c) Timeliness: the delay between the events measured and when the data become available should not be too great. Timeliness also includes the frequency of updates.

(d) Accuracy: sampling error is the most critical component for actuarial studies. For surveys there are issues of coverage, non-response and erroneous responses.

(e) Coherence: there should be both internal consistency in the data as well as consistency with regard to previous studies and those done by others.

(f) Interpretability: the data should lead to results which can interpreted by and be meaningful to users.

(g) Accessibility: the data and reports must be available to those who will use them.

As with all actuarial work, it is important to document what has been done. While this is noted above when communication is discussed, there are two other concerns. If the report considers only the task at hand, some features of the data may not be mentioned. However, data that is sufficient for the current task may not be reliable for other tasks in the future. Also, for audit or legal purposes, it is important to have careful documentation of the steps taken to obtain the final clean set of data used in any analyses.

10.2.9   Challenges presented by limited data

In many insurance applications there is an abundance of data. But that is not always the case. For example, liability insurance claims such as medical malpractice are fairly infrequent. This is particularly problematic when setting assumptions such as selecting a probability model. Having only ten or twenty observations can make this very difficult.

Options for obtaining more data include going back further in time or obtaining data from other sources. In both cases the additional data are not likely to be representative of the process being studied. This is particularly problematic in enterprise risk management. For example, when aggregating risks, correlations are critical, yet tend to be unstable over time. However, there is often no extended history regarding correlations of newer products. With regard to operational risk (sometimes defined as failures due to people or processes) there is limited data on failures (after all, in the history of a given firm, almost by definition a catastrophic failure has never happened). There is public information about major losses but each one occurs in a unique set of circumstances. For example, how many failures can be attributed to faulty or fraudulent auditing processes? The following is paraphrased from Samad-Khan, Moncelet and Pinch (2006).

When choosing between internal and external data, there are trade-offs that cannot be reconciled. When it comes to extreme events, there is likely to be little (if any) internal data. For operational risk events there will be even fewer data points. External data will be more voluminous, but usually must be scaled to reflect the risks of the particular organization. That is, the cost of a particular failure at company X may be $3 billion, but if the same event happened at our company it might cost $0.5 billion. The authors caution that the scaling should be only to firm size, and not by the risk manager's assessment of how the risk's specific impact would be altered by happening in his company. In the example, it can be inferred that our company is one-sixth the size of the company that had the failure. No attempt should be made to try and deduce the specific impact of that type of failure. An additional problem when using outside data is that the reporting basis may not be consistent.

Exercise 10.4

This exercise is from the Casualty Actuarial Society Committee on Professionalism Education (2008). Some of the words have been changed to be more consistent with usage in this text.

ETHICAL ISSUES FORUM – Working with what you got – a question of data quality

Kerry Komplete FCAS MAAA works as an analyst for Advanced Actuaries, LLC, a large consulting organization. For each of the past five years, Kerry has performed an annual reserve review (that is, the determination of reserves for claims yet to be resolved and those incurred but not yet reported) for GLRUS Inc., an insurer that provides liability coverage to mid-tier commercial clients. GLRUS is one of Advanced Actuaries' oldest and best clients. However, Kerry has been increasingly concerned about the financial position of GLRUS over the last few years.

As she does every year, Kerry requests updated data from GLRUS and places her annual call to Joe Honest, the executive in charge of claims, to find out if there have been any changes in claim handling. Joe tells Kerry that GLRUS laid off a large number of claims handlers about a year ago. Kerry expects the total annual payments and adjustments to case reserves (reserves for claims that are in process but the amount is yet to be determined) to be affected by this (with fewer claims handlers it is likely that there are more outstanding claims than in past years), but her initial review of the data does not show anything out of the ordinary.

Knowing that the total reserve liability could be greatly affected by a change in claim handling if she uses the same factors and methods, and that the financial position of GLRUS is uncertain, Kerry decides to verify, quantify, and, if necessary, adjust for the change. That analysis requires additional data and additional time.

> GLRUS tells Advanced Actuaries that the cost of obtaining the additional data is too high and that they will not provide it. They ask Kerry to work with the data that she has already received. In addition, they respectfully ask that Kerry try to keep her billable hours close to last year's level since they are trying to keep costs down during a difficult time.
>
> Should Kerry complete the analysis with the current data provided?

10.3   Assumptions

10.3.1   Why are assumptions critical to actuarial practice?

The dictionary definition of an assumption given earlier was "a fact or statement (as a proposition, axiom, postulate, or notion) taken for granted." There are two categories to consider when interpreting this definition:

- facts or statements which everyone agrees are true; and
- facts or statements with which not everyone may agree.

An example of the first case is the statement "The sun will rise in the East tomorrow." We all believe it to be a true statement and make decisions based on this statement. Of course, it is possible that a statement with which we all agree will ultimately be proved false (at one time everyone agreed that protons, neutrons and electrons were the smallest particles). The second case is far more interesting. Consider the following four statements:

- Inflation next year will be exactly 3%.
- The mortality rates on my company's superpreferred-ultimate-galactic life insurance policy will be exactly 50% of the standard valuation table rates.
- The times to death of each member of a married couple are independent.
- Insured lives who die between ages 90 and 91 all die at age 90.5.

All four statements are almost certainly false. For each of the first two, unless there is a remarkable coincidence, the true number will differ from that assumed. There is ample evidence that death times for spouses are positively correlated. At older ages, the average death age in an interval is probably prior to the halfway point. In these last two cases the actuary has made a simplifying (though wrong) assumption. It may be because the effect of being wrong is immaterial (likely the case for average death age) or because the resources are not available to construct a more complicated model (as is likely the case for correlated death times).

While an actuary may select different assumptions from those above (maybe a stochastic model for inflation or making allowance for dependence in mortality), two things should be clear. First, whatever assumptions are made, they will be wrong and second, it is not possible to proceed without assumptions about the processes that drive the cash flows.

It is important to differentiate assumptions from forecasts, predictions, or estimates. All of the latter terms imply a sort of precision that is not possible when approaching an actuarial problem. There are a lot of tools available to calibrate a model so that its output closely matches the past from which the data were taken. It is another matter to claim that the same model will closely match the future. As Niels Bohr said, "Prediction is very difficult, especially about the future[2]" and as Paul Valery said "The trouble with our times is that the future is not what it used to be.[3]" Pemberton (1999) asserts that "Actuarial science is concerned with the development of models which approximate the behaviour of reality and have a degree of predictive power, not the truth."

The rest of this section describes a control cycle process for setting assumptions. It is followed by an expansion of the first two steps of the cycle (the third step is covered in Chapters 17 and 18). The section closes with a discussion of the interdependency of assumptions.

10.3.2   The assumption-setting control cycle

The concepts of the control cycle can be applied to the assumption-setting process. There are three steps:

- Identify the assumptions. This is a qualitative step where a list is made of the assumptions required to complete the assignment.

- Quantify the assumptions. In this step, numerical values are assigned to each of the assumptions listed in the previous step.

- Monitor the assumptions. As experience is obtained, it can be used to make appropriate numerical changes to the existing assumptions. It may also reveal the need for additional assumptions to be added or for some to be altered beyond just changing the numbers (for example, a change to the type of probability distribution used).

The monitoring phase will be covered in later chapters. Monitoring can lead to changes either in the model (eg use a new probability distribution or change a deterministic assumption to stochastic) or in the assumptions (eg change the inflation rate or the effect of a deductible on average claim payments).

10.3.3   Identification of assumptions

The list of assumptions required will depend on the particular assignment. What is not so obvious is that for any given assignment, we will often have some choices about what assumptions to use, as well as how we quantify them. While it is not necessary to categorize assumptions into various types, it may help in understanding the range of possibilities.

One such categorization is by the source of the data used to set the assumption. Sources can include historical experience from:

- the same company and product;

- the same company, but different (though similar) products;

- similar products sold by other companies; and

- sources unrelated to the company or product.

It is also possible to combine data from the various sources. A decision will have to be made regarding relevance. For example, mortality data may be reasonably stable across companies and so a mortality study reflecting the combined experience of many companies

---

[2]   According to www.quotationspage.com/quotes/Niels_Bohr.
[3]   According to www.quotationspage.com/quotes/Paul_Valery.

may be appropriate. Lapse data tends to be more directly related to the particular terms of the policy (such as cash values or penalties for surrender) as well as the market in which the policies are sold. For economic assumptions, such as investment rates and expense inflation, it is more likely that external sources will supply the information needed.

Another breakdown is implicit versus explicit. Most assumptions are explicit, but at times simplification can be obtained by making assumptions that are not immediately obvious or stated. For example, consider an annuity with payments that increase with the inflation rate. An explicit approach would be to model separately inflation and investment earnings. An implicit approach is to note that if the investment rate minus the inflation rate is constant, then the correct present value can be obtained from a level payment annuity valued at that constant difference. There is now one explicit assumption (the size of the gap between investment rate and inflation rate) and an implicit assumption (that the gap is constant). A danger of implicit assumptions is that in the future the implicit assumption may be forgotten and trouble may ensue if it no longer holds. Assumptions that are not stated are also referred to as being implicit. For example, automobile insurance premiums might be increased to reflect inflation in claim costs. There is an implicit assumption that all other factors have remained unchanged.

Consider an analysis of a life insurance product. Depending on the model selected and the purpose of the analysis, it may be sufficient to assume a single, constant rate of investment return. Other possibilities are different assumptions for each of the various asset classes (needed if investment decisions are being made); the term structure of returns on each asset class (needed to study asset/liability risks); or maybe the investment earnings assumptions need to be set as random variables to be used in a stochastic model. For this last case probability distributions for investment earnings and the parameters of those distributions will need to be specified.

Exercise 10.5

You are the actuary responsible for performing calculations with regard to an employer-sponsored defined benefit pension plan. At retirement it provides a life-time annuity for an amount based on the employee's salary immediately prior to retirement. It also provides annuity payments to disabled employees. Make a list of assumptions required and identify possible sources of information on which calculations related to the present value of future payments may be based.

10.3.4   Quantifying assumptions

There are a variety of qualitative considerations to think about when assigning numbers to an assumption. Among them are the purpose of the assignment, regulatory or practice constraints, the quality of the data, materiality, and beliefs about the future.

Actuarial work often uses what is called the *best estimate*, at least as a starting point. It is best in the sense that it uses available information and appropriate techniques to arrive at the most accurate result. It is usually considered to be the expected value (ie the mean) of a distribution, using assumptions which are not deliberately optimistic or conservative. This is not to imply that different actuaries will all produce the same number, but their methodology should be defensible. There may then be a deliberate departure from the best estimate. A more cautious, or *prudent*, estimate can be reached either by making explicit additional margins for uncertainty, or by moving to deliberately conservative assumptions.

When performing analyses for regulatory, tax, or other governmental purposes, some of the assumptions may be prescribed. There may also be standards of practice that dictate what to do. This may be firm guidance, or a suggested safe harbor.

The quality of the data will have an impact on how refined the assignment can be. If the data is sparse or of low quality it should be made clear that the assumptions based on such data have more uncertainty than those based on data that is more plentiful and/or of higher quality.

The *materiality* of an assumption refers to how much impact a change in the assumption will have on the eventual results. Sensitivity testing can be used to evaluate materiality. For less material assumptions, fewer resources need be devoted to selecting the value. Sensitivity testing can also be used to identify the assumptions that require monitoring.

While an assumption may be a number, that number (or numbers) may be the parameters of a probability distribution. This illustrates where the boundary between model and assumption can become blurred. Consider, for example, the time from the insured's death until when the benefit is paid. The following might be considered, in increasing order of complexity:

(a) not considered in the model, so the time is effectively zero;

(b) modeled as a fixed time for all claims. Data is used to set the assumption as a number;

(c) modeled as a gamma distribution. Data is used to set the assumptions regarding the two parameter values; or

(d) modeled as a probability distribution with an unknown functional form. Data is used to determine both the type of probability distribution and its parameters.

In practice, case (a) will most likely be used as this assumption is probably not material. For cases (c) and (d) it is not clear if naming the probability distribution is an assumption or part of the modeling exercise. There is no practical need to decide this issue since in either case the choice of distribution should be monitored as part of the assumption-setting control cycle.

There is a compromise available between setting assumptions either as fixed numbers or as probability distributions. This compromise is the use of a set number of fixed scenarios. Here, various plausible values are selected and then the analysis is done for each one. Probabilities are not attached to the scenarios (or else it would be no different from assuming a probability distribution). Often, the point is to perform the analysis under each scenario to ensure that the outcome is favorable in each case. Another use is to postulate worst-case scenarios to learn how bad the outcome might be. This is different from sensitivity testing. The goal is not to evaluate the impact of having the wrong value for the assumption but rather to ensure that deviations can be tolerated.

If it is believed that the future will be different from the past, then assumptions should reflect that difference. For example, if highway speed limits are lowered, it is likely that there will be fewer accidents and therefore the frequency assumption for automobile accidents may be modified from one based on past experience.

Regardless of the method used, having appropriate data is likely to be more important than any statistical technique employed. For example, when evaluating historical workers compensation claim data the past payments will need to be modified to reflect medical and/ or salary inflation and to reflect what the payments would have been had the current policy terms been in force at that time.

In addition, our assumptions should not be totally constrained by data about the past. In the economic times in which this edition is being written, when the global financial system has seemed close to collapse, there are many references to "black swans," "perfect storms" and "unique circumstances." The term "black swan" is from the book of the same name by Nassim Taleb (2007). The title comes from the fact that Europeans believed that all swans were white, because that is all they had ever seen. Upon visiting Australia they discovered that swans can also be black. It now refers to situations where an event is totally unlike the past. The term "perfect storm" is from the book of the same name by Sebastian Junger (1997). The title comes from weather systems converging to create an extreme storm at sea. It now refers to any convergence of events that are individually plausible, but believed to be highly unlikely to occur simultaneously. It is very difficult to incorporate into assumptions or models events that are essentially unpredictable. When will the next bubble burst? How severe will it be? One way is to be prepared by understanding the environment (and not just rely on numbers produced by that environment in the past) and to be constantly thinking about ways in which extremely adverse results may occur and what steps can be taken to mitigate them.

10.3.5   Interdependency of assumptions

Interdependency applies in both deterministic and stochastic settings. In the former, assumptions need to be consistent with each other. For example, consider the case of economic variables. As seen earlier (with some detail provided in Chapter 9), investment and inflation rates bear some historical relationships to each other. When setting deterministic assumptions, that relationship should be reflected in the selected rates. In a stochastic setting maintaining this relationship can become complicated. For example, suppose an assumption is made that investment earnings follow some stochastic process and numerous scenarios are to be generated from that process. When setting the corresponding scenarios for inflation rates, the stochastic generator must be set up so that the relationship is appropriately reflected.

In addition to economic variables, many actions that are voluntary on the part of the policyholder will be sensitive to economic conditions. For example, policyholders are more likely to surrender their policies when the economy is poor (due to an inability to pay the premiums) or when a guarantee provided in the policy becomes advantageous (such as a guaranteed minimum withdrawal benefit).

Exercise 10.6

Consider your answer to Exercise 10.5. What dependencies do you expect exist among the assumptions you listed?

10.4   Practical implications for actuaries

Because actuaries are primarily concerned with uncertain future events, they must make assumptions about those events. These assumptions might be best estimate numbers or probability distributions and may also extend to a model that connects future cash flows. Actuaries not only must be prepared to choose from a variety of frameworks but also will be called upon to make decisions about the final choices. This requires both technical skill and professionalism. These decisions will not be made in isolation but rather in collaboration with others. This requires communication skills to ensure that the actuary's points are understood.

In order to set these assumptions, data is almost always needed. In addition, data will be needed as input to the actuary's models. While the actuary may not collect the data, ensuring its appropriateness and quality is a key actuarial function. While it can be a tedious task, data collection and cleaning can easily take up ninety percent of the time devoted to a given project. Exercise 10.4 and the accompanying solution provide a good example of some of the practical implications of the material in this chapter.

10.5 Key learning points

• As an applied science, actuarial work requires data. Data informs our understanding of the past and future cash flows of a financial system.

• There are many ways to collect data. Methodologies include studying the entire population or sampling. Data can be collected over time, over subjects or both.

• It can take considerable effort to ensure that the data is of high quality. There are many techniques that can be used and they can be tedious, but they are essential to ensuring meaningful results.

• Many jurisdictions have standards of practice that govern data issues. Even if your jurisdiction does not have one, reading them provides a means of ensuring you are taking appropriate steps.

• Whether arising from data or from other sources, actuaries must make numerous assumptions in order to solve problems.

• Some assumptions will be more important than others and a margin for conservatism may be appropriate.

• Assumptions can be set from a company's own experience, from the shared experience of many companies, from externally available sources, or from a combination of these.

• It is important to recognize assumptions that are interdependent and properly account for this.

CD Items

Actuarial Standards Board (US) 2004, Actuarial Standard of Practice 23 – Data Quality, American Academy of Actuaries, Washington.

Actuarial Standards Board (Canada) 2009, Standards of Practice – Section 1530 – Data, Canadian Institute of Actuaries.

Mailander, E. 2000, Some Guidelines on Data Quality Verification, Society of Actuaries Course 7 Study Note 7P-32-00, USA.

UK Actuarial Profession extracts from standards on data quality.

Chapter 10 Exercise 10.3 Data Spreadsheet

Chapter 10 Exercise Solutions

Chapter 10 Exercise 10.3 Solution Spreadsheet

References (other than CD Items)

Australian Bureau of Statistics 2009, 1520.0 ABS Data Quality Framework, May 2009, Australian Bureau of Statistics, Canberra, http://www.abs.gov.au/AUSSTATS/abs@. nsf/Lookup/1520.0Main%20Features1May+2009, accessed October 20, 2009.

Casualty Actuarial Society Committee on Professionalism Education (COPE) 2008, Ethical Issues Forum: Working with What You Got, used by permission of the Casualty Actuarial Society, first published in *Actuarial Review*, Volume 35, No. 3, August 2008.

Herzog, T.N., Scheuren, F.J. & Winkler, W.E. 2007, *Data Quality and Record Linkage Techniques*, Springer, USA.

Junger, S. 1997, *The Perfect Storm*, W. W. Norton & Company, New York.

Pemberton, J. 1999, The Methodology of Actuarial Science, *British Actuarial Journal*, Vol. 5, Number 1, pp. 115-196.

Private Placement Committee 2006, 1986-2002 Credit Risk Loss Experience Study: Private Placement Bonds Society of Actuaries, Chicago, http://www.soa.org/files/pdf/ Report2002.20060418.pdf, accessed October 20, 2009.

Samad-Khan, A., Moncelet, B. & Pinch, T. 2006, Uses and Misuses of Loss Data, *GARP Risk Review*, Vol 30, May/June, pp. 18-22.

Squire, P. 1988, Why the 1936 Literary Digest Poll Failed, *Public Opinion Quarterly*, Vol 52(1), pp. 125-133.

Taleb, N. N. 2007, *The Black Swan: The Impact of the Highly Improbable*, Random House, New York.

Fred's Coffee Shop – The Need for Capital

We now come to the need for capital. Capital is needed to finance the cash outflows when expenses are incurred earlier than revenue is received and, most importantly for a financial institution, to absorb risks. The central importance of capital is illustrated in Figure 11.1. The level of capital required is connected to all the other aspects of a company's operations.

Some of these aspects have been covered earlier in the book and others will be discussed later. Chapter 2 explained how the owners of capital accept the risk of making their capital available to an enterprise, in the hopes of earning a return. The greater the risk that is involved, the higher the expected reward that will be demanded. Chapter 7 explained why regulators are concerned that particular types of financial institution operate soundly. One way in which they try to ensure this is by setting rules for the amount and type of capital held by institutions. Chapter 8 on product design noted that more capital will be needed for products that involve more risk or are subject to high regulatory capital requirements. Since the providers of capital need to be compensated, there is a cost involved in holding extra capital; this cost must be taken into account when pricing, as will be discussed in Chapter 13.

Chapter 15 considers in detail how to set the appropriate level of capital. The providers of capital will want to judge whether the returns are in fact adequate compensation for their risks, so they need to measure the risk-adjusted performance. This brings us to the general problems of measuring profit and monitoring performance, which are discussed in Chapters 16 and 17. Finally, as you will learn in Chapter 18, one of the ways of responding to experience may involve raising further capital, or returning capital that is no longer needed.

The chapters we haven't mentioned explicitly here are also connected to capital. The tools and concepts that they discuss are needed to assess capital requirements and advise on capital management.

Chapter 11 considers why capital is needed and the forms that it can take. It points out that there is no single correct answer for the amount or source of capital and that different stakeholders will have different views. It therefore takes you through the perspectives of the main stakeholders. Since there is a fundamental connection between risks and capital needs, the chapter provides a brief overview of the types of risk faced by financial institutions.

How might this relate to Fred's coffee shop? Does Fred even need capital? He certainly does! He will have a lot of expenses before he sells his first cup of coffee. He doesn't need to be as cautious as an insurance company when assessing his capital needs, because the failure of a coffee shop is not going to cause the same damage as an insurance company failure. However, he should build in some margin in case his business does not become profitable as quickly as he might hope – that is, he should allow for risk and not be over-optimistic. As Chapter 11 points out, lack of sufficient capital is one of the most common reasons why small businesses fail.

If Fred doesn't have enough from his own savings, he has to find someone else to provide the necessary capital. A bank may lend him money but will probably require him to pledge assets as collateral. If he ever falls behind on an interest payment, the bank could take control of those assets and he could face serious financial loss. It would be safer to find a financial partner to put up the money in exchange for a share of the profits. If there are no profits and the coffee shop closes down, the partner only receives a share of whatever is left, however little that is, so Fred's risk is lower. But if the business becomes a great success, Fred will not reap the full benefits.

Thus, Fred has to decide how much capital he needs and whether to get it in the form of debt (a bank) or equity (a financial partner). The decision will depend on his assessment of the risks and his willingness to accept those risks.

Chapter 11:   The Need for Capital
by David Knox

11.1   Introduction: what is capital?

All business organizations need capital. In some cases, the capital requirements may be limited, such as a small business operating from home. However, even in this example, some initial capital will be required for equipment and costs (such as a computer, equipment, stationery and advertising) before the business earns any income. In addition, capital may be needed to pay wages and other costs in the early weeks or months of the business operation before any income is actually received. Additional capital is often needed as a business expands. In fact, one of the most common reasons for small business failures is insufficient capital. Optimistic owners and entrepreneurs often underestimate the amount of capital that it takes to establish and sustain a business and to withstand the shocks from unexpected events.

Example 11.1   A simplified example of a new business

Let us consider an example of a small business that expects to break even after four periods and make profits after Period 5. Table 11.1 shows the expected cash flows in the first six periods. You will note that Period 1 has relatively high expenses for the setup and that the income is small in the early periods. The expenses also grow, albeit more slowly than the income, as the business expands.

Table 11.1   Projected cash flow

Period	1	2	3	4	5	6
Income	0	25	100	140	200	280
Expenses	150	100	150	180	200	220
Net cash flow	-150	-75	-50	-40	0	60

Clearly, initial capital of 150 or even 300 would be insufficient for this new business. There is an expected shortfall in income for four periods, which may surprise the optimistic owner.

However capital is also required to enable the business to withstand unexpected events. As will be discussed later in this chapter, these events can be caused by a range of events, many of which are outside the control of the business. As an example, let us assume that difficult economic conditions arise at the end of Period 3, so that the income is 25 percent lower than expected in Period 4 and stays at this level for Periods 5 and 6. The projected income and expenses now look like those in Table 11.2.

Table 11.2   Projected cash flow under difficult economic conditions

Period	1	2	3	4	5	6
Income	0	25	100	105	105	105
Expenses	150	100	150	180	200	220
Net cash flow	-150	-75	-50	-75	-95	-115

The business is now in serious trouble. Not only does it need more capital but it must also reduce its expenses. Initial capital of 350 might have been considered more than sufficient under the expected business conditions shown in Table 11.1 but this would now be insufficient, even if some expenses are cut. This simplified example highlights the fact that capital is needed both for ordinary business operations and to enable the business to withstand unexpected shocks, which can arise from a variety of circumstances.

Although a small business is very different from the banks, insurance companies and funds managers in the financial services industry, these organizations must also have a strong capital base that is consistent with the risks present within their operations. In this chapter, we will also discuss how banks and insurance companies have special features which mean that they have additional capital requirements beyond those that apply to, say, a manufacturing company. In addition, we will consider the need for capital or reserves that can arise for superannuation or pension funds.

But, before proceeding, let us clarify what we mean by capital.

In broad terms, capital is the accumulated wealth of an organization. Some capital is derived from an organization's previous earnings but most organizations also raise capital by issuing financial instruments through the financial markets. Although there exists a wide variety of financial instruments, most can be classified as either equity or debt, or a hybrid of the two.

At this stage it is also worth noting that many financial services organizations use the term *economic capital*, which can be viewed as the amount of capital that the firm needs to ensure that it remains solvent over a certain time period with a specified probability. (See 2.12 for a description of economic capital.) As we will discuss in this chapter, economic capital is different from regulatory capital, which is normally set by the prudential regulator, who is concerned about the solvency and long-term sustainability of the entity.

11.1.1   Types of capital

Equity capital, provided by the owners or shareholders of the company, permits the investors to share in the financial fortunes of the organization. Hence, if the organization makes a profit, dividends may be paid to the shareholders or retained within the company. These retained earnings represent an increase in the net assets (or capital) of the company and therefore should cause an increase in the value of the shares. On the other hand, if the company goes bankrupt, the shareholders are likely to lose their money as they rank after those who have lent capital to the company through debt instruments.

In contrast to equity capital, *debt capital* normally requires a prescribed payment of interest and, in due course, repayment of the loan. Debt holders do not share directly in the profits of the company and rank ahead of the shareholders in the event of a winding-up.[1] There is a wide range of debt securities available including bank overdraft facilities, promissory notes, corporate bonds, mortgages, loans from associated companies and subordinated debt. As the name implies, *subordinated debt* refers to unsecured loans whose holders rank behind other debt holders but ahead of shareholders in the case of liquidation.

Companies with a high ratio of debt to equity capital are *highly geared*, or *leveraged*. In good times, highly geared companies deliver higher returns to the shareholders, but in difficult economic times, including global recessions, they may struggle to cover interest charges. They are more likely to fail than companies with less debt. The correct balance between debt and equity capital for an organization cannot be determined simply. In a perfect market, it can be shown that no combination is theoretically better than any other, as the market for shares and debt instruments will correctly allow for the different risks inherent in different capital structures. However, as will be discussed below, there are several factors that cause different capital structures to emerge in practice.

In addition, financial institutions such as banks and insurance companies should particularly aim for a very low probability of failure. Prudential regulations will usually require them to hold minimum amounts of equity capital. For the banking sector worldwide under Basel II,[2] this leads to the definition of *eligible capital* (types of capital which can be counted in deciding whether the institution meets the minimum capital requirement) as:

- *Tier 1 capital*, which represents the core measure of a bank's financial strength from a regulator's point of view, and comprises paid-up equity capital and disclosed reserves from post-tax retained earnings; and

- *Tier 2 capital*, which includes revaluation reserves, general provision for doubtful debts and various forms of capital instruments as approved by the regulator.

Tier 1 capital is permanent and does not impose any ongoing servicing costs on the bank while Tier 2 capital may have a limited life and/or ongoing servicing obligations. A bank must have enough Tier 1 capital to meet at least 50 percent of its required level of capital.

Clearly, such a regulation imposes restrictions on a bank's capital structure. There is no similar global definition within the insurance sector. In Australia, the capital requirements for life insurance companies must be effectively backed by 100 percent of Tier 1 capital whilst the above banking definition applies for general insurance companies.

---

[1] Companies may be wound up for many reasons, including insolvency. When a company is wound up, there may be insufficient funds to meet all of its debts, in which case a creditor's ranking becomes important. This is not an issue when a company is wound up with a substantial surplus to its debts.
[2] Basel II is the name given to recommendations on banking laws and regulations issued by the Basel Committee on Banking Supervision. The purpose of Basel II is to create an international standard that banking regulators can use when creating regulations about how much capital banks need to protect themselves against financial and operational risks. Generally speaking, these rules mean that the greater the risk to which the bank is exposed, the greater the amount of capital the bank needs to hold to safeguard its solvency and overall economic stability. Basel II uses a "three pillars" concept – (1) minimum capital requirements (addressing credit, operational and market risks), (2) supervisory reviews by the regulator and (3) market discipline which increases the disclosures required from the banks.

11.2   The reasons for capital

This section outlines some reasons for holding capital which apply to almost every organization.

11.2.1   Providing operational capital

As mentioned above, all organizations need capital to operate. This capital is used to provide the necessary infrastructure (such as premises, equipment and systems), as well as to provide working capital which can be used to pay wages and a range of other operating costs.

11.2.2   Withstanding fluctuations within ongoing operations

Every organization needs capital to withstand fluctuations that occur within its ongoing business operations. These events, which represent normal risks of business, include:

- the loss of a client to a competitor, thereby reducing income;
- an increase in input costs such as wages;
- increased price pressure in the market, thereby reducing income;
- increased interest rates affecting the cost of borrowing;
- mis-pricing of a contract due to inappropriate assumptions or an error;
- the financial failure of a debtor, so that the debt remains unpaid;
- a fraud within the operations of the organization;
- a poor investment in the financial markets or a general downturn in the investment markets;
- delay in the expected revenue from a new development;
- adverse currency movements, which have the effect of reducing sale prices relative to input costs for importers or exporters;
- adverse changes in the economic, social or legal environment which affect the company's financial position;
- adverse movements in the value of assets and/or liabilities (perhaps as a result of previously incorrect valuation); and
- for an insurer, an increase in claims, perhaps as a result of bad weather.

In each case, the organization will be adversely affected and may need to draw on its available capital. Without a sufficient level of capital, such events can pose a serious risk to the future existence of the organization.

Organizations or risks with a greater chance of significant cost from fluctuations in experience will generally require more capital.

11.2.3   Consumer confidence

Within most markets, consumers must have confidence in the provider of the service. A simple example is the restaurant industry where the consumer believes that the purchased food will be edible and not lead to food poisoning. A loss of this consumer confidence, which may be accentuated with adverse media coverage, leads rapidly to the demise of the restaurant.

This need for consumer confidence applies even more strongly within financial services. In the banking industry, depositors must believe that their money will be available when required by the customer and not at the bank's discretion. If that confidence is lost, a run on the bank may occur which can be detrimental to both the bank's future and the overall financial system. Similarly, insurance policyholders expect that the insurance company will continue to exist and be able to pay future claims whilst pension fund members expect their retirement benefits to be paid.

The existence of an appropriate level of capital represents an important factor in sustaining this confidence, particularly in financial services. In addition, organizations that are perceived to be strong may be able to charge more for their products or pay less interest on their deposits.

11.2.4 Withstanding unexpected shocks

A critical role of capital is to ensure (within reason) that the company's operations will survive a major financial shock from an unexpected event. These unexpected events are, by their very nature, difficult to predict. The terrorist attacks in the US on September 11, 2001 provided one such example that affected many industries including tourism, air travel and a range of financial services. More recently, the global credit crisis of 2008 represented a significant shock that caused several financial institutions around the world to fail.

Such unexpected events should be contrasted with the consequences of normal business events, as discussed in 11.2.2.

11.2.5 Ability to respond to future opportunities or capital needs

There will be occasions when capital is needed to respond to particular opportunities. These can arise for several reasons such as a change in government policy, the failure of a competitor, a growth in the market, or the opportunity to develop a new product or participate in a new development. In these cases, the existence of, or access to, readily available capital can provide the organization with the ability to respond to a situation that was not foreseen.

In other circumstances, financial projections will indicate the need for additional capital in the future. This may be driven by the future capital requirements of the existing business, as could occur with a portfolio of long-term life insurance business, a change in regulatory capital requirements or the known cessation of a stream of future income (eg a pharmaceutical company with a key drug approaching the end of patent protection). In these cases, it is critical that realistic financial projections are undertaken and that the organization responds with a clear process to raise the necessary capital.

11.2.6 Credit rating

Most governments and major companies, including banks and insurance companies, receive a credit rating from one or more of the major credit rating agencies,[3] such as Moody's, Standard & Poor's or Fitch. These credit ratings, which are determined by the agency's risk

---

[3] The rating structure used by different credit rating agencies can vary. It should also be noted that the value of such ratings has been questioned following the 2008 financial crisis.

assessment of the organization, directly affect its cost of borrowing. That is, a BB-rated organization will pay a higher interest rate on its debt than an AA-rated organization. In some sophisticated financial markets, credit ratings can also affect consumer confidence in the institution and thus the prices they can charge. For these reasons, many organizations elect to hold additional capital to improve their credit rating.

11.2.7   Stability and confidence in the financial system

Chapter 7 discussed the objectives of regulators. Prudential regulators require banks and insurance companies to hold minimum levels of capital not only to provide security for depositors and policyholders, as mentioned in 11.2.3, but also to engender stability in the financial system. Such stability provides confidence for consumers, business operations and investors and thereby provides positive economic benefits to the community.

Whilst the systemic importance of banks has been appreciated for many years due to their key role within the payments system, the relevance of this objective for insurance companies may be less obvious. However, the systemic involvement of insurance within a developed economy was highlighted with the failure of HIH in Australia in March 2001. The failure of this major insurance company contributed to disruption in several insurance markets, including public liability, professional indemnity and builders warranty insurance. Indeed, some building construction sites were closed for a period of time due to the lack of insurance.

Banks and insurance companies have a critical role in underpinning the financial stability of many sectors within a developed economy. Hence governments often require these organizations to hold a level of capital that is likely to be greater than they would otherwise choose.[4] This suggestion leads us to the issue of whether there is a correct level of capital for an organization.

Exercise 11.1

An entrepreneur has suggested that an evening newspaper should be available free during the evening peak hour in a major city. It would be distributed at major public transport centers and carry short news articles with a focus on entertainment and sport together with paid advertisements.

How would you determine how much capital is needed to start this newspaper? What are the major risks involved?

11.3   The need for capital: perspectives of different stakeholders

11.3.1   Introduction

There is no single answer as to the correct amount or type of capital that is needed by any organization. As we will discuss in this section, the amount of capital is determined by several influences, some of which operate in opposite directions.

---

[4]   We will discuss the relationship between economic capital and regulatory capital in 11.6.2.

Initially, let us recognize that the total market value of a company's issued securities (including debt, equity and hybrid securities) is determined by the future cash flows arising from the operations of the company's assets. This is consistent with the famous Proposition I of Modigliani and Miller (1958) who showed that, within perfect capital markets where there are no taxes, the total value of a company's securities is not changed by its capital structure.

At first sight, such a conclusion may be unexpected. Indeed, many companies increase their gearing through debt to apparently raise the expected earnings for their shareholders. However, as the company borrows more, there is also an increase in the risk for both the existing debt holders and the shareholders, which affects the market value of these securities. The 2008 global credit crisis highlighted this effect as the value of many companies with high gearing declined rapidly due, in part, to the difficulty of refinancing their debt.

This theoretical framework is complicated by the real world. First, there are tax effects on all the stakeholders including the company, the debt holders and the shareholders. In addition, these tax effects can differ within the same group of stakeholders. For instance, there may be shareholders who are higher-paying taxpayers and prefer capital gains whereas others are tax-free charities who prefer dividends.

Secondly, there are costs related to possible financial distress. A failure or liquidation of a company is not cost-free and it is the shareholders who lose out first, followed by the debt holders.

Thirdly, the decision between debt and equity is not always straightforward. In many cases, companies prefer to generate internal equity through retained earnings and lower dividends, thereby providing them with available capital and greater control over their financing choices, as well as less concern about the costs and uncertain effects of going to the market and raising either debt or equity.

However, such an approach may also lead to over-capitalization and an inefficient use of capital. With these concerns in mind, together with the increasing volatility in financial markets and greater competition, many banks and insurance companies are now placing greater emphasis on the concept of economic capital.

In the following sections, we will consider the views from the perspectives of different stakeholders and realize that, in fact, the level of capital selected is the result of a creative and positive tension between the desires of shareholders, the board of directors (the *board*) and management, regulators, customers, the rating agencies and the market. It is also affected by the time horizon of the organization and the realization that the presence of capital can provide an organization with some flexibility in times of stress.

Later, in 11.6, we will consider the question of the allocation of capital in the context of economic capital, regulatory capital and actual capital.

11.3.2   The shareholders (ie the investors)

The primary goal of the shareholders is to maximize the return on their equity capital invested, within an acceptable level of risk. However, even this objective creates its own pressures. After all, a lower level of equity capital can lead to a higher return but may also cause a higher probability of failure, due to a lower level of buffer capital. On the other hand, increased equity capital leads to greater financial strength, possibly a higher credit rating (which leads to a lower cost of capital), and possibly less volatility in the level of earnings. A higher level of equity capital can also lead to lower earnings per share, particularly if the prices in the market are relatively insensitive to the organization's capital position.

An important issue from the shareholder's perspective is to appreciate the level of risks associated with the company's business operations. For example, shareholders in an entrepreneurial company are likely to accept a higher level of risk and therefore a much higher probability of failure than would a shareholder in a major financial conglomerate. The entrepreneurial company may be willing to accept a one-in-five probability of failure whereas such a probability of failure would be totally unacceptable for an established insurance company or bank. Therefore, it is essential that the boards of all companies have a clear understanding of their risk appetite and use this to determine the appropriate level and sources of capital. Of course, within a fully informed and efficient market, the value of the company's shares should reflect these risks and be based on the expected cash flows arising from the company's assets and operations.

It is also worth noting that not all shareholders (or investors) of a particular company will have the same risk perspective. Some investors will be willing to accept a higher level of risk due to their diversified investment portfolios. That is, from a portfolio perspective, they may be willing to accept greater uncertainty of returns for a particular investment due to the existence of several other shares in their portfolio.

11.3.3   The board and senior management

As noted above, it is necessary for the board to have a clear appreciation of its risk appetite so that it can determine the appropriate level of capital and allocate it within the business accordingly. One approach is for the board to determine its tolerance toward certain negative results in respect of the whole group, certain business units or particular products. Questions that could be asked include – how willing is the organization:

- to have a return on capital below a given benchmark?
- to reduce its dividend (or even pay no dividend)?
- to breach its loan covenant?
- to lose market share?
- to lose money on a new product?
- to have a liquidity crisis?
- to fail?

The answers to such questions will assist the board to articulate its risk appetite, set targets for performance measures, influence the expectations of both investors and analysts and so, in turn, determine the appropriate sources and level of capital.

Figure 11.1 shows some of the relationships that exist in managing the company's risks, determining the capital needs and analyzing the returns to shareholders. It is apparent that the level of capital required will be strongly influenced by the board's strategic decisions in terms of the company's product offerings, selection of markets, as well as its growth and pricing strategies. Simply put, the board's risk appetite together with the risks inherent within the company's operations should determine the capital needs.

It is important to realize that the board and senior management should consider both the current and the projected capital requirements. Certain strategic decisions can increase the level of capital required in the future. This is particularly relevant for some insurance and financial contracts where contractual terms and/or payments can extend for many years. In this context, it is important for the company to fully appreciate the variations that may occur in respect of future capital requirements. The work of actuaries and other financial professionals is important here in endeavoring to quantify these future risks and their possible impact on projected capital requirements.

Figure 11.1   The relationship between shareholders, capital and risks

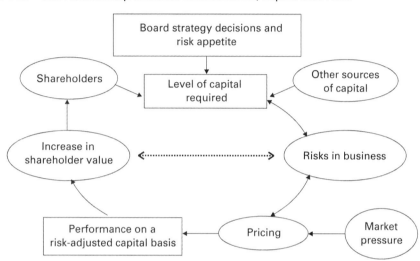

←→   indicates a two-way relationship, for example, the level of capital available affects the risks that an organization is willing to accept whilst the risks undertaken affect the level of capital required.
——→   indicates a one-way relationship, for example, market pressure can affect prices which, in turn, affect profitability or performance.
←→   indicates an indirect two-way relationship.

It is also possible that certain risks can be mitigated through various actions, such as reinsurance within the insurance industry, a well developed risk management strategy or changed behavior and culture, which can reduce the level of capital required. For example, the introduction of a reward system linked to performance and based on economic capital calculations can change behavior and reduce the risks within a business.

Of course, the company normally operates within a competitive market and, as will be discussed in Chapter 13, the pricing of its products will be influenced by the market. In some cases, this pressure may mean that the price that should be charged, consistent with the cost and risks of the product, cannot be used. Such an outcome, particularly over the longer term, can cause a company to fail if it does not withdraw from that market, unless it has sufficient capital to withstand the market pressure.

It is also important to note that the company's performance should be measured on a risk-adjusted basis. If this does not occur, there is a danger that the board, management and shareholders will be deceived by some recent results. For example, a 30% per annum return for two years may appear very positive. However, if it was generated by speculation in the capital markets, all stakeholders must recognize the risks taken and adjust the results accordingly. Hence, the increase in shareholder value that may arise from good performance must be assessed in the light of all the risks present within the business operations.

11.3.4   Regulators

The regulator in financial services will have a different primary focus from the shareholders or the company's board. In Australia, there is one integrated prudential regulator for banking, insurance and superannuation, namely the Australian Prudential Regulation Authority (APRA). It is interesting to note the mission of APRA, set out on its website,[5] namely:

> to establish and enforce prudential standards and practices designed to ensure that, under all reasonable circumstances, financial promises made by institutions we supervise are met within a stable, efficient and competitive financial system.

This mission has a number of interesting features, when viewed from the need for capital, including:

- the focus on the financial promises made to customers. This includes the promises of banks to repay deposits and insurance companies to pay claims, as defined under the contract. However, it does not cover investment performance on savings products unless the contract has a particular guarantee;

- that it is not an ironclad guarantee from the regulator. The standards are there to protect the customers in reasonable circumstances. It is impractical to offer these promises in all possible circumstances;

- the existence of prudential standards, which includes capital requirements; and

- the importance of stability, efficiency and competition within the system. This competitive element means that APRA recognizes the tension that exists between offering a stronger level of support to customers through higher capital requirements and the need to have a competitive industry within a global environment.

In summary, the regulator has a focus on protecting the individual customer and is not primarily concerned with the shareholders' return. Therefore, there is not a constant relationship between economic capital and regulatory capital. Indeed, often (but not always) the level of capital required by a regulator is higher than the level of economic capital determined by a financial institution. However, all stakeholders need to understand that an excessive regulatory requirement for capital is likely to promote inefficiency, less competition and a shortage of some financial products, as investors will withdraw from the industry if they cannot achieve a reasonable rate of return.

11.3.5   Customers

As in all markets, customers in the financial services industries are seeking the best quality product at the best available price. On the other hand, it should be recognized that most customers are unable to assess the financial condition of a financial institution. That is, there is asymmetric information and, without the existence of a third party (such as a regulator or rating agency), most customers are unable to assess whether a particular institution is likely to be there in future years to pay their insurance claims or retirement benefit.

---

5   http://www.apra.gov.au/aboutapra/

However, all customers have the expectation that the bank, insurance company or pension fund will continue to exist and meet its future promises. From the customer's perspective this promise should be backed by near certainty and this implies the need for a considerable level of capital. In periods of uncertainty or financial distress, there may be a *flight to quality* where organizations with stronger capital levels are deemed to be safer and therefore more likely to exist in the future. However, in more stable periods, this concern reduces and customers tend to consider that most financial organizations have a similar level of safety. This may lead to a disincentive for companies to hold capital above that required by the regulator, assuming that the regulatory requirement exceeds their own assessment of their economic capital requirements.

Again, how a company responds to its customers' desire for safety and security will depend on the board's business strategy, risk appetite and desired return on capital.

11.3.6 Rating agencies and market expectations

The goal of the rating agencies is to assess an organization's financial condition and its possibility of failure. It should represent an independent assessment, although it needs to be recognized that rating agencies are paid by the rated entity. Many organizations are willing to follow certain directions from rating agencies to improve their credit rating and so reduce their cost of debt capital.

In some cases, the expectations of the capital markets or the behavior of a competitor may cause an institution to carry additional capital. This external pressure may be short-lived (such as through an economic recession) or may introduce a new long-term benchmark.

Exercise 11.2

A non-government organization (NGO) plans to offer microfinance[6] loans at modest interest rates to small business operators in developing countries. It believes that it can raise funds from thousands of lenders through the internet where the lenders will receive their money back inside a 12-month period but at zero interest rate. The initial problem is that the NGO needs funds to set up its infrastructure and processes before the first loan can be made. This will require additional capital from its long-term shareholders who expect to receive a dividend.

Why is capital required? How would you determine this organization's risk appetite?

11.4 Financial institutions without shareholders

The previous sections have assumed the existence of shareholders who have provided equity capital. There are two important types of financial institutions which do not have shareholders: mutual organizations and superannuation or pension funds.

---

[6] Microfinance loans represent very small loans to those in poverty designed to encourage small business and entrepreneurship. These individuals normally lack collateral, steady employment and any credit history.

11.4.1 Mutual organizations

In a mutual organization or cooperative society, some or all of the customers become members and share in the financial performance of the organization. There are many types of mutual including deposit-taking institutions such as credit unions; life, general and health insurance companies; and friendly societies. Indeed, many of the largest life insurance companies in the world commenced their operations as mutuals.

Some of the issues of capital management which arise for a mutual organization are:

* as there are no shareholders in a mutual, permanent capital can only be accumulated from retained earnings. If a mutual finds it needs more capital unexpectedly, it may be forced to close or merge in situations where a shareholder company could use a rights issue to raise more capital. This may reduce the risk appetite of the mutual's board, in order to avoid such situations;

* the need to build up capital from retained earnings raises the question of equity between different generations of members. Shareholders can convert their right to retained profits to cash at any time by selling their shares in the market, without affecting the capital held by the company. On the other hand, members of a mutual have to wait for the organization to distribute its earnings. Since every organization needs some capital, it is likely that when their membership eventually ceases, some members will leave behind part of the earnings accrued during their membership;

* within mutuals, there are members participating in various activities. Examples include depositors and borrowers within a credit union and policyholders of different types of insurance within an insurance company. An important issue of equity arises as to how to share any operating surplus between these groups of members;

* as noted earlier, prudential regulators are primarily focused on the customers and not the shareholders. When these individuals are effectively one and the same group, the question arises as to whether the same regulations and capital requirements should apply; and

* many mutuals have a focus on a particular group of customers or geographical area which means that they are exposed to additional risks associated with this concentration.

One of the ways in which mutual life insurance companies have historically coped without the capital strength provided by having shareholders is to sell products which leave some of the risk with the policyholders. This was the origin of the traditional with-profit insurance which has been described in Chapter 4 (although with-profit insurance is also sold by shareholder companies, which may have lower capital requirements as a result of the flexibility thus provided). Chapter 18 will consider the issues of balancing the fair treatment of departing policyholders with the continuing capital needs of the organization and managing equity between different groups of members. The case study of the mutual insurer Equitable Life, described in "The End of the Equitable" on the CD, is worth reading at this point.

When the Equitable found that the guarantees provided under certain with-profit policies were beginning to bite (ie became close to being "in the money"), it sought to absorb the losses by exercising its discretion to reduce non-guaranteed bonuses. It turned out, however, that its directors did not have the full discretion to adjust bonuses that they thought they had under the Articles of Association. Their discretion was limited by their policyholders' reasonable expectations: expectations created both by the Equitable's past practices and by the practices of other companies offering similar products. Since the Equitable could not absorb the losses by adjusting the benefits, it had to meet them out of its capital. However, its capital was relatively low as the Equitable had followed a philosophy of distributing as much of its earnings as possible to each generation of policyholders. The Equitable was forced to close. Whilst a number of factors contributed to the Equitable's demise, this case study illustrates the particular difficulties facing a mutual organization.

In many economies, where there is a competitive and well-regulated financial sector, customers tend not to distinguish between the financial security of a mutual financial services organization and a shareholding organization. For example, a depositor with a credit union may believe that the security of that organization is similar to that of a small bank.

This public perception has led many prudential regulators to apply the same capital requirements for all organizations operating within the same financial industry. This means that it is now very difficult to establish a new mutual or cooperative organization, as a minimum amount of capital is required. For example, the minimum capital requirements for a life and general insurance company in Australia are A$10 million and A$5 million respectively.

We have also witnessed many demutualizations around the world, particularly in the life insurance industry, as companies have turned their retained earnings (held by the company as capital in the interests of its members) into shares which can be traded on the stock exchange. This removes the problem of balancing the interests of terminating members against the ongoing capital needs of the organization (although the result is usually a windfall to those who happen to be members at the time of demutualization and the decisions about how to allocate shares among those members can be highly controversial). This move has also provided these organizations with greater flexibility in responding to their capital requirements.

11.4.2 Superannuation funds

There are many types of superannuation fund. We will consider just two types here: an employer-sponsored defined benefit superannuation fund and a multi-employer (or industry) defined contribution superannuation fund.

Employer-sponsored defined benefit superannuation funds

In this type of fund, members are all employees or ex-employees of a single employer. They are promised retirement benefits based on their service and salary at or near to retirement and may also pay contributions equal to a fixed percentage of salary. Benefits on leaving service before retirement are often lower than the accrued proportion of the retirement benefit. The employer pays contributions as recommended by an actuary to meet the balance of the cost. The main stakeholders are the employer, the individual members and the trustees (or fiduciaries), who are responsible for the interests of the members as a group.

Such superannuation funds may be perceived to have added security, and therefore less need for capital, due to the presence of the sponsoring employer. However, if the fund is relying on future contributions rather than holding assets which are legally separate from the employer, then the members are subject to a double risk – a failure of the employer causes a loss of both their job and their retirement benefit. This has occurred in several notable failures in the US. It is generally considered prudent, and may be required by regulation, that funds should hold a minimum level of assets equal to the benefits payable if all members left service.

From the employer's perspective, there would usually be a preference to contribute at a rate that does not build up much, if any, buffer in the fund. The issue for the employer is that the money it contributes to the fund earns the return on the fund's portfolio of securities but is at more risk; is not available for investment in the employer's own business; and can be difficult or impossible to retrieve if it should prove excessive to the fund's needs.

The members would generally prefer to see a buffer of assets in the fund. However, the picture is not clear-cut. A fund might be in a position where it has a high level of assets compared to its liabilities, and thus a high level of security for the members' benefits, when the decision is taken to improve the benefits. The improvement may cost more than the surplus assets in the fund and be met in part by future contributions from the employer. The overall level of security of benefits is reduced but the members would probably be happy about the change because of the benefit improvement. If not all members receive the benefit improvement (eg only current pensioners), the trustees will have to consider issues of equity and weigh up whether the change is acceptable for those members who do not gain benefits but who will have less security.

However, the member is not the only stakeholder interested in the funding position of defined benefit funds. Under the pension accounting rules in many countries, the sponsoring employer must show the net financial position of the fund in its financial statements. These figures are normally determined by market conditions which can have a negative effect on the employer's financial position, particularly if there is a reduction in interest rates, which causes the accrued liabilities to increase, or a decline in asset values.

In addition, in countries where an agency exists to protect pension fund members (such as in the US and the UK), the fund's financial position affects the premium that the fund pays to this agency. That is, premiums increase with the level of any underfunding.

Multi-employer (or industry) defined contribution superannuation funds

In Australia and elsewhere, multi-employer (or *industry*) superannuation funds have been established where many employers make contributions on behalf of their employees to a single fund. In these defined contribution (or *accumulation*) superannuation funds, each member's superannuation account is adjusted to reflect investment returns and costs. On occasions, there is some degree of smoothing of returns, and small reserves may be built up to facilitate such smoothing. Otherwise, there is no capital backing these funds, which may be considered to be a form of mutual. Yet, while the members may appreciate that they are fully bearing the uncertain investment returns, the issue of operational risk remains.

A further issue occurs when the market is opened up to competition so that individual members can choose the fund that receives their employer contributions. Inevitably, such competition leads to marketing as many funds compete for the savings. Of course, such advertising is costly and requires the expenditure of some capital. Although the funds argue that this advertising is for the benefit of members, as it preserves or enhances the economies of scale and thereby reduces future unit costs, the source of such capital remains an important issue for the funds to consider.

11.5   Risks and capital needs in financial institutions

Chapter 6 discussed the relationship between risk and capital but it is worth revisiting this issue in this section.

The need for capital within a financial institution is strongly related to the risks present within its operations. Whilst the actual operations of a bank, life insurance company, general insurance company, superannuation fund or funds manager may be very different, it is helpful to consider the risks according to the following groupings:

- asset risks – events that may cause a reduction in the income generated from, or in the market value of, the assets;

- liability risks – events that may cause an increase in the size of liabilities;

- asset/liability risks – events that cause movements in the value of both the assets and the liabilities such that the net outcome is adverse; and

- operational risks – events that could cause a loss to the company as a result of inadequate or failed internal processes, people and systems, or from external events. These risks include legal risk but exclude systemic risk.[7]

Traditionally, banks have been more concerned with the risks associated with their assets (such as credit risk on their loans, and market volatility) whereas insurance companies have concentrated on liability issues (such as the variation in claim frequency or size). However, it is important to note that risks associated with the total operations (and hence the capital requirements) are not that straightforward and a more holistic approach should be adopted, as discussed in 11.6.

We will now discuss various types of risks that occur in each of these four groupings.

11.5.1 Asset risks

Default risks

All assets or investments have a probability of failure such that the investor may fail to obtain the expected return from the investment or, in some cases, may be subject to a total loss on the investment. A loss can also occur when the counterparty to a financial agreement defaults, such as with a reinsurance arrangement or financial derivative.

In the banking sector, credit risk is considered to be a major focus of the bank's risk management process. Fundamentally, the bank is attempting to minimize the probability of default on its loans. In some cases, a higher interest rate may be charged to compensate for the higher risk (or higher probability of loan default) but it should be recognized that when a borrower defaults, money is lost, whatever the interest rate charged.

From a capital perspective, riskier assets lead to a higher probability of default (because of greater volatility) and therefore a greater need for capital.

Market movements

Within a developed economy, interest rates and the share market move continually. Financial institutions often show the market value of their investments in their financial statements. The volatility in the value of certain assets can be significant and hence capital is required to protect the financial position of the institution from large falls in value.

---

[7] Systemic risks can affect each of the risks shown. However, they cannot be diversified away as they affect all players in the system and a particular organisation cannot remove their impact. Examples of systemic risk include legislative change and market conditions.

The level of capital required will be greater for institutions with more volatile or riskier investments (such as equities) and much lower, or even zero, for investments that are not subject to such variations, such as cash.

Concentration

Concentration risk occurs when the assets are not diversified. Examples include a major investment with a single company, or where a loan portfolio has a significant exposure to a single client.

The problems of concentrated assets have been highlighted with some failures of some small superannuation funds in Australia where more than 25 percent of the fund's assets were invested in a single property. If this property loses value, say because of its highly specialized purpose, then the overall investment return to fund members is adversely affected.

The lack of diversification always brings additional risks and therefore the need for additional capital. For similar reasons, a financial conglomerate should assess its exposure to a single client across all its business units and not just rely on each business unit maintaining its limits.

Liquidity

It is often assumed that all assets are equally liquid or marketable. This is not the case. There exists a range of assets that can be difficult to sell, particularly in difficult economic times. Examples include direct property, unlisted assets such as infrastructure and OTC[8] derivatives. In addition, there have been many instances when certain markets have been frozen for a period of time by the regulator for a variety of reasons. Even a well-developed equities market does not guarantee liquidity at all times. For instance, the stock exchange may suspend trading in a particular stock under certain circumstances.

Of course, the lack of liquidity in certain capital markets is more likely to occur at times when there are other economic pressures. This suggests that financial institutions should not assume that the level of liquidity available in the good economic times will always be present.

Other risks

There are several items that are normally recorded as assets in a company's financial statements which, in certain circumstances, may be of no or limited value. Hence, additional capital may be required in respect of these assets, including:

- loans to related parties – after all, in the case of failure of a financial group, the value of these loans is likely to be zero;

- future income tax benefits – this asset relies on future profits and, in the case of a winding-up, such profits will not occur; and

- goodwill – this item, due to an acquisition of another business or the company's reputation, becomes worthless in the case of a winding-up.

Regulators normally exclude these assets when assessing a company's financial position.

---

8   OTC = over the counter, ie not exchange-traded.

11.5.2 Liability risks

Pricing

The pricing of insurance and other long-term contracts can expose a financial institution to risks in respect of uncertain future events over which it has no control. For instance, fixed premiums for a long-term life insurance policy, or loan repayments based on a fixed interest rate, mean that the institution is exposed to future risks that it cannot pass on to the customer. Even in respect of general insurance policies that are renewed annually, there is a lag between the insurer becoming aware that the pattern of claims experience has changed and its ability to increase the premiums.

Hence, it is reasonable that if a portfolio has greater exposure to mis-pricing risks or has a greater level of guaranteed premiums or fixed repayments, then the capital needed to support these higher risks should be greater.

Valuation of liabilities

Insurance companies must set aside money to meet liabilities. There are many types of liabilities, including:

- long-term contracts, such as disability insurance or annuities, where premiums have been received but the frequency, timing and size of the future claims are not yet known;

- options embedded in long-term contracts, such as guaranteed insurability or guaranteed premium rates (including annuities);

- *outstanding claims*, where a claim has already been made but has not yet been fully paid due to the need for further investigation, negotiation or administration, or the fact that the claim will be settled by a series of payments;

- *Incurred But Not Reported* (IBNR) claims, where it is reasonable to suggest that claims will be made in respect of the past period but, due to a time delay in notification, the claims have not yet been reported; and

- *unearned premiums* or *unexpired risk*, which relate to the fact that an insurance premium has been received for a given period (say twelve months) but the insurance period has not yet been fully completed. Hence, a reserve is needed to ensure that funds are kept to match the future period of exposure.

In many of the calculations required to value these liabilities, long-term economic, demographic or social assumptions about the future are required. Examples include inflation levels, investment earning rates, mortality or sickness rates, claim escalation rates, possible court decisions and the growth in future expenses.

It is impossible to predict any of these variables with certainty and hence there is always the possibility that there will be significant changes in the liabilities from one year to the next. For example, a change in the underlying interest rate of two percentage points or more over a twelve month period is likely to have a significant impact on the level of liabilities. Capital is needed in respect of these uncertainties and the greater the risks, the greater the capital required. For example, within a general insurance company, there is the potential for much greater variability in the outstanding claims for long-tail business than for short-tail business. Similarly, in life insurance, an interest rate movement will have a much greater effect for an annuity portfolio than for term insurance. The value of pension liabilities is another example where a downward movement in the relevant bond rate can cause a significant increase in the liability on the sponsoring employer's balance sheet.

Experience

The actual experience of any financial institution will not be exactly the same as the assumptions that were used in pricing and the valuation of liabilities. These differences can occur in many areas including:

- the level of investment earnings;
- the frequency of claims or decrements (eg mortality, lapse rates);
- the average size of claims; and
- the level of expenses.

Again, capital needs to be held by the insurance company, so that it is available to support the financial position of the company should it suffer adverse experience. Such experience can occur in the short term or over the longer term. In this latter case, the recent experience may need to be reflected in assumption changes used for estimating liabilities and for pricing.

Concentration of liabilities

As with assets, it is possible for a company to have its liabilities concentrated with a particular client or within a particular geographical location. For example, if a general insurer concentrating on home and car insurance has 80 percent of its portfolio within a particular city, it is exposed to the risk of a major natural event (such as an earthquake, hailstorm or cyclone) affecting that city. In this case, the insurer could elect to protect its financial position from this concentration risk through additional capital or reinsurance.

A significant unexpected event

The valuation of a company's liabilities normally uses realistic assumptions, based on expected events, together with a prudential margin to allow for the expected variation in future experience. However, there are also unexpected events that may occur from time to time which can cause a significant increase in the level of claims or future liabilities. These events, which are beyond the control of the company, can include changes in government policy, court decisions, international events, acts of terrorism and major changes in economic conditions.

Whilst it is impossible to have capital that is sufficient to meet all unexpected events, it is reasonable that a company should consider how much extra capital (or ready access to capital) it needs for such unexpected events. Again, the level should be consistent with the board's risk appetite.

11.5.3 Asset/liability risks

Liquidity risk

All organizations must be able to meet their financial obligations as they fall due. This means that liquidity represents a financial risk for all commercial operations. However, it is particularly relevant for deposit-taking institutions (such as banks, building societies and credit unions) where a significant portion of their liabilities is at call. This means that depositors may seek to withdraw their funds at any time. Such possible payments mean that the banks must have sufficiently liquid assets to meet this possibility.

On the other hand, it is unrealistic for a bank to have all its assets in highly liquid short-term assets as this would limit the bank's lending and investment operations. Hence, in response to this liquidity risk, banks need to develop a liquidity management policy that provides sufficient short-term liquid funds to respond to the most likely scenarios but does not significantly limit the bank's opportunities. The balance between these two pressures will again depend on the level of risk appetite.

Liquidity risk can also exist in the operations of insurance companies, superannuation funds and funds managers. The causes may vary, but the consequence is always the same – that is, funds are needed now to meet financial obligations to policyholders or investors. Hence, all financial organizations need to have an appreciation of liquidity risk.

Some examples of incidents that can create pressure on the liquidity position of a financial organization are:

- negative media coverage in respect of a major life insurer so that large numbers of policyholders decide to surrender their life insurance policies or redeem their investment policies;

- the collapse of a major employer so that its superannuation funds are closed and all members are able to transfer their entitlements;

- a major hailstorm that means a general insurance company must meet very large claim payments in respect of motor vehicle and house insurance policies within the next two months;

- a major economic crisis that creates liquidity needs for an accumulation-based superannuation scheme as some members switch their investments into cash, other members transfer their benefits to another scheme (due to portability provisions) and/ or the need to cover a currency loss arising from a hedging contract; and

- a very poor investment performance for the last period for a major funds manager so that several major wholesale clients withdraw their investments immediately.

In each case, it is possible that the short-term liquid assets available will be insufficient to meet the cash payments. Hence, it is possible that longer-term assets may need to be sold, probably at unfavorable prices. Such a consequence may aggravate an already difficult situation.

Market risk

Movements in interest rates and market prices are likely to affect the value of both the assets and liabilities of financial institutions. For example, as interest rates fall, the value of long-term insurance liabilities is likely to increase. If the value of the assets supporting these liabilities does not increase by a similar proportion, then the interest rate movement in the market (over which the insurance company has no control) will lead to deterioration in the financial position of the organization.

It is therefore essential that financial institutions consider their investment policy in the light of their liabilities. In particular, the selection of assets according to the term and currency of the liabilities is an important risk management strategy. Of course, it is also possible to reduce the mismatching risk through the use of a hedging policy using derivatives rather than through the purchase of physical assets.

Many life insurance and superannuation products incorporate very long-term liabilities and it may be impossible to purchase assets to match these liabilities. In this case, it is important that the financial institution has available certain levers (or adjustment features) which can be used to vary the actual liabilities. If this flexibility is not available, then it is possible for a fixed liability to cause major problems in the future.

An example of this outcome was the demise of Equitable Life, which we mentioned in 11.4.1.

11.5.4 Operational risk

All organizations face *operational risk*, which can be defined as the risk of financial loss from inadequate or failed internal processes, people and systems, or from external events. Examples of internal events that can cause a financial loss include:

- administrative or transaction errors, eg errors in the calculation of unit prices, the overpayment of a benefit;

- the failure of part of the IT system, which can lead to a closure of part of the operations for a period of time, and then a loss of reputation and confidence;

- a mistake in an in-house software program, so that wrong results are produced which lead to incorrect decisions;

- fraud, mismanagement or inappropriate culture, which can lead to direct losses;

- compliance problems, which can lead to a breaking of the law, such as the securities law, and fines and a loss of public reputation; and

- poor quality controls or management, so that certain operations cause an inconsistency to develop between the assumptions in the pricing or product design and the actual outcomes (eg loan approvals in banking, underwriting in life insurance and claims management in general insurance).

In addition, contagion risks exist where an organization is a member of a larger group or conglomerate. In this case, the failure or distress of another group member can have negative flow-on effects for the organization.

Some of the internal risks can be ameliorated, but not removed, by improved control measures. Hence, it is suggested that the level of capital required to respond to these risks should be influenced by the compliance and control culture within an organization. Some of these risks may be greatly increased by sudden rapid growth in the company.

External shocks include court decisions, new legislation, the introduction of a major competitor or a totally unexpected event such as the September 11, 2001 terrorist attacks, which probably represents one of the greatest operational risk events yet seen, other than at a time of war.[9] In each case, the operating environment may change dramatically, which

---

[9] You can see the major impact of war by looking at the history of any significant German company in existence before WWII. For example, see the BMW history at http://www.bmwdrives.com/bmw-history.php.

can generate new risks. In general terms, the more unstable the legal-political framework, the greater the risk of an operational risk event.

Finally, it can be noted that most losses from operational risk events are small. That is, the frequency of such events may be relatively high but the average loss is small. However, there is always the small possibility of a very significant operational failure causing a major financial loss. The principal cause of the collapse of Barings Bank was the trading of Mr Nick Leeson. It is possible that greater controls on the operations of all traders within Barings may have prevented or limited the effect of Leeson's trading.

The Basel II capital requirements for banks, which commenced in 2008, require capital in respect of credit risk, market risk and operational risk. The amount of operational risk capital can be determined using one of three approaches, which are:

- the basic indicator, where the capital is 15 percent of a bank's gross income, averaged over three years;

- the standardized approach, where the capital is calculated by business lines, using a factor ranging from 12 percent to 18 percent of gross income for each business line; and

- the advanced measurement approach (which must be approved by the regulator), where the bank develops its own model using both qualitative and quantitative approaches.

A fundamental problem with the calculation of operational risk capital is the lack of data. In contrast to credit risk where a bank may have data in respect of thousands of commercial loans and millions of smaller loans (eg credit cards), the lack of comprehensive data about the cost of operational risk events of all sizes makes detailed modeling of operational risk capital problematical in most cases. Notwithstanding this shortcoming, the need for operational risk capital or reserves represents an important area for all financial institutions to consider carefully.

In late 2008 Mercer surveyed major not-for-profit superannuation funds in Australia about operational risk. A copy of the report is available on the CD. It is interesting to note that, although these "mutual" funds have no shareholders to provide capital, half of these funds have established an operational risk reserve to protect the fund from the potential financial consequences of unexpected events. The following case study highlights the advantage of such a reserve.

Example 11.2   Operational risk reserve case study

Some years after the Government Employees Superannuation Board (GESB) in Western Australia created an operational risk reserve, it found that a minority of members, including a few staff members, had been exploiting a loophole in the fund rules to gain a financial advantage. The total loss across the fund was $6.5 million. Although Michele Dolin, GESB's CEO, regards the episode as most unfortunate, she says that it "illustrated the real benefits of having an operational risk reserve – members didn't have to suffer." Larry Rudman, GESB's CFO, commented that "Many trustees of other funds are waking up to the fact that operational risks do exist and there is a need to protect members against them." Source: Superfunds, May 2008.

Exercise 11.3

A not-for-profit multi-employer superannuation fund providing accumulation benefits to its members wants to establish an operational risk reserve as it has become aware of the risk of such an event. It believes that should such an event occur it would be unfair for the members of the fund in that year to bear the full cost of that event.

What are the possible sources of capital for this reserve, which would be established over a three-year period?

11.6   An overall company perspective

The previous section considered the risks that confront a financial institution from the total company's (or group's) perspective. However, they are equally applicable to a particular business unit within a company.

For the company as a whole, there are a few obvious questions to address:

*   Given the capital needs of each business unit, what are the capital needs of the whole company? This is a question of the *diversification benefit*.

*   How does economic capital compare with regulatory capital and what are the implications?

*   What should the company hold in excess of regulatory capital? This is called *target surplus*.

*   How should the company allocate capital to business units?

11.6.1   Diversification benefits

Consider a business unit within a broader financial conglomerate. Taking into account the risks discussed in this chapter, this unit determines that it needs the level of capital for each type of risk within its operations depicted in Figure 11.2:

Figure 11.2   The capital for a particular business unit

Operational risks

Asset/liability risks (eg liquidity, matching)

Liability risks (eg pricing, valuing liabilities)

Asset risks (eg credit, market)

However, when it comes to assessing the total capital needed for the business unit, it is likely that some of the individual risks move in opposite directions when the same event occurs. For instance, an increase in interest rates affects the risk of loan defaults, the market value of the assets, the valuation of insurance liabilities and the matching of assets and liabilities. It is probable that the total capital required within a business unit is less than the sum of the capital required for the individual risks.

The diversification benefits arising from a range of risks are likely to be much greater when several business units are combined within a single financial institution. For example, the total capital needs of a financial conglomerate (comprising a bank, a life insurance company, a general insurance company and a funds manager) are less than the sum of the capital needs of the individual units. This result is represented in Figure 11.3.

Figure 11.3   The benefits of diversification

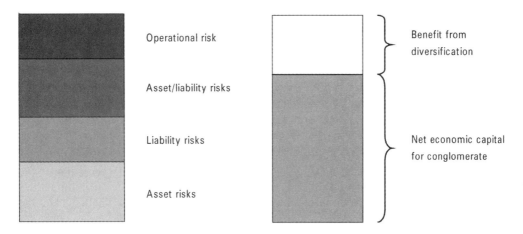

11.6.2   Economic versus regulatory capital

As we have seen, economic capital is the amount which the company decides is appropriate, having regard to the risks in the business, the company's access to further capital and its appetite for risk.

Regulatory capital is the amount calculated by applying the rules set down by the regulator, reflecting the regulator's view of certain risks in businesses in the same sector.

As previously discussed, regulatory capital may be greater than economic capital. Indeed, because the regulator is concerned to reduce the risk of failure of any business in the sector, it is likely that regulatory capital will be higher than economic capital; that is, the regulator will require the company (or business unit) to hold more capital than the company would otherwise consider necessary.

To the extent that diversification benefits exist, these are likely to exacerbate the position, because the regulator is unlikely to give as much credit to these benefits.

Sometimes (perhaps for a product line or a business unit), regulatory capital is less than economic capital. In effect, this represents a form of diversification benefit for the company.

It is important to note that, when regulatory capital is very far below economic capital, the company may not be well suited to competing in that market. This is because the company will require a return on economic capital when its competitors are probably committing less capital.

11.6.3 Target surplus

A key element of the company's overall capital management will be its desire to hold sufficient capital to satisfy the regulators. In many countries, regulators set capital requirements to help them to determine which companies require more attention. While regulatory attention can generally be managed (and is not of itself an indicator of pending insolvency), it is at best a distraction from operating the business.

Avoiding regulatory attention means being able to satisfy regulatory capital requirements in adverse circumstances. This means holding a capital margin over the regulatory requirements. Actuaries call this margin target surplus.

The amount of target surplus that a company decides to hold will depend on its view of its risks, its access to further capital and its appetite for risk (in this case, the risk of regulatory intervention).

11.6.4 Capital allocation

An organization needs to make a sufficient return on its capital to justify the cost of that capital. Therefore, in assessing the performance of its business units, a company will allocate capital (and a cost of that capital) to each business unit.

There are many possible methods of allocating capital between different businesses within a single organization. There is no single "correct" answer as it will vary according to the interdependence between the businesses, the extent of centralization (or decentralization) and the institution's internal culture. However, in all cases, one of the challenges is the allocation of those benefits from diversification (ie reduction of capital needs) which are achieved through the aggregation of risks. That is, should these benefits be allocated to each business line, held centrally or some combination of these two options? Factors that bear on this decision include the volatility of the diversification benefits over time; the complexity of cross-selling benefits and costs between business lines; and the overall strategy and objectives of the organization, as determined by the board.

Similarly, the allocation will be influenced by each business unit's regulatory capital requirements and the company's attitude to target surplus.

Finally, from the company's perspective, the net economic capital represents the capital that it deems necessary for its activities, given its agreed risk appetite. The importance of this conclusion is that, in assessing the financial performance of the total company, this generally represents the appropriate level of capital to use.

Exercise 11.4

What are the risks for a life insurance company that underwrites:

(a) Lifetime annuity business only?

(b) Term life business only?

(c) Participating endowment business only?

How would the sum of the economic capital for each of these companies be affected if these three companies merged into a single life insurance operation?

11.7   Practical implications for actuaries

An important component of an actuary's work is identifying and analyzing the risks faced by an organization. This should be carried out in the context of the whole organization and not restricted to part of the balance sheet. Within this holistic approach, the actuary must be willing to discuss the consequences of all risks with the relevant stakeholders, including the uncertainty of his or her assumptions, and their effects on an organization's capital. Actuaries also need to understand the role of economic capital in an organization's strategic decision making and its use in the assessment of risk-adjusted performance.

Actuaries often determine the level of an organization's reserves according to the regulator's requirements. In this context, actuaries need to recognize the differences between economic capital, minimum regulatory capital and the actual level of capital, which may include a buffer (or target surplus) above the minimum regulatory level.

It is important to recognize that there is not a single correct answer for the level of capital for a particular organization. Furthermore, the feasible answers will change over time with changes in the economic conditions, regulatory requirements and the organization's business. In addition, there will always exist a healthy tension between the various stakeholders as to the correct level of capital for an organization. The actuary needs to appreciate this tension in recommending the level of capital and/or reserves. In undertaking this task, the actuary must also take into account the equity considerations between the various stakeholders as well as between generations of members or policyholders.

11.8   Key learning points

*   All businesses need capital. The level and type of capital should be related to the risk appetite and strategy set by the board. There is a natural tension about the level of capital between the various stakeholders.

*   There is no "correct" balance between debt and equity in an organization's capital structure.

*   Economic capital represents an important measure to assess a company's risk-adjusted performance.

*   Economic capital and regulatory capital are not the same and serve two different purposes.

*   There are several reasons for an organization to hold capital. Each reason must be understood by the board and management.

*   The level of risks accepted by the company must influence its level of capital. These risks include those related to assets, liabilities, the asset-liability relationship and operations.

*   The allocation of capital between separate businesses within an organization represents an important management tool.

*   The allocation of the capital saving arising from the diversification of risks across an organization is not straightforward and can be carried out in several ways.

CD Items

Ferris, S. 2001, The End of the Equitable, *Actuary Australia*, March, Institute of Actuaries of Australia, pp. 12-13.

Mercer 2009, Point of View: Operational Risk Reserves, April 2009, Melbourne.

Chapter 11 Exercise Solutions

References (other than CD Items)

Modigliani, F. & Miller, M. 1958, The Cost of Capital, Corporation Finance and the Theory of Investment, *American Economic Review*, 48(3), pp. 261-297.

Fred's Coffee Shop – Valuing Liabilities

Fred has had an exciting week. His coffee shop has opened for business and customers have flocked to buy his products. Now that he has finished counting the takings, he finds that he has over $20,000 in cash. Time to upgrade his car to the latest model?

Probably not. Fred may have plenty of cash but he can't tell what money he has really made without working out what he owes. Out of the $20,000 cash, he has to pay the suppliers who have provided goods on credit, he has to pay wages to any employees and he needs to set aside money for tax and other bills. In other words, to understand his financial position, he needs to know the value of his liabilities.

In the case of a coffee shop, working out the value of the liabilities will mostly be straightforward. However, some liabilities may not be easy to value. One of Fred's customers burnt himself by spilling hot coffee and has threatened to sue. Fred can't be sure about the amount he might have to pay in compensation; when it might be paid; and indeed whether he will have to pay anything at all. Fortunately, Fred has the appropriate insurance policy and is confident that it will pay if the customer is successful in claiming damages. While Fred doesn't have to worry about setting money aside just in case, the insurance company does. But how does the insurance company decide how much money to set aside?

The actuarial profession has centuries of experience in helping insurance companies and other financial institutions deal with such problems, so actuaries have developed sophisticated approaches to valuing liabilities. Chapter 12 deals with this topic.

You may be surprised to find that Chapter 12 deals with the valuation of liabilities and we don't get to the topic of pricing until Chapter 13. After all, Fred had to set his prices before opening for business. The reason is that the valuation of liabilities affects the emergence of profit. In turn, this affects a financial institution's view of the prices that it should charge. In other words, the liability valuation basis is an important input to the pricing process and should be considered first.

Chapter 12: Valuing Liabilities
by Richard Lyon

12.1 Introduction

In this chapter, we consider how to place a value on liabilities. First, we need to think about general issues. In later sections, we consider some specific issues and how to handle them.

Much of the discussion in this chapter relates to concepts considered elsewhere in this book. This is consistent with the whole nature of the Actuarial Control Cycle. You should not need to refer to other chapters to understand the concepts in the context of this chapter, but you may find it helpful to do so.

Actuarial principles and techniques can be applied to a wide range of commercial and other problems involving uncertainty and/or the time value of money. However, this chapter will focus on insurance and retirement benefits, because these are the practice areas where actuarial valuation techniques and issues have become most developed.

12.1.1 A brief history

Actuarial practice in valuing liabilities developed first in life insurance, where actuaries have practiced since the 18th century.[1] Initially, the core issue was measuring the amount which could prudently be distributed to shareholders and/or policyholders, as deliberately high premiums far exceeded claims and expenses.

Actuaries devised formulae to enable them to perform these valuations reasonably efficiently, using limited data. With the advent of mechanical and then electronic calculators and computers, more complex valuations have developed, using more data. At the same time, valuations are often required to be more precise, with a view to measuring profit or releasing unnecessary capital. It is reasonable to assume that actuaries will continue to take advantage of increasing computational power and speed.

These days, actuaries routinely value liabilities in insurance and retirement benefits with techniques which can be extended to other businesses. Most valuations involve an explicit projection of future cash flows but the use of formulae is still common.

12.1.2 What are liabilities?

Very simply, you incur a liability when you promise to make a future payment. Typically, the promise is given in exchange for a payment made to you, but this is not always the case, eg a home owner makes a free (and implicit) promise to a visitor that the visitor will be compensated for any injury incurred while on the premises. The promise may depend on a future contingency, eg an insurer's liability to pay a death claim depends on the death occurring and a casino's liability to pay out on a bet depends on the success of the bet. In many cases, either or both of the amount and the timing of the future payment are uncertain, eg if a doctor is sued for negligence, the doctor's insurer will be uncertain as to both what the final payout will be and when it will be paid.

---

[1] Equitable Life is said to have created the first position of "actuary," when it was founded in the UK in 1762. For example, see http://www.actuaries.org.uk/knowledge/elas_archive/elas_importance.

In this chapter, we generally use the word *liability*, but several other names may be used in different jurisdictions and/or circumstances, including *reserve* and *provision*.

12.1.3   Liabilities in the accounts

While liabilities exist whether or not they are reported, actuaries are generally involved with liabilities in the context of financial statements, or *accounts*.

12.1.3.1   An accounting definition of liabilities

The Australian accounting profession defines liabilities as follows:

> A liability is a present obligation of the entity arising from past events, the settlement of which is expected to result in an outflow from the entity of resources embodying economic benefits.[2]

So, a liability relates to something which has already happened. You should note, however, that the past event may be the writing of an insurance contract which provides death cover for the next 40 years, provided that premiums are paid. So the claim need not have happened yet – and the premium relating to that claim need not have been received – but the liability still exists by virtue of the contract.

On the other hand, the liability must represent a current obligation. Non-life insurance policies are commonly one-year contracts. The fact that a very high proportion of customers renew their policies doesn't create a liability for the insurer in respect of claims not covered by current policies – generally, the claims which occur after the expiry of those policies.

12.1.3.2   Liabilities on the balance sheet

Pictorially, a company's balance sheet may be represented as:

Figure 12.1

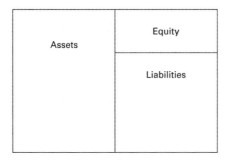

---

2   Australian Accounting Standards Board 2004, *Framework for the Preparation and Presentation of Financial Statements* 49(b). Other accounting bodies, eg the US Financial Accounting Standards Board and the International Accounting Standards Committee, have similar definitions. Unless otherwise indicated, all comments on accounting practice in the rest of this chapter refer to Australian standards. The intention is not to provide the reader with a summary of accounting practice, but to pick up on some important points which the accounting profession has tried to address and which are relevant to actuarial thinking on this subject.

So the value of *equity* (what the shareholders own) is the difference between the value of the company's *assets* and the value of its *liabilities*.[3] The size of the equity compared to the liabilities is often referred to as the strength of the balance sheet, and can be used as a very rough measure of the *solvency* of the company, ie how likely it is that the company will be able to meet its liabilities. Chapter 15 considers the topic of solvency in depth.

Of course, it doesn't have to be a company. Let's consider what an individual's balance sheet might look like. For ease of reference, we'll call this individual John.

Exercise 12.1

For the purposes of this exercise, assume that amounts payable or receivable in the future can be discounted at 5% per annum.

John's assets are a car (worth $5,000) and a bank account ($500 balance). What are his liabilities (and his equity) in each of the following situations?

(a) John borrowed from the bank to buy the car. The balance of what he owes is $250 and this must be repaid tomorrow.

(b) John borrowed from his parents to buy the car. The balance of what he owes is $1,050 and this must be repaid in a year's time.

(c) John owes his parents $1,050 for the car, payable in a year's time. His father is about to find out whether he has landed a major contract. If he does, he will forgive John's debt. John rates the probability of this occurrence at 25 percent.

(d) John has been taken to court in respect of a car accident in which another person was injured. He is not covered by insurance in this case. He estimates that there is a 5 percent chance that he will have to pay $52,500 in a year's time, a 50 percent chance that the case will be settled for $1,000 tomorrow and a 45 percent chance that he will not have to pay anything.

12.1.3.3   Liabilities in the profit and loss statement

Looking back at Figure 12.1, you should be able to see that the increase in equity over a period (eg a company's reporting year) is equal to the increase in assets less the increase in liabilities. Sometimes, changes are made directly to the equity (eg the raising of further capital by issuing shares, or the payment of dividends) but, after adjusting for such capital movements, the increase in equity over the period represents profit. So you can see that the change in liabilities is a key component of profit.

In simple terms, *Profit = Income – Outgo – Increase in Liabilities*.

---

[3]   You can think of the concept of "value" of liabilities as being the value of the assets which a company would need to hold in order to meet its obligations as they fall due. This value depends on the model and assumptions being used and would allow for expected future income such as contractual premiums and investment return.

Exercise 12.2

What is the increase in a bank's liabilities in relation to an individual bank account over the total period from just before the account is opened until just after it is closed?

What are the implications for profit in the accounting periods over which the bank account is open?

12.1.4   Measuring liabilities

In Exercise 12.1 you probably valued John's liabilities using:

$$Value = \sum (E[cash\ flow\ at\ time\ t]) / (1+i)^t$$

Actuaries would call the result the *best estimate* or *central estimate* of the liabilities. It is likely that John would take the same view of his financial position.

Now, suppose that John asks Jane to lend him $500 to install a better sound system in his car. Jane might prefer to err on the safe side in valuing John's liabilities. In the situation described in part (c), she might decide to ignore the possibility that John's father will forgive his debt. She is using conservative assumptions rather than the best estimate assumptions. We would say that she has added a *margin* to the best estimate valuation of liabilities or that she has made a *prudent valuation*.

So, the measurement of liabilities will depend on the measurer's perspective. Indeed, you will often hear actuaries say that the value of a liability depends on the purpose of the valuation.

While there are many reasons for measuring liabilities, they fall into two basic categories. Either we are trying to understand the company's financial position (its balance sheet) or we are trying to understand its financial performance (its profit and loss (P&L), or the change in its balance sheet).

Before we leave this overview, it is worth highlighting that we are valuing future cash flow. We generally expect the total value of this cash flow to be negative, ie a net liability, but it will probably include positive items. For example, future cash flows under a long-term insurance contract will include benefit payments and expenses but will also include premium income and investment return.

12.2   The nature of liabilities

A company's balance sheet is generally intended to present a "true and fair" view of its financial position. This requires the recognition of its liabilities and some attempt to place a sensible value on those liabilities. What constitutes a sensible value may depend on the significance of the liability and the underlying purpose of the valuation. For example, a balance sheet prepared to demonstrate solvency to a regulator may involve more conservative valuations of liabilities than one prepared for inclusion in the company's overseas parent's accounts.

In this section, we look at typical types of liabilities found on company balance sheets.

12.2.1 Short-term or long-term liabilities

Accounting standards generally require companies to identify the liabilities which fall due within the twelve months following the balance date. By comparing with short-term assets, the users of the accounts can assess whether the company has a short-term need for capital.

Long-term liabilities are identified separately and would be expected to be backed by long-term assets.

The types of liability typically found on balance sheets can be either short-term or long-term in nature, so judgment may be required in order to separate the components.

12.2.2 Types of liability

For convenience, liabilities can be considered as falling into four different types. While these types may be recognized separately in a company's balance sheet, the presentation of a particular liability is generally subject to the particular accounting rules applicable to the reporting entity and these rules are beyond the scope of this chapter.

12.2.2.1 Accounts payable

All companies are likely to have unpaid invoices from their suppliers, which would be recorded at face value. Companies in groups often owe each other money in relation to purchases made by one company on behalf of others. It would be highly unusual for such liabilities to be long-term in nature.

The purpose of recording these liabilities is to attribute the cost of supplies to the correct accounting period. After all, invoices are generally received after the goods or services have been provided, so the supplier is a creditor.

12.2.2.2 Tax liabilities

A profitable company can generally expect to pay tax and its liability for current tax is generally known (or can be closely estimated) and recorded on the balance sheet.

There may be aspects of the company's financial performance or financial position which give rise to a deferred tax liability. For example, most companies would be taxed on capital gains realized on the sale of assets but would not be taxed on the unrealized gain accrued while holding (and before selling) them. Typically, a company would record a deferred tax liability on its balance sheet equal to the tax which it would have had to pay if its assets had been sold at the balance date.

Recording tax liabilities ensures that the company's balance sheet reflects the tax effect of its financial performance.

12.2.2.3 Debt

Many companies borrow money. Generally, the amount of the debt is known at the balance date and it is easy to separate the total liability into short-term and long-term debt. Note that the criterion to adopt is the remaining term until repayment is required, not the original term.

Long-term debt may not be valued at face value, depending on accounting standards and/ or the purpose of the valuation. It is easy to see that two otherwise identical loans (in terms of repayment date, security, etc) with different coupon rates would have different values to an investor, implying different values to the borrower.

12.2.2.4 Provisions

Provisions are liabilities whose value cannot readily be ascertained as a matter of fact. Generally, their valuation involves the combination of uncertainty of one or all of occurrence, amount payable and timing.

Most companies will have provisions for amounts due to staff, including unused leave. As a rule, standard leave entitlements (eg annual leave and sick leave) are readily valued at face value. However, some obligations (such as long service leave[4] and retirement-related obligations) require the use of projection and discounting for a proper valuation.

A company may establish provisions in relation to its assets, including provisions for bad debts and provisions for unearned income. At the very least, this will generally require the exercise of judgment.

Much of the work of actuaries in relation to the valuation of liabilities concerns the provisions which are specific to particular types of financial institution. These typically require considerable judgment in the selection of valuation models and assumptions and include:

*   outstanding claims provisions for non-life insurers;

*   life insurance policy reserves; and

*   bad debt provisions for banks and other issuers or holders of large portfolios of debt assets.

Exercise 12.3

Obtain a copy of the accounts of five major companies in different industries (not just financial services) in your country. You should be able to do this via the internet.

Review the liabilities in each company's balance sheet and:

(a) note which types of liabilities are common to all companies;

(b) find out what the accounts say about the valuation approach used for each type of liability;

(c) identify the major liabilities for each company and how those liabilities relate to the company's business; and

(d) consider how each company's financial position might be affected by a change in the valuation of its major liabilities.

---

4   Long service leave is an employment-related entitlement in Australia, whereby employees with long service (usually more than ten years) are entitled to additional leave.

12.3 Measuring liabilities

In this section, we look in more detail at the process of measuring liabilities. This uncovers various issues which we address in later sections.

At the heart of any valuation of liabilities is the essential formula:

Liability = Present value of Outgo less *Present value of Income*

So, any valuation of liabilities is an attempt to determine the result of projecting and discounting future outgo and income. There are many ways of doing this and any approach may be valid if it meets the objectives of the valuation.

12.3.1 Best estimate liabilities

In many circumstances, a valuation of liabilities is required which has no margin for the risk of adverse deviations from the underlying assumptions, ie the *best estimate* or *central estimate* of the liabilities. Often, this liability is a component of a valuation which incorporates margins. We will discuss this concept in 12.3.2 and 12.3.3.

Reasons for a best estimate valuation might include:

- measurement of profit. From 12.1.3 you can see that the change in value of liabilities is a key component of profit. A valuation with no risk margins may be appropriate for this purpose. In 12.3.3 and 12.3.4, we consider other valuation approaches which may be used;

- measurement of capital employed. The difference between a company's assets and a realistic value of liabilities (excluding its long-term debt) is a measure of the capital employed. This, in turn, can be used to determine the return on capital employed (ROCE); and

- allocation of resources. Measuring profit and capital employed in each business segment[5] can help management to allocate scarce resources such as capital, IT development time and management time.

The Australian Prudential Regulation Authority (APRA) describes a best estimate liability as follows:

> The Best Estimate Liability is determined as the value of the expected future payments and receipts under the policy … based on obligations at the reporting date.[6]

APRA defines a central estimate liability for a general insurer as follows:

> The central estimate is intended to reflect the mean value in the range of possible values for the outcome (that is, the mean of the distribution of probabilistic outcomes). The determination of the central estimate must be based on assumptions as to future experience which reflect the experience and circumstances of the insurer and which are:

---

5   A business segment is any subdivision of the business, including a defined operating business unit, a product line or a geographic segment.

6   Section 5 of LPS1.04 Valuation of Policy Liabilities, APRA (2007).

(a)   made using judgment and experience;

(b)   made having regard to available statistics and other information; and

(c)   neither deliberately overstated nor understated.[7]

In effect, these definitions are equivalent as they are both intended to describe the (estimated) mean of the distribution of possible liability values.

Exercise 12.4

Under the then current prudential regime, a former Australian general insurer, HIH, accounted for its outstanding claims liabilities at central estimate. At the Royal Commission into the collapse of the company, this value was described as being as likely to be too low as to be too high.

Is this a reasonable description of the central estimate as set out above? Give reasons for your opinion.

12.3.2   Liabilities with margins

Often, a valuation of liabilities is required which incorporates an allowance for the risk of adverse deviations from best estimate assumptions. For example, this could be as a formal step in demonstrating solvency or a reflection of risk aversion.

The allowance may be explicit or implicit. An explicit allowance for risk may be achieved either through adding margins to an identified realistic valuation or through explicit adjustments to best estimate assumptions. For example, in Australia:

- APRA requires non-life insurers to add a risk margin to the central estimate of the liability. This margin is expressed as a percentage of the central estimate and is intended to result in a liability which has a 75% probability of being adequate; and

- by comparison, APRA's LPS3.04 requires life insurers to calculate a *capital adequacy liability* using best estimate assumptions adjusted to allow for the risk of adverse deviations. For example, the assumed mortality rates for insured lives should be increased by between 10 and 40 percent.

Risk margins are added to liabilities in similar ways to satisfy regulators in many other countries.

An implicit allowance would be obtained by performing the valuation using assumptions which were expected to give a valuation above best estimate but where the resultant margins could not readily be deduced from the valuation itself.

Examples of implicit conservatism include:

- a company may have a known non-interest-bearing liability payable at some time in the next few years. If it decides to hold this liability at face value, it has incorporated an implicit margin representing the time value of money over the uncertain term until the liability is paid; and

---

7   Section 18 of GPS310, APRA (2008).

- the liabilities of a superannuation fund (ie the value of future benefit payments and expenses) may be calculated on simplified assumptions which do not allow for employees leaving service before retirement. This unrealistic approach incorporates implicit margins representing the extent to which leaving service benefits are lower than the then present value of retirement benefits.

Exercise 12.5

In many countries, life insurance liabilities are calculated using a *net premium valuation* method.[8]

What form of margins does this approach incorporate? What are the benefits and risks of this approach?

You should note that margins may be incorporated in a valuation for reasons other than a prudent allowance for risk. In the next two subsections, we consider what these reasons might be.

12.3.3 Profit margins

Generally, when a company sells a financial product, it expects that product to be profitable, ie the present value of expected future income from that product is greater than the present value of expected future outgo. If the company accounts for its liabilities at their best estimate value, this means that as soon as it begins to include the product in its accounts it will be recognizing as profit the whole of the present value of the expected profits from that product.

There is a widely held view that profit should not be recognized until it has been *earned*. For example, clubs offer their members various services, often including the use of club facilities. They generally charge annual fees to cover the cost of these services. Some clubs (eg airline clubs) offer discounted prices for long-term membership, with a view to generating increased loyalty and/or raising cash. You may consider that these clubs should ensure that they do not recognize all the profit from these long-term memberships when the cash is received. This might be done by amortizing the fees over the period of the membership, ie establishing a liability equal to the *unearned* fee income. If the offer was profitable, this liability is higher than the expected cost of the services over the remaining term of the membership.

In 12.1.3, we saw that *Profit = Income – Outgo – Increase in Liabilities*. If future profit margins are included in the liability, the expected profit can be set to emerge in accordance with any desired pattern. For example, Australian and US life insurance liabilities are generally calculated so that the expected profit is spread over the term of the policies. This will be discussed further in Chapter 16.

---

[8] We assume that you have learned how to calculate liabilities on a net premium basis in an earlier stage of your actuarial education. This approach ignores many components of expected cash flows and gives arbitrary values to other components and to the discount rate. It is relatively simple to apply with limited computational resources and requires only basic, grouped, valuation data.

Exercise 12.6

What do you think are the advantages and disadvantages of spreading expected profit over the term of insurance policies?

12.3.4 Market value of liabilities

A best estimate liability doesn't include a cost for the risk of adverse deviations, while a prudent valuation may be too high for commercial purposes. In some cases, it is appropriate to place a value on a liability which is analogous to the market value of an asset. This may be for profit calculations or for assessing the value of the business.

Quite often, a liability has an obvious market value, since it is simply the inverse of a publicly traded asset. This would apply, for example, to corporate debentures and to most derivative contracts.

In many cases, however, there is no obvious market value for a liability. In that case, the concept of *fair value* may be applied.

Martin and Tsui (1999, p362) suggest the following definition of the fair value of a liability:

> The fair value of a liability is the value at which the liability could be settled or transferred between willing but not anxious parties, where:
>
> - both parties possess all material information relevant to the valuation of the liability;
>
> - any transfer parties are peers, who have a similar operational status, creditworthiness, and market access, and transact similar business in the same marketplace; and where
>
> - the fair value is determined on an 'as is' basis, ignoring special transferee or other restructure benefits that have not actually been offered by an identifiable party.

You should be able to see that this is similar to typical definitions of the market value of an asset.[9] Indeed, it is almost identical to the definition that Martin and Tsui use for the fair value of an asset.

A profit calculated from changes in the fair value of assets and liabilities should, itself, be a good measure of the tangible value added over the reporting period. This perhaps makes it unsurprising that the International Accounting Standards Board (IASB) is moving toward the use of fair value for assets and liabilities.

Exercise 12.7

In theory, a balance sheet prepared using fair values of assets and liabilities would place a fair value on the equity in the company.

Why might this value be different from the company's market value?

---

[9] But note that there is often confusion between market value and *fair value*, especially for assets such as listed shares. This will be discussed in Chapter 14.

12.3.5   Calculation methodology

Thus far, the discussion in this section has related to the philosophy behind the calculation of liabilities, rather than the nature of the calculation itself, although these two are clearly often closely linked.

First, we must consider whether to use a formula (with one or more parameters), a deterministic cash flow projection or a stochastic projection.

12.3.5.1   Formula valuations

Before computers, actuaries devised various formula approaches to valuing life insurance liabilities and such approaches are still in common use in many countries. The net premium valuation method is an obvious example.

Some liabilities are readily valued using formulae. For example, fixed-interest debt liabilities can be valued using basic compound interest formulae.

A formula method is also useful where a large number of calculations will be performed and the liability does not need to be precise. For example, suppose that we are making multiple projections of a portfolio of insurance policies under a range of scenarios. Within the projection program we may use a simple formula to determine policy liabilities.

Formula methods are also generally used in non-life insurance, relating the expected cost of outstanding claims to data about the historical development of claims costs. The formulae themselves are quite simple, with the complexity of the process being contained in the statistical analysis giving rise to the development parameters.

Finally, formulae (or at least, simple rules of thumb) may be used to provide a reasonableness check for valuations performed by other means.

The use of a formula is a simplification and the result will generally not bear any particular relationship to either a best estimate or a fair value liability. However, the choice of model (formula) and parameters will reflect the objectives of the valuation. Therefore, the actuary should have some understanding as to whether these objectives will be achieved, having regard to the characteristics of the liabilities being valued.

Similarly, the fact that formula valuations generally use limited data, often grouped to a fairly high level, should not prevent the actuary from checking that the data used is appropriate for the purpose.

Example 12.1

Consider a net premium valuation of traditional participating whole life insurance policies. Usually, an interest rate that is lower than the expected future investment return would be used, to allow for the addition of bonuses. Therefore, when long-term interest rates are around 5% per annum, using a discount rate of 3% might or might not be appropriate, but 10% is likely to be far too high. Also, a valuation which left out half the policies would be clearly wrong.

12.3.5.2   Deterministic cash flow projections

Most actuarial valuations are now performed using a deterministic cash flow projection.

This involves constructing a model of the behavior of future cash flows and setting assumptions for the parameters of the model, including discount rates.

A variation of this approach starts with a measurable (formula) value, such as account balance or surrender value, and uses a deterministic projection and discount approach to calculate an adjustment. One application of this variation is in an unbundled valuation (which we will discuss in 12.3.8).

Example 12.2

Investment-linked policies usually generate ongoing fee income which is higher than the associated administration expenses. Therefore, the best estimate liability is less than the account balance, ie number of units held × unit price.

Consider a policy with an account balance of $10,000, expected investment return of 10% per annum, annual fees of $110 and annual expenses of $44. The account balance after one year is expected to be $10,890, which is $10,000 \times 1.1 - 110$. If we expect the policy to terminate at that point, the present value of outgo (discounting at an interest rate of 10%) is $10,890/1.1 + 44/1.1 = \$9,940$. Therefore, the liability = $9,940, which is less than the account balance of $10,000.

In Example 12.3, we will see an example of a valuation approach which arrives at the same liability but starts from the account balance of $10,000.

12.3.5.3   Stochastic cash flow projections

Whether realistic or prudent, a deterministic valuation represents a single view of the future. Both the model and the assumptions may have been carefully chosen, taking into account the range of possible outcomes, the extent to which components of cash flow are correlated, likely management responses to experience, etc. Even so, the actuary would usually also run the model on different sets of assumptions, called scenarios.

However, running the model on different assumptions does not convey a measure of the probability of the particular scenario. Indeed, it does not even corroborate the intended strength of the base valuation, eg is this realistic valuation close to the mean of potential valuations, or is that prudent valuation pitched close to the target level of 75% sufficiency?

Increasingly, this information is so important that the actuary will use a stochastic model, ie one in which key drivers of cash flow are modeled as random variables and the process of projecting and discounting the cash flow is repeated many times to obtain a distribution of values.

This type of valuation generally requires significant computing power, since cash flows must be projected over a number of years and the projections repeated (with different randomly generated scenarios) many times. The information sought from the valuation may be critically dependent on the probability distributions used for the key drivers, the parameters assumed for these distributions and the degree of correlation assumed. The model may also incorporate rules which govern how, and how much, the company will react to changes in experience.

To reduce the scale of the computations required, actuaries may use stochastic models to help them select parameters to be employed in deterministic valuations.

For example, an electricity distributor may have entered into fixed-price contracts to supply electricity to a number of major industrial companies. Generally, the price that it will pay for electricity is low and fairly stable, but there are occasional spikes in price to extraordinarily high levels. It may not be possible to design a stochastic model which reasonably incorporates these spikes along with the other elements of variability in cash flow.

In that case, a stochastic model could be used to derive an appropriate basis for adjusting the expected cost of electricity to be used in a deterministic valuation model.

Exercise 12.8

Consider two examples of liabilities which are connected to you – that is, either they are your obligations to someone else or they are someone else's obligations to you.

Based on the nature of each liability, what would be an appropriate method to value the liability? Give reasons for your answer.

12.3.6 Valuing guarantees and options

Most liabilities incorporate some form of guarantee or option against the company. These must be properly allowed for when valuing the liabilities.

Often there is an obvious guarantee, such as the at-call account balance of a checking account or the agreed value[10] on a motor insurance policy. You should be able to see that the guarantees in these examples not only have value for the customer but also have a cost to the issuer.

Other guarantees and options may not be so obvious, or it may not be obvious that they have a cost. Examples include:

- *point of sale promises* – many countries effectively require companies to stand by representations made in advertisements, brochures, etc or by agents and other company representatives at or around the point of sale. Generally, this form of guarantee has a relatively minor cost. However, this is not always the case. In the UK, "pensions mis-selling" in the late 1980s cost companies large amounts of money in compensation[11] and in the US, "vanishing premium" sales in the 1980s led to major lawsuits in the 1990s;[12]

- *consumer protection legislation* – many countries have minimum standards of practice. For example, legislation in Australia restricts the fees which a product issuer can deduct from small superannuation account balances, and life insurance contracts have minimum surrender values. Outside financial services, a company's liability

---

[10] Under an agreed value policy, the insurer agrees to place a particular value on a car regardless of what condition it may turn out to be in at the time of a claim.

[11] See the first section of the article "Who Pays? The Aftermath of the UK Pensions Mis-selling Scandal" on the CD.

[12] See, for instance, the article "'Vanishing Premium' Litigation: The Plaintiff's Perspective" on the CD.

in relation to faulty goods or negligence is generally not avoided by any contract purporting to waive the customer's rights;

- *established practice* – discretions available to a company may be limited by the extent to which the company has exercised such discretions in the past. For example, traditional with-profit life insurance policies generally have non-guaranteed terminal bonuses payable on death or maturity. If the company has not actively adjusted these bonuses, it may find it hard to begin doing so either because it would adversely affect future sales or because a court would find that its established practice had created certain expectations;

- *out-of-the-money options* – many contracts have been issued with guarantees or options which appeared to have no cost because they were so far out of the money. Guaranteed annuity options on UK retirement savings products are a good example;[13] and

- *benefit definitions* – many life insurance products now pay benefits where the amount or even the fact of the payment depends on the claim satisfying a specific definition. Income protection insurance (based on a definition of inability to work) and trauma insurance (based on definitions of critical illnesses such as cancer and stroke) are obvious examples. In Australia, life insurers are not generally entitled to amend these definitions (except in the policyholder's favor) at any time over the term of the contract, which could be 40 years or more. This represents a significant guarantee which may not be fully mitigated by the offices' entitlement to change premium rates in future.

The first step in valuing guarantees and options in liabilities is to recognize that they exist. You would then need to determine whether they were likely to have a material cost. This would probably involve building at least a simplified valuation model, so you also need to decide what technical approach you will take to the valuation.

By themselves, many options can be valued using standard option pricing formulae, as set out in any modern finance textbook. However, it may be appropriate to adjust the results to reflect any correlation or interaction with other aspects of the liability. For example, the cost of a maturity guarantee on a life insurance policy will usually be mitigated by early terminations, because some policyholders will terminate their policies for personal reasons which will override the value of the guarantee that they are giving up.

Other options may require some form of branching or simulation approach to valuation, such as is recommended by Carrett and Wong (2002) for valuing executive options.

Finally, other options could be modeled by simple or complex allowance for future deterioration in experience. For example, some actuaries use multi-decrement tables, with take-up rates correlated to degree of ill-health, to value guaranteed future insurability options.

Whatever approach is taken, the important point is that options and guarantees have an intrinsic cost – even when well out of the money – so they should be identified and careful thought given to their effect on the liability valuation.

---

[13] For many years, most UK life offices included an option which allowed the policyholder, on reaching the end of the savings plan, to convert his/her policy to a lifetime annuity, at a guaranteed minimum rate. This minimum rate was calculated using interest rates far lower than those prevailing at the time that these policies were designed and issued. By the late 1990s, as a result of falling interest rates and improving mortality, most of these options were either in the money or close to being so. Companies had to set aside large sums of money in recognition of the high probability that the options would be exercised. Refer to "The End of the Equitable" article on the CD, for example.

Exercise 12.9

Considering contracts or other commercial relationships of which you are aware (eg contracts you have entered into yourself for insurance, banking, mobile phone service, etc), identify an example of each type of guarantee or option listed in the bullet points above.

12.3.7 Allowing for risk

We have discussed the need to allow for risk in many liability valuations. There are various technical issues associated with doing this, some of which we discuss elsewhere in this chapter.

In a stochastic projection, risk can be allowed for directly in the probability distributions applied to the various parameters modeled. A formula valuation is generally a simplified form of deterministic cash flow model, so the issue becomes one of how to allow for risk in a deterministic cash flow projection-and-discount valuation. It turns out that there are two basic ways to do this.

Risk-adjusted cash flows

Cash flows can be adjusted, either directly or by making more adverse assumptions. For example, a lifetime annuity valuation will be more conservative if the projected expenses are increased by x percent or the mortality assumption is lower than best estimate.

You should be able to see that an adjustment to the calculated value of the liability (eg calculating the best estimate liability then adding 20 percent) is equivalent to adjusting the projected cash flows.

Risk-adjusted discount rate

Whether or not the cash flows have been adjusted, it is also possible to adjust the discount rate to allow for risk. Where the cash flows being projected represent an excess of outgo over income, it will usually be conservative to use a lower discount rate.

As we shall see in 12.3.8, however, the liability may be calculated by subtracting the value of net future income from some base figure such as account balance. In such cases, it will usually be conservative to use a higher discount rate.

It may appear simpler to allow for risk in the discount rate, but there are two key disadvantages to doing so:

- a change in the discount rate won't change an asset into a liability (or vice versa);[14] and

- equivalent risk-based adjustments to cash flows for two different products will generally be mathematically equivalent to two different risk-based adjustments to the discount rate.

---

[14] Note that this statement may not hold if the periodic cash flows being discounted fluctuate between positive and negative, but this would be unusual.

Exercise 12.10

In what circumstances do you think that it may be appropriate to allow for risk in the discount rate?

12.3.8 Other considerations

12.3.8.1 Principles-based versus rules-based valuations

Whatever valuation method is used, an important consideration is any regulations or standards which must be followed. Liabilities valued by actuaries are generally material to the entity's financial position and financial performance. Therefore, their measurement is generally governed by accounting standards, prudential regulations and/or actuarial standards with which the valuer must comply.

These requirements may be very prescriptive, in terms of methodology and assumptions, in which case the resultant valuations are described as *rules-based*. For example, accounting standards may require that the liabilities under service contracts (such as gym memberships) be valued at no less than the membership fee multiplied by the outstanding proportion of the membership term.

Alternatively, the requirements may concentrate on the purpose of the valuation and the matters that must be considered, in which case they are described as *principles-based*. For example, an actuarial standard governing the valuation of long-term care liabilities may require the actuary to make appropriate allowance for all contingencies on which amounts may be payable.

12.3.8.2 Bundled versus unbundled valuations

The traditional actuarial approach to valuing liabilities is to project and discount all cash flows, either explicitly or implicitly. This *bundled* approach is clearly appropriate where there is one "owner" of all the cash flows, eg a non-life insurer.

For traditional with-profit whole life or endowment life insurance policies, the owner is a composite of the policyholders and the shareholders[15] and the bundled approach is generally appropriate.

For investment-linked life insurance policies, the company makes money from underwriting profits (life insurance charges less claims and expenses) and administration (fee income less expenses). The company's liability in respect of this business may be thought of as the total account balances less the expected value of net future income (with or without adjustments to allow for risk). This *unbundled* approach recognizes the fact that the policyholder "owns" the units underlying the account balance.

The advantage of an unbundled approach to valuing liabilities is that it avoids the unnecessary complexity which the bundled approach may introduce. It may be much simpler to produce a realistic projection of administration profits than to model all the details of the individual funds management contracts – and you can have more faith in the reliability of the model. As a guide, if the product is unbundled, ie fees and charges

---

[15] Here, the term *shareholder* includes the participating policyholders of a mutual life office.

are clearly defined and there is a clear account balance, it is likely that the liability can be valued by an unbundled approach.

Example 12.3

In Example 12.2, the policyholder "owns" the account balance of $10,000. The shareholders expect to receive fees of 110 from which to meet expenses of 44, giving an expected profit of $66. Discounting at 10% gives a present value of $60. Deducting this value from the account balance of $10,000 gives the value for the liability previously calculated, $9,940.

If we had added a risk margin of 10% to the expenses, the expected profit would have reduced to $61.60, with a present value of $56, giving a net liability of $9,944.

12.3.8.3   Deriving liabilities by valuing equity (the *indirect* approach)

As we have seen, the balance sheet shows how the total value of assets is subdivided into liabilities and equity. This means that the value of liabilities can be derived by deducting the value of equity from the total value of assets.

Actuaries generally use the expression *embedded value* to describe the calculated value of equity. In Chapter 16, you will learn more about calculating embedded values. However, you should be able to appreciate that you can project the expected cash flows (including interest on surplus assets) distributable to shareholders and that the present value of these cash flows is the value of shareholder equity.

If the valuation of shareholder equity contains risk adjustments (eg cash flows are discounted at a higher discount rate or using higher expense assumptions), the calculated liability will be greater than a best estimate liability.

You should be able to see that Example 12.3 is a very simple application of the indirect approach. This will usually be the case when an unbundled valuation is possible. However, the indirect approach will also work in more complex situations where the unbundled approach is unavailable.

12.3.8.4   Deferred acquisition costs and other assets

Often, the costs of acquiring a policy or customer (including promotional expenses, sales commissions, underwriting and new business processing) are considerably greater than the initial fee income generated by the sale. These costs are expected to be recovered from future income.

When valuing liabilities for the purposes of measuring profit, we generally want to reduce the liability by the amount of the unrecovered acquisition costs, so that profitable new business doesn't appear to make a loss.

There are two ways of doing this:

(a) reduce the liability by the value of components of future income considered to be set aside for the recovery of acquisition costs. You should be able to see that a best estimate liability implicitly does this because it allows for all future income; or

(b) establish a *deferred acquisition cost* (DAC) asset to offset part of the liability on the balance sheet.

A DAC may be considered to be the same as calculating a reduction in the liability; indeed, we could use the value of acquisition cost recovery components of future income in (a) as an explicit DAC in (b). However, a DAC is often calculated for a group of policies (eg all new business written in the past year) rather than at an individual policy level. Either way, it means that both the assets and the liabilities on the balance sheet are increased relative to the liability reduction approach.

Other income components can be shown as assets rather than serving to reduce the liabilities. One example is reinsurance, which can make a significant difference to the profile of risk insurance liabilities, both life and non-life.

Thus, a liability valuation cannot be considered in isolation from certain assets whose existence and value are connected to the liability.

Exercise 12.11

What issues might you take into account in deciding whether to show a negative component of the liability as an asset on the balance sheet? Consider your answer in the context both of a DAC and of reinsurance.

12.4   Profit and the liability valuation

It should be obvious that the extent to which margins are incorporated in the liability valuation will determine the likelihood that the valuation will prove sufficient if the underlying assumptions are not borne out in practice. That would suggest that we should prefer the valuation to be very conservative. However, the valuation also has an effect on profit. In turn, the amount and the rate of change in profit affect the company's share price and its standing in the market, both of which receive close attention from senior management!

In Section 12.1.3, we saw the simple formula for profit: *Profit = Income – Outgo – Increase in Liabilities*.

From this formula, it is clear that the valuation of liabilities is fundamental to the measured profit. Two factors particularly affect the valuation of liabilities and, hence, the measured profit:

- *the valuation objective* – the valuation may or may not be intended to incorporate risk margins, for example; and

- *the accuracy of the calculation* – the appropriateness of the valuation model and methodology, the availability and quality of the data and the accuracy of the assumptions can all have a significant impact on the valuation result.

In this section, we see the effect of these factors on the valuation and the consequences for profit.

12.4.1 The valuation objective

As we have seen, a valuation could be a best estimate or it can contain explicit or implicit margins, depending on the valuation objective. We now consider the impact of different valuation approaches, using a simple example product, details of which can be found on the CD.

Example 12.4 Example product[16]

Consider the investment-linked policy in Example 12.2, but now assume that it is a 10-year fixed-term policy, issued for a single premium of $10,000. Fees are 1% of account balance, deducted at the end of each year. Expenses are expected to be 5% of premium at issue and 0.3% of account balance, incurred at the end of each year. There will be no terminations during the 10-year term. The expected investment return is 10% per annum and there is no tax.

Table 12.1 shows how the account balance is expected to change over the period:

Table 12.1 Account balance for Example 12.4

Year[17]	Balance (Start)	Premium	Earnings	Fees	Payments	Balance (End)
0	0	10,000				10,000
1	10,000	0	1,000	(110)	0	10,890
2	10,890	0	1,089	(120)	0	11,859
3	11,859	0	1,186	(130)	0	12,915
4	12,915	0	1,291	(142)	0	14,064
5	14,064	0	1,406	(155)	0	15,316
6	15,316	0	1,532	(168)	0	16,679
7	16,679	0	1,668	(183)	0	18,163
8	18,163	0	1,816	(200)	0	19,780
9	19,780	0	1,978	(218)	0	21,540
10	21,540	0	2,154	(237)	(23,457)	0

From the company's perspective, the cash flows relating to the contract are as in Table 12.2:

---

[16] The tables in this example can be found on the CD in the file "Chapters 12 & 16 Valuation Model Spreadsheet."

[17] Note that we use a Year 0 in our projections. This is a very useful convention to separate those transactions which occur when a policy is issued from those in the rest of the first year. You will see later in this chapter (and in future chapters) how this highlights the initial capital requirement.

Table 12.2   Cash flows for Example 12.4

Year	Premium	Payments	Expenses[18]	Total
0	10,000		(500)	9,500
1	0	0	(33)	(33)
2	0	0	(36)	(36)
3	0	0	(39)	(39)
4	0	0	(43)	(43)
5	0	0	(46)	(46)
6	0	0	(51)	(51)
7	0	0	(55)	(55)
8	0	0	(60)	(60)
9	0	0	(65)	(65)
10	0	(23,457)	(71)	(23,528)

You will see that we have not included earnings or fees in this table, because they are incorporated in the accumulation of the account balance, which gives rise to the eventual payment.

Discounting at 10% per annum, the cash flows in the *Total* column have a present value of 169 at issue. You should be able to verify this.

Best estimate liability

The best estimate liability (BEL) is determined by discounting the expected cash flows at the expected interest rate. For example, at time 0 (the end of Year 0), when the premium has been received and the initial expenses incurred, the present value of the future cash flows is -9,331. Therefore, the BEL (the amount of money required in order to finance the future negative cash flows) is 9,331. Using this liability, the balance sheet immediately after issue will show 9,500 in assets and 9,331 in liabilities. Thus, the expected profit of 169 is fully recognized at time 0.

BEL + margin

We could calculate the liability with margins. For example, we could increase the projected expenses by 20 percent in the valuation. Then the liability at time 0 would be 9,388.

---

[18] In this example, we have determined the expenses before deducting the fees from the account balance. For example, the account balance at the end of Year 1 is 10,000 x 1.1 = 11,000 before deducting fees, so our assumed expenses are 0.3% x 11,000 = 33.

Margin on Services

A special case of a BEL plus margins liability is one where the margin represents the value of future profit. In this example, the present value of profit is about 17.71 percent of the present value of fees. (You should be able to verify this.)

We could calculate our liability as BEL plus 17.71 percent of the present value of future fees. This would be an example of a Margin on Services (MoS) valuation[19] and the liability at time 0 would be 9,500.

Account balance

If we adopted a liability equal to account balance, the liability at time 0 would be 10,000.

Account balance plus margin

Under many prudential regimes, a company issuing a product like this would have to hold additional capital, beyond the account balance. You should be able to see that the company would have to find an extra 100 at time 0 to finance a capital margin of one percent of account balance and that this would be released (with interest) when the policy terminated.

Account balance plus margin less DAC

If we established a DAC asset against the prudential liability, this would reduce the net liability.

The DAC would start at 500 at time 0, matching the acquisition cost. For the purposes of this example, we might allow the DAC to reduce linearly over the ten years, so that it was 450 at time 1, 400 at time 2, etc.

Table of liabilities

Assuming that the experience is in line with the best estimate assumptions, the liabilities calculated on the approaches described above will be as given in Table 12.3:

---

[19] The Margin on Services (MoS) valuation method was developed in Australia for valuing life insurance policy liabilities. The intent of a MoS valuation is that profit will only emerge when it has been earned, ie by providing the relevant service and receiving payment. The expected profit measured at issue of the policy is spread over one or more profit carriers, representing the major service(s) provided under the contract. For example, the major service under a level premium term insurance contract is coverage of the mortality risk, which will increase over the duration of the contract. If experience exactly matches the assumptions used when the policy is issued, profit will emerge as a constant proportion of the expected mortality cost.

Table 12.3   Liabilities under various schemes for Example 12.4

Year	Best Estimate	BEL + Margin	MoS	Account Balance	Acc Bal + Margin	DAC	AB + Marg less DAC
0	9,331	9,388	9,500	10,000	10,100	500	9,600
1	10,231	10,287	10,398	10,890	10,999	450	10,549
2	11,218	11,273	11,380	11,859	11,978	400	11,578
3	12,301	12,353	12,456	12,915	13,044	350	12,694
4	13,488	13,537	13,634	14,064	14,205	300	13,905
5	14,790	14,835	14,923	15,316	15,469	250	15,219
6	16,219	16,258	16,335	16,679	16,846	200	16,646
7	17,786	17,818	17,881	18,163	18,345	150	18,195
8	19,504	19,528	19,574	19,780	19,978	100	19,878
9	21,389	21,402	21,428	21,540	21,756	50	21,706
10	0	0	0	0	0	0	0

In the above example, you can see that the progression of liabilities varies according to the valuation approach. Recognizing that the product cash flow is unaffected by the valuation approach, we can see that a given year's profit will be increased by the interest on the liability at the start of the year and reduced by the increase in the liability during the year. Table 12.4 shows the contribution to profit on each valuation basis in Years 0, 5 and 10:

Table 12.4   Contribution of liability valuation basis to profit in Years 0, 5 and 10 for Example 12.4

Year	Best Estimate	BEL + Margin	MoS	Account Balance	Acc Bal + Margin	AB + Marg less DAC
0	(9,331)	(9,388)	(9,500)	(10,000)	(10,100)	(9,600)
5	46	56	74	155	156	76
10	23,528	23,543	23,570	23,694	23,931	23,876

Remembering that the cash flow in Year 0 is 9,500, you can see that the BEL valuation approach produces an expected profit of 169 in Year 0 (the present value of profit), the MoS valuation approach has no expected profit or loss and the Account Balance valuation approach results in an expected loss of 500 (from the acquisition cost). The final approach (Account Balance plus Margin less DAC) produces an expected loss of 100, which shows that the acquisition cost has been offset by the DAC and the remaining loss is the extra capital requirement.

We can graph the expected profits associated with a particular valuation approach. Such a graph is often called a *profit signature*. We can compare profit signatures to show how the valuation approach affects the expected emergence of profit. Remember that the valuation objectives inherent in each approach range from the immediate recognition of profit (best estimate basis), through the emergence of profit when earned (MoS) to the demonstration of capital adequacy (account balance plus a prudential margin). Figures 12.2 and 12.3 are taken from Chapter 16, which uses the same example product. These profit signatures are shown in two graphs to make them easier to see. All six are shown on the one graph in the workbook "Chapters 12 & 16 Valuation Model Spreadsheet" on the CD.

Figure 12.2   Three profit signatures for Example 12.4

Figure 12.3   Three further profit signatures for Example 12.4

It is important to remember that, regardless of the valuation basis adopted, profit will only emerge in accordance with the profit signature if experience is as expected. For many industries and/or products, actual experience can be quite volatile and the resultant effect on profit can overwhelm the expected pattern.

In the above examples, an unexpected doubling of expenses in Year 5 would reduce profit by 46, causing a substantial loss on valuation bases with low margins and even producing a loss on the MoS basis.

12.4.2   Liability valuation basis and total profit

As you can see from the graph (and the Excel workbook on the CD), the total profit is different on each valuation basis. This is because we have excluded the interest on any assets held above the valuation liability. If we include this interest, the profit in year t can be expressed as:

$$Profit_t = CF_t + iA_{t-1} - (L_t - L_{t-1})$$

where CF_t is the product cash flow, iA_{t-1} is the interest on total assets and L_t is the liability at time t.

Then total profit over the lifetime of the product is found by summing over t:

$$
\begin{aligned}
\Sigma\, Profit_t \quad &= \Sigma\, [CF_t + iA_{t-1} - (L_t - L_{t-1})] \\
&= \Sigma\, CF_t + i\Sigma\, A_{t-1} - \Sigma\, L_t + \Sigma\, L_{t-1} \\
&= \Sigma\, CF_t + i\Sigma\, A_{t-1} - (L_{10} - L_0)
\end{aligned}
$$

As $L_0 = L_{10} = 0$, total profit is independent of the valuation basis.

If we exclude interest on assets above the liability, thus focusing on the product itself,

$$\Sigma\, Profit_t \quad = \Sigma\, CF_t + i\Sigma\, L_{t-1} - (L_{10} - L_0)$$

and the liability basis clearly affects the total profit.

However, if we discount at the projection interest rate, the present value of profit can be found as:

$$
\begin{aligned}
PV(Profit) \quad &= \Sigma\, [CF_t + iL_{t-1} - (L_t - L_{t-1})] / (1+i)^t \\
&= \Sigma\, CF_t / (1+i)^t + \Sigma\, iL_{t-1} / (1+i)^t - \Sigma\, (L_t - L_{t-1}) / (1+i)^t \\
&= \Sigma\, CF_t / (1+i)^t + \Sigma\, L_{t-1} / (1+i)^{t-1} - \Sigma\, L_t / (1+i)^t \\
&= \Sigma\, CF_t / (1+i)^t + L_0 - L_{10} / (1+i)^{10}
\end{aligned}
$$

Again, $L_0 = L_{10} = 0$, so the present value of profit is independent of the valuation basis.

This means that: $\Sigma\, [CF_t + iL_{t-1} - (L_t - L_{t-1})] / (1+i)^t = \Sigma\, CF_t / (1+i)^t$

Therefore: $\Sigma\, [iL_{t-1} - (L_t - L_{t-1})] / (1+i)^t = 0$

This leads to a useful way to check projections for the life of a policy or group of policies: the present value of the interest on the liability should equal the present value of the change in the liability.

12.4.3 The accuracy of the valuation

Often, the valuation's effect on profit is not due to the expected pattern of profit emergence so much as to the accuracy of the valuation itself.

A company's profit may be a small percentage of its liabilities. For example, the profit of non-life insurers in Australia averaged about two percent of liabilities over the three years 1999 to 2001.[20] You should be able to see that a one percent error in measuring the liabilities of an average company would have changed the measured profit by 50 percent. (And note that shareholders react badly to earnings surprises – particularly negative ones.)

This is a particular issue for non-life insurers with long-tail business. Claims under long-tail insurance, such as product liability and professional indemnity, can take several years to become known and several years more to settle. Therefore, the insurer will have many years of claims on its books, including those which have not yet been reported, so the total liability can be substantial relative to expected profit.

If a business has large liabilities that are subject to high risk of valuation error, then it can expect to suffer volatile reported profits. However, even apparently small (or ignored) liabilities can have a significant effect on profit.

Example 12.5 Smoothing reserves

Sometimes, a company may use smoothing reserves to reduce the effect of volatile experience. Examples include *claims equalization reserves* and *investment fluctuation reserves*.

The rationale for such reserves is that short-term variances from the expected longer-term average experience are to be expected, that they are temporary and that it would be misleading to reflect them in full in the company's results.

However, the movement in these reserves can have a large effect on profit. Therefore, considerable judgment is required in setting them – and formal rules and constraints may also be imposed.

The subjective nature of these reserves is probably why the trend in regulation and accounting standards (such as those being developed by the International Accounting Standards Board) is not to permit them.

A liability valuation requires a determination, for each of the circumstances in which amounts are payable or receivable, of the likelihood of occurrence, the amount(s), the associated timing and the value at the valuation date.

Any or all of these elements can be very uncertain. Indeed, even the existence of a contract does not mean that we can be certain about whether liability exists for a particular event – and insurers often find themselves in court to establish the answer to this question.

Determining the present value of a future event (whether certain or contingent) involves discounting for the effect of earnings on the assets held to back the liabilities. This will be discussed in Section 12.6. For now, we will concern ourselves with the uncertainty relating to likelihood, amount and/or timing of payment. The following list illustrates some of the issues:

---

[20] Derived from Selected Statistics on the General Insurance Industry December 2001 (APRA, www. apra.gov.au). Pre-tax profit of direct insurers (ie not reinsurers) averaged 2.1% of liabilities in the three years covered by the document.

- Income claims in the course of payment, such as income protection claims or annuities, often involve well-defined payment amounts but the timing of cessation of payment may be very uncertain. Complex products may also introduce varying payment levels and additional contingent benefits, increasing the valuation challenge. If assumptions are based on past experience, it is easy to undervalue such claims during a period of deteriorating experience and to overvalue them as experience improves.

- Other known outstanding claims will be settled at some time in the future. Some amounts (such as legal fees and the costs of investigating the claim) will already have been incurred, but often the final cost of the claim will depend on future negotiations or will be decided in court. This means that the timing of payments is also unpredictable.

- In many cases, most notably non-life insurance but also for risk policies in life insurance, liability will exist for claims which have been incurred but have not yet been reported (IBNR). Estimating the value of such claims requires an understanding of past reporting patterns (and reasons why they might change). It is also possible that, once they become known claims, IBNR claims will behave differently in both size and timing of payments.

- Often, the liability being valued relates to a future contingent event which would give rise to a payment, part of which will be funded by future receipts. Examples include conventional endowment insurance policies and employer-sponsored defined benefit superannuation funds. Conventional endowment insurance policies pay the sum insured (and any bonuses) on death or the earlier maturity of the policy, in exchange for a fixed periodic premium and the expected value of future premiums must be allowed for in the valuation. In a defined benefit superannuation fund, different benefits are paid on different contingencies (including resignation, death in service and retirement) and allowance must be made for future employer contributions.

In all of these cases, actual experience will almost certainly be different from the valuation assumptions. Often, there are also issues with the data and/or the models being used. Any or all of these factors can have very significant consequences; corporate graveyards are full of examples.

Exercise 12.12

Using the CD and the internet as resources, find examples of corporate failures where liabilities had been significantly misstated. What do you think have been the major errors in the valuation of liabilities for these companies?

12.4.4   Intrinsic capital funding

Sometimes, the structure of a contract is such that additional capital is required at a future date – for example, to fund the issue of bonus units rewarding policyholders maintaining a policy for a particular period. If the basis of calculation of the liability does not make adequate allowance for this additional capital, some of the projected profits may be negative.

To avoid this, the liability basis could be changed or an additional component could be added, representing the present value of all additional capital requirements. In the UK, this component is called a *sterling reserve*, because it represents the future cash (sterling) demands of the contract.

12.4.5   Liabilities and pricing

The next chapter discusses pricing. As liabilities are a key determinant of profit, they must also be a significant input to the pricing process.

As part of the pricing process, profits can be projected on different liability bases in the manner of 12.4.1. For example, the profit at issue using a best estimate liability is one simple measure that some actuaries use in pricing. Projections using liabilities determined in accordance with profit reporting standards will show how the proposed new product will affect the company's reported profit.

For most financial products, issuing the product requires the allocation of capital to meet initial costs and to establish prudential margins in the liabilities. The pattern of usage and release of capital (with associated profits) can be seen in the profit signature for "AB Plus" in Figure 12.3. As the shareholders will require a higher return on this capital than the expected investment return (which they could obtain without taking the product risk), there is a cost associated with having this capital tied up in the product. This cost must be allowed for in product pricing. (And note that you cannot learn anything about this cost from determining the best estimate liability at issue.)

12.5   Practical valuation issues

We have seen how the approach to a valuation depends on its purpose and we have discussed the effect of uncertainty. We now turn our attention to some practical issues.

12.5.1   Materiality

Not surprisingly, a more precise liability calculation will generally require more time and effort. It is important to consider whether this would be justified.

Generally, where the liability is not *material* to the accounts (that is, a relatively large change in the liability will have only a small effect on the balance sheet or the P&L), a more approximate calculation will suffice.

12.5.2   Sensitivity

Often, the actuary is required to calculate liabilities which are material.

In these circumstances, it is important to understand how the choice of basis, data and assumptions (including discount rates) can affect the calculation. *Sensitivity tests* can be carried out by varying these choices and noting the effect on the liability.

Sensitivity tests can help the actuary to:

- select an appropriate valuation basis;

- determine how to analyze data (eg what groupings to use);

- identify key assumptions for which more research or more precision is required; and

- check that the valuation model is operating correctly – for example, there may be an error if it doesn't react as expected when assumptions are changed.

12.5.3   Data

Data was discussed in Chapter 10, but it is worth discussing specific issues in relation to liability valuations.

Data requirements depend on the model. Traditional actuarial valuation formulae were designed not only to minimize computations but also to be able to operate on limited, summarized data. Thus, for example, a net premium valuation requires data to be divided by entry age, original term and current duration and operates on the aggregate sum insured and attaching bonuses (dividends). It is often possible to group data even further, eg treat all 20-year endowment policies issued to people aged 20 to 30 as if they were all issued to 25-year-olds.

Models requiring projection and discounting of cash flows generally require more data. Each component of projected cash flow that will be derived from information about the business being projected needs to be fed that information. The information might be obvious, such as the level of premium being paid on a life insurance savings contract; or less obvious, such as date of last premium payment (if the model has a sophisticated mechanism for transferring policies from premium-paying to dormant). Similarly, where the projection depends on analysis of past data (such as in run-off triangles), the availability of more data is likely to enhance the projection – provided that the data is relevant and reliable.

Complex models generally don't allow much grouping of the data, because they require so much information from each record. The exception is where the complexity relates to the projection environment, rather than to the way in which rules apply to the business being projected. For example, a stochastic projection may have very complex rules governing future investment returns and the propensity of customers to make claims, withdraw funds, etc, but it could ignore or minimize differences in the rules governing individual contracts.

Exercise 12.13

This exercise requires you to do some research!

Actuaries have a long history of valuing liabilities in life insurance, non-life insurance and superannuation. Find out what data is required for valuing the following liabilities and discuss why these requirements are different:

(a) With-profit endowment policies valued by the net premium valuation method.

(b) Single premium investment-linked policies valued by the margin on services method.

(c) CTP (compulsory third party) claims valued by the Bornhuetter-Ferguson method.

(d) Defined benefit pension fund liabilities valued as part of a funding calculation using the Aggregate method.[21]

---

[21] Defined benefit superannuation funding calculations entail calculating the difference between assets and liabilities and determining the future contributions required to fund this difference. Different funding methods define and value the liabilities (and the assets) in different ways. In this exercise, we are interested in the liabilities which are taken into account in the Aggregate funding method, discussed in Chapter 13.

One major challenge facing most actuaries when valuing liabilities is the availability and quality of data. As we have seen, the more sophisticated and complex models generally require a lot of data. In turn, this means that such data must have been collected, validated, stored and adequately maintained; otherwise, it will have little or no value. Actuaries can have a critical role in ensuring that the necessary data is collected and that it is properly validated and maintained.

As with assumptions, a model will be more sensitive to errors in some data than in other data. For example, a valuation of investment-only life insurance liabilities is unlikely to be significantly affected by errors in the data relating to the age or sex of the policyholders. However, this is critical data for valuing risk-only life or health insurance liabilities.

Data also affects the model to the extent that it is used to derive assumptions. For example, most techniques for estimating outstanding non-life insurance claims require claims development patterns to be derived from past experience. If the data representing that experience is unreliable, both the starting point and the modeled claims development will be compromised.

The appropriate tests to validate data depend on the data itself, the sources of the data and the purposes for which it is to be used. These tests would include:

- *ratios and trends* – if the business is such that you would expect certain ratios to be similar from year to year or trends to be broadly maintained, then you can examine the data to see whether there are deviations. For example, you may expect the average claim size to be similar to that in previous years;

- *movement analysis* – you may have information about movements in the liabilities being valued, which you can use to validate this year's data. For example, you may know how many claims there were at the previous valuation, how many new ones arose during the year and how many were settled;

- *comparison with expected* – even without detailed movement information, you can often form a view about what the data should be like, based on market experience, the economic environment, the company's cash flows, etc; and

- *data integrity tests* – there are various tests, such as Benford's Law,[22] which can be applied to determine whether some or all of the data may be fake.

12.5.4 Projection assumptions

Chapter 10 addressed the general question of setting assumptions. As with any model, the assumptions used in valuing liabilities should be appropriate to the purpose of the valuation. However, this statement is both obvious and unhelpful.

In practice, in setting assumptions you need to answer a host of questions, including:

- what assumptions are needed? On one level, this question requires a list of parameters for which values are required. More importantly, however, it requires you to think about the nature of the parameter (eg is the assumed claim rate to be driven by lives or sums insured) and any implicit assumptions which you have made;

---

[22] Benford's Law was named for Dr Frank Benford, who noticed a pattern in the distribution of initial digits of sets of numbers from various sources, including tables of logarithms. In a large set of numbers not created from a specific random distribution, the probability that a number starts with the digit D is $log_{10}(1 + 1/D)$. This law can be used to highlight possible cases of artificial data. References include Matthews (1999) and Browne (1998).

- how accurate does this assumption need to be? The answer will depend on the sensitivity of the valuation to this assumption, the cost of increasing the accuracy and the nature and purpose of the valuation. Often, the important issue is how it relates to other assumptions, eg in calculating a superannuation liability, the gap between the investment return and salary inflation assumptions is usually far more significant than the absolute level of each assumption;

- how realistic or conservative must this assumption be? This is different from the previous question, because it relates to the way in which the assumption should differ from your best estimate. It will not always be obvious whether an assumption is conservative, either on its own or in conjunction with other assumptions;

- how will you derive this assumption? You need to consider how reliable the source is and how relevant it is to your valuation, eg claim rates derived from your company's own data should be more relevant than industry data, but the volume of data may be limited and past claims may relate to business written on different terms and/or subject to a different standard of underwriting. Also, having derived best estimate assumptions, it may be difficult to determine the margin to be added to achieve the desired level of conservatism; and

- what constraints apply? Often, the valuation is to be performed in accordance with actuarial standards, accounting standards, regulations and/or legislation, any or all of which might constrain the selection of assumptions. For example, many life insurance policy liability valuations under US GAAP[23] must use the original pricing assumptions, even if these are now clearly wrong.

As ever, the basic principles of the Actuarial Control Cycle apply to assumption setting.

Often, the liability valuation is an update of a previous valuation, so a set of assumptions already exists. This is generally a useful starting point and it may be appropriate to use many of the same assumptions, or the same processes for deriving them. However, you should always be prepared to challenge established practices.

Conversely, you may appear to have relatively little available as a starting point for setting assumptions. For example, you may be using a new model or performing a valuation under new standards or in a new business or industry. You can mitigate this problem by considering parallels in other areas, using plenty of reasonableness checks and sensitivity analyses and establishing mechanisms to enable you to review the emerging experience relative to the assumptions.

Exercise 12.14

You have been asked to value the liabilities of a forestry company. This company owns a pine plantation and has entered into a contract to deliver a quantity of timber at a fixed price in three years' time. For the purposes of this exercise, you can assume that it takes five years to grow pine trees to an appropriate size for timber harvesting and that the trees in the plantation were planted two years ago.

What assumptions will you need to make in order to perform this valuation? How will you set these assumptions?

---

[23] US GAAP (Generally Accepted Accounting Principles) applies to US companies and to many others which choose to report on this basis.

12.5.5   Discount rates

A valuation model comprises a projection and discounting of cash flows (whether explicit or implicit), so the valuation depends significantly on the discount rate(s) used. A full discussion on selecting the discount rate(s) could fill a book in itself, so this subsection is an overview of some of the key issues.

12.5.5.1   Same projection and discount rates?

Liabilities are often valued using the same rates of interest for projection and discount. This is the natural approach for calculating best estimate liabilities, which do not allow for the cost of the risk of adverse deviations from the assumptions.

Even where the valuation allows for risk, the projection and discount rates may be the same. This could be because the cash flows have been adjusted to allow for risk or because the nature of the liability (or the calculation) is such that there is no material gain in using differential rates.

If risk is being allowed for by using different rates, the discount rate(s) would be expected to be lower, since this should result in a higher liability. However, where the liability is being determined indirectly from an embedded value calculation, the discount rate(s) would be higher than the projection interest rate(s).

12.5.5.2   Allowing for tax

If you think of the value of liabilities as being the value of the assets which the company would need to hold to meet the liabilities as they fall due, you can see that all future cash flows, including tax, must be allowed for in the valuation.

Arguably, this means projecting after-tax cash flows and discounting at an after-tax discount rate. That is, if we expect the earning rate on assets to be 5%, with tax on these earnings at 30%, we would discount the after-tax cash flows at $(100\text{-}30)\% \times 5\% = 3.5\%$.

Consistent with this view, it is very common for liabilities to be valued using an after-tax discount rate and this is sometimes required by actuarial or accounting standards. However, Martin and Tsui (1999) give a very clear demonstration that this is equivalent to discounting those cash flows at the gross discount rate (5% in this example) and including a *tax cost liability*. The advantage of this approach can be seen when the *unwind*[24] of the liability discount is tax deductible. In that case, the tax on investment earnings is offset by the tax deduction for the increase in the liability resulting from the unwind of the discount and there is no tax cost liability.

---

[24] The unwind of the liability discount is the effect of removing one or more years of discounting of the cash flows. It is the amount by which the liability would be increased if that discounting had not applied.

Example 12.6

Martin and Tsui demonstrate their point with three-year projections, but it is also possible to see the effect over one year. For ease of comparison, we shall use the last year of their illustrations.

Consider an obligation to pay $1,000 in a year's time and assume that there are no other cash flows expected. If the appropriate gross discount rate is 10%, and tax is payable at 30%, then the net discount rate is 7% and the liability is 1,000 / 1.07 = $934.58.

Our valuation assumes a return of 10% on the assets supporting this liability, giving us pre-tax earnings of 934.58 × 10% = $93.46. If tax is payable at 30%, there will be a tax cost of 30% × 93.46 = $28.04. This gives after-tax earnings of 93.46 – 28.04 = $65.42.

Therefore, the projected assets are 934.58 + 65.42 = $1,000, which validates the liability calculation.

If we consider the liability as comprising a "payment liability" and a tax cost liability, we can calculate the payment liability as 1,000 / 1.10 = $909.09 and the tax cost liability as 28.04 / 1.10 = $25.49. This gives a total liability of 909.09 + 25.49 = $934.58.

Finally, if the unwind of the liability discount is tax-deductible, we find that the correct liability is the payment liability. Gross earnings on this liability will be $90.91, which is the same as the unwind of the discount rate (1,000 – 909.09). Therefore, any tax payable on the earnings will be offset by the tax deductibility of the unwind.

So, in summary, there is a clear theoretical basis for adopting a gross discount rate and calculating a tax cost liability to be included in the total liability. You should note, however, that it is often easier to use an after-tax discount rate when changes in the liability are not tax-deductible.[25]

12.5.5.3 Formula valuation methods

A formula needs to be relatively simple, so it will typically use a single discount rate for all future periods. Using traditional actuarial assurance and annuity functions, it is then straightforward to calculate liabilities. The net premium valuation is a good example of this approach.[26]

Apart from the constraints introduced by the particular formula approach being adopted (such as the implicit allowance for bonus rates in the discount rate in net premium valuations), the selection of discount rate(s) should not be affected by the fact that a formula is being used.

---

[25] You can see this by noting that the tax cost liability in Example 12.6 could not be calculated without knowing the total liability at the start of the year.

[26] For a net premium valuation, a lower interest rate produces a higher liability, so the calculation is generally expected to be conservative if it is performed with interest rates well below best estimate.

12.5.5.4 Cash flow projections

Where cash flows are projected and discounted, there is more scope to use multiple discount rates. It is quite common, for example, for outstanding claims estimates to be calculated using discount rates derived from the current yield curve of government bonds. That is, the projected cash flow in year Y is discounted at a rate of interest derived from the market yield on government bonds maturing in year Y.[27]

In general, a more accurate valuation would be achieved by using multiple discount rates. This would suggest that multiple rates would be used for best estimate and fair value valuations.

Conversely, a conservative or approximate valuation might be expected to use a single discount rate.

In practice, other factors also influence the choice. These factors include:

*   constraints of the valuation software programs – there may be no scope to use multiple rates even if you wanted to (but note that this may be a reason to use different software);

*   regulatory requirements – there may be an effective requirement to use a single discount rate;

*   the trade-off between complexity and accuracy – there may not be sufficient gain in accuracy to warrant the additional complexity; and

*   presentation of the results – at times, actuaries valuing superannuation liabilities have used different projection (and, hence, discount) rates in the first few years, because it is easier to explain the use of rates which are similar to current market yields.

12.5.5.5 Setting discount rates

So far, we have not really discussed how to set discount rates.

First, let us consider the situation where the discount rate and projection interest rate are the same. In this case, the question becomes one of how to set the projection interest rate.

Assuming that a realistic valuation is required, a common (but much criticized) approach would be to consider the mix of assets backing the liabilities and, based on some form of economic model, derive an interest rate.

For example, we might adopt a relatively simple model which starts with an assumed average inflation rate and assumes some relationships between inflation rates and short- and long-term interest rates and equity returns to progressively derive assumptions for average future cash, 10-year bond and equity returns. If we adjust these returns for tax and apply them to the expected asset mix, we have a projection interest rate.

This approach introduces two clear issues:

*   Do we have a sound basis for deriving the expected returns on various asset classes?

*   Is it appropriate that the value of the liabilities depends on the assumed mix of assets?

---

[27] Arguably, the discount rate to use for cash flows in year Y is the market yield for zero-coupon government bonds maturing in year Y. These can be derived from the yield curve of actual coupon-paying bonds, but often the market yield on those bonds is used as a proxy.

In both cases, the first question to consider is whether an apparently more appropriate approach will materially and cost-effectively affect the accuracy of the valuation. This is not just a question of the sensitivity of the answer to changes in the projection and/or discount rates. You would also need to consider the likely degree of error introduced by approximations in the model or the derivation of other assumptions.

Nevertheless, these are live issues and there is considerable debate among actuaries on the whole topic of setting discount rates. We consider this debate further in Section 12.6.

Exercise 12.15

Using the model on the CD for Example 12.4, find out how the value of profit changes when you change the investment return.

Why do you think this happens?

12.6   Financial economics and discount rates

As we have discussed throughout this chapter, there are many reasons why valuations should be as "accurate" as possible. We have also discussed the potentially critical role of the selection of discount rates and we have mentioned the current debate in this area.

Financial economics, including the concept of state price deflators, provides a theoretical framework for setting discount rates and actuaries cannot afford to ignore this; however, a full technical dissertation is beyond the scope of this chapter. Therefore, this section gives a brief overview of the key points. Jarvis et al (2001) present a good discussion of state price deflators and a very useful reference list. The concept of the *Capital Asset Pricing Model* (CAPM) and the distinction between diversifiable and non-diversifiable risk are discussed in Ashe (2010) on the CD.

The two key elements of financial economics are:

*   market prices are arbitrage-free; and

*   investors require a higher expected return for higher non-diversifiable risk.

12.6.1   Arbitrage-free pricing and state price deflators

An arbitrage opportunity exists in a market when it is possible to make a combination of transactions that give you something for nothing. Jarvis et al (2001, p4) give the following definition:

> An arbitrage opportunity exists when an investor can construct two different portfolios of differing price, which provide the same cash flows. Selling the more expensive portfolio and buying the cheaper portfolio with the proceeds produces an unlimited return without capital expenditure on the part of the investor.

In effect, this means that the value of a set of cash flows is the same as the value of a portfolio of assets (including negative assets) which replicates this set of cash flows. This holds true whether or not the cash flows are certain, provided that the replicating portfolio will replicate the cash flows under all circumstances.

An obvious example of such a condition is a 100 percent reinsurance contract, under which the reinsurer will pay the insurer any amount which the insurer, in turn, must pay under the terms of the policies covered by the contract.

Mathematically, it is possible to develop this line of thinking by considering theoretical assets which pay out one unit if a particular *state* holds true and nothing otherwise. By observing the market prices of real assets, and noting what their payouts would be in each state, it is possible to derive market prices for these *state assets*. These are known as *state prices*.

In turn, this enables us to value a new asset, provided only that we know what its cash flows will be in each state. We do not need to know the probability of each state occurring.

In fact, however, we can derive the probability of each state occurring from the market prices of the real assets. Since we also know the state price, we can then derive *state price deflators*, conceptually equivalent to the factor v^t in compound interest, to discount cash flows in each state back to the present day.

$$State\ Price = State\ Probability \times State\ Price\ Deflator$$

Example 12.7

Jarvis et al (2001) give an example of a two-state model where the future states are either "feast" or "famine." In their model, asset prices are such that it is possible to deduce the state price of feast as 0.35 and that of famine as 0.6. That is, an asset which will pay 1 in the feast state and 0 in the famine state would be worth 0.35 now. One which paid 0 in the feast state and 1 in the famine state would be worth 0.6.

In this model, a risk-free asset would pay 1 regardless of the state and have a value of $0.35 + 0.6 = 0.95$. This would suggest a risk-free discount rate of 5.26%.

If feast and famine are equally likely, the feast state price deflator = $0.35 / 0.5 = 0.7$ and the famine state price deflator = $0.6 / 0.5 = 1.2$.

12.6.2   The risk-return trade-off: CAPM

Disregarding state price deflators for the moment, the other key principle of financial economics is that investors demand a higher expected return for non-diversifiable risk.

Example 12.8

Consider two assets, both with a payoff in one year's time. There are two possible states at that time, "feast" with a 10% probability and "famine" with a 90% probability.

Asset A is certain to pay $100 while asset B will pay $190 in the feast state and $90 in the famine state. In both cases, the expected payoff is $100. However, an investor would be expected to be prepared to pay more for A than for B because B carries higher risk.

By extension, B would command a higher price than C, which pays $280 (feast) or $80 (famine). This can be validated by noting that B can be replicated by a portfolio of 50% A and 50% C. Since this portfolio must have the same price as B (otherwise an arbitrage is created) and A is more expensive than B, C must be cheaper.

You may consider that we have cheated with this example, because asset C is a linear combination of A and B. In fact, this will apply to all assets in this two-state model unless there is an arbitrage opportunity.

The example illustrates that as the risk increases so does the expected return required by the investor. Of course, this is not to be confused with the actual return.

This relationship between risk and expected return enables us to construct optimal portfolios of assets, which maximize the expected return for a given level of risk.

We can also see that some risk does not command a premium. Individual assets, whose payoffs are uncorrelated but have the same expected value, can be combined in a portfolio which has the same expected payoff and a lower risk. To avoid creating an arbitrage, the individual assets cannot be priced to yield a higher return than the portfolio.

By extension, no additional return can be expected for any risk which is diversifiable.

This leads to the CAPM equation:

$$E(r) = r_F + \beta (r_M - r_F)$$

That is, the expected return is the risk-free return (r_F) plus a factor (β) times the difference between the overall expected market return (r_M) and the risk-free return. β is the ratio of the riskiness of the asset to the riskiness of the overall market.

At this point, we can return to state price deflators. Remembering that the state prices simply reflect overall market prices, we can adjust the state probabilities so that the deflators all become the risk-free deflator $(1 + r_F)^{-1}$. These risk-adjusted probabilities could then be used to produce risk-adjusted cash flow projections which can be discounted at the risk-free rate.

What all this means is that there is always a set of risk-based adjustments to cash flows which would enable the results to be discounted at the risk-free rate. If these adjustments can be approximated by adjusting projection assumptions, we have a valuable practical model for valuations.

12.6.3   Actuaries and financial economics

As we have said, actuaries cannot afford to ignore financial economics. However, there are some practical issues which must be addressed.

Most actuaries probably derive economic assumptions from CAPM-inspired models like the simple one described in 12.5.5.5, ie starting with a base such as inflation or the risk-free rate of return and adding margins for risk, liquidity and the time value of money. A similar approach may be used to derive a discount rate for embedded value calculations.

This raises various issues, including:

- what is the risk-free rate of return, r_F? In some cases, this may appear obvious, but there is generally room for some debate;

- how much work is justified in deriving the market rate of return, r_M, and the β for each asset class? Given that liquidity premiums and other factors are also at work, a common practical approach is to start with observable differences in expected returns rather than attempting to calculate β etc. For example, a comparison of market yields on index-linked government securities and those on fixed-coupon bonds produces an implicit market expectation of future inflation;

- how relevant is the model over the long term? Many analyses of relative returns of asset classes show that equities have generally outperformed bonds over the long term. However, Fitzherbert (2001) has shown that there is no apparent long-term reward for risk within the class of Australian equities.[28] Furthermore, it is arguable that weight-of-money considerations are responsible for the past outperformance of equities;[29] and

- most projections require assumptions (generally implicit) about the returns available on future investments in various asset classes. Can these be determined using CAPM or state price deflators?

It is still standard actuarial practice, and sometimes required by regulators, to project and discount cash flows with reference to the expected investment return on the assets supporting the liabilities. On the face of it, this approach would appear to have been justified by the higher long-term returns achieved on equities.[30]

However, the move toward measuring liabilities at fair value clearly raises the issue of arbitrage-free pricing and the use of discount rates (or deflators) defined by the liabilities rather than the current asset mix. This, in turn, raises issues including:

- it is generally very difficult to determine an asset portfolio that replicates the liability. This makes it hard to identify the right discount rates or to derive state price deflators; and

---

[28] Note that this is not the same as saying that CAPM is "wrong." Fitzherbert (2001) simply asserts that CAPM is a single period model which is often used, uncritically, to justify long-term risk premiums in multi-period projections and that there is no evidence for a long-term risk premium.

[29] Higher equity returns can be explained by an argument that equities were mis-priced in the early days, when markets were inefficient and institutional investors didn't understand risk and largely ignored equities. As these barriers were removed, institutions sought to increase their exposure to equities. This increase in demand pushed up prices, which attracted further investment, further pushing up prices, etc.

[30] Short-term equity returns are, however, often lower than "risk free" returns. In periods of acute or sustained underperformance, allowance for higher long-term returns can be (at best) hard to explain.

- an apparent arbitrage can be sustainable if friction is high enough. In other words, if it costs too much (eg in transaction costs) to take advantage of the arbitrage, then the apparent arbitrage is sustainable. This may well apply to many financial services liabilities.

These difficulties may largely reflect the gap in practical applications of financial economics in this area, particularly the lack of insurance derivative products which would replicate typical liabilities and remove the friction costs of eliminating arbitrages. This has been the development path in other financial markets.

We can expect to see significant developments in actuarial thinking in this regard, to help actuaries to set discount rates in accordance with financial economics principles. With experience, including monitoring and review, our knowledge and practice will continue to improve. This is simply another demonstration of the control cycle principle.

Exercise 12.16

We have discussed the fact that actuaries must decide whether to allow for the expected earnings on the supporting assets when calculating a liability. One example is superannuation, where the actuary is recommending a contribution rate based on the difference between the assets and the liabilities.

Contributions to a defined benefit superannuation fund affect a company's profit. One major driver of the contribution rate is the net liability which is to be funded. Considering this and other relevant issues, what are the implications of:

(a) Allowing for an equity risk premium which does not eventuate?

(b) Allowing for risk-free returns which the fund significantly exceeds in practice?

12.7 Practical implications for actuaries

The valuation of liabilities is a core actuarial function[31] and this is the work that many actuaries perform every day. The change in liabilities is often a key component of profit. The accuracy (or, at least, the adequacy) of conservative liabilities affects the entity's perceived financial strength. However, many liabilities on a company's balance sheet are not routinely valued by actuaries. Moreover, the valuation of liabilities must be seen in the context of the valuation of assets, including deferred acquisition costs, which may be seen by the company as outside the actuary's scope. So, the actuary's valuation of liabilities cannot be viewed in isolation. The company's financial position is also affected by liability and asset valuations undertaken by others.

Thus, in valuing liabilities, the actuary must not only be aware of the purpose of the valuation (eg realistic profit or solvency) but also understand the context. This requires continual and effective communication with the rest of the entity's finance team.

---

[31] Legislation may require that certain liabilities, such as outstanding claims, must be certified by an actuary.

As the actuary's valuation is likely to have a significant effect on profit, it is important to keep management informed in a timely manner. You have not done a particularly good job if your valuation is technically perfect and your report is beautifully written but the number comes as a big surprise to management when your report is complete.

12.8   Key learning points

In this chapter, we have discussed the nature of liabilities and considered issues associated with their measurement.

- Reserves and provisions are established on the balance sheet for various different types of liability.

- The value ascribed to a liability depends on the purpose of the valuation; if the valuation is intended to be conservative, it can be expected to contain margins relative to a "realistic" valuation.

- Having determined the purpose of the valuation, there are usually several valuation methods available.

- When valuing liabilities, it is important to remember to allow for any guarantees or options.

- The valuation will affect reported profit; the effect can be largely an intended consequence of the valuation methodology or it can arise from uncertainties or errors in the valuation.

- Sensitivity tests are an important tool to help the actuary to understand and validate the valuation.

- For long-term liabilities, the selection of discount rate can be very important. This chapter introduces the reader to some of the issues surrounding this decision, including the role of financial economics.

- This chapter has close links to Chapters 9 (Modeling), 10 (Data and Assumptions), 11 (The Need for Capital), 13 (Pricing), 14 (Assets), 15 (Solvency) and 16 (Profit).

CD Items

Ashe, F. 2010, Investments.

Ferris, S. 2001, The End of the Equitable, *Actuary Australia*, March, Institute of Actuaries of Australia, pp. 12-13.

Ferris, S. 1999, Who Pays? The Aftermath of the UK Pensions Misselling Scandal, *Actuary Australia*, March, Institute of Actuaries of Australia, pp. 10-11.

Martin, G.C. & Tsui, D. 1999, Fair Value Liability Valuations: Discount Rates and Accounting Provisions, *Australian Actuarial Journal*, Vol 5, 3.

Pearson, E. 2002, General Principles of Establishing Outstanding Claims Provisions, The HIH Royal Commission, Background Paper No. 14.

Phillips, R. 1996, "Vanishing Premium" Litigation: The Plaintiffs' Perspective, www.smithphillips.com.

Chapters 12 & 16 Valuation Model Spreadsheet

Chapter 12 Exercise Solutions

References (other than CD Items)

Australian Accounting Standards Board 2004, *Framework for the Preparation and Presentation of Financial Statements*.

Australian Prudential Regulation Authority (APRA) 2002, *Selected Statistics on the General Insurance Industry*, December 2001.

Australian Prudential Regulation Authority (APRA) 2007, *Prudential Standard LPS1.04: Valuation of Policy Liabilities*.

Australian Prudential Regulation Authority (APRA) 2007, *Prudential Standard LPS3.04: Capital Adequacy Standard*.

Australian Prudential Regulation Authority (APRA) 2008, *Prudential Standard GPS310: Audit and Actuarial Reporting and Valuation*.

Browne, M. 1998, Following Benford's Law, or Looking Out for No. 1, *New York Times*, August 4, 1998, http://www.nytimes.com/1998/08/04/science/following-benford-s-law-or-looking-out-for-no-1.html, accessed January 14, 2010.

Carrett, P. & Wong, B. 2002, Executive Options: Valuation and Projection Methodologies, *Australian Actuarial Journal*, Vol 8, 1.

Fitzherbert, R. 2001, Volatility, Beta and Return – Was There Ever a Meaningful Relationship?, *Australian Actuarial Journal*, Vol 7, 4.

Jarvis, S., Southall, F. & Varnell, E. 2001, Modern Valuation Techniques, *Staple Inn Actuarial Society,* Paper 6, February 2001.

Matthews, R. 1999, The Power of One, *New Scientist*, Vol 163, 2194, July 10, 1999, p.26.

Fred's Coffee Shop – Pricing

Once Fred decided on the menu of coffee and light meals his coffee shop would offer, he had to work out what prices to charge. When he first started thinking about the sort of shop he would open, he wanted to offer the very best of everything: ingredients, surroundings, service. But when he added up all the costs, he found that he would have to charge $10 for a cup of coffee! This was more than most of his customers would be willing to pay. Fred's coffee shop, like any business, has to set prices that will both cover costs and be attractive to customers.

Chapter 13 describes a systematic approach for setting prices. This will involve repeated iterations, fine-tuning the combinations of product features and price by running them as inputs to the business model, on various assumptions, to find a combination that we believe will be competitive and meet our profit objective. Several different possible profit objectives are discussed.

The cost of the ingredients in a cup of coffee is tiny compared to the price a customer pays. Most of the price goes to cover fixed expenses (those that don't vary directly with number of sales) such as wages, rent and electricity. (Note that, once sales volume passes a certain point, Fred may need to put on extra staff and move to larger premises. So, strictly speaking, these expenses are "semi-variable" rather than fixed.) An important decision in pricing is how much each product should contribute to fixed costs. Fred might decide that a cup of coffee should have a loading of $2 above the cost of ingredients and any other variable expenses. Then, if he has 200 customers a day each buying a cup of coffee, the shop will generate $400 a day to cover fixed costs and profit. He could build the same loading into every product but this is not essential. It will help if he can get his customers to buy cake as well, even if the loading per cake is only 50 cents. With half of his customers buying a cake with their coffee, that's an extra $50 a day to cover overhead and profit.

However, if Fred structures his prices in this way, he will have to keep a careful eye on what he is selling, not just the total sales revenue. Suppose that his cakes are such excellent value that he sells twice as many as expected but he only sells half the coffee he had expected. You can see that he will have less to cover fixed costs and profit and may even end up operating at a loss. He may have to increase the loading on cakes to make a greater contribution or perhaps reduce the loading on coffee to stimulate more sales.

The actual costs may also turn out to be different from what Fred expected and he may have to adjust the prices for these reasons or make changes to the products. He will learn more about his customer preferences: maybe they are as willing to pay $4 as $3.50 for an item but very reluctant to spend more than $4, or perhaps they are price-sensitive on basic items and not on extras. So pricing is not a process that is done once and then set aside; it must be repeated at intervals as long as the product is offered for sale.

The first twelve sections of Chapter 13 consider setting prices when a company is providing a product and needs to cover its costs and make a profit. Section 13.13 looks at a related situation: deciding on the level of regular contributions to make into a fund to meet some long-term objective.

For example, suppose that Fred wants to buy the shop premises that he is renting at the end of ten years and sets up a fund in which to accumulate the projected cost. He might choose to spread the cost as evenly as possible over ten years, or he might decide to make no contributions for a few years and make higher contributions later on. In either case, he will need to check at intervals before the end of the period and adjust his contributions (and as he observes trends in real estate, he may have to adjust his target) to stay on track.

Now suppose that he has another fund, in which he is accumulating money to provide retirement benefits that he has promised to his staff. In this case, he probably won't have as much freedom about the level of contributions – his staff won't feel too confident of receiving the promised benefits if no contributions are made for the first few years. In fact, the staff (or regulations) will probably require Fred to get the advice of an independent actuary on the amount of contribution that should be made each year, so that the promised benefits are reasonably secure. Section 13.13 describes some of the methods that actuaries use for this purpose.

Chapter 13: Pricing
by Mark Rowley

13.1 Introduction

13.1.1 What is pricing?

In simplest terms, it is determining what a company will charge its customers to provide the product. For a simple insurance policy, the price would be the premium. For a long-term savings product, the price might be made up of a number of fees and charges and, perhaps, the rules governing the crediting of investment return. For a loan product, the price might include fees as well as the interest rate to be charged. The price includes additional fees which may be charged under certain circumstances, such as early withdrawal from a savings product or early repayment of a loan.

When you buy insurance for your car, to cover against the cost of accident or theft, you pay a premium that is set with regard to factors which might include the make, model, age and value of the car; where it is usually garaged or parked overnight; the usual driver's age, driving record and accident history; and the use to which the car will be put. Clearly, the premium is the price that you pay, but setting the rules and parameters determining how that premium is derived from these factors is *pricing*.

The answer to the question "What do actuaries do?" is that traditionally there are two things – price products and determine reserves. This is similar to a statement by Trowbridge (1989, p35):

> Actuaries have developed a generalized mathematical model for the interaction between a financial security system and its individual members. This model is employed in both rate making and the determination of reserves, two of the important functions that actuaries perform.

Chapter 12 discussed the valuation of liabilities – that is, the determination of reserves. We now come to pricing, which has always been fundamental to actuarial practice.

13.1.2 Pricing process: application of the Actuarial Control Cycle

The Actuarial Control Cycle is based on a simple problem-solving algorithm:

- understand the problem;
- develop and implement a solution;
- monitor the effectiveness of the solution; and
- repeat these three steps if necessary.

The pricing process is a good example of the application of the control cycle. In this chapter, we will primarily deal with the second and third aspects of the algorithm – develop and implement a solution, and monitor the effectiveness of the solution. In this context the company has identified the problem and understood that the solution is to develop a new product. To develop and implement the solution – the product – the following steps could be followed:

- A product, designed in a certain way, is proposed.

- Prices for the product are postulated.

- A model is built.

- Assumptions are set to use in the model.

- The profit of the product is tested by using the model.

- Sensitivity and scenario testing is done, to assess the vulnerability of the profit to adverse experience and the scope for additional profit.

- A report is written summarizing the results of the pricing including an analysis of the risks inherent in the product.

- Each of these steps is repeated until a decision is made to implement the product. For example, various designs, prices, assumptions and profit levels are considered. There will also be several drafts of the report written.

Different companies and actuaries do things differently, often in a different order than that suggested above. However, all these steps do need to occur if pricing is to be done well.

After the product is implemented, the cycle continues with a further step:

- The product is monitored based on how much of the product has been sold, the level of profitability and many other factors. Any aspect of the product could be changed, including designs, prices, assumptions and profit levels. An updated pricing report would also be written.

13.1.3   What is covered in this chapter?

This chapter addresses the various aspects of the control cycle in the pricing process. It is written assuming that the steps listed in Section 13.1.2 happen in that order, even though that doesn't always happen in actual pricing processes. First, however, Section 13.2 sets the stage with a description of the environment in which actuaries operate, which is important to understand as background for the Actuarial Control Cycle.

Sections 13.3 to 13.12 cover the pricing cycle set out in 13.1.2, including a section (13.7) that discusses expenses.

Much of the focus of the chapter is on life insurance, because this is where the full pricing process can be most clearly seen. Section 13.13 considers a variation of the pricing issue, namely the funding of long-term commitments such as defined benefit pension plans.

Section 13.14 discusses the professional and practical implications for actuaries.

Section 13.15 summarizes the key learning points in the chapter.

13.2   The environment in which actuaries operate

13.2.1   Pricing objectives – competitiveness and profitability

Prices should be low enough that customers will buy the product and high enough that the business can meet its profit goals. If the price is low enough it is *competitive* and if it is high enough the business can be *profitable*.

More broadly, if the price is competitive and profitable, the needs of the business's stakeholders can be met.

13.2.2 Stakeholders

There are many stakeholders involved with insurance and financial enterprises.

Owners of the business provide the capital needed to finance the enterprise. They need prices to be profitable so that they can meet their profit goals. Some owners need more profit than others. In Section 13.8, we will consider examples of profit objectives. Owners are also interested in prices being competitive so that sales goals are met. It is hard to earn enough profit if sales are low.

Sales intermediaries need prices to be competitive so that enough customers buy the product. This will allow them to earn an adequate commission from the sale of the product.

Customers also want prices to be competitive so that they can afford to purchase the product. They also want to believe that they are getting a good deal.

Governments and *regulators* want prices to be profitable so that insurance and financial enterprises stay in business. They want the businesses to be able to continue to serve customers. They also want prices to be competitive so that customers are treated fairly. Many regulators view their role to be one of protecting the consumer. It is challenging to manage these two objectives.

Employees of the business want the business to be profitable so that they can be confident that they will keep their jobs.

Insurers use *reinsurers* to help manage their risks and capital. Reinsurers want the insurers to set their prices to be competitive and profitable, since the reinsurers are subject to many of the same risks as are insurance companies.

13.3 Product design

The first step in the pricing process is to propose a product design. This was the subject of Chapter 8, where more detail may be found.

13.3.1 What is product design?

This depends on your perspective and is viewed differently by each stakeholder. To the customer, the *product design* is the benefits provided by the product and how they pay for the product. To the sales intermediary, it includes how much commission the product pays and how the commission varies by year. Owners of the business are interested in who is expected to sell the product, how the product will be marketed and how it will be administered. Actuaries are interested in all of these things and how the business's profits will change because of this product. All of these things are part of the product design.

13.3.2 Interaction of product design and pricing: an iterative process

As stated earlier, prices have to be low enough that customers will buy the product. In fact, the product has to be *competitive*, meaning that the customer finds the product design to have value at that price. It is common in the pricing process to consider several different product designs. The expected costs of each design are different and have to be incorporated into the pricing.

In this chapter, we assume that the first step in the pricing process is the proposal of a product design. The steps that follow will lead to the determination of a price that is designed to produce a reasonable profit. Another issue is how much of the product could be sold at the price determined.

The next step is the determination of whether this combination of product design and price is the best that can be done. There could be many reasons to change the design, including that:

- the marketing department doesn't think that sales goals will be met;

- there are too many competitors selling the same product; and

- the price that competitors are charging for the product will not result in an adequate profit.

If the decision is made to change the product design then the same steps are repeated to determine a new price that is designed to produce a reasonable profit. In most cases, the prices will be different because the design has changed. Also, another determination will be made as to how much can be sold with the new combination of design and price.

This process could occur many times. During the process, the right balance has to be found between the benefits provided by the product and the price. The product has to be competitive: the benefits have to be high enough and the price needs to be low enough.

13.4 Prices postulated

The second step in the pricing process is to postulate a price.

13.4.1 Setting and testing prices

Setting a price means choosing a price that will in turn be evaluated through *testing* – comparing the expected profitability against the objectives, as we will see later.

A price may be set using a *cost-plus* process. This means that prices are determined by evaluation of all the cost elements (such as claims and expenses) plus desired profit. This requires modeling to evaluate the expected level of all of these costs and the desired level of profit.

The key advantage of cost-plus pricing is that an expected profit margin is included in the price.

However, cost-plus pricing doesn't take into account the competitive position. In practice, it is common to set initial prices for testing by estimating what it would take to be competitive. For example, prices might be set at 95 percent of a particular competitor's prices, to allow entry into the market for a new product. While this can be a relatively easy way to set a price, we can't immediately tell how profitable it is.

The next step, therefore, is to test this initial price by modeling all the expected costs, which will allow for an estimate of resulting profits. In practice, several different prices are tested before a set of prices is chosen that best balances competitiveness and profitability.

13.4.2   Impact of prices and commission on sales

One important variable in testing is the level of sales, since lower prices typically lead to higher sales. The level of sales has an impact on how fixed expenses are considered in the pricing. We will consider this further in Section 13.7.

Another variable that can affect sales is the level of commissions paid to sales intermediaries. Chalke (1991, p162) discusses the impact of the price of the product (the *retail price*) and the commission (the *compensation structure*):

> With both of these independent price structures as variables during the pricing process, the insurer faces, not a demand curve, but a demand surface. As the compensation structure becomes more attractive independently of retail price, production is expected to increase. As the retail price increases independently of the compensation structure, production is expected to decrease. With one horizontal axis representing the retail price and the other horizontal axis representing the compensation structure, the demand surface might be similar to that shown in [Figure 13.1].

Figure 13.1   Chalke's product demand surface

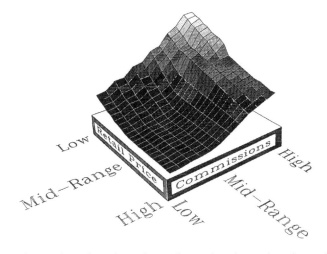

Chalke's product demand surface is a three-dimensional graph, where the independent variables are price and commissions and the dependent variable is sales. While in theory it is clear that price and commissions affect sales, it is hard to estimate the sales that will result from different combinations of price and commissions.

For more details, see Chalke's paper on the CD.

13.5   Modeling

The third step in the pricing process is to build a model. This was the subject of Chapter 9, where more detailed discussion may be found.

13.5.1 What is modeling?

A model is a representation of reality. Actuaries build models that approximate the financial implications related to products. Models are never precisely correct but they are useful in managing risk. Some models are very simple and some are very complex. Almost everything an actuary does involves a model, even if the actuary doesn't think about it in that way. Trowbridge (1989, p35) said it this way:

> By clearing away much of the distracting and confusing detail, a model reduces a complicated reality to its essential elements. A well-conceived model becomes an important and useful tool in the study of complex systems.

13.5.2 One pricing model

A model we will use in this chapter assumes that profit objectives are met whenever the present value of distributable earnings is greater than zero. In this case, the product is profitable enough if the present value of distributable earnings is greater than zero. We will discuss other possible profit objectives in Section 13.8.

A model is needed to work with the exercises in Sections 13.9 and 13.10 and the model used is intentionally simple for the purposes of this chapter. Improvements could be made to the model but they are not required in order to understand the key concepts in the chapter.

Distributable earnings means the amount earned by the product that can be paid to the owners of the business. If the distributable earnings are negative that means that the owners are investing capital. It is common for the owners to invest capital at the time policies are issued, and have capital paid back as a return in the subsequent years.

For the purposes of this model, profit earned at time t (PR_t) is defined as:

- premiums (P_t); less
- commissions (C_t); less
- expenses (E_t); less
- claims (CL_t); less
- change in reserve (CR_t); plus
- interest (I_t).

Distributable earnings (DE_t) are defined as:

- profit (PR_t); less
- change in target surplus (CS_t).

Note that *target surplus* here means the amount that the company wishes to retain in addition to its reserves to protect against adverse experience.

Each item in the model is adjusted by decrements (lapse rates, mortality rates etc) to reflect how many policies are still active.

This model can be found at Tab 13.1 in "Chapter 13 Pricing Model Spreadsheet" on the CD.

13.6 Assumptions

The fourth step in the pricing process is to set assumptions. One assumption that has to be set is the profit objective, which is discussed in Section 13.8. Assumptions are the subject of Chapter 10, where a more detailed discussion may be found.

13.6.1 What are assumptions?

Phillips (1998, p7) says:

> Actuarial assumptions are a representation of past or current experience in the parameters that affect a financial security system or the model it represents. [...] An actuarial model gives us a peek into how the future might be based on the actuarial assumptions that go into the calculations.

Assumptions include mortality rates, morbidity rates, incidence rates, claim amount distributions and per unit expenses; and the list could be much longer. When you consider the many types of insurance that exist, a great number of different kinds of assumption would be needed. Assumptions are needed to project claims, expenses, premiums, reserves and other amounts needed for pricing.

The projection of claims usually requires separate assumptions for incidence and severity, meaning that the actuary needs assumptions for both the probability of a claim being paid (*incidence*) and the amount of the claim given that a claim is paid (*severity*). Naturally, these assumptions will depend on the type of claim being projected and some products will require modeling of more than one claim type. For example, savings products may require projections of both withdrawals and deaths.

The projection of expenses requires assumptions for fixed, variable and semi-variable expenses. We will discuss these in Section 13.7.

13.6.2 What process is used to set assumptions?

The first step is to identify the need for an assumption, in other words to understand why the assumption is relevant. For example, it is relatively easy to understand why a mortality assumption would be relevant for life insurance and life-contingent annuities. A mortality assumption is needed to project claims costs and as a decrement.

The next step in setting an assumption is to obtain relevant data. This can be easy or very challenging. For common products, actuaries can easily find appropriate data from their own company or from industry studies. Finding data for new products can be much more difficult; and setting the assumption requires a lot of judgment.

The best data generally comes from a study on a more or less similar product. At times, however, directly relevant data is not available and data has to be obtained from other sources. Any source of data can be considered – it is common to use government or academic studies. In this case, the data has to be adjusted because the context can affect results. For example, mortality rates in the general population are different from mortality rates for life insurance, which are different from mortality for life-contingent annuities.

Some people apply for life insurance because they are relatively unhealthy and know that they have a strong need for the insurance. This leads insurance companies to *underwrite* applicants, meaning that good health has to be demonstrated. As a result, life insurance mortality tends to be lower than population mortality.

In some situations, insurance companies require significant proof of good health and the resulting mortality is a lot better than population mortality. This is sometimes called *full underwriting*. In other cases, less proof is required and the mortality is somewhat higher but still better than population mortality. This is sometimes called *simplified underwriting*. There are even situations where very little underwriting is done and the resulting mortality can be higher than population mortality. This is called *guaranteed issue*.

Mortality on life-contingent annuities is usually lower than population mortality because people who apply for annuities are relatively healthy. It makes sense that they would be healthy because they buy an annuity to receive income from the annuity as long as they stay alive; if they didn't expect to have a long life, it wouldn't be logical to purchase the annuity.

Another example of a relevant assumption for many products is the interest rate used. Interest rates are used in at least two ways: to estimate investment income on the assets used to support the product and to discount cash flows. We will discuss this latter use in more length in Section 13.8.

The interest rate or rates used to estimate investment income will often be derived from current interest rates being earned on new investments. To do this properly, it is important to understand the investment strategy that will be used for the product. Will ten-year bonds be purchased or thirty-year home mortgage loans? It may be that a variety of different assets will be a part of the investment strategy and the rates on all these assets need to be averaged. Another source of data could be the current investment yield on the assets already owned by the company. This might be appropriate if the strategy is to allocate investment income to all products in the company in the same way, as a proportionate share of all investment income.

The interest rate used to discount cash flows is often a return on capital rate that the owners of the company need to earn to be willing to invest in the company. A source of data for this assumption could be industry surveys as to what is commonly used. This rate is usually higher than the rate earned on new investments. It could also be estimated by stock brokers as the rate inherently used by purchasers of insurance company stocks.

It is important to confirm that the data is accurate. In many pricing efforts a very large amount of time is spent analyzing the data, correcting data that is in error and deleting data that can't be corrected. This is true regardless of the type of assumption being set; the actuary could be analyzing the size of claims or doing a study of the company's expenses.

In Section 13.10, we will discuss the importance of testing a variety of assumptions.

13.6.3   What is a margin?

A *margin* is a change to an assumption that considers the risk that the assumption will turn out to be worse than the expected value. For example, assume that the probability of claim for a new type of insurance product is estimated to be five percent, based on a statistical analysis of data from a similar product. There is a risk that the incidence rate in the new product will be higher than five percent. (Of course, if the distribution is reasonably symmetrical, there is about a 50 percent probability that the incidence rate will be higher than the mean.) Also, since this product is new, it may be that the underlying claims distribution is higher because of a factor that was not considered. If a pricing margin of 20 percent is added, then a six percent probability could be assumed. The risk that the incidence rate will be higher than six percent is most likely a lot less than the risk that it will be higher than five percent.

It is challenging to set assumptions and there is always a risk of adverse results. There is also always a chance that the assumption will turn out more favorably than expected. When there is a lack of relevant data, it is harder to determine the assumption and the risk is greater that the assumption is not set correctly. In many cases, this will lead to a greater margin being used. The idea is to compensate for the lack of data and reduce the risk that the assumption is too optimistic.

If a margin is added to assumptions that model claims, the result is that claims are projected to be larger. This can be done by increasing either the incidence rate or the severity assumption. In a similar way, if a margin is added to expenses, the result will be a projection of larger expenses.

There are times when including a margin in an assumption means that the assumption actually needs to be reduced. A common example is lapse rates, since it is true for many products that smaller lapse rates mean lower profits. This is especially true with lapse rates in the later durations of a product.

Two approaches that can be used in working with margins are:

- each assumption can be adjusted individually by a margin; or

- a single margin can be added to the entire pricing exercise, which has the same effect as increasing the profit objective.

If each assumption is adjusted individually by a margin, it may be difficult to evaluate how much margin exists in the total pricing. It may be that, in total, the pricing is very pessimistic. Said another way, it may be that there is so much margin that the pricing assumes a very extreme worst case scenario. If this is true, it is also probably true that this set of pricing assumptions would result in a very uncompetitive product. If instead only one or a few assumptions are adjusted by a margin, then the total margin is less likely to be larger than justified.

If a single margin is added to the entire pricing exercise, this should reflect the actuary's opinion of how risky the product is in total. What this means is that more profit is needed because the product is risky. This can be thought of as a risk/reward trade-off. We will discuss profit objectives in more detail in Section 13.8.

Example 13.1 Pricing a specialty health insurance product

Your company plans to introduce a cancer insurance product for women in a new country. The product will pay the insured $10,000 on proof of cancer. A premium is paid once a year and is higher for older insureds. The product can be renewed each year by paying the premium appropriate for that age. This is true whether or not the insured has had a claim and whether or not she currently has cancer. The premium is the same for a new customer who must prove that she doesn't have cancer and an individual who just renewed her policy, if they are the same age. The maximum that can ever be paid on the product is $20,000.

The only data available to help price this product is a study done by the government of the country as to the percentage of the female population, by age, that currently has cancer. The following table is extracted from the government data:

Age	45	50	55	60
Probability	2%	4%	7%	12%

The first thing that should be done is to evaluate whether this data is accurate. The actuary should read the report that came with this study and see if the author noted any concerns about the data. If there are issues with this data, the true value may be somewhat different from what was reported.

In this example, it is also clear that this data needs to be adjusted for the particular insurance context.

The applicants need to prove that they don't have cancer, so the probabilities need to be reduced to reflect that the applicants are healthier than the general population when they first buy the product.

However, the probabilities need to be different for the situation where the insured renews the product. Consider two 50-year-old women:

*   Anne, who has just proved that she doesn't have cancer; and

*   Belinda, who proved that she didn't have cancer when she bought the product a year ago.

It would generally be expected that Belinda has the higher probability of claim. Reasons for this include:

*   there is a chance that Belinda's health has changed for the worse in the year since she bought her policy; and

*   Belinda chose to renew the policy. It is more likely that she would make this choice if she thought that she had an increased chance of getting cancer.

To adjust for the insurance context, multiplicative factors are developed separately for women who have just proved that they don't have cancer and those who have just renewed their policies.

Assume that there is no data available to help determine these multiplicative factors. This is not an unusual situation. Experienced actuaries are often asked to use their judgment to deal with this kind of situation. Assume that the following factors are developed by the actuary:

Age	45	50	55	60
Factor for new policy	0.80	0.85	0.85	0.90
Factor for renewed policy	1.00	1.10	1.05	1.20

Combining the probabilities from the government study with these factors results in the following:

Age	45	50	55	60
Probability for new policy	1.60%	3.40%	5.95%	10.80%
Probability for renewed policy	2.00%	4.40%	7.35%	14.40%

Should a margin be added? An actuary would definitely want to add a margin given the lack of data and the need to develop factors based on judgment. There is plenty of risk that these probabilities could be too low. The margin could also serve as a profit objective. Since this is a new product, there may be very little competition. It may be possible to add a margin and still be able to meet sales goals. Let's use a margin of five percent of claims.

Assumptions also need to be set for commissions and expenses. A commission of $100 will be paid when a new policy is sold or a policy is renewed. Having completed a study of the company's expenses, it is decided that $75 per policy per annum is needed. In total, $175 needs to be included for commissions and expenses.

Premiums can now be set as the probability of claim, times 1.05 to add the margin, times $10,000 as the benefit amount, plus $175 for expenses. Here is the result:

Age	45	50	55	60
Premium for new policy	$343	$532	$800	$1,309
Premium for renewed policy	$385	$637	$947	$1,687

The last thing to do is to come up with one premium for each age, since the company plans to charge the same premium whether the policy is new or renewed. An assumption needs to be made as to the percentage of policies that will be sold as new and how many will be sold as renewed. This is a different kind of assumption than has been mentioned previously but it is a common type of assumption that actuaries have to set.

We will leave it to you to calculate what the premiums will be if it is assumed that half the policies at each age will be sold as new and half as renewed.

13.7   Expenses

Often, in pricing, one of the most important issues is how to allow for expenses. It is worth taking a side trip to consider this question.

This topic breaks into two components:

- analyzing expenses – that is, understanding how the different expenses in the business behave; and

- pricing for expenses – that is, deciding how to model expenses in the pricing.

13.7.1   Analyzing expenses

Expense analyses are often done by the accounting function. Each expense needs to be analyzed into fixed, variable and semi-variable. An expense that is *fixed* doesn't change as the number of policies administered or the number of policies sold changes. A common example is the salary of the chief executive officer. This can also be considered an *overhead* expense. Overhead expenses are fixed expenses not related to a particular function but not all fixed expenses are overhead expenses. For example, the salary of the chief marketing officer can be a fixed expense but might be classified as an *acquisition* expense (one associated with acquiring new business) rather than overhead.

An expense that is completely *variable* changes with volume, such as the number of policies administered or the number of policies sold. A good example is the commission paid to sales intermediaries, which might be modeled as a percentage of the premium paid by the customer. In this case, whenever a new policy is sold, this expense increases.

Some expenses are *semi-variable*. A good example is the salary of an administration manager. For example, a manager may be able to oversee the administration of up to, say, 100,000 policies. This person may receive the same salary whether the company administers 10,000 or 100,000 policies, meaning that the salary is fixed unless the company grows to more than 100,000 policies. Once the company has more than 100,000 policies, a second manager needs to be hired.

Example 13.2   Expense analysis

Consider the following expenses:

	Company has 50,000 policies	Company has 150,000 policies
Fixed Expenses	$100,000	$100,000
Variable Expenses	$100,000	$300,000
Semi-Variable Expenses	$100,000	$200,000
Total Expenses	$300,000	$600,000

Note that the fixed expenses don't change when the number of policies increases from 50,000 to 150,000. The variable expenses are $2 per policy no matter how many policies the company has. The semi-variable expenses are $2 per policy if the company has 50,000 policies and $1.33 per policy if the company has 150,000 policies. In total, expenses are $6 per policy if the company has 50,000 policies and $4 per policy if the company has 150,000 policies.

13.7.2   Pricing for expenses

The expenses of the company need to be considered in the pricing process. The method needs to consider all types of expenses: fixed, variable and semi-variable.

Some actuaries test pricing on a *marginal* basis using variable expenses and the change in semi-variable expenses. Others test using *fully allocated* expenses including variable and an allocation of fixed and semi-variable expenses. *Allocation* is often done by accountants and means to assign in a reasonable way all of the company's expenses across all of the company's products. The appropriate approach depends on the purpose of the pricing.

Testing on a marginal basis measures the amount that the product changes the total expenses of the business. One way to think about Example 13.2 is that a new product was added to increase the number of policies by 100,000, from 50,000 to 150,000. Total expenses increased by $300,000, from $300,000 to $600,000. On average, expenses increased by

$3 per policy ($300,000 divided by 100,000). This is $2 per policy for variable expenses, $1 per policy for semi-variable expenses, and $0 per policy for fixed expenses. When pricing on a marginal basis, fixed expenses don't matter, since they don't change. The pricing assumption in this example is $3 per policy, or $300,000 for the product in total.

When a marginal approach is used for all of a business's products then all the products can be combined and modeled together. In this "total company" model certain expenses will be considered separately, never being assigned to a particular product. The expenses handled in this way would be the fixed expenses and the part of semi-variable expenses that is not allocated to a product. This part of semi-variable expenses is treated the same as fixed expenses.

Example 13.3 Expense analysis (continued)

To continue with this example, an assumption could be made based on the analysis in the previous paragraph that the variable part of the semi-variable expenses is $1 per policy. This would mean the following:

	Company has 50,000 policies	Company has 150,000 policies
Fixed Expenses	$100,000	$100,000
Variable Expenses	$100,000	$300,000
Semi-Variable Expenses: Fixed Portion	$50,000	$50,000
Semi-Variable Expenses: Variable Portion	$50,000	$150,000
Total Fixed Expenses	$150,000	$150,000
Total Variable Expenses	$150,000	$450,000
Total Expenses	$300,000	$600,000

This is a simple example of an allocation technique that might be used where the result is to consider every expense as either fixed or variable.

Testing on a fully allocated basis allows for all profits of the company to be allocated to its various products and services. It reflects the idea that the pricing of products needs to cover all expenses. In Example 13.3, the pricing assumption would be $4 per policy ($600,000 / 150,000 policies). If expenses are fully allocated then there is no need to consider separately any fixed expenses.

The allocation of fixed and semi-variable expenses to products can be a difficult modeling process. If an expense is truly fixed then the allocation is mostly arbitrary based on some measure of the magnitude of the product, such as policy count, premium or assets. If an expense is semi-variable then at least a portion of the expense can be assigned to products in a way that is easier to explain. At times management allocates expenses strategically to emphasize certain products.

Robinson (2007, p3) makes the following points:

> Product pricing has everything to do with supporting a marketing program to maximize the product's contribution to the company's overheads and profit. It has little or nothing to do with notions of covering overheads or, equivalently, satisfying minimum product profit targets after overhead allowances – and it probably never did. Cost-plus pricing which builds on assumptions about unit overhead costs is the wrong starting point.
>
> [...]
>
> [A]pportionment of a company's overhead expenses to products, accounts or policies does not provide any useful decision-making information for product pricing – or product performance measurement for that matter.

Robinson doesn't find testing on a fully allocated basis to be useful. This doesn't mean that fixed expenses should be ignored. Instead, what it means is that it should be recognized that, by definition, fixed expenses don't change when the business becomes smaller or larger. On a company-wide basis it is critical to understand and manage all expenses, since they have a direct impact on company profitability.

In many cases, pricing expenses on a fully allocated basis will make it impossible to meet profit objectives, especially if a company has high per unit expenses. In this case Robinson would recommend pricing with as much of an expense allowance as possible. A common approach is to price for the per unit expenses that would be typical of a well-managed company. It is very helpful if the product makes some contribution to overheads, because any contribution reduces that which has to be made by the other products in the company.

Setting expense assumptions is challenging and involves more than doing a routine study of the company's expenses. It is critical to look at a "total company" model to see how much each product contributes to overheads and profit and also to evaluate the company's situation in total.

13.8   Profit objectives

The fifth step in the pricing process is to profit test the product to see if profitability criteria are met. The profitability criteria are the profit objectives.

Profit is the subject of Chapter 16 but it is a concept that is widely understood and it has already been discussed earlier in the book, including in Chapter 12. For the purposes of this chapter, we do not need to have considered the discussion in Chapter 16.

13.8.1   What are profit objectives?

In general terms, annual profit is the difference between revenue and expenses (with expenses defined broadly to include claims) less the increase in liabilities (called reserves in this chapter). *Profit objectives* are a measure of how much profit the owners of the business need in order to be willing to finance the company.

13.8.2   New business strain

Most products do not generate enough income at the time of sale to cover the initial expenses and the requirement to establish reserves and *target surplus*. Target surplus is the amount of capital that the company needs to hold, in addition to the reserves, so that stakeholders are confident that the company will stay in business.

The difference is often called *new business strain*. It is a good measure of the immediate cost of writing new business and forms the basis of several profit measures.

Example 13.4

Consider a simple bank product – a checking account. When a new customer opens an account, competitive pressures probably mean that there is no establishment fee, but the bank will incur costs to set up the account. It has also spent money on advertising and employed the consultant who sold the product to the customer in the first place. The bank also has to hold capital (above the balance of the bank account) in order to satisfy solvency requirements. The bank has suffered a new business strain through the sale of the checking account and will wish to make sufficient future profit to justify it.

13.8.3 Alternative profit measures

There are many different ways to measure profitability and each approach is appropriate in some situation. Some examples of different measures are profit margin, internal rate of return and return on capital. Sometimes products are priced to meet more than one profit objective.

Profit margin is the present value of profits divided by the present value of premiums. An important issue with this approach is the choice of interest rate used to calculate the present value. Two common choices are:

- the rate assumed to be earned on investments; and
- the rate expected to be earned by the owners of the institution.

The *internal rate of return* is the single interest rate that, when used to discount all the items projected in the pricing model (including the new business strain), results in a present value of zero. The items projected include premiums, claims, expenses and increases in reserves. An important issue is the extent to which the items also include changes in target surplus.

Return on capital is the single interest rate that, when used to discount all the items projected in the pricing model (excluding reserves and target surplus), results in a present value of the initial amount required to establish reserves and target surplus.

Internal rate of return and return on capital are measures that tie in well to how an investor thinks when considering financing or investing in a business. These measures don't work so well in situations where the initial investment required for a product is small, such as a situation where large commissions are not paid at the time a product is sold.[1] These measures also don't work well when pricing is done with marginal expenses, since investors expect products to have to cover some portion of fixed expenses. In these situations, profit margin is often used.

---

[1] You can see why this is so if you consider the effect of a small change in expected future profits.

The profit measure should be chosen to best reflect the goals of the stakeholders, especially the owners. It should also reflect what is common in the market where the business operates. For-profit enterprises often have the goal to maximize profits, while mutual insurance societies may wish to achieve certain profit targets without exceeding them. In this case, excessive profitability might be considered wasteful. In competitive markets, it is challenging for businesses to achieve a high level of profit.

13.9 Profit testing

13.9.1 What is profit testing?

The fifth step in the pricing process, *profit testing* is using the pricing model to measure the expected profit from the product and comparing it with the profit objectives. In this section, we illustrate this with a series of examples and exercises, using the workbook "Chapter 13 Pricing Model Spreadsheet" on the CD.

Example 13.5   Pricing a long-term care product

A long-term care (LTC) product in the US provides benefits primarily for less skilled levels of care than would be covered in most health insurance policies. Health insurance policies usually cover skilled nursing care while LTC products cover both skilled nursing care and custodial care. *Skilled nursing care* is complex enough that it needs to be provided by a trained nurse. *Custodial care* can be provided by individuals with limited or no medical training, and can include assistance with *activities of daily living*, such as transferring from a bed to a chair, eating and bathing. LTC products often pay for care whether it is provided in health care facilities (*nursing home benefit*) or in the insured's home (*home health care benefit*).

There are many aspects to the design of an LTC insurance policy. An insurance company that sells this kind of product must be aware of how its design compares to those of its competitors. Of course, the company also needs to be aware of how its price compares to competitors' prices.

The premiums for LTC insurance are designed to be level for life. Premiums increase with issue age. This largely reflects the fact that the average time until a claim is made reduces with issue age. Since it is a long-term product, the pricing requires assumptions to be made from the age at which the insured buys the product to a very high age such as 100 or 110. One important assumption is the interest rate used to discount premiums, claims, expenses, etc. In this example we will use a discount rate of 12% per annum, a rate that owners might use to model the profit required to justify investing in the product – the owners' required return on capital. Such a rate is generally higher than the interest rate earned on bonds or other investments. There is more information on various kinds of profit objectives in Section 13.8.

Premiums need to be set and tested for each issue age. The premiums for several issue ages should be tested against the competition. It is common that the premiums at some issue ages are more competitive and/or more profitable than the premiums at other issue ages. The most important thing is that, overall, the product is competitive and profitable, although there is a risk to having issue ages that are both competitive and unprofitable. This is because more of the product might be sold at these issue ages than expected.

Exercise 13.1 completes this example. In the exercise, we will only be setting and testing prices for issue age 65. We will compare the competitiveness and profitability of the issue age 65 premiums for two benefit designs:

- the standard product with nursing home and home health care benefits; and

- a proposed product with the same nursing home benefit but larger home health care benefits.

The pricing model for this exercise is the one that we set out in Section 13.5.2.

In this exercise and Exercise 13.2, input assumptions are stated as per policy. This means that this amount is appropriate for policies that at that point in the projection are still insured. To turn these into projected cash flows per policy sold, assumptions need to be made for lapse rates and, depending on the type of insurance, other decrements such as mortality.

Exercise 13.1

(a) This exercise uses Tab 13.1 of the workbook "Chapter 13 Pricing Model Spreadsheet."

(b) Verify that, with a $5,000 premium, the present value of distributable earnings is $3,966 (cell AO6).

(c) Use the spreadsheet to determine the present value of distributable earnings for the proposed product. Use a premium of $5,350 by changing the amount in cell H3. You also need to use the appropriate claims, which can be done by changing cell E12 to say "Proposed" instead of "Standard." You should get a present value of distributable earnings of $3,674.

(d) Your competitors have premiums that vary from $4,400 to $5,200 for the standard product design and from $5,000 to $5,800 for the proposed design. Your boss has told you that you can only do one of the designs. Which one do you propose? Why?

Example 13.6   Pricing a commodity product

A *commodity product* is a product that is sold by many competitors in a very similar form. Since all the competitors sell essentially the same product, the one that is sold for the best price would logically be chosen by the customer. For these products, price is the key differentiator among competitors.

In this situation, businesses would often need to reduce prices to meet sales goals. The two main approaches to do so and meet profit objectives for the product would be by:

- pricing with marginal expenses; and
- pricing with a smaller profit objective.

A company that sold only commodity products would find it hard to be profitable. Often, a company sells commodity products in the hope that this will lead to sales of more profitable products, such as niche products. Alternatively, commodity products may be sold to take advantage of spare capacity. Either strategy can work if the combination of all products leads to the company meeting its profit objectives.

A *niche product* is a product which meets particular needs (or the needs of a particular customer base) so that there aren't a lot of competitors that sell essentially the same product. In most cases, factors other than price drive a customer's decision to buy a niche product, so it is easier for a company to earn a higher level of profit. However, a niche product has a smaller market than a commodity product, so there may be higher costs involved in finding potential customers.

The pricing model that we will use in Exercise 13.2 is the same as that used in Exercise 13.1.

Exercise 13.2

(a) This exercise uses Tabs 13.2a, 13.2b and 13.2c of the workbook "Chapter 13 Pricing Model Spreadsheet."

(b) In Tab 13.2a, there is pricing for a 10-year term life insurance product for issue age 35. Verify that, with a premium of $163 (cell H3), the present value of distributable earnings discounted at 12% per annum (cell D7) is approximately zero (cell AO6). This means that, if all the assumptions are correct, this premium is expected to earn a 12% per annum return on capital.

(c) In Tab 13.2b, there is pricing for a whole life insurance product for issue age 35. Verify that, with a premium of $369 (cell H3), the present value of distributable earnings discounted at 12% per annum (cell D7) is approximately zero (cell AQ6). This means that, if all the assumptions are correct, this premium is also expected to earn a 12% per annum return on capital.

(d) The company has recognized that the 10-year term life insurance product is a commodity product and that the $163 premium is not competitive. If it is to meet its sales goals, it needs a lower premium. One way to price for a lower premium is to reduce the return on capital goal from 12% to the investment earnings rate of 5.5%. Change the discount rate in cell D7 to 5.5% and change the premium in cell H2 until you find a premium that results in a present value of distributable earnings of about zero.

(e) Another approach to price for a smaller premium is to price in lower expenses. The idea here is that only marginal expenses will be priced into the commodity product. Set the discount rate in cell D7 back to 12% and cut the per-policy expenses (C20, C21) from $200 in the first year and $25 in later years to $120 in the first year and $15 in later years. Now change the premium in cell H3 until you find a premium that results in a present value of distributable earnings of about zero.

(f) The last approach is to do both – set the return on capital rate to 5.5% and the expenses per policy to $120 and $15. According to these assumptions, what premium would result in a present value of distributable earnings of about zero?

(g) The company's strategy is to have the higher profits on whole life insurance make up for the lower profits on the commodity product, 10-year term life insurance. The company has decided that, to meet its sales goals on 10-year term life insurance, the product needs to be sold for a premium of $135. The company wants the combination of the two products to meet the return on capital goal of 12%, with expenses at $200 and $25. To test this, set the discount rate and expense figures in Tab 13.2a to their original values. Also put the premium of $135 into cell H3. In Tab 13.2c, the total distributable earnings for the two products is calculated, assuming that 67% of sales are from the commodity product and 33% from the niche product. If you have done this correctly, the present value of distributable earnings in Tab 13.2c should be -$68.

(h) The company assumes that it can increase the premium of the whole-life product without changing how many policies are sold, since it is a niche product. Change the premium in cell H3 of Tab 13.2b to get the present value of distributable earnings in Tab 13.2c to be approximately zero.

Example 13.7 Pricing a deferred annuity product

The pricing model we will use in this example is very similar to the one that was used in the previous exercises. We have simply replaced claims (CL_t) with death benefits (DB_t) and withdrawals (W_t).

Profit (PR_t) is defined as:

- premiums (P_t); less
- commissions (C_t); less
- expenses (E_t); less
- death benefits (DB_t); less
- withdrawals (W_t); less
- change in reserves (CR_t); plus
- interest (I_t).

Distributable earnings (DE_t) is defined as:

- profit (PR_t); less
- change in target surplus (CS_t).

A deferred annuity is a contract that enables the policyholder to receive an annuity from a future date. Commonly, the level at which the annuity will start is not fixed but will depend on the accumulation of savings up to the annuity date. There will usually be a rule for how the accumulated fund value converts to an annuity.

So, it is common for deferred annuities to have a fund value that works like a savings account, with premiums (also called deposits) increasing the fund value, interest increasing the fund value and withdrawals decreasing the fund value. In our example, a customer who makes a withdrawal in the early years of the annuity doesn't receive the full fund value because of the *surrender charge*, which is intended to recover some of the new business strain. The amount payable is called the *cash surrender value*. The full fund value is paid if the customer dies, meaning that there is no surrender charge.

In our example, it is assumed that the reserve is set using the simple formula:

reserve = (2 × fund value + cash surrender value) / 3

This means that the reserve is set closer to the fund value than the cash surrender value. This is an example of the formula approach to liability valuation in Chapter 12.

The key item that is priced is the *spread*, which is the difference between the interest rate earned on investments and the interest rate credited to the annuity. If the spread is increased, the profitability of the annuity is increased; and if the spread is decreased, the profitability declines. A smaller spread makes the annuity more competitive because it results in a higher crediting rate.

Exercise 13.3

(a) This exercise uses Tab 13.3 of the workbook "Chapter 13 Pricing Model Spreadsheet."

(b) In the spreadsheet, the spread for the deferred annuity is stated in basis points. 1 *basis point* (bp) is the same thing as 0.01%. The initial spread is 107 bp, which means the crediting rate is 4.43% = 5.50% − 1.07% (see cell H20). Note that 107 bp results in the present value of distributable earnings being approximately zero. The spread of 107 bp is in cell H18 and the present value of distributable earnings is in cell AQ6.

(c) What should the spread be if the profit objective was to make the present value of profit approximately zero? To determine this, change the spread (cell H18) until the present value of profit (cell AQ4) is approximately zero. This would be the result if it was decided not to price for any target surplus.

(d) What should the spread be if the profit objective was a profit margin of one percent? To determine this, change the spread (cell H18) until the profit margin (cell AQ8) is approximately one percent. This is the profit margin using a discount rate of 12% per annum.

(e) What should the spread be if the profit objective was a profit margin of one percent using a discount rate of 5.5% per annum? To determine this, first change the discount rate in cell D7 to 5.5%. Next, change the spread until the profit margin is approximately one percent.

13.10 Sensitivity tests

13.10.1 What are sensitivity tests?

The sixth step in the pricing process is to thoroughly test the pricing by doing sensitivity tests.

Sensitivity tests examine the impact of changing assumptions. You did some sensitivity testing in Exercises 13.1 to 13.3. Assumptions such as premium, expenses, profit objectives and spread were set at various levels and results were observed.

One way to think about these tests is that they are done to determine the specific changes in assumptions that cause profit objectives to not be met. Said another way, what would have to change so that the product wouldn't be as profitable as required? If we are setting the assumption for a variable where there is a lot of uncertainty about what the future values could be, several different values for that assumption should be tested to evaluate the range of results that is plausible. It is very important to document this range of results in the pricing report. The question should be asked as to whether the company is willing to take the risk that the results could be anywhere in the range.

It is also helpful to determine specific changes in assumptions that cause the product to be more profitable than expected.

For sensitivity testing, it is tempting to pick arbitrary changes to assumptions, such as increases and decreases of 10 percent. These are easy to understand but they don't tell you how likely the changes are.

There are alternatives. For example:

- Changes can reflect past experience. For example, the sensitivity range for an assumption could reflect a 95 percent confidence interval around the mean. However, this approach may not allow for extreme but plausible events or may be skewed by the nature of experience over the time being considered.

- Another approach is to have a story behind each sensitivity that explains why the assumption might turn out to be at a different value – perhaps one which seems quite extreme but is still plausible. This isn't always easy to do, but it is a very useful exercise to attempt. A story can also make it easier to communicate the sensitivity to others.

A special type of sensitivity test is called a scenario test. *Scenario tests* examine the profitability of the product using a particular set of assumptions. For example, the base pricing assumptions form one scenario. It is common to test plausible adverse scenarios, perhaps based on past experience such as a stock market crash or a recession.

Exercise 13.4

(a) This exercise uses Tab 13.1 of the workbook "Chapter 13 Pricing Model Spreadsheet."

(b) When you were doing Exercise 13.1, you may have noticed that there were sensitivity factors in cells D24 to D27. They were in the spreadsheet for this exercise.

(c) Assume that the company chose to sell the proposed product at a premium of $5,350. Change cell H3 to 5,350 and E12 to "Proposed." You should get a present value of distributable earnings of $3,674.

(d) To sensitivity-test the assumptions, we need to analyze the various assumptions. For some of the assumptions there will be more uncertainty than for others. All the assumptions could be tested, including the investment earnings rate, discount rate and required capital. In this exercise we will focus on the expenses, claims and lapse rates.

(e) Assume that the company has consistently had expenses close to $200 in the first year and $25 in years 2+. It is decided that an appropriate sensitivity test is to increase and decrease these assumptions by five percent and measure the present value of distributable earnings. To do this sensitivity test, change cell D24 to 1.05 first and then to 0.95. With higher expenses, the present value of distributable earnings decreases to $3,658 (cell AO6). With lower expenses, the present value of distributable earnings increases to $3,690. In the pricing report, the analysis would say that the expense assumption results in profitability ranging from $3,658 to $3,690. This might not even be worth including in detail in the pricing report, since the impact is so small. However, if the expenses were considered less predictable, both the range tested and the impact would be greater.

(f) Next we will analyze the claims assumption. Set cell D24 back to 1.00. Recall that claims are made up of incidence and severity. The company's study of incidence rates has shown a decline in recent years on the standard product, but it is unclear whether this same trend would happen on the proposed product. Also, there has been a slight trend upwards in severity. After analyzing all factors, the range of claims costs assumed is 95 to 110 percent of the base claims assumption. Set cell D25 to 1.10 first, and then 0.95. Distributable earnings should be $2,079 for the higher assumption and $4,471 for the lower assumption. The range, $2,079 to $4,471, is much wider than that for the expense tests. If the two tests are broadly equally plausible, it is clear that profit is more sensitive to reasonable variability in claims experience than to reasonable variability in expense experience.

(g) Next we will analyze the lapse assumptions. Set cell D25 back to 1.00. It is common to test early-duration lapses separately from late-duration lapses. For many products, high early-duration lapses are bad for profitability but the opposite is true for late-duration lapses. Early-duration lapses make it hard to recover acquisition expenses, such as commissions paid to sales intermediaries and other first year expenses. Late-duration lapses can benefit a product financially if a large reserve is eliminated or the payout is less than the present value of expected future claims.

(h) Assume that the lapse rates in the first five years are thought to have a range of 20 percent higher or lower than the base pricing assumption. (This range was determined after consulting with the director of marketing.) Set cell D26 to 0.8 and then to 1.2. The range of distributable earnings should be $3,501 (high lapses) to $3,849 (low lapses).

(i) Assume that the lapse rates in years 6+ are thought to have a range of 50 percent higher or lower than the base pricing assumption. (This range was also determined after consulting with the director of marketing.) Set cell D26 back to 1.00 and D27 to 0.5 and then to 1.5. The range of distributable earnings should be $2,902 (low lapses) to $4,233 (high lapses).

(j) As expected, higher early-duration lapses decrease profitability while higher later-duration lapses increase profitability.

(k) We could test some scenarios. For example, a favorable scenario would see claims at 95 percent, early-duration lapses at 90% and late-duration lapses at 120 percent of base. Verify that this gives a result of $4,811.

(l) Verify that a "worst-case" scenario, using all the adverse sensitivities in this exercise, would result in a present value of distributable earnings of just $1,131. If this scenario is plausible, the company may not be willing to take the risk of having profit this small.

13.11 Pricing report

The seventh step in the pricing process is to write a report that will be considered by those who decide whether to implement the product. In most cases, the actuary is not the final decision maker but is usually part of the team that makes decisions on product design and pricing.

A well-written pricing report (sometimes referred to as *product specifications*) describes the product design, the recommended prices, the key assumptions and the profitability. The profitability discussion needs to say whether profit objectives are met and what the risks are that could lead to different levels of profit – either better or worse. The risks generally have to do with different assumptions. As discussed in Section 13.6, it is difficult to set assumptions and it is very likely that some of the assumptions will turn out to be wrong.

A proper discussion of the risks requires the sensitivity testing described in Section 13.10 to be done. However, the first draft of the report may be written before this testing is done. The team making the decisions about the product would typically review the first draft of the report and suggest certain changes. These changes would require one or more of the previous steps in the pricing control cycle to be repeated and then a second draft of the pricing report would be written. The second draft of the report would be reviewed, which might lead again to repeating certain parts of the control cycle. At some point, the sensitivity testing would be done and all later drafts of the report would describe the results of these and subsequent tests.

In the pricing process, it is best not to label a pricing report "final" because:

*   the decision-making team might unexpectedly come up with additional changes; and

*   after the product is introduced, the report will be revised to reflect the monitoring of the product, which we will discuss in Section 13.12.

At times, the actuary needs to point out in the report that the product doesn't meet the company's standard criteria for pricing and profitability. It may be that the product only meets the criteria if an assumption is set in a way that the actuary doesn't believe is reasonable.

It is important to be clear in the pricing report who owns each assumption. If an assumption is directly based on the actuary's experience and/or research, then it belongs to the actuary. If this isn't true, then the actuary should make this clear in the report.

13.12   Product monitoring

This is the eighth step in the pricing process. It is important to compare the pricing assumptions to what has actually happened. Perhaps lapse rates have been high or claims have been lower than expected. Product monitoring is similar to the sensitivity testing done in Section 13.10, in the sense that the product is being profit tested with different assumptions.

Example 13.8   Monitoring a long-term care product

Suppose that it is now two years since the long-term care product in Exercise 13.4 was introduced. If claims and expenses are about as expected, but early-duration lapse rates are 20 percent higher, then the profitability will be at the lower end of the range measured in item (h) of that exercise. Of course, we do not yet know how later duration lapse rates may change, since all policies have been sold in the last two years. Also, even if claims have been as expected, there may be new theories about future claims. There may also be new sensitivities that should be tested. The pricing report should be updated.

Another aspect of monitoring is to analyze the mix of business. In Exercise 13.4, the only issue age illustrated is 65. In practice, the product would be sold at a number of issue ages and each issue age would not have the same profitability. An assumption that is set at the time of introduction of the product is the percentage of policies sold at each issue age. Overall profitability is measured by calculating the weighted average of profitability at each issue age. Allowing for the higher early-duration lapse rates, here is an example of the results:

Issue Age	Distribution	Present Value of Distributable Earnings
60	15%	$2,943
65	20%	$3,501
70	25%	$3,985
75	20%	$3,192
80	20%	$1,552
Average		$3,087

Suppose that the distribution of issue ages was actually as shown below:

Issue Age	Distribution	Present Value of Distributable Earnings
60	10%	$2,943
65	25%	$3,501
70	30%	$3,985
75	20%	$3,192
80	15%	$1,552
Average		$3,236

In this case, profit was better than expected, primarily because more was sold at issue age 70, which is the most profitable issue age.

The choice of two years in our example is arbitrary; different products need to be monitored at different intervals. Well-established products with stable results may not need frequent monitoring. New products, especially those where it was difficult to set assumptions, should be monitored more often. There are no simple rules about how often to monitor a product; actuarial judgment is required.

13.13 Pricing for long-term commitments

This topic was covered by David Service in section 16.5 of the first edition of this book. It is reproduced here with minimal changes.

13.13.1 What does it mean to price for long-term commitments?

In Actuarial Standard of Practice No. 4, the Pensions Committee of the Actuarial Standards Board (2007, p4) summarizes it this way:

> Measuring pension obligations and determining plan costs or contributions are processes in which the actuary may be required to make judgments or recommendations on the choice of actuarial assumptions, actuarial cost methods, asset valuation methods, and amortization methods.

This references only pension plans but there are other examples of long-term commitments, such as the funding of retiree medical costs. We will consider more examples in Section 13.13.8.

Pricing for long-term commitments is different from pricing most insurance products in that most financial institutions are established for the purposes of making profits and hence the measurement of profit is of fundamental importance. However, there are other situations where long-term commitments are made and the primary objective is not profit. Instead, the objective is to ensure that the expected future income equates to the benefits and expenses to be provided. The clearest example is defined benefit superannuation. Here, our task is to determine the minimum contributions required, together with the existing assets, to ensure that the benefits and expenses are paid.

In these situations, pricing is necessary to determine the appropriate level and incidence of contributions that will be made. The *funding method* (also known as *actuarial cost method*) chosen will determine the expected pattern of the contributions. Over the long term, the contributions have to be large enough, together with investment earnings, to fund all benefits and expenses. In this section, we will focus on funding methods rather than asset valuation or amortization methods.

13.13.2 Applying the Actuarial Control Cycle

In pricing for long-term commitments, the Actuarial Control Cycle is applied; however, the application is different from the other examples in this chapter. In Section 13.1.2, we were reminded that the Actuarial Control Cycle is based on a simple problem-solving algorithm, namely to:

- understand the problem;
- develop and implement a solution;
- monitor the effectiveness of the solution; and
- repeat these three steps if necessary.

In pricing for long-term commitments, the problem is to equate the future income to the future benefits and expenses. A funding method has to be chosen to develop and implement a solution. Monitoring is very important and is done every one to three years.

13.13.3 Funding methods in general

In deciding on an appropriate funding method, two criteria should generally be satisfied:

- member benefits should be fully funded by retirement; and
- the fund's assets should equal or exceed the minimum benefits payable if all members exited.

Funding methods generally fall into four groups. These are:

- *pay as you go* (PAYG) – do not fund in advance but pay benefits and expenses as they fall due for payment, which doesn't meet the criteria outlined above but is common in the public sector;
- *accrued benefits* – fund the present value of benefits which have accrued during the time period and pay current expenses;
- *projected benefits* – fund the present value of all future benefit payments and expenses; and
- *initial funding* – fund all benefits and expenses at the beginning, which is likely to require a lot of money at that time and can therefore be ignored for the remainder of this discussion.

Typically, we would recalculate the required contribution rate at regular intervals – such as every one to three years. This enables the contribution rate to vary to reflect deviations in actual experience from that assumed.

The required contribution rate is the solution to the equation:

$$PV(\text{contributions}) = PV(\text{benefits}) + PV(\text{expenses}) - \text{assets}$$

where PV() indicates present value and the contributions and benefits are calculated in accordance with our funding method.

13.13.4 Funding methods – accrued benefits

The major funding method in the accrued benefits category is the *projected unit credit* method. Under this method, the required contribution rate over the next year comprises two parts, both expressed as a percentage of one year's salary:

- the value of future benefits payable in respect of service accrued over next year; and
- one year's amortization of the difference between (a) the value of future benefits payable in respect of benefits accrued from service up to the valuation date and (b) the assets, where the amortization occurs over a relatively short period of time.

This method is required under US accounting rules for the determination of superannuation costs to be charged to the employer's accounts each year. As a result it is in widespread use.

> ### Example 13.9   Projected unit credit method
>
> WidgetMaker is a company with an annual salary bill of $10 million. The value of future benefits in respect of service accrued over the next year is $1 million. If accrued benefits are worth $15 million and the assets are $13 million, we also need to fund the $2 million deficiency. Amortizing over five years means that we must contribute $0.4 million this year. Therefore, the total contribution is $1.4 million.
>
> Dividing by total salaries gives a contribution rate of 14 percent.

13.13.5   Funding methods – projected benefits

The major funding method in the projected benefits category is the *aggregate* method. Under this method, the required contribution rate is calculated as:

*   the value of all future benefits payable, less the assets held;

    divided by

*   the value of all future salary payments to existing members.

> ### Example 13.10   Aggregate method
>
> Assume that the value of future benefits for future service of existing WidgetMaker staff is $22 million. Then the total value of future benefits for existing staff is $37 million. As the assets are $13 million, we need to fund $24 million.
>
> If the value of future salaries for existing staff is $200 million, the contribution rate is 12 percent.

13.13.6   Funding methods – projected unit credit versus aggregate

If actual experience precisely matches our assumptions, the contribution rate for an individual member under the projected unit credit method will generally commence at a lower rate than under the aggregate method. However, it will increase as the member's age increases until it exceeds that under the aggregate method, which will remain a fixed percentage of salary for the term of the member's membership.

In Examples 13.9 and 13.10, the projected unit credit method gave a higher contribution rate but you should be able to see that this was because of the need to fund an accrued benefit deficit. See how the answers would change if the assets were $15 million.

13.13.7   Responsibility and authority for making choices

This is a key issue because many countries have detailed laws, rules and regulations that need to be followed. Some of these are accounting rules.

Quoting again from Actuarial Standard of Practice No. 4 (p4):

> The actuary may have the responsibility and authority to select some or all actuarial assumptions, actuarial cost methods, asset valuation methods, and amortization methods. In other circumstances, the actuary may be asked to

advise the individuals who have that responsibility or authority. In yet other circumstances, the actuary may perform actuarial calculations using assumptions or methods prescribed by applicable law or selected by others.

13.13.8 Wider applications

These concepts are applicable to any problem where costs have to be spread over material time periods. The issues are all about how quickly funds should be built up to meet the benefits and how the system can respond to changes in experience.

Some other applications include:

- funding long service leave liabilities;
- funding higher education research students; and
- the financial implications of protecting timber plantations from the risk of fire.

Details will depend on the benefits to be met and practical ways of expressing the costs. In the case of superannuation, those costs are normally expressed as a percentage of salaries. In other cases it is usually better to express costs as a proportion of some ongoing relevant quantity rather than as a fixed monetary amount.

13.14 Practical implications for actuaries

13.14.1 What professional implications are most common in pricing?

A primary objective of being a professional is to serve the public and the public interest. However, pricing actuaries also have responsibilities to all the stakeholders mentioned in Section 13.2.2. The best actuaries are experts at balancing all of this, which is indeed very challenging. Actuaries need to help the company's mission of providing products that help the public. Balancing all these interests is easier if the products priced are both competitive and profitable.

Another important consideration is to ensure that you are qualified to price the product. Do you have the necessary knowledge and experience to handle the project? If you don't, the result may not benefit the public or the other stakeholders. In this situation it would be best to take the steps necessary to ensure that a qualified person supervises the project.

The actuarial profession has worked very hard over the years to build and maintain its reputation. Your goal should be to have your work have the same result.

13.14.2 Consideration of overheads in pricing

How should overheads be taken into account in pricing? This is an issue discussed at some length by Chalke (1991) and Robinson (2007). Robinson (page i) states the following:

> One outworking of this orthodox thinking is the common practice among pricing actuaries to apply the cost-plus paradigm (explicitly or implicitly, modified or not), to allow for a share of company's overheads in pricing, and to measure and rank products according to their profit performance on a full cost allocation basis.

In many cases, pricing expenses on a fully-allocated basis will make it impossible to meet profit objectives, especially if a company has high per-unit expenses. In this case, Robinson would recommend pricing with as much of an expense allowance as possible. While there are examples where pricing is done on a completely marginal basis, and it is possible that the other products the company sells can cover the fixed expenses, this is a risky strategy. Many companies have run into serious financial trouble by using a marginal pricing strategy. A common approach is to price for the per-unit expenses that are thought to be typical of an efficient company. It is very helpful if the product makes some contribution to overheads, because any contribution reduces that which has to be made by other products.

Setting expense assumptions is challenging and involves more than doing a routine study of the company's expenses. It is critical to look at a "total company" model to see how much each product contributes to overheads and profit and also to evaluate the company's situation in total.

It is not always wrong to price based on a fully-allocated approach. There are instances where it doesn't lead to the wrong strategic choices. And, after all, if the total overheads are to be covered then some products will have to contribute a higher share.

In fact, economics tells us that each product has an optimum price in each market. Relative to this price, if the price is increased (to increase unit profit) or reduced (to increase sales), the contribution to overheads is reduced. This lends support to Robinson's view that expense allowances in pricing should generally reflect competitive pricing.

For some products, this may mean that it is not possible to expect to recover even marginal costs from the product. If it is reasonable to expect sales of such products to lead to sales of very profitable products, it may be appropriate to price for a loss. However, it should be obvious that great care should be taken to limit the use of such *loss leaders*.

Note that "honeymoon" interest rates on mortgages and credit cards are an example of loss leaders actually built into a product design.

In the end, if the company's total expenses are not actually met from expense allowances and extra profit margins (above the product targets), it is not achieving its profit objectives and will need to find strategies to address this problem. This may include a revision of product pricing.

13.14.3 Actuarial assumptions and the future

This is the title of an article written by Phillips (1998). He states (p7):

> The actuary cannot and should not attempt to estimate or predict the future. This would reduce actuarial work to guessing. ... What then is the relationship of an actuarial model to the future? An answer is "none." What is the likelihood (probability) of the future turning out to be as depicted? Close to zero. So then can't a model predict the future? No! The future depicted is what it would look like if all the assumptions were fulfilled.

Along the same lines Trowbridge (1989, p67) comments:

> Actuarial assumptions often, though not invariably, relate to a long span of time, not infrequently fifty or more years. The ability of humans to predict even short-range future events is severely limited, and forecasting ability diminishes rapidly as the time span lengthens.

One thing that is certain about the projections in actuarial models is that they are wrong. The chance that the models will be exactly correct is zero. But they can still be useful. They are helpful in testing pricing, but it is important to know our limitations in projecting the future. Actuaries shouldn't suggest that they can do more than this!

13.15   Key learning points

- The pricing process is a good example of the application of the Actuarial Control Cycle.

- In pricing, there are two main objectives – competitiveness and profitability. The best actuaries are good at balancing these two goals.

- There are many stakeholders involved with insurance and financial enterprises. They all have their own goals, and actuaries need to be aware of all of them.

- *Setting* a price means to choose a set of prices. This can be done by choosing a price that is competitive or by solving for a price that considers a projection of claims, expenses and profit. *Testing* a price means to evaluate the financial implications of a set of prices.

- Developing a product, which is an iterative process, typically involves considering many different product designs and sets of prices before making a final decision.

- There are several different approaches to pricing for fixed expenses. It is important to keep in mind that truly fixed expenses don't change if the size of the business changes. It is common to price for something less than fully-allocated expenses. One approach is simply to use theoretical per-unit expense levels of a large, efficient company. In this case, unallocated expenses must be met from aggregate profit margins or managed down.

- When pricing a product, actuaries should consider the impact on sales of various sets of prices. If a change in pricing is expected to cause a large change in sales, the product is in the commodity category. If a change in pricing has little impact on sales, it is more of a niche product. Commission levels paid to sales intermediaries also affect sales. In theory, a three-dimensional graph could be constructed where sales are a function of price and commission levels. In practice, it is difficult to construct such a graph in an accurate way.

- It can be easy or very challenging to set assumptions. With common products there is usually much helpful data. With new products it can often be very difficult and actuaries have to be more creative. This can be very interesting work but it also means that there is more risk that the assumptions could be inaccurate.

- There are many ways to measure profitability; and each approach is appropriate in some situations. Profit objectives should be set to meet the needs of the owners of the business.

- A well-written pricing report describes the product design, the recommended prices, the key assumptions and the profitability. The profitability discussion needs to say whether profit objectives are met and what the risks are that could lead to different levels of profit – either better or worse. This report is what is relied upon by the team that decides whether or not to implement the product. Often the team will suggest changes, in which case the actuary repeats several of the steps in the pricing process, resulting in a new draft of the pricing report.

- Sensitivity testing is critical to understanding the financial risks of a product. This testing involves profit testing with various assumptions and could include scenario tests with particular combinations of assumptions. The results of these tests should be included in the pricing report.

- After a product is introduced, it is important to monitor the financial results of the product. This is similar to sensitivity testing in that profit testing is done with different assumptions. However, it is different in that the assumptions tested are based on how the product has performed since it has been introduced. The nature of the product determines how frequently it should be monitored.

- With long-term commitments, such as defined benefit superannuation, it is important to determine the appropriate level and pattern of contributions that will be made. In this kind of actuarial work, it is more important to equate the future income to the benefits and expenses than it is to focus on profit.

- In pricing, it is important to act professionally by serving the public and the stakeholders of the business. It is also important to ensure that you are qualified to price each product. If you are not qualified, there can be negative implications for you and the business that sells the product. It also harms the reputation of the actuarial profession.

- One thing that is certain about the projections in actuarial models is that they are wrong. The chance that the models will be exactly correct is zero; but they can still be very useful. They are helpful in testing pricing but it is important to know our limitations in projecting the future. Actuaries shouldn't suggest that they can do more than this!

CD Items

Chalke, S.A. 1991, Macro Pricing, *Transactions of the Society of Actuaries*, XLIII, pp 137-230.

Robinson, I. 2007, Pricing Wealth Products in Competitive Markets, Institute of Actuaries of Australia.

Chapter 13 Pricing Model Spreadsheet

Chapter 13 Exercise Solutions

References (other than CD Items)

Pension Committee of the Actuarial Standards Board 2007, Actuarial Standard of Practice No. 4: Measuring Pension Obligations and Determining Pension Plan Costs or Contributions, American Academy of Actuaries.

Phillips, W. 1998, Actuarial Assumptions and the Future, *Actuarial Futures*, Issue 18, pp7-9.

Service, D. 2003, Chapter 16 of *Understanding Actuarial Management: the actuarial control cycle*, Institute of Actuaries of Australia, pp395-397.

Trowbridge, C. 1989, *Fundamental Concepts of Actuarial Science*, Revised Edition, Actuarial Education and Research Fund.

Fred's Coffee Shop – Assets

In Chapter 14 an asset is defined as "something that you own and from which you can derive some value." What does Fred's coffee shop have in the way of assets?

While Fred may not own the building that houses his shop, it is likely that he will own the furnishings and equipment. Also, at any time he will have a supply of the ingredients for the food and drink he sells and he will have some cash on hand so that he can give customers change. These assets are a necessary part of running the business.

There are other assets where Fred has a degree of choice. When there is money left over at the end of the day, he may keep it in a checking account or call account ready to pay bills. If the bills are not due immediately, he may be able to earn a higher rate of interest by placing the money on deposit for a short term. Other funds may be put aside for long-term purposes, such as eventually buying the premises. In this case, Fred can choose from a wider range of assets, such as investments that have a longer term or are more variable in return. He can also use the choice of assets to manage his overall risk. For example, he may believe that the price of coffee beans will be increasing and so choose to buy a large supply today or to negotiate a contract for future delivery at the current price.

So Fred will have some regard to his outgoings when he makes choices about which assets to hold. However, for a coffee shop, this is only an incidental part of running the business. For many types of financial institutions, investment decisions are of fundamental importance. While a company's actuaries may not be directly involved in the investment process, they have an important role in understanding the interaction between assets and liabilities and in ensuring that their management is coordinated.

Fred will be required to complete financial statements in order to compute his tax payments and perhaps also to show his bank that his shop is solvent and the loan likely to be repaid. To do so, he will have to place a value on his assets. Depending on the accounting practices where he lives, there may be some flexibility available, such as with regard to depreciation schedules for his espresso machine. Even for a coffee shop, there can be different approaches to the valuation of assets, which can lead to somewhat different views of the financial position of the business. For a financial institution with long-term investments, the issue of valuation is very significant.

Chapter 14:   Assets

by Richard Lyon

14.1   Introduction

In this chapter, we consider assets.

Actuarial calculations, such as liability valuations and product pricing, are meaningless if the supporting assets do not exist or are not well managed.

In this chapter, we discuss the nature of assets (14.2) and their valuation (14.3). This discussion is quite brief, because it is supported by a more detailed paper by Frank Ashe[1] that can be found on the CD.

There are risks to the value of assets. These vary in likely impact according to the nature of the asset, as we will see in 14.4.

While these risks are interesting in themselves, the particular risks that most concern actuaries are those relating to the interaction between assets and liabilities. After all, we have not achieved a particularly good outcome in avoiding an asset risk if our liabilities have grown faster than our assets. We discuss asset-liability management in 14.5.

There are several constraints to asset management and asset-liability management, including legislative and regulatory requirements. We discuss these in 14.6.

We end the chapter with brief comments on the practical implications for actuaries (14.7) and recap the key learning points (14.8).

14.1.1   What are assets?

A simple definition of an asset is that it is something that you own and from which you can derive some value. For many individuals, assets will include a house and its contents, a car and financial assets such as cash, a bank account, some form of interest in a managed investment fund and perhaps a direct holding of corporate stock.

The assets of a business would include *tangible* assets like these and *intangible* assets such as registered trademarks and copyright from which the business expects to gain value.

14.1.2   Assets in the accounts

In Chapter 12, we saw how liabilities and assets fit in the financial statements or *accounts* of companies. It is worth repeating Figure 12.1 here:

---

[1] "Investments," which is based on his original Chapter 12 of the same name in *Understanding Actuarial Management* (2003).

Figure 14.1

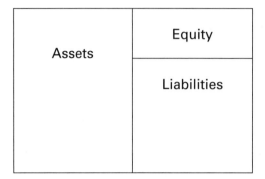

The same picture can be considered to apply to an individual asset. For example, your equity in your car is the difference between the value of the car and the amount that you owe on the loan that you took out to purchase it.

An accounting definition of assets

The International Accounting Standards Board (IASB, 2001) defines assets as follows:

> An asset is a resource controlled by the enterprise as a result of past events and from which future economic benefits are expected to flow to the enterprise.

Although there are technical niceties in the wording, this definition is close to our simple definition in 14.1.1.

14.1.3　Asset valuation terms

In discussing or reporting the value of assets, several different terms are used, including:

Cost price

As the name implies, this is the amount originally paid for the asset.

Book value (or carrying value)

Literally, this is the value at which the asset is held in a company's accounts. In this chapter, we use this meaning. However, note that other people often use this term to mean either cost price or a formula-based value derived from the cost price, for an asset that may be held at a different value in the accounts.

Amortized cost

For assets with a fixed term to expiry, the original cost price may be *amortized* over that term. Thus the amortized cost of a patent with 10 years of exclusivity remaining and acquired for $95,000 will be $85,500 after one year (assuming that there is no value at the end of the 10 years). Similarly, the amortized cost of a $100,000 bond, maturing in 10 years and purchased for $95,000, will be $95,500 after one year and $100,000 just before the principal is repaid. In these examples, we have used straight-line amortization, but other approaches are also possible.

Market value

The market value of an asset is the amount that can be realized by selling it at that time on the open market. Many assets are actively traded, so their market prices can be easily identified. Examples include *listed* company stocks (those listed on a stock exchange such as the New York Stock Exchange) and many government, semi-government and corporate bonds, which are traded *over-the-counter* (directly between buyer and seller) rather than at physical exchanges; but for which the current market price is always readily available.

Expert valuers can estimate the market value of assets, such as property, for which there is no objective market price. Valuations are typically based on recent sales of similar assets.

Fair value

While intended to represent the current value of an asset, market value as defined above may not represent the amount that would be paid by a willing buyer to a willing seller – the fair value.[2] If there is a significant surplus of buyers, market value is likely to exceed fair value, but it can also be well below fair value (and even effectively non-existent) when there are few or no potential buyers at the time. This is not uncommon for illiquid assets, but it can also be seen in market bubbles and busts, which cannot be rationally explained in terms of changes in the fundamental value of the assets.

Accounting standards increasingly require companies to show assets at fair value, or at least to ensure that they are not shown above fair value.

Useful value (or special value)

Some assets may have a demonstrably greater value to a company than their fair value or market value. For example, software may have been heavily tailored to suit a particular company's operations. It clearly has a significant value to the company, which would be unable to operate without it, but it may have very little value to any other company.

In some cases, an asset might have a special value to one potential acquirer. A common example is that the value (per share) of a listed company's stock to an intending purchaser of the whole company is greater than the market price of shares before a takeover bid is announced.[3]

Mark-to-model

When an asset is valued with reference to a pricing model, the valuation is referred to as *mark-to-model*. A valuation at market value is called *mark-to-market*.

Mark-to-model valuations are used where no obvious market value exists, perhaps because the asset is particularly complex or unusual. Arguably, they should also be used when market value is clearly different from fair value – but this argument doesn't address the question of how to tell that this is the case. When demand for an asset has collapsed, what is its fair value?

---

[2]   This definition is analogous to that set out in 12.3.4; refer to Martin and Tsui (1999) or accounting standards for a full definition.

[3]   This is because the purchaser expects to get extra benefit from full ownership of the company, such as the removal of a competitor or cost savings from combining duplicated back-office functions.

14.2   Types of asset

There are many reasons why the nature or value of assets is of importance to an actuary. For example, if an actuary is assessing the solvency of a company, all assets on the balance sheet should be reviewed.

14.2.1   Short-term or long-term assets

As with liabilities, accounting standards have traditionally required companies to divide assets into *short-term* (maturing within twelve months) and *long-term*. This gives users of the accounts a rather simplified perspective on how well matched assets and liabilities are. These days, however, more useful information is often available elsewhere in the accounts, with notes setting out the distribution of assets by duration and indicating the sensitivity of some liabilities to key assumptions including discount rates.

14.2.2   Non-investment assets

When considering financial management, we are generally most interested in long-term investment assets, especially in the context of the relationship between assets and liabilities. First, however, we shall consider the other forms of asset that can often be found on a company's balance sheet.

Cash

Companies hold money in bank accounts and even in physical cash on the premises. In fact, "cash" also includes short-term investments such as term deposits, bank bills and government securities due to mature within three months.

Cash represents the company's most liquid asset – indeed, liquidity is generally defined in terms of the ease and speed of converting an asset into cash. Like individuals, all companies need cash for day-to-day operations (to pay salaries and suppliers, for example) and to cover unexpected expenditure.

Accounts receivable

Many companies extend credit to their customers, allowing them time to pay their bills after the relevant goods or services have been provided. Debtors can be a significant asset on the balance sheet of consulting firms, who are rarely paid before providing the relevant service. Insurers can also have a large debtor asset, especially if they sell through brokers, who may have as long as 90 days before they have to pass on the premium. Reinsurance receivables can also be significant.

Inventory and raw materials

Manufacturers and retailers can accumulate large stockpiles of finished and unfinished goods. Their value may be very much dependent on the company's expectation of being able to make sufficient further sales, so a change in trading conditions (such as a recession) can have a major impact.

Capital assets

Many companies own capital assets, deployed in the business and ranging from computers and other equipment to factories and office buildings. These assets *depreciate*, meaning that their value reduces over time (without additional expenditure, such as a building renovation). Capital assets are held in the accounts at their depreciated value, which basically means the same as amortized cost, described in 14.1.3 above. The rate of depreciation is generally chosen to reflect the expected useful life of the asset. Chapter 16 discusses this in more depth.

For most financial services companies, even those that own their own office buildings, the value of capital assets is relatively small compared with their investment assets and their liabilities. However, for companies with major capital assets, there may be significant implications if the depreciated values are markedly different from the realizable values.[4]

Intangible assets

An intangible asset is a non-monetary non-physical asset. Common examples are trademarks, patents and *goodwill*. Goodwill, which is generally shown separately on the balance sheet, is the difference between the purchase price and book value of a company or line of business. It arises because the value of an entity is rarely the same as the book value of its net assets.

Intangible assets with finite useful lives (such as patents) are amortized over their useful life. Other intangible assets are generally held at cost, at fair value or at useful value.

Depending on the accounting standard being adopted, financial services companies may show a *deferred acquisition cost* (DAC) asset. This means that costs associated with selling a product that are not immediately recovered, but that are expected to be recovered from future income, can be treated as an asset. The accounting standard will have rules for testing if the costs are recoverable, and for how the DAC is amortized.

In many cases, the value of an intangible asset is dependent on the company continuing to trade – and even where the asset has an intrinsic value it may be less than its book value.

Tax assets

In most jurisdictions, operating losses and capital losses are deductible against operating profits and capital profits for tax purposes. Where a company has a net loss, it is generally able to deduct it from future profits, so it can expect a future income tax benefit (FITB), which would typically be shown in its accounts.

If past losses are too great or future profits too uncertain (eg major capital losses following a stock market slump or uncertain future profits for a new venture), the FITB may have to

---

[4] But note that IAS 36 requires *impaired* assets (those whose carrying value is greater than both fair value and value of future use) to be written down, so this is less of an issue for companies whose accounts comply with international accounting standards or similar.

be reduced or eliminated. And an FITB may have little or no value to an acquiring company or in the event of the company being wound up.

Other assets

Most companies possess other assets, which do not relate to their operations and are not long-term investments (although this view may be disputed by some). Such assets include collectibles such as art. Even if these assets are given a value in the accounts, it is unlikely to be material.

14.2.3   Investment assets

An investment asset may be a physical asset, such as a property or a mine, which can generate income for its owner(s) through rent or through the sale of outputs.

Other investment assets exist because someone has raised money for something. There is no limit to the ways in which such an investment may be structured, but we can usefully consider such assets as belonging to three main types, namely debt, equity and hybrid assets.

The very existence of assets enables the creation of derivative assets and the securitization of assets.

In total, this gives us six asset types,[5] which we discuss below.

Physical assets

Traditionally, ownership of land and its resources (including crops, meat, wool, fuel and metal ores) was the major source of wealth. Physical assets remain an important class of assets.

Physical assets generally require significant expenditure to maintain their capacity to generate earnings but they benefit from scarcity value; there are limited similar alternatives to a particular asset such as a prestigious vineyard.

Physical assets are not liquid assets and can be particularly difficult to sell during a market downturn. As each asset is unique in some way, these assets need to be valued individually. This process may happen once a year and the result is at best an estimate; between valuations, it may be extremely difficult to form a view of the value of the asset. This should be taken into account when considering the financial statements of entities holding such assets.

Debt

There are many forms of debt, but the essential characteristic is that the money borrowed is intended to be returned to the lender with interest.

---

[5]   See "Investments" on the CD for a more detailed description of the main subtypes of investment assets.

Debt instruments are distinguished by:

- the issuer;
- the way in which interest is paid; and
- whether the borrower provides *collateral* (giving the lender security in the event that the borrower is unable to make good on its promise to pay interest and capital) and, if so, the nature of that collateral.

Within a country, the national government is generally seen as the risk-free borrower, because it can print money.[6] State and municipal governments are considered slightly higher risk. Other issuers include non-government entities (such as the IMF) as well as financial institutions and other corporations.

Interest payments are generally *fixed* (the same coupon is paid in each period) or *variable* (a fixed margin or *spread* over a reference short-term interest rate). In some cases, the interest rate is *indexed* to some measure of inflation, so as to protect the lender against unexpected inflation. *Discount securities* or *zero-coupon bonds* are issued at a discount rather than explicitly paying interest, so that the only payment is the principal at maturity. *Certificates of deposit* (CDs) or *term deposits*, which are offered by banks and similar financial institutions, pay an agreed amount of interest at the end of a fixed term of between a few months and a few years (subject to a penalty if withdrawn early).

Debt may be secured against specific assets (often property, in which case the debt is a *mortgage*) or against a pool of assets or may be *unsecured*. There is also a *ranking* of creditors; higher-ranking creditors will be paid first, so their loans are more secure than those of lower-ranking creditors.

The value of debt assets depends on prevailing interest rates, the risk of default (*credit risk*) and the marketability of the debt – essentially, its *liquidity*.

Equity

Rather than lending money, an investor may prefer to share in the ownership of an enterprise and, therefore, in its profits. This offers the prospect of greater reward, but at greater risk, since all creditors must be paid before the owners are entitled to anything and *dividends* (the distribution of profit) cannot be paid if there is no current or retained profit to pay them from.

The concept of the *limited company* is fundamental to the ability to raise money through issuing shares, also known as *stock*. In a limited company, the liability of the owners for the company's debt is limited to the unpaid portion of their shares – and most shares are issued *fully paid*, meaning that there is no further liability.

A company may be *public* or *private*. Shares in a public company may be offered to anyone and, therefore, may be traded on a stock exchange. Shares in a private company are subject to rules agreed between the shareholders – and these rules will limit each shareholder's right to sell their shareholding.

---

[6] Note, however, that governments have occasionally defaulted in the past – for example, bonds issued by Tsarist Russia were not honored by the communist government after the 1917 revolution.

When we talk about *listed* shares in this chapter, we refer to those public company shares that are listed (and thus traded) on a stock exchange. Other public company shares and all private company shares (including *private equity*, which is described in "Investments" on the CD) are *unlisted*.

Public companies are subject to disclosure and governance requirements that vary from country to country but have the common aim of ensuring that individual investors are adequately informed and protected (without affecting the intrinsic risk in the enterprise). While private companies may be operated to the same standards, there are fewer legal obligations to do so.

Hybrid assets

Many assets exist that do not fit neatly into any of the above types. Often, they are hybrids – typically, a combination of debt and equity. Examples include:

- *convertible bonds*, which initially pay interest but can be converted to equity (generally at a set rate) after a certain time or on a certain contingency;

- *preference shares* (also called *preferred stock*), which are a form of equity but which rank ahead of ordinary shares and often receive a defined dividend rate (provided that there are profits from which to pay it); and

- *stapled securities*, where separate equity and debt instruments are issued together and cannot be unstapled.

Derivatives

For any real asset or set of real assets, it is possible to construct *derivative* assets based on the characteristics of the underlying real assets. Examples include the option to sell shares in company X at a fixed price within a set period (a *put option*) and a contract to deliver a quantity of wool at a certain price on a certain date (a *forward contract*).

There are three standard kinds of derivative:

- *forward contracts*, where one party contracts to supply the other with a certain amount of something at a certain price on a certain date – also called *futures contracts* when issued in a standardized form by the operator of an exchange such as the Sydney Futures Exchange;

- *options*, which are contracts giving one party the right, but not the obligation, to buy (*call option*) or sell (*put option*) an asset at a specified price (*strike price*) within or at the end of a specified period; and

- *swaps*, which are contracts to exchange cash flows, such as interest payments or payments in different currencies.

Note that it is also possible to have combinations of the basic types, such as futures options and *swaptions* (options on swaps).

Derivatives can be agreed between two parties (*over-the-counter*) or traded on an exchange operated by a clearing house (*exchange-traded*).

Where a contract requires the physical delivery of an asset, it can be closed out by buying the opposite contract (for receipt of the same asset), which means that far more money can be at risk in derivatives markets than is represented by the underlying assets. Indeed, some contracts, such as share price index futures and bond futures, can only be closed out in this way because they are written on indices rather than real assets.

Derivatives can be used to *hedge* profits or investment portfolios. For example, a UK company may have a major US subsidiary that is expected to deliver a profit of $500 million in six months. If the dollar falls against the pound in that time, the company's results (in pounds) will be adversely affected. However, if it takes out a forward contract to sell $500 million in six months for pounds at today's exchange rate, the company's profit will be unaffected by any movement in the dollar-pound exchange rate. A currency put option would have enabled the company to continue to benefit from appreciation of the dollar but it would have been more expensive.

Securitized assets

Many assets are not readily marketable. They can however be made marketable by turning them into securities – a process called *securitization*. Imagine for example that you have an office block worth $500 million. This is not very marketable, because you would need to find a buyer with $500 million to invest, and since the property would be unique, it would be hard to establish a market value. You could set up a company to own the property, whose shares are then available for sale. The shares would be smaller in value and identical to each other, so a market could be developed. The same effect could be achieved by creating a special purpose unit trust to hold the property, and issuing securities that give rights to the rents and other cash flows from the property. Other assets are not marketable because they are too small, and require a lot of administration. Home mortgage loans and credit card receivables fall into this category. The answer here is to pool a lot of mortgages or other small debts together in a special purpose trust, and then divide up the pool.

However, this may not be enough to make the securities marketable. For example, the purchaser of an A-rated bond has an immediate understanding, from the credit rating, of the riskiness of the investment. Because it would be prohibitively expensive to obtain an equivalently recognizable credit rating for an individual mortgage, there is no ready market for a slice of Mr & Mrs Smith's mortgage on 123 Acacia Avenue, Anytown.

The solution to this problem, which also applies to many loans other than mortgages, is *collateralized debt obligations* (CDOs). With a CDO (which may reflect underlying debt in the form of bonds, other loans or mortgages – a CBO, CLO or CMO respectively), the cash flows from a pool of loans can be repackaged into slices (known as *tranches*), as can the underlying collateral, or security, for the loans. As a result, after determining the ranking of the tranches, each tranche can be considered equivalent to debt with a particular credit rating.

On the basis that even the worst credit risks won't all fail together (an important assumption that should be viewed with extreme caution), A-rated CDOs can be created from very poor underlying risks. Of course, the residual tranches now have worse risk, but when credit is cheap (ie the market requires very small increases in interest rates for poorer credit risks) it is possible to find companies prepared to rent out their balance sheets to improve the rating. This is simply the corporate equivalent of parents standing guarantor for their children's loans, with all of the same risks on a much larger scale.

Exercise 14.1

Obtain a copy of the accounts of five major companies in different industries (not just financial services) in your country. You should be able to do this via the internet.

Review the assets in each company's balance sheet and:

(a) note which types of asset are common to all companies;

(b) find out what the accounts say about the valuation approach used for each type of asset;

(c) identify the major assets for each company and how those assets relate to the company's business; and

(d) consider how each company's financial position might be affected by a change in the reported value of its major assets.

14.3   Valuing assets

Valuation principles

Rationally, the value of anything is simply the value of the economic contribution that can be obtained from it. For example, the value of a discount security can be found by discounting the amount of the principal to be received at the end of the term, with an allowance for the risk of delay or default. This is merely a discounted cash flow (DCF) calculation.

The fact that an asset can usually be sold, today or at any time in the future, adds a further dimension to the determination of value. If our DCF calculation gives a lower value than today's market value, then the rational thing to do would seem to be to sell the asset. Similarly, the market value can be below the DCF value, making it rational to hold or buy the asset.

Of course, when excess demand drives market value well above the DCF value, an asset price bubble can develop. And when that demand collapses, the bubble bursts.

It is important to remember that the difference between our DCF value and market value effectively represents a different view of future cash flows, risk and discount rates. Nevertheless, many investment decisions are made on the basis of a view of fundamental value relative to market value.

In Chapter 12, we discussed discount rates in some detail and this discussion will not be repeated here. However, it is worth remembering that arbitrage opportunities exist if two assets or portfolios with the same future cash flows in all circumstances are given different values. This means that the same cash flow in the same future period should be discounted at the same rate. Thus, if we can risk-adjust projected future cash flows, we can discount each at the zero-coupon risk-free rate that applies for that term.

In the absence of a replicating portfolio, this approach should produce an estimate of fair value and a useful comparator to market value.

In practice, it is not possible to perform such detailed valuations of all assets in the time frame required for daily investment decisions. Therefore, investors often use proxy valuation methods. These rule-of-thumb approaches give investors a general sense of relative value and enable attention to be focused on a smaller set of asset valuations.

Below, we look at a few basic examples of these proxy valuation methods.

Bonds

The expected cash flow from a bond comprises the future interest payments (usually paid twice a year) and the return of the principal at the end of the term. The traditional approach to valuing a bond is to discount these cash flows at a single discount rate that reflects market interest rates having regard to the term of the bond and the creditworthiness of the issuer.

The market values of government bonds with different maturities imply a *yield curve*. From this, a "risk-free" yield can be deduced for a particular term. If you are valuing a non-government bond for that term, you can add market risk premiums for creditworthiness and liquidity and discount at that rate.

Further adjustments would be required to account for other differences from the basic government bond, such as variable interest rates or an option for the issuer to repay the principal early (a *callable* bond).

The greater the differences from the basic government bond, the more judgment is required.

Shares

The cash flow from a share comprises the future dividends (usually paid twice a year) that may be declared out of the company's profits.

Of course, it is not easy to project what these dividends will be. However, if the dividend, D, will grow at rate g in perpetuity and is discounted at rate d (where $d > g$), then (ignoring the timing of payments), the approximate value, A, of the income stream is given by:

$$A = D / (d - g)$$

If the ratio of the dividend to the annual earnings, E, is assumed to be constant, so that $D = rE$, then:

$$A = rE / (d - g)$$

If the price, P, is equal to the value, then:

$$P/E = r / (d - g)$$

P/E is known as the price-earnings ratio and is publicly quoted[7] for all listed shares.

In the short term, we may have a different view about the elements of this equation, primarily E, r and g, and this results in adjustments to valuations.

In practice, however, shares are frequently traded and so their prices often reflect speculation about short-term and medium-term price movements – which suggests that a valuation requires some understanding of feedback loops, behavioral science and game theory!

---

[7] For example, most major newspapers report P/E ratios along with price and trading information for shares listed on their national stock exchange.

Property

The expected cash flow from a property comprises the rent to be paid by the tenants less the costs of ownership, which include rates and taxes; utility costs; and repair and maintenance costs (to the extent that these are not charged to tenants). The building will require minor or major renovation from time to time.

In the short term, income is governed by the rental agreements with existing tenants. These will usually specify a monthly rent increased annually at a predetermined rate (but sometimes linked to an index such as CPI) and the basis of contribution to the costs set out in the previous paragraph. The rental agreement might provide for a period of reduced rent at the start of the tenancy, if the tenant has managed to negotiate such a reduction, or *incentive*. Usually, there is also an option for the agreement to be extended beyond its original term, on agreed terms.

In the short term, therefore, the net income to the property owner(s) is quite predictable – provided that the tenants continue to pay the rent. However, the longer-term projection needed for a DCF valuation requires assumptions as to future rental income and ownership costs. These may be estimated by considering other, reasonably similar properties. Thus, a full projection is possible, combining short-term and long-term income and expenses, and a DCF valuation can be performed.

In practice, a simpler approach is often adopted (or at least used as a reasonableness check). An experienced property valuer would be aware of the *rental yield* (the rent divided by the price paid) achieved on recent sales and would be able to estimate the adjustments required to reflect the particular characteristics and circumstances of this property. A value can be found by dividing the market rent by the estimated rental yield and then making any further adjustments required to reflect short-term factors such as the difference between current and market rent.

Derivatives

As with any other asset, the DCF valuation of a derivative requires the projection and discounting of cash flows. In turn, this requires an understanding of how the derivative reflects the cash flows of the underlying asset(s).

Futures and forward contracts, for example, are simply agreements to deliver (or purchase) a set quantity and quality of the underlying goods on a specified date at a set price, so the present value of the deliverable is always the settlement price, discounted at the risk-free rate (adjusted for dividend yields, storage costs, etc).

Options are not readily valued by DCF methods because of the asymmetric nature of the payoff. Financial economics points the way to two other valuation approaches, namely:

*   valuation by reference to a replicating portfolio of assets, which generates the same cash flows as the derivative in all circumstances; and

*   valuation using the Black-Scholes option pricing model and its subsequent variants.

Exercise 14.2

(a) What is the value, at 5% per annum (convertible half-yearly), of a bond with par value of 100, maturing in exactly five years, with a coupon of 6% per annum payable twice a year?

(b) ABC Ltd, with 100 million shares on issue, earns a profit of $20 million after tax. If its P/E ratio is 15, what is its share price?

(c) An office building has 12,000m² of lettable space, all leased out to a major government department, on a long lease, at $500 per m². Under the lease agreement, the lessee pays its own outgoings (electricity, etc) and a proportion of the lessor's outgoings in addition to the rent. If the lessor is left with outgoings of $1.1 million per annum, what is the value of the building on a 7% rental yield?

(d) The spot price of a 90-day stock index futures contract is $5,000. If the 90-day risk-free rate is 1% (4.12% per annum) and the estimated dividend yield over the period on stocks in the index is 0.75%, what is the forward price? You may assume that the dividend is paid at the end of the period.

14.4 Asset risks

As with any DCF valuation, the value of an asset can change for two reasons – either the expected cash flows or the discount rate(s) change. With cash flows, either the amount payable changes or there is a delay or default in payment.

In this section, we consider the key risks to the value of the asset types discussed in the previous section.

Bonds and other debt

For fixed-interest debt, the amount payable does not change, so the key cash flow risk is that of default. For a debt investor, the major concern is that the principal will be repaid, more or less on time. Lenders prefer some form of security, such as a mortgage over property, to provide a prospect of recovering the debt in the event of default.

The value of fixed-interest debt is sensitive to market interest rates. The greater the *duration* (the discounted mean term) of the debt, the greater the sensitivity of the value to changes in interest rates.

The risk of default is a similar concern for floating-rate debt, but cash flow is also affected by changes in interest rates. However, this means that the value of such debt is not usually sensitive to market interest rates.

Default risk is reflected in the value of both fixed-rate and floating-rate debt as the price of *credit risk*. Debt with a lower credit rating from a recognized rating agency will tend to be priced at a higher discount rate than otherwise identical debt with a higher rating. However, the margin is not constant: when the economy is strong and default rates are low, the price of credit risk can become very low – but there are times when extremely high prices are charged for credit risk.

Sometimes, the debt market is so risk-averse that it is almost impossible to sell debt with any credit risk. This, in turn, makes it very hard for businesses to raise or refinance loans and acts as a massive brake on economic activity. This phenomenon is known as a *credit crunch*. During a credit crunch, the market value of debt assets can be very much lower than their apparent DCF value.

It is important to remember that a credit rating is only a proxy for default risk. It is a subjective assessment, based on analysis of available (mostly historical) data. Assessment errors can be made – and, in any case, the default risk can change quite rapidly, as illustrated in the chart of TED spreads below. The TED spread is the margin between Eurodollar CDs (a good proxy for inter-bank lending rates) and US Treasury Bills (a proxy for the risk-free rate). Both rates are three-month rates. An increase in the TED spread represents an increase in banks' assessment of the risk of lending to each other.

Figure 14.2   TED spreads

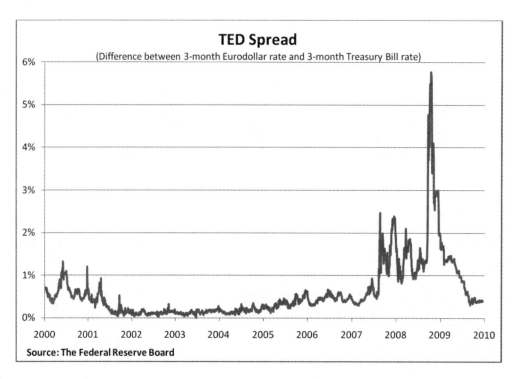

The chart shows the initial credit crunch arising from the unraveling of securitized subprime debt portfolios in 2007 and the crisis of confidence in banks in 2008, before governments around the world stepped in to guarantee deposits. This Global Financial Crisis is a powerful example of the speed with which things can change, also illustrating the difficulty in estimating the default risk of complex packaged and securitized debt.

Sometimes, borrowers have the option to repay early. Such repayment is likely to occur at a time that favors the borrower rather than the investor, such as when interest rates have fallen below the coupon rate. So investors face the risk of early repayment on loans where this is permitted.

Shares

Earnings are the key to the fundamental value of shares, so any event that affects the earnings prospects of a company must affect the value of its shares. The most extreme event is insolvency, which causes the shares to have no value, but market sentiment can magnify the impact of any event so that individual companies' share prices are generally far more volatile than their dividend payments. (On the other hand, a company can sometimes reduce its dividend or miss one altogether without any immediate change in the share price, if the market had already factored this into its view of the company.)

While the value of a portfolio of shares is less volatile than that of an individual company's shares, it is still greatly affected by market sentiment. In times of great uncertainty about the short-term direction of the economy (and hence of corporate profits), stock markets can see large daily movements in price indices.

In theory, changes to market interest rates should have a direct and predictable effect on share prices. After all, the projected cash flows are now being discounted at a different rate. Consider a share with a P/E ratio of 15. If 75 percent of earnings are distributed as dividends, then $(d - g) = 5\%$, so a 1% reduction in interest rates should reduce $(d - g)$ to 4%, giving a P/E ratio of 18.75, increasing the value of the share by 25 percent.

This doesn't happen, for reasons that include:

- d will be a risk-adjusted discount rate and, in practice, these rates are not perfectly correlated with market interest rates;

- a change in interest rates might affect the expected growth rate of dividends, g, perhaps because of implications for the economic outlook, so that $(d - g)$ does not move so much; and

- market sentiment is a more powerful driver of value than interest rates, because of the uncertainty of the future cash flows in a DCF valuation of the share.

Although listed shares are generally readily traded, the market price doesn't necessarily translate into the proceeds of a sale, especially if large parcels of shares are being sold into a falling market. This is the natural consequence of an open market, where every action forms part of the available information affecting participants' assessment of value.

Unlisted shares do not have an obvious market price and are therefore less sensitive to market sentiment. However, there will often be constraints on the investor's ability to sell them, making it harder to obtain a good price in the event of a forced sale.

Property

The key risk to the DCF value of a property is the loss of prospective rental income, such as the loss of a key tenant and any impediment to replacing that tenant. A property cannot be moved, so if the area becomes less attractive it will be harder to command the same rental income. And if the property itself is less attractive than local alternatives, the prospects for income are reduced.

As with shares, the market value of a property can be quite different from its DCF value, again as a result of market sentiment. Indeed, there are times when the market value seems to be independent of the rental income. Enterprising investors have been known to take advantage of this by acquiring properties with good-quality major tenants on long-term leases and splitting off the rental stream to create a new asset at virtually no cost.

Selling a property can take a long time and the sale price can be very different from expectations, especially if the seller needs to sell quickly. Properties can be held in collective vehicles such as unit trusts, either listed or unlisted, to make it easier to own and trade a portfolio of property exposures; this can mitigate the liquidity problem, at least in normal market conditions.

Derivatives

Derivatives provide a highly leveraged exposure to the volatility of the underlying assets, because they can be acquired at a fraction of the price. For example,[8] suppose that you have to make a margin deposit of $10 to buy a *contract for difference* (CFD) delivering the change in value of a BigCorp share currently worth $100. If BigCorp's shares are worth $110 tomorrow, a shareholder would have gained 10 percent but the derivative owner gains 100 percent. However, if BigCorp shares fall by 10 percent, the derivative owner has lost 100 percent.

So, one risk of derivatives is that the return is considerably less than anticipated – and even that it is highly negative.

Another risk is that the counterparty doesn't pay out on settlement, either because it claims that it is not required to (*legal risk*) or because it cannot pay (*credit risk*). These risks are greatly reduced by trading in derivatives on a registered exchange (*clearing house*), which uses standardized wording and requires each party to the contract to hold sufficient funds on deposit at the clearing house to enable it to close out its position that day, plus a margin. If that margin is eroded, the clearing house will make a *margin call* to top up the funds.

Margin calls introduce a further risk for derivative owners: there is a liquidity risk associated with temporary adverse movements in value.

Over-the-counter contracts are individually negotiated between the parties. Collateral may still be required and margin calls may be made on some contracts if market movements are sufficiently adverse. This would give rise to similar liquidity issues.

Note that option-holders would not face margin calls, because they can simply allow the option to lapse. The same does not apply to the issuers of those options.

To the extent that derivatives are used to hedge investment or operational risks, adverse movements in the derivative price should be offset by favorable movements in the underlying assets, provided that any margin calls can be met in the interim.

---

8   Note that this is a very simple example that ignores trading and holding costs, including brokerage and interest charges.

> ## Exercise 14.3
>
> In most countries, individuals have the opportunity to invest in managed investment vehicles such as unit trusts (mutual funds). Generally, the managers of these entities must produce a document that enables the investor to make an informed choice. Such documents give simple, but varied, descriptions of the risk profiles of the different investment options. These descriptions are intended to be meaningful and useful for potential investors.
>
> You should be able to find a few examples of such documents for products offered in your own country by searching on the internet. If not, try searching for investment "product disclosure statements" in Australia.
>
> Compare different issuers' descriptions of the risk profile of a range of single sector funds (such as "Australian shares") and composite sector funds (such as "balanced") and discuss how well they convey the relative riskiness of these funds.

14.5   Asset-liability management

While assets are interesting in themselves, they become particularly interesting when considered in conjunction with liabilities. Asset-liability management (ALM) – or, perhaps, *mis*-management – is at the heart of many corporate failures and very many more near misses. In this section, we look at the relationship between assets and liabilities and the nature of asset-liability risks. Then we discuss various approaches to managing these risks. As you will see, there is no single solution that applies to all situations. However, you should always bear in mind the fact that risk reduction usually comes at a cost, being a reduction in expected return plus, often, potentially significant execution and/or administration costs. An asset-liability manager will be looking for opportunities to reduce risk at relatively low cost and each possible strategy would be measured against that objective.

14.5.1   How assets relate to liabilities

Sometimes, assets exist because of the activities that gave rise to the liabilities. For example, a motor insurer collects premiums to pay for the risks being covered (loss or damage) and to meet its administration costs. After meeting current claims and expenses from premium income, there will be some money left over to cover the liabilities, including outstanding claims and unearned premium. In this particular example, the liabilities are primarily short-term in nature and the insurer's primary concern is the liquidity of its assets. Accordingly, it will probably hold most of its investments in cash and short-term fixed-interest securities.

As an extension to this example, an insurer of liability (casualty) risks – such as the risk that a person will suffer physical harm through the negligence of the insured – will have claims that take many years to emerge and be settled.[9] This means that the assets (and liabilities) on the balance sheet can be equivalent to several years' premiums. In a long-tail business such as this, there is a great deal of uncertainty as to the quantum and timing of

---

[9]   For example, mesothelioma (caused by exposure to asbestos) takes a long time to become apparent and the resultant claim often takes a long time to settle.

future claims payments. There are different investment approaches: many insurers regard their core business as insurance and invest in fixed-interest securities broadly matching the expected term of the liabilities, but some have quite significant proportions of their portfolios in "growth assets" (equities or property).

Many times, the liabilities exist because of the desire to own (and profit from) the assets. For example, an individual may decide to borrow money in order to invest in shares or property, in the expectation of gaining a higher return from the investment than the borrowing cost. Corporate examples include banks and mortgage originators, with a supply of borrowers; in turn, these companies need to borrow funds (perhaps by offering interest to individual savers) in order to have money to lend.

Long-term savings institutions, including life insurers, have a supply of potential savers, from whom they derive the funds for investment to meet their liabilities to the same group. In this case, the relationship between assets and liabilities depends on the nature of the product that the company offers to the savers. Traditional "with-profits" life insurance products such as whole of life and endowment policies comprise a capital-guaranteed element (the sum insured plus bonuses once they have been allocated) and the prospect of growth from non-guaranteed future bonuses. Life insurers have generally delivered the extra growth in these products by long-term investment predominantly in equities and property. In some countries, including the US, such products are called "participating" and are generally operated so as to pay dividends rather than accumulating bonuses. In those countries, funds backing these products are typically mainly invested in fixed-interest assets.

Since the 1980s, an increasing proportion of long-term savings business is investment-linked (variable universal life in North America), where the policy account balance is derived from the performance of the client-selected asset pool(s) in which the policy is invested.

14.5.2 Basic asset-liability risks

There are four basic risks associated with the relationship between assets and liabilities, namely that:

(a) the return on the assets (income and capital gains) is insufficient to enable the obligations to be met as they fall due;

(b) illiquid assets have to be sold cheaply to meet cash flow needs (a liquidity risk);

(c) it is not possible to reinvest surplus asset cash flows (interest, dividends and the proceeds of sale or maturity) – or, in reverse, to obtain refinancing – in a manner that avoids both (a) and (b); and

(d) the valuations of assets and liabilities will give rise to a deficiency, even where the assets may otherwise be thought to be sufficient.

In practice, as shown earlier in Figure 14.1, we would expect assets to exceed liabilities, providing a buffer against these risks. However, it is easier to understand the basic issues if we ignore this buffer (or *capital*) for the moment. In any case, asset-liability risks represent risks to capital and the fact that our assets still cover our liabilities is not sufficient if we no longer hold enough capital to be allowed to operate.

Risk of insufficient return

The risk of insufficient return can be 100 percent. Consider a savings institution that issues a one-year CD at 5% but can only invest one-year funds at 4.9%. And, of course, this risk is zero if the institution can invest securely at 5.1%.

The more usual situation is where there is volatility in either or both of the assets and the liabilities, so that there is a range of possible outcomes in which the return is insufficient – and other possible outcomes where it is sufficient. The risk of insufficiency may relate to income or capital gains (including the risk of default on debt) or to unexpected growth in the obligations.

Example 14.1

Consider a claim, currently in court, which will be paid at the end of the year. Let us suppose that there are two possible outcomes: there is a 20 percent chance that we will have to pay $85,000 and an 80 percent chance of $110,000, so we expect the claim to cost $105,000. We can invest $100,000 in a zero-coupon bond maturing for $105,000 in one year's time. If the outcome is favorable, the asset will prove more than sufficient (by $20,000). However, an unfavorable outcome would mean a shortfall of $5,000.

Now consider a hypothetical asset which is equally likely to pay $100,000 and $110,000 at the end of the year. The expected payout is therefore $105,000, the same as the zero-coupon bond. Ignoring the risk premium that would apply, this asset is also worth $100,000 today. The potential outcomes are:

Probability	Asset	Liability	Outcome
10%	100,000	85,000	15,000
40%	100,000	110,000	-10,000
10%	110,000	85,000	25,000
40%	110,000	110,000	0

You should be able to see that the expected profit is nil for both assets. However, the risk-free asset has only a 20 percent chance of being sufficient, while there is a 60 percent probability of the riskier asset being sufficient. Asset-liability risk is not necessarily reduced by using risk-free assets!

The insufficiency risk includes the risk of capital gains being too low. In the example, our asset could theoretically have been a 10-year zero-coupon bond, with a principal of $162,889 and a yield of 5% per annum. Assuming a flat yield curve, we expect a capital gain of $5,000 when we sell the bond in a year's time. If we happen to know that nine-year interest rates will then be either 5.57% or 4.46%, with equal probability, then we have our second set of scenarios, where the capital gain will be $5,000 less than expected or $5,000 more than expected.

Liquidity risk

As we have seen, the insufficiency risk includes the risk of selling an asset when its market price is low, thus reducing the investment return. For illiquid assets, however, the mere fact that the asset needs to be sold quickly may reduce its price. Consider, for example, the difference in the price that a house might fetch if it had to be sold by next weekend compared to its potential price if the owners could wait for the "right" offer.

At call bank accounts are an example of liquidity risk. With an at call bank account, the bank promises that cash may be withdrawn on demand. It uses the deposits to lend to other customers (the main source of its profits), only keeping enough cash to back a proportion of account balances (the *reserve ratio*[10]). Note that the customer loans are generally illiquid assets.

In normal times, the net level of withdrawals would be far less than the available cash. However, if there is a run on the bank, net withdrawal requests could exceed the available cash and the bank would need extra funds to meet them. As it would have limited capacity to generate cash from its loan portfolio, it would be in trouble, even though the total value of its assets might still exceed its liabilities.

Reinvestment/refinancing risk

For long-term liabilities, it is likely that a significant component of the future value of assets will depend on how income and sales proceeds are reinvested. Consider, for example, a portfolio of pensions or annuities. Even ignoring the uncertainty relating to the longevity risk, it is not usually possible to find a set of assets whose cash flows will match the annuity payments. Therefore, the investment strategy will most likely require reinvestment of assets. If interest rates are lower than expected when reinvesting, then the future returns will also be lower.

On the other hand, a lending institution may raise funding for its loans from the wholesale market rather than from individual depositors. In this case, it is likely that the institution will have to refinance maturing debt in large amounts and it will effectively have issued loans based on an assumed cost of mid-term refinancing of its funding. If markets move against it (either the general rate of interest or the specific terms available to the institution), the overall cost of its funds will be higher than it expected when pricing its loans.

This was a major factor in the collapse of several home loan originators in the credit crunch of 2007, including American Home Mortgage (US), Northern Rock (UK) and RAMS Home Loans (Australia).

Valuation risk

While it is arguable that the assets only need to be sufficient when the liabilities fall due, the reality is that a company cannot wait this long to discover that they are insufficient. After all, it has obligations to other parties, such as customers, lenders, trade suppliers and regulators. If the company ever finds that the value of assets is less than the value of the liabilities, it has a problem.

This problem can arise out of the risks described above. For example, the fact that we have had to sell an illiquid asset cheaply may mean that our remaining assets will clearly not be sufficient to meet future liabilities.

---

[10] In the US, the Federal Reserve has required a minimum reserve ratio of 10% since April 1992.

However, there are some other reasons why a valuation deficiency may arise, including:

- If the assets are not risk-free and the cost of default risk increases, the value of the assets will fall. For example, a corporate bond valued at risk-free + 5% would fall in value if the basis changed to risk-free + 7%.

- If the duration of the assets is different from that of the liabilities, their values will respond differently to changes in market interest rates. For example, if the assets are of a shorter duration than the liabilities and interest rates fall, the assets will increase in value by less than the liabilities.

- If the assets are, in fact, of a different structure than the liabilities, they will behave quite differently in response to changing market conditions. For example, liabilities of an annuity nature will behave like bonds; if the supporting assets are equities, they will behave quite differently and there is a high probability that their value will move in the opposite direction to that of the liabilities.

- If the valuation bases adopted for assets and liabilities are inconsistent, a deficiency can be measured even when none exists. For example, consider a term certain annuity portfolio (where payments are made for a specified period) matched by a bond portfolio with identical cash flows. If (for whatever reason) the bonds are valued at amortized cost and the annuities are valued by discounting at the risk-free rate, a fall in interest rates would result in the value of assets being measured as less than the value of liabilities.

To the extent that these valuation risks prove to be temporary, a company that accepts these risks will wish to be able to continue to trade as usual. This is a major reason to hold capital.

Of course, to the extent that the valuation risks prove to be permanent, the cause may then be categorized as insufficient return or reinvestment risk. As we have seen earlier in this book, risk does not neatly divide into distinct categories.

14.5.3 Cash flow matching

One way to reduce or eliminate asset/liability risk is to match cash flows. Clearly, if the assets' cash flow will be the same as the liabilities' cash flow in all circumstances, there is no asset/liability risk at all.

One example of cash flow matching is unit trusts (mutual funds in North America), because the liability is always derived from the value of the assets. Sometimes, fixed income products are sold that can be precisely matched by a portfolio of bonds.

Another cash flow matching technique is reinsurance, although it is unusual for the whole of the liability to be reinsured. Similarly, it is theoretically possible to construct a derivative to match any liability.

More complex cash flow matching techniques are sometimes employed where liability cash flows are reasonably predictable, as can be the case in an annuity portfolio. To the extent that reinvestment is required, these techniques may only provide a partial cash flow match, but the process of attempting to match assets also helps in establishing an appropriate price or liability. The approach requires the use of algorithms such as those set out by Kocherlakota, Rosenbloom and Shiu (1988).

Note that a more complete match can be obtained for an annuity portfolio if longevity insurance (or reinsurance) is purchased to cap the term of the liability.

14.5.4   Immunization

In 1952, the British actuary Frank Redington showed how a portfolio of business could be *immunized* against changes in interest rates by ensuring that the assets satisfied the following conditions:

- the present value of the assets equals the present value of the liabilities at the market rate of interest;

- the duration of the assets equals the duration of the liabilities; and

- the spread of the cash flow about the duration is less for the liabilities than for the assets.

This approach assumes a single interest rate at any point in time (a flat *yield curve*) and that all future liability outgoes and asset proceeds are known in timing and amount. This is unrealistic, but the theory is still very useful because it highlights the fact that asset/liability risk can be substantially reduced without full cash flow matching.

Furthermore, there are situations where the asset and liability cash flows may be considered effectively certain (again, annuity portfolios backed by fixed interest investments would be a good example), so the only remaining problem is the non-level – and varying shape – yield curve. In the very short term, the yield curve may be considered generally fairly predictable in shape, so immunization theory is in fact similar to the approaches taken to hedge portfolios.

14.5.5   "Appropriate" investment strategies

Another approach to managing asset/liability risk is to pick an investment strategy that is expected to be "appropriate" to the liabilities. This is clearly a looser objective than cash flow matching and immunization but it is essentially the standard approach.

One reason for the popularity of this approach is that, having selected a broad investment strategy, we can then focus on managing the assets in isolation from the liabilities. If we have the "right" mix of asset types, we can employ specialist asset managers and set them targets relating to relative performance within their sector.

This approach is also popular because it doesn't require the liabilities to be fully understood. A particular example of this is in the selection of investment strategies for individuals saving for retirement; financial advisers will discuss "risk tolerance" and general objectives but will usually not have a detailed understanding of the future liabilities (needs) of the individual. To be fair, the individual will usually have even less understanding of those needs.

Wealth management products, including the savings or investment policies issued by life insurers, have similarly unclear future liabilities.

While unclear in detail, most liabilities have general characteristics that can inform the selection of investment strategies. This is a topic that belongs in investment courses and textbooks, but we give a brief discussion here in the context of a few liability types.

At call savings accounts

Most savings accounts allow money to be withdrawn without notice ("at call") at face value. This suggests that a reasonable proportion of the assets backing such accounts should be liquid in nature. However, the financial institution would generally expect to earn a greater return on longer-duration assets, so it can afford to offer a more competitive interest rate on account balances if it does not just invest in cash and other liquid assets.

It is possible to smooth returns from portfolios containing significant proportions of volatile assets such as shares and property – but this will sometimes require subsidizing the interest paid, which is risky when the account holder can withdraw the subsidized balance at call. Long-duration debt assets pose a similar risk, especially if there is also credit risk. However, the volatility of debt assets is generally much lower than that of shares and property – and banks are experts at assessing and managing credit risk.

As a result, a proportion of the portfolio would be liquid, so that we can afford to meet expected withdrawals under most circumstances, and most of the portfolio would be medium-term and long-term debt assets. In the case of banks, these less liquid assets are often loans made by the bank to individuals and businesses.

Income claims (eg income protection or workers compensation)

In this case, the liability is a periodic (typically monthly or fortnightly) cash flow, replacing some or all of a person's income. The payments would be expected to grow in line with an inflation index (either prices or wages) and may or may not have a set termination date.

The assets will need to generate cash flow, so income-generating assets (debt, property or high-yield shares) are indicated. As the cash flow is reasonably certain, it is likely that the appropriate portfolio would be heavily weighted toward lower-risk bonds. In reflection of the inflation risk, inflation-indexed bonds may be considered.

Outstanding long-tail insurance claims

Public liability (PL) and professional indemnity (PI) claims can take a very long time to settle. Many of these claims, especially PL claims, relate to loss of income and/or the cost of services such as nursing care. Over the time it takes to settle the claims, the cost will grow with inflation. Quite often, there will also be super-imposed inflation as courts take a more generous approach to the items awarded or their valuation.

To keep pace with the face value of the claims, the supporting assets need to grow faster than inflation. Arguably, this is best achieved by investing a significant proportion in shares.

In practice, however, most long-tail insurers invest predominantly in high-grade fixed-interest assets. One reason for this would be that this makes the accounting position more robust: assuming that the duration of the assets is similar to that of the liabilities, a movement in interest rates will have a similar impact on the value of both the assets and the liabilities, meaning that there is a relatively small impact on the net asset position.

Defined benefit superannuation (pension) funds

Defined benefit funds generally have liabilities in excess of their assets, with the difference being made up by the value of future contributions, as shown below:

Figure 14.3

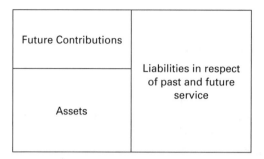

Retirement benefits are often expressed as a percentage of average salary times years of service, where salary is averaged over a period of years. Early leaving service benefits are usually considerably less generous. Therefore, liabilities accumulate during a member's employment with increases in salary and in the probability of a retirement payout and the reduction in the period over which that payout can be discounted.

If a pension is paid from retirement, this can last for many years.

If early leaving service benefits are not too generous relative to retirement benefits, the liquidity risk is not too high and the main issues are the need for the return on assets to exceed inflation by a reasonable margin and the extreme length of the term of the liabilities.

This liability profile suggests an investment strategy dominated by shares and other growth assets.

However, as we shall see in 14.5.6, there are reasons for adopting different strategies.

Products with performance guarantees

Some products contain guarantees of performance. For example, a product may offer a return based on that of a portfolio of shares but with an underlying capital guarantee.

The investment strategy would typically involve the use of derivatives. For example, put options may be purchased to protect the asset portfolio against loss in the event of a market fall.

14.5.6   Liability-driven investment

In recent times, particularly in the UK and Europe, a concept called *liability-driven investment* (LDI) has taken hold, especially in relation to pension funds.

For many companies with defined benefit pension funds, the fund's financial position is one of the key risks to the company's own financial position, because of the requirement to recognize it in the company's financial statements.[11] This becomes a particular issue when

---

[11] Where accounting standards do not require the fund's financial position to be reflected in the company's accounts, this is less of an issue, although the annual contributions to the pension fund will affect the company as they are made. However, international accounting standards require this recognition, so it can be assumed that the situation will become even more common.

the fund's assets fall sharply in value, even if the investment mix is thought appropriate in the long term.

LDI seeks to address this situation.

Note that there is no agreed definition of LDI, which may actually be thought of as a new name for asset-liability management. In broad terms, LDI can be described as "managing risk in assets with regard to the liabilities."

As the name suggests, LDI starts with the liabilities. There are various risks associated with the liabilities, including the asset-liability risks discussed in 14.5.2. In theory, each risk can be quantified in the context of each possible investment strategy. Because the risks relate to the liabilities, apparently "risk-free" investment strategies (such as holding 100 percent cash) do not minimize risk; the lowest risks come from the closest matching of the liabilities.

As with any risk management exercise, the optimal solution is one that maximizes expected reward while retaining an affordable level of risk. This solution will vary from case to case, both because the nature of the liabilities will vary and because of different attitudes to risk. For example, one pension fund sponsor may be especially concerned about the impact of the fund's financial position on the sponsor's accounts while another may be concerned about the level and volatility of cash contributions required.

In general, LDI solutions require the assets to be appropriate for the long-term and short-term risks in the liabilities, which are often conflicting objectives. In addition to close attention to duration risk, the solution is often found in the use of derivatives, such as swaps and options, to provide short-term protection to a portfolio selected for the long term.

14.5.7 Asset/liability modeling

Whatever approach is taken to managing the relationship between assets and liabilities, it is important to understand the implications and this requires a model.

Modeling is covered in Chapter 9 and Data and Assumptions in Chapter 10. However, for the purposes of the current chapter, it is worth noting that asset/liability modeling usually involves the simulation approach and that:

- minor errors in modeling assets (A) or liabilities (L) can have a material impact on $A - L$, which is relatively small;

- the modeled $A - L$ is sensitive to the assumed degree of correlation between A and L;

- much of the asset/liability risk relates to events in the tails of the probability distributions;

- there is not enough historical market data to form a robust view of a once-in-a-hundred-years asset event, let alone those further out in the tail; and

- both volatility and correlation change over time and quite large changes can happen when markets are under great stress.

As a result, it is easy for asset/liability models to understate the risks inherent in the way in which the relationship is being managed, but this may not become apparent under normal market conditions.

> **Exercise 14.4**
>
> Using the workbook "Chapter 14 ALM Spreadsheet" found on the CD, experiment with different asset mixes supporting the sample liability. What are your conclusions?

14.6   Asset-liability management constraints

In this section, we consider some of the constraints to the effective management of assets with regard to the liabilities.

14.6.1   Investment mandates

Whatever strategic approach to asset-liability management is adopted, someone will be responsible for managing the investments. This manager will have a set of instructions, or *mandate*. If different managers are responsible for different parts of the portfolio, each will have a mandate.

A mandate will set out what the manager is allowed to invest in and/or what investments are prohibited. For example, a mandate for an "ethical" fund will prohibit investment in companies involved in certain products or activities, perhaps including arms manufacture, tobacco and alcohol.

As an investment manager must not breach the mandate, it is important to ensure that it is not too constraining. However, the constraints must be effective and consistent with the intended objectives. For example, the use of derivatives may be permitted, in order to allow the manager to hedge positions to some extent, but the mandate should clearly state the limits on derivative exposure.

Note that many funds – including pension funds, special-purpose investment vehicles and academic endowment funds – may have investment constraints that should also be reflected in any investment mandates.

14.6.2   Investment product offerings

Investment-linked products sold by companies such as life insurers offer the purchaser the choice of several fund options. Generally, there are single-sector options (such as "Cash" and "Equities") and multi-sector managed options (such as "Balanced" and "Growth").

In many countries, consumer protection legislation requires that these options be properly described in product disclosure documentation – and the investment management must be consistent with the description. The expression "true to label" is often used to describe this requirement, which clearly constrains the investment manager.

14.6.3   Legislative constraints

The investment manager may also be constrained by legislation. For example, in order to access certain significant tax concessions, life insurers in Australia were once required to hold 30 percent of their assets in public securities, including at least 20 percent in government securities – the "30/20" rule. This rule is long gone, but it is a simple illustration of how legislation can constrain investment management.

14.6.4   Capital requirements

Regulators require companies to hold capital to reduce the risk of the liabilities exceeding the assets (*insolvency*). The requirements vary by country, by sector (eg banks versus insurers) and often by product. Generally, the requirements reflect the nature of the assets and of the liabilities, including any inherent guarantees. For example, a non-life insurer may be required to hold asset-risk capital as a percentage of its assets, where the percentage is higher for equities than for bonds and higher for B-grade bonds than for AA-grade.

Less often, the capital requirements explicitly or implicitly reflect the asset-liability risks. For example, life insurers may be required to test the effect on net assets of certain specified changes in asset markets.

The regulator's view of capital requirements may be quite different from the company's own view and can result in changes to the company's preferred investment strategy. However, even without the involvement of regulators, a well-run company would recognize the need to allocate capital to reflect the risk in each business unit.

14.6.5   Access to capital

The consequence of an adverse asset outcome relative to liabilities is that more capital is required to restore the position. While the availability of capital doesn't prevent the adverse outcome, it allows the company to manage it.

If capital is not readily available, this can be very serious; any remedial action is likely to be difficult and expensive. For example, it may be necessary to "de-risk" the assets by selling out of shares or property, but this is likely to crystallize losses and also means a lower exposure to any rebound in asset values. Sometimes, no remedial action can save the company.

Therefore, a key consideration in asset-liability management is the availability of capital.

14.6.6   The impact of tax and fees

Investment managers generally measure their performance against benchmarks relevant to their investment mandates. For example, the benchmark for a manager of an Australian Shares portfolio may be the S&P/ASX200 Accumulation Index.

Traditionally, the impact of tax and fees has not been considered to be particularly relevant to this comparison. However, the investor gets a return after tax and fees.

If taxation legislation distinguishes between different sources of income, such as capital gains versus revenue, the same pre-tax performance from two managers may generate quite different post-tax returns. And if different investors pay tax at different rates, they may also favor different components in the pre-tax return. For example, if unrealized capital gains are not taxed and dividend income carries a tax credit, a high-tax-paying investor would favor capital gains over income, while a low-tax-paying investor might prefer dividend income.

It is usual for an *active* manager (also known as a stock picker) to charge higher fees than a *passive* manager, who follows the index. In part, this reflects the extra cost associated with research, but the main reason for the higher fees is the active manager's expectation of beating the market.[12]

If the active manager beats the passive manager by more than the fee differential, this may be thought to validate the higher fee. However, active management introduces additional risk (at least relative to the benchmark), which requires a higher return. Also, the active manager could outperform on a pre-tax basis but underperform on a post-tax basis.

14.6.7 The impact of negative returns

As we have discussed, investment managers are given performance targets and benchmarks. They will measure their success in terms of performance against those targets and in terms of performance against similar funds.

Unfortunately, investors do not always view the delivered returns in the same way, especially when they are negative. Sometimes, this means that investors have not been properly educated in the nature of investment risk and the implications of their choices. Managers delivering negative returns face communication challenges and the possible outflow of funds, even when they have performed very well against the benchmark and their peers.

Some investment strategies are not expected to generate negative returns, usually because they employ a high proportion of cash. However, the pressure to outperform can lead to the development of "Enhanced Cash" funds, where additional risk is introduced. If this additional risk is not properly understood and managed, returns can go negative, sometimes catastrophically so. It is particularly sad to see massive losses accruing to investors who sought a "safe" 1% additional return by investing in such funds.

14.7 Practical implications for actuaries

Much of actuarial work focuses on pricing products and valuing liabilities. This work involves projecting and discounting cash flows, so there is a clear implicit assumption of a supporting asset portfolio generating returns.

The supporting assets cannot be taken for granted. If the assets are not managed properly, the product price or valuation liability is not valid. Indeed, asset problems are probably as big a cause of corporate failures as liability problems.

A good actuary does not need the stock-picking skills of an investment manager, but it is important to understand how the assets on your company's balance sheet affect its ability to meet its liabilities and generate the profits that will keep it in business (and paying your wages).

14.8 Key learning points

In this chapter, we have considered assets and their interaction with liabilities.

---

[12] While the *efficient market hypothesis* suggests that managers cannot expect to beat the market other than by chance, there are many claims that managers with rigorous approaches to stock selection have demonstrated an ability to outperform.

- Assets are the "other half" of the balance sheet.

- As well as its investments, a company will hold other assets; these may be quite significant in terms of the company's financial position, so they should not be ignored.

- Like liabilities, various approaches are used in valuing assets; these include market value, amortized cost and mark-to-model. The apparent financial position of a company can be significantly affected by this choice.

- For convenience, investment assets may be categorized as physical assets, equities, debt, hybrids, securitized assets or derivatives but there is no limit to the range of assets that could be constructed.

- Assets carry valuation risks, which can be broadly attributed to changes in expected cash flows (including defaults) or in discount rates. The likely impact is different for different assets.

- When considering the interaction of assets and liabilities, risk comes from the differences in cash flows. There is no risk of real differences arising if the asset cash flows are identical to the liability cash flows in all circumstances. However, even though the differences are not "real," constraints in the way assets or liabilities are measured can cause even identically matched cash flows to give rise to different values and this is another source of risk.

- Differences arise because it is not practical (or even possible) to match the liabilities or because a deliberate decision is taken to mismatch in the quest for profit.

- There are several ways to manage the asset-liability risks.

- Other constraints, including legislation and regulation, affect the management of assets.

CD Items

Accountants Super 2009, Product Disclosure Statement (January 12) and Supplementary PDS (July 1).

Ashe, F. 2010, *Investments*, based on Chapter 12 of *Understanding Actuarial Management*, 1st Edition, 2003, Institute of Actuaries of Australia.

Perpetual 2009, Product Disclosure Statement Part 2, October 2.

Suncorp 2009, WealthSmart™ Member Booklet and Product Disclosure Statement, April 17.

Chapter 14 ALM Spreadsheet

Chapter 14 Exercise Solutions

References (other than CD Items)

Federal Reserve Board interest rate data at http://www.federalreserve.gov/datadownload/Choose.aspx?rel=H.15, accessed on December 17, 2009.

International Accounting Standards Board (IASB) 2001, *Framework for the Preparation of Financial Statements*.

International Accounting Standards Board (IASB) 2009, *IAS 36 Impairment of Assets*.

Kocherlakota, R., Rosenbloom, E.S. & Shiu, E.S.W. 1988, Algorithms for Cash Flow Matching, *Transactions of Society of Actuaries*, Vol 40 Pt 1.

Martin, G. C. & Tsui, D. 1999, Fair Value Liability Valuations Discount Rates and Accounting Provisions, *Australian Actuarial Journal*, Vol 5, 3.

Redington, F.M. 1952, Review of the Principles of Life Office Valuations, *Journal of the Institute of Actuaries*, Vol 78 Part (iii).

Fred's Coffee Shop – Solvency

Fred has been in business for a while and friends often ask "How is the coffee shop doing?" Fred usually answers "Fine, thank you" without really thinking about it. But sometimes he does think about it. During a slow sales week, he might consider selling the shop and returning to his actuarial career. During a period of robust sales he may think of expanding his business. Any bank that he approaches for a loan will be interested in how his business is performing.

One measure of success is the profit the shop is making. Measuring profit is the subject of Chapter 16. Another measure of success is the degree of solvency. Solvency is defined in Chapter 15 as an organization's having an acceptable probability of meeting its obligations. The definition of "acceptable" can vary by industry and by the viewpoint of the person or agency determining solvency. Similarly, the methods for determining the probability can vary. Determining solvency is likely to be as challenging for Fred as it is for a financial services company.

There are three kinds of solvency. The first is *cash flow solvency*. Fred's shop is solvent in this regard as long as he has sufficient cash to pay his bills as they fall due. The second is *discontinuance* solvency and relates to Fred's thoughts about leaving the business. If Fred were to close down the shop would there be any money left after all the assets were sold and all obligations paid?

When Fred approaches a bank for a loan, the banker is more likely to be interested in the third view of solvency: *going-concern solvency*. If the shop stays open and follows its business plan, will it continue to be able to meet its obligations?

Meeting one type of solvency does not imply meeting either of the other two types. Shortly after opening the shop, it is likely to be insolvent were it to close. There is a lot of debt and few sales as the coffee-drinking public is not yet aware that Fred's is the place to go. However, as a going concern, the trends for increased future sales may all look good.

The reverse may also be true. If there is a downward trend in the demand for coffee drinks or the neighborhood is declining, the future for Fred's shop may look bleak but he may be able to close up now and walk away with some cash.

Conversely, Fred's long-term outlook may be good and his assets may exceed his liabilities, but he could still be in trouble. If most of his assets are in furniture and equipment, they cannot readily be turned into cash to meet payroll during a slow sales week.

One advantage Fred has over a financial services company is that there are few entities monitoring his solvency. Insurance companies and banks are continually scrutinized by regulators, stockholders and rating agencies, all of which are concerned about the firm's present and its future.

Chapter 15: Solvency
by Shauna Ferris

15.1   Introduction

An enterprise is solvent if there is an acceptable probability that it will meet its obligations.

Many people are interested in the solvency of an enterprise, including:

- customers and potential customers, particularly where the customer pays in advance or requires after-sales service;
- creditors, such as trade suppliers, landlords, the taxation authority;
- investors and potential investors, in both shares (stocks) and debt securities;
- directors, employees, agents and brokers;
- competitors, who may suffer from any general loss of confidence in their industry; and
- government and regulators.

The different parties may have different views about what is an "acceptable" level of probability of meeting obligations.

15.1.1   Deciding on the acceptable level of solvency

At the very least, a company must meet the legal minimum standards for solvency.

In many countries, companies are subject to corporate laws that forbid transacting business while insolvent. Most financial institutions are also subject to additional requirements that are suitable for their own particular industry, which are known as *statutory solvency requirements* (including *minimum capital requirements*) or *regulatory solvency requirements*. The background to such regulatory requirements is explained in Chapter 7.

The insolvency of financial institutions can be disastrous for their customers: depositors in banks, policyholders in insurance companies, beneficiaries of retirement plans. Third party claimants under insurance policies are also exposed to potential losses. And, as the events of 2007-09 have shown, widespread financial failures can affect the global economy. Given the severe consequences of such failures, there may be a temptation for regulators to aim for very high standards of solvency. Indeed, after a major collapse, there is normally a demand for stronger regulation.

However, it is important to realize that solvency comes at a price. It would be possible to create a very strict regulatory system where there is very little risk of insolvency – and historically, some countries have been quite successful in preventing failures. All you need is regulation that prevents the financial institutions from taking risks. This will however tend to mean higher prices, less innovation in products and the shifting of risks to consumers.

Exercise 15.1

Suppose that you were given the task of designing a regulatory system that would completely eliminate the possibility of an insurance company insolvency.

(a)   What restrictions would you impose?

(b)   What might be the consequences of each of these restrictions?

When the economy is in a recession, strict regulations may even have a counterproductive effect on the overall economy, by restricting the provision of financial services that are necessary for economic growth. Recognizing this problem, regulators may actually relax solvency standards temporarily in times of crisis. This is discussed further in 15.11.1 below.

Hence the regulators must find a balance: aiming to protect the security of consumers without impeding the efficiency of financial markets.

Directors of financial institutions will be mindful of the negative consequences of falling below the statutory solvency requirements. They will manage the business in a way that ensures that the company has a high probability of meeting the statutory minimums at all times – and this usually means that it is desirable to maintain a buffer of additional capital over and above the minimum.

In the case of insurance companies, their ability to sell products to the consumer is affected by the claims-paying ability or solvency rating assigned to the insurance company by rating agencies. (The CD contains a case study of General American, a life insurer that suffered the consequences of a rating downgrade.) When rating agencies are rating insurance companies, they consider the operations of the insurance companies, the risk management processes in place and the capital levels of the companies. In order to maintain a high rating, it may be necessary for an insurer to maintain capital reserves that are much higher than the minimum capital levels that are set by regulators.

15.1.2 Solvency management and capital

The need for capital was discussed in Chapter 11. Solvency is often assessed by looking at how much capital is available to absorb risks. However, it must be emphasized that no amount of capital is sufficient to ensure solvency under all eventualities, if an institution does not manage its risks appropriately. It is easy to lose a large amount of money in a very short time, if risk management controls are not effective.

Example 15.1

Think about these questions, make a guess, then check the answers at the end of the chapter.

- How long did it take for Nick Leeson to send Barings Bank into insolvency by unauthorized derivatives trading?

- How long did it take for Société Générale to lose 7 billion euros, as a result of unauthorized derivatives trading?

- How long did it take the once highly profitable Financial Products operation of AIG to drive the giant insurance company to require a US$150 billion bailout from the US government?

So, to assess solvency, as well as knowing the amounts of the assets and liabilities, we must have an adequate understanding of the nature of the assets, the nature of the liabilities, the relationship between the assets and the liabilities, and the risk management procedures in place.

The Bank for International Settlements (which sets international standards for banking regulation) has adopted a three-pillar approach to solvency regulation (BCBS, 1999):

- Pillar 1 – Capital. The financial institution must maintain adequate capital.

- Pillar 2 – Risk management. The financial institution must comply with corporate governance standards and implement effective risk management policies.

- Pillar 3 – Market discipline. The financial institution must provide adequate disclosure, so that the market can impose discipline on any company that fails to maintain adequate levels of solvency.

A similar framework has been adopted in many countries, in relation to the regulation of banks, insurers and other financial institutions.

15.1.3 Three views of solvency

According to the International Association of Insurance Supervisors (2002), "An insurance company is solvent if it is able to fulfill its obligations under all contracts under all reasonably foreseeable circumstances."

In this chapter, we examine three different sets of circumstances:

- *Cash flow solvency* (or *liquidity*): Will the company be able to pay its debts as and when they fall due?

- *Discontinuance solvency*: If the company ceased doing business today, would the company be able to cover its obligations?

- *Going-concern solvency*: If the company remains in business, following a specified business plan, will it continue to be able to meet its liabilities in the future?

Cash flow solvency is discussed in Section 15.2. Discontinuance solvency and going-concern solvency are discussed in Sections 15.3 onwards.

15.2 Cash flow solvency (or liquidity)

15.2.1 Liquidity risk in normal conditions

Cash flow management should be a normal part of daily operations. This requires careful planning in order to maximize profits. If you underestimate the amount of cash you will need, then you might have to borrow money and hence incur extra interest costs. But if you maintain excess liquidity, this will also affect profits. Liquid assets usually provide lower returns than less liquid assets.

A *liquidity ratio* can be used to monitor a financial institution's liquidity. This is calculated as the market value of liquid assets divided by the total of the liabilities falling due within a specified time frame. The management of the company should set an acceptable target range for this liquidity ratio, depending on the nature of the assets and liabilities. An unexplained low ratio, or deterioration in the liquidity ratio, provides a warning signal to regulators, rating agencies and consumers.

A cash flow model can be used to project expected cash flows under normal circumstances. To manage liquidity risks, it is necessary to identify the factors that might cause fluctuations in the cash flows, and to build these factors into the model. The model will produce current and projected future liquidity ratios under various scenarios. Cash flow testing is an essential risk management tool and is indeed a legal requirement for insurers in some countries.

Exercise 15.2   Identification of liquidity risks

Identify all the sources of cash flows into and out of a non-life insurance company over a year. Suggest factors that might influence each of these cash flows. For example, premium renewals might be affected by a marketing campaign, a change in the premium rates of a competitor, a credit rating downgrade, seasonal factors, or economic conditions.

Repeat this exercise with an employer-sponsored retirement plan.

Statistical analysis of historical cash flow data may be used to determine the sensitivity of the cash flow to various external events. The cash flow tests may also incorporate stochastic models of economic variables that may affect future cash flows (such as interest rates, inflation, and so on). This allows analysis of a wide range of plausible scenarios.

15.2.2   Liquidity risk in a crisis

Under normal conditions, an institution that is financially sound, and that has a good reputation, is unlikely to suffer prolonged liquidity problems. If there is an unexpected need for liquidity, such a financial institution would normally be able to borrow, using its good-quality assets as collateral. This could be expensive, but it may be less expensive than liquidating illiquid assets.

Hence, liquidity risk is more likely to be a problem for a company that is already in a weakened financial state. For financial institutions, fears about insolvency will lead to a net outflow of funds. Customers will withdraw their deposits from weak banks; policyholders will not renew their policies with a weak insurer, but will switch to another insurer; investors will withdraw savings from fund managers that have suffered investment losses. The normal sources of additional liquidity – eg borrowing – may not be available. Thus solvency fears can create liquidity problems.

And in a vicious cycle, liquidity problems can also create solvency problems:

*   A financial institution that needs to borrow money quickly may incur high interest costs. For example, when insurance giant AIG ran into liquidity problems in 2008, it was forced to borrow money from the Federal Reserve Bank at very high interest rates.

*   Money might be raised by selling assets – but a forced seller of illiquid assets may receive a price that is well below the normal market value. "Case Study of a Liquidity Crisis: General American" on the CD describes an example of this situation.

Any major dislocation in financial markets may also create abnormal liquidity problems. A sharp fall in asset values (such as a stock market crash or a fall in housing prices) will create concerns about the solvency of any financial institutions that have invested in such assets, and may lead to a rush to withdraw funds. A severe economic downturn may cause people to withdraw savings deposits, cancel insurance policies and fall behind on mortgage payments.

Liquidity problems are contagious. If one financial institution collapses, this can create a widespread loss of confidence. Any financial institution that has close links to the failed institution, or that is known to follow a similar business model, is more likely to suffer a run, even if these concerns are not justified. Furthermore, when financially sound banks see that other banks are suffering liquidity problems, they will take precautions to protect themselves by increasing their own liquid assets and refusing to lend money to other financial institutions. Typically, interbank lending rates increase, and the "flight to liquidity" depresses the value of non-liquid assets. In the extreme, certain types of assets may become virtually unsaleable. During 2007-08, the financial markets suffered through such a global credit crunch, which adversely affected many banks and other financial institutions – even ones that appeared to have satisfactory levels of capital and liquidity before the crisis.

Property-casualty insurance companies are likely to suffer liquidity problems when catastrophes occur, causing a spike in claim outflows. Reinsurers usually bear a substantial proportion of these losses and provide liquidity support for the insurer. So, when a reinsurer collapses there is a ripple effect throughout the insurance industry. Cash flow and solvency models should incorporate the risk that a reinsurer might fail to cover its obligations to the insurer.

When there are systemic liquidity problems, the government may alleviate the problem by providing extra liquidity for financial institutions. Typically, this is done via the central banks (such as the Federal Reserve Bank in the US), eg by lending money to banks against the security provided by the banks' holdings of non-liquid assets.

During the credit crunch in 2007-08, when many financial institutions were suffering from liquidity problems, many central banks around the world responded by expanding their lending programs: lending more money than normal, at lower interest rates, for longer terms, with more flexible collateral requirements and to a wider range of financial institutions.

15.2.3 Managing liquidity risks

The control cycle approach should be used for managing liquidity risks. Liquidity should be taken into account at every stage of the business process, from product design to capital management.

Product design

Liquidity risk increases if you create products with built-in liquidity options. For example, a life insurance company creates liquidity options if it offers guaranteed surrender values or policy loans at a fixed rate of interest.[1] For investment products (such as accumulation-type retirement savings), liquidity options arise if customers have the right to withdraw or transfer their funds at short notice. A derivatives trader bears liquidity risks if it is required to pay margin calls whenever the value of the underlying asset moves the wrong way.[2] A reinsurer faces liquidity risks if a reinsurance contract is cancellable whenever the reinsurer's credit rating is downgraded.

In some cases, liquidity risks can be alleviated by penalties for early withdrawal, and/or by giving the financial institution the option to defer payment, say for three or six months.

---

[1] High guaranteed surrender values caused significant liquidity problems for life insurers during the Great Depression in the 1930s. Loans on policies at guaranteed low interest rates caused problems during the 1970s, when interest rates on alternative investments were high, since policyholders had an incentive to borrow on their policies at low rates in order to invest at much higher rates.

[2] AIG ran into severe liquidity problems in 2008, when it was forced to pay billions of dollars on margin calls on credit default swaps it had written.

However, a deferral of this nature may be considered a sign of solvency or liquidity problems and may lead to increased requests for withdrawals.

Marketing

Liquidity risks in the product design will be exacerbated if the liquidity option is emphasized as a desirable feature of the product during the sales process. For example, if a life insurance company sells policies by offering higher guaranteed surrender values than the competition, then it will attract customers who are likely to take advantage of this feature.

Pricing

The price of the product should reflect the costs of providing any liquidity option. The company might need to hold a higher proportion of liquid assets, which generally provide lower returns; the company might need to pay a fee to maintain a line of credit; or the company might suffer losses due to forced sales of illiquid assets to meet unexpected cash outflows.

Risk management

As with other areas of risk, it is important to understand the nature of the risks and to be well diversified.

For example, the nature of the customers will affect liquidity risk. Large institutional customers are more likely to become aware of any perceived solvency problem, and to react quickly by withdrawing their investments or switching their insurance arrangements. Also, the loss of just a few large customers can cause liquidity problems. On the other hand, retail customers are more "sticky" as they are less likely to know about any problems (at least until it gets onto the TV news). Guarantees that compensate customers in the event of insolvency will also affect behavior in a crisis. For example, the Federal Deposit Insurance Corporation guarantees US bank deposits up to $250,000. Any customer with a deposit that is covered by this guarantee has less incentive to make a panic withdrawal. Customers with deposits above this limit are more likely to withdraw their savings if there is any doubt about the solvency of the bank.

The more diversified the customer base, the lower the risk. Liquidity risks are increased if all your customers are likely to act in the same way at the same time. For example, suppose that one brokerage or agency is responsible for a significant proportion of your sales – how would your business be affected if that broker loses confidence in your company? Clearly, it is prudent to diversify the sources of business.

Investments

A financial institution should ensure that it maintains an appropriate level of liquid assets, sufficient to cover cash outflows in the ordinary course of business, with a margin for safety. Of course, liquid assets generally provide a lower return, so judgment and modeling is required in determining the optimum level of liquidity.

Additionally, the liquidity of the overall portfolio should be assessed: for each asset, how much would be lost at a given time by selling on short notice? How much could be borrowed by pledging the assets as collateral? Is the holding of any particular asset so large that a forced sale would depress the market? Note that the liquidity of certain asset classes can change rapidly during an economic crisis. Prior to 2007, banks often assumed that they would be able to raise cash whenever necessary by securitizing their mortgages and credit card receivables, but in the aftermath of the subprime debt crisis, the market for these assets became very illiquid.

Asset-Liability mismatch

Borrowing short-term and lending long-term creates liquidity risks. Of course, maturity transformation is a key role for banks and other depository institutions: accepting asset-liability mismatch risks is simply part of their business. However the bank should have policies that set limits on the size of the mismatches.

Both assets and liabilities should be *laddered*, ie it is better to have a series of regular, small cash flows instead of infrequent large cash flows. For example, suppose that your company has issued bonds for X billion dollars. It would be better to spread the maturity dates for the bonds over several years, to avoid having to meet a disproportionately large refinancing requirement at any time. It could be disastrous being forced to raise a large sum at an inconvenient time, eg just after a rating downgrade.

Contingency plans

Each financial institution should have plans for accessing additional liquidity in an emergency, for example by arranging reliable lines of credit that can be drawn down at short notice if needed. In some countries, there are industry arrangements so that banks and other financial institutions will provide each other with support under specified circumstances.

Solvency

As noted above, a loss of confidence may trigger a liquidity crisis, so any company that has solvency problems has a higher liquidity risk. Since the credit rating agencies play a major role in informing the public of financial security, it is important to maintain a close relationship with the major agencies, and to heed their concerns. If there is a problem, the management should promptly explain the measures that have been taken to rectify the situation.

> ### Exercise 15.3
> Read the case study about General American (GA) on the CD. What factors contributed to the problems at GA?

15.3 Discontinuance solvency and going-concern solvency: general approach

15.3.1 Introduction

Cash flow solvency, as discussed in 15.2 above, is essential. But a company that is currently solvent in the short term, ie on a cash flow basis, may not be able to meet its obligations in the long term. A company that is in a very poor financial position may be able to keep meeting its obligations for a very long time, even as the situation is deteriorating. For example, consider a motor vehicle insurance company that is charging inadequate premiums. The low premiums will ensure a steady stream of new business; the new business premiums will be sufficient to cover the claims on existing business. The cash flow position may be fine for many years, as long as the company keeps growing. But as soon as growth stops, the company collapses.

Unfortunately, history is filled with numerous examples of such companies. These financial disasters motivated legislators to introduce more stringent solvency standards. What the regulators wanted to know was: If the institution ceased operations today, would the assets be sufficient to cover the liabilities? If the company remained in business, following a specified business plan, would it continue to be able to meet its liabilities in the future? In other words, the regulators were interested in discontinuance solvency and going-concern solvency.

Because of the interest of regulators in ensuring solvency, many of the issues for consideration will be addressed in regulatory solvency standards, and it is convenient to take the regulations as a starting point for our discussion. However, even if there are no regulatory standards, the same issues should be taken into account by any actuary advising a financial institution.

15.3.2   Alternative forms of discontinuance

To help you understand the discussion of discontinuance solvency, note that there are three possible courses of action when an entity ceases operations:

*   *Winding up:* The assets are sold and the proceeds are distributed among the creditors. This approach may cause problems for customers who have bought financial products, since there is no continuity of services. For example, a person in poor health may have difficulty finding replacement life insurance or health cover at a reasonable cost (or at all). The winding up process usually takes some time, and delays and uncertainty are likely to cause financial hardship for some customers.

*   *Run off:* The institution stops writing new business or renewing existing contracts, but continues to run off its existing liabilities in an orderly manner. This allows the assets to be sold off over time, in an orderly fashion, which is likely to produce better outcomes than an immediate forced sale. However, as the portfolio dwindles over time, and expense ratios increase, it may be more cost effective to transfer the business.

*   *Transfer of business:* Another stronger institution takes over the liabilities, along with sufficient assets to cover them. From a customer's perspective, this is usually the best option, since it provides continuity of cover and service. Therefore regulators will often do what they can to arrange a takeover by a stronger company, and may even provide financial support to facilitate this.

15.3.3   Measuring discontinuance solvency

To assess the discontinuance solvency of a financial institution, one would:

(a) determine the value of assets likely to be available to pay off the liabilities in a discontinuance situation;

(b) determine the value of liabilities in a discontinuance situation;

(c)   because (a) and (b) involve uncertainty, determine the minimum amount of additional capital that should be set aside to absorb losses if the assets turn out to be smaller or the liabilities turn out to be higher than expected; and

(d)   considering (a) and (b), assess the amount and quality of the capital that would be available to meet obligations. This was defined as *eligible capital* in Chapter 11; different terminology may be used in different countries.

Chapter 12 and Chapter 14 have described some methods used to value assets and liabilities. In 15.4 and 15.5 below we look at the specific issues that arise when the valuation is done for the purpose of measuring solvency. In the US, the principles for assessing solvency are set out in standards known as Statutory Accounting Principles (SAP). These are significantly different from the standards used for assessing profitability and general financial reporting, which are based on Generally Accepted Accounting Principles (GAAP). Regulatory authorities in other countries may also specify special principles for solvency valuations.

In 15.6 to 15.8 we discuss the determination of capital requirements, and in 15.9 we look at assessing the amount and quality of the capital.

The ratio of the amount of eligible capital available divided by the minimum capital requirement, ie

$$(d) / (c)$$

where (d) and (c) are the items in the list above, is often referred to as the *solvency ratio*. This is one measure of the ability of the company to meet its obligations.

Regulators and rating agencies will assess the financial strength of a financial institution by considering (among other things) measures such as liquidity ratios and solvency ratios, and trends in these measures over time.

A measure of solvency such as the solvency ratio described above is a point estimate. It gives a snapshot picture at a single point in time, although, as mentioned, the trend in the measure over time provides extra information. Although it is a measure at a point in time, the nature of the assets and, particularly, the liabilities for a financial institution require us to make assumptions about the future. For example, valuing the liabilities for a portfolio of lifetime annuities in a run-off situation requires a projection of mortality, expenses and investment returns for many years into the future.

15.3.4   Measuring going-concern solvency

When we measure the solvency of a financial institution on a discontinuance basis, we are examining its ability to meet its *existing* obligations, on the assumption that it will be winding up or going into run-off. We should also consider the solvency position on a *going-concern* basis, over a period of some years into the future, on the assumption that the institution will continue to accept new business.

The amount of capital required for an institution that continues in business is likely to be higher than for one that is in run-off, for two reasons. First, an institution that is writing new business is accepting more risk (including the risk of mis-pricing of new business), and incurring more expenses, even if the new business is expected to be profitable in the long term. Secondly, when measuring going-concern solvency, we are looking at solvency over a longer time frame. Hence there is an "expanding funnel of doubt," ie the longer the time frame, the greater the uncertainty about the future experience.

In many cases, going-concern solvency is assessed using projections of future experience, allowing for the impact of new business and allowing for a range of adverse scenarios. Actuaries will often be involved in making these projections. This is discussed in more detail in Section 15.10.7 below.

As noted in 15.1.2 above, going-concern solvency will also be addressed by risk management procedures and disclosure requirements. We return to this in 15.10 below.

In the following sections, we look at practical issues in the calculation for solvency purposes of (a) assets, (b) liabilities, (c) capital requirements and (d) eligible capital. When we discuss the valuation of assets and liabilities, we will begin by discussing the value in a discontinuance situation. This is because, as we noted, for financial institutions the measurement of discontinuance solvency is vital in itself, and in addition usually provides the starting point for the measurement of going-concern solvency.

15.4 Valuation of assets for solvency purposes

The value of the assets that appears in the company's accounts for general reporting purposes will usually need adjustment to arrive at the value for solvency purposes.

First, in some cases, the value of assets may be reported based on cost or using a discounted cash flow valuation method, rather than at market value. Although there has been a move to fair value accounting, which is based on market values, this has not been adopted in all countries for all types of financial institution and/or for all types of asset. However, if the assets have to be sold immediately, as may be the case in a discontinuance situation, then the market value of assets is an obvious starting point.

Secondly, the market value of assets in a discontinuance situation may well be less than the market value of assets under normal circumstances. In some cases, when assessing solvency, regulators will simply require the value of certain assets to be excluded – these may be denoted as *inadmissible* or *non-admitted* assets. In some cases, regulators will impose various restrictions on the inclusion of certain assets. Judgment may be required in order to assess the probable realizable value of certain assets in a winding up situation.

The following assets may be of little or no value in the event of winding up:

- intangibles, such as goodwill;

- assets whose value depends on the continued existence of the company, such as future income tax benefits, deferred acquisition costs and specialized computer software; and

- assets that may be difficult to collect if the company becomes insolvent, such as unsecured loans to directors, loans to employees and premiums outstanding from brokers.

Assets will usually not be admitted if there are any encumbrances, eg if the assets have been mortgaged and hence are not available to meet other liabilities.

Certain assets may be excluded to prevent double-counting. Suppose Insurer A owns Insurer B, and according to its accounts, Insurer B has equity capital of $10 million. For financial reporting purposes, we would consider that Insurer A owns an asset worth $10 million. But Insurer B might need $8 million for its own solvency requirements, to provide protection for its own policyholders. This sum cannot be used to meet solvency requirements for both companies, so Insurer A can only count $2 million of Insurer B's capital toward its own solvency requirements. The same would apply if the insurer owned any other type of company that had regulatory capital requirements.

Some regulatory solvency standards also exclude certain assets that are considered to be too risky. This often covers the situation of excessive exposure to a single counterparty, eg the rules might say that any investment in a single entity will only be admitted up to a value of x percent of total assets and any excess above this amount is inadmissible. Such a regulation encourages institutions to diversify their investments, and hence reduces risk.

The reliability of asset valuations is an issue. When a company is facing financial difficulties, there is always a temptation for the management to be overly optimistic in the assessment of asset values. Problems can arise from manipulation of market values, misleading transactions between affiliated companies and plain fraud. For a discussion of these and other contributing factors to insolvency, see "Empirical Studies of Common Factors in Insolvency" on the CD.

Asset values should be verified by an external auditor. It is essential that the auditor be:

- a person of integrity;

- experienced in the intricacies of the business under review;

- independent; and

- willing to question the company about doubtful valuations or unusual accounting practices.

The value of certain assets may be difficult to determine. For example, expert opinion may be required to assess the value of property, over-the-counter derivatives, private placements of debt and/or private equity holdings. Anyone who is responsible for the valuation of either assets or liabilities must meet the standards of integrity, independence and expertise.

The solvency legislation should provide sufficient powers for the auditor to draw any problems to the attention of the directors and, if necessary, the regulators. These are commonly known as *whistle-blower* rules.

In any review of the financial condition of a financial institution, it is sensible for the actuary to work closely with the auditor, to identify and discuss any issues involving asset valuations.

15.5 Valuation of liabilities for solvency purposes

As with the valuation of assets, we need to decide on the method of valuation and then make adjustments to allow for the impact of discontinuance.

15.5.1 Methods for the valuation of liabilities

Suppose that the regulator wishes to ensure full protection for the customers of a failed financial institution. For most policyholders of an insurance company, the best outcome would be a transfer of their policies to another insurer that is financially sound. In general, another insurer will only be willing to take over the liabilities if it also receives a transfer of assets equal to the fair value of the liabilities (as discussed in Chapter 12). Similarly, for pension funds, the interests of fund members would be protected if there is enough money available to buy an equivalent annuity from a financially sound life insurance company. This amount is sometimes called the *buy-out value*.

This leads to the conclusion that a valuation of liabilities for solvency purposes should be the fair value. This is higher than the central estimate (the expected value of the liabilities) because it allows for a reward for taking on the risks of the portfolio. The problem is that, for insurers, the fair value of liabilities is very difficult to determine. Fair values are relatively easy to determine for assets that are standardized, and traded in a liquid market where buy/sell prices are listed on an exchange every day (eg shares or money market securities). But insurance portfolios are not standardized; each contains a unique mixture of risks. And insurance portfolios are not commonly bought and sold – ie there is no liquid market for insurance liabilities – so there is little information available to estimate the "market value" of the liabilities.

The accounting profession and actuarial profession are both working on the development of standard methods for estimating fair value for insurance risks, but this is a very difficult issue and there is no consensus. Students who are interested in a more detailed comparison of these approaches may wish to refer to IAA (2009).

For solvency purposes, insurance and pension fund liabilities are often valued using one or a combination of the following methods:

* the *statutory valuation basis*;

* the *margin for adverse deviation method*; and

* the *probability of sufficiency approach*, also known as the *quantile method*.

We discuss each of these below.

15.5.1.1 The statutory valuation basis

In some countries, regulatory solvency standards require liabilities to be valued as the present value of expected future cash flows, calculated using methods and assumptions that are specified by the regulatory authorities. This method is commonly applied to life insurance companies, and may also be applied to retirement plans when determining minimum funding requirements. The regulations will set out the assumptions for mortality rates, interest rates (which may be determined by reference to an index such as AAA-rated corporate bond yields), inflation rates and expense rates.

The assumptions are deliberately chosen to be conservative, so that the value of liabilities includes an implicit risk margin. These assumptions should be updated regularly to reflect changes in the environment and the development of new products. Otherwise the standards may inadvertently become too strict or too weak.

The statutory valuation basis is objective, and hence difficult to manipulate, but it is not very sensitive to the differences between different companies, ie it does not reflect relative risk. For example, two life insurers might have quite different mortality experience (reflecting differences in product design, marketing methods, underwriting standards, etc), but both are required to use the same mortality tables for assessing solvency.

In non-life insurance there is much greater diversity of risks, so it is difficult to set standardized assumptions for the valuation of liabilities – judgment is required. Hence, the starting point for the valuation may be the actuary's best estimate of the future costs of outstanding claims (determined using recognized methods and models, based on an analysis of past experience). In some countries, the undiscounted value of these claim costs is used for the purpose of assessing solvency. This has an implicit margin equal to the difference between the present value of the expected claims cost and the undiscounted value. The size of the risk margin depends on the expected time until payment and the level of investment earnings. This is a rather ad hoc method of determining risk margins, which has been criticized for overstating the reserves required for long-tail claims in times of high interest rates.

15.5.1.2 The margin for adverse deviation method

The margin for adverse deviation (MAD) method allows for differences in the risks underlying each company's liabilities. Under the MAD method, the actuary works out a best estimate assumption for each element of the valuation basis, then adds a risk margin to each assumption, where the risk margin reflects the level of uncertainty in the estimate.

For example, suppose that the actuary is setting the mortality assumption for a life insurance portfolio. The best estimate might be determined after analyzing past experience. Then the actuary would consider the factors that might affect the reliability of that estimate for predicting the future, for example:

- the size of the portfolio (number of policies) and/or the number of death claims per annum;

- the number of years of past experience, and the stability of the experience over time;

- the mix of clients, including any changes that might arise from changes in marketing;

- the type of product, and any changes in the product design;

- the underwriting policy, including any changes in underwriting policy and/or practices; and

- the level of lapses and surrenders, which might create a deterioration in experience if there is selective withdrawal by healthy lives.

In general, when determining the appropriate margin for any assumption for any product, the actuary should consider:

- the credibility of past data (which determines parameter uncertainty in the model);

- the amount of stochastic variation in experience;

- the sensitivity of the outcomes to any changes in assumptions; and

- any changes in any aspect of the environment that would suggest that the past experience will not be a reliable guide to the future.

Exercise 15.4

Suppose that you are valuing the liabilities of a non-life insurer. Your best estimate of the liability is based on case estimates provided by the insurer's claims department. What factors would you consider when deciding on the margin for adverse deviation for this estimate? For guidance, see "Memorandum on Provision for Adverse Deviation for Property and Casualty Insurers" on the CD.

Of course this requires a thorough knowledge of all aspects of the business. Therefore the MAD method places great reliance on the judgment of the actuary. The MAD method has sometimes been criticized because a margin is added to *each* assumption. The combined effect arising from the interaction of all these margins may be more than necessary.

15.5.1.3   The probability of sufficiency approach

The probability of sufficiency (POS) approach is based on modeling the distribution of all possible outcomes for claims costs. The actuary aims to determine the amount of reserves that will provide an x percent probability of covering the claims, where the target value of x is determined by the regulator and/or by the board of directors of the insurer.

You may recognize that the POS approach is the same basic idea as Value at Risk (VaR), which was discussed in Chapter 6. VaR has been used for some time in the banking industry as a way to measure risk in trading portfolios. However the problems of implementing the approach are very different for insurance liabilities.

The POS approach was introduced in 2001 for non-life insurance liabilities in Australia. Prior to 2001, Australian actuaries would generally work out the present value of expected claims costs, ie a central estimate. The board of directors would then add a prudential margin to this central estimate, and this would be the value of liabilities reported in the financial statements, and used as the basis for measurements of solvency. However, this method was flawed, because there was no consistency in the determination of the size of the prudential margin. Financially weak companies (such as HIH, which had a large share of the Australian market and failed spectacularly in 2001) would have little or no prudential margin; other companies would vary the prudential margin from year to year in order to smooth reported profits, or to minimize tax liabilities.

In 2001 the Australian legislation was changed, to improve consistency in the determination of the prudential margin (which the legislation now calls a risk margin). The sum of the central estimate plus the risk margin must provide at least a 75 percent probability of sufficiency. Unfortunately, when the new regulations were introduced, there was no consensus within the actuarial profession on the best method of estimating the 75 percent probability of sufficiency. The actuarial profession has been hard at work to meet this challenge, and has made some progress in developing new statistical techniques, which are beyond the scope of this chapter.

The POS method is based on quantiles of the distribution of outcomes, which simply tells you the probability that your reserves will be insufficient to pay claims. This does not measure the amount of the potential shortfall. Others have suggested that other measures such as Conditional Tail Expectation (CTE) might be preferable when setting reserves. The CTE measures the expected value of the claim cost, given that the claims fall in the worst x percent of the loss distribution.

As with the MAD method, the risk margin under the POS approach must relate to the inherent uncertainty in the central estimate.

Some methods of valuation combine both the MAD approach and the POS approach. For example, in the US, the American Academy of Actuaries has proposed the adoption of *principle-based reserving*:

- For some products, actuaries would be able to use a "Deterministic Reserve" using *Prudent Best Estimates* (PBEs) for the assumptions. The PBEs are best estimates plus a margin that reflects the uncertainty in the best estimate (ie similar to the MAD approach).

- For products that contain risks that would not be captured by a deterministic approach, such as policyholder options that only become valuable in some scenarios, actuaries would determine a "Stochastic Reserve". The actuary would combine the PBEs for mortality and expense assumptions with stochastic models of interest rates and investment returns, in order to provide a range of different scenarios. The scenarios would be ranked from lowest to highest, and the reserve would be based on the average of the highest 35 percent of the outcomes (ie an estimate of the CTE).

15.5.2 Adjustments to reflect the impact of discontinuance on the liabilities

The value of the liabilities shown in the accounts is generally based on the assumption that the business will be ongoing. In the event of discontinuance, the liabilities may change, and adjustments will be needed. For example:

- In a life insurer, there may be a flood of policy surrenders. Therefore when assessing solvency, it is sensible to compare assets to the total of the surrender values on all policies.

- If an insurer is in run-off, it may suffer from selective cancellation: the good risks cancel their policies and obtain replacement cover elsewhere, while the poor risks remain, pushing up claims costs. The effect of this anti-selection can be cumulative. If the insurer increases premium rates to cover the increased risks, this only exacerbates the problem, as more good risks switch to a lower-cost provider; premiums have to be increased again, more good risks switch, and so on. Health insurers are particularly vulnerable to this spiral effect.

- In a retirement plan, if the employer-sponsor is facing insolvency, and the fund is winding up, it is likely that members will become eligible for enhanced benefits such as more generous early retirement provisions, which will increase the liabilities.

- When a financial institution goes into run-off, there are usually some additional expenses, such as terminations of staff. Expense ratios will increase, as any fixed costs will be spread over a reducing portfolio.

15.5.3 Dealing with discretionary benefits

The valuation process is even more difficult if the liabilities include discretionary benefits. In life insurance, policies that participate in profits receive discretionary amounts, referred to as bonuses in Australia and the UK, and as dividends in North America. In pension funds, benefits may be increased from time to time at the discretion of the trustees, in line with inflation.

Suppose that we are valuing a portfolio of participating life insurance business. The guaranteed benefit under the contract is the sum insured plus declared bonuses; there is often no legal entitlement to future bonuses that have not been declared yet. But many companies use bonus illustrations and sales material that would encourage policyholders to expect a certain level of future bonuses – and the premiums include a bonus loading. Hence, the policyholders develop reasonable expectations of future benefits. Should we allow for these discretionary benefits when assessing solvency?

This is a difficult issue, which is under consideration by various international standards associations. At present, different countries have adopted different approaches, reflecting differences in the types of products sold, the legal framework in each country, and the accounting standards of the country.

15.5.4   How can we be sure that the value of liabilities is correct?

We noted above that companies in trouble may be tempted to overvalue their assets, and there is a similar temptation to understate the value of their liabilities, for example, by using optimistic assumptions. Actuaries may find themselves under pressure to change the assumptions. Professional standards provide guidance for the determination of appropriate assumptions, and actuaries should resist any pressure to deviate from these standards.

The correct valuation of liabilities depends on the accuracy of the data, which may cause problems particularly when the work is done by external actuaries. Insurance insolvencies have sometimes revealed significant deficiencies in this area. For example, in the cases of the two failed insurance companies HIH (Australia) and Independent Insurance (UK), it appears that significant numbers of claims were simply not entered into the computer system. Some non-life insurers have deliberately reduced case estimates on outstanding claims in order to maintain a spurious appearance of solvency.

Exercise 15.5

(a) Do you think that actuaries are often asked to adopt more optimistic valuation assumptions? How should the actuary respond when a client suggests that the assumptions should be changed?

(b) Consult the Code of Conduct/Professional Standards/Standards of Practice for your own actuarial association. What guidance does it offer in relation to the setting of assumptions?

(c) Should an actuary do any checks to verify the completeness and accuracy of the data? What checks could you do?

(d) Actuarial reports normally include a description of the process used to choose the methodology and assumptions. This allows for peer review by another actuary. Some countries have already introduced peer review requirements. Do you think that peer review of liability valuations is necessary/desirable?

15.6   Capital requirements: the risk-based capital approach

15.6.1   Introduction to risk-based capital

By this stage, we have estimated the value of assets and liabilities for solvency purposes. These valuations include some risk margins that reflect our uncertainty about these estimates. But an explicit additional amount of capital is usually required for safety. There are different ways of calculating the required amount of capital.

In the past, many countries used a simple formula to set statutory capital requirements on a fairly arbitrary basis. For example:

- For banks, the regulator might require capital equal to 8 percent of the assets. The loans made to the bank's customers are its main assets, so this capital covered credit risks.

- For non-life insurers, the regulator might require capital equal to x percent of premiums and/or y percent of outstanding claims liabilities.

This approach has the virtue of simplicity, and it was considered suitable when companies generally sold similar products and had similar investment profiles. But as the financial markets developed, and a greater range of products was introduced (on both sides of the balance sheet), the inadequacies of this approach became apparent. The use of such arbitrary formulae ignores the differences in the risks accepted by each company, and hence may overestimate the amount of capital required for some companies, and understate the amount required for other companies.

There has therefore been a trend to develop detailed methods to calculate the minimum amount of capital a financial institution must hold, taking account of the risks faced by that institution. Methods of setting risk-based capital requirements (RBC) in statutory solvency standards were first developed in the banking industry, under the auspices of the Bank for International Settlements (BIS) meeting in the city of Basel in Switzerland. The standards proposed by the BIS (the *Basel Accords*) have been adopted by bank regulators in most developed countries.

The same concept has now been applied to other financial institutions, such as insurers. The International Association of Insurance Supervisors (IAIS) has suggested that capital requirements for insurers should be tailored to reflect the risks accepted by each company. RBC approaches for insurers have been adopted in jurisdictions including Australia, the US, Canada, Japan and Singapore. The European Union's (EU's) Solvency II regime also uses an RBC approach.

15.6.2   Creating a risk-based capital standard

How does a regulator create a risk-based capital standard? The steps in the process are:

- set objectives;
- identify all significant risks;
- decide which risks should be included in calculating the capital requirement;
- work out a measure of exposure to risk;
- ensure that the measures of exposure are objective and reliable;
- quantify the size of potential losses for each unit of exposure; and
- allow for diversification benefits.

We discuss each of these steps below.

Of course, the management of any financial institution will follow similar processes to make their own estimate of the amount of capital that is necessary to reduce the probability of ruin to an acceptable level. This is an essential part of capital management, as described in Chapter 11.

15.6.2.1   Set objectives

The first step in determining capital requirements is to specify the measurable solvency objectives. For example, in the EU's Solvency II system, the aim is to ensure a 99.5 percent probability of solvency over a one-year time frame.

Practical considerations play a role here. If the solvency standards are too strict, then some companies may be forced out of business. When introducing new RBC standards, or changes to parameters under existing standards, the regulator will usually test the effect by asking different companies to calculate their capital requirements under the proposed regime. If the new standard imposes too great an increase in requirements, it may be necessary to revise the standard and/or phase in the new requirements, thus giving companies time to raise new capital or reduce risks.

15.6.2.2   Identify all significant risks

Empirical studies into the failures of financial institutions are helpful in identifying the most significant risk factors. Some findings are summarized in the article "Empirical Studies of Common Factors in Insolvency" on the CD.

For example, for a bank, the most significant risks are credit risk, market risk, liquidity risk and operational risk. Of these, credit risk is by far the most common cause of bank failure.

For a life insurer, the risks may be divided into asset risks, pricing risks, asset-liability mismatch risk and operational risks. Pricing risks would include mortality, morbidity and expenses.

15.6.2.3   Decide which risks should be included in calculating the capital requirement

Risks that are relatively less significant may be excluded in the interests of simplicity.

Some risks may be excluded because they are difficult to quantify. To take banks as an example again, the first Basel Accord, issued in 1988, only covered credit risk, which was considered to be the most significant risk and the easiest to quantify. In 1996, the Accord was extended to include market risk. The second Accord, Basel II, issued in 2004, includes an allowance for operational risk. This has been controversial because it is very difficult to quantify operational risk.

Regulators usually have the right to require additional capital, over and above the amount required by objective application of the standard, in order to allow subjectively for factors that are difficult to quantify and to deal with entities that are unusual, for example those which have large exposures to what is normally a trivial risk. For example, in 2004 the Australian regulator increased the capital requirement for the National Australia Bank after an investigation into a loss of A$360 million from unauthorized derivatives trading revealed serious weaknesses in risk management and corporate culture.

15.6.2.4   Work out a measure of exposure to risk

Suppose that we have identified the main types of risk. How can we measure the exposure to risk?

Some risks can be measured using a formula approach. For example:

- In banking, under Basel I, the system for measuring credit risk was fairly simple. Each asset was classified into a broad risk category and given a weighting, from 0% for government securities to 50% for home loans secured by a mortgage, and 100% for commercial loans. The minimum capital requirement for credit risk was simply 8% of the total risk-weighted assets.

- In non-life insurance, outstanding claim liabilities can be classified by line of business, and each line of business is given its own risk weighting. Short-tailed business such as household insurance might require a margin of say 9%, whereas more risky long-tailed business such as product liability insurance might require a high margin of say 15%.

- In life insurance, the duration of assets and liabilities might be used to estimate asset-liability mismatch risk.

The formula approach can incorporate a stochastic model. For example, in banking, market risk can be measured using a Value-at-Risk approach. Under Basel II standards, stochastic models of interest rates and asset price movements are used to estimate the 99th percentile of the distribution of losses over a 10-day time frame.

A projection model may be used as an alternative to the formula approach for calculating RBC. The cash flows and balance sheet of the institution are projected under different scenarios, and the amount of capital at the start of the projection is varied to find the level required to provide a satisfactory level of solvency throughout the projection. A range of specific scenarios may be tested, and the capital set to achieve solvency in all of the scenarios. Alternatively, a stochastic model may be used to generate a large number of scenarios, and the capital level set so that solvency is maintained in an acceptable percentage of the generated scenarios.

The use of projection models is discussed further in 15.10.7 below.

The measure of exposure must be simple enough to be practical, but sophisticated enough to produce an adequate RBC level. If the RBC standard does not provide a reasonably accurate measure of risk, this may result in financial arbitrage and/or minimum capital requirements that are inadequate to ensure solvency. For example, under Basel I, all home loans secured by a mortgage were given a 50% risk weighting. This category was too broad. A bank that made home loans with low loan-to-value ratios to well-qualified borrowers would have the same minimum capital requirements as one that lent the full value of properties to subprime borrowers. Banks that wanted to make profits by taking on higher risks might switch into subprime lending, without having enough capital to cover potential losses. This business strategy led to the downfall of several banks during the late 1990s (BCBS, 2004).

The Basel II Accord has a much more sophisticated (and complex) system of categorizing loans. For example, under the new rules there are several different categories of home loans, depending on the loan-to-value ratio, level of documentation of the borrower's resources, adequacy of property valuation checks and mortgage insurance cover.

15.6.2.5 Ensure that the measures of exposure are objective and reliable

The measure of exposure must be based on objective and reliable values. For example, capital requirements for insurance risks are often a combination of percentages of the insurance exposure and the insurance liabilities. If insurers do not follow reasonably consistent methods in valuing the liabilities, then this will flow through to the estimation of the capital requirement. This will produce perverse results: a company that is over-optimistic in its valuation of liabilities will have a lower capital requirement than a company which adopts a more prudent approach. So a clearly defined method for valuing liabilities is a prerequisite for a sound RBC formula.

15.6.2.6   Quantify the size of potential losses for each unit of exposure

A formula-based RBC model requires parameters that reflect the size of potential losses for each unit of risk. For example, in Basel I, a home loan had a risk weight of 50%, and an unsecured personal loan had a risk weight of 100%. In non-life insurance, outstanding claims liabilities for household insurance might have a loading of 9%, compared to a loading of 15% for product liability cover. How were these risk relativities determined? Usually the parameters are based on some historical data, eg losses for each category of loan over at least one business cycle. Caution is needed in applying historical data: if economic or market conditions have changed, the historical results may require adjustments based on judgment. The parameters must be reviewed regularly and updated to reflect changes in the industry and the environment.

Example 15.2   Responding to changes in market conditions

During 2003, Australian house prices had increased sharply, and banks were making loans based on these high values. The regulators became concerned about the possibility of a downturn in real estate values, so they conducted stress tests to see if banks could survive a 20 percent fall in property prices. The study found that the banks would survive, but only because they had insured many of their more risky loans with mortgage insurers. This raised issues about the capital adequacy of the mortgage insurers. The regulators then ran stress tests on the mortgage insurers. As a result, in 2006 the minimum capital requirements for mortgage insurers were approximately doubled; and the capital requirements were adjusted to be more risk-sensitive to provide an incentive for improved risk management (Coleman et al, 2005). This helped to maintain the solvency of the Australian banking system during the subprime debt crisis in 2007-09, when default rates on loans increased.

15.6.2.7   Allow for diversification benefits

Suppose that a non-life insurance company faces just two major risks: an increase in the cost of outstanding claims, and investment risk.

The actuary has estimated that $1 million of capital would be enough to cover the outstanding claims risk, with a 99% probability of sufficiency.

The actuary has estimated that $2 million would be enough to cover the investment risk, with a 99% probability of sufficiency.

Now what is the total level of capital required, in order to attain a 99% probability of sufficiency for the company?

If we assume that these two events (increase in claims liability and decrease in investment assets) are quite likely to occur in the same period of time, then we might want to hold $3 million. That is, if the two risks are highly correlated, then we would want to set aside total capital equal to the sum of the individual amounts.

On the other hand, if we think that the two risks are independent, then $3 million would be excessive. If it is very unlikely that both events will occur in the same year, a reserve of $2 million might be adequate for a 99% probability of remaining solvent.

So in order to work out the total reserve, we need some idea about the correlation between different risks. In practice, this is a very difficult problem, and in some cases we can only use a rough rule of thumb such as the square root rule[3] used in the US insurance RBC rules.

The development of statistical models for the estimation of diversification benefits is currently a hot issue in actuarial research.

15.7 Risk-based capital: internal models

Many large financial institutions use their own internal risk models to explore various aspects of their business, including capital management. Regulators may (subject to certain conditions) allow the financial institutions to use their internal models to calculate the capital required for regulatory purposes. Basel II and Solvency II have adopted this approach. The advantages are:

- The model should be more accurate and more comprehensive. Each financial institution has its own sources of information, which would allow it to make more accurate assessments of risk than any arbitrary formula.

- If institutions are encouraged to develop their own models of risk, it might lead to improvements in internal risk management procedures. It might help the management to make wiser decisions about which risks to accept, and how different risks should be priced.

- Cost savings: many of the larger financial institutions already have their own risk management systems and it would be cheaper to have one system instead of two. The use of a more accurate internal system may enable a company to justify a lower capital requirement, so the cost of setting up a system may be worthwhile.

However, if a financial institution is allowed to assess its own capital requirements for regulatory purposes, there is obviously a potential for a conflict of interest. Therefore the regulator would need to examine the internal risk assessment system to make sure that it is applied consistently, is not too subjective, is based on accurate data, takes account of all relevant factors and is empirically tested and verified.

15.8 Integrating the capital management model into the control cycle

Ideally, the regulatory RBC rules should allow companies to reduce their capital requirements when appropriate risk mitigation strategies are in place. For example, the

---

[3] Under this rule, the insurer adds together the RBC amounts for risks that are believed to be correlated. The result is several RBC subtotals which are believed to be more or less uncorrelated. The required RBC total is the square root of the sum of the squares of the subtotals.

RBC rules should recognize the benefits arising from reinsurance of insurance risks and hedging of financial risks. This will motivate companies to implement such strategies.

From a management perspective, the output from the capital model should be used as an input for the decision-making process, to optimize the use of capital. For example:

- the product design process should take into consideration the capital requirements for providing various features such as capital guarantees and premium rate guarantees;

- the pricing of any product should include a loading that reflects the amount of capital required to support that product; and

- capital constraints should be considered before setting sales targets. Note that companies that grow too quickly often run into capital adequacy problems.

Of course, if a capital model does not assess risks accurately, or if it does not include all risks, it will not have the desired effect.

If the statutory capital requirements measure risks inaccurately, this creates an incentive for *regulatory arbitrage*, ie financial institutions find ways to achieve technical compliance with regulatory requirements, while undermining the intent of the regulations.

15.9   Assess the amount and quality of the capital

At this stage, we have placed a value on the assets and the liabilities for solvency purposes and calculated the additional capital that is needed to absorb unexpected losses. Our next step is to assess the amount and quality of the capital that the company has available to meet its obligations.

Such capital should ideally be a permanent and unrestricted investment of funds which is freely available to meet losses, which does not impose unavoidable charges on the earnings of the institution, and which ranks below the claims of those we wish to protect (policyholders, depositors, etc) in the event of a winding-up.

Shareholders' capital and retained profits fit this description. But there are other types of capital instruments that have some of the above characteristics, but not all. These are often debt/equity hybrid securities. For example, consider *mandatory convertible notes* and *subordinated debt* issued by an insurance company.

Mandatory convertible notes are initially classified as debt securities, since the insurer must pay interest on the notes each year. However, the face value of the notes will never be repaid. At the end of a specified term, say five years, each note will be converted into shares of the insurer. Hence in the long term, the money raised by the issue of these notes will contribute to capital. They provide a permanent source of funds, but in the short term they also impose an unavoidable charge on the company (ie the interest payments).

Subordinated debt is borrowed for a fixed term, say 10 years. The loan has special conditions: if the company becomes insolvent, the lenders will rank behind the policyholders. That is, the subordinated debt will not be repaid unless there is money left over, after all the policyholders have been paid first. Hence, during the term of the loan, the money raised by subordinated debt borrowing provides additional security for the policyholders. But this additional security disappears on the day the loan is repaid (ie at the end of 10 years in this example). Hence, this is not a permanent form of capital.

Subject to the approval of the regulator, debt/equity hybrids may be counted, at least partially, toward meeting regulatory capital requirements. They would usually be counted as *Tier 2* capital. The differences between *Tier 1* and *Tier 2* capital were previously discussed in Chapter 11.

Example 15.3

Suppose that a non-life insurance company XYZ has the following balance sheet. The values of the policyholder liabilities and the investments shown have been determined on a solvency basis.

Table 15.1   Balance sheet of general insurance company XYZ

Assets	$ million	Liabilities	$ million
Investments	36	**Policyholder Liabilities**	
Goodwill	1	Outstanding claims	20
Deferred Acquisition Cost (DAC) (see Chapter 12)	1	Unearned premiums	8
Loan to directors	1	**Other Liabilities**	
Reinsurance recoveries	4	Subordinated debt	3
		Mandatory convertible notes	2
		Short-term bank loan	1
		Shareholders' funds	
		Issued share capital	5
		Retained earnings	4
Total	43	Total	43

The admissible assets for solvency purposes may exclude goodwill, DAC, and loans to directors, if these would be of no value in a discontinuance situation, leaving $40 million.

The policyholder liabilities are $28 million.

Let's say the minimum capital requirement (as set by the regulators) is $7 million.

Is XYZ Ltd solvent? Would you say:

(a) Yes: the admissible assets of $40 million minus the policyholder liabilities of $28 million equals $12 million, greater than the required capital of $7 million;

   or

(b) No: the admissible assets of $40 million minus the total of policyholder
     liabilities ($28 million) and other liabilities ($6 million) equals $6 million,
     less than the required capital of $7 million?

The answer to the question lies in the concept of the "quality" of capital. In
Chapter 11 we saw that all companies need capital, and that they can raise capital
in the form of equity or debt. The capital, along with the money received from
policyholders, is invested in the various assets that appear on the left hand side of
the balance sheet above.

In this case, XYZ raised $5 million of capital by issuing shares, and over the
years it has retained some of its profits, totaling $4 million, so it has $9 million
of equity capital. Equity capital is the best quality capital from the point of view
of the security of the policyholders, because the shareholders are the last in line
to receive any money if the company winds up. To measure solvency we take a
cautious view of the assets, excluding those of doubtful value in a discontinuance
situation, which in this case has reduced the value of the assets by $3 million.
This notionally reduces the shareholders' funds, leaving us with the figure of $6
million of top quality capital. This corresponds to the situation in (b) above. If
we only count top quality capital, then XYZ does not meet the solvency standard.

XYZ has also raised money by issuing debt capital, of various forms. If we
considered that all the money is available to provide security for the policyholders,
then this would lead us to answer (a) above. However, this would be too optimistic
a view. Let's look at each of the "Other Liabilities":

•   Short-term bank loan: If the company gets into difficulties, the bank
     will demand repayment of its loan, reducing the money available to pay
     policyholders. So this capital has no protective value from the policyholders'
     point of view.

•   Subordinated debt is usually issued with the condition that it ranks behind
     the policyholders (which is why it is called "subordinated"). If XYZ
     becomes insolvent *before* the subordinated debt is repaid, then the money
     that was loaned to XYZ under the subordinated debt arrangement will be
     available to repay policyholders. However, suppose that the subordinated
     debt has a term of just one year. The debt will be repaid at the end of the
     year. If the insurer becomes insolvent at any time after that date, then that $3
     million will be gone, and will no longer be available to cover policyholder
     obligations. Furthermore, XYZ has to make interest payments on the debt
     for the term of the loan, which imposes a financial burden on the company.
     If interest payments are made when the company is suffering losses, then
     this will deplete capital.

•   The mandatory convertible notes are hybrid debt/equity securities. The
     terms and conditions for such hybrid securities vary from case to case, so
     the regulators will look at each situation individually. In particular, they will
     consider XYZ's obligations to the notes-holders in the event of the winding
     up of the company.

Let's say that in this case the mandatory convertible notes are not regarded as
capital that is available to protect the policyholders, but the subordinated debt is
counted as eligible capital.

> Then, the capital available to XYZ to protect the policyholders is:
>
> - $6 million of top quality equity capital ($9 million of issued shares and retained profits, less $3 million because some of the assets are not admissible); plus
>
> - $3 million of lower quality capital, money that was raised from borrowing the subordinated debt.
>
> The total capital available is thus $9 million, enough to meet the minimum capital requirement of $7 million. The solvency ratio = 1.29.
>
> The regulations may classify the $6 million of top quality capital as Tier 1, and the $3 million of lower quality capital as Tier 2. The classification is important, because the regulations may specify that some proportion of the minimum capital requirement must be met by Tier 1 capital.
>
> In the above example, we adjusted for inadmissible assets by deducting this amount from the total value of assets. As an alternative, we might simply increase the capital requirement to cover potential losses for some of these assets. That is, suppose we include $1 million of loans to directors as an asset. Then we increase the risk-based capital requirement by $1 million to cover potential losses if these loans cannot be collected. The RBC will be $8 million and the available capital will be $10 million (equity $9 million minus DAC and goodwill $2 million plus subordinated debt $3 million). The margin of spare capital is the same, $2 million, but the solvency ratio becomes 1.25 under this measure, and the amount of Tier 1 capital is higher. The exact methods of calculation for capital and solvency ratios will depend on the details of the regulation applying to XYZ.

Exercise 15.6

Under what circumstances do you think it would be reasonable to count subordinated debt as eligible capital?

Under what circumstances do you think it would be reasonable to count mandatory convertible notes as eligible capital?

15.10   The role of risk management and market discipline in solvency regulation

15.10.1   Introduction

We have noted above that holding adequate capital is only one pillar of a three-pillar approach to solvency regulation. The other pillars are effective risk management and market discipline.

In the past, when regulators were concerned about risky behavior, it was common to limit the types of risk that financial institutions could take. For example many jurisdictions imposed investment restrictions, pricing controls and reinsurance standards.

These days, in the face of international competition, there is a greater emphasis on letting financial institutions take risks but making sure that adequate mechanisms are in place to handle these risks. These mechanisms include:

- appropriate skills and expertise of management;

- effective internal risk management policies and controls;

- close supervision by the regulator, including reporting requirements, early warning systems and adequate powers of intervention;

- market disclosure, including ratings provided by credit rating agencies; and

- provision of risk management advice from professionals.

We will discuss some of these below.

15.10.2 Internal risk management

In recent years, there has been increasing emphasis on Enterprise Risk Management (ERM), as discussed in Chapter 2.

In order to promote ERM, regulators encourage financial institutions to develop a formal Risk Management Strategy (RMS). This is a high-level document, which is designed to take a holistic view of risk throughout the organization. The board of directors is given responsibility for approving the RMS, and it must be reviewed by the board annually. The RMS must be documented, and often a copy must be provided to the regulator.

Regulators may also issue "best practice" guidelines for managing specific types of risk.

Exercise 15.7   Risk Management Strategies

(a) What do you think should be included in an insurer's Risk Management Strategy about reinsurance?

(b) Many financial institutions outsource some of their work, eg computer systems, customer service, etc. What do you think should be included in a Risk Management Strategy about outsourcing?

(c) After the Australian non-life insurer HIH collapsed, a review found that HIH had excellent risk management policies – on paper. What are the obstacles that might prevent the effective implementation of a risk management strategy?

15.10.3 Reporting requirements and early warning systems

A regulator should monitor financial institutions, so that problems can be detected early, allowing action to be taken promptly, before losses multiply.

In many countries, financial institutions are required to provide detailed reports to the regulator, including annual reports, audited financial statements, details of assets classified by types of exposure, and so on.

These reports may be analyzed to look for danger signals. For example, in the US, the National Association of Insurance Commissioners (NAIC) developed the Insurance

Regulatory Information System (IRIS) and the Financial Analysis and Solvency Tracking System (FAST). Under the IRIS system, various ratios are calculated (based on regulatory returns) to evaluate the financial condition of the insurers. The ratios measure the level of reserves and trends in reserve levels, profitability, reliance on reinsurance, changes in the mix of business, investment returns and liquidity. There are different ratios for different types of insurers. Companies that have unusually large or small ratios would be given priority for further investigation. For example, if an insurer has unusually high growth rates, this may suggest that the insurer is underpricing. If the company has unusually high or low investment returns, this might prompt an examination of the company's investment strategy and asset allocation, to ascertain the reasons for such unusual performance. Unusually high returns may indicate that the company is taking on higher investment risks (for example junk bonds pay higher interest rates than AAA-rated bonds, but have a higher risk of default). Unusually low returns may indicate that the company is lending money to affiliated companies at below-market interest rates.

Exercise 15.8

Read the article "Empirical Studies of Common Factors in Insolvency" on the CD and draw up a list of signs that indicate that an insurer might be headed for trouble.

Some countries have also introduced early warning systems for banks. The best known is the CAMELS system, which was introduced in the US in the 1980s. Each bank is given a rating on each of six criteria:

> **C**apital;
>
> **A**sset quality;
>
> **M**anagement;
>
> **E**arnings;
>
> **L**iquidity; and
>
> **S**ensitivity to market risk.

Banks that earn high scores are subject to more frequent on-site visits, and may be subject to additional regulatory intervention.

15.10.4 Disclosure and ratings

Disclosure requirements form an important component of solvency regulation, for all types of financial institutions. Disclosure allows other market participants – potential investors, creditors, brokers, rating analysts and customers – to form their own opinion of the solvency of each organization. A company that is perceived to be in a poor financial condition may lose customers; may need to pay higher rates on borrowing; and may suffer a declining share price. The possibility of such market discipline creates a strong incentive for institutions to conduct their business prudently. When a company is in trouble, industry analysts are often the first to become aware of the problem. The result is often a falling share price, accompanied by adverse press reports. There are several credit rating agencies that provide ratings for many financial institutions. Regulators should be alert to the reasons underlying any downgrade in market ratings. The downgrade may itself exacerbate any existing problems, by making it more difficult and expensive for the company to raise new capital. The impact that a rating downgrade can have on a company is dramatically illustrated in "Case Study of a Liquidity Crisis: General American" on the CD.

15.10.5 The role of the professional

Regulators have limited resources, and hence may rely on professionals (such as auditors and actuaries) to provide early warnings.

The use of actuaries in life insurance has long been commonplace, while the use of actuaries in non-life insurance is less widespread but increasing. Many countries require the appointment of an "appointed actuary" or "responsible actuary" with legislated responsibilities. The role of the appointed actuary varies in detail, from one country to the next. Table 15.2 summarizes the position according to an IAIS survey (IAIS, 2003).

Table 15.2   Role of the "appointed actuary" or "responsible actuary"

Role	
Advice on valuation of liabilities	Required in all jurisdictions with an "appointed actuary" role in life insurance Very common in jurisdictions with an "appointed actuary" role in non-life insurance
Advice on items such as: the premiums to be charged; the terms and conditions of insurance contracts; the risk assessment policies; the adequacy of reinsurance arrangements; the investment policy	Required in some jurisdictions in both life and non-life insurance
Advice on the determination of the allocation of profits, distributions or bonuses to participating life insurance policyholders	Required in most jurisdictions with an "appointed actuary" role in life insurance
An important fiduciary role to represent the interests of the policyholders, particularly the participating policyholders, when decisions are taken within the insurer	Not a common regulatory requirement, but seen in some jurisdictions in life insurance
Dynamic solvency testing (as described below) and reports on the current and future financial condition of the insurer to assist the board of directors in developing risk management strategies	Some jurisdictions
Whistle-blower responsibilities to report to the regulator, if believed necessary in the interests of policyholders and/or to avoid contravention of the law	Some jurisdictions

---

Example 15.4   Example of appointed actuary responsibilities

The following summarizes the role of the appointed actuary under the Australian Life Insurance Act 1995 and accompanying prudential standards. There are similar roles in other countries.

A life company must not issue policies of a particular kind unless the appointed actuary has given the company written advice about the proposed terms and conditions, the proposed surrender value basis, and the method of unit pricing (if applicable).

A life company must not enter into a reinsurance arrangement unless the appointed actuary has given the company written advice as to the likely consequences of the proposed arrangement.

The policy liabilities must be valued in accordance with the actuarial standards (which are specified by the regulator).

The appointed actuary must make an investigation into the financial condition of the company at the end of every financial year and give the company a written report. This must include an assessment of the solvency and capital adequacy of the company. The Financial Condition Report is a comprehensive review of the company, and it must be conducted in accordance with the Institute of Actuaries of Australia's *Professional Standard 200*.

In order to perform his/her duties, the appointed actuary is given certain privileges. For example, if it is necessary for the performance of his/her duties, then:

- the appointed actuary may have access to any of the company's documents;
- the appointed actuary may request information from any employee; and
- the appointed actuary may attend board meetings, and may speak at board meetings on matters relating to solvency, capital adequacy, or any other matters about which she/he may be required to give advice.

The appointed actuary also has a responsibility to the regulator, who will be relying on the work done by the actuary in order to monitor the performance of the company. Therefore:

- the regulator is given a copy of the Financial Condition Report; and
- the regulator may request an additional investigation to be conducted if it is concerned about any aspect of the company's solvency.

The actuary has whistle-blower responsibilities. If the actuary thinks that action is required in order to avoid contravening the Act, or to protect the interests of the policyholders, then he/she must inform the directors or officers of the company. If the company fails to take action within a reasonable time, then the actuary must inform the regulator.

15.10.6   Financial condition reports

As noted above, in many countries actuaries are required to provide reports about the financial condition of a life insurer. These reports may be given to the board of directors or their representative, and they are often accessible to the regulator as well.

A financial condition report will usually include a comprehensive control cycle review of the company. Items covered will include: the company objectives, product design, pricing, customer mix, sales levels split by product, an analysis of past experience relative to expected experience, comments on trends in experience, a review of assets and investment performance, comments on the suitability of the investment strategy (including asset-liability matching and liquidity), a valuation of liabilities, an assessment of past and expected future profitability, an analysis of profit by source, assessment of capital levels, and a review of the adequacy of risk management controls. The aim is to identify the strengths and weaknesses, risks and opportunities for the company. A financial condition report will usually be required annually for life insurers, health insurers and non-life insurers. Similarly employer-sponsored defined benefit retirement plans are usually required to have periodic actuarial reviews.

15.10.7   Dynamic Solvency Testing

The actuary may also be required, by the regulator or by professional standards, to carry out projections of the business using *Dynamic Solvency Testing* (DST). DST is also known as *Dynamic Financial Analysis* (DFA) or *Dynamic Capital Adequacy Testing* (DCAT).

The following is a description of DCAT from the Canadian Institute of Actuaries (CIA, 2007). This note is included on the CD for further reference.

> DCAT is a process of analyzing and projecting the trends of an insurer's capital position given its current circumstances, its recent past, and its intended business plan under a variety of future scenarios. It allows the actuary to inform the insurer's management about the implications that the business plan has on capital and to provide guidance on the significant risks to which the insurer will be exposed. ...
>
> The principal goal of this process is the identification of possible threats to the financial condition of the insurer and appropriate risk management or corrective actions to address those threats. The process arms the insurer with useful information on the course of events that may lead to capital depletion, and the relative effectiveness of alternative corrective actions, if necessary. Furthermore, knowing the sources of threat, it may be advisable to strengthen the monitoring systems where the insurer is most vulnerable.

The projections will start with a base scenario, based on realistic assumptions. The actuary will model the cash flows from the existing in-force business, plus expected new business, based on the company's future business plans over the next few years (usually with a time frame of say five years). For each year, the model output would include a balance sheet, an income statement, and various measures of solvency.

The model may be used for sensitivity testing to identify the most significant risks, ie varying one assumption at a time to measure the effect of a change in, say, mortality rates or reinsurance costs.

Alternatively, the outcomes may be modeled for a range of plausible scenarios, allowing for ripple effects, ie where a change in the environment might flow through to affect a range of other assumptions (eg a recession that simultaneously affects interest rates, asset values, new business volumes, and discontinuance rates).

A *dynamic* model will take account of the management's response to any particular situation. For example, if the model assumes a drop in interest rates, it might be assumed that management would cut dividends/bonuses, or change the investment strategy. Chapter 18 will deal in more detail with the management's options for responding to experience.

Many DST models incorporate stochastic elements. A stochastic model defines some of the assumptions as random variables, which allows a probability to be assigned to the measurement of solvency, and may help to identify critical scenarios that may not have been recognized beforehand.

Professional standards may provide guidance on the range of risks that should be incorporated into the model. For example, the Canadian Institute of Actuaries suggests that actuaries should consider the following risks for a life insurer: mortality risk, morbidity risk, persistency rates, expenses, asset/liability mismatch, investment losses, reinsurance, political and regulatory risk, and off-balance-sheet[4] risks.

Under the Canadian regulations, the actuary must model at least three plausible adverse scenarios, after considering a range of different risks that are most applicable to this particular company. The actuary must then provide a report to the board of directors, presenting those scenarios that provide the most serious threat to the company, and advising on actions which might be taken to manage those risks.

DST/ DCAT is widely used for both life and non-life insurers in many countries.

15.11   Responding to solvency problems

From time to time, an actuary will be called upon to assist a financial institution that is facing solvency problems. As a starting point, it is sensible to identify the sources of the losses and take steps to prevent any further deterioration.

If there is a capital shortage, there are basically three approaches to alleviating the problem in the short term:

- Raise additional capital. This may be done by issuing shares or hybrid debt instruments, retaining profits (by reducing or suspending dividends to shareholders and reducing distributions of profits to participating policyholders), or borrowing by subordinated debt.

- Improve the quality of capital, eg by selling non-core businesses that have a goodwill component in the valuation, thus converting inadmissible assets to admissible assets.

- Reduce risks, for example by increasing reinsurance or switching to a more conservative asset allocation.

Note that changing the valuation assumptions, in order to improve *reported* solvency, is *not* recommended as an appropriate solution to the problem – although it is often the approach adopted by insurers that subsequently fail!

If these measures are not feasible, then the financial institution may be forced to seek a merger with another financial institution that can provide financial support.

If solvency problems are identified early, and appropriate action is taken, it is often possible to turn around the situation.

---

[4]   Off-balance-sheet risks are possible losses from items which do not appear on the balance sheet as assets or liabilities. Off-balance-sheet items may arise from new industry practices, when professional standards or regulations have not yet evolved to require their recognition on the balance sheet. CIA (2007) lists some examples.

If the management is slow to recognize and deal with its problems, then the regulator has a role to play, in encouraging, advising, and ultimately coercing appropriate remedial action. Legislation often gives the regulator the authority – and responsibility – to intervene at a fairly early stage, as soon as it appears that this is necessary to protect the public interest. Ideally, intervention should occur even before the solvency ratios deteriorate, as falling capital is a lagging indicator of problems. In the US, once an insurance company's capital falls below a specified level (as summarized in Table 15.3 below), the company is required to submit to the regulators a plan of action for dealing with the low capital level.

During the recession in the early 1980s, dozens of American banks fell into difficulties: some recovered, some failed. The banks that survived were generally those which made a serious effort to work with their regulator (OCC, 1988).

15.11.1   Deciding when to intervene

The regulator's first problem is deciding when to intervene.

Suppose a company is in a weak position, and the regulator is concerned. The management has a plan that *may* be successful in rectifying the situation – but there is a significant risk that the plan will not succeed. Regulators face a quandary: if they disclose their concerns publicly, this will inevitably hasten the decline of the company, destroying all chances of a recovery. On the other hand, if they allow the company to continue operations, and then the company fails, many customers may suffer even greater losses. A customer who pours money into a failing company, and loses it all, will be justifiably angry on discovering that the regulator was well aware of the risk but did not disclose it.

Regulators may be subject to political pressure to be lenient. If regulation is too strict, then the financial institution may threaten to move operations to another jurisdiction, where the rules are less strict. This may have a negative impact on jobs and on the local economy. In some cases, companies have persuaded politicians to exert pressure on regulators to relax the solvency rules, to give the company more time to recover. This was a problem during the US Savings and Loan crisis in the 1980s, as described in the article "The American Savings and Loan (Thrift) Industry" on the CD.

When the entire industry is facing difficulties, as a result of economic circumstances beyond the companies' control, the regulators may be more flexible. There is some debate about the desirability of varying capital requirements in the light of economic conditions. Critics have argued that risk-based capital requirements may be *procyclical*, that is, inflexible capital requirements may exacerbate the negative impact of economic downturns. For example, when equity values fell in 2001, many UK life insurers found it difficult to meet the solvency standards, and were forced to sell equities to improve their solvency position, switching money into lower-risk assets. This selling simply exacerbated the fall in share prices. To break this downward spiral, the regulator temporarily eased the solvency requirements (Bolger, 2001; MacIntosh, 2001; FSA, 2001). Similarly, in 2008-09, when the subprime debt crisis adversely affected the solvency levels of many institutions, there were calls for a relaxation of regulatory capital requirements for banks and insurers in the US and UK (Felstead, 2008; Zuill, 2008; Scism, 2009; Perkins, 2009).

The pros and cons of regulatory forbearance have been hotly debated. However, the evidence suggests that delays in taking action can be dangerous – too often, the situation deteriorates, making the eventual resolution efforts more difficult and more expensive, with the possibility of becoming more widespread and systemic. For example, many experts believe that delays in taking action against failing US Savings and Loan societies during the 1980s significantly increased the ultimate cost to the community.

As a result, some countries have passed legislation that *requires* the regulator to take prompt corrective action when regulatory capital standards are breached, in both banking and insurance. For example, US insurers must calculate and report annually the risk-based capital required according to regulatory formulae (NAIC, 2009). This is compared to the company's actual capital. The comparison will result in one of the five outcomes shown in Table 15.3 below.

Table 15.3   Intervention levels for US insurers

	Company's Capital level	**Action**
	Capital ("Total Adjusted Capital") > 200% of required RBC ("Authorized Control Level Risk-Based Capital")	No action is required.
Company Action Level	Capital < 200% of RBC	The company must submit a plan to the regulator.
Regulatory Action Level	Capital < 150% of RBC	The company must submit a plan to the regulator; the regulator may (if it considers it necessary) take corrective action.
Authorized Control Level	Capital < 100% of RBC	The regulator may (if it considers it necessary) take control of the company.
Mandatory Control Level	Capital < 70% of RBC	The regulator must rehabilitate or liquidate the company.

15.11.2   Deciding how to intervene

Ideally, the legislation should give the regulator considerable flexibility in choosing the most appropriate course of action, ie the one that will minimize the cost to the public and minimize systemic risk. In choosing between various courses of action, accurate information is essential. Legislation should give the regulator wide powers to investigate and obtain specialist reports (such as actuarial reviews) when necessary.

Initially, when a company falls below the minimum capital standards, the regulator may require the company to obtain additional capital. However, improving the capital position merely addresses the symptoms; the regulator should, at the same time, address the underlying causes. For example, if the loss was caused by speculation in derivatives, the regulator would seek assurances that risk management procedures would be improved.

If the regulator believes that a company can be salvaged, it may simply impose various conditions on the company.

If the basic problem is poor management, the legislation may permit the regulator to put the company under the management of a more competent person. For example, under Australian legislation, a life insurance company may be placed under judicial management, described as a "halfway house between the life and death of a company." To date, this has only occurred once, in the winding up of Regal and Occidental. Two actuaries involved in this process have written a useful account of the problems encountered and the steps that were taken to protect the policyholders (Edwards and Martin, 1994).

The regulator may seek assistance from the other companies in the same industry, to arrange financial assistance. The other companies may be willing to assist, in order to avoid the negative publicity that will affect the entire industry. But if the losses are large – and more particularly, if the losses are unquantifiable because the accounts have been falsified or market conditions are unstable – then the other companies may be understandably reluctant to pour money into a black hole. The histories of Long Term Capital Management, Barings Bank, Confederation Life, and Lehman Brothers all give some insight into the desperate negotiations that may occur behind the scenes in an attempt to save a failing financial institution. (For LTCM see Lowenstein, 2001; for Barings see Fay, 1996; for Confederation Life see McQueen, 1996.)

If the company is beyond redemption, the regulator will often seek to minimize the impact on customers, by arranging for another stronger institution to take over some or all of the liabilities. A fair price must be negotiated; otherwise the acquisition of a weak company might drag down a previously sound company. Many companies have become insolvent after taking over a weaker company – particularly when the weaker company fails to make a full disclosure of its position. Run-off often produces a better outcome than winding-up, but is not always possible.

Exercise 15.9

Suppose the sponsoring employer of a retirement plan that pays pension benefits is going out of business and will not be making any further contributions. According to the actuary, the value of assets is about 98 percent of the value of liabilities, on a best estimate basis. The trustees of the plan might decide to sell the assets of the plan and buy an annuity (deferred or immediate) for each member from a life insurer. Alternatively they might decide to continue administering the funds and pay the accrued pension entitlements as and when they become due. Which option should be adopted? Why?

15.12   Guarantee funds

When a financial institution becomes insolvent, many innocent members of the public may be adversely affected: this may include both the customers of the financial institution, and third parties. For example, if a medical malpractice insurer becomes insolvent, people who have a legitimate complaint against a medical practitioner may be unable to obtain compensation.

To alleviate the effects of any insolvency, it is often considered desirable to set up a guarantee fund, that will provide financial assistance to customers and third party claimants. Guarantee funds might be set up by the government, or by industry groups. They may be funded by taxes, or by levies on the industry.

15.12.1   Arguments for and against guarantee funds

The advantages of guarantee funds are:

- the financial burden of the failure is spread across the wider community; and

- guarantee funds provide reassurance to the public, and hence help to improve the stability of the financial system. For example, a banking system with deposit guarantees is less vulnerable to runs.

Many countries do have such funds: they may be called deposit insurance (for banks and other savings institutions), or policyholder guarantee funds (for insurers), or benefit guarantee funds (for retirement plans).

Some people argue that such funds are undesirable, because they create a *moral hazard*. When such protection exists, the management of a financial institution may be inclined to take more risks; the customers may be inclined to choose the cheapest insurance provider or the bank account paying the highest interest rate, without any regard to the underlying solvency of the company; and the regulator may be inclined to be more lenient with a weak company that is breaching the minimum solvency standards.

The article "The American Savings and Loan (Thrift) Industry" on the CD illustrates how deposit insurance can cause a problem.

The introduction of a guarantee may have unexpected and unintended side effects, by distorting the market. In 2007-08, during the global financial crisis, many banks suffered liquidity problems. In response, to allay panic, several countries extended and strengthened their deposit guarantees. Since banking is a global industry, this immediately put pressure on other countries to follow suit – otherwise, there might be an outflow of deposits to the safer havens. Financial institutions that were not covered by the guarantees were at a comparative disadvantage.

Example 15.5   The Australian experience with deposit guarantees

On October 12, 2008, the Australian Government announced the establishment of a deposit guarantee scheme to cover banks and other financial institutions that accept deposits. The Minister announced that: "The arrangements are designed to promote financial system stability in Australia, by supporting confidence and assisting Authorised Deposit-taking Institutions – banks, building societies and credit unions – to continue to access funding at a time of considerable turbulence. They are also designed to ensure that Australian institutions are not placed at a disadvantage compared to their international competitors that can access similar government guarantees on bank debt." (Media Release, Treasurer Wayne Swan, November 28, 2008).

This was a relief for some of the weaker banks, which were having trouble raising money – especially those banks that had a greater dependence on wholesale funding sources. For example, before the guarantee was announced, Suncorp Metway Bank (Australia's fifth largest bank) was reportedly having difficulties and was looking for another larger bank to take it over. Shortly after the government guarantee was announced, the bank announced plans to raise funds by relying on the AAA rating of the Australian government (Johnston, 2008).

However, the scheme caused difficulties for other institutions: there was an outflow of funds from other investment vehicles, such as property trusts and retirement funds, as worried customers moved their money into banks. As a result, several large property trusts were forced to freeze redemptions. This created problems for customers of those property trusts, who were unable to access their savings.

The lobby groups that represent the financial services industry sometimes advocate the formation of guarantee funds, to help build confidence in their industry. Indeed, sometimes schemes are set up by industry bodies themselves.

Often, however, the financial institutions are opposed to the creation of guarantee funds. They argue that, because of the moral hazard mentioned above, these funds may encourage imprudent practices such as underpricing in insurance.

Furthermore, the guarantee funds are often funded by levies on the entire industry: effectively, the stronger companies are forced to provide funds to bail out the policyholders of their cut-rate competitors. Naturally the stronger companies are likely to object!

Despite these objections, it is very difficult for governments to resist the public pressure to provide assistance to those affected by the collapse of financial institutions. Even when there is no explicit (statutory) guarantee, there is often an implicit guarantee, because the government simply cannot afford to allow a loss of confidence in the financial system.

Example 15.6

When British steelworkers lost 90 percent of their pension benefits, due to the insolvency of their employer-sponsored fund in 2002, they ran a very effective publicity campaign to blame the government for inadequate pension fund regulation. Public opinion polls showed that more than 80 percent of people thought that the government should compensate them. The government eventually relented and provided compensation for the protesting workers. And in 2005, the UK government set up the Pension Protection Fund to provide similar protection for members of all UK pension funds (The Guardian, 2009).

15.12.2 Design of guarantee funds

There are several questions to consider when designing a guarantee fund:

- Under what circumstances should compensation be provided? Sometimes assistance is restricted to losses caused by fraud or dishonest conduct – is this a good idea?

- Who should be eligible for compensation? Should compensation be limited to local residents? Should certain types of policies receive a higher level of compensation than others? Should the assistance be targeted to certain sectors of the community?

- Should there be limits on the amount of assistance? For example, some funds will only compensate the customers for 80 percent or 90 percent of their loss, subject to a maximum amount. Other funds might guarantee the full amount but restrict the availability of any payment for a period of time. As well as limiting the cost, this might reduce the moral hazard: customers might be more careful in choosing where to put their money, if they are at risk of losing up to 20 percent of it or not seeing their money for years.

- Who should pay? Should the money be provided from general government revenue (ie all taxpayers), or should it be funded by a levy on other financial institutions within the same industry (ie other policyholders who may also benefit from the guarantee in later years)? Naturally the industry lobby groups will argue that the government should bear the cost, but the government may not agree with this view!

- If the money is to be raised by a levy, should it be funded in advance (by collecting a premium from each financial institution every year) or should the levy be collected only when needed?

If the levy is collected only when a company collapses, and several companies collapse in one year, this may impose an unexpected demand on other companies in the same industry (which may themselves be suffering from the same weaknesses). Hence it may be advisable to limit the amount of the levy to be collected in any one year, and/or have a mechanism for spreading the costs over time.

- If the money is to be raised by a levy, how should the amount of the levy be determined? Should it be based on a fixed percentage of assets? Or would it be more reasonable to impose a higher charge on companies that are more likely to become insolvent? Risk-based charges create an incentive for the weaker companies to improve their solvency. However, it may be difficult to determine an appropriate measure of risk.

During periods of economic downturn, when the number of failures is unusually high, there may be heavy demands on the guarantee fund and the guarantee fund itself may need careful financial management.

If a government-funded guarantee fund is created, then this immediately gives the government a greater financial incentive to prevent insolvencies. Hence the creation of a guarantee fund may be associated with closer supervision and/or tighter regulation of financial institutions. Some of the government-run guarantee funds have early warning/early intervention programs designed to minimize the ultimate cost of the bailout.

Example 15.7   Problems at the PBGC

The Pension Benefit Guaranty Corporation (PBGC) guarantees the benefits of members of defined benefit pension plans in the US. The PBGC is owned by the US government, but funded by levies on all pension plans covered under the scheme.

Initially, the PBGC levies were a flat rate per member. This was changed so that the rate per member varies depending on the level of funding. The lower the level of funding, the higher the levy. This provided some incentive for plans to increase their funding levels – but not enough.

The guarantee system creates a moral hazard. Employers can promise generous benefits to employees, but they don't have to fully fund these benefits. As the PBGC director points out, "there is little to prevent financially weak employers from creating unfunded pension costs that they can shift to the insurance system if the company fails" (Belt, 2005).

In the years up to 2005, the PBGC began to accumulate large deficits. The PBGC regularly monitors funding levels in all the pension plans it guarantees, and it was concerned that many plans were seriously underfunded. It asked for an increase in the levy rate and stricter minimum funding rules for defined benefit plans. An increase in levies was approved (Belt, 2005).

However, many employer lobby groups have opposed any increase in funding levels, arguing that they could not afford to pay any more; if they were forced to increase funding, this would only lead to job losses. The government partially acceded to these requests (Halonen, 2009).

In September 2008, the PBGC had a deficit of about US$11 billion. As a result of the global financial crisis, the projected deficit as at March 2009 had increased to US$33 billion. And this is expected to increase in the future.

15.13   Practical implications for actuaries

The financial system is based on trust. Customers hand over their hard-earned cash – insurance premiums, bank deposits, pension fund contributions – and in return they receive a promise. Customers rely on financial institutions to pay the promised benefits when they fall due, which may occur many many years later. No financial institution can survive for long if the customers doubt its ability to fulfill its promises; and ultimately, insolvencies may undermine confidence in the entire financial system.

Therefore solvency is *the* fundamental essential requirement for any financial institution.

Actuaries have long been entrusted with some of the responsibilities involved in assessing and maintaining solvency. Historically, the primary role of the actuary was to value liabilities. But these responsibilities have expanded, and the actuary's role may now include cash flow projections, dynamic solvency testing, provision of financial condition reports, determination of risk-based capital requirements and the design of risk management controls.

In meeting these responsibilities, the actuary must comply with both professional standards and regulatory guidelines. In many ways the discipline of solvency measurement is still evolving, and continuing professional development is necessary to ensure that actuaries continue to meet best practice standards.

The management of solvency cannot be divorced from the overall management of the business. At every stage of the Actuarial Control Cycle – from product design to profit distribution – the potential impact on the company's solvency must be a prime consideration for decision-makers.

15.14   Key learning points

*   Solvency can never be measured simply by comparing two numbers (the assets versus the liabilities). A financial institution cannot survive for long unless it has adequate risk management processes to identify, monitor and manage all relevant risks.

*   The management must consider a range of situations and assess solvency under different scenarios: will the company be solvent on a cash flow basis, on a discontinuance basis, and on a going-concern basis?

*   Ensuring cash flow solvency involves structuring the assets so that they are available to meet the obligations when required, and understanding the liquidity risks in the business. Liquidity management needs to be considered both in normal situations and in a crisis.

*   When assessing solvency in a discontinuance situation, we must start by valuing the assets and the liabilities. The valuations should be adjusted to allow for the adverse impact of break-up, and should always be performed by competent, independent, experienced professionals who follow accounting standards and/or professional standards (as applicable). Despite strong pressures to assume otherwise, optimism is out of place in a solvency valuation.

*   Since financial institutions are in the business of accepting risks, there will always be a need for capital to cover potential losses. The level of capital required will vary, depending on the risk profile of each company. Risk-based capital standards may be

used to help regulators set statutory minimum capital requirements. Some companies may use more sophisticated internal models for this purpose.

- Capital requirements are part of the control cycle, ie a system with feedback. As managers become more aware of the capital required to support a particular line of business, they might respond by changing the risk profile: changing product design, changing pricing structures, and/or changing asset allocations.

- Despite advances in modeling risks, the development of fair, objective, practical and consistent regulatory capital standards is no easy task; and regulators are still struggling to set solvency standards that will allow for a high degree of security for the public, without imposing excessive burdens on the financial institutions.

- Although capital requirements are an essential component of solvency management, no amount of capital can protect a company that is poorly managed. Auditors and actuaries have a vital role to play in providing expert advice to management. Financial condition reports can pinpoint potential problems before they arise, and dynamic asset/liability models can assist in strategic planning for the future. They model the institution as a going concern, allowing for future new business. These are useful tools for management, and for regulators. Regulators are now using a variety of sources of information to get early warnings of insolvencies – and actuaries and auditors also have a vital role to play in this regard.

- Not all risks can be managed successfully, and regulation is never perfect. Major insolvencies will occur from time to time, and it is often considered desirable to set up safety nets to protect the public from the ill effects of such collapses. However, such programs must be designed carefully in order to avoid moral hazard and other adverse effects on the industry.

- The science of solvency assessment and management is evolving. Actuaries in this area need to keep up to date with the latest changes as part of their continuing professional development.

Answers to questions in Example 15.1

Q. How long did it take for Nick Leeson to send Barings Bank into insolvency by unauthorized derivatives dealing?

Barings was the oldest merchant bank in London (established in 1762).

At the end of 1993, Barings' accounts showed that shareholders' equity was over £400 million.

But by January 1995, Barings was insolvent. Barings was ultimately sold to ING for £1.

How did this happen? In 1993, Barings appointed a young man named Nick Leeson to trade in derivatives in their Singapore office. Leeson was supposed to do low-risk arbitrage trading, but he soon started to take unhedged positions, exposing the bank to much more risk. Initially his losses were relatively small, but the losses accumulated over time as Leeson took on larger and larger risks.

Leeson also had control over the "back office," ie the record-keeping and accounting staff who did the paperwork for the derivatives deals. This allowed

Leeson to disguise his losses by setting up a secret account. The head office of Barings had no idea that he was losing money – in fact Leeson made sure that the accounts showed that he was making substantial profits (hence Leeson earned large performance-based bonuses).

Leeson invested in derivatives based on movements in the Japanese Nikkei stock market index. In January 1995, there was an earthquake in Kobe, Japan. The Japanese stock market fell sharply. As a result, Leeson suffered severe losses on his derivatives trades. His losses amounted to £827 million, which wiped out Barings' capital (refer to Ambit ERisk, 2010).

The UK's Board of Banking Supervision conducted an enquiry into the collapse of Barings which identified numerous weaknesses in the bank's risk management controls. (For more information on the deficiencies of the risk management controls, see BBS, 1995.)

Q. How long did it take for Société Générale to lose 7 billion Euros, as a result of unauthorized derivatives trading?

According to newspaper reports, the employee alleged to have carried out the trades had profits of about 2 billion Euros in December but was facing losses of about 5 billion Euros by February. So it took about two to three months to lose 7 billion Euros. This suggests significant deficiencies in risk management (which was the conclusion of both the internal review and the regulator's review).

(For a brief account of the incident, see Gauthier-Villars, 2008.)

Q. How long did it take the once highly profitable Financial Products operation of AIG to drive the giant insurance company to require a bailout from the US government?

The Financial Products Group dealt in credit default swaps.

• In August 2007, an AIG executive said that he did not expect to lose a single dollar on any of these transactions.

• By November, AIG admitted that the estimated losses were US$352 million.

• By December, the losses were up to US$1.1 billion.

• In February 2008, after queries by the SEC about their valuation methods, AIG announced that losses were more than US$11 billion.

• By the end of 2008, AIG needed a bailout from the government, amounting to about US $150 billion, in order to survive.

(O'Harrow and Dennis, 2008)

CD Items

Canadian Institute of Actuaries (CIA) 2007, *Educational Note on Dynamic Capital Adequacy Testing.*

Canadian Institute of Actuaries (CIA) 1993, *Memorandum on Provision for Adverse Deviation for Property And Casualty Insurers.*

Ferris, S. 2003, *Case Study of a Liquidity Crisis: General American.*

Ferris, S. 2003, *Empirical Studies of Common Factors in Insolvency.*

Ferris, S. 2003, *The American Savings and Loan (Thrift) Industry.*

Ferris, S. 1999, Who Killed Confed Life? Book Review, *Actuary Australia*, March.

National Association of Insurance Commissioners (NAIC) 2009, *Risk-Based Capital: General Overview.*

Chapter 15 Exercise Solutions

References (other than CD Items)

Actuarial Standards Board (Canada) 2009, Standards of Practice Number 2300: Valuation of Policy Liabilities: Life and Health (Accident and Sickness) Insurance.

Ambit ERisk 2010, Case Study: Barings, http://www.erisk.com/Learning/CaseStudies/Barings. asp, accessed on February 2, 2010.

American Academy of Actuaries 2005, Conceptual Framework of a Principle-Based Approach for Life Insurance Products from the American Academy of Actuaries' Universal Life Working Group, presented to the NAIC Life and Health Actuarial Task Force, June 2005.

Australian Prudential Regulation Authority (APRA) discussion papers, http://www.apra.gov. au.

Bain, J. 2001, *The Remarkable Roller Coaster Ride*, HarperCollins Publishers, Sydney.

Basel Committee on Banking Supervision (BCBS) 1999, A New Capital Adequacy Framework, *Consultative Paper*, http://www.bis.org.

Basel Committee on Banking Supervision (BCBS) 2004, Bank Failures in Mature Economies, *Working Paper 13*, http://www.bis.org.

Belt, B.D. 2005, *Testimony of Bradley D. Belt Executive Director Pension Benefit Guaranty Corporation Before the Committee on Finance United States Senate*, PGBC.

Board for Actuarial Standards (UK) 2006, *Guidance Note 1, The Prudential Supervision in the UK of Long-Term Insurance Business.*

Board of Banking Supervision (BBS) 1995, Report of the Board of Banking Supervision Inquiry into the Circumstances of the Collapse of Barings, July 1995.

Bolger, A. 2001, Move to aid Life Insurers in Falling Markets, *Financial Times*, September 12, 2001.

Buchanan, R. A., Bell, I. F., Goodsall, D. M. & Partridge, S. M. 1993, Solvency and Capital, *Transactions of the Institute of Actuaries of Australia*, Vol II, pp.761–813.

Coleman, A., Esho, N., Sellathurai, I., & Thavabalan, N. 2005, Stress Testing Housing Loan Portfolios: A Regulatory Case Study, *APRA Working paper*, http://www.apra.gov.au/ Policy/upload/Stress-Testing-Housing-Loan-Portfolios-A-Regulatory-Case-Study-Sep-2005.pdf , accessed January 15, 2009.

Davidson, R. 2001, Risk Assessment Tools Available to Regulators, *Journal of Insurance Regulation*, Spring.

Edwards, B. A. & Martin, G. C. 1994, Judicial Management, *Transactions of the Institute of Actuaries of Australia*, pp.579–672.

European Commission reports, http://ec.europa.eu/internal_market/insurance/solvency.

Fay, S. 1996, *The Collapse of Barings: Panic, Ignorance and Greed*, Random House, London.

Felstead, A. 2008, FSA relaxes grip on capital requirements, *Financial Times*, London, October 15, 2008.

Financial Services Authority (FSA) 2001, Further relaxation of Resilience Test for Life insurance Companies, Press release September 24, 2001, http://www.fsa.gov.uk/Pages/Library/Communication/PR/2001/121.shtml, accessed January 15, 2009.

The Guardian 2009, Money: What happens when it all goes wrong?, April 11, 2009.

Gauthier-Villars, D. 2008, Société Générale Details Lapses - Probe Says Staff Entrusted To Verify Kerviel's Trades Failed to Dig Deep Enough, *The Wall Street Journal*, February 21, 2008.

Halonen, D. 2009, Corporations and PBGC square off; Plans and government go toe-to-toe over need for funding relief, *Pensions and Investments*, June 15, 2009.

HIH Royal Commission 2001-2002, *Transcripts of Evidence to the Royal Commission*, Commonwealth of Australia.

International Actuarial Association (IAA) 2009, Measurement of Liabilities for Insurance Contracts: Current Estimates and Risk Margins, *An International Actuarial Research Paper*, prepared by the ad hoc Risk Margin Working Group.

International Association of Insurance Supervisors (IAIS) 2002, Principles on Capital Adequacy and Solvency, January 2002.

International Association of Insurance Supervisors 2003, The Use of Actuaries as Part of a Supervisory Model, *Guidance paper*.

International Association of Insurance Supervisors 2007, *Summary of IAIS Positions on the Valuation of Technical Provisions*, October 2007.

Johnston, E. 2008, Sun Sets Over Sale Plans for Suncorp, *The Age*, October 27, 2008; and Suncorp-Metway Chief Rides Out the Storm, *The Age*, October 31, 2008.

Lowenstein, R. 2001, *When Genius Failed: The Rise and Fall of Long Term Capital Management*, Fourth Estate, London.

Macintosh, J. 2001, FSA Allows Insurers to Lower Reserves, *Financial Times*, September 25, 2001.

McQueen, R. 1996, *Who Killed Confederation Life?*, McClelland & Stewart, Toronto, Ontario.

Milhaupt, C. J. 1999, Japan's Experience with Deposit Insurance and Failing Banks: Implications for Financial Regulatory Design?, *Washington University Law Quarterly*, Vol 77, pp.399-431.

National Association of Insurance Commissioners (NAIC) publications, http://www.naic.org.

O'Harrow, R. & Dennis, B. 2008, Downgrades And Downfall: How could a single unit of AIG cause the giant company's near-ruin and become a fulcrum of the global financial crisis?, *Washington Post*, December 29, 30 and 31, 2008.

Office of the Comptroller of the Currency (OCC) 1988, *Bank Failure: An Evaluation of the Factors Contributing to the Failure of National Banks*.

Perkins, T. 2009, Nobody's Saviour, *The Globe and Mail*, April 24, 2009.

Scism, L. 2009, Crisis on Wall Street: Life Insurer Rules Aren't Eased, *The Wall Street Journal*, January 30, 2009.

Zuill, L. 2008, US State Regulators Mull Easing Life Insurer Rules, Reuters, December 2008.

Fred's Coffee Shop – Profit

Before Fred opened his coffee shop, he spent a year selling coffee and cakes from a mobile van. He made $41,282.47 profit from that venture. He can be very precise about how much profit he made because he put an initial sum of money into a bank account, paid all expenses out of that account, paid all revenues into that account and, at the end of the year, returned the rented van and all the equipment, gave away all remaining supplies and took back his initial investment. What was left was clearly the profit made over the year.

Now that Fred has the coffee shop and plans to run it indefinitely, it isn't quite so simple. He can't wait until he has sold his last coffee to count his profits. It is likely that other stakeholders, such as business partners or lenders, or the tax authority, will want to know every year how the shop is doing. Fred needs to know for his own benefit – if he is making losses year after year, he needs to make changes now, not just carry on blindly until he has no money left.

The problem in working out the profit for the shop is that at the end of the financial year, there will be various items of unfinished business. For example, suppose that last year Fred bought enough takeout cups to last for two years. Boxes of cups labeled "Fred's fabulous coffee" don't have much resale value, so it might seem reasonable to place a zero value on the cups in the end-of-year balance sheet, even though they cost $1,000. But, by doing so, all the cost of the cups falls into the past accounting year. Last year will seem less profitable by $1,000 than it really was; and next year will seem more profitable, because no money will have to be spent on cups. Using a conservative value for the balance sheet creates a distorted picture in the profit and loss account.

So Fred decides to place a value on the cups. Even so, he may still have decisions to make. Should he use the $1,000 that the cups cost him, or the $2,000 that the same quantity of cups will now cost? There is no strictly correct answer, although accounting rules may specify a standard approach in an attempt to make accounts more comparable across companies. None of the decisions affects the actual profit but they do affect the way in which it is allocated between years.

For Fred, these decisions are not of major importance. Most of his transactions are carried out within the financial year – the coffee beans are bought, roasted and sold within a short period of time. For a company that has long-term contracts, such as a life insurance company, decisions about how to treat the ongoing contracts have a major impact on the profit that is reported in the accounts each year.

Chapter 16 introduces several approaches that can be used to determine the profit that is reported. It also points out an important distinction between *reported* profit (that which appears on financial or regulatory reports) and *distributable* profit (that which can safely be taken out of the business).

Chapter 16:   Profit

by David Service and Richard Lyon

16.1   Overview of profit

For any business, there are three views of profit. Suppose the owner(s) of the business keep all transactions separate from any other parts of their lives. When the business closes or is sold, they can compare how much money they have to what they had when the business started. This difference will be called *ultimate profit* and requires no assumptions or accounting rules. Before this time, various parties are keenly interested in how the business is performing. For example, it is likely that the owners do not want to wait until the end to claim (and enjoy) the profits. Each year they would like a measure of the share of the ultimate profit earned that year. This *distributable profit* measures the amount that could be safely withdrawn from the company. It is likely to be calculated conservatively to ensure that the ultimate profit is not jeopardized. Others, such as the banks that have lent money to the owners, are interested in a more realistic version of the company's status. *Reported profit* is the result of a formal process, often constrained by accounting or regulatory rules. In this chapter, *profit* will always refer to a measure of gain over a specified period, usually one year, and the distinction between distributable and reported profit will be made when necessary.

In general accounting terms, profit is determined as the difference between *income* and *expenditure* for a specific time period, where both income and expenditure are those attributable to that time period.

In this context, income and expenditure are not simply cash amounts received or paid but include:

- *income* – cash received or receivable, the value of new net assets recognized and the increase (or decrease) in the value of existing assets (eg unrealized capital gains on invested assets held); and

- *expenditure* – cash paid or payable, depreciation of fixed assets and the increase (or decrease) in provisions or liabilities for costs of future services, benefits or expenditures that the entity is obliged to incur.

Profit in respect of the existing insurance operation of an insurer can be expressed as:

$$income = \text{premiums} + \text{investment income}$$

less

$$expenditure = \text{claims} + \text{expenses} + \text{tax} + \Delta \text{ policy liabilities.}$$

You can see that the determination of *policy liabilities* will have a material impact on the amount of profit in this calculation. However, as we have seen in Chapter 12, policy liabilities will have no impact on the ultimate profit because they always start and end at zero.

The determination of other items can also be important, for example:

- how unrealized capital gains on investment assets are (or are not) taken into account;

- how expenditure on items such as computer systems or advertising is recognized, ie whether it is recognized in the current year or spread over, say, three or five years; and

- consistency in the way in which the assets and liabilities are measured.

While these definitions of profit seem relatively simple, there are three key issues which we will explore in the following sections:

- the difference between *reported* and *distributable* profit. Generally, not all reported profit is available to be distributed because some needs to be retained to provide funding for capital expenditure or to meet growing requirements for regulatory capital;

- when does profit arise in long-term contracts? Can we recognize the present value of all future profit when we write the contract or should we wait until we progressively deliver the services under those contracts? and

- are we measuring the profit arising from the provision of services to customers in the period or are we measuring the change in economic value of the company arising from actions taken in the period?

The chapter will conclude by looking at how appraisal values are calculated and their use as a profit reporting measure.

16.2   Profit measurement

For any business the general accounting model of profit measurement will nearly always involve a need to estimate some quantities. For example:

- the value of invested assets of any financial institution (which affects investment income);

- the expected economic life of a machine or of the benefits of an advertising campaign (which affects expenses); and

- the policy liabilities of an insurer (which affect the change in policy liabilities).

Where the nature of a business is short-term, involving substantial cash turnover and little in the way of assets and liabilities that span profit reporting periods, the measure of operational profit may be considered to be relatively reliable. However, as the assets and liabilities (or other items) increase in relative size, any measure of profit becomes increasingly dependent on the reliability of the measurement of these items.

This feature is at the heart of the difference between two historic paradigms for profit reporting for long-term insurance business.

The insurer has certain accounting objectives, while the user of the corresponding financial reports has certain requirements. Ideally, an accounting approach will be adopted that satisfies these objectives and requirements. In fact, insurers report on a number of different bases. Insurance supervisors will focus on a statutory accounting approach that stresses solvency aspects; investors and shareholders will be interested in the accounting treatment; and the insurer's management will need the operational information and the value-added insight of managerial accounting for decision-making purposes. *Reported profit* will refer to the net income or loss produced by the accounting system defined by the generally accepted accounting rules and practices in the jurisdiction where the insurer is domiciled.

16.2.1 The traditional view of profit

Traditionally, profit had no meaning until the last of the business had gone off the books and all outstanding claims had been finalized. It was then possible to calculate, in retrospect, the ultimate profit generated by that business. The standard actuarial textbook by Fisher and Young (1965, p. 21) said "Profit could only be determined when the last survivor of a group of contracts had gone off the books and all claims and expenses applicable to the group had been paid."

Calculations in the intervening periods produced estimates of *surplus*. Generally defined as the excess of assets over liabilities and typically measured on a conservative basis, surplus was vigorously differentiated from any concept of "realistic" profit. A prime reason for this position was the uncertainty of the estimates of future experience and the resulting impact on the value of policy liabilities which, of course, was a key determinant of the amount of either profit or surplus. This view underlies the general accounting practice within Lloyd's, under which the accounts for each year's written premium are typically held open for three years during which time no profit is recognized.

In this traditional view, the increase in surplus in a period may be viewed as the "profit" in that period. Over the life of a group of contracts, the total increase in surplus would be the same as the ultimate profit from those contracts, so this view seems quite reasonable.

However, surplus will typically be measured for purposes other than an assessment of the financial performance over the past year. If, for example, the measurement is quite conservative, the surplus arising in the early years of a group of contracts is likely to be lower than the total modern profit described in 16.2.2 below. Therefore the surplus which will then arise over the remainder of the contracts' life is greater than the remaining profit under 16.2.2.

This means that it may not be very easy to tell how traditional profit in a period is likely to compare to modern profit. Certainly, the fact that the surplus may be determined on a conservative basis doesn't mean that the increase in surplus is a conservative measure of profit.

16.2.2 The modern view of profit

Differing from the traditional view is a more modern approach which holds that while the estimation of policy liabilities (and therefore profit) is uncertain, a current measure of profit is nonetheless essential for shareholders, regulators, policyholders and other users of financial statements to measure the realistic progress of the business. It is also necessary for the equitable treatment of stakeholders (for example, policyholders versus shareholders).

The modern view recognizes that uncertainty in estimating future experience for insurers is, conceptually, no different from the uncertainty inherent in profit measurement for many other industries. What, for example, is the life of a mine and how should the development costs be written off against future revenue? How quickly should you depreciate a steel mill in measuring its annual profit?

The calculation of profit for an insurer is now considered to be accepted practice.

16.2.3   Profit measurement versus solvency

While the modern view of profit may be considered to be self-evident and the traditional view somewhat quaint, it is important to understand the critical tension between realistic profit measurement and questions of solvency or financial stability.

The traditional view reflects an environment in which the actuary determined the *distributable profit,* ie the amount that could be prudently distributed to policyholders (eg as bonuses) or to shareholders (eg as dividends). The priority was to ensure that there was sufficient surplus to maintain the solvency of the company into the future. Having done this, the second objective was to be equitable in distributing profit, both between policyholders and shareholders and between different groups of policyholders. There was no particular demand for the calculation of a realistic profit.

The modern view recognizes a clear distinction between *reported profit* and distributable profit. As the measurement and reporting of an institution's distributable profit becomes increasingly comprehensive and separate from the profit reporting basis, the profit reporting basis can be freed to focus on determining a measure that gives a best estimate of profit.

Without this clear distinction, it is hard to resolve the tension between measuring a realistic profit and establishing how much profit may be prudently distributed. You should note that the financial reporting bases of many industries (and some financial institutions) do not clearly distinguish between reported and distributable profit.

16.3   The emergence of profit

16.3.1   Sources of profit

In any business, profit can be thought of as having been generated from three sources:

* investment earnings on the net shareholders' funds of the business held in cash deposits or other financial instruments (eg bonds, shares or property);

* the profit margins built into the pricing of products; and

* deviations of actual experience from that which was expected in the product pricing.

For example, the owner-operator of a coffee shop may expect, based on budgeted sales and costs, to make a profit of 20 percent of turnover.[1] In practice, sales and costs will be different from budget and the actual profit margin will most likely not be 20 percent.

In most businesses in which actuaries are involved with the measurement of profit and/or liabilities, the change in liabilities will generally be at least as significant a component of profit as the difference between actual experience and the pricing assumptions.

In some businesses, profit is affected by the change in value of depreciating assets such as a new computer system or the costs incurred in a mine before ore can be extracted and sold. To the extent that there is flexibility in the pattern of depreciation or amortization,[2]

---

[1]   We use the term *turnover* here in its sense of the total income from sales, net of sales taxes but before deduction of any expenses.

[2]   The terms *depreciation* and *amortization* are conceptually interchangeable, although the former is generally used with reference to tangible assets while the latter relates to intangible ones.

the approach taken will dictate the expected contribution to profit from these assets. Look at the accounts of a mining company for examples of the impact of depreciation and amortization.

In the case of life insurance, the change in *policy liabilities* is one of the most important inputs into the calculation of profit. We can, therefore, link the profit outcome with the methods and assumptions used in calculating policy liabilities.

The three sources of profit mentioned above relate to the assumptions made in pricing but not to the assumptions made in the calculation of the liabilities. As we have already discussed, the assumptions and methodologies used in determining liabilities will affect both the reported profit and the distributable profit but not the ultimate profit. If these assumptions and methodologies are not the same as was expected in the pricing, this is a fourth source of profit. Unlike the other three, it is not a source of ultimate profit.

Therefore, we can contemplate the following definitions:

- *real profit* is represented by the three sources listed at the start of this subsection;

- *measured profit* is the real profit adjusted by the effect of the differences between pricing and liability assumptions; and

- the *emergence* (also called *recognition*) *of profit* is a description of the way in which the measurement approach allows the real profit to emerge.

When the last policies have terminated, the total measured profit since the first policies were issued will be equal to the total real profit over the same period, ie the ultimate profit. However, the pattern of emergence of measured profit will have been shaped by the liability basis and assumptions adopted along the way.

So, to recap:

- the ultimate profit reflects the prices charged and the actual experience and is not affected by the liability basis or assumptions;

- the pricing assumptions determine the total expected profit but they do not affect the total real profit (the ultimate profit) because any difference between pricing assumptions and actual experience appears in the total experience profit; and

- along the way, the emergence of profit is shaped by the liability basis and assumptions.

We can use the insight we have gained in this subsection to enable us to determine how to calculate policy liabilities so that realistic profit emerges in a particular manner. Now we are ready to move the discussion on to questions around the nature of profit and the appropriate timing of its emergence or recognition.

16.3.2   Timing of profit recognition

There has been, and will continue to be, much discussion about the way in which profit should be measured for long-term contracts. If we assume that the premiums charged include profit margins over and above the expected cost of benefits and expenses then when should those margins be recognized as profit? The possibilities range from recognizing the present value of expected future profit margins when the contract is sold through to recognizing the initial capital requirement as a loss, so that there is no net profit until the contract has terminated. In practice, the way in which those possibilities are turned into reality revolves around the manner in which the liabilities are calculated.

We can see the effect of different approaches by considering the following examples, which draw on Example 12.4 in Chapter 12. The contract is a 10-year fixed-term investment-linked policy, issued for a single premium of $10,000. Fees are one percent of account balance, deducted at the end of each year. Expenses are expected to be five percent of premium at issue and 0.3 percent of account balance, with the latter incurred at the end of each year. There will be no terminations during the 10-year term. The expected investment return is 10 percent per annum and there is no tax.

We will ignore assets held in excess of the liability in the same way as we ignore other products, to make it easy to see the effect of the liability calculations on the emerging profit of this policy. Since we are only considering the assets held to cover the liabilities, interest on assets and interest on liabilities become identical.

In our examples, we note that we can determine profit (ignoring interest on capital held in excess of the liability) as:

profit = cash flow[3] + interest on liability at start of year – increase in liabilities.

Note that *increase in liabilities* could be either positive or negative.

Example 16.1   Immediate recognition of future profit

The best estimate liability (BEL) is determined by discounting the expected cash flows at the expected interest rate. As this allows for all future profits, the expected profit is all recognized in Year 0 as shown in Table 16.1.

Table 16.1   Profit pattern when all profit is recognized at time 0

Year[4]	Cash Flow	Interest on Liability	Increase in Liability	Profit
0	9,500		(9,331)	169
1	(33)	933	(900)	0
2	(36)	1,023	(987)	0
3	(39)	1,122	(1,083)	0
4	(43)	1,230	(1,187)	0
5	(46)	1,349	(1,302)	0
6	(51)	1,479	(1,428)	0
7	(55)	1,622	(1,567)	0
8	(60)	1,779	(1,719)	0
9	(65)	1,950	(1,885)	0
10	(23,528)	2,139	21,389	0

After Year 0, the interest on the liability is sufficient to fund the negative cash flow and the increase in the liability.

---

[3] Cash flow is as shown in Example 12.4.
[4] As explained in Chapter 12, it is a useful convention to show the transactions at the point of issue in a separate "Year 0," because it makes it easier to see the immediate implications of selling a policy or product.

16.3.2.1   What about risk margins?

From Chapter 15, you will be aware of the need to hold a margin for risk on top of a best estimate of the liabilities. A similar approach could be adopted for our simple example. (For example, we could add a margin of 20 percent to our expense assumption.) To the extent that the risk margin varies from the profit margin reflected in the product pricing, a profit or loss at policy inception (or renewal) will be reported.

Example 16.2   BEL + margin

If our valuation liability is more conservative than best estimate, the valuation margins can be expected to be released over the life of the contract.

This liability basis (assuming that the cash flows are as originally projected) leads to a somewhat reduced initial profit and a small expected profit thereafter. This reflects profit being held back initially to finance the valuation margin and this margin being released over time. You should be able to see from Table 16.2 that each year's projected profit after issue is equal to 20 percent of the expected expenses.

Table 16.2   Profit with margin equal to 20 percent of expected expenses

Year	Cash Flow	Interest on Liability	Increase in Liability	Profit
0	9,500		(9,388)	112
1	(33)	939	(899)	7
2	(36)	1,029	(986)	7
3	(39)	1,127	(1,080)	8
4	(43)	1,235	(1,184)	9
5	(46)	1,354	(1,298)	9
6	(51)	1,484	(1,423)	10
7	(55)	1,626	(1,560)	11
8	(60)	1,782	(1,710)	12
9	(65)	1,953	(1,874)	13
10	(23,528)	2,140	21,402	14

16.3.2.2   Margin on Services profit

The *Margin on Services* (MoS) valuation method was developed in Australia for valuing life insurance policy liabilities. The intent of a MoS valuation is that profit will only emerge when it has been earned, ie by providing the relevant service and receiving payment. The expected profit measured at issue of the policy is spread over one or more profit carriers, representing the major service(s) provided under the contract. For example, the major service under a level premium term insurance contract is coverage of the mortality risk, which will increase over the duration of the contract. If experience exactly matches the assumptions used when the policy is issued, profit will emerge as a constant proportion of the expected mortality cost.

In the example above (16.2), you should be able to see that the profit at issue would reduce to zero if the risk margin was set at about 59 percent of expenses. However, for a MoS valuation it would be more usual to express the margin as a profit margin on fees (17.7 percent in this case). In this example, there is no difference between these two approaches, as you can see by adjusting the Excel model on the CD. However, the choice of *profit carrier* (fees in this case) will usually affect the expected shape of emergence of profit.

16.3.2.3   What about capital?

All financial institutions are required by the relevant regulatory authorities to have at least a minimum amount of capital to support the business they write. That capital may be separately identified, as an amount of net assets that must be retained in addition to the published liabilities. For example, for a bank the amount of capital required is usually calculated with regard to the risks inherent in the bank's assets, liabilities and operations and the published net assets must exceed this amount.

For many years, and still in some jurisdictions, the capital for life insurance business was not separately identified but was included by way of minimum standards for the calculation of policy liabilities. This means that any calculation of profit using these liabilities will include the movements in capital requirements. This is a very limited way of calculating profit. For a growing business, it appears to show losses that are, in reality, merely the representation of the additional capital required to support the new business. For a declining business, high levels of profit emerge as the margins in the liabilities are released.

Example 16.3   Distributable profit

If we adopted a liability equal to account balance, the projected profits would become as illustrated in Table 16.3.

Table 16.3   Profit with liability equal to account balance

Year	Cash Flow	Interest on Liability	Increase in Liability	Profit
0	9,500		(10,000)	(500)
1	(33)	1,000	(890)	77
2	(36)	1,089	(969)	84
3	(39)	1,186	(1,055)	91
4	(43)	1,291	(1,149)	99
5	(46)	1,406	(1,252)	108
6	(51)	1,532	(1,363)	118
7	(55)	1,668	(1,484)	128
8	(60)	1,816	(1,617)	140
9	(65)	1,978	(1,760)	152
10	(23,528)	2,154	21,540	166

> The expected profits on this valuation basis reflect the initial expenses being financed by the company[5] and then recovered (together with a profit) from future fees less ongoing expenses. These profits would be distributable if no additional capital was required to be held.
>
> In many countries, additional capital would be required. As the account balance is 10,000 at time zero, a requirement to hold an extra one percent of account balance would increase the liability at that date by 100, increasing the loss at issue to 600. The increase in liability in Year 1 would be increased by 9, but the interest on the Year 0 liability would be increased by 10, so the profit in Year 1 is increased by 1. You should be able to see that similar small increases in profit would apply in Years 2 to 9, with a large increase in profit in Year 10 when the margin (now 215) is released.

16.3.2.4 Amortized assets

Similar issues relating to the emergence of profit arise when considering the amortization of assets. There are several industries in which companies invest significant amounts of money in a project in anticipation of future earnings. Examples include property development, mining and infrastructure companies.

A key amortization issue is the manner in which these acquisition expenses are amortized over the life of the business acquired through that expenditure. As with our example product, it may be considered misleading to show a loss as a result of this investment if the project or product can be expected to be profitable over its useful life. Therefore, the original acquisition expenses may be treated as an asset (the *Deferred Acquisition Cost* (DAC) discussed in Section 12.3.8), to be written down (*amortized*) against future earnings. You should be able to see that the rules or principles adopted in amortizing the asset will affect the emergence of profit in an equivalent manner to the liability-driven examples in the tables above. Different accounting systems may impose different rules as to the amount able to be amortized and the manner in which that amortization should be done. The same issues apply to some other major assets on many companies' balance sheets. For example, when a company acquires another company, it will often pay more than the target's net assets. Therefore, when the target is consolidated into the acquirer's balance sheet, the acquirer needs to show an additional asset, called *goodwill*, in order to avoid making a loss on the acquisition. Again, this asset is expected to be justified by future earnings. The way in which it is amortized (if at all) can have a significant effect on the emergence of profit.

Finally, a company may purchase major tangible assets with limited useful lives. Examples include buildings, manufacturing equipment and computer systems. Such an asset is *depreciated* over its expected useful life. Generally, this depreciation occurs either on the straight-line method (where the asset is written down by the same amount each year) or on the declining-balance method (where the asset is written down by a constant proportion of its remaining value each year), but several other approaches are possible.

---

[5] The negative initial profit on this basis is often referred to as new *business strain*. This concept was discussed in Chapter 13.

Example 16.4   DAC-adjusted profit

Continuing our example, remember that the initial expenses are 500. If we adopted a liability equal to account balance plus a one percent margin, we might also establish a DAC asset of 500 for reporting purposes. Our projected loss at issue would reduce by 500 to become 100.

If we amortize our DAC linearly over the 10-year life of the policy, it will reduce by 50 each year. For example, after four years the DAC is expected to be 300.

Our projected profits (with DAC offset against the gross liability) are illustrated in Table 16.4.

Table 16.4   DAC-adjusted profit

Year[4]	Cash Flow	Interest on Liability	Increase in Liability	Profit
0	9,500		(9,600)	(100)
1	(33)	960	(949)	(22)
2	(36)	1,055	(1,029)	(10)
3	(39)	1,158	(1,116)	3
4	(43)	1,269	(1,211)	16
5	(46)	1,390	(1,314)	30
6	(51)	1,522	(1,427)	45
7	(55)	1,665	(1,549)	60
8	(60)	1,819	(1,683)	77
9	(65)	1,988	(1,828)	94
10	(23,528)	2,171	21,706	348

This pattern is different again. There are losses in Years 1 and 2 as well as at issue. If we compare with Table 16.3 where the liability was the account balance, the initial loss of 100 is less than the previous initial loss of 500 because of the prudential margin and the initial DAC.

In Year 1, our prudential margin increases by 9 (from 100 to 109) but our DAC reduces by 50 (from 500 to 450), so our net liability increases by 59 more than the account balance (949 compared with 890). As the net liability after Year 0 was 400 lower than account balance (9,600 compared with 10,000), the interest earned in Year 1 is reduced by 40. Overall, the profit in Year 1 is thus 99 lower than in the previous table (a loss of 22 compared to a profit of 77).

At the end of the term, the prudential margin will be released, partly offset by the final year's amortization of DAC.

16.3.2.5 Profit signatures

A graph of expected profits is often called a *profit signature*. It can be used to compare different products or different valuation bases. In this case, we can compare the profit signatures from Examples 16.1 to 16.4 (including the variations described in those examples) to show how the valuation basis affects the expected emergence of profit. These examples cover the range from up-front recognition of profit to passing the full capital implications through to profit and also show the effect of DAC.

Comparing these profit signatures shows the effect of the difference between the pricing assumptions and the various liability assumptions, which is the fourth source of profit given in Section 16.3.1.

Figures 16.1 and 16.2[6] show the pattern of expected profit for each valuation basis. It is important to remember that the actual measured profit will reflect the deviations of actual experience from expected. That is, actual profit = expected profit + experience profit. So, if experience is volatile, if the assumptions are unrealistic or if expected profit is small, the experience profit could make a significant difference.

If, for example, we recognized the present value of expected future profit margins at commencement, the measured profit each year thereafter would simply reflect the deviations of actual experience from that expectation (and we can certainly expect that there will be some deviation in actual experience).

Figure 16.1   Three profit signatures for Examples 16.1 to 16.4

Figure 16.2   Three further profit signatures for Examples 16.1 to 16.4

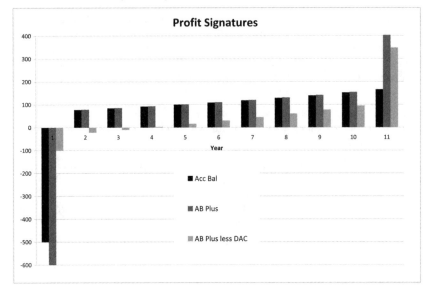

Exercise 16.1

Consider a company whose products are all the same as the example product described above. Considering the profit signatures shown in Figures 16.1 and 16.2, and ignoring assets held in addition to the policy liabilities, describe how profit would be expected to emerge in the following circumstances if liabilities are valued on (i) best estimate, (ii) MoS and (iii) account balance plus a margin:

(a) The company is growing rapidly; new business is at a much higher level than is required to replace the maturing policies.

(b) The company is stable; new business is at a level which replaces maturing policies.

(c) The company is declining; new business is insufficient to replace maturing policies.

How would your answers be affected if you included assets held in addition to policy liabilities (so that total assets were unaffected by the liability valuation basis)?

Exercise 16.2

This exercise requires you to do some research.

Find the accounts of three major companies outside financial services (generally available on the internet) and, in each case, read the note which explains the approach taken to valuing intangible and depreciating assets. Compare these approaches and discuss their effect on the companies' reported results.

16.3.3 Measurement issues

We have seen how the emergence of profit is affected by the choice of methods to value liabilities and to amortize or depreciate certain assets. We have also briefly discussed the fact that the reported profit will differ from the expected profit because actual experience will differ from expected experience.

Other factors may also affect the calculation of components of the profit and, hence, affect the total reported profit.

Accounting rules can have a major impact on reported profit. To the extent that companies can interpret these rules, a comparison of profit between companies may require particular caution. Even when options are limited, the same experience may generate quite different results under different accounting regimes.

Example 16.5   Accounting treatment of bonds

If a company purchases a corporate bond (eg a debenture), we would expect that the value at the time of purchase would equal the purchase price, or *cost price*. A bond has a fixed schedule of interest payments at a *coupon* rate of interest and is expected to be repaid at its *face* or *par* value on maturity.

Between purchase and maturity, the market value of the bond (ie the price at which the company could expect to be able to sell this asset) will depend, primarily, on the term structure of risk-free interest rates and the credit risk margin associated with the issuer of the bond.

Depending on the applicable accounting rules and the options available to the company, it may choose to value the bond during this period using methods such as:

- *market value* – profit is affected by the full impact of changes in interest rates and credit spreads;

- *amortized value* – the bond is valued on the purchase interest rate, so the contribution to profit is as would have been expected when the bond was purchased; and

- *adjusted cost price* – the bond is valued at the cost price, except where this is clearly too high. Unless interest rates rise too much, the yearly contribution to profit will generally be the interest payments, except at maturity when the bond is effectively written up or down to its face value.

Note that accounting rules may sometimes provide that changes in the value of an investment affect the balance sheet without affecting profit.

Investment return is also affected by the value placed on investments with no independently verifiable market value such as property and unlisted equities. For some companies, in some years, the values placed on these assets can have a significant effect on measured profit.

Issues can also arise in valuing liabilities. Valuation issues are discussed in Chapter 12, but the key point to recognize is that a conservative valuation approach may not produce a conservative liability (and hence a conservative profit) if there are deficiencies in the data or the assumptions.

Indeed, data deficiencies in general can have a large effect on reported profit. If a company's operating or recording processes are inadequate or its risk management is ineffective, the data in its financial systems may be very inaccurate. Several high-profile corporate failures occurred after reported profits were inflated by undetected errors, whether or not fraud or other deliberate intervention was involved.

Finally, reported profit is affected by timing issues, including the question of which accounting period a particular item of income or expense belongs to. For actuaries, the most significant timing issues generally relate to delays in the reporting of claims. As such, an allowance should be made for incurred but not reported (IBNR) claims to reflect the true experience in a particular period.

16.4   Profit versus value

Running across the emergence of profit issue discussed above, there is a general issue that goes beyond the difference in the use of pricing or liability assumptions and/or pricing or liability profit/risk margin determination. This relates to a fundamental profit recognition issue. It is the difference between:

> *earned profit* – for example, booking the profit margin within an insurance premium as the risks under the insurance product pass and the premium is earned;

and

> *economic value accrued* – for example, booking the value of the difference between the future premiums to be received and the future benefits and expenses, created on the day the business is written.

These alternative views of profit are reflected in the currently competing accounting frameworks of:

- *deferral-and-matching* – under this framework, the focus is on determining a meaningful measure of profit. The assets and liabilities on the balance sheet are measured in a way that aims to achieve a match in the timing of the recognition of income and expenditure; and

- *asset-and-liability* – under this framework, the focus is on determining a meaningful balance sheet. Profit is then the change in the value of the balance sheet's net asset position[7] over time.

Proponents of the deferral-and-matching model are concerned with trying to distill a measure of the underlying profitability of a business process. Profit reporting based on liabilities set on the pricing assumptions would be broadly consistent with this approach. Some typical insurance accounting approaches that may apply under a deferral-and-matching basis would be holding unearned premium reserves (so premium is earned over time) and policy acquisition costs amortized over the life of the policies. Under this approach, assets are sometimes recorded at historic cost although the trend now is for assets to be measured at market values with liabilities measured in a consistent manner.

---

[7]   Net assets are the difference between assets and liabilities.

Proponents of the asset-and-liability model are concerned that the deferral-and-matching approach fundamentally involves artificial balance sheet items (for example, deferred acquisition costs or devices designed to match profit release with measures of services provided). Under the asset-and-liability model, an insurer could value assets at current market value and report policy liabilities on a present value basis based on current best estimate assumptions (or measured on a *fair value* basis – the market price at which the liabilities could be transferred to another party at the reporting date). If movements in such a "true" balance sheet disclose large volatility in profits, then this reflects the underlying reality of, and risks inherent in, the business. The volatile profit is not wrong; rather, a comprehensive analysis of the drivers of the profit is needed in order to properly understand the business.

In practice, most reporting bases reflect elements of both of these approaches. For example, under MoS reporting, assets are reported at market value and liabilities are calculated on current assumptions and discount rates. However, MoS defers the recognition of future profit margins until the service is provided. This treatment of profit margins has the effect of amortizing (deferring-and-matching) the main insurance profit margins and acquisition cost recovery.

16.5   Appraisal values

An actuarial appraisal value (AV) is a discounted cash flow valuation technique. It represents the present value of all future distributable earnings from one or more blocks of business. In determining the AV of a financial institution, we will value all of its blocks of business. The AV includes the future cash flows from existing business and from future new business.

AVs were first used by actuaries for life insurance companies but their use has now extended to non-life insurers, funds managers and other financial institutions. The concepts are equally applicable to any business but, to date, there has been little application to companies outside the financial services sector. AVs are used as the basis for sale of insurance companies as well as a measure of profit.

In the discussion that follows, we will use the term "company" but remember that a single block of business can have its AV calculated using the same approach.

16.5.1   Overview of appraisal values

We are valuing the company from the perspective of the shareholders. It is, therefore, the future earnings that can be paid to those shareholders that determine value. Hence we are focused on distributable earnings (ie after changes in capital requirements), rather than just profit. The relationship is captured in this formula:

$$distributable\ earnings = profit - \Delta\ capital$$

For an expanding business, the capital requirement is usually increasing, meaning that distributable earnings are less than profit. However, if we are not allowing for new business additions (eg the block of business is assumed to be closed to new business) then the distributable earnings will be larger than profit because capital is released as the business which it supported exits.

While an actuarial AV is a sophisticated approach that takes account of the major characteristics of the business and its future earnings, the general concept of relating value to the future earnings is to be found in valuation approaches for a wide range of businesses. The most obvious example is the use of a price/earnings multiple in valuing equities. If the price (ie the value) is some multiple of earnings, the multiple can be decomposed into the following formula:

$$multiple = (1 + g) / (r - g)$$

where:

> g = expected growth rate of future earnings (excluding growth from reinvestment of profits);
>
> r = discount rate for future earnings;

and the earnings are assumed to continue in perpetuity. Earnings may be the latest reported profit or they may be adjusted to represent *maintainable* earnings.

16.5.2   Components of an appraisal value

A typical discounted cash flow valuation projects the total operations of a business. However, under the common actuarial AV approach, the AV is calculated via three components:

- *net worth*, ie net assets;

- *value of in-force* – the value of future distributable earnings from existing business; and

- *value of new business* – the value of future distributable earnings from future new business.

These three components can be put together to create two different measures. The first – Embedded Value (EV) – combines net worth and value of in-force. This measure is used in a number of jurisdictions as a profit measurement tool. It measures only the existing business and gives no value to the company's ability to write future business. The second – Appraisal Value (AV) – combines all three components. It measures not only the existing business but also the company's ability to write future business. It is used both as a profit measurement tool and as a measure of the value of the company.

16.5.2.1   Net worth

While a major part of the AV is the future distributable earnings from current and future business, all financial institutions will have material amounts of net assets to provide the necessary capital adequacy required by the regulators. These net assets will, themselves, provide future earnings. As we noted in the earlier discussion on profits, the liabilities in respect of a financial institution's business can already contain margins over the fair value of those liabilities. To the extent that these margins exist, the net assets shown in the balance sheet will be understated.

Notwithstanding these differences in treatment, adopting the balance sheet net assets as the net assets for AV purposes ensures consistency with the balance sheet for this particular item.

16.5.2.2 Value of in-force

Value of in-force (VIF) is the value of future distributable earnings from existing business. There is some question as to what constitutes existing business and what constitutes new business. For example:

- is the renewal of an existing non-life insurance policy existing or new business? Typically these are treated as part of existing business;

- are increases in the sum insured on a yearly renewable term policy new business? Automatic Consumer Price Index increases are generally treated as existing business, otherwise increases are generally treated as new business; and

- are future deposits to a personal retirement benefit unit trust new business? These are often treated as existing business if generally consistent with past customer behavior, otherwise they are new business.

Calculation of these distributable earnings is simply a matter of projecting the business until its expiry allowing for all necessary characteristics. The earnings distributable to shareholders is:

$$distributable\ earnings\quad = [premiums - claims - \Delta\ liabilities]\ \textbf{or}\ [fees]$$
$$- expenses$$
$$- \Delta\ capital$$
$$+ investment\ income$$

The alternative in the first term depends on whether the business is insurance or funds management in nature – or, in the terminology of Chapter 12, whether we are looking at our business in a *bundled* or an *unbundled* manner.

Capital relates to the capital requirements of the business over and above the liabilities allowed for in the first term. It is essential to confirm that the sum of the liabilities used in the first term and the capital used in the third term is equal to the regulatory requirement. If an unbundled approach is adopted, then the capital is the amount that must be held by the shareholders in addition to the account balance held on behalf of policyholders.

The value to the shareholders of their capital in the company is less than its face market value. The market value assumes that the shareholder has complete freedom to use that capital for another purpose. However, for regulatory capital that is not the case. The capital remains committed until the business that it supports exits. Its true value to the shareholder is the present value of the future return of that capital. The difference between the market value of the assets representing the capital and the present value of the future return of capital is the cost of the commitment of capital to the business. The profits earned by that commitment of capital are captured in the present value of the future cash flows from the business.

Generally, companies will need to keep more capital than the regulatory minimum. In the context of a life insurer, this excess is referred to as *target surplus*. While opinion varies, many AVs only allow for the cost of regulatory minimum capital. The view is taken that the target surplus is at the discretion of the company and could be reduced to zero at any time.

However, as we have included the release of capital over time in the above present value calculation, and the current capital amount is also reflected in the net assets above, the current capital amount needs to be excluded from VIF (or deducted from net worth) in order that it is not double counted.

If capital is deducted from the value of the in-force business, this gives:

$$VIF = PV(\text{in-force earnings}) - capital(0)$$

$$EV = \text{total assets} - \text{liabilities} - capital + VIF$$

16.5.2.3   Value of new business

In an AV, Value of new business (VNB) can be interpreted in two ways. Either it is the value of the infrastructure that allows the company to be able to write profitable business in the future or it is the value of the best estimate of the profit to be achieved from writing future new business.

In the former case, the infrastructure is the company's product range, distribution channels, brand, competencies, technology platforms and physical infrastructure. While we could value some of these items at the cost of replacement (eg technology platforms and physical infrastructure), how does one value the replacement cost of a brand? An alternative method of valuing this infrastructure is to calculate the value of the future profits from one year's new business and then apply some multiple to that figure. This approach asserts that the value of the infrastructure is best measured by the value of the future new business it allows the company to write. However, while the value of the profits from one year's new business can be readily calculated, what is an appropriate multiple? Clearly, there is room for much debate on the answer.

The other approach makes no attempt to value the infrastructure. It values all future new business, with volumes and profitability calculated, like the in-force value, using best estimate assumptions. This method is more consistent with other valuation approaches. For example, the price/earnings multiple approach values all future business (albeit implicitly) as it assumes future profits in perpetuity.

There is one crucial point to note when interpreting the value of future new business. Since we are allowing for the capital which may be required to write that new business and its subsequent return as the business exits, the value of future distributable cash flows must equal zero if the business returns the risk-adjusted discount rate on the capital invested in the new business. Unlikely as it may seem, and difficult as it is to explain to many observers, a zero value of future new business is not an unreasonable situation. And a negative value does not mean new business is unprofitable. It is simply not earning the risk-adjusted discount rate. These outcomes do not necessarily lead to sound decision-making. If the value of new business is zero then there is no apparent impact whether we write no new business or enormous volumes. However, decisions of this type inevitably affect other areas, eg if we write no new business it is almost certain that our expense rates will rise and our overall profitability will decline. Therefore, VNB should be treated with caution when business decisions are to be made.

In projecting future new business volumes, we need to make sure that the rate of growth is consistent with our overall economic assumption set, eg low inflation rates are likely to mean lower growth rates than high inflation rates. While it is also usual to assume that future profit margins will decline as competition intensifies, it should be noted that the evidence for this assumption is not consistent across all product groups.

Exercise 16.3

The concept of Appraisal Value for life insurers is well-established because of the long-term nature of life insurance policies. Considering the components of value, how would you determine the appraisal value of:

(a) a non-life insurer;

(b) a simple savings bank, offering deposit accounts and mortgage products; and

(c) a mining company?

16.5.3 Appraisal value as a profit measure

In 16.1, profit was defined as the outworking of the financial transactions relevant to the particular time period. An alternative view of profit is to view it as the value added by the operations of the business over that time period. The value added is the difference between the present value of future profits, with allowance for any capital requirements, at the end and the beginning of the time period. This present value is, of course, the AV.

This approach has merit as a way of measuring the overall effectiveness of the management performance over a time period, because it captures the potential long-term impact of decisions taken. However, it may not take account of the uncertainty of the estimates of future business behavior; it is potentially volatile; and it can be crucially dependent on the discount rate used.

Nevertheless, while not using this method as their headline profit figure, many institutions use the change in AV as an important internal measure of performance. As a result, AV has become an essential measurement tool. When used in this manner it is important to distinguish the change in AV arising from assumption changes from the changes that arise from management activity. This latter component might be properly referred to as *value added*.

In the UK, for example, the change in embedded value is often used as a measure of reported profit. In Australia the requirement to value the assets of a life company at market value means that, if one life company owns another life company, the subsidiary will appear in the balance sheet of the owning company at AV, this being the most useful surrogate for market value.

16.6 Practical implications for actuaries

Companies' owners and managers cannot afford to wait until actual profit can be reliably measured on long-term contracts or in other situations where there is a significant timing mismatch between income and associated expenses. Profit (ie measured profit) is generally the way that both groups assess the company's performance, so anything that might affect a component of profit is itself of significance. Therefore, actuaries involved in valuing assets or liabilities need to understand the potential consequences of their valuations. This is not to say, of course, that they should be prepared to amend their valuations to suit the company; rather, there will be situations where the valuation will cause a substantial change to the previously-forecast profit and the actuary must be prepared to communicate the likely impact in a timely and effective manner.

Measured profit emergence also provides an early indication of the actual performance of products which the actuary may have priced. So, actuaries may have a keen interest in understanding profit in order to validate (or provide grounds to review) pricing assumptions.

Finally, businesses which consistently do not make profits (or surplus, in the case of mutual and other non-profit organizations) are not sustainable. As an adviser or as an employee, the actuary therefore has another interest in profit, regardless of any technical role. You should be able to see that this introduces a potential conflict of interest in relation to actuarial work with a profit impact.

16.7   Key learning points

In this chapter, we have discussed profit and considered issues associated with its measurement.

- Profit is the difference between income and expenditure.

- To the extent that the measurement of components of income or expenditure is uncertain, measured profit is only an estimate of true profit, which can only be known after all contracts have terminated.

- Expenditure includes the change in liabilities, which can largely dictate the pattern of emergence of profit, as can the pattern of amortization of some assets.

- Both income and expenditure can be affected by how components are measured, whether because of accounting rules or for other reasons. In turn, this will affect measured profit.

- Profit can represent the change in the economic value of the business or be some measure of the underlying profitability of the business processes.

- An appraisal value (AV) is a measure and valuation of future distributable profits from a company or line of business. It has three main components, being the value of in-force business, the value of future new business and the value of net assets. Movement in AV can be used as a measure of profit.

- This chapter has close links to Chapters 12 (Valuing Liabilities), 13 (Pricing) and 14 (Assets).

CD Items

Chapter 12 & 16 Valuation Model Spreadsheet

Chapter 16 Exercise Solutions

References (other than CD Items)

Appraisal Values Subcommittee 1993, Guidelines for Actuarial Appraisals of Life Insurance Business, *Transactions of the Institute of Actuaries of Australia*, Vol I.

Burrows, R. & Lang, J. 1997, Risk Discount Rates for Actuarial Appraisal Values of Life Insurance Companies, *IAA Centenary Convention*, Vol IV.

Burrows, R. P. & Whitehead, G. H. 1987, The Determination of Life Office Appraisal Values, *Journal of the Institute of Actuaries*, III, pp.114.

Carrett, P. & Stitt, A. 2001, The Valuation of Retail Funds Management Companies, *Australian Actuarial Journal*, Volume 7, Issue 2, pp.251-335.

Coleman, A. M., Edwards, B. A. & Torrance, D. M. 1992, Maintainable Earnings and Actuarial Methods for Valuing Life Insurance Companies, *Transactions of the Institute of Actuaries of Australia.*

Fisher, H. F. & Young, J. 1965, *Actuarial Practice of Life Insurance*, Cambridge University Press.

Hill, T. E., Bean, M., Prince, W.S., Stiefeling, C. & Von Shiling, E. 2001, Stochastic Pricing, *Record of the Society of Actuaries*, Vol 27, No 2.

Mehta, S. J. B. 1992, Allowing for Asset, Liability and Business Risk in the Valuation of a Life Office, *Journal of the Institute of Actuaries* 119, III, pp.385-455.

Melville, G. L. 1987, Some Comments on a Paper by R.P. Burrows and G.H. Whitehead Entitled 'The Determination of Life Office Appraisal Values', *Transactions of the Institute of Actuaries of Australia*, Vol 1.

Perrott, G. 1993, Stochastic Analysis of Universal Life Products, *Proceedings of the 3rd AFIR International Colloquium*, Rome.

Truslove, A. L. 1997, Risk Discount Rates for Market Valuation of Life Insurance Business, *Australian Actuarial Journal*, Vol IV.

Fred's Coffee Shop – Monitoring Experience

As you already know, monitoring experience is one of the key stages in the Actuarial Control Cycle. In fact, monitoring – and then responding – is fundamental not just in actuarial work but in almost everything we do; and every enterprise needs to monitor how its business is going.

Let's consider monitoring Fred's coffee shop. What do you think Fred should monitor? How could he do this?

Think about this for a few minutes and make a brief note of any ideas. Then read on.

The first thing that Fred wants to know about his shop is whether it is making a profit. If not, then he should either close the shop and get out of the business as soon as possible or start doing things differently. You learned about measuring profit in Chapter 16. This means that he needs an accounting system that not only satisfies the needs of others (such as the tax authority, those from whom he has borrowed funds and any partners) but also helps him understand his business.

Suppose Fred measures his profit and finds that, for the last year, he made a profit of $2,000. Would he think, "Fantastic! A profit!"? The answer depends on what he was hoping for. If his business model had projected a profit of $100,000 in that year, he could be very disappointed. On the other hand, if he has only just started out in business, maybe $2,000 for the first year is a good result. So Fred is interested not just in how much profit he made but also on how it compares to what he expected.

Fred will also want to understand how his total profit is made up, so that he understands his business and can maybe improve it. If he has collected the right data, he can break the figure down in various ways, including the following:

- He could look at the profit from different areas of the business. Maybe he is making a large profit on coffee but a loss on food. If that is the case, he might be better off just selling coffee. Or he might be able to change his food prices or offerings to make that part of his business profitable.

- He could analyze the different factors affecting the income and outgo that combine to produce the final profit figure. For example, throwing away stale food will reduce the income from sales and so reduce profit. Therefore Fred will want to know how much is thrown away. If the amount of waste is significant then he may want to investigate further – are particular items more likely to be thrown away? Do the prices reflect this or is he losing money on (say) desserts, after allowing for waste? If he doesn't throw away much at all then he might not bother investigating.

How could Fred carry out the monitoring? Consider the following:

- Fred has to decide how often, or over what period, to do his analysis. He won't give up the business just because of one bad day. But, if he only analyzes profit once a year, he won't find out if he makes a profit in summer and a loss in winter.

- Suppose that Fred wants to measure the wastage of dessert items. To get a meaningful measurement, he needs to know how many are thrown away; he also needs to know how many he bought in the first place – that is, he needs a measure of the exposure. He needs a system that will produce this data, such as making a record of each bin full of discarded stale desserts.

Monitoring is especially important for a financial services firm, because of its reliance on long-term contracts with numerous factors that contribute to profit.

Chapter 17: Monitoring Experience

by David Service

17.1 Introduction

A major component of the Actuarial Control Cycle is the regular comparison of expected outcomes with experience, ie the actual outcomes. Analysis of actual experience is an essential element of this comparison.

17.2 Why do we analyze experience?

17.2.1 Introduction

We analyze experience for a variety of reasons, although all fit into the overall control cycle process. The reasons include:

- reviewing assumptions;
- providing understanding of the drivers of the emerging experience;
- developing a history of experience over time;
- aiding in an analysis of profit and its sources;
- providing information to management;
- providing information to shareholders and third parties;
- satisfying regulatory requirements;
- aiding public relations purposes, including communicating with clients/customers; and
- satisfying disclosure requirements in a listing or acquisition.

Each of these reasons may have a different audience for the results of the analysis. It is important to recognize that each audience will have its own objectives for the analysis. These differing objectives may lead to variations in focus – what is important – and frequency of analyses. The discussion that follows should be interpreted with this caveat in mind.

17.2.2 Reviewing assumptions

Every time period for which we collect and analyze experience provides additional data on which to base our new assumptions. If our previous assumptions were appropriately set as best estimate, then the interperiod experience provides us with independent data against which we can compare our previous assumptions.

When we compare the actual outcomes with the expected outcomes we immediately gain information on the appropriateness of our previous assumptions. The detailed analysis of the experience will be an important piece of input into the review of the previous assumptions.

17.2.3 Providing understanding of the drivers of the emerging experience

The analysis of experience is more than comparing actual to expected. It also includes studying the likely causes of the emerging experience. For example, a decrease in persistency of motor vehicle insurance may be caused by a decision to increase prices leading to customers switching to competitors. Every change in experience has a cause (or causes) although we may not be able to confidently identify each one.

We need an understanding of the reasons for the experience that has occurred in order to propose solutions in cases where the experience is adverse. For example, a deterioration in disability experience could be due to worsening incidence rates or lengthening claims durations. Measures to counter the deteriorating experience will be different depending on the cause.

It may also be the case that the deteriorating experience is due to the results of a particular subgroup in the business. Examination of experience by subcategories is a way of revealing just where the changes have occurred. For example, a life insurance company experiencing worse mortality than expected should review the experience of all categories of business – substandard, standard, and preferred. The company may discover flaws in its underwriting of its preferred business, say.

17.2.4 Developing a history of experience over time

Analyzing data over successive time periods gives a picture of the changes in experience over time. This may highlight trends or seasonality. It may also show spikes in the experience that can be related to specific events.

17.2.5 Aiding in an analysis of profit and its sources

One of the ways we can validate the profit is by analyzing the profit into its various sources. Many of those sources will be relevant to the difference between actual and expected experience and the financial impact of that difference.

Measuring the financial impact of the experience assists in assessing the materiality of the outcome. This informs us as to the necessity for action in response.

17.2.6 Providing information to management

One of management's tasks is to change behavior and strategy so as to adapt to changing market circumstances. Observed experience is an important input into the decision-making process for determining the appropriate actions. The critical part of the input from the experience is the knowledge of the drivers leading to the observed experience. Without that knowledge, management is severely constrained in its ability to respond appropriately. The proper analysis of the experience is, therefore, a central part of this process.

Providing information to management and analyzing the sources of profit are usually closely related. Some parts of management will have particular business segments for which they desire analysis, eg distribution channel, product group or geographic area. Other parts of management may have a different focus, eg expenses, mortality or investment performance. It is often sensible to conduct the analysis using a matrix approach so that both types of information request can be accommodated.

17.2.7 Providing information to shareholders and third parties

As the disclosure requirements of good corporate governance increase, the pressure on companies to provide adequate information to shareholders will similarly increase. The analysis of experience will become more important as a source from which to extract information for disclosure to shareholders. Generally, information provided to shareholders is highly aggregated to provide a broad overview. This requirement can usually be met easily by aggregating analyses already performed to satisfy other audiences.

Third parties who are affected by the company's performance might also require information. This group would include reinsurers and creditors.

17.2.8 Satisfying regulatory requirements

The various regulatory environments in which financial services institutions operate all require a variety of information to be submitted. Some is publicly available but some is confidential to the regulator. Often the data which the regulator requires will be data about experience. Our analysis of the experience is then a required piece of input for the submission of information to the regulator.

17.2.9 Aiding public relations purposes

As well as making disclosure to shareholders, companies provide information to stock market analysts, market researchers, the media, etc for the purpose of improving the company's image. Clients/customers, potential clients/customers, politicians, etc are part of this target audience. In some cases the data needed to support such information disclosure will come from the experience analysis.

17.2.10 Satisfying disclosure requirements in a listing or acquisition

When companies list on the stock exchange or are involved in acquisitions, either as buyer or seller, information must be disclosed by way of a prospectus or by passing the information to the other party. In many of these cases, the data required will be found in the output of the experience analysis. For example, in an acquisition the seller will often provide detailed information to the potential buyer as the buyer prepares a bid or completes due diligence prior to confirming the acquisition.

17.3 What do we analyze?

17.3.1 Introduction

While, in principle, we could analyze all items of experience, in practice we will only analyze those that are important in a particular situation. Normally "important" is determined by the financial impact that variations in experience have on the problem with which we are dealing. In deciding which experience items are important we will initially review each one and, with the aid of sensitivity testing, determine which ones can lead to material financial impacts. In subsequent work we will often rely on these first sensitivity tests. It is important, however, not to lose sight of the fact that an item, which may not initially show itself to be important, can change over time. An accumulation of small changes, a change in the product design or some change in the external environment can cause a previously minor item to become material. It is sound actuarial practice to review periodically all the minor experience items to confirm their continued immateriality.

The experience items for analysis fall into six main groups:

- product-specific, ie contingencies specifically relating to the product, such as:

    ○ performance on risks accepted (eg claims under insurance, defaults on loans, promotional salary increases in retirement benefits based on final salaries, etc); and

    ○ persistency;

- economic;

- investment performance;

- expenses;

- new business volumes and mix; and

- profit and return on capital.

There are obviously links between many of the experience items. The major one is the link between profit and each of the other items. Variations in any experience item will impact the profitability of the business. But there are other less obvious links. In retail funds management, poor investment performance may lead to worse persistency. In disability business, deteriorating economic conditions may lead to deteriorating claims experience. Lower volumes of new business can lead to higher expenses per unit.

Across different types of institutions, the importance of the same item can vary markedly, eg investment performance is normally a minor issue for term life insurance but is a major factor in defined benefit superannuation.

In the next few subsections some observations relating to various types of business will be made and in 17.4 detailed discussion of the techniques and issues relating to each type of experience item will take place.

17.3.2   General insurance

Persistency in the general insurance context is the rate at which policies renew. Even though general insurance contracts are one-year contracts the costs of selling the contract will be much more than the expense loadings in one year's premium. Hence the rate at which existing customers renew has a marked impact on profitability.

Clearly, the item of most importance is claims experience. This includes the rate at which new claims arise and, for long-tail business, the rate and amount at which claims ultimately settle. The rate of inflation, both general and superimposed, is also a part of the long-tail claims experience.

For some types of general insurance, eg crop insurance, weather conditions and seasonality may be important factors. The cyclical climatic pattern known as El Nino may be a driver of claims experience. Climate change is likely to have a major impact, although the evidence of its effect on general insurance claims may take some time to emerge.

17.3.3 Life insurance

Persistency in the life insurance context is the extent to which policies do not terminate by lapse or surrender. There is also the related phenomenon of partial withdrawals from investment products.

Life insurance business divides into two major types of business – risk and investment.

For risk business the claims experience is a major issue. Expenses are relatively more important in life risk business than in general insurance, because the claim rates are normally much lower, meaning that more of the premium is charged to cover expenses.

For investment business the expense rates and persistency are crucial. Investment performance is of central importance only for products with guarantees, where the insurance company accepts some or all of the investment risk. For investment-linked business, where the customer accepts all of the investment risk, investment performance will drive profitability by its impact on total funds under management, which is normally the prime driver of fees charged to customers.

17.3.4 Funds management

The extent to which investment performance drives business volumes and persistency for funds management is unclear. There are suggestions that investment performance is material for wholesale business but much less so for retail business. However, in the longer term, poor investment performance will have an impact on the retail business.

In these circumstances, the major driver of profitability will be expenses and, in the case of retail business, persistency.

17.3.5 Superannuation

In this context, superannuation refers to the actual superannuation scheme, not the institutional product which may be used as the vehicle. Such products fall under either funds management or life insurance.

For defined benefit superannuation the issue of supreme importance is the relationship between investment performance and the inflation rate that applies to benefits. This relationship is often referred to as "the gap." If the gap is greater than that assumed when calculating contribution rates, they will be more than adequate and vice versa. Contribution rates are highly sensitive to this item.

In the case of defined contribution superannuation, all the investment and inflation risks are borne by the members unless there is an element of capital guarantee. The major risk for the fund is that of expenses being greater than charged to members.

17.3.6 Banking

In many ways a bank's accounts run in reverse to those of an insurance company. For a bank, the "claims" experience, ie the losses from default on various loans, affects assets rather than liabilities. It is one of the most important experience items. Not only is it driven by the particular underwriting approach adopted when granting credit but it is strongly correlated to economic conditions. The other crucial experience item is the interest margin, ie the difference between the interest rate a bank has to offer to obtain deposits and the rate it is able to charge on its loan book. The overall interest margin will, itself, be affected by the makeup of the bank's deposits, ie retail versus wholesale, and the makeup of its loan book, ie housing loans versus corporate lending versus credit cards.

As with all financial institutions, expenses have a major impact on profitability. Hence, one of the published measures of bank performance is the cost to income ratio, ie how much of the interest margin is taken by expenses, after allowing for other charges to customers.

17.3.7   Health insurance

Health insurance is conceptually another form of risk insurance. Therefore, the key issues are persistency and claim rates. A major driver of claim costs is inflation of medical expenses and catastrophic claims.

The overall health regime in a particular jurisdiction is a most crucial determinant of the form which health insurance may take. Insurers may face controls on policy design and on pricing. They may be very constrained in their ability to set premiums which fully reflect risk factors such as age, sex or medical history. This is important when considering the mix of business, which is discussed in 17.4.6 below.

Premiums for health insurance are almost always a matter of political importance. Hence, the credibility of experience analyses, which are relied on to justify rate increases, is of more importance than in some other lines of business.

17.4   How do we analyze experience?

17.4.1   Introduction

Before dealing with specific techniques for performing an analysis of experience, we will consider the overall approach. Each analysis will involve the following steps:

- establish the objectives – as we noted earlier, different audiences may have different objectives. Before conducting an analysis we must be confident that the specific objectives will be satisfied;

- collect the data – if the particular analysis is being carried out for the first time or is being extended or amended, this step will include specifying the required data;

- ensure data quality – the adequacy of the data should be assessed, errors in the data should be identified and dealt with, and the impact of approximations should be determined;

- perform the analysis – this includes appropriate and detailed documentation of the process;

- validate the results; and

- explain the results – the results are documented and communicated, including the reasons for those results together with their implications.

Establishing the objectives has been discussed earlier in Section 17.2. It is essential that the specific objective will be satisfied by the analyses conducted.

The issues involved in ensuring data quality have been discussed in Chapter 10 and are revisited in Section 17.5.

The performance of the analysis is discussed below in Sections 17.4.2 to 17.4.7. While there are many common elements to the methods we use to perform the analysis of experience, we will deal separately with each of the six groups of items set out in 17.3.1.

The validation of the results is a crucial phase of the process. The results need to be compared with other relevant information, eg industry studies, other internal analyses (such as annual persistency studies versus monthly lapse data) and any published analyses. If the comparisons are materially different and the explanation is not obvious, then the possibility of errors must be carefully considered. Alternatively, the implications of what would be exceptional results must be dealt with.

Finally, the experience analysis is not complete until the results have been explained. This starts with identifying reasons for the deviation of actual experience from that expected. However, in many cases it will not be possible to fully identify all the reasons. The financial consequences of the deviations should also have been calculated. It is not enough to produce a figure for the ratio of actual versus expected. The financial effect of that difference on the profit for the period under investigation must also be determined. This is usually a by-product of preparing the analysis by amount rather than by number of policies or contracts. We then have actual financial outcomes versus expected financial outcomes. The resulting financial impact is clear and the reasons for the deviation have, as far as possible, been identified.

17.4.2 Product-specific

The analysis of product-specific items generally follows one of two methods:

*   calculate actual versus expected; or
*   calculate the actual rates.

The more common of these is actual versus expected. We calculate the expected outcome, using a specified set of assumptions, for some measurable quantity over some defined time period, eg the number of policies renewing during a quarter, or the amount of claim payments in the calendar year. This is then compared with the actual outcome for the same quantity over the same time period.

Such experience analyses are always conducted for a fixed period of time. A major issue this raises is how to deal with events that occurred during the time period but were reported after the period has ended. We can handle this in two ways. We could delay the analysis until a sufficient time has elapsed to allow all events to have been reported, or we can make specific allowance for the late reporting. The difficulty with the first is how long do we wait? In some cases events can be reported years after the event. In such a case, the analysis is useless by the time it would be available. It is also true that rarely do we know how long we need to wait, even if it is a comparatively short period of time.

Generally we use a combination of the two approaches. We wait a short period to allow reporting with a short delay, eg one month, to have occurred and then make a specific allowance for incurred but not reported (IBNR) events. You have probably learnt some techniques for estimating IBNR claims, but note that such an allowance may be required in all analyses, not just those relating to claims. The validity of our allowance should be regularly compared with the emerging experience of reporting delays. The allowance itself is one of the product-specific items to be analyzed.

Calculating actual rates from an experience analysis is rare. We generally do not have sufficient data to allow us to derive a reliable set of smooth rates. And, even if we have sufficient data, the prime purpose of experience analyses is to compare our original models and assumptions with the actual experience. We can then use the control cycle approach to refine our models and assumptions. In these circumstances some form of comparison of actual and expected is essential.

To be true to the Actuarial Control Cycle, our expected is normally calculated using the assumptions adopted for the most recent iteration of the particular problem. It can also be valuable to calculate our expected using a consistent set of assumptions over successive analyses, to show the trend in experience over time.

The most difficult decision to make when analyzing experience is the extent to which the block of business being analyzed should be broken down into subgroups corresponding to particular characteristics (and combinations thereof). At one extreme we could treat each policy or contract as a subgroup and at the other we could treat the whole block as one single group with no distinction made by any characteristic.

While we normally use the characteristics which are distinguished in our assumption set for calculating the expected, eg age and duration for decrements, we do not necessarily produce comparisons of actual versus expected for each of those characteristics. For example, we would normally distinguish by age and duration when calculating our expected numbers of death claims, but show the actual versus expected only for the whole portfolio, not for each age and duration.

This lack of detail in the analysis is often forced on us by the paucity of the data. If we used all possible cells we would have relatively few observations in each cell and valid conclusions would be hard to draw. However, decisions on how to cut the data are critical for proper analysis as failure to distinguish between characteristics can lead to improper conclusions. The following example demonstrates the danger.

Example 17.1

A life insurance company has two blocks of term insurance – one is yearly renewable term (YRT), the other is an older block of level term business. Both blocks have premium rates differentiated by smoking status. The latest mortality analysis shows the following results, where expected is calculated using the most recent pricing assumptions.

For the YRT block, actual versus expected (A/E) = 95%, while for the level term block, A/E = 84%. The obvious conclusion is that the YRT block has worse mortality experience than the level term. This conclusion is supported by some qualitative reasoning. For YRT, the lives in good health can switch to another company with cheaper rates so leaving us with worse lives. However, this option is not usually attractive to those with level term. The premium rates for their attained age will usually be much higher than they are currently paying. Hence we could expect to see higher mortality for the YRT block than for the level term block.

But suppose that the composition of the two blocks is materially different. In the YRT block, 75% of the business is nonsmoker, while in the level term block, only 25% of the business is nonsmoker. This difference in composition immediately exposes us to the possibility that it is the relationship between smoker and nonsmoker mortality which has changed and not the overall mortality experience.

In our pricing basis, smoker mortality is assumed to be 190% of nonsmoker mortality. When we break down the analysis of the two blocks of business by smoking status, we discover the following A/E results:

	Nonsmoker	Smoker
YRT	100%	79%
Level Term	100%	79%

The interpretation of the results is radically different. It is the smoker experience which has improved – it is now 150%, ie 0.79×190% of nonsmoker mortality compared to the assumed 190% – rather than the two blocks having different experience. In fact the two blocks have identical experience.

It is not only the way we cut the data that is relevant. The particular characteristics that we analyze will impact the way we interpret the results. In analyzing general insurance claims data there are two key measurable characteristics – the claim incidence rate and the final cost of claim settlements. The proper interpretation of the results of any claims analysis depends on these two characteristics being separated. The response to deteriorating claims experience will be different if the cause is a rise in incidence rates or an increase in final claim settlement amounts. Hence, the claims experience analysis needs to distinguish these two characteristics. Not only is the final claim settlement amount important, but also the delay between claim incidence and claim settlement. This is particularly relevant for long-tail claims.

Where there are many potential characteristics that may influence experience we can use generalized linear modeling techniques to measure the impact of each characteristic. This approach avoids us having a multitude of single-dimension analyses, each of which has only small amounts of data. It is particularly useful in many lines of general insurance where there are a large number of rating factors, eg motor vehicle insurance. Instead of a single value for actual versus expected, this technique will show us how well the most recent experience fits our prior model and will also identify which particular characteristics are causing a poor fit.

Section 17.2.4 commented that one reason for analyzing experience is to develop a history of experience over time. For many institutions it is not possible to analyze the experience with the required number of characteristics from the data of a single time period, eg one year. In some situations it is not possible to analyze even the aggregate data over a single time period, eg mortality where the number of expected claims from even a material number of policies is still relatively small. So we aggregate experience over several time periods to obtain sufficient data for analysis. There are two main dangers in this approach. The first is the potential for hiding trends in the data over time. The second is the extent to which changes in the environment, eg economic conditions or changes in underwriting standards, are likely to invalidate conclusions drawn from data from earlier time periods.

Standard time series analysis identifies four components of a data set:

- *trend*, long-term fairly steady changes in one direction;

- *seasonal*, short-term fluctuations that occur each calendar year with similar timing and intensity;

- *cyclical*, rises and falls that are repeated over a longer and less regular pattern than seasonal effects, such as changes related to the business cycle; and

- *random* or *error*, everything else.

The existence of cyclical or seasonal components in a typical experience data set depends on the type of data we are analyzing. Insurance dependent on the weather, eg pluvius insurance or crop insurance, may well be expected to show these components. The probability of rain is quite seasonal and the propensity for drought or flooding can depend on longer cyclical weather patterns such as El Nino. For disability insurance we may find some correlation with economic conditions and for lending we definitely find an increase in bad debt experience when the economy turns down.

Extraction of the components of the time series represented by our experience data is covered in any standard statistics text on time series. These techniques are entirely appropriate for use with our typical experience data.

17.4.3 Economic

Most headline economic data such as GDP, general price inflation and remuneration inflation will be available from various official sources. The key economic items that reflect our individual experience are the rates of inflation experienced by our expenses and affecting any benefits paid or payable in future, such as general insurance claims or pensions linked to inflation. The general economic conditions will, of course, have an impact on business volumes. It is also asserted that claim rates in some classes of business are affected by the state of the economy. The measurement of the inflation incurred in our own expense inputs is dealt with in 17.4.5. The rate of inflation applying to benefits may emerge from the analysis of actual to expected payments, or, in the case of index-linked benefits, will be observed from the published index.

The general economic conditions are usually measured by items such as growth in GDP, retail sales and various surveys of consumer and business confidence.

17.4.4 Investment performance

While it is sometimes argued that investments are "different," the reality is that all the processes described in this chapter are as relevant to the measurement of investment performance as they are to any other experience item. The results of measuring investment performance can be very important in selecting, and sometimes remunerating, investment managers. This has led to the development of Global Investment Performance Standards. For further information, see http://www.gipsstandards.org.

Three key issues are dealt with in this section. These are:

- the objective of the performance measurement;

- the calculation of that performance; and

- the analysis of the reasons for the performance deviating from expected.

These are, of course, drawn from the general process discussed in 17.4.1.

Investment performance is, in the first place, of crucial importance to those whose money is being invested. They want to know how well or badly they have fared due to the performance of the investments. It is also relevant to compare actual investment performance with that expected; to compare different products available on the market;

and to compare different investment managers. These various objectives require different calculations of performance.

The calculation of the performance from the perspective of the person or entity whose money is being invested is known as the *Money Weighted Return* (MWR).

To determine the MWR, calculate the internal rate of return of the cash flows over the period under analysis.

Define

α Time at beginning of period [measured in years or fractions thereof]

β Time at end of period [measured in years or fractions thereof]

CF_{t_k} Cash flow at time t_k, $k = 1, ..., n$, $\alpha = t_1 < t_2 < \cdots < t_{n-1} < t_n < \beta$

M_t Market value at time t before cash flow at time t is included

$MWR_{\alpha, \beta}$ Money weighted rate of return over the period α to β

Then

$MWR_{\alpha, \beta}$ is the rate r at which

$$\sum_{k=1}^{n} CF_{t_k} \times (1+r)^{\beta - t_k} + M_\alpha \times (1+r)^{\beta - \alpha} = M_\beta$$

The time parameters need to be expressed on the same basis (most likely years).

This is the effective rate of investment earnings that has been earned over the period, taking into account the times at which the cash flows occurred.

However, in order to make comparisons (between products or between managers, for example) it is necessary to remove the impact of the timing of the cash flows. This then enables these required comparisons to be done with truly comparable results.

This calculation is known as the *Time Weighted Return* (TWR).

Define

$TWR_{\alpha, \beta}$ Time weighted rate of return over the period α to β

$t_{n+1} = \beta$

Then

$$TWR_{\alpha,\beta} = \left[\prod_{k=1}^{n} \left(\frac{M_{t_{k+1}}}{M_{t_k} + CF_{t_k}} \right) \right]^{\frac{1}{\beta - \alpha}} - 1$$

Note that these formulae assume that we know the exact dates of cash flows and also, for the TWR, the market values at the time of every cash flow. In practice, the calculation is usually done using market valuations at regular intervals and assuming that all cash flows occur at the beginning of each interval. Provided that the intervals are short enough, eg monthly, this does not normally cause a problem unless the cash flows are large compared to the amount invested at the start of the investigation.

These approaches are illustrated in the following example.

Example 17.2

Two portfolios are invested in the same underlying assets, but the cash flows are very different. Table 17.1 shows the dates when the cash flows occur and the value of the assets at each date.

Table 17.1

Date	Index of Asset Value	Cash flow		Market Value	
		Portfolio A	Portfolio B	Portfolio A	Portfolio B
January 1, 2009	1.00	5,000	1,500	5,000	1,500
March 31, 2009	1.40		1,500		3,600
June 30, 2009	1.20				3,086
September 30, 2009	1.00		2,000		4,571
December 31, 2009	1.10			5,500	5,028

The two different investment performance measures give the results in Table 17.2:

Table 17.2

Portfolio	Money Weighted Return	Time Weighted Return
A	10.0%	10.0%
B	0.9%	10.0%

The underlying investment performance in both portfolios was the same, as indicated by the TWR. However, the performance in each quarter was very different. Hence, the timing of the cash flows made a dramatic difference in the actual result delivered to the investor, as illustrated by the MWR.[1]

A major idea in this chapter is to explain, as far as possible, the reasons for any deviation from expected. This same approach is adopted for dealing with investment performance and is the third issue noted above. The technique, developed by Brinson, Hood and Beebower (1986), is known as *attribution analysis*. It breaks up the difference from expected into that which is attributed to:

---

[1] In practice, the use of TWR does not completely solve the problem of performance comparison. The process of investing cash inflows, or realizing assets to meet cash outflows, can incur transaction costs in terms of moving the market. In the example, the manager of Portfolio B, where cash flows occur more often, could be disadvantaged in comparison with the manager of Portfolio A.

- the asset allocation decision;

- the performance of the individual assets in each asset class in the asset allocation; and

- the interaction between those two.

Example 17.3

Assume that we have a portfolio with three asset classes and with an expected set of allocations to each class as in Table 17.3:

Table 17.3

Asset Class	Allocation
Equities	70%
Cash	10%
Fixed Interest	20%

The actual allocations maintained over the period and the actual performance for each asset class are given in Table 17.4:

Table 17.4

Asset Class	Allocation	Actual performance of our portfolio	Performance of benchmark
Equities	75%	25%	20%
Cash	15%	10%	8%
Fixed Interest	10%	10%	12%

The actual overall performance was 21.25%, while the performance of the benchmark using the expected asset allocations would have been 17.2%. The actual was 4.05% greater than the expected. We now want to understand the reasons for the difference.

Using the three categories described above to explain the difference, we have the following formulae:

WP_i = Actual allocation to asset class i

WB_i = Expected allocation to asset class i

RP_i = Actual performance for asset class i

RB_i = Benchmark performance for asset class i

$$\text{Difference due to asset allocation} = \sum_i [(WP_i - WB_i) \times RB_i]$$

$$\text{Difference due to asset class performance} = \sum_i [(RP_i - RB_i) \times WB_i]$$

$$\text{Interaction} = \sum_i [(RP_i - RB_i) \times (WP_i - WB_i)]$$

> If we now complete the arithmetic, we find that the contributions to the overall difference of 4.05% are:
>
> | | |
> |---|---|
> | Asset allocation | 0.20% |
> | Asset class performance | 3.30% |
> | Interaction | 0.55% |
>
> This leads to the conclusion that the prime reason for the better-than-expected performance was the asset class performance, principally in the equities class.

A typical investment issue is relating actual performance to the risk taken to achieve that performance. The measurement of risk is an open question. However, the common definition is that risk equals variance. As a measure of risk, the variance lacks several desirable characteristics, but it is the measure most often quoted. Hence, in measuring the extent to which performance is related to risk, the formulae assume this definition. There are three measures often used. Each of these measures assumes that CAPM is applicable.

CAPM, you will remember, asserts that the return expected from a particular investment i can be defined as

$$R_i = R_F + \beta_i \{R_M - R_F\}$$

where

R_F is the expected risk-free return

R_M is the expected return from the market

β_i is $cov(R_i, R_M)/var(R_M)$ and is a measure of the systemic risk in investment i

The three measures set out below use the following symbols:

R_P is the expected return from the portfolio

σ_P is the standard deviation of the portfolio return

Sharpe

This measures the excess return of the portfolio – compared to the risk-free return – relative to the variance of the portfolio return.

$$(R_P - R_F)/\sigma_P$$

Treynor

This measures the excess return of the portfolio relative to systemic risk. Diversifiable risk is ignored.

$$(R_P - R_F)/\beta_P$$

Jensen

This measures the return added by the portfolio compared to a passive benchmark portfolio. Of the three measures, this is the only one which is absolute, the other two being relative.

$$R_P - (R_F + \beta_P(R_M - R_F))$$

While there is some question as to the definition of risk used in these measures, if CAPM is adopted as an appropriate theory then each provides useful information as to the "risk" involved in the portfolio relative to its return.

Exercise 17.1

An accumulation superannuation fund with assets of $4 billion uses external managers for its investment management. The fund has a strategic asset allocation of 60% equities, 15% property, 20% fixed interest and 5% cash. The property and cash are 100% invested in Australian assets. The overseas proportion of the equities and fixed interest are at the discretion of the managers. Each equities manager is allowed to hold up to 15% of its allocation in cash for the purposes of short-term trading opportunities.

The equities are split evenly between three managers. The relevant performance data is set out in the spreadsheet "Chapter 17 Exercise 17.1 Data Spreadsheet" on the CD.

(a) Calculate the TWR and the MWR for the benchmark and the three managers.

(b) You are the asset consultant retained by the trustees and are preparing your annual review of the performance of the equities managers. Analyze the performance of each manager and prepare your report.

17.4.5 Expenses

In most financial services companies, expense experience is a major contributor to profitability. It is, therefore, appropriate to subject it to very serious analysis. It is also true that expenses are the one item that the company has very material control over. Hence, the effort normally put into expenses analyses. Most of the other experience items are substantially outside the direct control of the company, although companies can often take action which will lead to changes in that experience over time.

The actuarial analysis of expenses is directed at understanding the drivers of those expenses. This enables future expense cash flows to be projected in such a way as to closely approximate the expenses that will arise from a given pattern of business. Those drivers must be able to be related to the key statistics and characteristics of future business. We are not trying to do the job of the cost accountants.

Expense data in an organization will come in a two-dimensional form. One dimension is the type of expense, eg salaries, premises and advertising. The other will be the organizational unit. While the types of expenses are similar over different institutions, the size and structure of the organizational unit for which expense data is available will vary significantly.

The conduct of an expense analysis follows these three steps:

*   division of expenses by function and product;

*   allocation of items; and

*   comparisons and conclusions.

We will illustrate the process with two examples. Example 17.4 carries out the first two steps using data from an insurance company. Example 17.5 repeats these steps for a credit card business.

Step 1:   Division of expenses by function and product

The first step in the expense analysis is to divide the expenses according to function and product group. The functions we are interested in are those that relate directly to products, eg sales, marketing, investment management, claims administration and underwriting, and those relating to overhead, ie not directly related to products. The breadth of the range of individual products which are included in a single product group is quite variable. The main consideration is the extent to which the significance of the particular product as a driver of expenses will be different to other products. Where the significance is very similar, it would be appropriate to group those products together.

We always find that in some organizational units there are either multiple functions or multiple product groups. In those cases it is usual to attempt the internal allocation of expenses by using staff surveys to identify the proportion of time that is spent on each product or function. The smaller the organizational unit the less likely it is that such allocations will be necessary.

We also find that some organizational units provide services to other units but have, themselves, no product or directly product-related function, eg IT or HR departments. Then there are the overhead units, eg the CEO. As a result of the existence of these service units some of the expense types that appear for an organizational unit may already have been the result of an allocation. For example, the HR costs may have been allocated in proportion to each organizational unit's remuneration costs. For those units we have designated as overhead we may not attempt to allocate them to products or functions at this stage.

In an accounting sense expenses can be divided into two categories – fixed and variable. Variable expenses will vary directly with business volumes while fixed expenses are largely independent of business volumes. While this division makes sense in the short term, most expense analyses suggest that in the longer term there is no such thing as fixed expenses. As the business grows the fixed expenses also grow, perhaps not in direct proportion to the business volumes but steadily nevertheless. The rest of this expense discussion ignores the distinction between fixed and variable expenses, but you should remember that in some situations this distinction remains important and should be retained. In pricing a new product with large development costs, eg computer systems, the fixed nature of that expense must be considered when running the profit tests. In such a situation the development of sufficient business to cover the development expenses in an appropriate time frame should be part of the pricing paradigm. This particular paradigm should be recognized when performing the expense analysis used to derive relevant expense assumptions.

After this first step we end up with a two-dimensional table showing the total expenses for each product group and function with overheads shown separately. A typical set of results is shown below in Table 17.5, using data based on that derived from an insurance business.

Example 17.4

Table 17.5   Insurance company: expenses by function and product group

Function	Overheads $m	Product A $m	Product B $m
Commissions – Initial		40.5	35.4
Commissions – Renewal		14.7	12.1
Commissions – Volume Bonus, etc	30.0		
Policy Admin – New Business		9.8	18.0
Underwriting		3.6	3.9
Policy Admin – Renewal		12.5	6.1
Marketing	25.0	18.0	5.5
Sales Management	44.0		
Finance	11.0		
Claims Management		6.2	1.7
Investment Management	4.5		
General Management	10.4		

Step 2:   Allocation of items

The second step is to relate these results to an appropriate set of business statistics. Here, we are attempting to identify those business statistics that will appropriately represent the key drivers of expense when related to business volumes. In making the decisions as to appropriate drivers, we are sometimes limited by the statistics that are (or will be) available in respect of the business.

The way in which such decisions are made is more easily described in an example than in the abstract. We start with the insurance company example. The data from Table 17.5, showing the total expenses by product group and function, will be used together with the relevant business statistics for the same period (one year), set out in Table 17.6 below.

Example 17.4   continued

Table 17.6   Insurance company: business statistics

		Aggregate	Product A	Product B
Start	Policies		240,000	100,000
	Annual Premium ($M)		165	87
	Avg Sum Insured ($)		95,000	155,000
	Funds under Mgt ($M)	1,010		
End	Policies		250,000	135,000
	Annual Premium ($M)		175	113
	Avg Sum Insured ($)		96,000	167,000
	Funds under Mgt ($M)	1,250		
New	Policies		40,000	45,000
	Annual Premium ($M)		35	50
	Avg Sum Insured ($)		110,000	180,000

We then take each of the expense items from Table 17.5 in turn.

Commissions

Commissions are normally the easiest item to calculate business statistics for because the commission rules are known. As a result, the drivers of basic initial and renewal commissions can be derived directly from these rules. In some cases the complexity of the rules may require approximations.

The other commission items, such as volume bonuses and persistency bonuses, are based on the performance of the whole business introduced by a particular distributor. The rules for calculating these other commission items are almost always too complex for us to relate them directly to the business statistics. One way of proceeding is to assume that, on balance, the amount of basic initial and renewal commissions earned by a distributor is a good estimator of the underlying drivers of these other commission items.

In this example (using the expenses in Table 17.5), we would then load each of the basic commission rates by 29.2% [30.0/(40.5+35.4+14.7+12.1)]. This is the "Volume Bonus, etc" item divided by the sum of the initial and renewal commissions.

Policy administration expenses

It is usual to assume that the costs of policy administration are fundamentally driven by the number of policies. The costs of processing renewals are asserted to be independent of the policy size. Taking this approach gives the following $ per policy (using the figures in Tables 17.5 and 17.6):

Product A

> New Business   245.00   [NB Admin Expenses/No. of new
>   policies = 9,800,000/40,000]
>
> Renewal   51.02   [Renewal Admin Expenses/Ave. No.
>   of policies over year = 12,500,000/
>   (240,000+250,000) × 0.5)]

Product B

> New Business   400.00
>
> Renewal   51.91

Note that the manner in which we have calculated the renewal expense rates assumes that renewal expenses are incurred in the first policy year in addition to the new business expenses.

Underwriting expenses

Underwriting expenses will be driven by those policy characteristics that demand the most underwriting. Those characteristics will depend on the particular products. Sum insured is normally at least one key characteristic. There may be other factors, but in the end we should bear in mind the purpose of our expense analysis as described earlier. Additional complexity may not add a great deal in those areas, like underwriting, where the expenses are a small proportion of the total expenses. In this case we make the reasonable assumption that underwriting increases as the sum insured increases. This assumption leads to these results in $ per $1,000 sum insured (using the figures in Tables 17.5 and 17.6):

> Product A   0.82   [Underwriting Expenses/(Ave. Sum
>   Insured × No. of new policies) =
>   3,600,000/(110,000 × 40,000)]
>
> Product B   0.48

Claims management expenses

Claims management expenses will be driven by those characteristics of claims that require most investigation. Like underwriting expenses, this will depend on the characteristics of the particular products. We could reasonably assume that the major driver of claims management expenses is actual claim costs. Since projections of future claims cash flows will allow for the various product and customer characteristics that drive those claim costs, this approach will lead to appropriate projections of future claims management expenses.

Investment management expenses

We normally regard investment expenses as driven by the volume of funds under management by asset class. This allows for the fact that a portfolio of property, for example, is more expensive to manage than a portfolio of passively-managed equities. In this example we do not have funds under management broken down by asset class, but we can assume that investment expenses will still be driven by funds under management. This would lead to an investment expense of 40 basis points $[4.5 \times 2/(1010+1250)]$.

So far the drivers of expenses have been moderately obvious. The remaining four functions – sales management, marketing, finance and general management – introduce a much wider range of possibilities. As in this example, these functions often have a material proportion of expenses attributed to them. The decisions made about appropriate drivers will, then, be important in the analysis of expense performance.

Sales management expenses

It is easy to assert that sales management expenses are driven by those issues that relate to producing sales. However, which issues? The number and complexity of the various distribution channels and the number and size of individual distributors will be important factors. It is likely that those drivers of sales management expenses could be represented by commissions. But, if so, what about distribution channels which are not remunerated by commissions? Given the data, it would certainly be a good step to subdivide the sales management expenses by distribution channel. The best focused sales management team would be driven by the profitability of new business and would direct its efforts to those activities that led to increases in the profitable volumes of new business. This would lead to using this measure as the driver for expense projections. In practice, new business volumes are often used as the driver. When different products have different profitability there may be some attempt to adjust the raw volumes in order to get a better surrogate for profitability.

Marketing expenses

In our example, marketing expenses are divided between overheads and both products. This is quite usual. Some marketing expenses can be ascribed directly to particular products, eg brochures and product development, while others are applicable to the whole marketing effort. For those marketing expenses ascribed to products the issue is choosing the appropriate driver. As with sales management, it would be reasonable to view the profitability of new business as the appropriate driver. In practice, new business volumes are often used as the drivers of product-specific marketing expenses. For marketing overheads the discussion on sales management is equally relevant and the same drivers are often used for both categories of overheads.

Finance and general management expenses

Finance expenses can cover a wide range of activities and it is necessary to gain full understanding of their components in a particular situation before reliable drivers can be determined. In most cases there will, however, be a material component that is best described as related to the business as a whole, eg preparation of published accounts and other shareholder information, capital management and contribution to overall strategy. This component is in the same category as the general management expenses which are clearly related to the business as a whole. There is a wide range of potential drivers, eg profit, premium volume or funds under management. One approach is to assert that the time of general management will be usually divided according to the importance and size of the various organizational units. A measure of size could be taken as the expenses of that organizational unit. In most financial services companies this measure of size will be closely related to staff numbers. In general, the more staff in an organizational unit, the greater share of the overall business success attributed to that unit. Such an approach would lead to the expenses of each organizational unit driving the allocation of general management expenses.

Example 17.5

We now illustrate the process of expense analysis with a second example: the credit card business unit of a bank. The data from Step 1 is shown below in Table 17.7. Step 1 involves dividing the expenses by function and product group, but in this case, the expenses are not divided by product, as there is deemed to be no material difference in expense drivers for the various credit card products.

Table 17.7   Credit card business: expenses by function

Function	$ million
Transaction processing	16.7
New card issuing	14.8
Marketing	8.4
Internal commissions paid to branches on new cards	12.4
Sales costs for merchants	6.4
Business unit management	3.5
Information technology	9.5
Contribution to bank management overhead	10.0
Costs of pursuing defaulters	3.1

The relevant business statistics are shown in Table 17.8:

Table 17.8   Credit card business: business statistics

Item	Number of Cards	Amounts ($ million)	Amount Type
Start	1,458,520	5,104.0	Balance
End	1,565,926	6,107.0	Balance
Purchases on Cards	29,450,900	13,750.0	Purchases
New Cards	137,200	1,029.0	Limits
Cards Cancelled by Customers	24,568	221.0	Limits
Cards Cancelled by Bank for Default	5,226	49.6	Balance Written Off

The expense allocation process follows a similar logic to that for Example 17.4. The discussion will, therefore, be rather shorter.

Transaction processing is driven by the number of transactions, ie purchases [16,700,000/29,450,900 = $0.57 per transaction].

New card issuing is driven by the number of new cards issued [14,800,000/137,200=$107.87 per card issued].

The sales and marketing activities for credit cards are directed at two very different types of customers – the individuals who may take the card and the merchants who may use the bank as their credit card processor. However, the business statistics do not readily distinguish between these two. The amounts involved are 17.5% of total expenses. These sales and marketing activities are not just directed at new customers but very much at ensuring that existing customers continue to use their cards. It would, therefore, be reasonable to allocate these according to the average balances over the year

[(8,400,000+6,400,000)/(0.5×(5,104,000,000+6,107,000,000)) = $2.64 per $1,000 of balance].

Commissions paid to branches for new cards clearly relate to new cards only. As with the life insurance example, the rules for commissions would be known. We assume here that commissions are based on the credit limit offered to the new customer. These expenses would then be allocated according to the limit [12,400,000/1,029,000,000 = 1.2% of the credit limit].

As was argued in Example 17.4, the business unit management and the contribution to bank overheads are best allocated to a measure of the overall size of the unit. For credit cards this would be the average balances outstanding [(3,500,000+10,000,000)/(0.5×(5,104,000,000+6,107,000,000)) = $2.41 per $1,000 balance].

Information technology is most likely driven by the transaction volume rather than the amounts. This volume will be made up of processing of purchases, processing of payments and statement preparation. A suitable surrogate for this overall measure would be the average number of cards over the year [9,500,000/(0.5×(1,458,520+1,565,926)) = $6.28 per card per annum].

The costs of pursuing defaulters will be driven by the number of defaulters and the amount of their default. It is easy to imagine that the larger the outstanding balance the more effort might be expended. However, the vast majority of credit cards have, in absolute terms, relatively low amounts outstanding, so the extra complexity in performing calculations by amounts may make little difference in practice. It may, therefore, be appropriate to allocate the cost of pursuing defaulters by the number of defaults rather than the amounts involved [3,100,000/5,226 = $593 per card in default].

Step 3: Comparisons and conclusions

After the first two steps are completed we will have a set of expense drivers and the actual expense rates for each of those drivers. We can then compare the latest period with prior periods and draw reasonable conclusions as to the source of the difference between actual and expected expenses. The reasons for the differences can be many. In a particular case it would be necessary to understand whether those differences are due to:

- the expenses being different, eg higher than expected increases in remuneration;

- the business volumes being different, eg lower new business; or

- a combination of these two.

It is only after examining the detailed differences that a conclusion can be drawn. When business volumes increase the expenses will also increase. But the result may overall be positive, ie lower unit costs. When volumes decrease it is often the case that expenses do not drop at the same rate so that unit costs increase – even if actual expenses do decrease. Comparing expenses without consideration of business volumes almost always leads to misleading conclusions.

Exercise 17.2

A medium-sized university operates in a developed country.

Full details of the university's financial data, staffing and enrolment statistics are set out in the spreadsheet "Chapter 17 Exercise 17.2 Data Spreadsheet" on the CD.

Carry out a full expense analysis.

17.4.6   Business volumes and business mix

Analysis of business volumes should cover new business and inforce separately. The analysis of in-force volume is primarily an outworking of a proper analysis of the product-specific factors discussed in 17.4.2. The other item that is relevant is the rate at which customers have increased their insurance cover or their deposits to investment contracts.

Most insurance contracts encourage customers to keep their level of cover increasing so that in real terms it remains constant, eg buildings and contents insurance should increase at the rate of increase in building costs and inflation of household goods. The in-force volume will be impacted by the extent to which customers follow the company's encouragement. Our models should have an expected take-up rate of increases offered, and an analysis of actual versus expected appropriately segmented will provide information for updating the models.

For investment contracts our models should have allowed for an expected rate of change in annual deposits (or premiums) independent of rates of persistency. For example, in retirement savings products an increase in contributions consistent with the rates of increase in remuneration would be expected. For the self-employed, the rates of contribution to retirement savings is likely to have some relationship to the profitability of the customer's business. Customers with flexible investment contracts, ie with no requirement to continue paying premiums, will show some rate of dormancy, ie no premiums (or deposits) paid during the time period. Again, an analysis of actual versus expected for each of these items is required to complete a proper examination of experience.

The new business *mix* refers to how the volume of new business is made up of customers with different characteristics. This is particularly important if pricing does not fully reflect risk factors. For example, suppose that legislation requires a health insurer to charge the same premiums to young and old customers, even though it believes that older customers will cost more. If the new business contains a higher proportion of customers at the older ages than expected, then claims will be higher than expected, even if the age-specific experience is exactly as expected.

The reliability of our models of new business volume and characteristics is a matter of fundamental importance in any projection of future cash flows. We need to understand the reasons why the actual new business differs from that expected on the basis of our models. Our analysis should focus on two issues – the profitability of the new business and its requirement for capital. Volumes, by themselves, can be a very misleading indicator. A large increase in volume in a low profit product can be completely negated in terms of profitability by a small fall in the volume of a high profit product. Similarly, a small increase in volume in a product may lead to a disproportionately large increase in risk-based capital requirements if the increased sales in the product are to the high-risk customers. An analysis of volume alone will not show such an outcome.

When the various characteristics of the actual new business are examined, we have a set of useful indicators of other problems or happy outcomes. Customer preference for a particular product variant may indicate a strong competitive position or it could indicate a serious mis-pricing problem.

The particular characteristics that should be analyzed include product set (and variants), distribution channel, case size, and customer characteristics. The customer characteristics of interest will depend on the product type. For life insurance, age and sex will be of key importance, whereas geographical location would be important in other types of insurance.

A typical analysis of new business compares this period with the previous period. While this may show some useful information the more valuable analysis is comparing actual with expected, and highlighting the reasons for the difference. Only this type of work gives pointers to the actions required to maximize future outcomes.

In two areas there are potential interactions between new business and other experience analyses. These are capital requirements and expenses. The management of capital is one of the most important responsibilities of the executive team. Understanding why the anticipated capital requirements differ from the actual is a key input to the process. Capital demands from new business are a major contributor to this difference and are, therefore, a key part of the capital analysis which is discussed in 17.4.7.

Generally, the necessary infrastructure for the projected volumes of new business needs to be in place before the business arrives. As a result, if the volumes are below those anticipated, the expenses will not be recovered. There is, therefore, a close relationship between new business volumes and profit.

17.4.7   Profit and return on capital

The difference between planned and actual profit is, of course, the outworking of all the other experience items. However, we want to understand the profit result in some other ways. In particular, we usually want to analyze profit according to business unit or product. We may also want to segment profit by distribution channel, customer segment or geographic area.

The principal difficulty in segmenting profit comes with the allocation of expenses and capital.

As noted in 17.4.5, the allocation of many categories of expense cannot be done on a basis that is other than arbitrary. As a result, using profit that is based on such expense allocations will inevitably lead to arguments as to alternative measures of profit. Given that profit can be a crucial input to many performance measurements, such uncertainty as to the actual amount of profit is unhelpful. An alternative approach is to analyze profit, at the lower levels of the organization, on a basis that excludes those expenses which have no direct basis of allocation. Instead of trying to measure profit, we measure "contribution to overheads and profit." Such an approach is more closely a true reflection of the performance of the particular sub-unit.

The extent to which the allocation of overheads impacts the apparent profit of a sub-unit will determine whether this alternative approach is required. However, at a product level a material component of expenses is likely to come from this source.

It is, however, necessary to calculate the after-all-allocations profit as well as the contribution to overheads and profit; otherwise it may not be apparent that large contributions may be offset by similarly large consumption of overhead resources, even if the allocation of the latter can only be approximate. We are trying to provide the most useful information from the analysis and both pictures are likely to be required to get the full picture. A reporting structure of the following type may be appropriate:

+	Direct Revenue
−	Direct Expense
=	Contribution to Overheads and Profit
−	Allocated Overheads
=	Calculated Profit

In the case of capital, the issue is the extent to which the overall reduction in capital caused by the size of the organization as a whole, and the existence of benefits from business diversification, can be attributed to an individual sub-unit. Since most performance measurement is based on return on capital, the extremes of these expense and capital allocations lead to very different outcomes. At one end of the spectrum we have a full allocation of overheads used in calculating profit but we use the capital required assuming the particular sub-unit is totally independent. This will give a materially lower return on capital than excluding overheads and only allocating capital according to the organization's overall capital requirement.

There are no simple solutions to this problem. The main issues are, first, to ensure that in all comparisons, whether of expected to actual profit or of different business units or products, like is compared with like. Secondly, the limitations of the particular approach should be noted, and alternative measurements calculated where the differences in outcomes would be material.

The analyses of the financial impact of the individual experience items will provide us with an analysis of profit according to source. This provides the key financial indicator as to the importance of the particular experience item and hence the extent to which deviations from expected require corrective action.

We can conduct this analysis in a multi-dimensional fashion, eg experience item, business unit, product, distribution channel, customer segment and geographic area. However, such an approach rapidly provides more information than we can easily comprehend. We need to limit the cells in our analysis to those where the financial impact is material.

The analysis of the change in capital required follows similar lines to the multi-dimensional analysis of profit but some items are of more importance. New business is often the most significant contributor to the difference between planned and actual capital required. And profit itself, of course, may be a major source of the change in available capital.

Exercise 17.3   Profit analysis for a bank

A bank has structured itself into three business units and a range of central service units.

The business units are:

* Retail Deposits;
* Retail Lending; and
* Commercial Lending.

The analysis of the bank's profitability by business unit for 2009 shows the results given in Table 17.9. The figures are $ million. Note that, for simplicity, all ratios are based solely on the figures in the table, eg ROC is Profit/Capital. In reality, capital would be averaged over the year.

Table 17.9

Item	Retail Deposits	Retail Lending	Commercial Lending	Shareholders' Funds	TOTAL
Revenue	110	58	14	11	193
Expenses	103	50	11	2	166
Profit	7	8	3	9	27
Capital	118	82	61	0	261
ROC	5.9%	9.8%	4.9%	N/A	10.3%
Assets	0	1,635	613	261	2,509
Liabilities	2,248	0	0	0	2,248

The expenses of the Central Service Units have been allocated to the business units in proportion to their unit's expenses before the allocation. No expense allocation is made to Shareholders' Funds. The amount allocated in 2009 was $45 million.

The bank's target capital is a minimum of 10% of liabilities. In the table, the assets and liabilities have been simplified to show only the external assets (loans) and liabilities (deposits).

Capital is allocated to business units as follows:

Retail Lending	5% of assets	[Assumes 50% risk weight]
Commercial Lending	10% of assets	[Assumes 100% risk weight]
Retail Deposits	The balance	

> Since all the funds that the lending business units have to lend are funded by retail deposits, those two business units pay the Retail Deposits unit 4% of their assets. The Retail Deposits unit treats this as revenue and the lending units treat it as negative revenue. In addition, Retail Deposits charges its customers fees which are included as revenue.
>
> Analyze these profit and capital figures and determine which business unit is the most profitable.

17.5   Data issues

Data is discussed in depth in Chapter 10. Here we concentrate on the issues arising in collecting and using data to analyze experience.

All analyses of experience are dependent on the quality of the data used as the foundations. Since for most data used the experience analysis will be a secondary use of the data, the expected quality will vary depending on the primary use of the data. Data used in producing audited accounts, eg expenses, can reasonably be regarded as of high quality. Business statistics may be similarly regarded if they are the basis for regulatory reporting. However, some data has no real primary use. The recording of a continuing claim as closed may often have no impact for any other purpose. If the claim payments have ceased then the recording of the claim status as closed may be solely an administrative issue. Often this task is given low priority by those doing the work, particularly if general workloads are high. But if the experience analysis relies on this status the possibility of erroneous conclusions is clear.

In those areas where the primary purpose is not sufficiently close to the experience analysis purpose it is essential to ensure other checks are made. In the example cited it would be desirable to check the date of the last claim payment for each open claim (or for a representative sample). This would indicate whether potential problems were present in the data.

The problem of primary or secondary use is not the only source of error in the data. Data validation is an important part of any experience analysis. Validation of data against an independent source can be a crucial test. At a simple level the comparison of in-force regular premium against the regular premium income in the accounts for the same period can easily provide an alert for a potential problem with the premium data.

Often the exact data required is not available and approximations must be accepted. These are often in the form of grouped data or a surrogate for the actual desired data. The error introduced by these approximations in the analysis needs to be considered. If at all possible, a comparison of exact and approximate data, even if only on a small sample, should be conducted.

When first defining the data collection mechanism, the best approach is to collect all the data that is available even if it is not immediately needed. It is almost impossible to subsequently collect additional historical data when the scope of the investigation expands or data relationships are desired to be examined. Generally, collecting data, provided it is available, is not a problem when it is first specified. The work in doing the collection is often substantially independent of the volume of data items to be collected.

We need to decide on the frequency of data collection. In most cases monthly collection is appropriate but for some items, eg unit prices, a daily collection may be needed. The same principle enunciated in the previous paragraph is a good place to start provided serious regard is given to the problems of data storage and processing with collection at very frequent intervals. Collection at a greater frequency than monthly would, in most cases, need to be particularly justified.

17.6   Practical implications for actuaries

In practice, experience analysis can easily become a routine technical task. It is often given to one of the junior analysts. However, there is much information available when the analyses are done rigorously and comprehensively, which requires a more seasoned perspective.

It is particularly important to understand the reasons for the deviations from expected experience. The implications which emerge from such understanding can be of great importance to the business executives. The actuarial advice which can be provided will provide insight as to what is happening with respect to customer behavior and this is the core driver of actual experience.

A key theme in experience analyses is the statistical significance of the results. If the results are not statistically significant they should be used as the basis of business decisions only with very great caution. However, if they are significant, then they should be regarded as central pieces of information that should be given great weight in decision making.

It is often the case that some items of the experience such as claims are regarded as "actuarial" but the other items are not. This approach should be firmly resisted. All areas of the experience are credible targets for "actuarial" analysis and the results of such analyses will be well worth the effort.

The analysis of experience is an essential item to feed back into the management of the business in the future. It should therefore receive the time and other resources required to perform the analysis to an acceptable standard. In many cases actuaries will face additional pressure on this process when the recent results have been poor and the client or employer wants a quick fix.

17.7   Key learning points

The essential learning points can be grouped under three headings:

*   why we analyze experience;
*   what we analyze; and
*   how we do the analysis.

Why?

We analyze experience in order to provide the information necessary to satisfy the requirements of one or more of the following:

*   reviewing assumptions;
*   providing understanding of the drivers of the emerging experience;
*   developing a history of experience over time;

- aiding in an analysis of profit and its sources;
- providing information to management;
- providing information to shareholders and third parties;
- satisfying regulatory requirements;
- aiding public relations purposes, including communications to clients/customers; and
- satisfying disclosure requirements in a listing or acquisition.

Each of these is discussed in Section 17.2. Each requires particular types of information. However, the methods used in the underlying analyses do not change. It is only the *What* which may change and the method of presentation of the results.

What?

The items that we analyze fall into one of the following categories:

- product-specific:
    - performance on risks accepted;
    - persistency;
- economic;
- investment performance;
- expenses;
- new business volumes and mix; and
- profit and return on capital.

The particular items for analysis will depend on the context of the business and product. Some different contexts are discussed in 17.3.

How?

The main learning issue is the *How Process*.

Every analysis of some piece of experience follows the same process:

- establish the objectives;
- collect the data;
- assess data quality;
- validate the data;
- perform the analysis, including documentation of the process;
- validate the results; and
- explain the results.

Each item in the process is discussed in Section 17.4.1. Following the process is a guaranteed way to produce quality experience analyses.

It is the *perform the analysis* step where there are important differences in methods according to *what* item of experience is being analyzed. These methods and examples are discussed in Sections 17.4.2 to 17.4.7.

The essential issues are:

- Product-specific

  Usually measured by Actual/Expected.

- Investment Performance

  Understand the difference between Money Weighted and Time Weighted rates of investment return and the circumstances in which each is the preferred approach.

  Make sure you can perform an attribution analysis. This is a critical piece of analysis for understanding the reasons for the investment performance experience observed.

- Expenses

  Expenses are one of the most important items to analyze. Pay particular attention to the determination of which business statistics are the appropriate expense drivers.

- Profit

  Understand the suggested method of showing the profit contribution made by each segment of the business before allowing for capital and before allocating overhead costs. Make sure you can articulate the various methods of allocating capital to individual segments.

CD Items

Chapter 17 Exercise 17.1 Data Spreadsheet

Chapter 17 Exercise 17.2 Data Spreadsheet

Chapter 17 Exercise Solutions

Chapter 17 Exercise 17.1 Solution Spreadsheet

Chapter 17 Exercise 17.2 Solution Spreadsheet

References (other than CD Items)

The most useful references are the extensive published analyses of industry experience. The Institute of Actuaries of Australia produces analyses of mortality experience, disability experience and group life experience. The Faculty and Institute of Actuaries UK produce the Continuous Mortality Investigation Reports which, despite the name, cover disability as well as mortality. The Society of Actuaries (SOA) produces Reports that contain many experience analyses. All these analyses relate to life insurance although occasionally the SOA Reports have other analyses, eg Credit Risk Loss Experience. It is an unfortunate fact that very little public analysis of general insurance experience is published.

A limited selection of other references is listed below.

Albert, F., Bragg, D. G. W. & Bragg, J. M. 1999, Mortality Rates as a Function of Lapse Rates, *Actuarial Research Clearing House*, Vol. 1.

Beard, R. E. 1951, Some Notes on Graduation, *Journal of the Institute of Actuaries*, Vol 77, pp. 382-431.

Beard, R. E. 1961, A Theory of Mortality Based on Actuarial, Biological and Medical Considerations, *International Population Conference*, Vol 1, pp. 611-625.

Bragg, J. M., Albert, F. & Jones, B. L. 1998, Mortality and Lapse Rates, Session 31PD, *Record of the Society of Actuaries*, Vol 24, No 3, New York Annual Meeting, October.

Brinson, G. P., Hood, L. R. & Beebower, G. L. 1986, Determinants of Portfolio Performance, *The Financial Analysts Journal*, July/August.

Carter, L. & Lee, R. D. 1992, Modeling and Forecasting US Mortality: Differentials in Life Expectancy by Sex, *International Journal of Forecasting* 8, No 3 (November), pp. 393-412.

Daw, R. H. 1946, On the Validity of Statistical Tests of the Graduation of a Mortality Table, *Journal of the Institute of Actuaries*, Vol 72, pp. 174-202.

Daw, R. H. 1974, A Study of the Variance of Mortality Rates, *Journal of the Institute of Actuaries*, Vol 101, pp. 415-434.

Gutterman, S. 2007, *A Comprehensive Guide to Measuring and Managing Life Insurance Company Expenses*, Society of Actuaries.

Jones, B. L. 1998, A Model for Analyzing the Impact of Selective Lapsation on Mortality, *North American Actuarial Journal*, January, Vol 2, No 1.

Lee, R. 2000, The Lee-Carter Method for Forecasting Mortality, with Various Extensions and Applications, *North American Actuarial Journal*, Vol 4, No 1.

Lewis, W. J. D., Dipaolo, F. P. & Eckert, R. J. 1975, Impact of Inflation on Life Insurance Companies – Discussion, *Record of Society of Actuaries* 1975, Vol 1, No 2.

Pollard, A. H. 1970, Random Mortality Fluctuations and the Binomial Hypothesis, *Journal of the Institute of Actuaries*, Vol 96, pp. 251-264.

Redington, F. M. 1969, An Exploration into the Patterns of Mortality, *Journal of the Institute of Actuaries*, Vol 95, pp. 243-317.

Redington, F. M. & Michaelson, R. L. 1940, An Aspect of the A Priori Theory of Mortality, *Transactions of Twelfth International Congress of Actuaries*, Lucerne, I, p. 225.

Renshaw, A. E. & Haberman, S. 1986. Statistical Analysis of Life Assurance Lapses, *Journal of the Institute of Actuaries*, Vol 113, pp. 459-497.

Seal, H. L. 1943, Tests of a Mortality Table Graduation, *Journal of the Institute of Actuaries*, Vol 71, pp. 5-67.

Fred's Coffee Shop – Responding to Experience

Now that Fred is monitoring various aspects of his business, what can he do with the results? Generally, there will be five areas he can look at to improve his results, namely:

- expenses – can they be reduced without other consequences?
- prices – can they be increased without other consequences?
- products – can they be modified, discontinued, or supplemented?
- systems – can operating procedures be changed? and
- capital structure – can he refinance his loans or look elsewhere for financing?

For example, Fred may currently run his shop with one person taking orders and a second person preparing the coffee. He notes that it takes longer to prepare a gourmet coffee drink than to take the order. Expenses may be reduced if an employee serves a given customer from beginning to end. However, quality may suffer as Fred will have to ensure all his employees are adept at making fancy coffee.

By carefully observing what products sell well and which do not, as well as by surveying his customers, Fred may choose to alter his product mix.

By tracking business throughout the day, Fred can determine the best hours for the shop to be open. Similarly, he can track the effectiveness of various advertising schemes to determine which ones work best.

While running a coffee shop is challenging work, Fred has one advantage over a financial services company. He can rapidly adjust his business. Should customers learn about the high calorie content of some of his drinks, it is easy for him to introduce low-fat, low-carb versions. Should a character in a popular movie only drink coffee made from a particular bean, Fred can quickly lay in a supply.

Financial services companies make long-term commitments and may have fewer options for changing direction if experience is unfavorable. Nevertheless, they must know where the problems are and where improvements can be made – and do their best to act on that information.

Of course, it isn't all bad news. We hope that there will be profits to allocate. In Fred's case, the decision will be whether to sink profits into the business or to take them out. Financial services companies may have products that share in profits and therefore have to decide how to distribute the profits.

Chapter 18   Responding to Experience
by Bruce Edwards

18.1   Introduction

This chapter discusses how experience results are interpreted and applied in practice in a variety of actuarial assignments. The common theme is reviewing the experience of an entity and making appropriate decisions in response to the experience. Sometimes the response is unexciting – eg leaving premium rates unchanged or maintaining bonuses at the same level as last year. On other occasions, the experience may require a material change to past practice.

Some specific examples are given on allocating investment earnings to accounts; unit pricing; the review of the pricing of an insurance product; setting contribution rates in a superannuation fund; and the allocation of profit to participating policyholders of a life insurance company.

18.2   Role of the actuary

For many professional assignments, the role of the actuary is advisory, whether the actuary is an employee or a consultant. The actuary makes recommendations to the governing body of the employer or client but the decisions on, and implementation of, the recommendations are the responsibility of that body. In formulating actuarial advice, it is important to identify who is the client and what is the exact scope of the work. Clarifying this as early as possible can save time later in the process.

When responding to experience, the actuary needs to understand any limitations in the data and systems used to produce and report the experience. This may involve analysis by the actuary, or discussion with staff members or consultants who are familiar with the data and systems. The actuary needs to have regard to any such limitations in formulating responses to the experience.

The outcome of an assignment may be different from what was initially expected by the client. The best response to an unprofitable product may be not an increase in prices but a tightening of the terms or conditions of the product or a change in the way the product is managed or sold.

Responding to experience often requires careful consideration of the fairness and equity of alternative solutions. This is an important part of the role of the actuary. Many assignments call for the involvement of actuaries primarily because the parties wish to achieve a fair and equitable outcome. This includes government and regulators in drafting legislation and regulations.

In seeking to achieve fairness and equity, the actuary should be mindful of the broad spectrum of interested parties. These may include the client; its governing body and executives; customers or members; government including the tax office; the industry; financial analysts; the media; and the community generally.

Good communication, both written and oral, is essential in most actuarial assignments. Unless the actuary's suggestions and recommendations are clearly expressed, they may be misunderstood and/or not implemented.

18.3   General considerations

When responding to the experience of a financial entity, various general considerations apply across a range of assignments. These include:

- legal constraints – this encompasses specific legislation and regulations relating to the client entity, other legislation and regulations covering business behavior (eg non-discrimination, competition and selling methods) and relevant case law;

- the taxation consequences of proposed responses;

- professional standards and guidance notes which apply to the situation – this includes non-actuarial standards (eg accounting standards), where relevant;

- fairness and equity – actuarial assignments often require the actuary to seek outcomes which are fair and equitable between different groups involved in an enterprise (eg the shareholders and policyholders of a life insurance company). This usually requires a good understanding of the financial contribution made by each group over time;

- business plans and objectives – in responding to experience, the actuary should have regard to the business plans of the client or employer and, where possible, develop recommendations which are consistent with those plans;

- competition – most financial entities operate in a competitive environment. The actions of competitors must be considered when responding to experience, especially when the experience affects the whole industry. There is often a tension between the best outcome for the entity and the need for the entity to remain competitive; and

- capital requirements – most financial entities need to retain a proportion of annual profit to build a buffer against future adverse experience. The amount of the capital required is a function of the level of risks borne by the entity, its size and profitability and any regulatory requirements. The cost of the capital must be allowed for in many aspects of the actuary's work, including pricing and the allocation of profits between stakeholders.

Frequently, there are several possible ways of responding to particular experience. It may be appropriate for the actuary to discuss the alternatives with the client or employer, presenting the advantages and disadvantages of the possible courses of action.

It is often important to understand the true causes of the result. This may involve examining the results in more detail than is initially available. Understanding the causes of the experience allows a more targeted solution to be developed. For example, are high processing expenses caused by low volumes, poor systems or low productivity? Is poor claims experience caused by a worsening trend or by temporary factors such as high motor vehicle claims during wet weather?

18.4   Managing the business

18.4.1   Business plans

For most businesses, the business plan and risk management framework are developed by management and approved by the board of directors (the *board*). The planning is usually carried out annually and relates to the year ahead or several years ahead. The planning process identifies the expected income (from the expected volumes of new and existing business), the expected outgo (including the employment costs of the expected workforce) and the major risks in achieving these results. The resulting projections of profitability and capital requirements and risk assessment can then be tested against the board's financial objectives and risk appetite.

The actual experience of the business is usually different from the assumptions made in the business planning. It is therefore essential in a competitive world to make frequent checks of actual versus expected results (often monthly). This information enables management to respond to the experience by making operational changes to correct for any adverse trends in the business (and to take advantage of any favorable trends) as soon as they are identified.

More frequent reviews of actual versus expected experience may be required for products that are particularly sensitive to market conditions. For example banks issuing term deposits to wholesale customers review their interest rates daily to reflect changes in market interest rates and the volumes of term deposits written in the recent past. Special one-off reviews of experience may also be appropriate when there are sudden material changes in market conditions.

Usually it is important to understand the underlying cause of experience variations so that appropriate actions can be taken.

The following paragraphs outline control processes that companies use to manage their businesses and give some examples of responding to the emerging experience.

18.4.2   Financial control systems

Financial control systems help organizations monitor their financial progress and take action to address impending issues in a proactive way. Ideally such systems are designed to meet the needs of each organization but they often cover areas such as producing good quality financial statements (annually and monthly), managing the collection of receivables in a timely manner, forecasting cash / liquidity needs for the period ahead and ensuring the availability of sufficient capital to meet operating needs.

Progress is often monitored by producing monthly management reports. Approximations may be used to produce monthly reports where year-end processes are complex or expensive. These systems provide an early warning of emerging problem areas so that they can be addressed before they become more serious.

Financial control reports are usually unaudited and produced under time pressure. The actuary should therefore understand how these reports are produced and their limitations before making use of the results. Actuaries are often in a position to design or suggest improvements to financial control systems and a useful by-product of many actuarial assignments is suggestions for changes to the financial control systems. Changes need to be cost-justified given the frequency of the reporting.

Similar considerations apply to other management information reports used to monitor the experience of the major business drivers and high-risk areas for each organization. These might include new business, management expenses, lapses and redemptions. More specific examples were given for different types of businesses in Chapter 17.

Example 18.1

A direct marketing company sells its products by television advertising which invites potential customers to phone in to complete the purchase. The company has identified *number of phone calls per $100 of media spend* as a major business driver and monitors this measure each month. In recent months the results have been declining and on further investigation it was noted that the results from advertising in major cities in the evening were poor relative to other demographics.

The company's response was to redirect its media spend in subsequent months to regional television stations and non-peak viewing times, where the number of phone calls per $100 of media spend was higher.

18.4.3   Audit controls

18.4.3.1   External audit

The published financial reports of most companies are audited annually or six-monthly by an external audit firm.

The external audit is a form of control cycle in its own right. Usually the auditor begins by assessing the business to be audited and identifying likely risk areas. These may be discussed with the board and management of the company and an audit plan developed. The audit is carried out and the auditor reports to the board and management with recommendations for improvement. Areas of weakness identified in one audit may receive more attention during the next audit while identified areas of strength may receive less attention.

The reporting from the external auditor is valuable because of its independence and companies can improve their performance by responding constructively.

18.4.3.2   Internal audit

Most companies also have some form of internal audit process. This is usually directed at the broader activities of managing the business, not just the financial reports. The focus is to ensure that the everyday functions of the business are being conducted efficiently and in line with any internal manuals or standards. The internal auditor may be an employee or an external consultant. The internal auditor may report to the senior management of the business or to the audit or compliance committee of the board.

The internal audit process usually consists of an agreed program of separate audits of the activities of each department in the organization. It is also a form of control cycle and the reports from the internal auditors are useful to the company as an early warning of developing problems.

Example 18.2

An insurance company requested a review by its internal auditor of its reinsurance policies and systems. The company had grown by acquiring other companies and as a result it had inherited a large number of reinsurance contracts which were inconsistent with each other and complex to administer. The internal auditor found that many errors were occurring in the calculation of reinsurance premiums and claims because staff members were confused by the complexity of the arrangements.

The company responded to this advice by undertaking a comprehensive review of its reinsurance arrangements to make them simpler and more consistent. Once in place, the new arrangements reduced the calculation errors and also reduced administrative costs.

18.4.4 Expense controls

18.4.4.1 Measuring expense performance

Management expenses are usually a key component of business plans and a key driver of profitability for most commercial enterprises. They are also the component most easily controlled by management.

Most businesses prepare an expense budget for the year ahead and then compare actual expenses against budget on a monthly basis. This may be done at a divisional level within an entity to encourage each division to take responsibility for its own expense management.

The preparation of the budget may start with each department of the organization planning its own staffing needs and preparing its own budget for expenses. This needs to have regard to expected business volumes and activity levels envisaged in the business plan. The departmental budgets can then be aggregated to give a *bottom-up* estimate of budgeted expenses for the year ahead. Senior management will then usually check the result by using *top-down* tests such as whether the resulting profit budget for the year is acceptable and whether the product-related expenses from all departments are covered by the expense margins included in the product pricing. Often this leads to an iterative process whereby departmental expense budgets and overall expense budgets are adjusted until an acceptable outcome is achieved.

Exercise 18.1

Refer back to the insurance company example in Section 17.4.5.

(a) Express all the expenses in that example in the form of *unit costs* (a percentage of new or in-force premiums, a dollar per policy cost for administration expenses, etc). The discussion in Chapter 17 provides some suggestions about how to do this but you will need to decide for yourself what the most relevant expense drivers are for each type of expense. For example, you might decide that commissions are most likely to relate to premium volumes. When you have expressed all the expenses as unit costs, check that you can re-confirm the total expenses by applying the unit costs to the business volumes.

(b) Assume that the expense analysis in (a) relates to the most recent year of operation of the insurance company. Now consider the expense budgets for next year. Make an estimate of the expenses for next year by applying the unit costs from your answer to (a) to the projected business volumes in the table below. You will need to adjust any $-per-policy unit costs for inflation at the rate of 4% per annum.

Business Statistics – Next Year

		Aggregate	Product A	Product B
Start	Policies		250,000	135,000
	Annual premium ($M)		175	113
	Average sum insured ($)		96,000	167,000
	Funds under management ($M)	1,250		
End	Policies		250,000	175,000
	Annual premium ($M)		175	155
	Average sum insured ($)		98,000	167,000
	Funds under management ($M)	1,450		
New	Policies		35,000	55,000
	Annual premium ($M)		30	60
	Average sum insured ($)		115,000	190,000

(c) The various departments of the insurance company have prepared their own budgets for next year. When these budgets are consolidated, they show a total expense budget for the company of $350 million. What steps would you take to reconcile this expense budget with your own estimate in (b)? Your aim is to set a reliable budget for next year's expenses.

In financial services companies, expense control usually involves a measure of actual versus assumed expenses by expense category. The actual expenses are those incurred by the business during the period of the investigation as determined from an expense analysis. Assumed expenses are the planned level of expenses built into the business plan, or those which would result from applying assumed unit costs to the actual volumes of business. Categories of expenses would usually include product lines, distribution channels, and acquisition and maintenance expenses.

Methods of analyzing and monitoring management expense are covered in Chapter 17.

18.4.4.2 Improving expense performance

It is usually a key objective of management to improve the expense performance of the business. In a competitive market this results in increased profits or better customer benefits or both. Some methods of improving expense performance are:

- increasing volumes of new business to achieve economies of scale – this may involve offering sales incentives or investing in distribution which may increase expenses in the short term;

- retaining more business, on the basis that renewing business is usually more cost-effective than obtaining new business – this may involve offering better service, for example telephone follow-up of outstanding premiums;

- increasing sales of high-service products where the pricing reflects the services provided;

- business review processes which result in lower costs; and

- a combination of all or several of the above.

Business review processes are worthy of a whole book on their own. Reducing expenses by streamlining procedures requires care and can be counter-productive if not managed well. Savings are available by reducing duplication of procedures or by introducing better technology. One business review process consists of process mapping where work flows are presented in a flowchart. Work flows are then simplified to avoid multiple handling and to streamline the process.

Not all expenses are bad! Expenditure which may generate business benefit and which, following review, it may be appropriate to *increase* includes:

- customer service – may support higher prices;

- advertising – may generate more business;

- major project (eg new IT system) – justified on the basis of expected future expense savings;

- financial risk control (eg underwriting, claims management and credit control) – may reduce business costs/losses; and

- risk management, including ERM – may reduce likelihood of major loss.

> ### Example 18.3
>
> A life insurance company found that errors in its policy database resulted in several departments carrying out their own accuracy checks on the data before using it. This was a duplication of effort and increased the costs of running the business. In response, the company invested in a more rigorous data entry system to ensure the accuracy of policy data from the outset. This reduced the overall costs of checking and correcting data – and also reduced reporting times.

Expense reductions need to be carefully targeted to achieve the desired result. For example, claims investigation expenses often reduce the ultimate costs of claims by several times the investigation expense. Yet claims investigation expenses may be reduced when a general reduction in expenses is applied across the board. This can lead to increased claims costs more than offsetting the expense savings.

Another example is advertising. Sales are often influenced by brand strength. Reducing advertising may result in lower sales with the result that the expense problem is increased, not reduced.

For most organizations there are no easy expense savings because any such savings have already occurred. Usually it is necessary to make an initial investment in technology or process change in order to achieve sustainable long-term expense savings.

18.4.4.3 Outsourcing

Sometimes, management expenses can be reduced by outsourcing administrative functions to a specialist manager. For example, a company might outsource computer system management to another company with specialist staff and greater economies of scale in its area of specialty. However, it is arguable that outsourcing rarely achieves significant cost savings and that the benefits of outsourcing relate to focus – the ability of the business to focus on core activities and the fact that the specialist manager brings focus and special skills to the outsourced function.

Whatever your view about the ability to achieve cost savings, outsourcing needs to be carefully managed to achieve its aims.

18.4.5 Claims controls

The aim of claims management is usually to ensure that the numbers and types of claims admitted are consistent with the expectations in the product design and pricing.

Claims are monitored by number, by average size, by type and by distribution channel to identify any developing problem areas or opportunities. Methods of comparing actual against expected claims have been covered in Chapter 17.

Claims experience can fluctuate significantly from year to year even for relatively large insurance companies. So the credibility of past experience must be considered and care should be exercised in responding to experience over relatively short periods.

Judgment is usually required because often there are not enough claims to provide conclusive proof of an emerging problem.

In the case of long-tail general insurance business, actuaries form a view about the ultimate claims cost quite early in the claims' development. Subsequent short-term variations in experience, if extrapolated to the ultimate claims cost, can result in widely fluctuating estimates of the liabilities and the profitability of the portfolio. While management will welcome good news, adverse changes will be scrutinized. This can place the actuary in a difficult position because the ultimate claims cost is always subject to estimation error.

Companies may respond to a worsening claims experience by one or more of the following actions (but note that product terms and conditions or regulations may limit the scope to take some of these actions):

- increasing premium rates, if the increased claims are considered to be an industry-wide problem;

- tightening contractual terms, if the claims are outside the intended coverage of the product;

- tightening underwriting procedures, if there is evidence of anti-selection;

- improving claims management procedures, if there is evidence that claims management decisions have not been in accordance with contractual terms or have been unduly delayed; and

- reviewing sales through a particular distribution channel which may have generated a disproportionate share of the claims.

Improving claims management has more relevance for some products than for others. There is little potential to improve death claims by better claims management but disability income experience can be improved by increasing recovery rates through rehabilitation or a gradual return to work.

Example 18.4

An insurance company noticed that the profitability of one of its products was worsening over time because of increasing claims. On further investigation it was found that a high proportion of the claims arose from policies generated by one agency. The agency was actively seeking business from high-risk customers who up to that time met the company's underwriting standards. The response was to explain the results to the agency and limit the proportion of future business from the high-risk group to a small percentage.

The agency, which had not realized that the business was unprofitable, redirected its marketing efforts toward lower-risk customers and continued to produce business for the insurance company.

18.4.6 New business and termination controls

Changing volumes and product mix of new business can have a significant effect on profitability and on capital requirements. This is particularly true when there is a mix of high capital products and low capital products or where there are cross-subsidies between products. A surge in production of one product or from one source may be a cause for further review to ensure that the pricing and underwriting remains appropriate.

Alternatively, where sales of a profitable product are low, it may be appropriate to increase commission or to review the way in which the product is advertised or marketed.

Attracting new customers is usually time-consuming and expensive and retaining existing customers can be beneficial. This is particularly true for products with high acquisition costs, such as mobile phone (cell phone) contracts and some life insurance policies. The pricing of these products allows for the recovery of the acquisition costs if the contracts, on average, remain in force for a significant term. If the termination rate is higher than expected then the profitability is reduced. Where termination rates are unduly high, for a product or a particular sales source, remedial action is necessary.

Ways in which companies may seek to improve customer retention include:

- direct (eg telephone) contact to re-sell to terminating customers;
- loyalty bonuses; and
- adjusting commission scales to reflect persistency rates.

18.4.7   Capital management

The need for capital has been discussed in Chapter 11.

Capital management generally involves maintaining the appropriate level of capital in the business and sourcing the capital in a form most suitable for the business (ie equity or debt or a combination).

Financial services companies monitor their capital position frequently, perhaps monthly, to ensure that the actual capital exceeds the regulatory requirements and their own targets. This is important because capital strength can erode quickly in the event of a surge in new business or a downturn in asset values.

18.4.7.1   Charging for capital

While capital efficiency is a common business objective, it is usually possible to raise more capital so long as there is an adequate return to the provider of the capital. For example, offering stronger investment guarantees to customers is more risky for the product manager and requires a higher level of capital support. This is viable if the customers recognize the value of the guarantees and are prepared to pay higher fees to fund the required return on the capital.

Capital management is also applied at product level. Well-managed companies understand which of their products are more risky and therefore require higher capital support. Return on capital can then be monitored for each product. This helps to ensure that products are soundly priced to provide an appropriate return on the capital required to support the risks inherent in the product design.

18.4.7.2   Optimizing capital requirements

Business risks and resulting capital requirements are not static but change over time as a result of changes to product terms and conditions, product mix, underlying profitability and changes in economic conditions. If capital efficiency can be improved then the return on capital to shareholders is improved or benefits can be improved for customers.

Optimizing capital does not necessarily mean minimizing capital because higher capital levels may be necessary to support products that are attractive to customers and to demonstrate financial strength. Reducing capital usage may result in lower margins for commodity products or higher costs for increased risk sharing – eg reinsurance.

However, the experience of a business may suggest ways to improve capital usage, for example:

- reduce business risks – eg increase the level of reinsurance for risk insurances or use derivatives to hedge investment or currency risks;

- reprice products with declining profitability to ensure that safety margins are maintained;

- review product terms and conditions and develop new, less capital-intensive products – the aim is to retain guarantees only where the pricing supports the cost of capital required; and

- increase the diversity of the business through higher volumes, wider product range, different distribution systems, etc.

Example 18.5

For many years a bank offered an annuity product that provided customers with an attractive interest rate guarantee for the duration of the annuity. The market for such products was very competitive and the bank had achieved only a modest market share.

The product had an inherent investment risk because market interest rates provided to customers could not be supported by risk-free investments.

The bank achieved a positive return on capital from the portfolio but not high enough to provide an adequate return on its risk capital. Extensive scenario testing was carried out to determine the optimum way to manage the capital requirement for this product. The conclusion was that an acceptable return was unrealistic in the competitive market that existed.

As a result the bank closed the product to new business and sold the existing portfolio to another financial services group. The bank lost the contribution to overhead expenses that the product had provided, but closing the product allowed the capital to be re-deployed to support other products where the bank had a stronger competitive position.

18.5   Allocating interest to accounts

Many financial businesses involve the distribution of investment income. The same basic process is followed for all financial products:

- *determine* the amount of investment income;

- *allocate* this between customers (or members) and any shareholders and between different groups of customers; and

- *distribute* the income consistently with the allocation.

Particular attention is required when the investment income includes realized and unrealized capital gains and losses.

A common method of allocation and distribution is by using an interest rate declared on an account balance. This method is used by banks, many superannuation funds and also for investment account policies sold by life insurance companies.

The simplest arrangements are where the full investment return is distributed to customers or members each year. The investment return is then allocated by a *mean funds* formula, meaning a formula of the form $i(AB_0 + CF/2)$, where i is the crediting rate, AB_0 is the account balance at the start of the year and CF is the net cash flow allocated to the account during the year.

Exercise 18.2

An investment fund distributes investment earnings to members by means of an annual interest credit to their accounts (the *crediting rate*). Last year the fund had only three members:

Alex had an account balance of $5,000 at the start of the year and made new investments of $6,000 midway through the year and $6,000 at the end of the year.

Kim had an account balance of $15,000 at the start of the year and made redemptions of $2,000 midway through the year and $2,000 at the end of the year.

Pip had an account balance of $10,000 at the start of the year and made no new investments or redemptions during the year.

The fund had retained earnings (not allocated to members) of $2,000 at the start of the year. The investment earnings for the fund for the year amounted to $1,700.

Show that the fund investment earnings rate for the year is 5%. (You may assume that mid-year cash flows earn half a year's interest.) Assuming that the crediting rate is also 5%, allocate the investment earnings to the members' accounts and to retained earnings.

What equity issues can you see in this method of allocating investment earnings to the members' accounts?

For this exercise and Exercise 18.3, it is recommended that you construct your own spreadsheet to help you to understand the issues.

The investment return is not usually uniform throughout the year, so care is needed with cash flows (new funds or withdrawals) which take place during the year. Practical considerations often result in the use of an overall interest rate for all customers or members for the year, irrespective of the actual returns earned during the months they were invested.

Redemptions are often catered for by declaring an interim earnings rate in advance to apply until the final rate for the year is declared. The interim rate may need to be adjusted under changing economic conditions – especially if the underlying assets are sensitive to market fluctuations.

Apart from considerations of equity, managers of such funds do not wish to unduly discourage new investment or encourage withdrawals.

18.5.1.1 Smoothing of returns

Some managers smooth the returns to their customers or members by averaging the actual investment returns over a number of years. Many different formulae have been used in practice for such smoothing. Sometimes, smoothing is used to provide more predictable returns irrespective of the level of market interest rates. At other times, smoothing may be used to avoid or defer declaring unpopular negative interest rates during unfavorable market conditions.

Smoothing is usually managed by holding back part of the return during good years and using this to subsidize rates during periods of poor returns. The alternative of over-declaring interest during bad years and hoping to recover the deficit in later years has the practical difficulty of discouraging new investment and encouraging withdrawals during the period of the deficit, which can compound the problem.

Exercise 18.3

Consider the investment fund referred to in Exercise 18.2.

Make a five-year projection of this fund from the end of the year in Exercise 18.2, initially assuming no further investments or redemptions. Assume that fund investment earning rates for the five years are 5%, -5%, 5%, 5% and 5% respectively for each year. Assume that the crediting rate for each year is determined as the geometric average of the investment returns declared in the previous three years and that the fund investment earning rate was 5% in each of the two years preceding the projection.

Show that the level of retained earnings at the end of the five years has grown to $2,425.

Now allow for new investments and redemptions at different points in time. Test out what is the best and the worst time for new investments and redemptions from the viewpoint of the investor and the fund manager.

What can you conclude from this exercise?

Clearly there are equity issues when smoothing is used. The main problems arise if retained earnings are allowed to become negative to support higher crediting rates than could otherwise be declared. The risks are increased if the investment fund is open to wholesale investors (such as larger superannuation funds, institutional investors and endowment funds). Wholesale investors are often quicker to take advantage of opportunities to switch investments when it suits them.

Funds with negative retained earnings hope to reverse the position by paying crediting rates in future which are lower than the investment earnings rates. This may not be possible in a competitive market where competitors can offer higher returns and the fund is exposed to increased redemptions.

Having said this, many investment funds continue to use the smoothed crediting rate approach. The approach is most practical where:

- the crediting rules do not allow retained earnings to fall below zero;

- redemptions are subject to redemption fees which discourage customers and members from redeeming funds at times of low investment values;

- the investors in the fund are retail rather than wholesale in nature; and

- the fund communicates its approach to crediting investment returns in a clear way to its customers and members.

Funds that build up larger retained earnings have the capacity to increase long-term returns by investing in more market-sensitive investments, such as longer-term fixed-interest securities and equities. Stochastic methods can be used to determine the probability of negative returns in a particular year for a given combination of investment mix and level of retained earnings.

18.6   Unit pricing

An alternative is to fully distribute actual returns by using a unitized method. Customers or members are allocated units in a pool of investments and the unit price reflects subsequent investment earnings including capital gains and losses. At any point in time, the unit price is calculated as the value of the investments in the pool divided by the number of units. New investments or withdrawals require the purchase or sale of an appropriate number of units at the unit price on the day of the transaction.

Example 18.6

An investment fund operates on a unitized method. Today the assets of the fund amount to $13,000 and there are 10,000 units on issue to the current investors in the fund. The unit price for today is therefore $1.30 ($13,000 / 10,000).

Today a new investor invests $2,600 in the fund and an existing investor redeems $1,300. At today's unit price the new investor receives 2,000 units and the redeeming investor redeems 1,000 units.

After these transactions the number of units on issue is 11,000 (10,000 + 2,000 - 1,000). The assets in the fund amount to $14,300 ($13,000 + $2,600 - $1,300). The unit price remains at $1.30 ($14,300 / 11,000).

Unit prices can normally go up and down, so the customers or members receive the full market value investment returns without any smoothing. The above example shows that the unit pricing method deals equitably with new investments and redemptions, which are based on current market values at the time of the transaction. Continuing members are unaffected by the transactions. Unlike the annual interest credit method, customers or members are treated equitably for the exact time they are invested in the fund.

Unit pricing may be used for a wide range of different asset classes or a mixture of asset classes but it works best where the market value of the assets can be readily identified on a day-by-day basis. If the investment assets are short-term deposits or similar, the manager of the investment pool may guarantee that the unit price will not fall, so the unitized method can also be used for cash management accounts.

If the unit pricing mechanism works efficiently, including daily pricing, there is no need for intervention – ie there is no need for a response to the experience. Otherwise, some intervention will be required to handle sudden and severe volatility in markets.

In practice, the unitized method has its own design and management issues. Unit pricing errors are not uncommon and these do require a response.

Key design and management issues in unit pricing are:

- Transactions can be made at unit prices determined *in advance*[1] or *in arrears*.[2] If the unit prices are determined in advance, the customer can exercise an option against the fund. If in arrears, the customer may not understand why the applied price is different from the published price on the day of the transaction. Common practice is to use unit prices calculated daily in arrears.

- Transaction costs, such as brokerage and stamp duty, may be charged to customers who are buying or selling, through the use of differential buying and selling unit prices. An alternative approach is to charge them to the fund as a whole, which means that they are largely borne by continuing customers. Both methods are used in practice.

- Transactions may be backdated, where promises are made to intending customers but there is some delay in processing the transaction.

- Current market prices for some assets are not available at the time that unit pricing is done. For example, there may be delays in getting the prices of units held in pools managed by other investment managers, such as specialist international funds.

- Unit pricing includes an allowance for income tax payable on investment income and net realized gains. Usually, this allowance is calculated at the standard rate of income tax applicable to the policies. The actual tax ultimately paid will differ from the amount allowed for, for various reasons including the sheer complexity of tax legislation. Some companies will adjust unit prices to reflect this difference when it emerges. Others may view this as a shareholder profit (or loss) allowed for in the product pricing.

- Unit pricing also includes an allowance for deferred tax, because unrealized gains and losses will give rise to tax liabilities or benefits when ultimately realized. The tax liabilities or benefits are future events and therefore worth less than face value. A discounted value may be applied but there is no standard approach. The approach used will affect equity between generations of customers.

- Sophisticated systems are needed to enable accurate unit pricing on a daily basis.

Because of the need for precision in unit pricing, unitized funds require tight management control including regular and frequent reconciliations of investments and units on issue.

Unit pricing errors occur from time to time, especially where the management controls are not adequate. The actuary may need to recommend what remedial action should follow. Where unit prices are too high, withdrawing unit holders are paid too much, while new unit holders do not receive enough units. The converse happens if unit prices are too low. If the pricing errors are minor and short-term in nature it may be appropriate to take no action other than adjusting the unit price back to the correct level over a short time period. The continuing unit holders will then gain or lose relative to the new and withdrawing unit holders.

Regulations in some countries prescribe narrow tolerances for unit pricing errors, above which the errors must be rectified for all affected customers. This can be a complex task and it is carried out at the expense of the fund manager.

---

[1] Also known as *historic pricing*, where units are purchased at the latest published price, which does not take account of subsequent market price movements.

[2] Also known as *forward pricing*, where unit prices are calculated based on market price movements before applying the day's contributions and withdrawals, so that these cash flows do not affect the unit price.

18.7   Review of insurance pricing

18.7.1   Pricing review cycle

Companies review the pricing of their products at regular intervals and when specific issues arise. The purpose of this exercise is to test the profitability, capital efficiency and competitiveness of products in the light of experience, market changes and assumption changes since the previous review.

If the claims experience is different from expected, it may be appropriate to adjust the premium rates but this is not always the case. This section considers a range of possible responses to changing experience. Pricing theory, methods and assumptions were covered in Chapter 13 and are not repeated here.

Experience includes not only claims experience but also lapses, withdrawals, expenses, new business volumes, capital requirements and overall profitability. The analysis of experience was covered in Chapter 17.

Competition is an ever-present consideration in pricing and this applies equally to pricing reviews.

18.7.2   Pricing changes

After reviewing the experience, the actuary should be able to develop test pricing which covers expected claims and includes appropriate margins for management expenses, cost of capital and profit, in line with the business plan.

The test pricing is first compared to the existing pricing of the product.

If the test pricing is lower than the existing pricing, consideration may be given to retaining the existing pricing and using some of the margins to improve policy benefits or increase commissions or profit margins. Reduced pricing may be quickly copied by competitors and may start a pricing war in the industry.

If the test pricing is higher than the existing pricing, consideration needs to be given to the attitude of existing customers and potential new customers. For example if the pricing for an existing portfolio is increased in response to a poor claims experience, it is likely that the best risks in the portfolio will insure elsewhere, leaving behind the poorer risks who may find it more difficult to switch insurers. The claims experience may deteriorate, rather than improve, albeit on lower volumes.

For life insurance policies, life companies need to consider whether to apply the new pricing to existing customers or just to new customers. Term life premium rates tend to reduce over time, reflecting ongoing mortality improvements in the community. Some companies prefer to retain the higher margins on existing business despite the switching of some existing customers to the new premium rates. Other companies prefer to operate on a single (current) table of premium rates for administrative efficiency and as a customer service.

18.7.3   Pricing response

In practice, in a competitive market, it is rare for the initial best estimate pricing to also meet the competitive requirements of the product. Further work is usually required to achieve a satisfactory balance between profitability and competitiveness. This may include consideration of other responses to experience such as:

- a review of the terms and conditions of the product in response to unsatisfactory claims or to reduce expensive litigation;

- a review of brokerage and commission arrangements, including allowances for good quality, high-volume producers;

- changes to underwriting procedures – eg asking for more information on application forms or strengthening underwriting procedures where unsatisfactory claims were identified;

- changes to the risk classifications where an undue proportion of claims related to particular risk categories – eg transferring occupations between occupation classes in disability income insurance and transferring models of cars between rating categories in motor vehicle insurance;

- changes to claims management practices – eg claims costs in workers compensation and disability income insurance can be reduced by helping the claimant to return to work as soon as possible. Motor vehicle accident claims costs can be reduced by adopting standard repair assessments and by the use of insurer-owned workshops; and

- a review of discounts for wholesale arrangements which reduce the administrative costs of the insurer.

Example 18.7

A life insurance company writing disability income business experienced claims about 125% of expected. On further analysis, it was found that the poor experience related entirely to blue collar customers despite the high loadings in the premiums for these occupations. Many of the claims related to transport or work accidents. At this level of losses, the company realized it would need to increase premium rates as well as tighten underwriting and the benefits under the policy.

In consultation with the reinsurer, the company narrowed the range of acceptable occupations for new policies, tightened the somewhat generous benefits for accident claims and increased premiums for blue collar occupations only.

The outcome was that the mix of business shifted toward white collar occupations and the product returned to profitability.

It is often worthwhile to examine claims experience at the lowest levels of risk classification permitted by the data. Sometimes, this may be at the level of individual claims, to understand exactly where the claims are coming from. It may be appropriate to reprice (or take some other remedial action) for specific risk classifications rather than repricing for the product as a whole.

Similarly, lapse or withdrawal experience may vary markedly between distribution channels and this may lead to a management response for a particular channel, rather than a repricing of the product.

Exercise 18.4

The claims experience of the public liability product of a large general insurance company has averaged about ten percent lower than expected in the pricing for some years, although there have been variations in the claims experience from year to year. The CEO of the company has received a letter from a large broker suggesting that the company's premiums for this product are no longer competitive and need to be reduced. What issues do you see in this situation and what additional analysis would you recommend before the company replies to the broker?

18.7.4   Experience refunds

Some wholesale products provide an experience refund to the customer in years when the claims experience is better than expected. This has the benefit to the insurer of giving the customer a financial interest in adopting risk management practices to minimize claims.

The financial effect of such refunds is that in good years part of the profit is returned to the customer, while in bad years the insurer suffers the losses. The cost of experience refunds must therefore be included in the pricing of the product, and it is usual to use stochastic methods for this exercise.

Exercise 18.5

For an insurance portfolio there is a 75 percent probability of total claims this year of $80 and a 25 percent probability that total claims are $160. So the risk premium for this portfolio is $100. There is an experience refund to the insurance client of 50 percent of profit, where profit is defined as the excess, if any, of premiums over claims for the year. What is the risk premium required to cover the cost of the claims and the experience refund?

18.8   Defined benefit superannuation

18.8.1   The actuarial review

Defined benefit superannuation schemes provide benefits expressed in terms of members' salaries at or near retirement. These benefits are funded by regular employer and employee contributions. While the employee contributions are defined, the employer contributions are periodically reassessed with the aim of building up sufficient assets to meet the benefits as they fall due. This reassessment takes place through actuarial reviews, typically once every three years.

The actuarial review of funding requirements for defined benefit superannuation funds is a classic example of responding to experience. The contribution rate recommendation at the current review date is a function of the current membership, current assumptions and the current assets of the fund. At the next review it is likely that membership will have changed, assumptions will have changed and the assets and valuations will be different from expected. So assessing the required employer contribution rate for a defined benefit superannuation fund is like constantly adjusting your aim when you are shooting at a moving target.

18.8.2 The pace of funding

At one extreme, an employer could choose to fund the benefits for a new employee by putting aside an amount equal to the present value of all future benefits for the employee. This would provide good security of benefits for the employee but would be an unreasonable charge against the employer's profits at that point of time. At the other extreme, an employer could fund the benefits when they fell due – eg at the retirement of the employee. This defers the cost to the employer but provides no security for the employee.

For private sector superannuation funds, an intermediate approach is usually chosen which provides for a more even charge to the profits of the employer and which secures benefits for members progressively during their service with the employer. For example, benefits might be funded by employer contributions set as a level percentage of salaries during members' employment with the employer. There are various funding methods used in practice, resulting in a faster or slower buildup of funds to meet the eventual benefits. The speed of the buildup is often referred to as the *pace of funding*.

There is often a minimum level of funding established by regulations or generally accepted practice. For example, funds may be required to hold sufficient assets to cover the amount of current termination benefits for all members.

18.8.3 Responses to the actuarial review

The primary purpose of the actuarial review is to set the employer contribution rate for the period until the next review. So the primary response to experience is to adjust the employer contribution rate.

If experience has been favorable then the employer contribution rate may be reduced, so long as the funding level does not fall below minimum levels. Sometimes the experience is so favorable that the employer can cease contributing for a period of time or even indefinitely. This is known as a *contribution holiday*.

If experience has been unfavorable then the employer contribution rate may be increased. This may take the form of an increase in the long-term contribution rate or a special increase designed to achieve target funding levels within a chosen time frame. If the funding position has fallen below minimum levels then a short-term funding boost to return the fund to satisfactory funding levels is a likely outcome.

There are also other actions that can be considered following the review. These include:

- changes to the investment policy or investment manager(s);
- updating of, or other changes to, fund benefits, often affecting only benefits accruing for service after the date of the change;
- improvements in administration procedures; and
- changes to the level of insurance of death and disablement benefits.

Sometimes experience gains are used to fund improvements in benefits for members. Employers are usually happy to improve benefits for their employees if they do not need to increase the employer contribution rate. Some care is needed because it can be expected that there will be periods of favorable and unfavorable experience. If benefits are improved when the experience is favorable and the employer contribution rate is increased when experience is unfavorable, the result may be that benefits become excessive in terms of the objectives of the employer.

The possible responses may be interrelated. For example, a superannuation fund in a strong funding position can take a more aggressive approach to investment policy, and can afford to carry more of the insurance risk, than a fund which is close to minimum funding levels. A more aggressive approach can, in turn, result in lower employer contribution rates over the longer term.

Often, defined benefit funds have a high proportion of "growth" investments (shares and property) to maximize long-term returns. This means that the relative performance of investment returns and salary increases in a three-year period can be quite variable. For newer funds, this may not result in unduly variable employer contribution rates because the experience gains or losses can often be funded over a long period of time. For well-established funds with longer-serving members, the effect of experience variations will be greater but the risks can then be reduced by adopting a less aggressive investment strategy.

Also, a fund whose members are approaching retirement, or which is closed to new members, is likely to be invested more conservatively than one with a strong flow of new members. At the extreme, the investment policy might move toward fixed interest securities with terms roughly matched to the expected retirement dates of remaining members.

Exercise 18.6

A defined benefit superannuation fund has experienced better than expected investment returns over the last three years and salary increases have been generally in line with expectations. The trustee is considering how to deal with the resulting surplus.

On further analysis it has been found that the investment performance was largely due to good timing decisions by the investment manager.

What options do you think are available to the trustee in dealing with the surplus? What further information would you seek before making a recommendation to the trustee?

18.8.4   Returning excess funds to the employer

One option not considered so far in this discussion is to return excess funds from the superannuation fund to the employer. Usually, when a substantial surplus arises in a defined benefit superannuation fund, it is because the employer has contributed more than required to fund the benefits. This can happen if the employer has chosen a fast pace of funding or where the funding assumptions have proved to be conservative. So returning such a surplus to the employer seems a fair and reasonable response.

In many countries, superannuation funds are established as trusts or other entities separate from the employer and the trustees or directors of the fund have responsibilities to consider the interests of both the members and the employer. So a decision to benefit the employer at the expense of reduced security of members' benefits is not taken lightly. There may also be legal constraints on transferring excess funds to the employer.

Sometimes, transfers to the employer must be sanctioned by a court of law. In practice, this may mean a negotiation between the employer and the fund members – for example, the members may agree to a transfer of a portion of the excess funds to the employer so long as the remainder of the excess funds is used to improve the benefits for members.

This is an option which needs care.

18.9 Participating life insurance

18.9.1 The origins of the actuarial profession

Traditional life insurance policies were designed to provide savings and insurance benefits over long periods of time. The mechanism for dealing with ever-changing economic conditions was to charge customers a little more than the theoretical premiums and to pay bonuses reflecting the actual investment and experience outcomes. Rather than developing complex policies to cover every possible outcome, the industry used simple policies and relied on the actuarial profession to formulate equitable methods of allocating the experience profits to the various interest groups.

The profession has a substantial body of research on which present-day practice is based. This chapter contains an introduction to this subject as a classic example of actuaries responding to experience.

18.9.2 Participating policies

Participating policies (also known as *with-profit* policies in some countries) are policies that participate in the profits of the life insurance company. Usually the life insurance company is a mutual company or was a mutual when these policies were first issued.

The profits of the company are distributed to the participating policyholders by means of bonuses, dividends or interest credits depending on the country and the form of the participating product. For convenience, we will use the word "bonus" to represent all such forms of distribution to policyholders. Originally, bonuses were used to distribute unplanned mortality profits but, over time, they became the main vehicle for distributing long-term investment returns to the policyholders.

Usually participating policies share in all the profits of the life insurance company: investment returns, mortality, management expenses and other sources. Bonuses are increased if experience is good but reduced if it is poor. The existence of the participating policyholders has thereby stabilized the operations of companies during changing economic conditions over long time periods.

The term *participating policies* includes a range of product types. The *conventional* participating products are whole life and endowment assurance policies, which have a contractual sum insured payable on death or, in the case of endowment assurance, at the maturity date of the policy. Profits are distributed by declaring reversionary bonuses, which are increases in the sum insured. Variations include products where profits are distributed by means of cash dividends, by interest credits to investment accounts and by increased unit values for unitized participating policies.

The principles involved in achieving equitable outcomes for these variations are similar to those for conventional policies, so in this chapter we have focused on the conventional products.

18.9.3 Allocation and distribution of profit

As part of the annual actuarial review of a life insurance company, the actuary makes recommendations about how investment and other experience profits are allocated and distributed to participating policyholders. *Allocation* is used to describe the determination of the quantum of profits to be allocated to each group while *distribution* refers to the method used to pay out the allocated profit.

> ### Example 18.8
>
> A company may decide to allocate $5 million of profit to type A participating policies and $10 million to type B policies, and carry forward $5 million. It might distribute this to type A policies by reversionary bonuses and to type B policies by reductions in next year's premiums.

18.9.4 Allocation of profit

A first consideration in allocating profits is the legal requirements. In many countries the insurance regulations specify that a minimum proportion of the profits earned in respect of participating business must be allocated to the participating policyholders, with the balance to shareholders. The constitution of the company is also important as it may specify a higher minimum allocation for policyholders.

Subject to the legal constraints, in making recommendations about allocating profit, the actuary has a legal and professional responsibility to seek a fair and equitable allocation as between the various interest groups involved. These include:

- shareholders and policyholders;
- different classes of policyholder – eg by type of policy, duration of policy, age of life insured;
- different generations of policyholder; and
- those who surrender and those who continue.

Actuaries have developed principles for achieving equity and these are outlined below.

18.9.5 Fair and equitable

Achieving equity requires the exercise of considerable judgment. In making these judgments, actuaries often have access to more detailed information and analysis than others. In making recommendations it is important that actuaries provide good explanations of the process, so that equitable results are achieved and are seen to be achieved.

There is no single definition of equity, only some basic principles. There is always a range of solutions that are acceptable as reasonably equitable, so the answers are not black and white. The actuary should seek a solution which is practical to implement, as there is sometimes a trade-off between strict equity and the cost of implementation.

A simple test of equity is whether all the interested parties feel that they have been fairly treated. This is of course the ideal situation but it is very difficult to achieve in practice! Another test is whether you yourself feel comfortable about the allocation that you have recommended – could you defend it to another actuary? Some concepts used to test equity include:

- meeting reasonable expectations;

- fair return in relation to risks accepted; and

- generational equity.

These are now considered in turn.

18.9.5.1 Reasonable expectations

The traditional actuarial view is that the *reasonable expectations* of policyholders are met if reasonable benefits are paid to them having regard to all the circumstances of their policies, including economic conditions during the term of the policies. This is interpreted in the context of a full knowledge of the nature of the policies and the experience of those policies. It is difficult for average policyholders to determine reasonable expectations for their policies. Rather, an independent professional view is required.

Factors that need to be considered in determining reasonable expectations include:

- point of sale benefit illustrations and other sales material – the bonuses will not necessarily be declared at the same bonus rate used in illustrations, but they should be consistent with what was promised, allowing for the difference between actual and expected experience;

- established company practice;

- the policy terms and conditions;

- the constitution of the company; and

- the general economic and business environment.

Of key importance in interpreting reasonable expectations is a good understanding of the sources of profits and the relative contribution of the different groups of policyholders. Profit may arise from one or more of the following:

- experience variations from the pricing assumptions;

- profit loadings in premiums (intended to go to shareholders as reward for their risk and their provision of capital);

- bonus loadings in premiums (intended to go to policyholders as bonuses); and

- investment earnings on capital and retained profits including unrealized gains and losses.

If the experience is better or worse than expected then the participating policyholders should share in that experience by way of increased or reduced bonuses.

While the term *reasonable expectations* is generally applied to policyholders, it can equally be used to judge the outcome for shareholders.

18.9.5.2   Fair return in relation to risks accepted

This test requires returns for each of the interested parties that reflect the relative risks borne by each of them. For example:

- shareholders require returns to compensate for the capital provided and the entrepreneurial risk in operating the business of the life insurance company;

- participating policyholders require bonuses or other returns to compensate for the increased premiums they have paid and their contribution in sharing in the experience risks of the life insurance fund;

- participating policyholders with benefit guarantees accept lesser risks than those without guarantees and this should be reflected in the profit allocation; and

- non-participating policyholders do not share in the experience of the business because their benefits are contractual, so they do not generally share in allocations of profit.

18.9.5.3   Generational equity

This test requires each generation of policyholders to make a fair contribution to the capital and retained profits of the company (also referred to as the company's *estate*). Note that *generation* is not tightly defined because there is always overlap between policyholder groups based on age, policy type and duration.

For a mutual life insurance company, the first generation of policyholders establishes the estate, which provides the financial buffer for later generations and allows the company to increase returns for later generations by taking a longer-term investment strategy. Subsequent generations contribute to the growth of the estate to enable the company to continue to grow, thereby achieving economies of scale in management processes.

In a proprietary company, the issue relates more to making an appropriate charge to the policyholders for the use of the capital supporting their policies.

In some circumstances, it is argued that subsidies between generations are fair if they are in line with reasonable expectations. For example, if policyholders are led to expect smooth bonus rates irrespective of economic conditions, then there should be cross-subsidies between policyholders at different stages of the economic cycle.

18.9.6   Distribution of profits

Once the profits have been allocated to the interested parties, the next question is the amount and form of the distribution. Some general factors to consider are:

- capital requirements, which may limit the distribution of profits;

- competition, where a company tries to match the distributions of competitors. Note that care is required because distributions not supported by experience can lead to financial difficulty;

- consistency with legal requirements and past practice; and

- simplicity and practicality – the proposed distributions must be practical to administer and readily explained to policyholders and distributors.

18.9.7 Methods of distribution

For conventional participating policies, surplus is distributed by means of:

- uniform reversionary bonuses – either simple, compound or super-compound; and
- terminal bonuses.

18.9.7.1 Uniform reversionary bonuses

Profits on traditional whole life and endowment assurance policies may be distributed by uniform reversionary bonuses, which are additions to the sum insured payable on death or maturity. These may be either:

- *simple* – $x\%$ of sum insured each year;
- *compound* – $x\%$ of (sum insured plus accumulated bonuses) each year; or
- *super-compound* – $x\%$ on sum insured + $y\%$ on accumulated bonuses, where $y > x$.

The rates ($x\%$ and $y\%$) may be the same for all policies in a product group or they may vary according to year of issue (especially if premium rates changed at some past date) or by maturity age.

Once the bonus is declared, it is a legal liability of the company.

The compound reversionary bonus method is more equitable than the simple reversionary bonus in distributing profits arising from excess investment earnings but it does not work as well in dealing with other types of profits – eg from mortality experience or expenses. However, these are usually relatively small amounts compared with the investment profits.

The super-compound method favors longer-term policies. When combined with a terminal bonus, it is considered to be most suitable for conditions of high interest rates, growth-type assets and high capital requirements for new policies. It is now widely used in practice but it is a little harder to explain than the compound bonus system.

18.9.7.2 Terminal bonuses

Terminal bonuses are a percentage addition to the amount of a claim, including reversionary bonuses. The terminal bonus rate applies to claims paid within a stated time frame (eg within the next year) and may be changed for subsequent claims. The terminal bonus method was developed to deal equitably with the more volatile returns from equity investments.

Until around the 1950s, only dividends and realized capital gains were included in profits for distribution. Unrealized gains were not included. This was inequitable to policyholders who surrendered before the capital gains were realized. Equities were then a relatively small proportion of investment assets, so the inequities were not material.

As equity investment increased, a new method was needed to deal with unrealized gains. Life insurance companies did not want to pay reversionary bonuses using unrealized capital appreciation because the bonuses, once allotted, were guaranteed, whereas the capital appreciation could disappear if markets fell. The terminal bonus method was the solution. Those policies which terminated when markets were high received a terminal bonus to reflect the unrealized gains, but the terminal bonus rates could be reduced if markets subsequently fell.

Some companies declare terminal bonuses that are adjusted gradually to reflect policyholder expectations of smoothed returns, at the expense of strict inter-generational equity.

Exercise 18.7

A life insurance fund containing participating policies has just made a large unexpected windfall gain, perhaps from realizing a large investment or from the sale of computer software or other intellectual property. The source of the gain has been held by the life fund for many years but its value was not previously recognized.

What options would you consider for distributing the surplus from this windfall gain to the participating policyholders? What further information would you seek before arriving at a conclusion?

18.9.8 Asset share methods

One test of equity is whether the amount paid out or set aside for each policy, including the value of the bonuses declared to date, matches the *asset share*, which is the amount of money accumulated for each policy.

The amount of money accumulated for each policy sounds like a simple concept but the calculations are complex. The asset share is calculated by accumulating the cash payments for a group of policies over the entire lives of the policies using the actual experience over this period. The cash payments include premiums, investment earnings, expenses and claims payments.

It is reasonable to reduce asset shares to allow for the cost of capital required to support the policies.

By using *actual* cash flows in the accumulation, the asset share represents the actual experience of the policies, including investment earnings, expenses and mortality. Actuaries try to achieve equity for these policies by reflecting this actual experience in the bonus rates declared.

Asset share methods can be used to test the equitable treatment of terminating policies by comparing current asset shares with current termination values (including the value of bonuses declared).

Asset share methods can be used to test the equitable treatment of continuing policies by comparing current asset shares with the current values of continuing policies (including the value of bonuses declared). The current values of continuing policies may be determined by a discounted cash flow of the future benefits less the future premiums.

This method is widely used to assess bonus allocations and distributions. If the asset shares for some groups of policies are higher than the policy values then the life insurance company may enhance bonuses for these groups – and vice versa for groups where the asset shares are lower than the policy values.

Differences in applying the asset share technique reflect companies' different bonus philosophies.

18.10 Practical implications for actuaries

Responding to experience is a central part of the Actuarial Control Cycle and a central part of the work of many actuaries. In formulating responses, actuaries must be careful to consider the alternatives before choosing or recommending a particular course of action.

The client or employer may not take appropriate action if they do not fully understand both the actuary's recommendations and the analysis and reasoning that support those recommendations. So, communication is very important here. The actuary should think carefully about how best to communicate to the client or employer. The actuary's written report might be supplemented by presentations, discussions and face-to-face meetings with those directly affected by any proposed changes.

Actuaries are recognized as having expertise in achieving equitable financial outcomes even outside the traditional practice areas. If the profession is to maintain this reputation, it is important that all actuaries take such assignments seriously and avoid superficial analysis and responses. We have discussed some general principles in this chapter but each assignment needs to be considered in the light of the circumstances surrounding the particular case. It is often helpful to discuss these situations with colleagues before presenting a final view.

18.11   Key learning points

* Appropriate response to emerging experience is a critical success factor in managing an organization.

* The business plan and the risk management framework provide the basis for understanding and responding to the experience of an organization.

* Careful analysis is usually required to determine the optimal response.

* Financial control systems and audits provide early warnings of potential problem areas.

* Expenses, claims and capital management are of particular importance for insurance companies.

* Investment earnings may be distributed to customers by means of smoothed or unsmoothed crediting rates but there are practical and equity issues to consider.

* Unit pricing is potentially more equitable but there are several practical considerations.

* Changing premium rates is only one of the possible responses to the emerging profitability of an insurance product.

* An actuarial review of a defined benefit superannuation fund is a classic example of responding to the experience of the fund.

* For participating life insurance business, actuaries have developed a framework for achieving equity between shareholders and different groups of policyholders.

* Achieving fairness and equity is often a key consideration when actuaries advise organizations about responding to experience.

CD Items

Chapter 18 Interest Crediting Spreadsheet

Chapter 18 Expense Analysis Spreadsheet

Chapter 18 Exercise Solutions

Fred's Coffee Shop – Applying the Actuarial Control Cycle

You have now reached the last chapter in this book. This is a time to reflect on what you have learned. For Fred, it is also a time to reflect. His coffee shop has been a great success and he has expanded into a chain of five similar shops. When Fred thinks about it, he realizes that all of the aspects of the Actuarial Control Cycle covered in this book have contributed to his successful approach to business. In Chapter 19 we will be looking at some other applications of the Actuarial Control Cycle.

Chapter 19   Applying the Actuarial Control Cycle
by the Editors

19.1   Introduction

Now that you have completed a study of the elements of the Actuarial Control Cycle, it is time to reflect on what you have discovered.

In this chapter, we illustrate the principles of the earlier chapters by four real world examples of actuarial work.

The earlier chapters focus to a large extent on examples from insurance and pensions or superannuation. These are the practice areas where actuarial principles were first developed and they often provide the most suitable examples for your initial study. However, actuarial practice is by no means restricted to these contexts. In this chapter we have deliberately chosen four applications from outside these areas, to help you recognize how actuarial techniques and the control cycle approach can be used for all sorts of practical problems. You will see that all four have modeling as a common theme (which should be no surprise) but they each address a different aspect of an actuarial problem.

19.2   Advising on the viability and financing of a fiber optic cable project

Tony Coleman (Director, Lonergan Edwards & Associates) talked to Clare Bellis about one of the projects he worked on as a consulting actuary and partner at PricewaterhouseCoopers.[1]

19.2.1   Background

The task for Tony's firm was to advise on the feasibility of building and project financing a new fiber optic cable for a major telecommunications company ("telecom") operating in Australia.

The proposal was to build a cable from northern Sydney, where there was a major link to the telecommunications network at the Australian end, across to Japan. That would allow the telecom concerned to link into cables, in which it already had rights, connecting Japan to the US West Coast. This would give it an alternative capability for delivering extra internet services across the Pacific.

The context for the project related particularly to its timing: in the middle of the internet boom at the start of the 21st century. Tony commented that this raised several fascinating issues:

- A competing consortium was building a cable directly across the Pacific: Sydney – Auckland – Hawaii to the US West Coast. This would mean a significant increase in capacity on the route.

---

[1] The transcript of the interview, which also covers some other interesting projects, is in "Cables, Toll Roads and Forests" on the CD.

- The motivation for the new cables was the massive growth in the volume of traffic. Internet traffic between Australia and the US had roughly doubled in each of the three prior years. It was difficult to make assumptions about future growth rates, since obviously the growth would not continue at that level forever.

- The telecom was physically running out of capacity for its operations. It needed the extra capacity. Other solutions were available, such as connecting via Singapore, but would be considerably less efficient.

- Pricing pressure in the market for telecommunication services generally meant that the price that could be charged was dropping rapidly. The net effect was that, while the volume was going up rapidly, the total revenue was actually only growing at around 7% or 8% per annum above the inflation rate.

Traditionally, such projects have been financed using project finance. Project finance relies on the cash flows generated by the project itself without financial guarantees or support from the parent. Lenders decide whether to lend based on the inherent risk profile of the project.

19.2.2   Developing a solution

The consultants' task was to make sure that the cable could be financed. This required an assessment of the fundamental economics of the project. As Tony explained, that meant having a view about two crucial things: first, the revenue stream and its quality and second, the cost of building the cable and the technical difficulties of building it.

The revenue side was investigated by a series of scenario tests. For example, if the internet traffic was not doubling every year but only going up by 50% per annum, what happened? What was the effect of the competing cable going into the ground? The models had to take account of the factors driving the price changes in the market. For example, what guaranteed contracts could the sponsor put in place with customers to feed base demand? On what terms and conditions would customers be prepared to sign up? The sponsor was keen not to sell too much of the capacity of the cable at fixed prices, because it thought that it would be able to sell it at much higher prices later on. On the other hand, the banks financing the project were keen to see contracts with customers in place that locked in revenue at levels that would repay their loans.

The actuaries' model had to allow for these different factors and for the trade-off between the various interests: for example between what the banks would want if they were providing project finance and what the sponsor would want in terms of maximizing its return from the project. Another complication was that a cable like the one proposed won't only have one equity partner involved, because what drives the value of the cable is the ability to feed traffic down it. When building a cable to Japan, the ideal partner is a big Japanese telecom. So the modelers had to start thinking about what would attract the Japanese partners, giving them another set of stakeholder interests to balance.

What Tony's team was looking for was a financial structure that worked whether capacity or demand doubled or halved, or the price halved or fell by 75 percent – because, in this type of business, such huge swings are possible. The business and financing model had to be robust in a rapidly changing environment. This involved trying different combinations that varied the design of the business and the nature of the financing. In this context, the design was the contracts and prices for customers; and the financing considerations involved the balance between debt and equity, and the level of guarantees and risk. For example, large customers could be offered some equity in the cable to lock them in.

After arriving at a business structure that looked feasible, the actuaries tested it on a range of scenarios to see if it held up. A list of criteria was developed, and the results evaluated against those criteria. Using this feedback, the design was adjusted and the set of scenarios run again to see if it produced a better result.

The second part of the model – the cost side – was in some ways the easier part. The technology for laying cables was relatively well known, as were the sorts of things that could go wrong and how to deal with them. However, there was another complicating factor to the technology. Once the cable was laid, it would be relatively inexpensive to boost its capacity massively by adding units at each end of the cable to compress the data going down the cable. So, after the cable had been installed, it would be possible to increase its capacity in steps to up to 16 times the original capacity. And, furthermore, new cable technology was coming which meant that the cable itself was probably going to be technically obsolete within four or five years, because the next generation of cable would be capable of even greater capacity increases again. This created choices beyond the straightforward decision to invest or not: for example, waiting for the new technology to enable a superior cable for a similar cost in three or four years time, or going ahead now but factoring in future additional investments to increase capacity.

Real options inherent in an investment decision have value. For example, the option to increase an existing cable's capacity if needed to meet increasing demand had a real value because the sponsor was not locked in to making the extra investment required to lift capacity if the demand (in the form of both volume and the price that customers will pay) did not occur as quickly as might originally have been expected, if at all. The option of making a smaller investment that could be increased later versus a larger initial investment could be evaluated using option pricing theory and carefully considered assumptions about the probabilities attaching to different levels of revenue that might arise in the various scenarios being contemplated.

Tony concluded his description of the task by saying "So, we did all this work and we wrote a report which said, in essence, that it is viable and can be done in certain ways and we recommend you go ahead with it in a particular way. And in fact they did pretty much as we recommended. It was an interesting job. I learnt a lot about international telecommunications, that I would never have known any other way!"

19.2.3   Comments on the fiber optic project

Let's see how this project illustrates the application of the various topics in this book.

The first stage is to understand and clearly specify the problem. The various parties involved in this project were each concerned about their risk/return from participation in the project. The consulting actuary's role was to help structure the optimal solution, which requires a clear framework for managing risk. The actuary would approach the work in a professional way. The project would make use of various financial products, such as different forms of debt and equity finance. The context in this case was the market for internet capacity at that particular time – the internet boom – and that particular place – across the Pacific. The various risks had to be identified and managed.

Exercise 19.1

We comment above that the actuary "would approach the work in a professional way." Reviewing Chapter 3, what do you think this sentence means?

Exercise 19.2

(a) What were the contrasting objectives of the various stakeholders in the project?

(b) What are the sources of risk in the project?

The actuary can then begin to design the solution. Various tools could be used to manage the uncertainties, such as locking in some revenue by selling a proportion of the capacity at long-term fixed prices. The design of the project financing would no doubt have been influenced by rules around taxation and accounting standards. The viability of the project depended on the design of contracts for internet capacity that could be sold at the outset or in the future, and the pricing of these products. Model building was obviously a very important part of the work, and the resultant projections of cash flows required an understanding of the nature of assets and liabilities. The parties providing debt finance would be keenly interested in the solvency of the project, and the actuarial models could provide them with a clearer picture of the security of their investment under different scenarios. The consortium would need advice on interpreting the results of the cash flow models – would the profits be sufficient to make the project viable?

Finally, although there was no ongoing monitoring and responding to experience involved, because of the one-off nature of this consulting assignment, we can see that the same skills that are involved in monitoring and responding were in this case applied in the process of model refining and modification of the structure of the project. In addition, the consultant could advise on what aspects need to be monitored by the client, and might also expect to be re-engaged in a few years to assess subsequent developments and recommend adjustments.

Exercise 19.3

Projects to lay fiber optic cables under the Pacific Ocean don't come along every day. Can you think of other sorts of projects that raise similar issues to this example?

19.3 An application of the Actuarial Control Cycle to marketing problems

Clare Bellis talked with David Isaacs, consulting actuary at Quantium, an Australia-based consultancy that specializes in the analysis of customer data and the application of quantitative techniques to marketing problems. They discussed examples of how Quantium used the Actuarial Control Cycle in its work.

19.3.1 Interview

CB: What is your background?

DI: I'm an actuary. I have been at Quantium for about seven years, and before that I was at the consulting firm Trowbridge Deloitte. I have worked in general insurance and spent a lot of time thinking about how general insurance and other actuarial techniques can be applied to a wider range of problems.

CB: Can you give me an example of your work where you use the Actuarial Control Cycle?

DI: One example would be media effectiveness modeling. Here we are advising a client how to make the best use of different combinations of marketing methods. The approach we use mirrors the Actuarial Control Cycle: we understand the data, build a model, use that to recommend a strategy and then, perhaps six to twelve months down the track, we use new data to refresh the model. Suppose a client has historically advertised in press, on TV and online but has not used radio. We can evaluate the past results to come up with an optimal allocation across the existing media and then we might recommend applying, say, five to ten percent of the budget to radio. This enables us to enhance the marketing strategy, but in a controlled manner. This then feeds back into the model. It is important to see what works well in aggregate, not just in isolation. The length of the cycle might vary but it is a process of continual refinement. I think that is something that makes our approach different from what many marketers do.

CB: In terms of the model building, do you use actuarial techniques?

DI: Yes, we use techniques such as GLMs (Generalized Linear Models). At a high level, it is similar to modeling claims cost or demand in general insurance but there are a few additional technical subtleties to take account of factors that do not exist in the general insurance environment. We develop a historic picture of media exposures and sales results with a lot of granularity. For example, with television, we do not just consider what program was shown but how it rated with different demographics, to build a geographic and demographic footprint of the historic media exposure. The richness of these media footprints means that we can identify subtle differences in exposure to media that can be used to explain the marketing impact in terms of enquiries and sales. Then we have developed an optimization system that interrogates the models, allowing a lay person to make decisions about how to allocate their investment in marketing.

We also use valuation techniques to look at lifetime customer value. Many businesses still measure success in terms of numbers of sales. As actuaries, it is second nature to develop strategies that take full account of the potential value of the customers they are trying to attract. For example, we did some work for Jetstar, a low-cost airline. Sydney-Melbourne flights are less profitable than Sydney-Perth return flights. We helped Jetstar to understand where they should spend their marketing dollars to generate the best return measured by future profits, not just customer numbers.

19.3.2 Comments on the marketing application

Quantium's work particularly illustrates the points made in Chapters 10 and 17. Data is of fundamental importance, and collecting data in a way that enables analysis along different dimensions gives valuable insights. This application also highlights the importance of context, of mastering the detail but also looking beyond the detail to recognize the broader issues. Quantium's actuaries originally gained experience in modeling techniques in the context of non-life insurance but they have applied those same techniques in a very different environment.

Exercise 19.4

Of the three phases of the Actuarial Control Cycle, which will provide the greatest challenge to an actuary working on non-traditional problems?

19.4 Risk management consulting

Stuart Klugman interviewed Vinaya K. Sharma and Samuel J. Keller about the application of actuarial skills to enterprise risk management problems.

19.4.1 Background

In recent years, actuaries have become involved in enterprise risk management (ERM). This is a natural fit within the insurance industry as actuaries often have a broad knowledge of the company's operations and also possess the modeling tools to address risk-related issues. The actuarial profession has recognized this by creating a special designation for actuaries with an ERM skill set. The CERA credential[2] was created by the SOA in 2007; and, in November 2009, a treaty was signed by thirteen worldwide actuarial organizations for each to recognize and eventually offer this designation.

As actuaries honed their ERM skills within their traditional employment areas, it became apparent that those same skills would work in broader financial services and beyond. The two actuaries interviewed work for a consulting firm that provides enterprise risk management consulting to a variety of financial services organizations.

Vinaya K. Sharma FSA CERA PRM graduated from university in 1993 with a degree in actuarial science. He spent several years working for two insurance companies and for an actuarial consulting firm. In 2006 he joined his current employer.

Samuel J. Keller FSA MAAA graduated from university in 1997 with a degree in actuarial science and worked as a pricing actuary over a range of life insurance and annuity products for an insurance company until 2003. In 2003 he joined the actuarial practice of a Big Four accounting firm, where he focused on audit and advisory engagements covering financial reporting and modeling. In 2007 he joined his current employer.

19.4.2 Interview

SK: What does ERM mean in the context of your job?

VKS: ERM means an integrated view of (generally financial) risks. In many organizations, one department may be responsible for managing interest rate risk, another manages credit/obligor risk, and yet another manages the equity markets. Alternatively, an organization may manage its risks by business unit (fixed annuities, variable annuities, life insurance, etc).

---

[2] CERA stands for Chartered Enterprise Risk Analyst, and more detail is available on http://www. ceranalyst.org. However, in Australia it is proposed that CERA will stand for Chartered Enterprise Risk Actuary.

The ERM function brings the various risks/units (and their associated transactions) together to see how they interact with each other in the same economic environments. For example, for capital management purposes, the economic environment that is bad (99th percentile) for variable annuities might not be so bad for life insurance. In fact, there might be some offsetting risks, thus leading to a lower overall capital requirement than simply summing up the capital necessary for each business unit or each type of risk. I work with clients to help them determine the amount of capital necessary for the amount of risk/return they are willing to tolerate. It is not uncommon to see potential capital reductions of 10 percent just by integrating the risks in a single view compared with a "silo" approach to risk management.

SK: Can you give an example of an ERM project you have worked on?

VKS: I started the ERM program at a large insurance company in the early 2000s. The task was formidable since nothing formally existed and staff was very limited. My position had three distinct roles:

- Aggregation/integration of various financial risk profiles (from different parts of the organization) into a consolidated reporting platform and measuring against company limits/tolerances (that I helped establish).

- Discussion with various areas of the organization on a regular/consistent basis to understand what risks they were dealing with, and in several cases, help to quantify the impact/exposure. Many of the discussions were with areas that actuaries are not normally exposed to, such as Marketing, Legal and Human Resources. By understanding concerns from all parts of the organization, I could see possible synergies, (avoidance of) duplication of work, as well as synthesize risks for senior management in a single coordinated fashion.

- Quantifying ad hoc events on an as-needed basis (for example, I coordinated very preliminary information and came up with a potential risk position by late in the day of September 11, 2001[3]).

SJK: I assisted an investment risk management department with expanding its analysis of embedded financial markets risks. This organization was most interested in the evolution of its financial asset positions covering a range of deterministic and stochastic scenarios over a three- to four-year horizon. The financial asset position ranged from straightforward non-callable corporate bonds to complicated structured (securitized) assets and interest rate derivatives such as swaps and caps. Embedded in this analysis was a range of assumptions determined from experience studies such as credit quality migration and mortgage prepayments that varied with interest rate environment, which would impact the structured assets' ultimate performance.

We modeled a variety of investment strategies including moving to higher or lower credit quality and longer or shorter maturities, duration hedging approaches using interest rate derivatives and a migration away from the complicated structured assets. Key measures investigated were the development of market values to book values under each scenario, the portfolio effective duration over time, as well as simply cash flows spun off from the potential investment portfolios and hedges.

---

[3] You are probably familiar with this date: terrorists hijacked commercial airliners and flew them into New York's World Trade Center, resulting in its collapse; they also attacked the Pentagon and attempted to attack another target, believed to be the Capitol or the White House.

SK: Were there any roadblocks to bringing the various parts of the organization together? Or, conversely, was there any key factor that smoothed your pathway?

VKS: What I am about to say is the common response in the literature but in this case it really is the most important point: without strong and active support from the organization's leader, the effort will fail. It is simply not enough for a consultant or Chief Risk Officer to extol the benefits of ERM.

SK: How did your actuarial training help you succeed?

VKS: My actuarial training is a huge help in the ERM world. Through various rotations as an actuarial student, I was exposed to various types of "traditional" actuarial risks, along with asset-liability management, which was relatively new at the time. My knowledge of the "right hand side" of the balance sheet (liabilities) naturally grew from these rotations. That knowledge was particularly helpful in starting an ERM program since I had much more exposure to various (life insurance company) risks than others, knew how to model and manage those risks, as well as communicate them. Starting the ERM program gave me insight into the asset side of the company, an area I was not too familiar with. The exposure proved valuable since it enabled a change in career path to a leading ERM consulting firm, where I help clients manage both sides of the balance sheet (with an emphasis on credit/asset modeling and capital management).

SJK: Actuarial training and background brings a discipline to quantitative analysis that is particularly helpful in financial and enterprise risk management. My actuarial training has driven a natural curiosity toward the problem-oriented mathematics that drives the movement of the risk measures we analyze. This drive to understand the cause-and-effect relationship between management actions, market movements and the ultimate riskiness of a company's financial position ultimately produces better analysis and hopefully the capacity to make better decisions.

19.4.3   Comments on the risk management interview

This example obviously relates closely to Chapters 2 and 6, which deal with risk management. It also brings out how risk is related to capital. Organizations that manage risk at an enterprise level can identify the diversification benefits and therefore may be able to hold less capital. A full understanding of risk requires attention to the asset side of the balance sheet, to the liability side of the balance sheet and to how the two sides of the balance sheet interact. And finally, in this example as in the previous ones, it is not enough for the actuary to build a model, come up with some answers and hand over a solution. The actuary needs to be able to deal with other people, from understanding the problem, to cooperating in building a solution, to communicating the solution and tailoring it to meet the client's needs. All this is part of doing a professional job.

Exercise 19.5

In the interview above, Samuel J. Keller stresses the importance of understanding "the cause-and-effect relationship between management actions, market movements and the ultimate riskiness of a company's financial position." Give examples of such relationships.

19.5   A football tipping model

Richard Lyon interviewed James Sullivan, from actuarial consulting firm Taylor Fry, about the use of a statistical model in a newspaper's tipping competition. Apart from promoting the firm (and actuaries in general), the experience demonstrated the value and limitations of modeling and the importance of continual monitoring and frequent review.

19.5.1   Background

Australians follow several different types of football, including Australian Rules Football. This fast, skillful game is played on an oval ground (often a cricket ground) 135 to 165 meters long and 110 to 155 meters wide. The object of the game is to kick the ball (quite similar to a rugby ball or an American football) between four posts – the two middle posts are called *goal posts* and the outer two are called *behind posts*. Kicking the ball between the two goal posts scores six points, while kicking the ball between a goal post and a behind post scores one point.

Teams in the Australian Football League (AFL) averaged between 76 and 108 points per game in the 2009 season.

Not only do Australians like to play and watch sport, but they are also very happy to gamble on the results of matches. Sophisticated options are available, including betting on both the winning team and the margin, but a popular pastime is the "tipping competition," in which participants attempt to pick the winners of each match, every weekend of the season. The one with the most correct tips over the season is the winner. Many workplaces run such competitions, as do radio stations (among others).

Newspapers, including the *Sydney Morning Herald* (SMH), invite a panel of celebrities to nominate their tips for each weekend's round. In 2009, the panel included "The Computer," introduced by the SMH as follows:

> Taylor Fry Consulting Actuaries – normally in the business of advising government and corporations – have developed a statistical model to pick winners based on several factors including venue, team and recent and long-term form using generalised linear modelling. So confident is The Computer that Taylor Fry has promised to donate $500 to charity for every tip it is behind the winner – if any – at the end of the season.

Over a cup of coffee (good, but no match for Fred's!), Richard Lyon discussed the model and the experience of the tipping competition with James Sullivan, the model's developer.

19.5.2   Discussion

James described how the model was used to predict the margin between the two teams (and hence the winner) in each match. He said that the model used a range of modeling techniques, including generalized linear modeling and tree-based data mining techniques, using readily available data in a manner that would be familiar to many actuaries and actuarial students, especially those working in general insurance.

Part of the skill and judgment in the process lay in the selection of splines to fit to the data. For example, in assessing the contribution of recent form, they would consider the total win/ loss record in each team's last five matches – a score of five would mean that the team had won its past five matches; a score of four would mean that it had won four and lost one; and so on. In addition to statistical tests, it would be a matter of judgment as to whether one fitted a linear spline or a more complex function to the data. For example, teams that have lost all five previous matches may not be significantly different from those that have lost four out of five. Similar considerations apply for teams that have won four or five out of five.

James said that the firm had a policy of testing its models by deriving parameters from a randomly-selected 75 percent of the available data and using the remaining 25 percent to measure the quality of fit and, hence, the usefulness of each selected variable. So, in fact, there was not one model but a collection of models from which the best was selected. For the football tipping, it was not possible to isolate part of the data at random in this manner, not least because of the importance of recent form trends. Instead, a range of models was built using data excluding the 2008 season. These models were then tested against each other using 2008 data. Statistical tests were used to choose the best-performing model, which was then used for 2009.

This detailed and iterative approach to building a model and selecting parameters is clearly consistent with the application of the Actuarial Control Cycle. However, the team didn't stop there.

As well as being updated weekly with the latest data, the model was periodically reviewed and recalibrated. This was essential, because some teams' performance in 2009 was markedly different from pre-season expectations. Any delays in recalibration meant that the model had systemic biases that resulted in poorer quality predictions. James was able to illustrate these biases by comparing actual to expected performance for each team, as illustrated in Figures 19.1 and 19.2.

Figure 19.1   Model performance before review

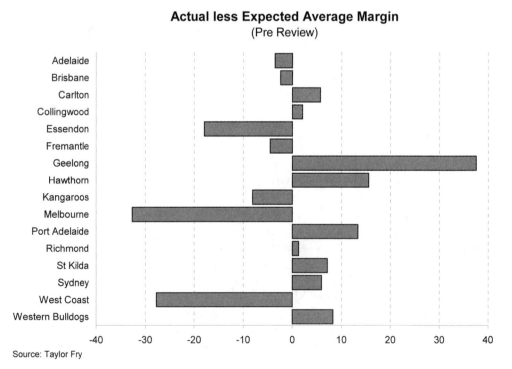

Actual less Expected Average Margin
(Pre Review)

Source: Taylor Fry

In Figure 19.1, we can see that predictions were relatively poor for some teams, especially Melbourne, Geelong and West Coast. This could indicate bias within the model or the availability of more information within the data with predictive power. Either the model's parameters needed to be recalibrated or a further variable needed to be introduced.

In Figure 19.2 (below), we can see the benefit of a recalibration of parameters; the larger prediction errors have reduced considerably, meaning that the predictive power is much improved.

Figure 19.2   Model performance after review

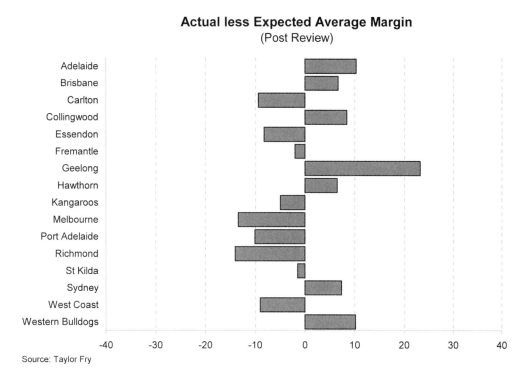

Source: Taylor Fry

For the tipping model, we would expect to see some residual error, partly because of random (or at least completely unpredictable) events and partly for obvious reasons that cannot readily be modeled. For example, the latter category would probably include the availability (or otherwise) of key players, for which reliable and consistent data would be hard to obtain. Alternatively, it may be relatively straightforward to obtain predictive data that explained past results but that would not be available in time for the panel's tipping deadlines. Such data might include the weather conditions.

Even at optimum performance, therefore, the model would not be expected to beat the outliers from a large group of tipsters in any one year. However, the model would be expected to produce good results year after year and thus outperform many tipsters over several years. James says that this has been their experience when using the model in large tipping competitions over the past few seasons.

Thus, among the SMH panel of ten in 2009, The Computer might reasonably have been expected to rank in the top two or three. James blames a delay in initial recalibration for the fact that it ranked tied for fourth place, five points (and $2,500 to charity) behind the winner.

19.5.3 Comments on the tipping example

Many situations in life require decisions to be taken in relation to uncertain future events. The Actuarial Control Cycle is all about enabling such decisions to be taken – and learning from experience to improve those decisions in future.

In situations like the tipping model, frequent decisions are required, so it is important to learn from past experience and to ensure that models stay up-to-date. Availability of data is critical in adjusting the models in a timely manner. There is also a tight deadline for decisions, which means that the decision-making process needs to be timely and efficient.

Exercise 19.6

The football tipping example involves relatively frequent decisions, with short deadlines. Another area where actuaries have had to cope with rapidly changing information is in the energy markets. On the CD, you will find two articles describing such applications.

Can you think of some examples, outside financial services and energy markets, where quick but accurate decisions are required? What about decisions which require much more time but must be made with more precision?

19.6 Conclusion

Each of our four examples in this chapter has special characteristics:

- The fiber optic project deals with the evaluation and management of an essentially irreversible major decision. The strategy for addressing it is twofold: first, make the decision as well-informed as possible and, secondly, build into the solution as much flexibility as possible, to make it relatively future-proof.

- The marketing application is an analytical situation, which involves modeling, the use of data and setting assumptions. Future assignments would build on past experience.

- The risk management discussion is about the relevance of a deep knowledge of life insurance practice. It demonstrates the need to consider assets and liabilities together and the capital benefits that result from an integrated approach to risk.

- The tipping competition is about monitoring and responding to experience. The modeling is important but what is distinctive in this example is the need to be very dynamic.

They are applications in very different contexts. What they have in common is that they are all practical problems. Much of the work that actuaries do requires them to sort through a great deal of information and knowledge to determine what is relevant to the particular situation and then arrive at a practical solution. We need to understand the theory – and its limitations – and make sure that the solution is a workable one that takes account of the stakeholders' needs.

You should now see that the Actuarial Control Cycle is not a prescription that you should try to force to fit every situation but that it can offer insights into the way to tackle a very wide range of problems. It is also a model for how you can approach your own career. Your life will be full of opportunities to gain experience, learn from it and adapt the way you proceed in future. We wish you all the very best on that journey.

CD Items

Burge, A. 2001, Energy Markets, *Actuary Australia*, September 2001, pp. 8-9.

Coleman, T. & Bellis, C. 2003, Cables, Toll Roads and Forests, Transcript.

Driussi, A., Stevenson, C. & Davis, T. 2007, An Actuarial Approach to Optimising the Trade-Off Between Media and Price Promotions, Institute of Actuaries of Australia.

Hinton, B. 1999, Energy Market Actuaries, *The Actuary*, March 1999, Institute of Actuaries.

Chapter 19 Exercise Solutions

Notes on Editors and Contributors

Editors

Clare Bellis BA MA FIA CertHEd
Senior Lecturer in Actuarial Science, University of Kent, Canterbury, UK

Clare Bellis has over ten years' experience in teaching actuarial management using the Actuarial Control Cycle framework to many hundreds of students in Australia, the UK and, via the internet, around the world. She worked in life insurance, investments and pensions consulting in England and Australia for ten years before becoming a full-time academic in 1989, first at Macquarie University in Sydney and then at the University of Kent from 2007.

As well as her actuarial qualifications, Clare has a degree in history from the University of Cambridge, and is the author of a book on the history of the Australian actuarial profession, *The Future-Managers: Actuaries in Australia 1853-1997*. She has served on the Council of the Institute of Actuaries of Australia and on many Institute committees. Clare was also Editor of the Australian Actuarial Journal from 1999 to 2001.

She was a member of the education committee of the International Actuarial Association, and has also served as the Australian liaison representative on the education task forces of the Society of Actuaries and the Institute/Faculty of Actuaries.

Clare has co-authored a number of papers on educational topics, including:

Bellis C. S. & Felipe M. A. 2002, Actuarial Education in 2002 and Beyond: A Global Perspective, *Transactions of the 27th International Congress of Actuaries*.

Goford J., Bellis C. S., Bykerk C. D., Carne S. A., Creedon S., Daykin C. D., Dumbreck N. J., Ferguson D. G. R., Goodwin E. M., Grace P. H., Henderson N. S. & Thornton P. N. 2001, Principles of the Future Education Strategy, *British Actuarial Journal*, Vol 7, No 3, pp. 221-240.

Bellis C. S. & Clarke S. M. 2001, Teaching Actuarial Management Internationally, Using the Internet, *Internationalising the Curriculum*, Macquarie University, Sydney.

Bellis C. S. & Shepherd J. A. 1993, The Education of Australian Actuaries: Improving the quality of learning, *Transactions of the Institute of Actuaries of Australia*, Vol II, pp. 883-921.

Richard Lyon MA FIAA
Principal, Professional Financial Solutions Pty Ltd and CFO, Invivo Medical Pty Ltd, Sydney, Australia

A graduate of the University of Cambridge, Richard Lyon has almost 30 years' experience of actuarial practice, mostly in Australia. He has been the Chief Actuary of a medium-sized life insurer, a director of a master trust operator and a partner of a major accounting firm. He now divides his work time between actuarial consulting and the financial management of a medical malpractice underwriting agency.

Richard has served on the Council of the Institute of Actuaries of Australia and on many Institute committees and taskforces.

He has been involved with the education of actuaries for longer than he cares to remember and has chaired the Education Management Committee and Council Education Committee of the Institute. He has also been a tutor and an examination marker and is a former member of the CPD Committee.

Richard is closely connected with the subject of this book, having been there at its birth when chairing the committee which launched the Actuarial Control Cycle in the paper "Actuarial Education for the Next Century" (Bellis, C.S., Lyon, R.H.S., Aa, M.J., Carter, J., Harslett, G., Hart, D.G., Kerr, D.I.C., Knox, D.M., Miles, S.P. & Tender, R. 1994, *Transactions of the Institute of Actuaries of Australia*, 1994, pp. 469-521). He was also an editor of the first edition of this book.

Stuart Klugman FSA CERA PhD
Staff Fellow – Education, Society of Actuaries, Schaumburg, IL, USA

Stuart's actuarial career has been mostly involved in education. He was an actuarial professor at The University of Iowa (1974-1988) and Drake University (1988-2009) and currently works in the Education Department of the Society of Actuaries (SOA).

He is co-author of the books *Loss Distributions* and *Loss Models* (now in its third edition), which have been required reading for SOA and Casualty Actuarial Society examinations for the past 25 years. He co-created the SOA Intensive Seminar on Applied Risk Theory in the 1990s and was instrumental in the creation and teaching of the SOA Seminar in Applied Modeling in the 2000s.

While serving as an SOA Vice-President he co-chaired the committee that re-designed the examination system in 2005 and implemented the Fundamentals of Actuarial Practice course, for which this text is a key component. In addition to his education efforts, Stuart has also published numerous research articles with a focus on statistical modeling of insurance losses and on credibility theory.

Authors

Anthony Asher BBusSc PhD FIA FASSA FIAA
Principal, Deloitte Actuaries and Consultants, Sydney, Australia

Anthony Asher provides actuarial advice particularly in relation to life insurance capital issues and in the development of appropriate products and advice for life insurers and superannuation funds. He also has experience with social security, regulatory reform and unit pricing issues. He has previously worked with the Australian Prudential Regulation Authority and was Professor of Actuarial Science at the University of the Witwatersrand, Johannesburg from 1989 to 2002. Before that, he was Chief Actuary of Prudential Assurance in South Africa and has also served in a number of non-executive positions. His publications have largely been in relation to the social impacts of actuarial work – ranging from investments to social security.

The opinions expressed in Anthony Asher's chapter are his own and do not necessarily reflect the opinions of his employer.

Jeffrey Beckley FSA
Co-Director, Actuarial Science Program, Purdue University, West Lafayette, IN, USA

Jeffrey Beckley spent the first eight years of his actuarial career as a practicing actuary working for life and health insurance companies. He spent the next 17 years as a consultant in life and health insurance. Since 2004, he has taught at Purdue University.

Jeff has been an active volunteer for the Society of Actuaries working on education and exam committees as well as in research. He is currently on the Board of Directors of the Society of Actuaries.

Bruce Edwards BSc MA FIA

Bruce Edwards established an actuarial consulting practice in 1984 which later became KPMG Actuaries. He was Managing Director until retiring from the firm in 2001. He is now a director of an insurance company and a superannuation fund trustee and teaches the Actuarial Control Cycle at Macquarie University.

Bruce has served on the Council of the Institute of Actuaries of Australia and on numerous Institute committees.

Shauna Ferris BA MComp FIAA
Senior Lecturer, Actuarial Studies Department, Macquarie University, Sydney, Australia

Shauna Ferris has been teaching the Actuarial Control Cycle at Macquarie University since 1996. She has been involved in the educational processes of the Institute of Actuaries of Australia for many years; she has previously edited the Part III Superannuation course notes and acted as examiner in the Part III Investments course.

Shauna has published papers on a number of topics relating to risk management, solvency and regulation in the financial services industry.

David Knox BA PhD FIA FIAA
Senior Partner, Mercer Australia Pty Ltd, Melbourne, Australia

David Knox is Mercer's Senior Actuary in Australia and is currently the actuary to the Victorian and Tasmanian governments and the Western Australian public sector superannuation plan and was the industry expert of the three-person team that conducted a review of Military Superannuation for the Australian Government in 2007.

David has had a varied career with his more than two decades in academia culminating as the Foundation Professor of Actuarial Studies at The University of Melbourne. He has spoken and written widely and has served on many government and industry committees.

David was an independent board member of the Australian Prudential Regulation Authority from 1998 to 2003 and President of the Institute of Actuaries of Australia in 2000.

Ian Laughlin BSc FAICD FIA FIAA
Convenor, Risk Management Practice Committee, Institute of Actuaries of Australia

Ian Laughlin has extensive experience in executive, board and audit committee positions in the financial services sector in Australia, the UK and Hong Kong, and has also worked in New Zealand.

His risk management experience includes a number of years as managing director of a group of life insurance companies in the UK that was in some difficulty when he was appointed in 2002. He and his management team oversaw a major transformation of the business, built on robust risk management.

Ian is a fellow of the Australian Institute of Company Directors, holds a diploma in financial planning and a BSc, and is a qualified actuary in Australia and the UK.

Mark Rowley BSBA FSA MAAA
Vice President, Managing Actuary, EMC National Life Company, Des Moines, IA, USA

Mark Rowley is the only credentialed actuary at a small life insurance company. Mark has 25 years of actuarial experience with large and small insurance companies and has also worked as a consulting actuary.

He has served as an adjunct professor at Drake University and as a member of the business faculty for the Society of Actuaries' Course 7. He also wrote several case studies that were used in the Course 7 curriculum.

David Service FIAA Grad Cert (Higher Ed.)
Senior Lecturer, Actuarial Studies, Australian National University, Canberra, Australia

After working with a number of different companies in increasingly senior roles including Chief Actuary and Chief Executive, David Service joined the Commonwealth Bank of Australia in 1987 with the task of establishing the bank's own life insurance company. After five years it had become the most successful of the bank-owned life insurance companies in Australia.

He joined Trowbridge Consulting in 1993 as a partner and consulted extensively in the financial services marketplace, specializing in distribution issues and mergers and acquisitions. David joined the Australian National University (ANU) in 1999 and was the founding director of the Centre for Actuarial Research. He has responsibility for teaching the Control Cycle at ANU. David has served on the Council of the Institute of Actuaries of Australia and has been the course leader for Commercial Actuarial Practice since its commencement in 2005.

John Shepherd BA MHEd GradDipEd AIAA

Honorary Associate, Learning and Teaching Centre, Macquarie University, Sydney, Australia

John Shepherd recently retired from Macquarie University after 25 years teaching thousands of actuarial students. In 2006 he received a Carrick Award for Teaching Excellence, one of three for Law, Economics, Business and Related Studies at Australian universities. He has taught in Canada, the US, Singapore, Kazakhstan, Malaysia and several cities in China (Beijing, Shanghai, Chengdu, Hefei and Hong Kong), as well as in Australia.

John taught the Actuarial Control Cycle subject at Macquarie University from its inception in 1996 until his retirement. He is a member of the Education Council Committee of the Institute of Actuaries of Australia, and has taught for the UK Actuarial Profession and for the Society of Actuaries. John has also given many presentations on actuarial education and teaching at actuarial conferences around the world.

John was one of the three editors of the first edition of this book.

Andrew D Smith BA

Partner, Deloitte LLP, London, UK

Andrew is well-known internationally for his portfolio of ground-breaking client assignments and extensive published research in the actuarial field. He leads Deloitte's capital market modeling team, and advises clients on all aspects of financial models. His award-winning papers include "How Actuaries can use Financial Economics," "Market Consistent Valuation of Life Assurance Business," "The Cost of Capital for Financial Firms" and "Modelling Extreme Market Events." He was a co-author with Jon Exley and Shyam Mehta of the definitive (but then deeply unpopular) 1997 paper "The Financial Theory of Defined Benefit Pension Schemes" which, as reported in *The Economist* in 2006, "laid the foundations for a completely new actuarial school."

In 2008, the Institute of Actuaries awarded Andrew a Finlaison Medal, in recognition of Andrew's contribution to actuarial science.

Andrew has a first class degree in mathematics from the University of Cambridge.

Craig Thorburn BEc ASA FIAA

Senior Specialist, World Bank, Washington DC, USA

Craig is responsible for relations with standard-setting bodies and technical assistance to countries on regulation, supervision and financial sector development. He has led and participated in Financial Sector Assessment Program (FSAP) assessments in Latin America, the Caribbean, Asia, Eastern Europe, and the Middle East. He has written on supervision and market development and is a former chair of the IAIS Solvency Subcommittee.

Prior to joining the World Bank, Craig held a number of positions in the private sector then was appointed as Australian Government Actuary in 1996, Chief of Life Insurance Supervision in 1998, and a senior supervisor of financial conglomerates from 1999. He qualified as an actuary in 1987 and is a member of Australian and North American Actuarial Associations.

Stuart F. Wason FSA FCIA MAAA

Senior Director, Actuarial Division of the Office of the Superintendent of Financial Institutions Canada (OSFI), Toronto, ON, Canada

OSFI is an independent agency of the Government of Canada and reports to the Minister of Finance. OSFI supervises and regulates over 450 banks and insurers, and some 1,300 federally registered private pension plans. Stuart Wason manages and directs OSFI's actuarial expertise as applied to Federally Regulated Financial Institutions.

He has over 30 years of actuarial, financial reporting and insurance company management experience. Prior to joining OSFI, Stuart was Senior Actuary at Assuris, a not-for-profit corporation, funded by the Canadian life and health insurance industry, that protects Canadian policyholders against loss of benefits due to the financial failure of a member company. He is a former Director of Mercer Oliver Wyman.

Stuart has been actively involved in the work of the actuarial profession. He served as chair of the Solvency Subcommittee of the International Actuarial Association (IAA) for several years until 2009. Currently he is a member of the International Association of Insurance Supervisors' Insurance Groups Subcommittee and a member of the Joint Forum. Stuart is also a Past President of the Canadian Institute of Actuaries (1999-2000). He is a frequent speaker at international insurance and actuarial conferences on the topics of risk management and solvency frameworks.

The opinions expressed in Stuart Wason's chapter are his own and do not necessarily reflect the opinions of his employer.

Steering Committee

Chair	Martin Stevenson BSc FIA FIAA *Worldwide Partner, Mercer Australia Pty Ltd, Sydney, Australia*
Members	John Evans MBA Syd, FIA Lond, FIAA, ASA *Associate Professor, University of New South Wales, Sydney, Australia*
	Tim Higgins BA BSc GradDipStats FIAA *Senior Lecturer, Australian National University, Canberra, Australia*
	John Shepherd, BA MHEd GradDipEd AIAA *Honorary Associate, Learning and Teaching Centre, Macquarie University, Sydney, Australia*
	Stephen Wright BCom (Management), MEd (Adult Learning) *Director of Professional Education, Institute of Actuaries of Australia*
Secretary	Carol Dolan BEc MBA FIAA *Actuarial Education Consultant, Institute of Actuaries of Australia*

Reviewers

Earlier drafts of the text were reviewed extensively, both as individual chapters and as a complete text. Sincere thanks to the following individuals who each provided feedback on the whole book.

Tim Birse MA FIA
Deputy Chairman, Board of Examiners, The UK Actuarial Profession

Stephen Britt CFA FIAA
Senior Manager, Insurance Australia Group (IAG), Sydney

Hsiu-Mei Chang FCAS MAAA
Assistant Director & Actuary, Aon Global Risk Consulting, USA

Marcus Robertson FCIA FSA
Robertson, Eadie & Associates Ltd, Ontario, Canada

Sincere thanks are also extended to the following individuals who reviewed various chapters of the text.

Kemi Akinyemi	Ryan Anderson	Simon Andersson
Ashley Andrews	Doug Andrews	Huda Ansari
Carlos Arocha	Colleen Atchison	Mona Auji
Waswate Ayana	Elizabeth Baker	Greg Baker
Michael Bannister	Richard Beauchamp	Roger Bevan
Mike Blakeney	Sebastien Blondeau	Gordon Boronow
Aaron Bruhn	Yang Buqing	Sally Calder
Donald Campbell	Margaret Cantwell	Dennis Chan
Rudy Chan	Kuan Kiat Cheah	Chao Chen
Ruoshu Chen	Rob Clover	Ding Dai
Peter Davies	Shiliang Deng	Christian DesRochers
Giovanni Di Meo	Kate Dron	Peter Duellman
Peter Duffett	Steve Eadie	Stephen Edwards
Jill Falkenberg	Jui Fan	Lei Feng
John Ferguson	Harvey Feuer	Charlie Ford
Guy K. Fors	Robert J. Foskey	Harshawardhan Gavankar
Jessica Gilbert	Andrea Gluyas	Michele Goldberg
Monika Gontarek	Scott Haglund	Timothy Harris
Mark Heller	Wendy Ho	Walter H. Hoskins
David Hotchkies	Xing Hu	Mai Mohamed Farid Hussien
David Ingram	Trevor Jack	Andrew Jackson
Nicholas Jacobi	Jay M. Jaffe	Dhruvi Jain
Nitin Jain	John Kaspar	Kun Khim
Barry Koklefsky	Vladimir Kustov	James Lang
Wilfrid Law	Theresa Lee	Edward Li
John Lin	Chris Logan	Bronwyn Loong
Zhou Lu	Chris Z. Makomereh	Dorothy Margrave
Scott Martin	Bonnie Maxie	Sian McAlpin
Jacob O. McCoy	Sean McDermott	James McDonald
Kelly McKeethan	Gaurang Mehta	Andreas Milidonis
John Millett	Ryan Morgan	Richard Muckart
Shams Munir	Chris Murphy	Jamala Murray

George Nassios
Shivani Obhrai
Andrew Patterson
Bill Sakaria
Neha Singh
Lindsay Smitherman
David Strey
Mike Thornton
George Tyrakis
Paul Wharram
David Wilmot
Fan Yang
Aurelia Zeng
Sihong Zhu

Louis Ng
Kurt O'Brien
Kevin Pledge
Michael Schleis
John Smith
Anita Solow
Pawel Szeszko
Joseph Tiong Kiat Lim
Andrew Vallner
Alan Whitelock-Jones
Jill Withers
Grace Yeo
Hong Zhang
Marina Zompatori

Andrew Ngai
Harmit Atulkumar Patel
Brett Roush
Steve Sherman
Steven Smith
Randall Stevenson
Siqi Tang
Jim Toole
Shihui Wang
Sam Wills
Qi Yafei
Kevin Yung
Vicki Jingjing Zhang

Glossary

Note: This glossary is designed to help if you encounter an unfamiliar expression when you are reading this book. Many concepts cannot be defined accurately within the few lines available here, so please do not treat the descriptions below as complete definitions. Often you will find a more detailed explanation in the book itself – refer to the index.

401(k) plans, public offer superannuation funds or personal pensions	pooled arrangements whereby individuals can save for retirement, taking advantage of tax concessions
accounts receivable	an asset shown in the balance sheet of an enterprise representing the amount owed by customers
accumulation-type retirement savings	superannuation where the retirement benefit is the accumulated value of contributions from the employer and employee; more commonly called defined contribution or money purchase
acquisition expense	an expense associated with obtaining new business
active manager	an investment manager who aims to beat the market return by actively selecting stocks or by timing movements in and out of the market
adverse selection or anti-selection	making the decision to purchase or retain a product (eg term insurance) while presenting a higher than average risk – for example, a person diagnosed with cancer will pay the renewal premium for a YRT policy while a healthy one may decide to lapse; in consequence, adverse selection can be expected to drive claims costs up
affiliated companies	companies associated (often through common ownership) with the one in question
agreed value	the amount agreed between the insurer and the insured as being payable in consequence of a specified event, such as the theft of a motor car
allocated annuity or allocated pension	a form of variable annuity sold as a retirement income product in Australia
ALM or asset-liability management	understanding the interaction between assets and liabilities and managing them in a coordinated way; note that the acronym ALM is often used for asset-liability modeling, ie building a model which shows both asset and liability cash flows and their interactions
amortized cost or amortized purchase price	the original cost adjusted up or down to move toward the final value at maturity
annuity	a periodic payment (often monthly), made for the remainder of the recipient's life or for a fixed term
anti-discrimination legislation	laws banning differential treatment of individuals on the grounds of certain characteristics such as age, gender, ethnicity and state of health; such laws may incorporate some form of conditional exemption for insurers

anti-selection or adverse selection	making the decision to purchase or retain a product (eg term insurance) while presenting a higher than average risk – for example, a person diagnosed with cancer will pay the renewal premium for a YRT policy while a healthy one may decide to lapse; in consequence, adverse selection can be expected to drive claims costs up
anti-trust or anti-monopoly regulation	laws designed to prevent the abuse of monopoly power
appointed actuary or responsible actuary	an actuary who has a formal responsibility, generally enshrined in legislation, in relation to the financial condition of a company
appraisal value (AV)	one measure of the value of a company, calculated as the value of net assets plus the present value of future distributable earnings from existing business plus the value added by future new business from existing capacity
arbitrage	the simultaneous purchase and sale of two equivalent assets at different prices, allowing a risk-free profit
asset-liability management (ALM)	understanding the interaction between assets and liabilities and managing them in a coordinated way; note that the acronym ALM is often used for asset-liability modeling, ie building a model which shows both asset and liability cash flows and their interactions
asymmetric information	where one party to a contract has significantly more information material to the contract – for example, a major financial institution is better informed about the risks inherent in its products than is the typical purchaser
auditor	a person who checks a company's processes and/or disclosures (eg financial statements)
Authorised Depository (or Deposit-taking) Institutions	financial institutions, such as banks, building societies, credit unions and savings & loan associations, that are granted the right to take retail deposits subject to certain standards and prudential supervision
automobile insurance or motor insurance	insurance covering loss or damage to the policyholder's vehicle and, possibly, damage caused by the insured's vehicle to the person, vehicle or other property of any third party
back testing	using past experience to test a model
Bank for International Settlements (BIS)	an international organization of central banks – see http://www.bis.org/
Basel Accords, Basel I, Basel II	widely-adopted recommendations on banking laws and regulations issued by the Basel Committee on Banking Supervision
best estimate	an estimate (eg of an assumption or a liability) that is not intended to be either optimistic or conservative
best estimate liability	a liability calculated with no margin for the risk of adverse deviations from the underlying assumptions

bonus (in relation to life insurance policies)	an addition to the sum insured, which may be guaranteed (reversionary bonus) or only allocated to policies terminating in the immediate future (terminal bonus)
book value or carrying value	strictly, the value (of an asset) shown in the company's accounts (its "books"), but often used to mean the amortized purchase price as distinct from the market value
building society or savings & loan association	(also known as a thrift) a non-bank financial institution that accepts deposits and makes mortgage loans to people to buy homes
business interruption insurance	insurance against loss of revenue arising as a consequence of other losses
business model	the way in which the company in question does business – for example, some companies set out to have the lowest prices and others provide comprehensive advice or service
buy-out value	(in relation to an annuity) enough money to buy an equivalent annuity from a financially sound life insurance company
callable bond	a debt security where the borrower has the option to repay early
capital	the amount held (or required to be held) by a company in order to cover expected and potential losses; also, more generally, the resources (both debt and equity) which finance the business
capital guaranteed	(in relation to an investment) where the product issuer has promised that the account balance will not be reduced by investment losses
carrying value or book value	strictly, the value (of an asset) shown in the company's accounts (its "books"), but often used to mean the amortized purchase price as distinct from the market value
cash	any instrument that can be immediately converted to money with no loss of value (eg money held in an "at call" bank account)
cash flow matching	choosing investments so that the cash inflow from the assets exactly matches, in timing and amount, the cash outflow on liabilities
cash management trust, also called money market account	an investment trust whose assets are cash and very short-term securities and that appears, to the investor, very similar to a bank account
cash value or surrender value	the amount payable to a policyholder if s/he decides to terminate the policy
CD (as in "on the CD")	the CD-ROM that accompanies this textbook
CD (when referring to an investment)	certificate of deposit or term deposit, ie an investment where the issuer (usually a bank) agrees to pay a fixed amount of interest at the end of the term, which is typically between three and 12 months but could be longer
CDO (collateralized debt obligation)	a security created by packaging together the cash flows from a pool of debt

central estimate	the expected value of the liabilities
certificate of deposit (CD) or term deposit	an investment where the issuer (usually a bank) agrees to pay a fixed amount of interest at the end of the term, which is typically between three and 12 months but could be longer
checking/cheque account or current account	a bank account against which the account holder can write checks (or cheques)
civil code	codified, written law – as opposed to common law
clearing house	an organization that improves the efficiency and reliability of settlement of transactions by standing between the two parties as the counterparty
client	(in the context of actuarial advice) the person or company soliciting the advice – including the actuary's employer
collateral	assets used as security for a loan
collateralized debt obligation (CDO)	a security created by packaging together the cash flows from a pool of debt
commission	payment made to an intermediary, on an agreed basis, as a reward for securing or retaining business
commodity product	a product that is sold by many competitors in a very similar form
common law	law made by judges and established by precedent (on the basis that the same facts should give rise to the same outcome)
commutation	taking a lump sum payment in exchange for all or part of a pension or annuity
compulsory third party (CTP) insurance	insurance that is required by many governments as a condition of registration of a vehicle and that covers death, disability and medical costs of a third party injured by the insured's vehicle
conditional tail expectation (CTE) or tail value at risk (TVaR)	the expected loss in a specified period, given that the loss exceeds the VaR – generally regarded as a more useful measure than VaR because it uses more information about the tail of the risk distribution
contagion risk	the risk that an adverse event in one institution has a negative impact on other institutions, affecting others in turn, causing a much larger and more widespread problem (a domino effect)
conventional or traditional life insurance	generally with-profit or participating whole life or endowment policies
convertible bonds or convertible notes	debt instruments that can be converted to equity under specified conditions and in a specified manner – for example, conversion may be at the holder's option at the end of five years, at a rate of six shares for every $100 of principal

counterparty risk	the risk that the party on the other side of a transaction, particularly an entity to which a risk has been transferred, fails to meets its obligations
court decisions and precedent	judges interpret the written law (if any) in relation to the matter brought before the court, having regard to precedent (the desire to be consistent with previous decisions based on similar facts)
credit crunch	a sudden and prolonged reluctance to lend to potentially risky borrowers so that many businesses have great or extreme difficulty raising the funds required to continue operating, with the result that economic activity is reduced
credit default swap	a swap contract with a payoff in the event that the subject loan suffers a defined event such as a payment default
credit insurance (for businesses) or trade credit insurance	insurance sold to cover payment defaults by customers
credit insurance (for individuals)	insurance sold to cover the individual's repayments on loans in various circumstances
creditor	a person or company to whom money is owed
credit risk	the risk of loss from non-payment of an amount that is due; can also apply to the risk of a fall in market value caused by a downgrading in the credit rating of a loan
critical illness insurance, trauma insurance or dread disease insurance	a contract paying a fixed schedule of benefits in the event of the diagnosis (or treatment) of one of a number of conditions listed in the contract
current account or checking/ cheque account	a bank account against which the account holder can write checks (or cheques)
debt capital	capital that is to be repaid with prescribed payments
debtor	a person or company owing money
declared bonuses	amounts credited to policies as a result of a distribution of profit
decreasing term insurance	term insurance with decreasing sum insured, generally designed to repay a mortgage or other decreasing debt with a lump sum
deductible or excess	the amount of a claim that must be met by the policyholder – used to reduce the claims cost and, hence, the premium by eliminating the need to administer small claims and by encouraging the policyholder to manage the risk of a claim
default	a failure to fulfill an obligation, especially in relation to loans
deferred acquisition cost (DAC)	an asset established on the balance sheet, representing costs incurred at the point of sale (especially commissions) that are expected to be recovered from associated future revenue; by establishing this depreciating asset, the acquisition costs are charged to profit as the relevant income is earned

deferred annuity	strictly, an annuity that starts after a set term (eg when the annuitant turns 65) but deferred annuity policies generally provide the option to take cash rather than the annuity at maturity and are therefore usually sold and operated as savings contracts
defined benefit pensions or defined benefit superannuation	superannuation where the retirement benefit is defined, usually in terms of years of service and final salary or salary averaged over a period
defined contribution or money purchase superannuation	superannuation where the retirement benefit is the accumulated value of contributions from the employer and employee
derivative instrument	a security whose cash flows are based on the price of some underlying asset or index
directors and officers (D&O) insurance	insurance against liability incurred as a consequence of the insured's position in a company or enterprise
disability income insurance (DII), permanent health insurance (PHI) or income protection	a contract that pays an income stream on disability as defined in the contract
discontinuance solvency	the expectation that a company would have sufficient assets to meet its liabilities if it were wound up today
distributable earnings	amount earned by a product that can be paid to the owners of the business
diversifiable risk	a risk that can be mitigated by diversification
diversification benefits	the benefits, generally relating to reduction in risk, of spreading exposure – eg the risk of losing half of your investment is reduced by investing in 20 different stocks rather than just one
dividend (in relation to life insurance policies)	a distribution of profit to participating or with-profit policyholders
domino effect	the collapse of one institution can create a widespread loss of confidence, leading to a cascade of further collapses
dread disease insurance, critical illness insurance or trauma insurance	a contract paying a fixed schedule of benefits in the event of the diagnosis (or treatment) of one of a number of conditions listed in the contract
driver	a thing that has an impact on something else – for example, investment income is a driver of profit
duration	in immunization theory, the discounted mean term
dynamic model	a model that takes account of the likely response to any particular situation – for example, if an iteration of the model assumes a drop in interest rates, it might be assumed that management would therefore cut dividends/bonuses, or change their investment strategy

Dynamic Solvency Testing (DST) or Dynamic Financial Analysis (DFA) or Dynamic Capital Adequacy Testing (DCAT)	projecting a company's solvency under different assumptions, to assess its ability to withstand adverse experience
economic capital	the amount of capital needed to ensure that a firm remains solvent over a certain time period with a specified probability
eligible capital	capital of a form considered by prudential supervisors to be appropriate to be taken into account in assessing financial strength – for example, it would generally exclude temporary capital (such as most debt) and items of doubtful value in the event of insolvency (such as goodwill and other intangible assets)
employers liability insurance or workers compensation	insurance for liability of employers for compensation of employees for injuries and death associated with employment
embedded value (EV)	one measure of the value of a company, calculated as the value of net assets plus the present value of future distributable earnings from existing business – unlike an appraisal value, no allowance is made for future new business
endowment insurance	a policy that pays the sum insured (including any bonuses) on the death of the life insured during a specified term or on the insured's survival to the end of the term
enterprise risk management (ERM)	an expression in general use, meaning risk management across a business (enterprise)
equity (as a principle)	literally "moral justice," a core principle adopted by actuaries in relation to discretionary decisions such as the allocation of profit
equity (as an investment)	shares (stock) in a company
equity (on a balance sheet)	the excess of assets over liabilities – also referred to as available capital
equity capital	capital provided by the owners or shareholders
estate	that part of the capital of a with-profit fund that does not clearly belong either to policyholders or to shareholders; the estate provides support for guarantees and other risks borne by the with-profit fund for the benefit of policyholders
excess or deductible	the amount of a claim that must be met by the policyholder – used to reduce the claims cost and, hence, the premium by eliminating the need to administer small claims and by encouraging the policyholder to manage the risk of a claim
exchange-traded funds (ETFs)	derivatives that are equivalent to a unit trust passively invested in a particular index
external forces	forces that affect the product, service or scheme on which the actuary is working but that are outside the actuary's control or sphere of influence

extreme event	an event with a very low frequency and very high severity
fair value	the value of an asset or liability at which it would change hands between well-informed, willing but not anxious parties – note that market value, where available, is often used as a proxy
fair value accounting	an accounting approach that seeks to value both assets and liabilities at fair value, in order to arrive at a useful assessment of financial position and performance
fiduciary	(from the Latin *fidere*, to trust) one who holds anything in trust; refers to an actuary having a responsibility to act on behalf of others as if being a trustee
financial condition report (FCR)	a wide-ranging actuarial report, often required by legislation or regulation, on the financial position of a company, having regard to matters including its financial statements, its business plans, its access to capital and its risk management
financial underwriting	the act of verifying that the benefits under an insurance contract will not exceed the financial loss to the policyholder, thus reducing the risk of moral hazard
fitness and propriety	a test to determine whether a person should be allowed to hold a responsible position such as appointed actuary
fixed expense	an expense that does not change as the number of policies administered or sold increases
fixed-interest mortgage	a mortgage where the interest rate is fixed for a period of time; early repayment of such a mortgage is an option against the lender and therefore may carry a penalty
floating rate	an interest rate that varies along with rates on similar products issued by the lender – and often maintains a broadly consistent relationship to the official cash rate
fund members	members of a fund – eg employees who are members of their company's superannuation fund
funding method	a method of determining periodic contributions that are sufficient, with interest earned, to pay anticipated benefits and expenses
futures contract	a derivative enabling future transactions to be entered into at agreed prices
(highly) geared or leveraged	having a high ratio of debt to equity capital
general insurance, property and casualty insurance (P&C) or non-life insurance	indemnity insurance usually covering risks other than life and health, with contracts which are usually reviewable at least annually
Generally Accepted Accounting Principles (GAAP)	the name given to any standard accounting framework – generally qualified with a descriptor for the jurisdiction in which it applies, such as US GAAP

global financial crisis (GFC)	the period of financial turmoil, beginning with a credit crunch in 2007, that saw the collapse or bail-out of high-profile financial institutions (including banks) around the world and large falls in stock market indices – and massive financial stimulus by the governments of major economies in a bid to limit recessionary consequences
going-concern solvency	the expectation that a company will continue to be solvent, based on its business plan – but note that going-concern solvency does not mean that the company would have sufficient assets to meet its liabilities if it were wound up today
goodwill	an accounting concept, representing the difference between the amount paid for an asset and its contribution to net assets after purchase – for example, a company that has paid $100 million for another company with net assets of $60 million would show a goodwill asset of $40 million in its balance sheet (provided that it could demonstrate at least $40 million of future value)
granularity of data	the repeated subdivision of data in accordance with its characteristics makes it ever more granular
GST ("goods and services tax")	an Australian consumption tax, equivalent to VAT in the UK and Europe and sales taxes in most US states
guaranteed investment contracts or investment account policies	capital guaranteed life insurance policies with interest credited periodically
health insurance	insurance providing at least partial payment of medical costs
health maintenance organization (HMO)	an organization that pays health care professionals an amount for each person covered, with the aim of reducing claims costs by providing an incentive to keep people healthy
heat map or risk heat map	a diagram that places each risk based on its likelihood and financial impact
hedging	the use of derivatives or other instruments to protect against loss under certain conditions
home and contents insurance	insurances covering damage to the building and loss or damage to the contents respectively
hospital cash	a simple form of medical insurance, paying a fixed amount for each day the insured spends in hospital
HR	human resources – the department of an organization that looks after staff-related issues
human capital	the accumulated set of skills, knowledge and experience that equips people to earn an income
hurdle rate	the minimum rate of return required by an investor in order to be prepared to invest in a project

index-linked annuity/pension	an annuity or pension where the payment increases in line with an index such as the consumer price index (CPI)
illiquid assets	assets which generally cannot be sold without a delay or a loss in value
immediate annuity	an annuity that starts when the purchase price is paid (or within the next year at the latest)
inadmissible or non-admitted assets	assets that are excluded from eligible capital for solvency purposes
income protection, disability income insurance (DII) or permanent health insurance (PHI)	a contract that pays an income stream on disability as defined in the contract
indemnity cover	where insurance covers the loss incurred by the insured, rather than a fixed amount, such as an agreed value
industry fund or multi-employer fund	a superannuation fund covering employees from different companies or organizations in the same industry
inherent risks	risks that are present prior to risk mitigation and risk control
insolvency	a situation where a company is unable to pay its debts (or where it has less capital than the minimum required by regulators) and may be required by law to cease trading
insurable interest	the person buying the insurance has an insurable interest if s/he will suffer a loss if the insured event occurs
intangibles	identifiable assets, other than monetary assets, that are not physical assets – examples include brand value, DAC and goodwill
interbank lending rates	the interest rates at which banks lend to each other through the interbank lending markets
internal rate of return	an interest rate that, when used to discount all cash flows, produces a present value of zero
International Association of Insurance Supervisors (IAIS)	see http://www.iaisweb.org/
International Financial Reporting Standards (IFRS)	financial standards adopted by the International Accounting Standards Board (see http://www.iasb.org/) and adopted by many countries as shown at http://www.iasplus.com/country/useias.htm
investment account policies or guaranteed investment contracts	capital guaranteed life insurance policies with interest credited periodically
investment-linked	used to describe savings products where the investment return is linked to the performance of an underlying pool of assets
investment-linked life insurance or variable life	a life insurance policy that delivers investment returns through an investment-linked mechanism

joint life policies	life insurance which pays out on the death of either the first-to-die or the last-to-die
junk bonds	high-risk, high-yield bonds with a very low credit rating (below investment grade and generally BB or less) – attractive during periods of relatively low market default
key risk indicator	a measure that is monitored to highlight the level of the risk
laddered	relates to a series of regular, small cash flows as opposed to infrequent large cash flows
lagging indicator (and leading indicator)	a readily-available measure whose movement indicates the direction of something else such as the economy – for example, consumer sentiment is a leading indicator of the economy (typically changing direction before GDP does) and the unemployment rate is a lagging indicator (providing confirmation that an observed change in direction in GDP may be genuine)
lapses	termination of policies by policyholders before a surrender value has accrued – often used loosely to include surrenders
(highly) leveraged or geared	having a high ratio of debt to equity capital
liability insurance, including professional indemnity, medical malpractice, public liability and directors and officers (D&O) insurance	insurance against claims arising as a consequence of unsafe workplaces or products or negligent practice
liability, provision or reserve	except where clearly indicated, these words are often used interchangeably to denote the amount set aside to meet a company's obligations (or the value of those obligations)
life insurance	a contract that pays out on the death of the life insured during a specified term or, where there is a savings element, at the end of that term
lifetime annuity	an annuity that lasts for the remaining life of the annuitant
liquidation (of assets)	the conversion of illiquid assets to liquid assets, generally by sale
liquidation or winding up	the termination of a business, including the settlement of debts (as far as possible) and the distribution of any surplus assets
liquidity ratio	the market value of liquid assets divided by the total of the current liabilities (generally those falling due within a year)
liquidity, liquid assets	cash, or assets readily convertible to cash without delay or significant loss in value
listed shares or listed stock	shares (stock) in a public company that are listed on a stock exchange
long-tail insurance	insurance where the claims typically take a long time to settle (and may even take a long time to emerge in the first place)

long-term care insurance	insurance that covers the costs of assistance with the needs of everyday living
mandatory convertible notes	convertible notes where the conversion to equity is mandatory by a certain date
margin calls	a demand, usually from a clearing house and as a result of adverse experience, for additional funds to be deposited to continue to give the counterparty to a contract (such as a futures contract) comfort that the contract will be honored
margin for adverse deviation method (MAD)	a valuation method where a risk margin is added to the best estimate assumptions
margin on services liability	a liability calculated with margins where the margin represents the value of future profit
margin, for an assumption	a change to an assumption that considers the risk that the assumption will turn out to be worse than expected
marine insurance	insurance that covers ships, aircraft and goods in transit
market risk or systematic risk	a risk that arises from exposure to a system or market and that cannot be reduced by diversification within that system or market
market value	the amount that can be realized by selling the asset on the open market
master trust	a unit trust that invests in other unit trusts
materiality	how much something matters, how much difference something will make to the final outcome
maturity transformation	the role that banks and similar institutions play, by borrowing for short terms and lending for long terms
medical insurance or private health insurance	indemnity cover for medical expenses
medical malpractice insurance	liability insurance for medical professionals against claims arising as a consequence of alleged negligent practice (the doctors' equivalent of professional indemnity insurance)
microinsurance	insurance with small premiums and benefits
model office	a computer model that represents the cash flows and financial statements of an insurance operation
money market fund or cash management trust	an investment trust whose assets are cash and very short-term securities and that appears, to the investor, very similar to a bank account
money purchase or defined contribution superannuation	superannuation where the retirement benefit is the accumulated value of contributions from the employer and employee

moral hazard	the situation that people will make less effort to avoid the risk of adverse events if someone else will compensate them if the event occurs; also used to describe the risk that insurers and lenders face that their customers will take unfair advantage of their contracts
morbidity risk	the risk of becoming sick or disabled, either temporarily or permanently
mortgage	a loan against the security of property; strictly speaking the document that assigns the security to the lender, but generally used to refer to the loan
motor insurance or automobile insurance	insurance covering loss or damage to the policyholder's vehicle and, possibly, damage caused by the insured's vehicle to the person, vehicle or other property of any third party
multi-employer fund or industry fund	a superannuation fund covering employees from different companies or organizations in the same industry
mutual fund or unit trust	a legal trust that pools investors' interests in one or more assets
mutual insurance company	a company that is owned by its policyholders
National Association of Insurance Commissioners (NAIC)	the association of insurance commissioners for the US states and territories – see http://www.naic.org/
National Insurance contributions	in the UK, a levy on employers (on behalf of employees) to fund certain welfare and state pension benefits
new business strain	the difference between net income generated at the time of sale and the initial liability
niche product	a product that meets particular needs in a market without many competitors selling similar products
no claims bonus or no claims discount	a reduction in premium reflecting the fact that a lack of recent claims suggests a lower risk – generally used as much as a marketing tool as a mechanism to reward lower risk, but note that small claims may be reduced because of the fear of losing this discount
non-admitted or inadmissible assets	assets that are excluded from eligible capital for solvency purposes
non-life insurance, property and casualty (P&C) or general insurance	indemnity insurance usually covering risks other than life and health, with contracts which are usually reviewable at least annually
off-balance-sheet risks	possible losses from items that do not appear on the balance sheet as assets or liabilities
operational risk	risk of financial loss from inadequate or failed internal processes, people and systems, or from the failure to manage external events
option contract	a derivative providing one party with the option to buy or sell an asset at a future date at an agreed price

options	unless referring to derivatives, usually refers to customer choices eg to withdraw cash
Organisation for Economic Co-operation and Development (OECD)	an international organization helping governments to tackle the economic, social and governance issues of a global economy – see http://www.oecd.org
outstanding claims	the value placed on claims that have been incurred but have not been paid – may include IBNR (incurred but not reported) and IBNER (incurred but not enough reported) components
overhead expense	a fixed expense not related to a particular function
over-the-counter	contracts that are negotiated between two parties, as opposed to standardized contracts that are traded on an exchange
pandemic	an epidemic of an infectious disease that spreads on a wide geographical front
parsimony	in statistics, using the simplest model that provides a reasonable explanation
participating or with-profit policies	life insurance policies that share in the distribution of profits, usually by the addition of bonuses to the sum insured or by cash dividends or premium reductions
peer review	the process of having another professional review a piece of work, mostly with the aim of ensuring that it complies with professional standards and with any requirements that the firm or the client may have set
pension funds, superannuation funds or provident funds	savings vehicles established for the purpose of providing lump sums or pensions at retirement
pension	an annuity payable after exiting the workforce (generally by retirement but also by proxy, such as a spouse's pension) – usually payable for life but may be constrained, such as a means-tested state pension
permanent health insurance (PHI), disability income insurance (DII) or income protection	a contract that pays an income stream on disability as defined in the contract
persistency rates	the "opposite" of lapse or surrender rates, being the proportion of policies that renew or continue in force
personal accident insurance	life or disability cover limited to losses caused by accident
personal pensions, public offer superannuation funds or 401(k) plans	pooled arrangements whereby individuals can save for retirement, taking advantage of tax concessions
pluvius insurance	insurance against losses caused by adverse weather, usually rain; it is typically taken out to cover spectator events

policyholders' reasonable expectations (PRE)	a principle applied by the courts, especially in the UK, in adjudicating on the exercise (or intended exercise) of discretion by a life insurer – recognizing that the disclosures and other statements made to policyholders, together with the insurer's past practice, create a reasonable expectation as to how the insurer will act in future
pooled superannuation trusts	a form of unit trust providing an investment vehicle for superannuation funds
preference shares or preferred stock	shares (stock) that receive distributions of profit (ie dividends) ahead of ordinary shares (common stock), with these dividends generally being limited to a set amount per share; there may also be preferential treatment in the event of a winding-up of the company
primary legislation (Acts, laws)	law developed by the relevant legislative body (for example, the national, regional or provincial parliament)
primary markets (for securities)	a market for the issuing of new financial securities
principles-based reserving	reserving based on requirements that concentrate on the purpose of the valuation and the nature of the risks being undertaken – as opposed to prescriptive, rules-based reserving
private equity	investment provided from pools of funds contributed by wealthy individuals and generally not subject to the same scrutiny as listed companies
private health insurance or medical insurance	indemnity cover for medical expenses
private placements of debt	loans made by insurance companies (or others) directly to corporations; such loans are not publicly traded
probability of sufficiency approach (POS)	a method that sets reserves to provide a given probability of covering claims
procyclical	something that acts to reinforce a cycle – such as solvency regulation that leads to forced sales of stocks after a stock market crash
professional indemnity insurance	liability insurance against claims arising as a consequence of alleged negligent practice
profit signature	the expected profits, year by year, associated with a particular valuation approach – could be measured at the level of an individual policy or for a group of policies
profit testing	using a pricing model to measure expected profit and comparing it with the profit objectives
property and casualty insurance (P&C), general insurance or non-life insurance	indemnity insurance usually covering risks other than life and health, with contracts that are usually reviewable at least annually
provident funds, superannuation funds or pension funds	savings vehicles established for the purpose of providing lump sums or pensions at retirement

provision, liability or reserve	except where clearly indicated, these words are often used interchangeably to denote the amount set aside to meet a company's obligations (or the value of those obligations)
prudential regulation	regulation that tries to ensure that institutions are operating soundly
prudential supervisors	regulatory bodies responsible for overseeing the financial institutions and administering the prudential regulation
public liability insurance	liability insurance against claims arising as a consequence of allegedly unsafe workplaces or products
public offer superannuation funds, personal pensions or 401(k) plans	pooled arrangements whereby individuals can save for retirement, taking advantage of tax concessions
pure endowment	a policy that pays the sum insured (including any bonuses) only on survival of the life insured to the end of the term and, generally, a return of premiums on earlier death
rating agencies	organizations, such as Fitch, Moody's and Standard & Poor's, that investigate the creditworthiness of companies' obligations – including debt and the payment of claims – and assign one of a series of ratings (eg AAA to C) to help investors or policyholders to decide whether to invest or insure
rating downgrade	a reduction in credit rating by a rating agency – eg from A- to BBB+
recession	a period when the economy is shrinking in real terms
(make) redundant or retrench (in relation to employment)	lay off (staff), terminate employment
regulatory arbitrage	a situation where institutions find ways to be regulated under a different set of requirements, in order to achieve technical compliance with regulatory requirements, while undermining the intent of the regulations
regulatory solvency requirements or statutory solvency requirements	legal minimum standards for solvency
reinsurance	insurance for insurers
reinsurance recoveries	money expected to be received from reinsurers in relation to outstanding claims
reserve, liability or provision	except where clearly indicated, these words are often used interchangeably to denote the amount set aside to meet a company's obligations (or the value of those obligations)
residual risks	risks that remain after risk mitigation and controls have been put in place
responsible actuary or appointed actuary	an actuary who has a formal responsibility, generally enshrined in legislation, in relation to the financial condition of a company

retirement benefit plan	an arrangement between an employer and its employees that provides benefits to the employee after retirement
retrench or make redundant (in relation to employment)	lay off (staff), terminate employment
return on capital	an interest rate that, when used to discount future cash flows, produces a present value equal to the new business strain
reversionary bonus	a permanent addition to the sum insured on a traditional life insurance policy, resulting from a distribution of profit
risk appetite	the amount of risk an entity is prepared to take, usually expressed qualitatively and at a high level
risk heat map or heat map	a diagram that places each risk based on its likelihood and financial impact
risk premium	the extra return required by an investor to compensate for the extra risk in the investment
risk tolerance	a translation of risk appetite into meaningful limits for operational purposes
risk-based capital	the capital required by a company having regard to the nature of its risks
rules-based reserving	reserving based on prescriptive requirements that are objective and thus the same for all companies – as opposed to principles-based reserving
run off	an institution stops writing new business or renewing existing contracts, but continues to handle its existing liabilities in an orderly manner
run (on a bank)	an overwhelming rush to withdraw deposits
savings & loan association or building society	(also known as a thrift) a non-bank financial institution that accepts deposits and makes mortgage loans to people to buy homes
scenario	a set of assumptions used to test pricing or future solvency; a possible future situation
scenario test	a sensitivity test that uses a specific scenario or set of scenarios
secondary markets	markets for buying and selling existing financial securities
securitization	the process of making assets more marketable – by dividing the entitlement to cash flows from large assets (or pools of small, reasonably similar assets) into equal shares, sometimes with the assistance of credit enhancement techniques
selective withdrawal	the decision by a healthy policyholder to lapse a policy (perhaps finding cheaper cover elsewhere) while an unhealthy policyholder would retain his/her cover both because it now represents better value and because it might be difficult to obtain cover elsewhere

sensitivity test	a test that examines the impact of changing assumptions
service unit	a department of a company that does not generate revenue but that provides services to the business units that do generate revenue
share or stock	a certificate of ownership of part of a company, usually entitling the holder to a share of profits and to vote at owners' meetings
short-tail insurance	insurance policies for which claims tend to be settled quickly
social assistance	a government-sponsored scheme that does not require contributions
social insurance	a government-sponsored scheme that involves contributions by or on behalf of the covered person
Solvency II	the name given to the solvency regulations for insurers operating in the EU
solvency ratio	generally, the ratio of available capital (often eligible capital) to the minimum amount required to satisfy solvency regulations
solvent	an enterprise is solvent if there is an acceptable probability that it will meet its obligations
special purpose vehicle (SPV) or special purpose entity (SPE)	a legally separate entity created for a specific purpose, enabling both the parent company and investors to benefit without exposing either the parent or the SPV to the risks of the other
sponsoring employer	(in relation to a superannuation fund, generally a defined benefit fund) the employer making contributions to fund the employee's benefits
(interest rate) spread	the difference between the interest rate earned on investments and the interest rate credited to an insurance product
stakeholder pensions	personal pension schemes with fees limited by UK legislation
stakeholders	parties that have a financial or psychological interest in the outcome of some process (such as the operation of a company)
Statutory Accounting Principles (SAP)	used in the US for assessing solvency; differ from standards for profitability and financial reporting
statutory solvency requirements or regulatory solvency requirements	legal minimum standards for solvency
statutory valuation basis	an objective (rules-based) valuation approach where assumptions and formulae are specified by the regulatory authority
stochastic model	defines some of the assumptions as random variables
stock or share	a certificate of ownership of part of a company, usually entitling the holder to a share of profits and to vote at owners' meetings
subordinated debt	debt that is not repaid unless there is money left over after all policyholder obligations have been met

subprime	refers to borrowers who do not meet the highest, or prime, standard of creditworthiness
subprime debt crisis	the surge in 2007 of defaults on mortgage loans to subprime borrowers, particularly in the US but affecting institutions around the world, and the ensuing global financial panic
superannuation funds, pension funds or provident funds	savings vehicles established for the purpose of providing lump sums or pensions at retirement
Superannuation Guarantee levy	in Australia, a compulsory deduction from earnings that must be saved for retirement and is directed by the employee to his/her chosen fund
surplus	the excess of assets over liabilities (effectively, capital), or the increase in this amount over a period (effectively, profit); the expression "surplus" is often preferred in the context of mutual life insurance or pension funds
surplus arising	the correct name for the increase in surplus over a period – but "surplus" is often used instead
surrender	the voluntary termination of a contract, initiated by the policyholder
surrender value or cash value	the amount payable to a policyholder if s/he decides to terminate the policy
swaps and swaptions	respectively, derivatives used to convert cash flows (usually borrowings) to more acceptable structures or currencies and options on such derivatives
systematic risk or market risk	a risk that arises from exposure to a system or market and that cannot be reduced by diversification within that system or market
systemic risk	the risk of collapse of a system or market; note, however, that the words "systemic risk" and "systematic risk" are often used as if they were interchangeable
tail value at risk (TVaR) or conditional tail expectation (CTE)	the expected loss in a specified period, given that the loss exceeds the VaR – generally regarded as a more useful measure than VaR because it uses more information about the tail of the risk distribution
takaful	a type of insurance that is compliant with Islamic law
target surplus	amount of surplus needed to be able to satisfy regulatory capital requirements in adverse circumstances
term certain annuity	an annuity that lasts for a fixed term
term deposit or certificate of deposit (CD)	an investment where the issuer (usually a bank) agrees to pay a fixed amount of interest at the end of the term, which is typically between three and 12 months but could be longer
term insurance	a contract that pays on death before the end of a fixed term but not at the end of the term and has no surrender value

terminal bonus	an addition to the sum insured on a traditional life insurance policy, resulting from a distribution of profit but only allocated to policies terminating in the immediate future
third party claimants (under insurance policies)	people or entities other than policyholders that stand to benefit from an insurance company payout, for example a person injured in an accident caused by the policyholder and for which the policyholder is covered by the policy
Tier 1 and Tier 2 capital	two types of eligible capital defined under the Basel Accords; Tier 1 is of higher quality
total & permanent disablement (TPD) insurance	an insurance contract that pays a lump sum on proof of permanent disability
trade credit insurance or credit insurance (for businesses)	insurance sold to cover payment defaults by customers
traditional or conventional life insurance	generally with-profit or participating whole life or endowment policies
tranche	one of a number of related securities offered as part of the same transaction (from the French *tranche* or slice) – used, for example, to refer to a slice of a CDO
trauma insurance, critical illness insurance or dread disease insurance	a contract paying a fixed schedule of benefits in the event of the diagnosis (or treatment) of one of a number of conditions listed in the contract
trust	in the sense of a dedicated investment trust, a vehicle for pooled investments
underwriting	generally, the process of selection and pricing of risk within a set framework – for example, the higher risk presented by an unhealthy 40-year-old proposing for term insurance may result in a 50% loading on the premium; can also refer to the acceptance of risk (and the consequences of that decision), especially in the context of general insurance
unit trust or mutual fund	a legal trust that pools investors' interests in one or more assets
unitized with-profit policies	participating policies similar to investment account policies
unit-linked life insurance	the same as investment-linked life insurance; the name derives from the use of "units" to allocate investment return to the policy
universal life	a life insurance policy consisting of an investment contract with a term insurance rider
unlisted shares or unlisted stock	shares (stock) in a company that is not listed on a stock exchange

Value at Risk (VaR)	the minimum loss suffered in the worst specified percentage of outcomes in a specified period – eg a one percent one-year VaR of $100 million means that there is (according to the assessment) a one percent chance that the loss over the next year will exceed $100 million; note that this measure does not use any information about the shape of the tail of the risk distribution
variable (or floating rate) mortgage	a mortgage where interest rates can vary – usually in response to changes in the general level of interest rates in the economy
variable annuities	investment-linked policies that provide income from assets held on behalf of the policyholder, often with some form of guarantee of returns, and that can be sold as deferred annuities (and therefore as savings products)
variable expense	an expense that changes with the volume of policies administered or sold
variable life or investment-linked life insurance	a life insurance policy that delivers investment returns through an investment-linked mechanism
whistleblower	someone with inside knowledge who informs superiors, regulators or other interested parties when something is seriously "wrong" in a company; even where such behavior is protected by law, this can be an extremely difficult thing to do
whole life insurance	a level premium contract, providing permanent life cover, that can be surrendered for cash; may or may not be participating
winding up or liquidation	the termination of a business, including the settlement of debts (as far as possible) and the distribution of any surplus assets
with-profit or participating policies	life insurance policies that share in the distribution of profits, usually by the addition of bonuses to the sum insured or by cash dividends or premium reductions
workers compensation or employers liability insurance	insurance for liability of employers for compensation of employees for injuries and death associated with employment
wrap fund	similar to a master trust except that the underlying assets are held in the investor's own name
yearly renewable term insurance (YRT)	term insurance with premium rates that change each year over the term of the policy, to reflect the relationship between age and mortality risk

Index

A

Account balance liability valuation, 337–8
Accounting standards, 124
    prudential regulation, 192
Accounts receivable, 396
Accumulation-type retirement savings, 94, 302
Active manager, 419–20
Actuarial Control Cycle
    applying, 6, 559–71
    assumption-setting, 281
    feedback mechanism, 109
    framework, 3
    illustration of, 5–6
    marketing, application to, 562–4
    modeling, role of, 255–6
    risk management process, 22
Actuary
    Appointed, 60, 452–3
    Chief, 37–8
    definition, 1–2
    financial security systems role, 69, 101
    legislated roles for, 59–60, 192–3
    training, 565
Administration of product, 220–1
Administrators
    operational risk, 39
    risk management, interest in, 39
Adverse selection see also Anti-selection, 209, 220, 238
Advisers
    risk management, interest in, 39
Affiliated company risk, 143
Agents, 121–3
    multi-agents, 122
    sole agents, 121
Agreed value, 85, 329
Akaike Information Criterion, 244
Allocated annuity, 96–7
Allocated pension, 96–7
Amortization
    bonds, amortized value, 483
    deferred acquisition cost (DAC), 479
        DAC-adjusted profit, 480
    profit affected by, 474, 479–80
Amortized cost, 394
Annuities, 95
    allocated, 96–7
    deferred, 90

    pricing, 377–8
    immediate, 95
    index-linked, 96
    lifetime, 96
    retirement income from, 229
    term certain, 96
    variable, 96–7
Anti-competitive behavior, 182
    compulsory financial products, 185
Anti-discrimination legislation, 119, 180, 185
Anti-selection see also Adverse selection, 76, 145, 161
Anti-trust regulation, 182
Application risk, 17
Appointed Actuary, 60, 452–3
Appraisal value (AV), 485–9
Arbitrage, tax and regulatory, 80
Arbitrage-free pricing, 350
Asset-liability management (ALM), 409–17
    actuaries' role, 420
    asset-liability modeling, 417
    asset-liability relationship, 409–10
    capital requirements, 419
    cash flow matching, 413–14
    constraints, 418–20
    defined benefit funds, 415–16
    immunization, 414
    investment strategy, 414–16
    legislative constraints, 418
    liability-driven investment (LDI), 416–17
    negative returns, 420
    outstanding long-tail insurance claims, 415
    performance guarantees, 416
    product design, 221
    product disclosure requirements, 418
    risk, 143
Asset-liability mismatch risk, 150, 431
Asset/liability risks
    capital needs and, 303, 306–8
    definition, 303
    insufficient return risk, 411
    liquidity risk, 306–7, 411–12
    market risk, 307–8
    reinvestment/refinancing risk, 412
    types, 410–13
    valuation risk, 412–13
Asset risks
    bonds, 405–7
    capital needs and, 303–4

Asset risks (*continued*)
   concentration, 304
   debt assets, 405–7
   default risks, 303
   definition, 303
   derivatives, 408
   discount rate change, 405
   liquidity, 304
   market movements, 303
   property, 407–8
   shares, 407
Asset share methods, 554
Asset valuation, 394–5, 402–4
   amortized cost, 394
   Black-Scholes model, 404
   bonds, 403
   book value, 394
   cost price, 394
   derivatives, 404
   discounted cash flow (DCF), 402
   double counting, preventing, 434
   fair value, 395
   market value, 395, 434
   mark-to-model, 395
   principles, 402
   property, 404
   reliability, 435
   shares, 403
   solvency purposes, for, 434–5
      discontinuance situation, 434
      inadmissible/non-admitted assets, 434
   useful value, 395
   verification, 435
Assets
   accounts, in, 393–4
   accounts receivable, 396
   capital assets, 397
   carrying value, 394
   cash, 396
   convertible bonds, 400
   debt, 398–9
   definition, 393, 394
   derivatives, 400–1
   equity, 399
   hybrid, 400
   inadmissible, 434
   intangible, 393, 397
   inventory, 396
   investment, 398–401
   laddering, 431
   liquid assets, level of, 430
   long-term, 396

   mandatory convertible notes, 446
   margin calls, 408
   non-investment, 396–8
   options, 95
   physical, 398
   preference shares, 400
   raw materials, 396
   securitized, 401
   short-term, 396
   stapled securities, 400
   tangible, 393
   tax assets, 397
   types, 396–401
   valuation *see* Asset valuation
Assumption reinsurance, 167
Assumptions
   assumption-setting control cycle, 281
   best estimate, 282
   "black swans", 284
   categorization, 281
   control cycle concepts, 281
   data for, 268, 365
   definition, 268, 280, 365
   economic, 282
   estimates, differentiated from, 280
   explicit, 282
   false, 280
   forecasts, differentiated from, 280
   identification, 281–2
   implicit, 282
   importance of, 280–1
   incidence and severity, 365
   interdependency, 284
   liability valuation, for, 345–6, 436, 437
   margins, 366–7
   materiality, 283
   monitoring, 281
   mortality study, from, 281
   overview, 267–8
   "perfect storms", 284
   predictions, differentiated from, 280
   pricing, 365–9, 387
   probability distribution, 283
   quality of data, 283
   quantification, 281, 282–4
   reviewing, 495
   setting, 365
   taken for granted, 268
AS/NZS 4360, 21
Asymmetric information, 183
   market failure, source of, 183
At call savings accounts, 412, 415

Attribution analysis, 506
  see also Investment performance
Audit
  audit committee, 37
  business operations, 32
  external, 532
  internal, 532, 533
  risk management process, 32, 37
Auditor, 435
Australian Prudential Regulation Authority
    (APRA)
  best estimate liability definition, 323
  capital, regulating level of, 298
  mission, 298
Automatic reinsurance treaty, 167
Automobile insurance *see* Motor vehicle
    insurance
Autoregressive model, 234, 235

B

Back testing, 241
Bank for International Settlements (BIS)
  Committee on Banking Supervision (Basel
      Committee), 190
  first Basel Accord, 442, 443
  second Basel Accord, 129, 291, 442, 443
  solvency regulation, 426–7
Banking
  monitoring experience, 499
  risk identification, 151–2
Banks *see also* Financial institutions
  capital management, 539
  capital needs, 294, 309
    operational risk, 309
  deposit guarantees, 459
  profit analysis, 521
Barings Bank collapse, 309, 463
Basel Accords, 441
  Basel I, 442, 443
  Basel II, 129, 291, 442, 443
Basis risk, 143
Bayesian method
  Bayes Information Criterion, 244
  model calibration, 241
Benefit definitions, impact on liability
    valuation, 330
Benford's Law, 345
Best estimate, 282
  assumptions, 282
  liability (BEL), 320, 323–4, 326, 336
    BEL plus margin, 336, 338, 477

immediate recognition of future profit,
    476
  profit, timing of, 476–7
  prudent best estimate, 282, 438
Black-Scholes model, 249, 404
"Black swans", 284
Board of directors
  business plan, 531
  capital, view of level of, 296–8
  corporate structure, place in, 13
  culture, 36
  responsibilities, 36
  risk management
    policy, 34
    responsibilities, 36, 531
    stake in, 35
Bonds, 82
  accounting treatment, 483
  adjusted cost price, 483
  amortized value, 483
  callable, 403
  convertible, 400
  junk, 451
  market value, 483
  valuing, 403, 483
Bonuses *see also* Dividends on insurance
    policy, 90, 549, 553
Bootstrapping, 250
Brokers, 122
Building society, 12
  terminating, 78
Bundled liability valuation, 332
Business credit risk, 142
Business environment, 120–3
Business mix, 518–19
Business model, 16, 21, 171, 252
Business needs
  equity or capital, 78–9
  financial life cycle, 78–80
  regulatory arbitrage, 80
  risk management, 79
  tax arbitrage, 80
Business plans, 530, 531
Business risk, 17, 79
Business volumes, 518–19
Buy-out value, 436

C

CAMELS system, 451
Capital
  adequacy liability, 324
  allocation, 312, 519–22
  assets, 397, 419

Capital (*continued*)
  availability, 419
  banks, 294, 309
    operational risk, 309
  board's perspective, 296–8
  business funding, 78, 289
  charging for, 538
  consumer confidence and, 292–3
  credit rating and, 293–4, 295
  customers' perspective, 298
  debt capital, 291
  debt/equity hybrid securities, 446, 447
  debt to equity ratio, 291, 295
  diversification benefits, 310–11
  economic capital, 40, 290, 311
    regulatory capital, differentiated from,
      311
  efficiency, 538
  eligible capital, 291
  equity capital, 290, 295
  financial institutions without share-holders,
    299–302
  financial stability, for, 294
  fluctuations in operations, withstanding,
    292
  future opportunities or needs, for, 293
  gearing, 291, 295
  initial, 289
  insurance companies, 294
  management, 538–9
  market expectations, 299
  minimum amount, 192, 291
  mutual organizations, 300–1
  need for, 289–313
  new business, 289
  operational capital, 292
  operation risk and, 303, 308–10
    banks, 309
  overall company perspective, 310–12
  over-capitalization, 295
  pricing and, 305
  product design, for, 206
  profit and, 478
  providers' risks, 40
  prudential regulation, 192, 291, 298
  rating agencies' perspective, 310–12
  reasons for holding, 292–4
  regulating level of, 298
  return on, 373
    monitoring experience, 519–22
    profit, measure of, 373, 519
  risk and, 31, 296, 297, 302–10
    diversification, benefits of, 310–11

risk-based, 40
  solvency, requirements for *see*
    Solvency
senior management's perspective, 296–8
shareholders' perspective, 295–6
shareholders, relationship with, 297
solvency, requirements for *see* Solvency
subordinated debt, 291, 446
superannuation funds, 301–2
  operational risk, 309
target surplus, 312
Tier 1, 291
Tier 2, 291
types, 290–1
unexpected events, withstanding, 293
what is, 289
Capital Asset Pricing Model (CAPM), 350–3
  assumptions from CAPM models, 353
  investment performance, 508
  risk-return trade-off, 351–2
Capital guaranteed, 94, 410
Capital management, 538–9
  charging for capital, 538
  optimizing capital requirements, 538
Capital market risks, 143, 152
Cash flow matching, 413–14
Cash flow solvency, 427–31
  liquidity risk *see* Liquidity risk
Cash flow testing, 427, 428
Cash management account, 82, 542
Cash value, 171, 228
Catastrophes *see* Extreme events
Census data, 272
Central bank role, 81, 98, 184, 429
Central estimate, 320, 436, 576
Certificate of deposit, 81, 399
Chalke's product demand surface, 363
Checking account, 16, 329, 373
Chief Actuary, 37–8
Chief Risk Officer (CRO), 37
Civil code system, 177–8
Civil law, 180
Claims controls, 536–7
Claims management
  expenses, 513
  improving, 537
Claims risk, 141
Clearing House, 400, 408
Client, 3, 7
Climate, 113–14
Code of conduct, 54–5
  application, 57
  monitoring, 56

Coinsurance, 167
Collateral, 82, 163
Collateralized debt obligations (CDOs), 401
Commissions, 123, 512
Commodity product
    definition, 375
    pricing, 375–6
Common law system, 177–8
Communication
    documentation, 32–4
    professionalism in, 64
    project management, 208
    reports, 6–7, 32–4, 64
    stakeholders, with, 32–4
Commutation, 115, 147
Compensation schemes *see* Guarantee funds
Competition, 124–5
    anti-competitive behavior, 182
    pricing, 210–11, 360, 544
    product design and, 210–11, 361
    regulation promoting, 182, 184
    responding to experience, considerations,
        530
Compulsory financial products
    regulation of, 185
    third party insurance, 185
    workers compensation, 185
Concentration risk, 143
Conditional tail expectation (CTE), 438
Confidence level, 156–7
Conflicts of interest, 61
Consumer confidence
    capital and, 292–3
    credit rating affecting, 294
Consumer protection
    discretionary amounts, 58
    legislation, 329
        liability valuation and, 329
    market failure, after, 188
    role of actuary, 58–9
Contagion risk, 308
Contents insurance *see* Home insurance
Context, 105–31
Conventional life insurance, 342, 576
Convergence, 121
Convertible bonds, 400
Convertible notes, 446
Corporate governance, 13–14
    prudential regulation, 192
Corporate structure, 13, 78–9
Cost/benefit analysis, 31
Cost-plus pricing, 362
Counterparty risk, 30

Court decisions, 179
Credit card business
    expense analysis, 516–17
Credit crunch, 406
Credit default swap, 93, 168, 429, 464
Credit insurance, 83, 86, 89
Credit rating
    capital affecting, 293–4, 295
    consumer confidence and, 294
    rating agencies
        capital, perspective on need for, 299
    solvency management, 451–2
Credit risk, 16, 142, 399, 405
    banking sector, 303
    capital needs and, 303
    data checks, 275–6
Creditor, 78, 291, 321, 399
Criminal law, 179
Critical illness, 74, 86, 113, 330
Cross-sectional data, 273
Culture
    corporate culture context factors, 127–8
    risk management, 18, 36, 38, 40
Currency risk, 142
Customer expectation risks, 150–1
Customers
    capital, perspective on need for, 298–9
    pricing needs, 361
    protection *see* Consumer protection
    risk management, reliance on, 38
Current account, 86

D

Data
    ability to process, 269
    accessibility, 278
    accuracy and completeness, 278
    assumptions based on *see* Assumptions
    Benford's Law, 345
    census, 272
    checks, 274
    coherence, 278
    collaboration in collection of, 269
    collection costs, 256
    cross-sectional, 273
    definition, 268
    deterministic checks, 274
    error correction, 273, 277
    error detection, 273
    error prevention, 273

Data (*continued*)
  experience data, 153–4, 522–3
    collection, 500, 522
    components, 503–4
    cyclical component, 504
    economic, 504
    quality, 500, 522
    random/error component, 504
    seasonal component, 503
    trend component, 503
    validation, 522
  exploratory checks, 274–5
  exploratory data analysis, 239–40
  external, 272, 279
  extreme events, 146–7
  grouping, 272, 344
  high quality, obtaining, 273–4
  importance of, 268–70
  inadequate, 277
  individual or grouped, 272
  institutional environment, 278
  insurance companies collecting, 269
  integrity tests, 345
  internal, 272, 279
  interpretability, 278
  liability valuation, for, 344–5
    comparison with expected, 345
    integrity tests, 345
    movement analysis, 345
    quality, 345
    ratios and trends, 345
    validation tests, 345
  limited, challenges presented by, 278–80
  longitudinal, 273
  missing, 277
  modeling, for, 271
  necessity for, 267, 268–70
  overview, 267–8
  quality, 273–4
    ABS framework, 278
    liability valuation, for, 344–5
    standards of practice, 277–8
    verification, 274
  reasonably accurate, 267
  relevance, 278
  repair, 273, 277
  sampling, 272
  sources of, 272–3
  specifying requirements, 270
  survey, 272
  timeliness, 278
  whole population study, 273

  Y2K problem, 270
Debt capital, 291
  debt to equity ratio, 291
  mandatory convertible notes, 446
  solvency requirements, 446
  subordinated debt, 291, 446
Debt/equity hybrid securities, 446, 447
Debtor, 89, 292, 396
Declared bonuses, 439
Decreasing term insurance, 84
Deductible, 86, 209
Default risk, 303, 405
  capital needs and, 303
  credit rating, 406
Deferral-and-matching framework
  profit measurement, 484, 485
Deferred acquisition cost (DAC), 397
Deferred annuities, 90
  pricing, 377–8
Defined benefit superannuation fund, 91, 148
  actuarial review, 546
    responses to, 547–9
  asset/liability management, 415–16
  contribution holiday, 547
  contribution rate, adjusting, 547
  data to determine value of benefits, 271,
    344
  excess funds, returning to employer, 548–9
  funding calculations, 344
  funding requirements, 546
  growth investments, 548
  monitoring experience, 499
  pace of funding, 547
  responding to experience, 546–9
  risks, 148–9
Defined contribution fund, 91, 148
  monitoring experience, 499
  risks, 149
Demographic structure and trends, 117
Deposit-taking institutions, 307
Depreciation
  profit affected by, 474, 479
Derivatives, 94–5, 400–1
  asset risks, 408
  contracts for difference (CFDs), 95
  exchange-traded funds (ETFs), 95, 400
  futures contracts, 94, 400
  margin calls, 408
  option contracts, 95, 400
  risk mitigation, 204
  swaps, 95, 400
  valuation, 404
Deriving liabilities by valuing equity, 333

Deterministic cash flow projections in valuing liabilities, 327–8, 331
Directors and officers insurance, 89
Disability
definition, 84
income risk, 73–4
Disability insurance
disability income insurance (DII), 85
income protection, 85
lump sum disability, 85
payout ratios, 86
total and permanent disablement (TPD), 85
waiver of premium, 85
Disaster risk, 144
Disasters
extreme events, 146–7
man-made, 115
natural, 113–14
Disclosure
informed markets, ensuring, 189
modeling and, 261–2
regulation compared, 189
solvency management, 451–2
Discontinuance solvency, 427, 431–3
forms of discontinuance, 432
run off, 432
transfer of business, 432
winding up, 432
measuring, 432–3
valuation of assets, 434
valuation of liabilities, 439
Discount rates
after-tax discount, 347
arbitrage-free pricing, 350
Capital Asset Pricing Model, 350, 351
cash flow projections, 349, 402
financial economics and, 350–4
formula, 348
liability valuation, 347–54
projection rates and, 347
risk-adjusted, 331
risk-return trade-off, 351–2
setting, 349
state price deflators, 350–1
tax, allowing for, 347
tax cost liability, 347
unwind of discount, 347
Discounted cash flow (DCF), 402
Discretionary amounts
customer protection, 58–9

Distributable earnings, 364
Distribution
channel, 203
new, need for new product, 201
product design, affecting, 203–4
direct, 123
intermediary, through, 203
method, 203
product design, 217–18
distribution channel, 203–4, 217
distribution method, 203
marketing, 217–18
new channel, need for new product, 201
Distribution risk, 144
Distributors
information asymmetry, 183
Diversification
benefits, 310–11
capital needs and, 310–11
Dividend policy
modeling, 228
Dividends on insurance policy, 162
Divorce, 75
Documentation
report types, 32–4
risk management policy, 34
risk management strategy, 34
Domestic banking risks, 151
Domino effect see Contagion risk
Double counting
assets, of, preventing, 434
evidence, of, in modeling, 245
Dread disease, 86
Driver, 495, 533
Due diligence, 169–70
Duration, 145, 396, 405
Dynamic Capital Adequacy Testing (DCAT), 454–5
Dynamic model, 454
Dynamic Solvency Testing (DST), 454–5

E

Earnings, distributable, 364
Economic capital, 40, 290, 311
regulatory capital differentiated from, 311
Economic environment, 116–20
Economic environment risk, 142
Embedded value (EV), 333, 486

Employer
  group superannuation and insurance
    100–1
  pricing needs, 361
  risk management, interest in, 39
  sponsored superannuation fund, 91
Employers liability insurance *see* Workers
    compensation
Employment patterns, 118–19
Endowment insurance, 90
Enterprise Risk Management (ERM) *see also*
    Risk management
  actuaries, implications for, 41–2
  board role in, 36
  Chartered Enterprise Risk Analyst
    (CERA), 564
  consultation, 564–6
  definition, 19–20
  example of ERM project, 565
  forces supporting, 20
  global financial crisis lessons, 171–2
  integrated view of risk, 564
  need for, 20–1
  overview, 18–19
  planning, integration into, 21
  risk management framework, 11–12, 561
  solvency risk management, 450
  success of
    factors for, 40–1
    measurement of, 41
Enterprise risks, 137
Equity, 78–9, 319, 399–400
  embedded value, 333
  private, 400
Equity and property risk, 142
Equity capital, 290
  debt to equity ratio, 291
  minimum amounts, 291
  shareholder's perspective, 295–6
Equity law, 180
Established practice in valuing liabilities, 330
Estate, 552
Estimates
  assumptions differentiated from, 280
  best estimate *see* Best estimate
Ethical behavior, 60–1
Event risks, 144
Excess *see* Deductible
Excess reinsurance treaty, 167
Exchange-traded funds (ETFs), 95
Exclusion periods, 161
Expense analysis, 509–18

Expense controls
  improving expense performance, 535–6
  measuring expense performance, 533–5
  outsourcing, 536
Expenses over life cycle, 69–70
Expense performance
  improving, 535–6
  measuring, 533–5
Expense risks, 74–7, 144
  measure of exposure to, 442
  solvency testing, 455
Expenses, 369–72
  acquisition, 370
  analyzing, 509–18
  fixed, 369, 371, 510
  fully allocated, 370–2
  monitoring experience, 509–18
  overhead, 369
  pricing for, 370–2
  variable, 370, 510
Experience
  adverse, affecting capital needs, 306
  analyzing *see* Monitoring experience
  data, 153–4, 522–3
    collection, 500, 522
    components, 503–4
    cyclical component, 504
    economic, 504
    quality, 500, 522
    random/error component, 504
    seasonal component, 503
    trend component, 503
    validation, 522
  monitoring *see* Monitoring experience
  product design, 207
    updating for experience, 201
  reasons for analyzing, 495–7
  refunds, 546
  responding to *see* Responding to
    experience
  sharing, 162
Exploratory data analysis, 239–40
External forces *see* Context
Extreme events, 146–7
  and GFC, 169

F

Facultative reinsurance treaty, 167
Fair value
  asset, of, 395
  liability, of, 326

Fair value accounting, 434
Family income benefits, 84
Fiber optic cable project
    applying Actuarial Control Cycle, 559–62
Fiduciary, 180, 452
Financial Action Task Force (FATF), 191
Financial condition reports, 453–4
Financial control reports, 531
Financial control systems, 531–2
Financial economics
    actuaries and, 353–4
    arbitrage-free pricing, 350
    discount rates and, 350–4
    risk-return trade-off, 351–2
    state price deflators, 350–1
Financial institutions *see also* Banks
    convergence, 121
    customer protection, 58–9
    deposit guarantees, 459
    guarantee funds, 458–61
    liquidity risk, 428–31
    monitoring experience, 500
    prudential supervision, 57–8
    risk management, service providers'
        interest in, 39
Financial life cycle
    businesses, 78–80
        risks, 79
    capital, 78–9
    equity, 78–9
    exceptions, 72
    expense, 69–70
        risks, 75–7
    families role, 97–8
    household income and expense studies, 73
    income, 69–70
        risks, 73–4
    overview, 69
    risks and volatility, 73–8
    savings, 70–1
    socio-economic class, 72
Financial markets
    failure *see* Market failure
    market conduct regulators, 39
    regulation, 181–4
        fitness and propriety of participants,
            183
        primary markets, 182
        secondary markets, 182
Financial planners, 122
Financial products, 80–97
    administration of, 220

compulsory, regulation of, 185
design *see* Product design
distribution, 121–3
long-term savings *see* Long-term savings
    products
monetary products *see* Monetary products
Financial Sector Assessment Program (FSAP),
    191
Financial security
    actuarial role, 69, 101
    employers' role, 100–1
    families' role, 97–8
    governments' role, 98–100
Financial services regulators
    risk management, interest in, 39
Financial Stability Board (FSB), 191
Financial underwriting, 219
Fitness and propriety, 183
Fixed-interest mortgage, 76, 82
Floating rate, 76
Football tipping model, 567–70
Forecasts
    assumptions differentiated from, 280
Formula liability valuations, 327
401(k) plans, 92
Funding method, 383, 384–5, 547
Fund members, 38, 301
Funds management
    monitoring experience, 499
    risk identification, 149–51
Funds under management (FUM), 149–50
Futures contract, 94–5, 400, 404

G

Gearing, 291, 295
General insurance, 87–9
    liability valuation, 341
    monitoring experience, 498
    risks, 145–7
Generally Accepted Accounting Principles
    (GAAP), 124, 346, 433
Generalized linear models, 563
Global financial crisis (GFC), 167–72
Globalization, 128–9
Going-concern solvency, 427, 431, 433
    measuring, 433–4
Goods & Services Tax (GST), 175
Goodwill, 397, 479
Government
    guarantee funds funded by, 461
    money, 98

Government (*continued*)
  policy effect on regulation context, 111
  regulation *see* Regulation
  retirement provision systems, 100
  social assistance, 99, 112–13
  social insurance, 112–13
  statutory insurance schemes, 99–100
  taxation, 112
Granularity of data, 256–7
GST, 175
Guarantee funds, 458–61
Guaranteed investment contracts (GIC), 94
Guarantees, 329–30
  point of sale promise, 329

H

Hazard risks, 17
Health insurance
  anti-selection, 76, 145
  critical illness insurance, 86–7
  dread disease, 86
  exclusion periods, 161
  health maintenance organizations (HMOs),
    87
  hospital cash, 87
  income protection insurance, 85
  long-term care insurance, 87
  medical costs, 76, 86
  monitoring experience, 500
  permanent health insurance (PHI), 85
  pricing product, 367–9
  risks, 145
  trauma, 86
Health maintenance organizations (HMOs), 87
Heat map *see* Risk heat map
Hedging, 79, 162–3
  external, 205
  hedgeable risks, 79
  internal, 204
  profits, 401
  risk mitigation, 204
Highly geared companies, 291
Home insurance, 88
Hospital cash, 87
Human capital, 70
  risk, 143
Human resources (HR), 610
Hurdle rate, 40, 237
Hypothesis testing, 242–4
  multiple hypotheses, 254
  theoretical ambiguities, 254

I

Illiquid assets, 395, 411–12
Immediate annuities, 95
Immunization, 414
Inadmissible assets, 434
Income cycle, 69–70
Income protection insurance, 85
Income risks, 73–4
Incurred but not reported (IBNR) claims, 305
  analyzing experience, 501
  profit measurement, 484
  valuation of liability, 342
Indemnity agreements, 167
Indemnity cover, 85
Indirect liability valuation, 333
Industry associations, 125–6
Industry environment, 120–3
Industry fund, 92, 302
Inflation
  annuities not protected against, 230
  assumptions, 282
  expense risks, 76–7
  interest rates, relationship with, 229–36
  super-imposed, 147
Information asymmetry, 183
Information collection, 63
Information criterion, 244–5
Inherent risk, 31
Innovation
  financial services, 200
  insurance industry, 200
  product design, 199–200
Insolvency *see* Solvency
Insurable interest, 219
Insurance
  administration of product, 220
  agreed value, 85, 329
  business, 79, 89
  business interruption, 89
  competition in market, promoting, 182,
    184
  contract, writing of, 215–17
  credit, 83, 86, 89
  customer protection, 58–9
  design features to control risk, 209
  directors and officers, 89
  disability *see* Disability insurance
  general, 87–9, 145–6
  health *see* Health insurance
  home, 88
  indemnity policy, 85
  insurable interest, 219
  insurable risks, 79

Insurance (*continued*)
  Islamic, 119–20
  legislated roles for actuaries, 60
  liability, 89
  life *see* Life insurance
  long-tail, 147
  long-term care, 87
  marine, 89
  medical costs *see* Health insurance
  medical malpractice, 278, 458
  motor *see* Motor vehicle insurance
  personal accident, 89
  pluvius, 504
  product design *see* Product design
  professional indemnity, 89
  property and casualty insurance (P&C), 87–9
  public liability, 75
  risk selection, 218–20
  statutory insurance schemes, 99–100
  trade credit, 89
  underwriting, 219–20
  unemployment insurance, 86
  waiting period, 85
  workers compensation, 89
    regulation of, 185
Insurer
  credit risks, 16, 142
  policyholder guarantee funds, 459
  risk identification, 140–7
  underwriting risks, 17–18, 141–2
Interbank lending rate, 429
Interest payments, 399
Interest rate
  assumptions, 366
  discounting cash flows, for, 366
  floating, 76
  inflation, relationship with, 229–36
  investment income, estimating, 366
  risks, 76, 142
  spread, 378
Intermediaries
  distribution of products through, 203
  risk management, interest in, 39
  sales intermediaries
    commissions, 363
    pricing needs, 361
Internal model, 154
Internal rate of return, 373
International Accounting Standards Board (IASB), 190
International Actuarial Association (IAA), 53

International Association of Insurance Supervisors (IAIS), 190
International banking risks, 151–2
International Financial Reporting Standards (IFRS), 190
International Monetary Fund (IMF), 191
International Organization of Securities Commissions (IOSCO), 190
International regulatory organizations, 190–1
  core principles, 192
International regulatory standards, 190–1
Intrinsic capital funding, 342
Invested asset credit risk, 142
Investment
  entrepreneurs' capital risk, 72
  income, distribution of, 539–42
  liquidity risk management, 430
  rate, assumptions, 282
  savings risks, 77–8
  smoothing of returns, 540–2
Investment account policies, 94
Investment-linked, 92–3
Investment management expenses, 514
Investment performance
  attribution analysis, 506
  Capital Asset Pricing Model (CAPM), 508
  Global Investment Performance Standards, 504
  Jensen measure, 508
  measuring, 504–9
  money weighted return (MWR), 505, 506
  Sharpe measure, 508
  time weighted return (TWR), 505, 506
  Treynor measure, 508
Investment risk
  hedging instruments used to mitigate, 204
  modeling, 228
  risk management consultation, 565
  solvency testing, 455
Investor due diligence and GFC, 169–70

J

Jensen measure, 508
Joint life policies, 83
Judicial decisions, 113
Junk bonds, 451

K

Key risk indicator, 33

L

Laddering assets and liabilities, 431
Lagging indicator, 456
Lapses, 220, 282, 499, 545
Law *see also* Regulation
  civil, 180
  civil code system, 177–8
  common law system, 177–8
  criminal, 179
  equity, 180
  financial sector, influencing, 180
  precedent, 179
  work of actuaries, influencing, 180
Legal risk, 144
Legislation *see also* Regulation
  primary legislation, 178
  roles for actuaries, 60, 192–3
  subsidiary legislation, 178–9
  taxation legislation, 181
Leveraged, 291
Levies, 181
Liability-driven investment (LDI), 416–17
Liabilities
  accounts, in, 318–19
  accounts payable, 321
  balance sheet, on, 318–19
  capital adequacy liability, 324
  concentration of, 306
  debt, 321–2
  definition, 317–18
  incurred but not reported (IBNR) claims, 305, 342
  laddering, 431
  long-term, 321
  long-term contracts, 305
  measuring *see* Valuing liabilities
  options, 305
  outstanding claims, 305, 342
  pricing and, 343
  profit and loss statement, in, 319
  projections using, 343
  provisions, 322
  short-term, 321
  tax liabilities, 321
  types, 305, 320–2
  unearned premiums, 305
  unexpired risk, 305
  valuation of *see* Liability valuation
Liability insurance, 89
Liability risks
  capital needs and, 303, 305–6
    concentration of liabilities, 306
    definition, 303
    experience, 306
    pricing, 305
    significant unexpected event, 306
    valuation of liabilities *see* Liability
      valuation
Liability valuation
  account balance, 332, 337
    plus margin, 337, 338
    plus margin less DAC, 337, 338
  accuracy, 334, 341
  actuarial history in, 317
  after-tax discount rate, 347
  allowing for risk, 331
  arbitrage-free pricing, 350
  assumptions, 345–6, 436, 437
  benefit definitions, 330
  best estimate (BEL), 320, 323–4, 326, 336
    BEL plus margin, 336, 338, 477
    margin on services, 337, 477
  bundled, 332
  capital adequacy liability, 324
  Capital Asset Pricing Model (CAPM), 350, 353
    assumptions from CAPM models, 353
    risk-return trade-off, 351–2
  central estimate, 320, 323–4
  conditional tail expectation (CTE), 438
  consumer protection legislation, 329
  core actuarial function, 354
  data, 344–5
    comparison with expected, 345
    integrity tests, 345
    movement analysis, 345
    quality, 345
    ratios and trends, 345
    validation tests, 345
  deferred acquisition cost (DAC), 334
  deriving by valuing equity, 333
  deterministic cash flow projections, 327–8, 331
  discount rates, 347–54
    after-tax discount, 347
    arbitrage-free pricing, 350
    Capital Asset Pricing Model, 350–3
    cash flow projections, 349
    financial economics and, 350–4
    formula, 348
    projection rates and, 347
    risk-return trade-off, 351–2
    setting, 349

Liability valuation (*continued*)
  state price deflators, 350–1
  tax, allowing for, 347
  unwind of discount, 347
established practice, 330
fair value, 326
financial economics
  actuaries and, 353–4
  arbitrage-free pricing, 350
  discount rates and, 350–4
  risk-return trade-off, 351–2
  state price deflators, 350–1
formula valuations, 327
guarantees, 329–30
incurred but not reported (IBNR) claims,
  305, 342
indirect approach, 333
intrinsic capital funding, 342
long-tail business, 305, 341
margin for adverse deviation (MAD)
  method, 437–8
  POS method combined with, 438
margin on services (MoS), 337, 477
margins, 320, 324–5, 334
market value, 326
materiality, 343
methodology, 327–9
non-life insurers, 341
  long-tail business, 341
objective, 334, 335–9
options, 329–30
out-of-the-money options, 330
outstanding claims, 305, 342
overview, 305, 323
point of sale promises, 329
practical issues, 343–50
pricing and, 343
principles-based, 332
probability of sufficiency (POS) method,
  438
  MAD method combined with, 438
  VaR, compared to, 438
profit and, 334–43, 483
  accuracy of valuation, 341
  different valuation approaches, 336–8
  liability valuation basis and total profit,
    340
  table of liabilities, 337, 338
  valuation objective, 334, 335–9
profit margins, 325, 336
profit signature, 338, 339
projection assumptions, 345–6

projection interest rates, 347
prudent valuation, 320, 326
risk affecting capital needs, 305
risk margins, 324–5
risk-adjusted cash flows, 331
risk-adjusted discount rate, 331
rules-based, 332
sensitivity tests, 343
smoothing reserves, 341
solvency purposes, for, 435–40
  accuracy, 440
  discontinuance, adjustments for, 439
  discretionary benefits, 439
  margin for adverse deviation (MAD)
    method, 437–8
  methods, 435–9
  principles-based reserving, 438
  probability of sufficiency (POS)
    method, 438
  prudent best estimates, 438
  statutory valuation basis, 436
  stochastic reserve, 439
statutory valuation basis, 436
sterling reserve, 342
stochastic cash flow projections, 328–9,
  331
tax, allowing for, 347
tax cost liability, 347
unbundled, 332–3
Life insurance
allocation of profit, 550–2
  fair and equitable, 550–2
  fair return in relation to risk, 552
  generational equity, 552
  reasonable expectations, 551
Appointed Actuary, 60
asset share methods, 554
bonus, 90, 549
conventional, 549
decreasing term, 84
design features to control risk, 209
distribution of profits, 550, 552–4
  terminal bonuses, 553
  uniform reversionary bonuses, 553
endowment, 90
family income benefits, 84
guaranteed surrender values, 429
history of actuarial involvement, 549
investment account policies, 94
investment-linked policies, 93
joint life, 83
life insured, 83

Life insurance (*continued*)
  liquidity options, 429
  longevity risk, 145
  monitoring experience, 499, 502
    investment business, 499
    risk business, 499
  overview, 83
  participating policies, 90, 410, 549
  pure endowment, 90
  responding to experience, 549–54
    allocation of profit, 550–2
    distribution of profit, 550, 552–4
    participating life insurance, 549–54
  reversionary bonuses, 553
  risks, 145
  term insurance, 83–4
  traditional savings products, 90
  unit-linked, 115
  universal life, 94, 200
  variable life, 93
  whole life insurance, 84
  with-profit, 58
  yearly renewable term, 84, 167
Lifetime annuity, 96
Limited companies, 399–400
Liquidation *see also* Winding up, 291, 295
Liquidation value risk, 143
Liquidity, 427–31
  see also Solvency
Liquidity options, 429
Liquidity ratio, 427
Liquidity risk, 16, 143, 428–9
  asset-liability mismatch, 431
  capital needs and, 304, 306–7
  contingency plans, 431
  crisis, in, 428–9
  financial institutions, 428–9
  incidents influencing, 307
  investment and, 430–1
  laddering assets and liabilities, 431
  liquidity options, 429
  managing, 429–31
  market dislocation causing, 428
  marketing and, 430
  pricing and, 430
  product design and, 429
  property-casualty insurance companies, 429
  risk management, 430
  solvency problems, 428–31
  vicious cycle, 428
Listed shares/stock, 395, 400

Loans
  administration of product, 220
Longevity risk, 145
Long-tail business, 147
  asset-liability management, 415
  claims control, 536
  liability valuation, 305, 341
  risk identification, 147
Long-term care insurance, 87
  monitoring, 382
  pricing, 374–5
Long-term commitments
  funding methods, 383, 384–5
    accrued benefits, 384
    aggregate, 385
    initial funding, 384
    pay as you go (PAYG), 384
    projected benefits, 384, 385
    projected unit credit, 385
  pricing for, 383–6
    Actuarial Control Cycle, applying, 383
    actuarial cost method, 383
    funding methods, 383, 384–5
    responsibility for choices, 385
Long-term savings products, 90–5
  deferred annuities, 90
  derivatives, 94–5
  direct investment, 94
  endowment insurances, 90
  investment account policies, 94
  investment-linked arrangements, 92–3
    life insurance policies, 93
  master trusts, 93
  overview, 90
  pooled superannuation trusts (PSTs), 93
  superannuation funds, 90–2
  traditional life insurance savings products, 90
  unit trusts, 92
  universal life, 94
  wrap funds, 93
Longitudinal data, 273

M

Management control risk, 143
Mandatory convertible notes, 446
Margin calls, 408
Margin for adverse deviation (MAD) method, 437–8
Margin on services (MoS)
  liability valuation, 337, 477

Margin on services (MoS) (*continued*)
  profit, 477–8
Margins
  assumptions adjusted by, 366–7
  in liability valuation, 320, 324–5, 334
  profit *see* Profit margins
  risk, 324–5
Marine insurance, 89
Mark-to-model, 395
Market conduct regulators
  risk management, interest in, 39
Market efficiency
  regulatory interference and inefficiency,
    188
  self-referential models, 246
Market failure, 181–4
  anti-competitive behaviour, 182
  asymmetric information, 183
  consumer protection after, 188
  market misconduct, 182
  sources, 181
  systemic instability, 184
Market misconduct, 182
Market research
  product design, 202
Market risk, 15, 16, 142–3
  capital needs and, 303, 307–8
Market value of assets, 395
Market value of liabilities, 326
Marketing
  advertising, 218
  applying Actuarial Control Cycle, 562–4
  brokers, use of, 217
  direct, 218
  expenses, 514, 517
  liquidity risk management, 430
  product design and, 217–18
Markets and models, 260–1
Master trusts, 93
Materiality, 62
  assumptions, 283
  liability valuation, 343
Maturity transformation, 431
Maximum likelihood method
  model calibration, 240
Measure of exposure to risk, 442–4
  first Basel Accord, 442, 443
  objectivity, 443
  projection models, 443
  reliability, 443
  risk-based capital standard, creation of,
    442–4

second Basel Accord, 442, 443
  Value-at-Risk approach, 443
Medical costs
  expense risks, 75–6
  insurance *see* Health insurance
  national health schemes, 76
Medical insurance *see* Health insurance
Medical malpractice insurance, 278, 458
Mergers
  prudential regulation, 187
Microinsurance, 119
Middle management
  corporate structure, place in, 13
  risk management responsibilities, 38
Misaligned incentives and GFC, 168
Model calibration, 240–1
  Bayesian method, 241
  calibration error, 248
  frequentist/classical framework, 240
  maximum likelihood method, 240
  past data, to, 255
Model office, 251
Model risk, 146
Modeling
  Actuarial Control Cycle, role in, 255
  advocacy, for, 259–60
  asset-liability, 417
  automobile insurance, 227
  back testing, 241
  Black-Scholes model, 249
  blend-test evaluation, 241
  bootstrapping, 250
  Box's dictum, 254
  calibration of model, 240–1, 255
    Bayesian method, 241
    error, 248
    frequentist/classical framework, 240
    maximum likelihood method, 240
  challenging fitted model, 237–8
  commercial, 255–62
  computational classification, 250–3
  computer spreadsheets, 257
  computer technology development, 247–8
  costs, 256–7
  data *see* Data
  defensive programming, 248
  deterministic, 27, 251
    stochastic differentiated from, 252
  disclosure, 261–2
  dividend policy setting, 228
  double counting of evidence, 245
  dynamic, 454

Modeling (*continued*)
  error, causes of, 248–50
  estimating tail events, 255
  evaluation of model, 229
  examples, 227–9
  exploratory data analysis, 239–40
  fit to evidence, 241–2
  fit to theory, 245–6
  fitted models, 236–8
    challenging, 237–8
    using, 236–7
  football tipping model, 567–70
  generalized linear models, 563
  governance and control, 258–9
  graveyard, 245, 262
  hypothesis testing, 242–4, 254
  inflation and interest rates, case study, 229–36
    actuarial problem, 230
    autoregressive model, 234, 235
    data analysis, 231–5
    data sources, 230
    fitted model, 236–8
  information criterion, 244–5
  insurance price fairness, 227
  internal model, 154
  investment risks and returns, 228
  markets and, 260–1
  model error, 248, 249
  model estimation, costs, 256
  model office, 251
  model output, costs, 257
  model testing, 247–8
  model, what is, 229
  Monte Carlo models, 252–3
  mortality improvement, 228
  motor vehicle insurance, 227
  noise parameter, 245
  normative approaches to, 238–53
    limitations, 253–5
      practical difficulties, 253–4
      theoretical ambiguities, 254
      unexpected events, 255
  operational error, 248, 250
  out-of-sample evaluation, 241
  parameter error, 248, 249
  parsimony, 244–5
  pension benefits valuation, 228
  physical sciences, 239
  price testing, 363
  pricing process, 364–5
  probability distributions, 252

  probability generating function, 252
  process error, 248, 249
  project management, 257–8
  projection, using models for, 248–50
  regression testing, 247
  risk models, 27–8, 154–5
  robustness, 257–8
  savings product, 227
  scenario modeling, 27–8, 560
  self-referential models, 246
  sense-checking model outputs, 247
  social behaviour, 229
  social sciences, 238–9
  statistical inference, 239
  stochastic model, 252
    data collection, 271, 272
    deterministic model differentiated from, 251
    Monte Carlo models, 252–3
  survivorship bias, 248, 249
  testing routine outputs, 247
  testing software functionality, 247
  theory, fitting to, 245–6
Modified coinsurance, 167
Monetary products
  annuities, 95
  bonds, 82
  borrowing instruments, 82–3
  credit, 82
  debentures, 82
  government role, 98–9
  long-term savings products, 90–5
  money, 81
  mortgage loans, 82
  overview, 80
  retirement income products, 95–7
  securitization, 83
  short-term savings products, 81–2
  transaction services, 81
Money market funds, 82
Money purchase structure *see* Defined contribution superannuation
Monitoring
  assumptions, 281
  product design, 221
Monitoring experience
  actual rates, calculating, 501–2
  actual vs expected outcomes, 495, 501
    incurred but not reported (IBNR) claims, 501
  Actuarial Control Cycle, 495, 502
  analysis techniques, 500–22

Monitoring experience (*continued*)
banking, 499
profit analysis for bank, 521
business mix, 518–19
business volumes, 518–19
case study, 562
data, 153–4, 522–3
collection, 500, 522
components, 503–4
cyclical component, 504
economic, 504
quality, 500, 522
random/error component, 504
seasonal component, 503
trend component, 503
validation, 522
developing history of experience over
time, 496, 503
disclosure requirements, satisfying, 497
economic data, 504
expenses, 509–18
analyzing *see* Expense analysis
explanation of results, 501
funds management, 499
general insurance, 498
health insurance, 500
investment performance, 504–9
items for analysis, 498
life insurance, 499, 502
management, providing information to,
496
new business mix, 518–19
objectives, 495–7, 500
product-specific items, 501–4
profit, 519–22
profit analysis, aiding, 496
public relations purposes, 497
reasons for, 495–7
regulatory requirements, 497
response *see* Responding to experience
return on capital, 519–22
reviewing assumptions, 495
sensitivity testing, 497
shareholders, providing information to,
497
superannuation, 499
third parties, providing information to, 497
time series analysis, 503–4
understanding drivers of emerging
experience, 496
validation of results, 501
what is analyzed, 497–500

Monte Carlo models, 252–3
Moral hazard, 71, 83, 85, 86, 88, 459
Morbidity rate
assumption, 365
Morbidity risk
measure of exposure to, 442
solvency testing, 455
Mortality rate
assumption, 365
improvement, modeling, 228
life-contingent annuities, 365, 366
life insurance, 365
Mortality risk
measure of exposure to, 442
solvency testing, 455
Mortality study
assumptions from, 281
data, 276
Mortgage, 82, 399
Motor vehicle insurance, 88
calculation of premiums, 227
compulsory third party (CTP), 88
regulation of, 185
modeling, 227
underwriting, 219
Multi-employer fund, 92, 302
Mutual enterprises, 12
Mutual funds, 92
Mutual organizations
capital needs, 300–1
demutualizations, 301

N

National Association of Insurance
Commissioners (NAIC), 190
Financial Analysis and Solvency Tracking
System (FAST), 451
Insurance Regulatory Information System
(IRIS), 451
prudential regulation, 190
National Insurance contributions, 99
Net retention risk, 142
New business
capital needs, 289
controls, 537–8
mix, 518–19
strain, 372–3, 479
value of, 486, 488
Niche product
definition, 376
pricing, 376

Noise parameter, 245
No claims bonus/discount, 88
Non-admitted assets, 434
Non-life insurance *see* General insurance

O

Off-balance sheet risk, 143, 455
   solvency testing, 455
Operational risk, 17, 143
   capital needs and, 303, 308–10
      banks, 309
   definition, 303, 308
   external influences, 308
   internal influences, 308
   regulation, arguments for, 189
   superannuation funds, 309
Option contracts, 95
Options on policies *see under* Liability
   valuation
Organization for Economic Co-operation and
   Development (OECD)
   financial sector regulation, 191
Outsourcing, 536
   expense control, 536
Outstanding claims, 305, 342
Overhead expense, 369
Over-the-counter, 395, 400

P

Pandemics, 114–15
Parsimony, 244–5
Peer review, 56
Pension benefits
   index-linked, 96
   valuation, modeling, 228
Pension fund *see* Superannuation fund
Pensions *see* Annuities
"Perfect storms", 284
Permanent Health insurance, 85
Persistency, 204, 220, 445
Personal accident insurance, 89
Personal pensions, 92
Physical environment, 113–16
   climate, 113–14
   man-made disasters, 115
   natural perils, 113–14
   pandemics, 114–15
   technological developments, 115–16
Pluvius insurance, 504
Point of sale promises, 329

Policyholder behavior risk, 142
Policyholders' reasonable expectations (PRE),
   216, 551
Political risk, 142, 144
   solvency testing, 455
Pooled superannuation trusts (PSTs), 93
Precedent, 179
Predictions, 280–1
   assumptions differentiated from, 280
Preference shares/stock, 400
Pricing
   Actuarial Control Cycle, 359–60
      applying, 383
   actuarial cost method, 383
   arbitrage-free pricing, 350
   assumptions, 365–9, 387
      data for, 365
      margins, 366–7
      setting, 365
   business owners' needs, 361
   capital needs and, 305
   Chalke's product demand surface, 363
   changes, 544
   commission on sales, 363
   commodity product, 375–6
   competitiveness, 360–1, 544
   cost-plus pricing, 362
   customers' needs, 361
   deferred annuity product, 377–8
   employees' needs, 361
   expenses, 369–72
      acquisition, 370
      analyzing, 369–70
      fixed, 369, 371
      fully allocated, 370–2
      overhead, 369, 386–7
      pricing for, 370–1
      variable, 370
   forward pricing, 543
   funding methods, 383–5
      accrued benefits, 384
      aggregate, 385
      initial funding, 384
      pay as you go (PAYG), 384
      projected benefits, 384, 385
      projected unit credit, 385
   governments' needs, 361
   health insurance product, 367–9
   historic pricing, 543
   insurance products, 210
   liabilities and, 343
   liquidity risk management, 430

Pricing (*continued*)
  long-term care product, 374
    monitoring, 382
  long-term commitments, 383
    Actuarial Control Cycle, applying, 383
    actuarial cost method, 383
    funding methods, 383, 384–5
    responsibility for choices, 385
  manufacturing costs, 210
  modeling, 364–5
    distributable earnings, 364
    target surplus, 364
  niche product, 376
  objectives, 360
  overheads, 369, 386–7
  overview, 359
  postulation of price, 362
  process, 359–60
  product design and, 210–11, 361–2
  product monitoring, 382–3
  profit measures, 373
    internal rate of return, 373
    profit margin, 373
    return on capital, 373
  profit objectives, 372–4
    new business strain, 372–3
  profit testing, 374–5
  profitability, 360–1, 544
  regulators' needs, 361
  reinsurers' needs, 361
  report, 381
  response, 544
  review, 544–6
    changes, 544
    cycle, 544
    insurance pricing, 544–6
  sales intermediaries
    commissions, 363
    needs, 361
  sales, impact on, 363
  sensitivity tests, 379–81
  setting price, 362
  stakeholders' needs, 361
  testing, 363
    changes after, 544
    fully allocated basis, 370–2
    marginal basis, 370, 371
  underwriting, 365–6
  unit pricing, 542–3
  what is, 359
Pricing committee
  fitted model presented to, 237
    challenging, 237–8
    role of, 237
Pricing risk, 141
  capital needs and, 305
Primary markets, 182
Principles-based reserving, 332
Private equity, 400
Private health insurance *see* Health insurance
Private placement of debt, 275
Probability distribution
  assumption, 283
  modeling, 252
Probability of sufficiency (POS) liability
    valuation method, 438
Product design
  actuarial department expectations, 212
  administration of product, 220–1
  administrative requirements, 212
  asset-liability management, 221
  capital requirements, 206
  communication between parties, 208
  company experience, 207
  competition and, 210–11, 361
  consumer expectations, 213
  contract, 215–17
  control cycle, 199–221
    stage 1, 199–207
    stage 2, 207–14
    stage 3, 214–21
    stage 4, 221
  distribution, 215–18
    channel, 203–4, 217
    marketing, 217–18
    method, 203
    new channel, need for new product, 201
  financial viability of project, 208
  innovation, 199–200
  launch of product, 214
  liquidity risk management, 429
  market needs driving, 205
  market research, 202
  marketing, 217–18
  marketing department expectations, 212
  marketplace, understanding, 211
  monitoring, 221
  need for new product, identifying, 199–202
    entry into new market, 201
    innovation, 199–200
    market research, 202
    new distribution channel, 201

Product design (*continued*)
    regulation or tax law changes, 201
    updating for experience, 201
  objectives of project, 208
  policyholders' expectations, 213, 216
  pricing, 210–11, 361–2
  product strategy, 202–7
  project management, 207–9
  provider's expectations, 212
  regulators' expectations, 213–4
  reinsurance, availability of, 205
  resources, identification of, 205–7
  retailer expectations, 213
  risk
    design features to control, 209
    evaluating ability to mitigate, 204
    identification, 204–5
    selection, 218–20
  sales material, 215–17
  stakeholder expectations, 212–14
  timeline, 208
  what is, 361
  writing of contract, 215–17
Product design risk, 141
Product monitoring, 382
  long-term care product, 382
  pricing process, 382–3
Profession
  benefits of membership, 49
  changes to concept of, 50
  characteristics, 48
  definition, 48
  international differences, 50–1
  standards of practice, 55–6
  theory of, 49–50
Professional body
  code of conduct, 54–5, 57
  European Actuarial Consultative Group
    (Groupe Consultatif), 53
  guidance, 54–7
  international, 52, 53
  International Actuarial Association (IAA),
    53
  Mutual Recognition Agreements, 54
  national, 54
  practice, standards of, 55–7
  role, 48, 50–1, 52–3
Professional indemnity insurance, 89
Professionalism
  approach to work, 62–4
  communicating results, 64
  competence, 63

  conflicts of interest, 61
  defining the task, 63
  ethical behavior, 60–1
  information collection, 63
  knowledge, 63
  materiality, 62
  reasonableness, 63
  reliance on other experts, 62
  third parties, consideration of, 61
  whistle-blowing, 60, 61
Profit
  accounting rules, 483
  amortization affecting, 474, 479
  appraisal values, 485–9
  asset-and-liability framework, 484, 485
  bonds, accounting treatment, 483
  capital and, 478
  change in policy liabilities, 475
  deferral-and-matching framework, 484,
    485
  deferred acquisition cost (DAC), 479
    DAC-adjusted profit, 480
  depreciation affecting, 474, 479
  distributable profit, 471, 474, 478
    reported profit differentiated from, 472,
    474
  earned profit, 484
  economic value accrued, differentiated
    from, 484
  emergence of, 475
  formula, 319, 334, 471
  immediate recognition of future profit, 476
  income less expenditure, 471
  incurred but not reported claims, 484
  internal rate of return, 373
  liability valuation and, 334–43, 483
    accuracy of valuation, 341
    different valuation approaches, 336–8
    liability valuation basis and total profit,
    340
    profit margin, 325, 336
    profit signature, 338, 339
    table of liabilities, 337, 338
    valuation objective, 334, 335–9
  long-term business, 472
  margin on services profit, 477–8
  margins *see* Profit margins
  measured profit, 475
  measurement, 373, 472, 483–4
    accounting rules, 483
    appraisal values, 485–9
    asset-and-liability framework, 484, 485

Profit (*continued*)
    deferral-and-matching framework, 484, 485
    solvency differentiated from, 474
    measures of, 373
    modern view, 473
    monitoring experience, 519–22
    new business strain, 372–3, 479
    overview, 471
    policy liabilities, impact of, 471
    pricing assumptions, 475
    real profit, 475
    reported profit, 471
        distributable profit differentiated from, 472, 474
    return on capital, 373, 519
        monitoring experience, 519–22
    risk margins, 477
    short-term business, 472
    signatures, 338, 339, 481–2
    sources of, 474
    surplus, estimate of, 473
    target surplus, 372–3, 487
    testing, 374–5
    timing of recognition, 475–82
    total measured profit, 475
    traditional view, 473
    ultimate profit, 471
    value differentiated from, 484–5
Profit margins, 325, 474
    definition, 325, 373
    liability valuation, 325, 336
    pricing, 373
    source of profit, 474
Profit objectives
    definition, 372
    new business strain, 372–3
    pricing process, 372–4
Profit signatures, 338, 339, 481–2
Profit testing
    definition, 374
    pricing process, 374–5
Project management
    communication between parties, 208
    financial viability of project, 208
    modeling, 258
    objectives of project, 208
    product design, 207–9
    responsibility, 208
    timeline, 208
Projection
    assumptions *see also* Assumptions

incidence and severity, 365
    valuing liabilities, for, 345–6
    error, causes of, 248–50
    interest rates, 347
    liabilities, using, 343
    models, using for, 248–50
Property
    asset risk, 407–8
    expense risk, 75
    valuation, 404
Property and Casualty (P&C) Insurance *see* General insurance
Provident fund *see* Superannuation fund
Provisions *see* Liabilities
Prudential carveout, 191
    WTO agreements, 191
Prudential regulation, 186–8
    accounting standards, 192
    Australian Prudential Regulation Authority (APRA), 298
    capital, amount of, 192, 291, 298
    core principles, 192
    entry and exit rules, 187
    international organizations, 190–1
    international standards, 190–1
    licensing, 187, 192
    mergers, 187
    regulators, 39
    roles for actuaries, 192–3
    solvency margin, 192
    supervisors, 57–8, 186, 193
    supervisory authority, 192
    winding up, 188
Prudential regulators, 39
    risk management, interest in, 39
Prudential supervision, 57–8, 193
Prudential supervisors, 186
Prudent valuation, 320, 326
Public liability insurance, 75
Public offer superannuation funds, 92
Pure endowment policy, 90

Q

Quota share treaty, 167

R

Rating agencies, 299
Rating downgrade, 452
Recession, 116
Redundancy, 86, 91, 99

Regulation
  arguments for, 189
  arguments for minimising, 188
  circulars, 179
  civil code systems, 177–8
  common law systems, 177–8
  competition, promoting, 182, 184
  compulsory financial products, 185
  core principles, 192
  cost, 188
  court decisions, 179
  definition, 177
  disclosure alone compared to, 189
  economic objectives, 184
  inefficiency from market interference, 188
  inflexibility, 188
  international organizations influencing, 190–1
  international regulatory standards, 190–1
  law-making structure, 177
  law, types of, 179–80
  legal systems, 177–8
  legislated roles for actuaries, 59–60, 192–3
  levels of, 178
  markets and companies, 181
  objectives, 184
  precedent, 179
  primary legislation, 178
  professional body role in, 50–1
  prudential see Prudential regulation
  regulations, 178
  self-regulatory organizations, 179
  sources of law, 177
  standards, 179
    international, 190–1
  structure of, 193
  subsidiary legislation, 178–9
  supervision differentiated from, 177
  taxation legislation, 181
  third parties, disclosure to, 59
  unforeseen implications, 188
  world regulatory practice, 189
Regulators
  financial services, 39
  market conduct, 39
  pricing needs, 361
  prudential, 39
  risk management, interest in, 39
Regulatory arbitrage, 80
Regulatory risk, 144
  solvency testing, 455
Reinsurance, 165–7

product design influenced by availability of, 205
  recoveries, 447
  retrocession, 166
  solvency impact, 455
  types, 167
Reinvestment risk, 143
Reporting
  CAMELS early warning system, 451
  financial condition reports, 453–4
  financial control reports, 531
  incident register, 33
  key risk indicators, 33
  risk heat map, 26, 33
  risk management assessment, 32–3
  risk register, 33
  solvency problems, 450–1
  summary reports, 33
Reputation risk, 144
Reserves see Liabilities
Reserving risk, 142
Residual risk, 31
Responding to experience
  allocating interest to accounts, 539–42
  audit controls, 532–3
  business plans, 530, 531
  capital management, 538–9
  capital requirements, 530
  claims controls, 536–7
  competition and, 530
  defined benefit superannuation, 546–9
  expense controls, 533–6
  experience refunds, 546
  fairness and equity of solutions, 529, 530
  financial control systems, 531–2
  general considerations, 530
  investment income, distribution of, 539–42
  legal constraints, 530
  life insurance, participating, 549–54
    allocation of profit, 550–2
    asset share methods, 554
    distribution of profit, 550, 552–4
    participating policies, 549
  limitations in data and systems, 529
  managing business, 531–9
  new business controls, 537–8
  pricing changes, 544
  pricing review, 544–6
  professional standards, 530
  role of actuary, 529
  smoothing investment returns, 540–2
  termination controls, 537–8
  unit pricing, 542–3

Responsible Actuary *see* Appointed Actuary
Results, communicating, 6–7
Retirement benefit plan
  benefit guarantee funds, 459
  valuation, modeling, 228
Retirement income products, 95–7
  allocated annuities, 96–7
  government systems, 100
  lifetime annuities, 96
  term certain annuities, 96
  variable annuities, 96–7
Retrenchment *see* Redundancy
Retrocession, 166
Return on capital, 373
  monitoring experience, 519–22
  profit, measure of, 373, 519
Reversionary bonuses, 553
Reward and risk, 15
Risk
  allowing for in liability valuation, 331
  analysis *see* Risk analysis
  appetite, 23–4, 40
  application, 17
  business, 17
  capital needs and *see* Capital needs
  concentration of risks, 19
  contagion, 308
  credit, 16, 142
  definition, 14, 135
  diversifiable, 15, 19
  evaluation, 29
  expense risks, 74–7, 144
  financial, 16
  gross, 31
  hazard risks, 17
  identification *see* Risk identification
  implementation, 17
  income risks, 73–4
  inherent, 31
  interaction between risks, 19, 28
  liquidity, 16, 143
  management *see* Risk management
  market, 15, 16, 142–3
  measure of exposure to, 442–4
    first Basel Accord, 442, 443
    risk-based capital standard, 442–4
    second Basel Accord, 442, 443
  net, 31
  non-financial, 16
  operational, 17, 143
  product design and *see* Product design
  residual, 31

reward, balance, 15
savings risks, 77–8
strategic, 17, 143
systematic, 15
systemic, 14
tolerance for, 24
treatment of *see* Risk treatment
types, 15–18
underwriting, 17–18, 141–2, 152
Risk-adjusted cash flows, 331
Risk analysis, 25–8, 152–7
  confidence level, 156–7
  experience data, 153–4
  impact, 25, 27
  likelihood, 25
  modeling risk, 27–8, 154–5
  new risks, 28
  qualitative, 25, 153
  quantitative, 26, 27, 153
  risk heat map, 26
  risk measure, 156
  stress testing, 28
  terminal provision, 157
  time horizon, 155
  unmeasurable risks, 28
Risk appetite, 23–4, 40
Risk assessment *see* Risk analysis
Risk-based capital, 40
Risk-based capital requirements (RBC)
  control cycle and, 445–6
  internal models, 445
  procyclical, 456
  risk-based capital standard, creation of,
    441–5
    diversification benefits, allowing for,
      444
    identification of risks, 442
    measure of exposure to risk, 442–4
    objectives, setting, 442
    quantifying risks, 442
    quantifying size of potential losses,
      444
  solvency, for, 440–5
Risk committee
  fitted model presented to, 237
    challenging, 237–8
  role of, 237
Risk evaluation, 29
  allowing for risk in liability valuations,
    331
Risk heat map, 26, 33

Risk identification, 24–5, 138–9
  banking risks, 151–2
  funds management risks, 149–51
  insurer risks, 140–7
  product design, 204–5
  superannuation risks, 147–9
Risk impact, 25, 27
  reducing, 30
Risk likelihood, 25
  reducing, 30
Risk management *see also* Enterprise Risk
      Management (ERM)
  ad hoc, 11
  analyzing risks, 25–8
  audits, 32
  board of directors
      policy, 34
      responsibilities, 36, 531
      stake in, 35
  capital providers, 40
  communication, 32–4
  consultation, 32–4, 564–6
  context, establishing, 22–3
  culture, 18, 36, 38, 40
  definition, 18
  ERM *see* Enterprise Risk Management
      (ERM)
  evaluating risks, 29
  execution, 34
  external environment, 23
  framework, 11–12, 561
  identifying risks *see* Risk identification
  internal environment, 23
  liquidity risk, 430
  middle management responsibilities, 38
  monitoring, 32
  policy, 34
      implementation, 34
  process, 21–32, 41, 136
  regulators' responsibilities, 39
  review, 32
  senior management responsibilities, 37
  service provider interests in, 39
  shareholders stake in, 35
  solvency regulation *see* Solvency
  standards, 21
  strategy, 34, 158
  success of
      factors for, 40–1
      measurement of, 41
  systematic, 11
  treatment of risks *see* Risk treatment

Risk management committee, 36–7
Risk management framework (RMF)
  case study, 561
  definition, 11–12
  enterprise risk management *see* Enterprise
      Risk Management (ERM)
Risk management policy, 34
Risk management strategy, 34, 158
Risk margins, 324–5
  profit, timing of, 477
Risk measure, 156, 169
Risk metric, 156, 169
Risk mitigation *see* Risk treatment
Risk models, 27–8, 154–5
  see also Modeling
Risk premium, 353
Risk selection *see also* Underwriting
  definition, 218
  product design, 218–20
Risk tolerance, 24
Risk transfer, 30
  counterparty risk, 30
Risk treatment, 29–31, 157–67
  avoiding the risk, 30, 159–60
  exploiting the risk, 30, 165
  issues, 30–1
  net risks, 31
  reducing the risk, 30, 162
  reinsurance, 165–7
  retaining the risk, 30, 160–1
  transferring the risk, 30, 162–5
Rules-based reserving, 332
Run off, 432
  discontinuance solvency, 427, 431–3
Run (on a bank), 189, 412, 428

S

Sales management expenses, 514
Sampling, 272
Savings cycle, 70–2
Savings and loan association, 12
  crisis, 456
Savings products
  investment guarantee, 227
  long-term *see* Long-term savings products
  modeling, 227
  monetary products *see* Monetary products
  short-term, 81–2
Savings risks, 77–8
Scenario modeling, 27–8, 560
Scenario tests, 379, 381, 560

Secondary markets, 182
Securitization, 83, 401
    global financial crisis lessons, 169–71
Selective withdrawal, 437
Self-regulatory organizations, 179
Senior management
    capital, view of level of, 296–8
    Chief Actuary, 37–8
    Chief Risk Officer (CRO), 37
    corporate structure, place in, 13
    culture, 37
    risk management responsibilities, 37
Sensitivity tests, 379–81
    claims assumptions, 380
    experience, monitoring, 497
    lapse assumptions, 380
    liability valuation, 343
    pricing, 379–81
    scenario tests, 379, 381, 560
Service units, 510
Shares, 399–400
Share value, 407
Shareholders
    capital, view of level of, 295–6
    corporate structure, place in, 13
    monitoring experience to provide
        information to, 497
    risk management, stake in, 35
Sharing experience, 162
Sharpe measure, 508
Short-tail business, 145
Smoothing investment returns, 540–2
Smoothing reserves, 341
Social assistance, 99, 112
Social behavior modeling, 229
Social environment, 119–20
Social insurance, 112
Social sciences
    modeling, approach to, 238–9
Solvency, 425–64
    acceptable level of, deciding, 425–6
    actuaries, role of, 452–3
        financial condition reports, 453
    BIS approach to regulation of, 426–7
    CAMELS early warning system, 451
    capital requirements, 426, 427, 440–5
        amount and quality of capital, 446
        banks, 441
        BIS standards, 441
        control cycle and capital model, 445–6
        debt/equity hybrid securities, 446, 447
        improving quality of capital, 455

        mandatory convertible notes, 446
        non-life insurers, 441
        raising additional capital, 455
        regulatory arbitrage, 446
        risk-based *see* risk-based capital
            requirements *below*
        statutory requirements, 425, 446
        subordinated debt, 446
    cash flow solvency, 427–31
    cash flow testing, 427, 428
    consequences of insolvency, 425
    credit rating and, 451–2
    directors' responsibility, 426
    discontinuance solvency, 427, 431–3
        forms of discontinuance, 432
        measuring, 432–3
        valuation of assets, 434
        valuation of liabilities, 439
    Dynamic Capital Adequacy Testing
        (DCAT), 454–5
    Dynamic Solvency Testing (DST), 454–5
    equity compared to liabilities as measure
        of, 319
    Financial Analysis and Solvency Tracking
        System (FAST), 451
    financial assistance, 458
    financial condition reports, 453–4
    going-concern solvency, 427, 431, 433
        measuring, 433–4
    guarantee funds, 458–61
    Insurance Regulatory Information System
        (IRIS), 451
    intervention, 456–8
    liquid assets, level of, 430
    liquidity, 427–31
    liquidity ratio, 427
    liquidity risk *see* Liquidity risk
    market discipline, 427
    minimum capital requirements, 425
    people interested in enterprise's, 425
    problems, 428–31
        responding to, 455–6
    profit measurement versus, 474
    reducing risks, 455
    regulatory solvency requirements, 425
    reporting requirements, 450–1
    risk-based capital requirements (RBC),
        440–5
        control cycle and, 445–6
        internal models, 445
        procyclical, 456

Solvency (*continued*)
    risk-based capital standard, creation of,
       441–5
       diversification benefits, allowing for,
          444
       identification of risks, 442
       measure of exposure to risk, 442–4
       objectives, setting, 442
       quantifying risks, 442
       quantifying size of potential losses,
          444
    risk management, 427, 449–53
       actuaries, role of, 452–3
       credit rating, 451–2
       disclosure, 451–2
       early warning systems, 451
       enterprise risk management (ERM),
          450
       financial condition reports, 453
       internal, 450
       liquidity risk, 430
       reporting requirements, 450–1
       strategy (RMS), 450
    statutory solvency requirements, 425
    testing, 454–5
    valuation of assets, 434–5
    valuation of liabilities, 435–40
       accuracy, 440
       discontinuance, adjustments for, 439
       discretionary benefits, 439
       margin for adverse deviation (MAD)
          method, 437–8
       methods, 435–9
       principle-based reserving, 438
       probability of sufficiency (POS)
          method, 438
       prudent best estimates, 438
       statutory valuation basis, 436
       stochastic reserve, 439
Solvency margin, 192
Solvency ratio, 433
Solvency II, 18, 129, 171
Sovereign risk, 142
Special purpose entities (SPE), 163–4
Special purpose vehicle (SPV), 83, 163–4
Spread (interest rate), 378
Spread risk, 142
Staff
    corporate structure, place in, 13
    risk management responsibilities, 38
Stakeholder pensions, 92
Stakeholders

advice, consideration of effect on, 61
communication and consultation with,
    32–4
corporate governance, and, 13
definition, 126
elements of context, 126–7
product design and expectations of, 212–
    14
risk, attitude to, 23, 30
Standards of practice, 55–6
    data quality, 277–8
    monitoring, 56
Standards, regulatory, 179
    altering, 179
    force of law, 179
    international, 190–1
State price, 351
    deflators, 350–1
Statistical inference, 239
Statutory Accounting Principles (SAP), 433
Sterling reserve, 342
Stochastic model, 252
    cash flow projections, 328–9, 331
    data collection, 271, 272
    deterministic model differentiated from,
       251
    Monte Carlo models, 252–3
Stocks *see* Shares
Strategic planning, 21
Strategic risks, 17, 143
Subprime debt crisis, 431, 444, 456
Subprime loans, 211
Superannuation
    defined benefits *see* Defined benefit
       superannuation fund
    monitoring experience, 499
    risk identification, 147–9
Superannuation funds, 90–2
    capital needs, 301–2
       operational risk, 309
    defined benefits *see* Defined benefit
       superannuation fund
    defined contribution *see* Defined
       contribution fund
    employer-sponsored funds, 91, 301
       capital needs, 301–2
       group superannuation and insurance,
          100–1
    industry funds, 92, 302
       capital needs, 302
    multi-employer funds, 92, 302
       capital needs, 302
    operational risk, 309

Superannuation funds (*continued*)
    pooled superannuation trusts (PSTs), 93
    public offer funds, 92
    risk identification, 147–9
    risk management, employer's interest in,
        39
Superannuation Guarantee Levy, 175
Super-imposed inflation, 147
Supervision, prudential, 57–8
Surplus, 473
Surrender, 284
Surrender value, 84, 429
Survey data, 272–3
Survivorship bias, 248, 249
Swaps and swaptions, 95, 400
System risks 143
Systematic risk *see* Market risk
Systemic connections and GFC, 168
Systemic instability, 184
    market failure, source of, 184
Systemic risks, 14, 303

T

Tail value at risk (TVaR), 156
Takaful, 119–20
Target surplus
    appraisal value, 487
    capital needs, 312
    definition, 372–3, 487
    new business strain, 373
    pricing models, 364
    profit, 372–3
Tax arbitrage, 80
Tax assets, 397
Tax liabilities, 321
    liability valuation allowing for, 347
    tax cost liability, 347
Taxation
    changes in law creating new market needs,
        201
    effect on context, 112
    legislation, 181
    levies, 181
    responding to experience, considerations,
        530
Technological developments, 115
Term deposit, 81, 396, 399
Terminal bonuses, 553
Terminal provision, 157
Third parties
    advice, reliance on by, 61
    disclosure to, 59

    experience monitoring providing
        information to, 497
Third party claimant, 425, 458
Tier 1 capital, 291
Tier 2 capital, 291
Time horizon, 155
Total and permanent disablement (TPD), 85
Trade credit insurance, 89
Traditional coinsurance, 167
Tranche, 83, 401
Transfer of business, 432
    discontinuance solvency, 427, 431–3
Trauma insurance, 86, 87, 145
Treynor measure, 508
Trusts *see* Unit trusts

U

Unbundled liability valuation, 332–3
Uncertainty risk, 146
Underwriting
    credit risk, evaluating, 218
    definition, 218
    expenses, 513
    financial, 219
    full, 366
    insurance, and, 219–20, 365
    product design and, 218–20
    simplified, 366
Underwriting process risk, 141
Underwriting risk, 17–18, 141–2, 152
Unemployment
    income risk, 74
    insurance, 86
Unitized with-profit policies, 94
Unit-linked life insurance, 115
Unit pricing, 542–3
    errors, 543
    forward pricing, 543
    historic pricing, 543
    transaction costs, 543
Unit trusts, 92
Universal life, 94, 200
Unlisted stock/shares, 400

V

Valuation of assets *see* Asset valuation
Valuation of liabilities *see* Liability valuation
Value at risk (VaR), 156, 438, 443
Value of in-force, 486, 487
Value of new business, 486, 488
Variable annuities, 96–7

Variable mortgages, 76
Volatility risk, 146

W

Warehousing risk, 152
Whistle-blowing, 60, 61, 435
Whole life insurance, 84
Whole population study, 273
Winding up, 432
    discontinuance solvency, 427, 431–3
    prudential regulation, 188

Withdrawals, selective, 437
Work patterns, 118–19
Workers compensation insurance, 89
    regulation of, 185
World Bank, 191
World Trade Organization (WTO), 191
Wrap funds, 93

Y

Yearly renewable term insurance (YRT), 84,
    167